Intercultural Communication in the Global Workplace

Fifth Edition

Iris Varner

Professor Emerita, Illinois State University

Linda Beamer

Emerita Professor, California State University, Los Angeles

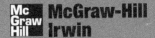
McGraw-Hill Irwin

McGraw-Hill
Irwin

INTERCULTURAL COMMUNICATION IN THE GLOBAL WORKPLACE, FIFTH EDITON

Published by McGraw-Hill, a business unit of The McGraw-Hill Companies, Inc., 1221 Avenue of the Americas, New York, NY 10020. Copyright © 2011 by The McGraw-Hill Companies, Inc. All rights reserved. Previous editions © 2008, 2005, and 2001. No part of this publication may be reproduced or distributed in any form or by any means, or stored in a database or retrieval system, without the prior written consent of The McGraw-Hill Companies, Inc., including, but not limited to, in any network or other electronic storage or transmission, or broadcast for distance learning.

Some ancillaries, including electronic and print components, may not be available to customers outside the United States.

This book is printed on acid-free paper.

3 4 5 6 7 8 9 0 QVS/QVS 19 18 17 16 15 14

ISBN: 978-0-07-337774-2
MHID: 0-07-337774-0

Vice President & Editor-in-Chief: *Brent Gordon*
Vice President EDP/Central Publishing Services: *Kimberly Meriwether David*
Publisher: *Paul Ducham*
Sponsoring Editor: *Laura Hurst Spell*
Editorial Coordinator: *Jane Beck*
Associate Marketing Manager: *Jaime Halteman*
Project Manager: *Erin Melloy*
Design Coordinator: *Margarite Reynolds*
Cover Image Credit: *© Photodisc*
Production Supervisor: *Nicole Baumgartner*
Media Project Manager: *Suresh Babu*
Composition: *S4Carlisle Publishing Services*
Typeface: *10/12 Times Roman*
Printer: *Quad/Graphics*

Library of Congress Cataloging-in-Publication Data

Varner, Iris I.
    Intercultural communication in the global workplace / Iris Varner,
Linda Beamer.—5th ed.
      p. cm.
    Beamer's name appears first on the previous ed.
    ISBN 978-0-07-337774-2
    1. Communication in management—Social aspects. 2. Business
communication—Social aspects. 3. International business enterprises—Social
aspects. 4. Intercultural communication. I. Beamer, Linda. II. Beamer, Linda.
Intercultural communication in the global workplace. III. Title.
HD30.3.B4 2010
658.4'5—dc22   2009054446

www.mhhe.com

For Carson and David

Preface to the Fifth Edition

Welcome to the fifth edition of *Intercultural Communication in the Global Workplace.* The fourth edition has been used around the globe. We are grateful for the reception of the earlier editions, particularly the many comments and suggestions users have given us. We have incorporated those comments into the fifth edition and are confident that this book presents a valuable tool in your understanding of the impact of culture on international business communication.

The effects of culture on human behavior in general and on global business activities in particular make headline news almost every day. More than ever businesspeople cite cultural understanding as the single most important factor in international success. Prof. Dr. Marion Debruyne is quoted as saying "Culture is the real power of globalization."[1] Dramatic changes in communication technology—the growth around the planet of satellite and cellular telephony—since our first edition have made international communication commonplace.

When we wrote the first edition, e-mail was just starting to be used widely, but it was almost impossible to attach files to an e-mail. We used FedEx to send book chapters to each other for comments and suggestions. Today, files can be sent easily all over the world; we can talk to each other and even see each other on our computer screens. Blogs, Facebook, and Twitter have revolutionized communication. Technology allows us to use rich channels that do not just transmit text but also our gestures, facial expressions, and pauses. We can communicate over vast distances as if we sat in the same room. Companies have embraced this new technology to facilitate communication among their employees from around the world. A survey of new media published in *The Economist* magazine in April 2006 reported that thanks to broadband technology, mass media are being replaced by personal media created by the users of the Internet.[1] Since 2006, personal media devices have developed further, and offer, in addition to a chance to speak and listen, the capability to receive and transmit data to and from mobile devices. "Nowadays, YouTube streams more data in three months than all the world's radio stations plus cable and broadcast television channels stream in a year."[2] It's a long way from the development over 40 years ago of technology to allow internetworking—the origin of the "Internet"—to exist.

The technological revolution means that organizations need intercultural communication skills even more today than they did when this book was first written. The fifth edition of *Intercultural Communication in the Global Workplace* has updated discussions of globalization and new technology in business communication. The discussion of multicultural teams in the workplace has been expanded.

What else is new? The fifth edition has a new discussion about the study of communication in different cultures, and the study of communication between cultures. It also shows how intercultural communication research fits within the dominant research paradigms, and includes an analysis of their strengths and weaknesses. The descriptions of religions and their influence on intercultural business communication has been expanded. The concept of Cultural Intelligence (CQ) is now discussed in greater detail throughout the book. Chapter 3 has a new section on culture's influence on how people reason, and Chapter 4 has a new section on self-identity and self-construal in relation to culture. Chapter 8 includes an expanded discussion about culture's effect on conflict management.

Chapter 12 ties together the concepts discussed in all the other chapters. It applies updated intercultural knowledge to the case of DaimlerChrysler and examines the cultural reasons for the failure of the merger within just seven years of its beginning. This chapter also introduces the role diverse teams play in the success of international business. Two in-depth cases in the Appendix to Chapter 12 provide an opportunity to apply intercultural knowledge to specific problems.

Throughout the book we have added more short cases, and kept the introductory vignettes to each chapter to illustrate the issues covered in that chapter. New illustrations and examples have been added, often drawn from cultures not mentioned in the earlier editions.

Users of earlier editions will notice that the appearance of the fifth edition is more user-friendly, as we continue to improve the book's layout and add new exhibits.

These changes reflect our continued commitment to provide a source for readers that addresses culture and cultural variations, communication across cultures for business purposes, and the way culture affects organizations.

Many new books have arrived in the marketplace since we finished our fourth edition, but we are convinced this one is unique: It addresses the issues of culture and communication within the context of international business.

The fifth edition of *Intercultural Communication in the Global Workplace,* like the first four editions, provides examples of how cultural values and practices impact business communication. We explore the relationships among the cultural environments of the firm and the structure of the firm. We look at how companies and individuals communicate. Throughout the discussions about specific communication tasks, we concentrate on the underlying cultural reasons for behavior. This approach, as we asserted from the very first edition, we confidently believe will help the reader develop an ability to work successfully within an environment of cultural diversity both at home and abroad.

We have continued to strive to avoid specific cultural viewpoints in this book but have come to realize since the first edition that total cultural neutrality is not possible. Nor is it desirable in a sense; every human has some cultural filters through which she or he views the world. And comments from users have confirmed this. Nevertheless, the framework we develop here applies to all readers regardless of their native cultures. This book is for anyone from anywhere around the globe who wants to develop and improve intercultural business communication skills. Intercultural business communication is an exciting field, and we are proud to be able to contribute to a broader understanding of it.

Notes

1. *The Economist,* April 2006.
2. "The Internet at 40," *The Economist*, September 4, 2009, http://www.economist .com/sciencetechnology/displaystory.cfm?story_id=14391822.

About the Authors

Iris I. Varner is the Director for the International Business Institute and a Professor Emerita in international business at the College of Business, at Illinois State University, where she taught the cultural environment of international business and international management. Her PhD, MBA, and MA are from the University of Oklahoma. She has the Staatsexamen and Assessorenexamen from the Albert-Ludwigs-Universität, Freiburg, Germany.

Varner has extensive international experience. She grew up in the former East Germany and studied in Germany, France, Great Britain, the United States, and Taiwan. She has given seminars and lectures around the globe, including New Zealand, Russia, France, Belgium, Japan, Germany, and China and has spent time in many other countries. She is an ad hoc professor at the University of Lugano, Switzerland, where she teaches in the Executive Masters Program for Corporate Communication Management and at Shanghai University, China.

Varner is the author of over 80 articles in the area of intercultural managerial communication. Her research, which she has presented at regional, national, and international conventions, has focused on the connections between culture, communication, and business practices. She has been honored with the Outstanding Membership Award and the Meada Gibbs Outstanding Teaching Award of the Association for Business Communication. She was named a Fellow of the Association for Business Communication and a Caterpillar Scholar and State Farm Fellow by Illinois State University.

As a president of the Association for Business Communication in 2000 to 2001, she contributed greatly to the internationalization of the organization. She was chair of the Ethics Committee and is an active member of the International Committee. Varner is a member of the Academy of Management and the Academy for Human Resource Development. She also serves as a reviewer for a number of scholarly publications and consults for a variety of national and international firms.

Linda Beamer is an Emerita Professor of California State University, Los Angeles, where she taught undergraduate business communication, intercultural communication, and diversity in the workplace, and courses in high-performance management and international business in the MBA. She received the honors students' Professor of the Year award in 2001, and in 2002 she received the Outstanding Professor award from her campus, followed by a Distinguished Woman award in 2005. She subsequently taught intercultural communication to undergraduate and postgraduate students at Unitec New Zealand, where she and her husband make their home.

She has taught and consulted in the United States, Great Britain, Canada, the Middle East, China, Argentina, Mexico, Hong Kong, Japan, and New Zealand. Her BA is from the College of Wooster in Ohio (with one year in Scotland at Edinburgh University), and her MA and PhD are from the University of Toronto. The latter led to dual U.S.–Canadian citizenship.

Her research, resulting in about two dozen publications and 70 presentations, has focused primarily on the effects of culture on business communication, with a special interest in Chinese communication issues. She has served on the Editorial Board of *Business Communication Quarterly* and was Associate Editor of the *Journal of Business Communication;* she frequently reviews for other publications as well. She served as President of the Association for Business Communication in 2004, as Chair of the Intercultural Committee of the Association for Business Communication, and as a member of the Board of Directors. In 2005, she was honored with the Fellow award. She was also voted a Fellow of the International Academy of Intercultural Research at its inception in 1997.

Beamer has been the recipient of several research grants and received the Outstanding Publication award from the Association for Business Communication. She held a six-year Visiting Professor appointment at Unitec New Zealand before moving to Auckland, and held a three-year Visiting Professor appointment at Shanghai University until 2009. She taught at Chuo University in Tokyo in 2004 and 2010, and has been a guest lecturer at many campuses around the world.

Acknowledgments

Intercultural Communication in the Global Workplace is the result of many years of work. Although this book is based to a great extent on our professional research and personal experiences, we also want to acknowledge the suggestions and advice we have received from our families, friends, clients, colleagues, and students. We are particularly indebted to the users of previous editions for giving us valuable feedback. Many people have been generous in sharing information with us, and we are grateful for their support.

We give special thanks to the reviewers who carefully read the fourth edition and offered their insights and suggestions.

Last, but not least, we thank the people at McGraw-Hill/Irwin, and particularly Jolynn Kilburg, the developmental editor. Their work and support made this edition possible.

Introduction

The Need for Intercultural Business Communication Competence

What does culture have to do with business? In the past, many business majors and practitioners immersed in questions of financial forecasting, market studies, and management models did not examine culture and the way it affects business. Unlike the hard data from measurable issues, culture is soft and, at times, slippery. Although it can be elusive, culture is still undeniably important. It's often easiest to spot culture at work when something goes wrong, when a key element of culture is overlooked. Here is an example:

> Mickey Mouse took up residence in Hong Kong in 2005, but Mainland Chinese visitors to the new theme park seemed unsure about the meaning of the Happiest Place on Earth. Disney film characters like Cinderella, Snow White and the Seven Dwarfs, and Tinkerbell are based on fairy tales and stories from Europe that are unfamiliar to children in China. Disney television shows with cartoon characters for children haven't been aired in China for decades, as they have in the United States. Meanwhile, visitors who were puzzled by the theme park wandered aimlessly up Main Street and had their pictures taken with Marie the Cat—a character from the 1970s movie *The Aristocats,* whose appeal is in her appearance: It is remarkably similar to the hugely popular Japanese figure, Hello Kitty.
>
> However, in early 2006 sparse crowds were replaced by hordes, and visitors' mild bafflement turned to outrage. Hong Kong Disneyland was deluged by crowds. Three times during the "Golden Week" of the Chinese New Year the gates to the park were closed after the first 30,000 visitors came through, and thousands more visitors with paid tickets in their hands were turned away. Many parents who had spent large sums of money on travel to the promised holiday treat were photographed attempting to climb the fence or toss their child over it. Disappointed patrons threatened to sue Disney.
>
> Disney made a public apology. The problem of too many visitors had come about because Hong Kong Disneyland, worried about lack of sales, had sold tickets that were good for up to six months. Many bought their tickets and then held on to them until the New Year holidays, something the Disneyland managers hadn't anticipated. The chairman of the rival Ocean Park was quoted as saying it was a mess: "Many of the problems 'were things that somebody who did their homework should have realized and understood.'"[1]
>
> Nor was the Golden Week debacle the first cultural bump in the road for Hong Kong Disneyland. Initially, a park restaurant planned to serve shark fin's soup, a Chinese delicacy that was later withdrawn from the menu because of animal rights protests. Local celebrities were invited for public relations appearances, but they subsequently complained they weren't treated well by Disney executives from the United States. Disney also had learned that Chinese visitors to parks preferred places for taking photographs over roller coaster rides, so they put fewer rides into this park, which is the smallest of the six worldwide. As a result, shortly after it opened the park was criticized for being too small.

Other culture-related issues that plagued the opening of Hong Kong Disneyland were the danger to children's health from people smoking in nonsmoking areas, and the threat to sanitation from some visitors' practice of urinating on the flowerbeds near food areas.

Hong Kong Disneyland isn't an isolated instance of cultural misunderstandings. The history of the Disney theme park in France is notorious. Euro Disney had similar problems with unplanned crowds when it first opened. Locals who had postponed their visits during the summer tourist season surged to visit in September 1992. French critics called Euro Disney an example of U.S. cultural imperialism, and hundreds of employees left their jobs after a few days. The Disney prohibition on the sale of alcohol in its theme parks did not fit with the French custom of drinking wine with meals. But by 2006 it had become France's number-one tourist destination with 50 million visitors a year.[2]

Similarly, the future of tourism in Hong Kong is bright, and Disney has adapted to take advantage of it. The people of Hong Kong may have had more patience with the U.S. company than the French did. Chief Executive Donald Tsang said when the theme park opened: "We have to remember that Disneyland is a new organization [in Hong Kong] . . . It may need time to understand the situation of Hong Kong and especially the culture of Hong Kongers and figure out how to make all its employees happy."[3]

More and more organizations with strong success records at home, like Disney, are finding themselves involved in communication between cultures, either because they are doing business in unfamiliar foreign countries, or because they are sourcing from another country and seeking financing and a workforce from another country.

Companies around the world have increasingly multicultural workforces. In the United States, for example, Latinos (from Mexico and Central and South America) have become the biggest minority group. In Europe, the composition of the population is changing as more and more people emigrate from Africa, Asia, and the Middle East. In the Middle East, many workers come from India, the Philippines, and Southeast Asia. Countries like Holland and Australia are considering an examination system to see if immigrant applicants are culturally suited to living in those countries. As a result of these migrations, people with diverse cultural backgrounds and different languages are working side by side in many countries, creating a workplace that is multicultural.

Business communication today is intercultural communication. To communicate with people from another culture, one needs to understand the culture. To do that, one needs a method. This book offers an approach to unfamiliar cultures that makes understanding easier and consequently makes business communication with those cultures more effective. We believe intercultural business communication skills can be learned.

At its lowest level, business communication with unfamiliar cultures means simply finding a translator for conducting discussions in a foreign language. However, as more and more corporations are finding out, communication must take into account unarticulated meanings and the thinking behind the words—not just the words alone. To be effective, communication must be culturally correct, not merely grammatically correct.

To understand the significance of a message from someone, you need to understand the way that person looks at the world and the values that weigh heavily in that person's view of the world. That view includes meanings that are assumed to be universal (even when they are not), the importance of the words that are used, and the way the message is organized and transmitted. You also need to know what to expect when someone engages in a particular communication behavior such as making a decision known, negotiating a sales agreement, or writing a legal contract. And you'd be wise to know something about the organization that person works in and the way its structure—a result of culture—affects communication.

In applying intercultural communication skills to practical business concerns, this book makes an important contribution. Most books about doing business with people from other cultures come from one of two areas, either intercultural and cross-cultural communication scholarship and its near relative, intercultural training, or international business. Intercultural and cross-cultural communication scholarship is grounded in a body of theory but has little direct application to business communication. Intercultural training draws from psychology and related fields and specializes in preparing people for sojourns in foreign countries for development work, such as for the Peace Corps, for studying abroad, or for working in an expatriate posting, but this training typically has little application to business communication.

Books on international business, in contrast, concentrate on business functions such as finance, management, marketing, shipping and insurance, and accounting. They tend to ignore the importance of the all-encompassing communication tasks and the skills necessary to complete them successfully. They also tend to ignore the different priorities in other cultures that affect the act of communication and its outcomes.

This book connects business communication and understanding of cultural priorities with actual business practices. Of course, business practices themselves, as the book points out, are culturally based.

By combining intercultural communication skills with business, this book helps you become a successful communicator in culturally diverse workplace environments both at home and abroad. As more and more firms are finding out, effective intercultural communication is crucial for success domestically and internationally.

Intercultural Business Communication Competence and Growing Domestic Diversity

All over the world, nations are trying to come to terms with the growing diversity of their populations. Reactions range from a warm welcome, to conditional acceptance, to mere tolerance, to rejection. As migrations of workers and refugees have increased globally, some countries are trying to control diversity by establishing strict guidelines for emigration from other countries. Other countries are attempting to develop government policies concerning the rights of immigrants to preserve their own cultures in their adopted homelands. Canada is an example of a bicultural (English and French) country where federal and provincial governments have ministers of multiculturalism to protect the cultural "mosaic" pattern that immigrants bring to Canada. New Zealand is an example of a country that has issues of biculturalism (Māori and non-Māori) to work through and that needs additional energy and resources to attend to the increasing cultural diversity of immigrants.

The United States historically afforded a home to people of diverse cultures. But even in the United States, with its ideals of equality and tolerance, the advantages and disadvantages of acknowledging diversity are debated hotly. Social critics in the United States have voiced opposition to measures that preserve immigrants' cultural differences. They say the insistence on diversity separates Americans from one another by forcing them to focus on what differentiates them. This view holds that the "melting pot" that has been alleged to describe American culture depends on the fusing of all cultural identities into one, in keeping with the American ideal of offering equal American-ness to everybody. Furthermore, they warn that multiculturalism may threaten the very characteristic that is so American: the union of one from many.

We don't subscribe to this view. We do acknowledge that uniformity is easier to deal with than diversity. Diversity is difficult, although it also can be very rewarding. Often the impulse to deny cultural differences comes from embarrassment at focusing on difference, since frequently to be different is to be excluded. It isn't polite to point out that someone looks different, talks differently, wears different clothes, or eats different food. Thus, many times, out of a concern to avoid making someone feel uncomfortable, difference is played down.

This attitude may be motivated in the United States by a sincere desire for equal behavior toward people regardless of their ethnic or cultural background under the all-encompassing umbrella of the ideal of equality. After all, most people who call themselves "American" have ancestors who were immigrants. Today, many still have a strong desire to include newcomers in a friendly and tolerant national embrace and to affirm the high priority of equality in American culture. This is also true of some people in other countries with recent immigrant populations, such as New Zealand, Canada, Argentina, and Australia, as communities struggle to reconcile national identity with newer cultures.

People from different cultures really are different (as well as similar) in how they see the world. That's a great thing about being human, and a potential source of delight and wonderment as much as a source of fear and suspicion—the choice is ours. As people of different cultures we begin with different databases, use different operating environments, run different software and process information differently to get to what are often different goals. To pretend we're all alike underneath is wrong and can lead to ineffectual communication or worse. The way to deal with diversity is not to deny it or ignore it but to learn about differences so they don't impair communication and successful business transactions.

We also need new models to describe diverse populations. The description of the United States, for example, as a "melting pot" is neither an accurate description of the reality nor an ideal that many of the more recent immigrants embrace. Even the immigrants from Europe of a previous century did not "melt"; they created a new culture with distinct differences based on cultural heritage. Some have described this integration as a salad or a pizza or a stew, in which each element retains a recognizable identity but contributes to the flavor of all. The combination gains something from each ingredient. The United States' value of tolerance has in some cases given immigrants to that country the freedom to keep their own identities while becoming part of a new culture. In other countries, similar cases exist, and they represent a goal to which all can aspire.

Cultural differences don't prevent us from working with each other or communicating with each other or transacting productive business with each other. Indeed, we must learn to work with each other. The future of any organization depends on it. When connections are formed with people from other cultures, similarities appear. We weave fabrics of cooperation in which we see recurring common threads. It's a source of delight to realize someone from a culture very different from one's own has the same attitude or value or behavior. Furthermore, to see and accept different priorities and views can provide strength and create new synergies.

The essential ingredient for a successful cultural mix is skill in putting into operation the knowledge you acquire about another culture; this is intercultural communication competence. Many companies around the globe, such as Hewlett-Packard in the United States, have discovered the value of intercultural communication skills and the increased productivity they bring. These organizations have instituted diversity programs to train employees.

Changes in Communication Technology and Political Structures

The 20th century nurtured unprecedented change in communication technology. The first decade of the 21st century brought even faster change. International communication that only a few decades ago took days, if not weeks, now takes nanoseconds. With e-mail, faxes, the Internet, satellites, cellular telephones, and conferencing software we contact our international partners at a moment's notice. If we want a more personal exchange, audio and video desktop technology, video teleconferencing, and Skype bring the other person right into our office.

Today's techno-developments are in the realm of participatory communication. In the first decade of the 21st century, words like "blog," "wiki," and "podcasting" appeared in our dictionaries. Podcasting ("pod" coming from the Apple product the iPod, for downloading music and audio as well as video from the Internet, and "casting" from broadcasting) allows podcasters to record anything and then upload it to the Internet where it can be downloaded by other users. Every garage band can play to unknown listeners. Every orator can declaim to the globe. At sites like Second Life, people create virtual identities for themselves, called avatars, and engage in creative ventures such as making films. How this kind of participative communication will impact the entertainment industry, such as Disney with whom we began this introduction, remains to be seen.

The variety of channels of business communication has also increased. Instant Messaging, wikis in the workplace, blogs and texting by mobile phone, Black-Berry, iPhone, or other smartphone devices carry written messages. They also can transmit still and moving visual images. Voicemail, podcaster feeds, and Skype systems carry audio and video messages. The choice of which channel to use in a particular situation is influenced by cultural priorities and values, and those choices are multiplying.

The changes in technology have facilitated the exchange of ideas, but they also have magnified the possibilities for cultural blunders. It is so easy to assume that the person on the other end of the connection communicates just as we do. After all, he or she uses the same technology and maybe even the same business terminology.

In addition to changes in technology, political and economic changes affect business communication internationally. China, the world's largest market for mobile telephony, is adopting more and more Western practices and a market economy. India is a technological powerhouse. Small industrialized countries jostle with big ones. Non-Western countries are becoming more assertive and protective of their cultural values and behaviors and do not accept Western dominance in business practices any longer. These new voices are increasingly powerful. Not long ago an elite group of industrialized countries could more or less dictate economic practices. This is changing. Today, the first-world "overconsumers" are being forced to take into consideration the cultural values and practices of "sustainable consumers."

As a result, understanding other cultures is more important than ever. If we consider that people with the same economic, political, and cultural background have problems communicating effectively, we can appreciate the difficulties and challenges that people from diverse cultures face when trying to communicate. Misunderstandings will always be a part of intercultural communication. One of the goals of this book is to minimize misunderstandings through an awareness of the priorities and expectations of business partners.

International Business and Corporate Responses

Managers in the past talked about the need for faster and more efficient communication, as if speed guaranteed effective communication. They paid lip service to the need for good intercultural communication, but staffing decisions typically were based on technical knowledge rather than good intercultural communication skills.

Now with growing competition and increasing globalization, that attitude is beginning to change. International experience in more countries is becoming more important for making it to the top of the corporate ladder. The car industry is a good example for worldwide alliances, mergers, and joint ventures that have required an increasing understanding of international business practices and intercultural communication dynamics.

The trend toward a global business environment is not restricted to car manufacturers or big industrialized countries such as the United States, Germany, Japan, France, Canada, and Great Britain. Nor is it restricted to large cities or trade centers on the coasts. Global business involves geographic locations that just a few years ago were considered to be wholly engaged in domestic business. Many small towns in the landlocked states of Mexico, for example, are involved in international business today. Chinese investments in Africa show that international business has new players today who are not only based in the Western world.

Local firms may export or import; they may be owned by foreign firms, or foreign firms may establish subsidiaries. People who never dreamed of going into international business may work side by side with recent immigrants from different cultures. The salesperson in a small business in a small town in any one of a hundred countries may have to answer inquiries from around the world. The salesperson doesn't have time to think about how to deal with a foreigner. She or he must be ready to communicate on the spot.

The Foundation for Intercultural Business Communication

The first step in effective intercultural communication involves self-analysis, self-awareness, and understanding. You can't understand the other party unless you understand yourself.

The next step is the understanding and acceptance of differences. That does not mean we have to agree with another culture's viewpoint or adopt another culture's values. It does mean we (and they) must examine our (and their) priorities and determine how we all can best work together, being different. In the process, we will realize that a person entering another culture will always have to adapt to a number of cultural conditions. That doesn't mean turning one's back on one's own culture or denying its priorities. Rather, it means learning what motivates others and how other cultural priorities inform the behavior, attitudes, and values of business colleagues. This approach means adding to one's own culture, not subtracting from it. For example, a businessperson from New Zealand going to Japan must adapt to many Japanese practices, just as a Japanese businessperson going to New Zealand must adapt to a variety of New Zealand practices.

In attempting to understand another culture's perspective, we will gain greater ground if we take off our cultural blinders and develop sensitivity in the way we speak and behave. That is not always easy. We are all culturally based and culturally biased.

For example, people in the United States refer to themselves as "Americans." They often say that they live in "America." Most Europeans use the same terminology. Germans, for example, refer to the country of the United States as *die Staaten* (the States) or as USA, but they always refer to the people as *Amerikaner* (Americans). The French call the people of the United States *les americains* (Americans); they refer to the country as *les Etats Unis* (the United States) or *l'Amerique* (America). The Japanese refer to people from the United States as *america-jin*. But these are not precisely accurate terms; they constitute an example of cultural bias. People from Central America and South America call themselves "American," too, and call people from the United States *yanquis* (Yankees). "North Americans" are people from Canada, Mexico, and the United States.

As residents of the United States, accustomed to using the word American to refer to people of the United States, we have struggled with the terminology in the writing of this book. We have attempted to distinguish between other Americans and those in the United States. But no exclusive term exists for the people of the United States—such as Statesians or USians—comparable to Mexicans or Canadians. We use the United States when referring to the country and often use the phrase people of the United States and United States businesspeople to refer to the people. But occasionally, when we feel the context is clearly the United States, we also use the term *Americans* to denote the people.

The third step in intercultural competence is to challenge the knowledge we have gained about other cultures and to see our understanding as flexible and incomplete. In any intercultural encounter, variations will occur. What we expect won't be exactly what we get. Openness and willingness to learn characterize the skilled person in intercultural communication.

The fourth step is analysis of communication behavior to reach conclusions about what has been successful and what has not. This book offers many examples of both success and failure. Specific communication tasks presented in the following chapters help with learning beyond stereotypes. Business correspondence, greeting behavior, conflict management, face-to-face and technology-mediated communications, and negotiations appear in the book, and they offer us an opportunity to model the analyses a good intercultural communicator must make.

The final step in intercultural communication competence is enacting what one has learned. You know as a newcomer to a culture when you have done something that is culturally incorrect; you also know when you can behave in accord with the other culture. At that point, you are walking in the shoes of the other culture. That is the ultimate goal of learning about a culture and learning the skills to communicate with that culture: to behave as if you are of that culture. In addition to this individual-level goal, you can also apply these principles to business organizations, as illustrated in the cases at the end of the book.

The Organization of This Book

This book has three major parts:

1. An understanding of culture and how to get to know unfamiliar cultures for business, and how to understand culture's impact on communication.
2. The application of intercultural communication skills to specific business communication tasks.
3. The implications of intercultural business communication for the domestic multicultural/international/global firm.

Part One

This section begins with an introduction to culture followed by the first steps in developing intercultural communication skills and a look at the way culture affects communication. A discussion follows about the study of communication across cultures. Chapter 2 examines the issue of language in communication with an unfamiliar culture and discusses the important role of the interpreter. Chapters 3 and 4 present a structure for understanding the dimensions of an unfamiliar culture by posing specific questions. The questions are in five different categories, and they cover the priorities or values of any culture that are important for business. Examples show how these priorities affect business transactions.

Part Two

Chapter 5 discusses the influences of cultural values and language patterns on the organization of business messages. Chapter 6 looks at the role of nonverbal communication across cultures. Chapter 7 discusses what happens when people from different cultures encounter one another in specific social contexts that have different meanings for each party, and also touches on ethics across cultures. Chapter 8 examines the impact of cultural priorities on information gathering, decision making, problem solving, and conflict managing—all activities that involve certain communication tasks. Chapter 9 concludes this section on the application of intercultural communication skills to business negotiations across cultures and to multicultural teams.

Part Three

Chapter 10 explores the legal environment and the communication implications for the international/global manager. Chapter 11 ties intercultural business communication practices to the organization and structure of the international/global firm. A broad variety of examples illustrates the impact of structure on communication. The last chapter applies the concepts from all the previous chapters to the case of DaimlerChrysler. Through this case analysis, you can see how culture affects real business decisions in the real world. This chapter also discusses how companies can use the work of intercultural teams to take advantage of the potential synergies of diverse groups in achieving corporate goals.

In connecting intercultural communication theory and international business concerns, this book presents a unique approach. It probes the reasons for cultural priorities and behavior and identifies the major applications in intercultural business communication tasks. In this process, it establishes a framework that will help readers ask the right questions and identify cultural issues so they can communicate effectively in new cultural settings.

This book is based on many years of research and experience living and working in a variety of cultures. The many examples make the book particularly valuable for anyone who wants to be an effective player in international business.

Notes

1. Bruce Einhorn, "Disney's Mobbed Kingdom," *BusinessWeek Online,* February 6, 2006, Academic Search Premier database (retrieved April 25, 2006).
2. "Introduction to Disneyland Paris," *Frommer's.* www.frommers.com/destinations/disneylandparis/0796010001.html (retrieved August 15, 2006).
3. Paul Wiseman, "Miscues Mar Opening of Hong Kong Disney," *USA Today,* Section: Money, November 10, 2005, p. 5b, Academic Search Premier database (retrieved April 25, 2006).

Contents in Brief

Contents

Chapter 9
Intercultural Negotiation Teams   329

Chapter 10
Legal and Governmental Considerations in Intercultural Business Communication   365

Chapter 11
The Influence of Business Structures and Corporate Culture on Intercultural Business Communication   403

CHAPTER ONE

Culture and Communication

Martin Walpert is the president of a family-owned business called Walpert Industries Ltd. in Montreal, Canada, that produces Christmas crackers. The company, located in French Canada, is one of the world's top five suppliers of the product (mainly to consumers in English-speaking countries), and exports two-thirds of its output to the United States. Walpert estimates that the international market for crackers is about $150 million, with the majority sold in Great Britain.

Crackers are paper tubes with small trinkets inside. When the twisted ends of the cracker are pulled, it pops or "cracks," causing the contents to spill out. Crackers are a tradition dating from Victorian England, and they are still very popular in England and in the countries Britain dominated in the 19th century.

The story of British crackers begins with an English confectioner in France, who saw Parisians selling paper twists of candy and brought the idea back to England. Instead of using candy, he filled his twists with little novelties and romantic verses. The result was a 19th-century success story of intercultural adaptation, because crackers became a tradition among British Christmas revelers. Today, crackers often have jokes instead of poems, a funny paper hat to wear at dinner, and prizes ranging from gimmicks and noisemakers to small watches. (In J. K. Rowling's book, *Harry Potter and the Sorcerer's Stone,* for instance, Harry Potter pulled crackers that emitted a loud explosion and produced mice and admirals' hats.) Crackers are colorful—usually red, green, and gold—and are typically laid alongside place settings at Christmas dinners or hung on Christmas trees.

Like many companies today, product manufacture at Walpert Industries Ltd. spans several countries. While its home office is in Canada, its crackers are manufactured in China, where in 1997 the company invested in a plant outside Beijing. Locating in China has given Walpert a competitive edge because labor costs are lower there than in Canada. However, due to the transnational nature of his company's production, Martin Walpert was soon to learn a valuable lesson regarding the role of culture in business.[1]

In December 2002, when some Canadian families opened their Christmas crackers made by Walpert, they had an unpleasant surprise. They discovered tiny plastic panda bears wearing military-style caps with a swastika on them. Some were saluting.

Martin Walpert is well aware that the swastika is the symbol used by the German Nazi party in the mid 20th century, and represents the horrors the Nazis perpetrated against Jews and other groups in World War II. A swastika was the last thing he wanted in his Christmas crackers. He wondered if he was the victim of a deliberate attempt to sabotage the company's business.

After receiving complaints and seeing newspaper articles about the swastika-wearing pandas, Martin Walpert launched an investigation. He already knew that in China panda bears are a cute, positive symbol appropriate for a holiday, especially a holiday for children. Furthermore, he knew that when Walpert Industries in Montreal approved the design of the red, green, and gold crackers, the panda bears did not wear swastikas. The swastikas, Walpert concluded, had been added by someone in China. But why?

Through his investigation, Walpert learned that the swastika, so negative in European cultures today, is a very old and positive Buddhist symbol of prosperity in Eastern cultures. In fact, the swastika has been used by many ancient cultures all over the world. In Greece, it is known as the G cross (*crux gammata*), because the Greek letter *gamma,* which looks like an upside-down L, appears as the four arms of the symbol. In Hindu culture, the swastika is associated with the god Ganesh.

Celts, Romans, and ancient Germanic peoples also used the swastika. In the early 20th century, English-speaking people believed it to be a good luck symbol, and the four L arms stood for luck, light, love, and life. The swastika also has been found in central Asia, as well as in Mayan and southwestern U.S. native cultures. The unauthorized addition of the swastika to the panda bears in the Christmas crackers was well-intentioned, not sabotage.

However, Martin Walpert's customers primarily saw the meaning of the swastika as negative, and his company has made sure that no more swastikas appear on its products.

The Importance of Learning about Cultures

Why learn about foreign cultures when you are doing business internationally? Because understanding others' cultures is important to success.

Understanding foreign cultures is not only important for companies that operate in more than one global area and market internationally. It is just as important for organizations at home that employ workers from more than one culture. Workplaces are increasingly multicultural around the world as employees are recruited globally. In the workplace, companies need to understand the cultural basis of behavior for everyone, and culture's role in the way people make meaning.

Understanding culture is also important for individuals who work in the global workplace. Often culture comes to our attention when something goes wrong at work. Something we feel is important seems to be overlooked or set aside. Or perhaps we know a little bit about another culture, but what we know makes us puzzled. We may hear people speak or see their actions and not comprehend it.

The two important reasons for understanding culture are to learn how others make sense of their environment, and to prevent mistakes and miscommunication.

Making Sense of Our World

An example of the challenge of making sense of our world occurred when Disney opened a theme park in Hong Kong that many visitors from China went to experience. In Hong Kong, children watch TV programs made by Disney, the American entertainment giant. For many years, Hong Kong children have grown up with these cartoon characters in their stories. Many characters are animals who act like humans—Donald Duck, Bugs Bunny, Mickey Mouse—and other characters come from children's stories and folklore, like Aladdin. But the people in mainland China were not familiar with the characters. The cartoon characters had not been on their TVs. They wandered around Hong Kong Disneyland unable to make sense of it. When they encountered people in the costumes of Disney characters, they were baffled.

A similar experience awaits visitors from Europe or North America who go to Dubai and visit the Ibn Battuta shopping mall. The largest themed mall in the world, it has six sectors, each representing a region Ibn Battuta visited in his unparalleled world travels: Andalusia, Tunisia, Egypt, Persia, India, and China. If you don't know who Ibn Battuta is, however, the costumed host who greets you will baffle you, or have no meaning. To make sense of the theme of the Dubai shopping mall, you need to know something about the culture.

In Focus

Ibn Battuta, a young Islamic law scholar, was curious to travel and learn about the world. Shortly after his 21st birthday in 1325, he set out on a journey to Mecca, on the Muslim pilgrimage called the *hajj*. He returned to his home in Tangiers, Morocco, 24 years later, after traveling through almost the whole of the Islamic world. He still wasn't finished, though. He made further journeys, only coming back to Morocco for good in 1354. He has been called "the world's greatest pre-modern traveler."[2]

Like many young adults, Ibn Battuta wanted to experience the world. However, unlike most students today, he traveled more than 75,000 miles, acquired a number of wives on the way, had narrow escapes from death and imprisonment, and served many of the 14th century's most important rulers.

Fortunately, he dictated his travels to a scholar named Ibn Juzayy, at the court of the Sultan of Morocco. The resulting book, *Rihla* (the Journey), tells how Ibn Battuta first went to Mecca through North Africa and Egypt, then to Syria and Palestine. His next journey was to Iraq and Mesopotamia, then back to Mecca again. Then he traveled to Yemen, Aden, Mombasa (in east Africa), Kulwa, Oman, Hormuz, Bahrain, and back to Mecca for his third *hajj*. His fourth itinerary was to have been to India, but instead he revisited Egypt and the Middle East, then modern Turkey, the Black Sea, and the southern Ukraine to Constantinople. Then he turned east and eventually crossed the Hindu Kush mountains into Afghanistan, Pakistan, and India. He next made a roundabout journey from Delhi to China, passing twice through the Maldives Islands in the Indian Ocean, and finally reaching Canton (southern China) via Sumatra (Indonesia), Malaya, and Cambodia. His long journey back from China took him to India, and then to Muscat (Oman), then through Iran, Iraq, Syria, Palestine, and Egypt, to Mecca again for his seventh and final *hajj*.

(continued)

When he arrived back in Tangier, he learned his mother had passed away in the Black Death pandemic. His father had died earlier. He decided to travel again, this time to Andalusia, the part of southern Spain under Muslim rule, and his final journey was by camel train across the Sahara to Niger and Timbuktu in central Africa.

Ibn Battuta described for Ibn Juzayy his culture shock, his impressions of the local scene, the people he met, and the ways of life he experienced. You can read more about him[3] and also watch trailers for the BBC television series about Ibn Battuta on YouTube.

Even if you haven't traveled to other countries, you may have met or observed people from other cultures and felt baffled. You may have been unable to figure out what their behavior meant or what meaning lay behind their symbols. If you haven't yet met people from other cultures in your work, you will. When you do, you will want to understand them. This is why we study culture. *Culture explains how people make sense of their world.*

The World Is Becoming Increasingly Diverse

All over the world, nations are experiencing more and more people from other cultures coming into their countries. Some people give newcomers a warm welcome. Some are less warm, but allow foreigners to thrive. Some reject those who come from a different culture. Tourism is expanding, migration is increasing, and people are moving in large numbers. Some governments (for example, Australia and the Netherlands) are proposing to manage immigration by having newcomers take tests to see how likely they are to fit into those nations. Other countries (Canada, for example) are trying to develop government policies to help immigrants keep their own cultures.

The United States has a long history of offering a home to people from many other countries. But in spite of its ideals of equality and tolerance, some people in the United States argue against allowing immigrants to keep their own language—in school, for instance. They say recognizing difference actually *separates* people, rather than enables people to tolerate others who are unlike them.

Because people from different cultures get jobs all over the world, you will experience cultural difference when you go to another country. At the same time, if you stay home, you will likely be working with people from other places and cultures. In order to do your job, you will need to make sense of other people's cultures.

People around the World ARE Different

People from different cultures really are different (as well as similar) in how they see the world. Cultures are the amazing products of human imagination, and that is a reason to celebrate differences. We people of this earth have created many interesting cultures throughout human history. They are a source of delight and wonder. The variety of cultures expresses what it means to be a human being.

Preventing Mistakes

The Walpert case that opened this chapter is one example of how a lack of cultural understanding can create problems for businesses. It also shows that cultural mistakes can be unconscious or unintentional, but damaging nevertheless.

Documented cultural mistakes in international business are easy to find on the Internet. The blunders-and-bloops literature is full of instances in which the error was fatal and the deal came apart, as well as instances in which the error was laughable. Many cases have led to a loss of business. The failures usually result because someone didn't understand the reasons why people think as they do and value what they do.

Today, businesses are looking for markets, suppliers, associates, partners, subsidiaries, joint-venture partners, customers, employees, and a favorable image in more than one country. Successful businesspeople must be able to communicate interculturally both at home and abroad.

Donald Hastings, chairman emeritus of Lincoln Electric, attributed many of his company's mistakes abroad to the attitude that since the company's practices were successful in the United States, they certainly would succeed in other countries.

In Focus

Donald Hastings had been chairman of Lincoln Electric, a leading manufacturer of arc-welding products, for only 24 minutes on the July day when he first learned the company was suffering huge losses in Europe. The losses meant the company might not be able to pay U.S. employees their expected annual bonuses. Since the bonus system was a key component of the manufacturer's success, with bonuses making up about half the U.S. employees' annual salary, this was a much more significant threat than simply a disappointing performance by the company. For the first time in its 75-year history, it looked like Lincoln would have to report a consolidated loss.

Lincoln Electric, based in Cleveland, Ohio, had expanded hugely, spending about $325 million to acquire foreign companies. But according to Hastings, lack of knowledge about the cultures of the acquired companies, and the cultures of the countries where they operated, was a critical factor in the company's financial nosedive.

First, the company didn't realize that a bonus system was not an incentive to European workers, who were hostile to the idea of competing with co-workers for their annual pay. Their pay scales were negotiated by labor leaders. The idea that some workers, based on individual performance, might earn more or less than the agreed income was unacceptable to European workers.

Second, Lincoln Electric learned that products not made in a European country would not be able to penetrate a European market that easily because of a cultural loyalty to domestically produced goods.

A third problem was that executives of the recently acquired European companies wanted to deal only with Lincoln's top executives, not with lower-level people sent over from Ohio. This status issue arose primarily in Germany, from the cultural characteristic of hierarchy in German culture.

A fourth cultural issue was that workers in Germany, France, and other European countries typically have a month of vacation in the summer, and so production gears down during that slow time. Lincoln wasn't used to that in its U.S. operation.

A fifth and fundamental problem was that nobody in the executive ranks at Lincoln had had international experience or had lived abroad. The Chief Executive Officer didn't even have a passport, and a last-minute panic occurred when the company scrambled to get one for him for an urgent trip to Europe. Finally, Hastings realized that he could not hope to bring Lincoln back to profitability without moving to Europe, where he could be at hand to deal with problems immediately, while learning what he and the other executives needed to know about that culture.

The U.S. workers of Lincoln Electric, who had been fully informed of the company's negative financial situation in Europe, rallied to help the company. Their enormous efforts paid off. At the same time, the chairman and executives painfully learned the lessons of culture they needed to know to operate overseas.[4]

Most businesspeople want to act appropriately and avoid offending their counterparts in foreign countries. They want to know what people in other cultures value, if only for the sake of making a sale. One researcher suggests that McDonald's is successful in 118 countries because it practices a localized approach. McDonald's succeeds because it offers what local people want.[5] That means being sensitive to the cultural needs of the immediate market.

Responding to Different Cultures

When members of different cultures find themselves face to face, a number of responses are possible. History shows that one response is to clash and struggle for dominance of one set of values over another. History also shows conflict is not the only result.

Contact and communication between people from different cultures is as old as human existence on earth. Consider, for example, the life of Moses (*Musa* in Arabic). Moses was born about 1228 B.C.E. when his mother, an Israelite, was a slave in a foreign country, Egypt. Her son was adopted into the family of the ruler, the Pharaoh. Thus, Moses was raised in two cultures. He married a woman from yet another culture, the culture of Midian, where he lived for eight to ten years. (Midian today is variously identified as southern Jordan or Ethiopia or northwest Saudi Arabia. In any case, the Midian culture was a different culture from either the culture of the Israelites or the culture of the Egyptians.)

According to some accounts, when Moses led the Jews out of Egypt, he and the children of Israel encountered Amalekites, Canaanites, Edomites, Ammonites, Moabites, and Midianites. Reports tell how Moses' people interacted with the people of these different cultures. Some encounters were in *battle* (Amalekites, Canaanites), some were in *making efforts to avoid hostility* (Edomites, Ammonites, Moabites at first), and some encounters involved sexual seduction by women (Midianites, whom the Israelites later slaughtered). The responses ranged from hostility to cooperation to close personal relationships.

Thus, the life of one person who lived long ago shows us that encounters with people from different cultures are not new, and neither are the various responses to difference. They have been going on even longer than records tell.

Hostility to Difference

Hostile responses to immigrants show up in the histories of many countries. Immigrants speak languages that may be unrelated to the host culture's languages; they may write in systems the hosts cannot decipher; they often have worldviews that have been developed without reference to the host culture. It is sometimes a shock to realize that far from wanting to become part of the dominant culture, some immigrants reject it out of fear they will lose their own culture. Immigration stories from every continent include experiences of hostility.

In the past few years, hostility toward immigrant groups has made the news in France, Belgium, Germany, Spain, and Italy, along with countries in the Middle East, Asia, and all the nations of the "new world."

In companies, too, people of one culture may experience hostility from people of another culture. But hostility is by no means the only inevitable response to members of other cultures.

Curiosity about Difference

Ibn Battuta was curious to experience other cultures. Seven hundred years later, people all over the world are still curious about people from other cultures. The Internet and sites like Facebook and YouTube bring us more closely together than ever before on a larger-than-ever stage. An open, respectful interest in learning about another culture motivates many people to connect around the globe and at work with members of other cultures.

In addition to satisfying one's curiosity, another reason to learn about a culture is to establish connections with people who think differently. Close personal relationships can endure between people from different cultures, to the mutual enrichment of both. Along with the connection may be a wish to compute the meanings of things by using a different mental operating environment and running different mental software. To connect with someone who is different is to affirm something that is importantly human.

Denying Difference

In some cultures, showing curiosity about difference is not good manners. Furthermore, some argue that emphasizing difference separates people, and does not help us get along with each other. They support a denial of difference, whether out of a misguided but well-meaning wish to avoid conflict, or out of fear and lack of skills for finding out about difference. Denial of difference is the opposite of curiosity.

> The productive way to respond to cultural difference is not to deny it exists, but to learn about difference and how to communicate about it.

Assumptions of Superiority

A common human response to differences in cultures is "Of course they're different, but we're better. If they really knew our culture, they'd prefer to be one of us."

English-speaking cultures encode this assumption of superiority by using words such as *backward* and *primitive* to criticize those whose cultures are different. Other languages have their own terms for the same thing. Of course, such evaluations are one cultural view, not an absolute assessment. They really say more about the person holding the opinion than about the persons being criticized.

For instance, the Japanese think of outsiders as barbarians; the Chinese call their country the Middle Kingdom and for centuries considered only Chinese to be "cooked" and all outsiders to be "raw" (uncivilized, because not familiar with the Chinese culture). Your culture has its terms for outsiders, and its attitudes—not always acknowledged—about the superiority of your culture. All groups tend to look at their own culture as superior, and others as inferior.

Ethnocentrism

"The Germans live in Germany, the Romans live in Rome, the Turks live in Turkey, but the English live at home."[6]

You generally can depend on this: Members of other cultures, deep down in their heart of hearts, are convinced their own culture is the *normal* one. People everywhere tend to assume their own culture has got things right, and they tend to assess all other cultures by how closely they resemble their own.

The *self-reference criterion* is an important concept that explains this behavior. Through the self-reference criterion, people tend to evaluate everything they see and experience on the basis of their own background and then act on their evaluations accordingly.[7] People in all cultures use this self-reference criterion in considering other cultures. It's a kind of mental comparison that goes on consciously and unconsciously.

Those with little experience of other cultures are especially inclined to believe that their own culture (ethnicity) is normative and at the center of human experience—hence *ethnocentrism*. The further from our own another culture is, the more it seems to belong on the fringe, to be peripheral and not normal. Conversely, the closer to our own culture another culture is, the truer it seems to be. Along with a preference for cultures that are similar to our own is the view that difference is dangerous. It threatens the norm. It's only a small step from there to viewing difference as dismissible, or even *wrong*.

For this reason, ethnocentrism can lead to a complacency about one's own culture, a lack of interest in understanding another culture, and actual discrimination against people of other cultures.

Assumptions of Universality

One of the comments people often hear from travelers to foreign countries is, "They may talk (dress, eat) differently, but underneath they're just like us." This notion is profoundly incorrect. People underneath are *not* alike. Culture is the whole view of the universe from which people assess the meaning of life and their appropriate response to it, and those views are not the same. Let's put this another way: People begin with different operating environments and run different software. They have different databases and process information differently, with different goals for their information processing. They arrive at different results.

To pretend we are all alike, or should be, can lead to miscommunication or failed communication. The future of businesses and indeed of the world may well depend upon people who think differently acting together.

Cooperating with Difference

Cultural differences don't prevent us from working together. We can communicate and have productive business relationships even though we are different. Indeed, we *must* work together.

Geert Hofstede, the Dutch researcher who laid the foundation for cross-cultural studies, advises: "The principle of surviving in a multicultural world is that one does not need to think, feel, and act in the same way in order to agree on practical issues and to cooperate."[8]

We can agree to be different and to celebrate diversity. The more we know about other cultures, the more we will know about our own. Then we can begin to explain why people from different cultures behave the way they do in business situations. Their behavior *will* differ even if their workplace is in the same culture.

When connections form between people from different cultures, similarities appear. Together we weave a fabric of cooperation, in which we see common threads. It is a source of delight to realize someone from a different culture has the same idea as you. It is very satisfying to connect in friendship and cooperation with someone who has a different culture but similar goals.

We don't have to become like people from other cultures. We don't have to adopt their customs. We don't even have to like them. But we do have to learn about what makes sense in their culture, and how to communicate effectively with them.

Three things are necessary in order to minimize and prevent mistakes across cultures. Knowledge about one's own culture is the first step. With this, knowledge about another culture is easier to learn. The second requirement is motivation—the drive to know and to use the knowledge. The third step is implementing knowledge, and behaving in a way that makes sense in the other culture, the one in which you want to do business.

Understanding Culture

Culture is difficult to define because it is a large and inclusive concept. Over 500 definitions of culture exist. Some are not helpful, because they are too general, such as "everything you need to know in life to get along in a society." Culture involves learned and shared behaviors, values, and material objects. It also encompasses what people create to express values, attitudes, and norms of behavior.

Culture is largely undiscussed by the members who share it. E. T. Hall wrote:

> Culture [is] those deep, common, unstated experiences which members of a given culture share, which they communicate without knowing, and which form the backdrop against which all other events are judged.[9]

Culture is like the water that fish swim in—a reality that is taken for granted and rarely examined. It is in the air we breathe and is as necessary to our understanding of who we are as air is to our physical life. Culture is the property of a community of people, not simply a set of characteristics of individuals. Societies are shaped by culture, and that shaping comes from similar life experiences and similar interpretations of what those experiences mean.

If culture is mental software, it is also a mental map of reality. It tells us from early childhood what matters, what to prefer, what to avoid, and what to do. Culture also tells us what ought to be.[10] It gives us assumptions about the ideal beyond what individuals may experience. It helps us in setting priorities. It establishes codes for behavior and provides justification and legitimization for that behavior.

In order to understand another culture, you need to understand your own. Culture determines business practices, for instance. Business practices are not neutral or value-free. Neither are communication practices. You need to understand the cultural values you transmit when you interact with someone from another culture, as well as understand the other person's cultural values. You also need to recognize the likelihood that there will be gaps in your comprehension, and holes instead of connections, in your interaction.

From among the many definitions of culture, here is the definition this book will use.

> **Culture is the coherent, learned, shared view of a group of people about life's concerns, expressed in symbols and activities, that ranks what is important, furnishes attitudes about what things are appropriate, and dictates behavior.**

This definition merits a closer examination. First, it contains three characteristics of culture—coherent, learned, and shared—and then it outlines three things that culture does.

Culture Is Coherent

Each culture, past or present, is coherent and complete within itself—an entire view of the universe. A pioneer researcher into the study of cultures, Edward Tylor, said in 1871 that culture is:

> . . . the outward expression of a unifying and consistent vision brought by a particular community to its confrontation with such core issues as the origins of the cosmos, the harsh unpredictability of the natural environment, the nature of society and humankind's place in the order of things.[11]

The fact that different groups of human beings at different times in history could develop different visions is a cause for wonder. Often, as we shall see, different cultures develop different behaviors but have similar visions. The incredible variety of cultures fascinates historians, anthropologists, travelers, and nearly everybody else. It makes all our lives richer when we glimpse, and even claim, a bit of this treasure of human achievement.

Regardless of how peculiar a fragment or single thread of a culture seems, when it is placed within the whole tapestry of the culture, it makes sense.

The completeness of cultures also means that members looking out from their own seamless view of the universe probably do not see anything lacking in their unifying and consistent vision. This is the source of ethnocentrism.

Here is a hypothetical case to illustrate the coherence of culture. Let's imagine that a boat full of south-coast Chinese sets sail for San Francisco, which has been known as "Old Gold Mountain" in China from the 19th century, a place where immigrants can acquire gold. But a storm blows the boat off course and wrecks the navigation instruments. Eventually the Chinese make landfall off the coast of

Mexico, although they don't know where they are. It is the last week of October, much later than their intended arrival in San Francisco. They wearily go ashore to the nearest town. To their horror and dismay, in every store window and every home's doorway are images of skeletons, skulls, and graves. In China, death is not mentioned, let alone broadcast by images everywhere. "What sort of people live here?" they ask each other.

The Chinese voyagers have arrived in Mexico at the time of *el Dia de los Muertos,* the Day of the Dead. It is a fiesta with deep meaning for Mexican families. It emphasizes family ties that reach beyond the grave, as departed family members are remembered and brought to join the living family through a celebration. The skulls and skeletons in the windows are made of candy and bread, and are meant to be eaten, to show how unimportant death is, and how the people are not afraid of death as the end of family relationships.

In fact, the Chinese traditionally hold a celebration with a similar objective, called *Qing Ming,* on the fifth day of the fourth month, or April 5. They too visit the graves of departed family members to reaffirm their family union in spite of death. If the Chinese were able to learn *why* Mexicans display skulls and skeletons everywhere, they would understand the Mexicans' attitudes toward death symbols. But if they were to see only the cultural fragment—a bit of behavior—they would regard it as bizarre, unnatural, and odious.

Culture Is Learned

Culture is not something we are born with; rather, it is *learned.* Much of what is learned about one's own culture is stored in mental categories that are recalled only when they are challenged by something different. We all have to be taught our culture. The process begins immediately after birth—and perhaps even earlier, according to some.

If culture is learned, it is also *learnable.* That means nobody has to remain for a lifetime locked inside only one culture. If you want to understand other cultures, you can learn them—not just learn about them but actually get inside them and act according to what is expected. Many people have learned more than one culture and can move comfortably within and among them. When circumstances dictate, they make the transition from one culture to another easily. Businesses don't have to accept failure in another culture simply because they do not have an employee who grew up in that culture.

This book is about how to learn other cultures. We believe it is not only possible to do so but also interesting, rewarding, and necessary.

Culture Is the View of a Group of People

A culture is shared by a society. Members of the society agree about the meanings of things and about the *why.* Along with everyone from whom they have learned their culture—family, teachers, spiritual leaders, peers, and legal, political, and educational institutions—they have interpreted life experiences in ways that validate their own culture's views. They agree about what the important things are—the things that truly merit respect. They agree without having to talk about it.

Societies are motivated by common views, which are a dynamic force enabling them to achieve goals such as protecting economic resources and developing alliances.

People in a culture share symbols of that culture. The most obvious set of symbols is language. Much more will be said about the role of language (in Chapter 2) and communication (later in this chapter). Visual symbols such as company logos, icons, religious images, and national flags form the visual vocabulary of a culture.

Thus, the three characteristics of culture are that it is coherent, learned, and shared. Now we'll look at three things culture does.

Culture Ranks What Is Important

Cultures rank what is important. In other words, cultures teach **values** or priorities.

What is of paramount importance to one group may be virtually meaningless to another. For instance, consider the amassing of wealth. In one Pacific Island culture, the Guru rumba of Papua New Guinea, a rich man is required to expend all the fortune he has spent long years accumulating—in this case, pigs—in the lavish entertainment of the members of his society. Being able to entertain this way is the real meaning of wealth, because it means that the giver is owed and therefore has great prestige. Try to explain that to a businessperson in the United States or Hong Kong or Italy who has spent his or her life amassing monetary wealth! Usually in these cultures, resources are saved and increased, not depleted in one big blowout. To be sure, businesspeople in these cultures often make generous charitable and philanthropic donations, but their cultures teach them to value personal wealth as something to cultivate, like a garden, and make it grow.

The term *values* crops up frequently in books about intercultural business, as does the term *attitude*. What is the difference? Values are standards we use to judge what is important. Values are mental constructs that underlie specific attitudes and that determine attitudes as well as behavior. They enable us to *evaluate* what matters to us or apply standards to our attitudes and behaviors. People go to war over values and conduct business by values.

Because values tell us how to weigh the worth of something, they indicate a relative hierarchy. We can talk about values as cultural priorities. Within a culture, values may be of greater or lesser importance. For example, a culture may

In Focus

A story is told of the Sultan of Brunei, one of the world's wealthiest men, who was shopping in a department store in Manhattan. When he made a purchase, he was asked for identification. However, he carried no identification. "I'm the Sultan of Brunei," he stated. The salesperson insisted that he had to show identification. A quick-thinking aide to the sultan darted forward, put his hand in his pocket, and pulled out a bill in the currency of Brunei. All the money in Brunei has the Sultan's picture on it. What values in the Brunei culture does this story suggest?

put a high value on honesty and a low value on making only a minimal effort. Values or priorities vary from culture to culture: Progress reports about the delivery of a component may be of great value to a Dutch firm associated with a business in Japan but of little value to a Japanese firm awaiting the delivery of a component from Holland.

Culture Furnishes Attitudes

Attitudes are learned tendencies to respond to phenomena (events, people, experiences) in a consistent way. Attitudes are feelings, positive or negative, about something, based on values. Attitudes can change, although changing some attitudes can be difficult. You can have an attitude toward eating raw fish, for example, that is positive and is based on the belief that expert preparation of *sushi* and *sashimi* by Japanese chefs results in culinary delicacies. Or you may have an attitude that is negative, based on the belief that raw fish can contain parasites that cause unpleasant consequences in the human digestive system. You can even hold both attitudes at the same time. If you do, you probably *value* both fine eating experiences and physical health.

Attitudes are based on beliefs as well as on values. **Beliefs** are convictions or certainties that come from subjective and often personal ideas rather than on proof or fact. **Belief systems,** or religions, are powerful sources of values and attitudes in cultures. We will look at religions in more detail in Chapter 3.

Attitudes vary according to how important something is (its value). In Mexican culture, when an aunt dies, the family expects that business associates understand the family has suffered a significant event. A boss is expected to have an understanding attitude toward an employee who is unable to get a report done by the deadline because of the funeral and family needs. In Britain, the attitude toward a business associate's loss of an aunt is that this is a private affair, regrettable and perhaps very sad, but something that may not affect the relative's ability to get a report done by the deadline. In fact, for a businessperson in the UK, handling the situation well means keeping it from having an impact on work.

Culture Dictates How to Behave

Behavior refers to actions. To continue the example in the previous discussion, a brief expression of sympathy by a businessperson to a bereaved work associate is appropriate British behavior. Co-workers may send a card, if they have worked together for a time. In Mexico, in contrast, much more than an expression of sympathy is appropriate behavior. Business associates may attend the funeral, send flowers, offer services such as transporting family members, and visit the family's home to show respect.

Behavior comes directly from attitudes about how significant something is—how it is valued. Values drive actions. We're back at the point made earlier: Cultural priorities motivate business behavior.

In intercultural interactions, cultural differences usually make themselves known first by behavior, which is related to attitudes and which springs from values in the culture.

Table 1.1 illustrates briefly how values, attitudes, and behaviors are related.

TABLE 1.1
Relationship of
Values, Attitudes,
and Behavior

Value	Attitude	Behavior
Honesty	Telling lies is wrong.	Lying
Family	Family events come first.	Choosing to attend a family party rather than go out with friends
Status	High status means one has better control over events and people.	Dressing expensively to show high status
Achievement	Achievement deserves praise.	Giving recognition for an accomplishment
Harmony	Dissent causes disruption in groups.	Refraining from disagreeing

In Focus

A Japanese employee in Tokyo has not written a report that's due to his boss. The deadline has arrived. The situation is that problems at home with his wife have encouraged him to spend his evenings drinking with fellow employees and going home very late. The result is a raging hangover that makes him unable to concentrate on writing the report. He goes to his boss and explains all this. For the Japanese worker, neither the excessive drinking nor the domestic problem is a source of shame, and his expectation is that the superior's attitude will be acceptance and a paternalistic concern for the employee's plight. The superior's behavior is probably to counsel the employee and inquire into the domestic situation in subsequent weeks.[12]

When this scenario is presented to businesspeople in the United States, however, their reaction is that an employee who explained that he had failed to complete a report because of a hangover from excessive drinking (whether or not it was to escape domestic problems) probably would be in double trouble with his superior. He would be criticized for drinking too much, and for not completing the report on time.

In the United States, the superior's behavior would probably be to tell the employee to get a grip on himself and seek some help, or else expect unpleasant consequences. The employee in the United States may be just as debilitated by a hangover as his Japanese counterpart, but he will offer some other reason for not being able to get the report done. He may stay home, telling the boss he's ill.

The Japanese employee with a hangover illustrates the *value* of group membership: The employee goes out drinking with co-workers and expects his boss to be sympathetic to his family problems. Another *value* is hierarchy: The boss is in the position of parent or counselor, one who has the ability to forgive a missed deadline. An *attitude* is the way the employee views his own situation regarding the missed deadline and his hangover: It couldn't be helped because he is struggling with problems at home, and his excessive drinking is excusable (another attitude) because he has these problems. A *behavior* is drinking until late at night with co-workers.

Onstage and Backstage Elements of Culture

Onstage culture is the behavior we display. It is what people who are in contact with one another find easiest to observe and discuss. Onstage culture involves actions such as shaking hands, bowing, or kissing upon meeting. It includes traditional ways of celebrating with food and dances, costumes and music. When people are asked to describe another culture, they often refer to onstage behavior.

By contrast, *backstage* culture is not so visible. Backstage culture is values. Backstage culture underlies what others see onstage. The actors themselves are not always aware that their onstage behavior is culturally driven; they think their backstage culture is simply normal. Backstage cultural aspects include the ways people make decisions, respond to deadlines, accomplish tasks, rank events by importance, and conceptualize knowledge. If you can explain backstage behavior, you understand the *why* of culture.

In Japan, a foreign observer can see young people who dress like young people in the United States or Western Europe, listen to the same music, and go to the same new cinema releases. Onstage images are virtually interchangeable. The backstage cultures of Japan, the United States, and Western Europe, however, are very different. A foreign observer can misattribute reasons for onstage behavior, thinking the reasons are the same in different cultures because the observable behaviors *look* the same.

The *why* is the essence of a people's culture. If you understand why people value some things, you can make good guesses about why they value other things. If you understand why they behave a certain way, you can interpret other behavior with some degree of accuracy. Once you have insight into what people think is important and how they behave, you can do business with them. You know what makes them the way they are.

Transactional Cultures

What happens onstage when members of different cultures interact? What do we see? Does each person act out a script for behavior that is from his or her culture?

Sometimes this is exactly what happens. A person initiates an exchange that is based on expectations that come from his or her backstage culture. The following provides an example.

A businessperson from Saudi Arabia, who wants to show willingness to get to know a businessperson from England, stands close during a conversation. The English person politely maintains a distance to show respect for the Saudi. A kind of dance results in which the conversing pair move across a room. The English person backs up and the Saudi moves forward.

In another example, at an initial meeting a Mexican businessman holds out his hand to shake a Japanese businessman's hand, while the Japanese simultaneously attempts to bow toward the Mexican. We can see that each is following a script from his own culture.

But keep watching the stage. What we are likely to see next is that the Japanese quickly holds out his hand, while the Mexican attempts a bow. What happens onstage when members of different cultures interact may be *different* from their usual behavior in their own cultures. The new behavior may be temporary, compared with their enduring backstage cultures.

Consider, for example, the experience of several Western businesspeople who had taken seminars to prepare them for negotiating business deals in Saudi Arabia. As they sat down at the negotiating table, they heard the Saudi executive say,

"We can do business either the Western way or the Arab way. What's your choice?"[13] The Saudi was talking about onstage cultural adaptation, or in other words, creating a *transactional culture.*

A transactional culture exists when interactants respond to cultural cues and modify their own behavior, creating—or co-creating—a new, temporary culture. In this transactional culture, the participants can perform behaviors and act upon attitudes that are shaped primarily by the interaction. The context of the interaction becomes more important for molding actions than the individuals' cultural backgrounds. Transactional culture exists when interactants are sensitive to, and knowledgeable about, another culture, and adjust their behavior. The amount of adjusted behavior depends on several factors, including their level of knowledge about the other culture, their willingness to experiment with new behaviors and attitudes, and their previous experience with successful intercultural interactions.

For instance, a Canadian businessman may put his hands together at the palms, fingers up, to give a *wai* greeting to a Thai businessman, although the Canadian would not *wai* to a fellow Canadian. A Taiwanese businesswoman with experience of Brazilian culture may kiss the cheek of a Brazilian businessman at their first meeting but would not kiss the cheek of a Taiwanese man or woman. They have learned to act as if they were members of the other culture when interacting with the other party. Transactional cultural behaviors are transitory and last only as long as the interactants are involved in communication together.

Adopting Another Culture's Behavior

When members of a culture adapt permanently to another culture, they function as members of that culture. They may retain their old culture, but it is not activated either backstage or onstage, until they are again with members of their original culture. Adopting a new culture has historical precedents, as Kongo shows.

In Focus

In the year 578, a carpenter named Kongo, with special skills in constructing temples made of wood traveled, from Korea to Japan. He and his sons began constructing the Shitennoji temple in Osaka for the emperor. Over succeeding generations, sons worked with fathers from the Kongo family in the business of building Buddhist temples and Shinto shrines in Japan for successive emperors.

Today, the company, Kongo Gumi, is still going strong following the calling of *miyadaiku* (temple builders). They continue to be the carpenters who maintain the Shitennoji temple. The current chief executive, Masakazu Kongo, says that as the only son he wasn't allowed to go skydiving or do anything that might endanger his ability to carry on the family business, which is thought to be the oldest continuous family business in the world.

The company is strong, and in a modern twist, the CEO looks forward to having the more than 1,400-year-old family business carried on—by his oldest daughter![14]

Some sources for intercultural communication offer lists of behavioral dos and taboos as guides for success in other cultures. These lists are popular and offer some pragmatic help, such as this one governing nonverbal communication:

- Never refuse an offer of coffee from a businessman in Kuwait.
- Be very careful not to point the sole of your foot at someone in Thailand.
- Remove your jacket and work in shirtsleeves in Japan only after your Japanese colleagues do so first.
- Never help yourself to food when you are the guest of honor at a banquet in China.
- Do not become irritated if you find yourself waiting half an hour or more for an appointment with a businessperson from Venezuela.
- Use business courtesies in Dubai, such as shaking hands when introduced, except when females are involved.
- Do not offer your host gifts for his wife or children when doing business in Saudi Arabia.
- Plan to spend about two hours on lunch in France.

Dos and taboos lists are usually accurate, but their helpfulness is limited because they focus only on onstage behavior. One-sentence advice on behavior is like seeing a snapshot from a movie. It is accurate, but without the context of the whole movie, the snapshot's significance may not be understandable. Lists of dos and taboos don't explain *why* you should or should not behave in a particular way in a particular place. They don't tell you anything about backstage behavior. Even if a business traveler has a very long list, who can consult a list for every situation in every different country?

Once you begin to build a picture of a culture's priorities, you can draw fairly accurate deductions about what kind of behavior will be offensive and what kind will be pleasing. Chapters 3 and 4 discuss what questions to ask to gain an understanding of a culture that will enable you to do business effectively.

Culture Shock

Culture shock is an inevitable result of immersion in a new and unfamiliar culture. It happens to everybody. It's important to know that culture shock and its symptoms are normal and to be expected.

Culture shock is the sense of dislocation and the problems—psychological and even physical—that result from the stress of trying to make the hundreds of adjustments necessary for living in a foreign culture. Actually, the term *culture shock* is not accurate, because it refers to a range of responses that take place over time. However, it isn't a single jolt. Culture shock is experienced in four stages.

The first stage of experiencing a new culture is usually **euphoria.** Everything about the exciting new adventure is wonderful. This stage generally lasts no longer than two weeks, and some people skip it altogether. Some short-visit travelers go home before they have progressed to the next stage. All who stay for more than a short visit go on to the second stage.

The second stage is a downturn as **disillusionment and frustration** arise. This is usually the stage people refer to when they use the term *culture shock.* It is a feeling of not being in step with the members of the culture. It results from finding out that there are inadequacies in your understanding, your mental road map for navigating this new culture. You don't know what you don't know. Finding out what you don't know is exhausting, even when it is also exciting. Inevitably, there are disappointments in yourself and in others; inevitably, you make mistakes. When the adjustment to a new culture means an upward change in status, people feel good about the new culture. When the adjustment means a downward change in status, people quickly feel unhappy.

Most sojourners—travelers who stay for a longer time than a few days—experience psychological symptoms of culture shock. Some people find themselves becoming depressed. They may experience long periods of homesickness. Some are very lonely and may get involved in relationships that they wouldn't form if they were in their own culture. Nearly all sojourners and temporary residents in a new culture experience dissatisfaction with the way things are. Things that seemed acceptable when they first arrived become irritations. Sojourners can become aggressive and exhibit unpleasant behavior that they would not use at home. They may get angry easily and express hostility and suspicion toward members of the host culture. Frequently, culture shock shows itself when sojourners believe that native members of the culture are trying to take advantage of them—to overcharge them, for example—because they are foreign.

Physical symptoms also can result from this stage of culture shock. They include aches and pains in limbs, headaches, chronic fatigue and lack of energy, loss of appetite, inability to get a good night's sleep, stomach upsets, and frequent colds or flu. This stage can last longer than the first euphoric stage—perhaps months.

The third stage is **adjustment.** As the sojourner learns more about the backstage culture and how the other culture works, he or she is able to cooperate more effectively with members of the host culture. Some successes occur, and solutions are found for some of the problems that seemed so hard to resolve in stage two. At this stage, business probably can be conducted successfully.

The fourth stage, **integration,** occurs when a sojourner becomes fluent enough in the other culture to move easily within it and not be thrown by the different attitudes, beliefs, and values, and the behaviors they generate. Often, linguistic fluency helps to get to this stage. Now the sojourner is able to identify with the host culture.

Most people who work, live, study, or visit for any length of time in another culture, regardless of the length of the stay, experience all four stages of culture shock. Furthermore, the longer one stays, the more cycles one goes through. The fourth stage, in which one feels comfortable in the new culture, leads to another euphoric stage, followed by frustration and disappointment, followed by adjustment, and so on.[15]

Reverse Culture Shock

A similar adjustment period with its accompanying symptoms usually occurs when a sojourner returns home. This is often called reverse culture shock. People often don't realize that it is normal. After all, it's somewhat ironic: The sojourner has been longing to return to the old, familiar culture of home. But once home, the sojourner finds many things to criticize and often asks why the old culture can't be more like the one so recently encountered. Friends and family members typically find the traveler impatient with things that never used to cause complaint. Another factor in reverse culture shock is that nobody wants to hear about the wonderful adventure the sojourner has had.

Returnees find that people at home have had new experiences, too, and the returnee must adjust. Things have changed at the company, and people have been promoted, achieved successes, retired, left for another employer, and so forth. The returnee is something of an outsider even after returning "home" and may have a new job to get used to as well as new contacts to make. Returnees feel they have been working for the sake of the corporation, usually at some (nonmonetary) cost and personal sacrifice, but upon returning, often they feel they are not valued. Some companies provide mentors and training programs to ease re-entry.

Businesspeople who return from years abroad often feel they have a greater problem with reverse culture shock than they had with culture shock when they were adjusting to the other culture. It may be that an inverse relationship exists between the ease of adjustment to living in an unfamiliar culture and the degree of reverse culture shock: The easier it is to adjust initially to a foreign culture, the harder it is to readjust to home.

The discussion of culture shock leads us to a key aspect of understanding cultures: self-knowledge.

Self-Knowledge and Understanding One's Own Culture

As we have seen, the best response to cultural diversity for communication across cultures is openness. The same openness needs to be applied to oneself and one's own culture. Sun Tzu, the Chinese martial philosopher, said about 2,000 years ago:

Know yourself; know your enemies: One hundred battles; one hundred victories.

Researchers have shown that having a good understanding of one's own culture's values, attitudes, and behaviors—including communication behavior—is the best foundation for developing the ability to understand the communication behavior of people from other cultures.

If you know what your own culture believes is normal and natural, you will be able to figure out where other people's ideas are different, and what is behind other people's behavior. You will be less likely to judge other cultural values as inferior to yours, but will see them simply as different. You won't be surprised at different behavior.

Knowing one's self is not simple. As Hall says in describing a man in a foreign environment, "The more that lies behind his actions . . . , the less he can tell you."[16] For example, take an accountant. She operates with mental processes and parameters that she learned through accounting courses and through practice; they constitute her mental software about accounting. But she uses a set of values and ideas about how to act that are not only part of the accountancy software in her mind but

In Focus

What is "normal" business attire? (Also see Chapter 7.) In Indonesia, a businessman wears a loose cotton shirt over pants. A male proprietor of a small firm may not wear pants at all, but a skirt-like wrap. In Saudi Arabia, a businessman wears a long robe over his trousers and shirt, while in Japan a businessman wears a dark suit with a white shirt. In each of these countries, expectations are that a serious, responsible businessman in that culture will dress like that.

Businessmen from the United States often dress informally, in sweaters and slacks or in short-sleeved shirts without jackets. When they are in very warm countries they may wear shorts for leisure activities. This attire can be acceptable in certain situations, but it also can appear disrespectful toward the other culture's attitudes.

Recently, a U.S. automobile parts manufacturer was shown on television trying to make a sale to some Japanese automobile firms. He was dressed in a boldly patterned cardigan sweater; his hosts were all in dark suits and white shirts. The camera caught one of the host party, a woman, repeatedly looking at his sweater with something like alarm in her eyes and looking away again. The sweater could indeed have been a factor in his reported failure to get a single sale.

The salesman in this episode was acting in accordance with ideas about dress that seemed appropriate to him from his cultural windows. He may have considered the informality of his dress as signaling a willingness to put aside rigid rules of behavior and be friendly. He may have been cold and enjoyed the warmth of a large sweater. He may have spent the previous 20 hours on a plane without a chance to change his clothes and may have gone straight to the trade show because, to him, being there was more important than being dressed a certain way.

also part of the larger operating environment of unconsciously held values, attitudes, and behaviors from her society. It's easier for her to look at what makes up her view of accounting than to look at what makes up her view of life.

Most people assume that what they take for granted as *natural* and *normal* is what everyone on the planet also considers natural and normal. Most people discover only when they come into contact with something different that the ideas they hold as absolute truths are actually culture-based positions. At the same time, to assume that you know how someone else is thinking based on how you see things is called *projected cognitive similarity*. It occurs when you think you know someone else's perceptions, judgments, attitudes, and values because you assume they are like your own. In other words, it is an example of the self-reference criterion that was discussed earlier. Assuming you know what someone else is thinking can lead to disrupted communication and even conflict. Even when people may agree on goals—for example, the corporate goals of an organization—they may expect to reach those goals by different methods.

Mental Representations

One way of understanding our own culture, as well as another, is to use mental categories that hold information items grouped together.

Mental representations change with the introduction of new information. They are dynamic and can be altered to form new mental categories as more data come in. Everyone has a large data bank of mental representations. To understand yourself, you need to be aware of your own data bank and its categories. Then, when you encounter someone from another culture, you can understand how your mental category is being transformed by reality. You can be open to new awareness and have a dynamic experience of the transformation of your mental categories.

Even incomplete, sketchy mental representations that are based on objective observation usually contain some truth. That's why they can be useful: for example, "Latin American businesspeople often talk about their families before getting down to business"; "Japanese negotiators use silence a lot more than Europeans do."

Generalizations like these have some kinship with stereotypes, which are discussed in Chapter 3.

Prejudice

Generalizations that are based on limited knowledge, and that express an *evaluation—usually negative*—are **prejudices**. In other words, they are *prejudgments*. They come from people who make up their minds before they have all the facts. "Chinese always give you a fish-eye look; they don't feel any emotion"; "Irish have hot tempers and get angry easily; they can be really difficult to deal with." It may be one's experience that Chinese people do not show emotion readily, but that doesn't equal *coldness,* which is a negative evaluation. It is judging Chinese character, not simply observing behavior. It may be one's experience that Irish people easily find words to express emotion. But *hot-tempered* is a negative judgment. Prejudice, or prejudging before all the facts are known, is leaping to an evaluative conclusion, usually based on limited knowledge, without gathering information about the individual, the culture, and the context.

Prejudice often is accompanied by suspicion, fear, hatred, or contempt. Business communicators need to be aware of prejudices and consciously avoid acting on them.

Racism is one form of prejudice that leads to behavior that excludes or sidelines people on the basis of their perceived race. Sexism is another. *Ageism* is prejudice in favor of younger or older individuals that leads to older workers' being laid off or not hired because of their age, or causes favoritism of older people to the exclusion of younger, less experienced workers. *Homophobia* is a term usually used to mean prejudice against homosexuals, although it really means a phobia or irrational fear of being sexually aroused by someone from the same sex. It leads to the persecution and exclusion of homosexuals at work.

These prejudices are carried into intercultural business dealings. Not only are they often unrecognized by the people that have them, but in foreign surroundings people's prejudices can come to the forefront. People who would not allow themselves to express their prejudices in their own culture may do so in an unfamiliar culture. This is a well-documented result of culture shock, as was discussed earlier.

Eighty years ago the social psychologist E. S. Bogardus began to research the effects of prejudice. In an interesting experiment, he asked people to rate, on a social distance scale from 1 to 8, how favorably they felt toward groups of people according to their national identity.[17] The most favorable rating, number 1, indicated a willingness to have a daughter or son marry someone of that group. An 8 meant not being willing to allow someone of that group into the country, let alone into one's home. The interesting thing was that the list of more than 60 nations included three fictitious ones: Danireans, Pireneans, and Wallonians. Bogardus found that the people who were unwilling to admit members of other, known nations also were unwilling to admit members of the unknown nations. Conversely, tolerance toward people of many nations included tolerance toward the three unknown (and nonexistent) nationalities. This finding suggests that intolerant people are intolerant across the board, and tolerant people are tolerant even of members of unknown countries.

Bias

We all have biases, and we are ready to acknowledge many of them. You may have a bias toward tough disciplinary measures for dealing with those who break the rules, a bias toward a work environment where the superior is approachable and low-key, or a bias toward a four-day workweek. A bias *for* something is really nothing more than a preference. A bias *against* something is a negative attitude that ranks it low. Many biases are recalled from long-term memory only when forced by an external challenge. For instance, you may not realize you have a bias against French cars or lime-flavored soft drinks until you are given no other choice at a car rental agency or restaurant.

Studies of job interviews show that interviewers are biased toward interviewees who appear to come from their own cultural background—who have an accent that indicates membership in the same ethnic group, for example. When other factors remain constant, the accent is the factor that determines which candidate gets the job from which interviewer.[18] In this case, the bias has an easily understandable basis; we prefer what is known and familiar because it poses little threat. Those who understand the self-reference criterion discussed earlier and who are open to making adjustments in their evaluations are likely to become more aware of their own cultures while they are learning about other cultures.

We need to be aware of our biases and be open to changing them. In addition, we need to be ready to discover unrecognized biases within us that can influence the way we understand another culture.

Discrimination

When biases or prejudices are *acted on,* the actor is showing discrimination. Discrimination is the act of sifting out and selecting according to bias toward something or someone, and treating them differently. We say someone has "discriminating taste" as a compliment because that person is able to sift carefully through a mass of items and identify the best. To be undiscriminating is to lack judgment and be unable to discern the best from the second best or the inferior. In the United States, discrimination became a widely used term for racism, the identification of others as worse based solely on their perceived racial membership. Discrimination occurs in all cultures, where negative behavior is shown toward groups.

Cultural Intelligence

Anyone with some experience of another culture has observed that people are not alike in how well they adapt to another culture. Even those who show sensitivity and delicacy when interacting with people in their own culture may fail to show the same ability to adapt in a new culture. *Cultural Intelligence* (*CQ*) is the term some have used to explain how certain people seem able to fit into another culture more easily than others.

> Cultural Intelligence is the capability of an individual to learn and understand another culture and then act accordingly.

It is called CQ because of an analogy to reasoning-based and logic-based intelligence that is measured on tests to achieve a numerical score expressed as a quotient. Logic-based intelligence is called IQ, which stands for Intelligence Quotient.

Psychologists also recognize different kinds of human intelligence. These include:

- EQ (Emotional Intelligence, the ability to read others' and one's own emotions and act accordingly)
- SQ (Social Intelligence, the ability to understand social needs and expectations, and act accordingly)
- PQ (Practical Intelligence, the ability to accomplish daily living tasks efficiently and effectively)

Furthermore, studies have shown the definitions of intelligence are culturally defined.

Cultural intelligence, "a person's capability for successful adaptation to new cultural settings, has three main components."[19] We have already encountered these three components on page 9. They are the necessary components to have in order to understand another's environment and prevent cultural mistakes:

- **Cognition**, or thinking processes, including knowledge about the culture and about what to do in a new culture
- **Motivation**, or desire to adapt successfully
- **Behaviors**, or appropriate actions

Exhibit 1.1 shows the CQ model.

CQ has three main components: (1) *cognition* involving both knowledge about a culture and knowledge about how things are done that together enable one to think and solve cultural problems, (2) *motivation* to adapt to a new culture, and (3) *application,* putting one's desire to adapt and one's knowledge and ability to solve cultural problems into action. In summary, knowledge, desire to adapt, and behavior appropriate to the new culture together make up cultural intelligence.

Obviously, for people whose work takes them to other countries, high CQ is valuable. These are people who get along well. They pick up on what is important

EXHIBIT 1.1
Model of Cultural
Intelligence (CQ)

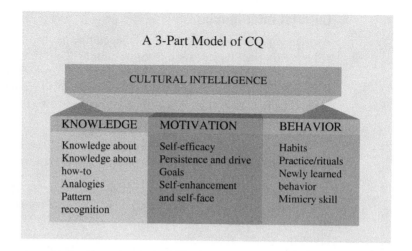

A 3-Part Model of CQ

CULTURAL INTELLIGENCE

KNOWLEDGE	MOTIVATION	BEHAVIOR
Knowledge about Knowledge about how-to Analogies Pattern recognition	Self-efficacy Persistence and drive Goals Self-enhancement and self-face	Habits Practice/rituals Newly learned behavior Mimicry skill

(values) and what the cultural attitudes are, and they learn to behave according to the expectations of that culture. Because they adapt successfully, they also manage to accomplish many of their goals in the new culture.

The Question of Change in Cultures

Are Cultures Merging into One Global Culture?

Predictions often are made in the popular business press that all cultures are becoming alike. However, the evidence does not suggest that one global culture will one day dominate the planet.

A glance at the events in recent decades in the former Yugoslavia shows how far ethnic groups are willing to go to defend their cultures. Yugoslavia was created in 1929 when the kingdoms of Serbs, Croats, and Slovenes that had come together after World War I changed their name to Yugoslavia. After World War II, the country was ruled by a communist government under Marshall Tito. But following Tito's death and the end of Soviet rule in Eastern Europe in 1991, individual cultural groups began to break away: Slovenia, Croatia, and Macedonia each splintered off, followed by Bosnia-Herzegovina in 1992. Today, all these groups are independent of Yugoslavia. Although Serbia and Montenegro, original components of Yugoslavia, tried unsuccessfully to coerce the others militarily into a Greater Serbia, today they stand alone. They also used armed force to expel cultural Albanians from the Serbian province of Kosovo, prompting international military intervention. Today, Kosovo is governed by a United Nations mission, but old cultural divisions continue to disrupt the governance of the state. Cultural priorities lead people into devastating armed conflict because of the strength of their allegiance to their cultures. Cultural divisions can last centuries.

Clashes of cultures are not always bloody. French Canadians who wanted to defend their culture nearly succeeded in separating from the rest of Canada in 1995 when a national referendum on the question failed by a tiny margin: less than half of 1 percent. As societies achieve more economic stability, rallying around their cultures seems to increase in importance, not decrease. In spite of spreading global technology, in spite of the availability of the same consumer goods in many countries, and even in spite of changing tastes and fads that sweep from continent to continent, the deep values of cultures remain unchanged.

Europe gives us examples, too. For example, observers in 2007–8 saw Belgium come close to breaking apart into two nations, one Flemish-speaking and the other French-speaking. Regarding the larger region, countries in the European Union still exhibit a desire to protect national cultures. For instance, the French have blocked the purchase by Italy of a French utility, in the name of national security and interest. Since countries want to protect their own labor pools, the EU is finding labor mobility a tricky issue. The EU won rulings in the World Trade Organization (WTO) that uphold the protection of brand names associated with specific national locations, including Parma ham from the Italian province of Parma, and *feta* cheese from Greece. Thus, national cultures so far are not disappearing into one European culture.

Ever-Changing Popular Taste

Much is written about the constant change cultures undergo. Global companies such as Pepsi, Sony, and Microsoft are said to be changing cultures. It is true that *popular taste* changes; fads come and go, especially in the marketplace, which is driven by changing tastes. Korean students who think of McDonald's as a Korean restaurant are no less Korean because they eat fast food that originated in the United States. Sufferers from migraine headaches in Argentina who consult acupuncturists are no less Argentine for seeking a traditional Chinese treatment. These are instances of popular taste.

Popular culture, which includes consumer products—for example, music, food, hairstyles, clothing, recreational activities and their equipment, styles of cars, and furnishings—constantly changes. But backstage culture—the values, attitudes, and cultural dimensions that have been learned from birth—change very little and very, very slowly.

Sometimes the shifting emphasis of existing values in a culture is mistaken for cultural change. As if a spotlight first illuminates one situation and then fades while another event is highlighted on the stage, circumstances—geopolitical, economic, and religious—focus attention on some values as others recede.

All cultures include values that can be in opposition to each other. In the United States, the value of independence is sometimes in conflict with the equally held value of respect for personal property. In Singapore, the value of belonging to a group is sometimes at odds with the value of asserting one's position to accomplish a task. But these values are in the culture all the time. Certain situations bring out one value or another. What looks like a change in the culture, seen in the short term, is actually a shift in emphasis.

Significant change in social organization occurs with economic change. China is a country in which offspring have always shown respect to, and eventually cared for, their parents. The behaviors are associated with the Confucian value of filial piety. In traditional China, the eldest son and his family always lived with his parents. However, economic change created a shift in family structure. Rather than a son bringing his wife to his parents' home, married couples increasingly lived on their own. This change came about because neither parents nor young couples could afford housing large enough for everyone. However, this change in housing doesn't mean that filial piety is no longer valued in China. Filial piety is apparent in ways offspring arrange care for their parents, either having someone check on them regularly, or finding a care-giving facility for them. As more wealth is created by families in China, the traditional model is re-emerging: Parents live with their children and grandchildren.

Research will be necessary to demonstrate that backstage culture actually is changing in China, or any other culture, and that the change consists of more than proceeding and receding emphases on values that already exist within the culture. In the short term, the older members of a culture always deplore the way values seem to be abandoned by the young. When those children become parents and grandparents, the cultural values they were taught as youths often reassert themselves.

Technology often is identified as an agent of cultural change. ***Technology is the way humans relate to their physical environment.*** For example, technology has altered the way space and time affect human communication: Cell phones and e-mail have reduced both time and space constraints to almost nothing. Microchips are making smart machines possible in a wide range of applications. The constraints of the human body and the physical environment are disappearing, and activities that were not possible except through great effort and expense now occur with ease. Activities as different as online shopping and online academic research are changing the marketplace and the university. Medical innovations include the possibility of surgically embedding microchips in humans who have been physically unable to do certain things. But this marvelous technology does not change the cultural imprint of the culture on its members. Individuals still carry a map of their culture in their minds and hearts no matter what technological innovations they implement.

The Study of Communication across Cultures

Culture and communication are closely connected. Culture is learned and shared through communication, and communication is based in cultural norms. What is communicated and how it is communicated are both determined by culture.

Language is the tool for communicating and it is also related to thought processes and mental categories. But learning another language alone cannot help us understand another culture.

The study of communication and culture is relatively young, and has its roots in the United States. In 1959, American anthropologist Edward T. Hall wrote about how culture affects communication in his book *The Silent Language*. The silent language is, of course, culture. The study of cross-cultural communication began with the United States' interest in sending people to other countries and having them succeed because of their cultural training beforehand. Edward Hall worked for the United States Foreign Service Institute (FSI). After the Second World War, the United States decided to study foreign cultures and train people in languages and cultural knowledge for working in other countries. As a result, the FSI developed training programs.

Three Characteristics of the Discipline of Cross-cultural Communication

This beginning has led to three major characteristics of the study of cross-cultural communication.

- To a very great extent, for the FSI trainees the American culture was the normative culture and other cultures were compared to it—an ethnocentric approach. Research has been **American-dominated** in the field of cross-cultural communication.
- The study of foreign cultures was based almost entirely on **observed behaviors**—onstage culture. The study of cultural values came later.
- The early study of communication and cultures was multidisciplinary—a characteristic that is still true today. Psychology, anthropology, sociology, communication, linguistics, and language training all play a part in the study of culture. More recently, management studies also have contributed to the understanding of communication and culture, along with political studies, economics, and geography.

Study of the Communication of Groups versus the Study of Individuals' Communication

Researchers gather two general kinds of information about communication. Some research looks at the way groups and cultures communicate, while other research looks at the communication of individuals. **It is important to keep these two ways of studying communication separate.** When an entire culture is the subject of study, information is gathered by very large surveys, and the results lead to generalizations about the way the culture communicates. Statistical means and averages describe the entire culture, but may not describe every person in that culture. In fact, we err if we believe that just because a person comes from a particular culture, therefore they will inevitably communicate in a certain way. People's behavior is determined by many factors, of which culture is one.

In the other approach, when individuals are the focus of study, the individuals are interviewed and observed, and the result is rich, complex information about the individuals, but that information cannot be generalized to a whole culture.

Now we will look at the difference between the two terms *intercultural* and *cross-cultural*.

Intercultural and Cross-cultural Communication Study

These two terms are often used interchangeably, which can cause some confusion. However, they can be used to mean different kinds of study. An understanding of their different use can be helpful.

Cross-cultural Communication

According to William B. Gudykunst,[20] the approach called *cross-cultural communication* **involves a comparison.** Communication within one culture is the focus first, and then communication within a second culture is the next focus, so the two can be compared.

For example, consider the communication styles of the United States and of Oman, one of the Gulf states on the Arabian peninsula. Americans usually greet someone from another culture with a casual and personal greeting. Americans often communicate with direct statements and questions to get information and avoid ambiguity and misunderstanding. Americans often freely give their opinions without being asked, and usually show a desire to be liked.

What about communication in the Omani culture? Omanis usually use formal greetings, following established formulas, especially when first meeting someone from another culture. Politeness takes precedence over an open declaration of opinions, since Omanis usually try not to give offense and to maintain harmony in social situations. In order to have a pleasant conversation, Omanis may use indirectness to avoid saying things that could make the other person feel angry or disrespected.

Each culture's communication style is analyzed in terms of its own cultural values and practices. Then the communication is compared, and differences and similarities appear. For example, consider the language that members of different cultures use to articulate their accomplishments, perhaps in a job interview. Some cultures expect claims of expertise, even when the communicator's experience is slight. Other cultures expect modesty, not claims of expertise, even when that applicant has had recognized success. What might be called "giving yourself credit" in one culture is called boasting in another. In the culture of New Zealand, making claims for oneself is considered to be in bad taste, and one who does so is called a skite. Mothers teach children from a young age to avoid "skiting" (boasting about accomplishments) or seeking the limelight.

In Focus

In New Zealand, the game of rugby is a fervent national pastime. Rugby teams attract large crowds of loyal fans, and games are popular events. Faithful followers recall a game with Australia in which a player on the New Zealand All Blacks team got his hands on the awkward ball and plowed past the opposing team members to churn toward the goal line 35 yards away. The crowd roared with delight as he drove alone and unimpeded to the goal, but then as he got closer to scoring, the roar began to diminish until finally one All Blacks fan could be heard to yell, "Bloody skite!"

Intercultural Communication

Intercultural communication occurs when **people from two or more cultures interact.** Using the American–Omani example, we can consider what happens at the point where an American and an Omani interact. As a result of the cultural differences, the Omanis could feel somewhat insulted by the bluntness of Americans. Americans may feel the Omanis are not open and candid.

Since initial greetings are different in their formality, to the Omanis the Americans may seem too informal and therefore not serious about developing a relationship. At the same time, to the Americans the Omanis may seem too formal and therefore not serious about developing a relationship. Americans communicate with openness and want to be friendly, but often they are not sensitive about how their statements are received. Omanis may seem evasive or even deceptive when they do not declare their positions, although that is not how they want to be perceived. Both cultures value successful social interactions. Americans want to be friendly, so they disclose information about themselves, while Omanis want to be friendly, so they avoid disclosing too much about themselves in a first meeting.

Intercultural communication involves analysis of what is happening at the point when communication is taking place. Of course, the analysis involves information about each culture, which means that an understanding of each culture is necessary. That sounds very much like the first step in the cross-cultural approach. The line between *cross-cultural* study and *intercultural* study is not precise.

However, some situations clearly are intercultural. For example, when teams from different cultures are engaged in negotiation, intercultural communication is taking place. When a manager from one culture is meeting with an employee from another culture, intercultural communication is taking place.

On the other hand, when a television network is planning how to reach markets in more than one culture, cross-cultural communication is being considered.

Table 1.2 shows a summary of different categories of research within cross-cultural and intercultural approaches.

Each of these areas of research has produced theories for understanding the relationship between culture and communication.

Now we will look at two basic approaches to communication research.

Two Broad Approaches to Communication Research in the Social Sciences

Some authors say that approaches to research in "social science" differ because one approach emphasizes "social" and the other approach emphasizes "science."

The "**science**" approach is also called **positivist** or **functionalist.**

The "**social**" approach is also called **interpretivist** or **humanist.**

See Table 1.3 for the key differences in the two paradigms or models.

Positivist Research Design

The positivist approach:

- **is based on a philosophical position that what is being studied is objective.** It has an objective reality.
- **collects data through observation by the researcher (who is impartial) and by questionnaire.**
- **produces studies that can be replicated**—that is, another researcher who is equally unbiased and impartial and who observes the same phenomenon can repeat the study. (In social science, a phenomenon usually means a human behavior.)

TABLE 1.2
Some Areas
of Research in
Cross-Cultural
and Intercultural
Communication

Cross-cultural	Intercultural
• Compares communication in different cultures	• Examines communication interactions between people of different cultures
— Treats culture as a theoretical variable	— Uses cultural variables/dimensions in explaining interactions
— Includes cross-cultural psychological processes; e.g., perception and emotion	— Includes intercultural psychological processes; e.g., identity management, facework
— Compares nonverbal communication and other communication behaviors	— Focuses on outcomes of communication interactions and processes (such as acculturation, conflict management, teamwork, negotiation)
— Looks at verbal (language) communication differences across cultures	
— Contrasts facework negotiation behaviors; compares conflict management approaches	— Studies adaptation and accommodation of groups in other cultures
	— Examines communication networks

TABLE 1.3
The Two General
Research Paradigms
in Business and the
Social Sciences

	Functionalist Research Paradigm	Interpretivist Research Paradigm
View of reality	Objective and can be observed by researcher	Subjective, is constructed by human mental activity
View of researcher	Impartial, observation does not affect what is being studied	Involved to some degree with what is being studied, and impacts what is being studied
Objective of research	Describe and predict communication behavior	Describe communication behavior and reasons as reported by subjects under study
Methods of study	Observation	Field research (e.g., interviews, ethnography)
What study produces	Identification of cultural variables in behavior; conclusions that may be generalizable to other cultures	Explanations of culture and communication in a social context

For example, a researcher may study the behavior of members of a culture who are responding to a request for charitable gifts for an orphanage. The behavior could be, for example, the donation of money from the reader's pocket. The researcher may want to know which key words are most effective in moving the person to make a donation. The researcher can observe and can also ask the subject at what point, if any, the decision was made to donate money.

Researchers who use the positivist approach believe their study of the phenomenon does not directly affect it. In other words, positivists believe that the behavior of the participants is not affected by the researcher doing the study.

The objective of the positivist researcher is to describe the behavior and predict it. In order to predict that certain words are successful in getting donations, the researcher has to generalize from what has happened during the study. Let's say that 40 percent of the time people who were asked to give money *did* give money. And let's say the researcher found by using a questionnaire that among several phrases that achieved that response, the most frequently successful phrase—according to the respondents—was "you will feel a reward for what you have done." Of the 40 percent who gave money, 70 percent said that phrase was what convinced them.

If the researcher has this kind of information, the researcher can predict that in the future, the phrase "you will feel a reward for what you have done" will generate donations, and may expect the phrase to work with 70 percent of the people. In other words, the positivist researcher usually gathers **quantitative** data—information that is in numerical form. Questionnaires provide responses that can be added, averaged, that can have percentages found, and so forth. The positivist researcher counts responses and analyzes data numerically. Some statistical analyses are quite sophisticated, well beyond the simple percentage figures in the example.

Now consider a positivist study involving culture and communication. Let's say the researcher wants to find out whether the phrase "you will feel a reward for what you have done" works to stimulate donations in one culture compared to another culture, and at what rate. With the results of this positivist study, a researcher may draw conclusions about the cultures represented in the study and charitable giving, and may predict the success of the phrase in a third culture.

Interpretivist Research Design

The interpretivist approach:

- **is based on the philosophical position that reality is subjective, created by the minds of people according to the way things make sense to them.** Reality, and what it means, comes from the conceptualization shared by a group of people.
- **collects data by observation and perhaps by questionnaire, but mainly by interview and focus groups.**

In this case, the researcher wants to explore reality with the subjects in the study, and that means asking questions to get as much information as possible about how the subjects see the world and where meaning comes from. The researcher often uses interviews that give the subjects a chance to talk about what they understand. The interpretivist researcher usually wants to know *why* the participants in the study act in a certain way.

That means the interpretivist approach:

- **Studies one group in depth.**
- **Believes the act of gathering information impacts the information** since having an interviewer ask questions makes people think about associated meanings and reasons.

The objective of the interpretivist's research is to describe the phenomenon and to find out the reasons for it as reported by the participants in the study. Not every participant may have the same reasons, so the researcher may end up with a list of reasons not shared by everyone. The researcher cannot generalize from these findings, because another group of participants might have different reasons, more reasons, or fewer reasons. So the interpretivist researcher is not interested in predicting behavior in the future, but rather in carefully explaining the reasons for the conclusions in this specific study.

The **context** is part of how the researcher explains the conclusions of an interpretivist study. In a positivist study, the findings are generalized, and specific characteristics of a particular context are not taken into account.

Combined Approach

These two general approaches to research, positivist and interpretivist, are usually used in some kind of combination in communication research. Human communication behavior is complex in its motivations and often lends itself to more than one explanation. That is why the interpretivist approach is a frequent choice.

At the same time, numerical data help give an overall picture, and quantitative analysis can shed light on what the data mean, especially in large studies, so positivist elements often figure in a research project.

The Merits of Positivist Research

- **Positivist research uses data that can be generalized,** so predictions can be made about communication in other contexts (this is particularly useful in comparing communication in different cultures).
- Often data are numerical and are measurements (questionnaire responses, counts of behavior), so statistical analysis is possible. The positivist approach is also often called **quantitative** research, because the data collected are expressed in numbers.
- **Studies have high *reliability*.** Reliability is an important quality in research. It is the degree to which a study can be *replicated* (that is, repeated or reproduced) at another time, by the same or a different researcher.

We have already discussed the example of a research project about culture's impact on communication that asks for charitable donations. Let's explore this in more detail as a positivist research study.

A positivist researcher could choose several phrases that ask for donations and put them on a questionnaire. Then the researcher could use the questionnaire to ask members of a culture to select the phrase that is most likely to make them want to give.

Next, the researcher would take the same phrases and ask the same questions in a questionnaire for another culture. The researcher would try to have the two cultural groups be as alike as possible in every way except culture, so other variables besides culture would not be factors in their answers. Other variables could be age, gender, income, location (in a city or countryside), experience with previous requests for donations, and so on. The researcher would want a large number of respondents from both cultures.

The analysis of the responses would look at how many people from each culture chose which phrase most frequently, which second most frequently, and so on. The analysis of the findings would lead the researcher to conclude which one phrase works best. It might be the same phrase in both cultures, or it might be a different phrase in each.

Then the researcher would predict which phrase will work in each culture in the future. The researcher might also predict which phrase would be most effective in a third culture.

Now let's look at the weaknesses of the positivist approach.

The Overall Weaknesses of the Positivist Approach

- **Separating out the other variables among respondents is difficult.** Even if age, gender, income, and so on are similar in both groups, people are not identical. The factors that generate communication behavior are not all the same among people of one culture.
- Respondents may choose one phrase in one situation, and another phrase in another situation, but the researcher is probably asking for one response. Questionnaires cannot ask for responses to every situation. This means **a positivist study is low in *validity*.** Validity is the degree to which research truly finds out about what it says it is studying.

In our example, a respondent about which phrase moves her to make a donation to charity might be affected by the emotions she felt when she read a story in the newspaper that day about someone in need, and her choice might be different today from what she would have chosen yesterday. Next month, she may not remember the story in the newspaper when asked the question about which phrase moves her, and her answer may be different. A questionnaire is unlikely to ask her about her emotions that day. **The positivist researcher has no way of exploring the context for the respondent's answer.**

The Merits of Interpretivist Research

The merits of interpretivist research include:

- **Rich, detailed data can be gathered from the sample.** Interpretivist research is often called **qualitative research.** That is, when researchers talk to respondents, they can uncover more information than they had expected. Respondents can reveal interrelated ways they see reality. The researcher may not even have thought of some factors influencing the respondents' behavior and attitudes, and the researcher needs to be open to finding something different from what was expected.

- Because the researcher can explore how the participants behave, along with their reasons for doing so, **the *validity* of interpretivist research is high;** the complexities involved in information about behavior, values, and attitudes can be explored.
- The research context can be addressed. Besides the gathering of qualitative data, the analysis of data can also be qualitative.

In our example about what triggers a charitable donation, an interpretivist researcher will interview participants in the study. Together they will explore meanings, behavior, and reasons. The interviewer will probe to make sure he or she understands the participants as fully as possible. Factors affecting the participants' answers will also be investigated. The result of such a study would be a comprehensive description of the participants' responses to a certain communication.

But the interpretivist approach also has weaknesses.

Weaknesses of Interpretivist Research

The weaknesses of interpretivist research include:

- **The findings are subjective,** since the researcher/observer is also to some extent a participant. This means the researcher's opinions form part of the conclusions. The researcher and the participant collaborate to interpret the phenomena being studied. The extent of collaboration varies from project to project.
- As a consequence of the subjectivity, **interpretivist research has low *reliability*.** Because the data collected refer to one specific group, the study cannot be replicated exactly.
- Furthermore, **the results of interpretivist research cannot be generalized to any other context or group** than the one in which the study takes place. That means **predictions cannot be made** based on findings from interpretivist research, which is interested in describing behavior and interpreting it.

The Rhetorical Approach: A Kind of Interpretivist Study

Before we leave this discussion of the two primary paradigms in social science research, we need to mention one key approach in communication studies: the rhetorical approach. Rhetoric forms the basis of an important kind of *interpretivist* research for communication. Rhetoric dates from the 5th century B.C.E. and involves examining written texts or oral utterances in order to explain attitudes, values, and behavior. The goal of rhetorical research is to interpret meanings of what people have said or what they have written down, in their original context. Context plays an important role in rhetorical research.

Study of Culture and Communication: Individuals or Cultures

In this book, we are focusing on the role of culture in communication for business. Cultures have preferences about communication, and that leads to differences from one culture to another. Individuals have preferences about communication, too, although not always the same preferences their culture has, and individuals communicate differently depending on their personalities and interaction skills. Intercultural communication researchers recognize this distinction between a focus on individual members of a culture and how they communicate with individuals in another culture, and a focus on how cultures behave.

Intercultural Business Communication

Intercultural business communication is communication by members of different cultures for business or workplace purposes.

Business activity involves specific communication acts, products, and communicators, and the field of intercultural business communication focuses on people of different cultures. People in various roles such as negotiators, writers of business messages, team members, meeting hosts and guests, and co-workers generate communication acts including meetings, memos, e-mails, letters, reports, proposals, presentations, speeches, advertisements, public relations documents, and interpersonal conversations. Culture affects all these communications.

Perception and Communication

Communication is the perception of verbal (worded) and nonverbal (without words) behaviors and the assignment of meaning to them. It takes place whether the sending of signals is intentional or unintentional. Communication even takes place when the verbal or nonverbal behavior is unconscious, as long as it is observed and meaning is assigned to it. When a receiver of signals perceives those signals, decides to pay attention to them as meaningful, categorizes them according to categories in his or her mind, and assigns meaning to them, communication has occurred.

Perception is a process that can break down at any of these steps. This is true when communication takes place between members of the same group, who share values, attitudes, experiences, behavioral expectations, and even a history together. When communicators come from different cultures, however, the challenges are much greater. Perception involves four options as Exhibit 1.2 shows.

Communication signals can be verbal or nonverbal or a combination of both. Imagine a glance from someone, accompanied by a noise in that person's throat. When you encounter something unfamiliar, you have several choices: (1) You can assume it is nothing. It fits no category known to you and means nothing. At this point, you have perceived a signal but have chosen not to attend to it. (2) You can assume it is simply a variant of something familiar that is already in a mental category. It may seem that the noise in the throat is a prelude to speech that will be directed at you since the person is looking at you. In this case, you have categorized it and assigned meaning to it, but both may be wrong. The glance may, in fact, be directed past you to someone or something else, and the noise in the throat may actually be words in a language you don't understand. (3) Another option is that you can choose to perceive the signals as unfamiliar and therefore not to be matched with existing mental categories; thus, you

EXHIBIT 1.2 Perception Model of Choices about Communication Signals

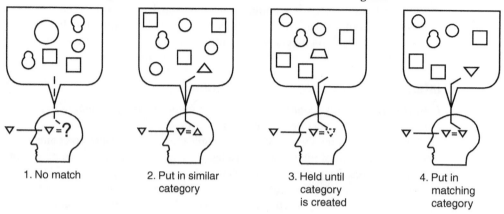

| 1. No match | 2. Put in similar category | 3. Held until category is created | 4. Put in matching category |

reject them or hold them until you can relate them to something already familiar. It's hard to keep the uncategorized and unmeaningful in your mind for very long unless you have learned to do so. Finally, (4) you have the option of altering your mental category to accommodate the new information and assign it a new meaning. This is how categories are constantly being revised and increased. Meaning is assigned to verbal and nonverbal behavior based on one's accumulated experience and understanding— one's mental data bank of meanings, from one's culture.

To have good communication with someone from another culture, you need to understand meanings in that culture.

A Schemata Model for Intercultural Communication

The mental categories we create in order to make sense of the world can be called *schemata*. Among the schemata are those that categorize what we know about cultures other than our own. If you are asked to summon up what you know about a culture, say, the dominant culture of Ethiopia, you may not have many data in your schema; indeed, you may have to create a new schema because this is the first time you've thought about Ethiopia.

We can model our expanding knowledge of another culture and how we communicate with it.[21] Exhibit 1.3 shows your culture as Culture A, Ethiopian culture as Culture B, and your projection or schema about Ethiopian culture as B[1] (B *prime*).

If you imagine yourself traveling to Ethiopia for business, you now may be able to make further projections, based on the categories in your schema, of what you can expect to find. What food will you be offered by your business contacts there? What will unlikely be offered? Would it be acceptable for you to refuse refreshment? You will observe Ethiopians eating with their fingers. Why? What will you do? If the businesspeople you spend time with represent one company, what else may they have in common?

Whatever you know about Ethiopia, based on these few facts and questions or on your prior knowledge, unless you are Ethiopian, your mental schema will

EXHIBIT 1.3
Communication Is
with Schemata, Not
Actual Culture

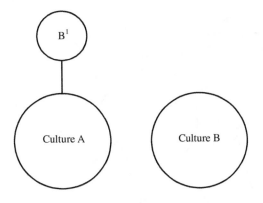

EXHIBIT 1.4
Communicators Send
and Receive Messages
through Schemata

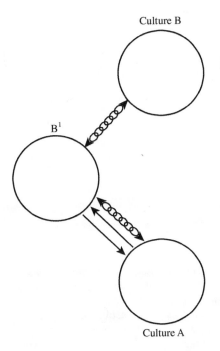

not reflect accurately the reality that is Ethiopian culture. Furthermore, if you attempt to communicate with Ethiopian counterparts for business purposes, you probably will be communicating with your mental projection of Ethiopian culture. Exhibit 1.4 describes this process.

When you communicate, you are sending messages to B^1, the schema of Ethiopian culture. When you receive messages from a member of that culture, they are understood by you after being filtered through your B^1.

EXHIBIT 1.5
**Schema Modified
and Coming Closer
to Actual Culture**

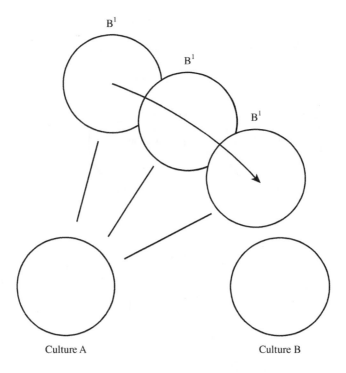

Culture A   Culture B

In Focus

If you know Ethiopia is a country in Africa, you may make certain additions to your schema, which may or may not be accurate. Does it help to know that over 100 different ethnic groups live in this country?

Here is some more information. The dominant culture is Amharic, which is also the official language. Ethiopia is one of the oldest countries in the world. The capital is Addis Ababa. Businessmen typically wear a white robe (*shamma*) over their shirts and trousers and may stand closer to people in conversation than Europeans do. Bureaucracy flourishes; a strong chief or leader dominates business organizations. Families are strong units, and family members may be business partners. People tend to make distinctions based on social and economic position. Business encounters are formal; hospitality is valued highly. Businesspeople are not afraid to stand up for their individual rights, but at the same time they show sensitivity to the rights of others. They have the ability to endure adversity with patience. Age is respected.

About 45 percent of the people are Muslim, and 40 percent are Ethiopian Orthodox Christians. Formerly, the highest levels of society were mostly Christian, but since the political upheavals in Ethiopia in past decades, Muslims as well as Christians occupy all levels. Women often own small businesses, and unlike some other Muslim cultures, the Muslim women of Ethiopia do not wear a veil or *chador*. Ethiopians are Semitic people (like Jews and Arabs). Coffee is a major export product.

The more you learn about Ethiopia, the more you can revise and adjust your mental projection of B^1, and the closer it can come to the reality (B) that is Ethiopian culture. Exhibit 1.5 shows this process as a result of induction, or the accommodation of new data that alter the schema.

The more you understand about another culture, the closer your schema will be to the reality that is the other culture and the better your communication will be. You will have fewer misunderstandings of the kind that arise when messages are assigned different meanings and different categories.

Summary

This chapter began with two reasons why intercultural business communication matters to organizations: Communicators can make sense of their interactions with people of other cultures, and understand *why* people think and behave the way they do, and then they can prevent miscommunication more often.

Next, the chapter considered how we respond to foreign and unfamiliar cultures: hostility, curiosity, denial, and cooperation.

Culture is defined as coherent, learned, and shared, using an agreed set of symbols to rank what is important, furnish attitudes, and dictate behavior for a society. Onstage culture is observable behavior; backstage culture is the deep values and meanings that give rise to behavior. Transactional culture is temporary, and is co-created between people from different cultures.

Culture shock and reverse culture shock are normal reactions to the many adjustments people must make when they find themselves in an unfamiliar culture.

Self-knowledge is critical for understanding people in other cultures and communicating successfully with them. Assessment of one's Cultural Intelligence, or CQ, is a good place for self-knowledge to start; its components are cognition, motivation, and behavior.

Cultures appear to change very little on a deep level, although popular culture and popular taste do change.

The study of communication and culture, which began in the United States, is based on the two main social science research paradigms: positivist and interpretivist. Studies can focus on groups or individuals, and can be cross-cultural or intercultural.

Finally, the chapter looked at perception and communication, and a schemata model for intercultural communication.

Learning about culture will be discussed in more detail throughout the book. The most obvious issue for communication across cultures, of course, is language, and that is the subject of the next chapter.

Notes

1. Peter Diekmeyer, "Walpert Greets Yuletide with a Bang," *Montreal Gazette,* December 16, 2002, B1; Canadian Press News Wire, *Canadian Business and Current Affairs,* 2002. Micromedia Limited, D, December 29, 2002; Catherine Yronwode, http://www.luckymojo.com/swastika.html.

2. D. Singer, "The Voyages of Ibn Battuta," S*eattle Pacific University Response,* 26:2, 2003, p. 1, http://www.spu.edu/depts/uc/response/spring2k3/voyages .html.

3. See *Ibn Battuta,* by L. P. Harvey (2008), published by I. B. Tauris. An excellent source is a book by R. E. Dunn, *The Adventures of Ibn Battuta: A Muslim Traveller of the 14th Century* (University of California Press, 2004).

4. Donald F. Hastings, "Lincoln Electric's Harsh Lessons from International Expansion," *Harvard Business Review* 77, no. 3 (May/June 1999), pp. 163–175.

5. James L. Watson, "China's Big Mac Attack," *Foreign Affairs,* May–June 2000, pp. 120–134, http://www.mcdonalds.com/corporate/press/financial/2003/05132003/index.html.

6. J. H. Goring, 1909 nursery rhyme, quoted in Geert Hofstede, *Cultures and Organizations: Software of the Mind* (London: McGraw-Hill, 1991), p. 235.

7. Iris Varner, "The Theoretical Foundation for Intercultural Business Communication," *Journal of Business Communication* 37, no. 1 (2000), pp. 39–57.

8. Geert Hofstede, *Cultures and Organizations: Software of the Mind* (London: McGraw-Hill, 1991), p. 237.

9. Edward T. Hall, *The Hidden Dimension* (New York: Anchor Press/Doubleday, 1966).

10. Richard Mead, *International Management,* 2nd ed. (Malden, MA: Blackwell, 1998), p. 8.

11. Raymond Cohen, paraphrasing Tylor's *Primitive Culture.* In *Negotiating across Cultures* (Washington, DC: United States Institute of Peace, 1991), p. 8.

12. Hiroko Sakomura and Sue Winski, unpublished case from Transform Corporation, Tokyo, in an unpublished paper, SIETAR International Congress, Denver, 1988.

13. Molouk Y. Ba-Isa, "Learning to Do Business the Arab Way," www.executive-planet.infopop.cc, posted Friday, May 23, 2003; retrieved May 26, 2003.

14. George Nishiyama, "14-Century-Old Japanese Firm's Longevity Secret: Sticking to Basics; Kongo Gumi Hasn't Branched Out Too Far beyond Building Temples since Its Founding in 578," *Los Angeles Times,* Business, Part 3, May 23, 2003, p. 6. Retrieved from Lexis-Nexis database on June 22, 2003.

15. Read more about culture shock in Colleen Ward, Stephen Bochner, and Adrian Furnham, *The Psychology of Culture Shock,* 2nd ed. (New York: Routledge 2001); Elisabeth Marx, *Breaking through Culture Shock* (Nicholas Brealey Intercultural, 2001); and the *Culture Shock! Guides* series of Graphic Arts Center Publishing, by country.

16. Edward T. Hall, *Beyond Culture* (New York: Anchor Press/Doubleday, 1976), p. 116.

17. Emory S. Bogardus, *Social Distance* (Yellow Springs, OH: Antioch Press, 1959).

18. Larry Copeland and Larry Griggs, *Going International* (video).

19. Christopher Earley, Soon Ang, and Joo-Seng Tan, *CQ: Developing Cultural Intelligence at Work* (Stanford, CA: Stanford University Press, 2006), p. 5.

20. William B. Gudykunst, "Forward," *Intercultural and Cross-cultural Communication* (Thousand Oaks, CA: Sage, 2003) p. vii.

21. Linda Beamer, "A Schemata Model for Intercultural Communication and Case Study: The Emperor and the Envoy," *Journal of Business Communication*, 32 (April 1995), pp. 141–161.

CHAPTER TWO

The Role of Language in Intercultural Business Communication

The Language Barrier and Its Consequences: Real and Perceived

Eric Moore, the owner of a medium-sized electronics company in Denver, Colorado, and Hiromitsu Sodomori, the manager of a small Japanese electronics company in Tokyo, met at a trade show in Frankfurt, Germany, a few weeks ago. A mutual friend from the Netherlands had introduced them. Both were looking for possible international expansion, and they decided to explore how they could benefit by working together. Moore had worked for a large company before going out on his own. He had done business in Western Europe and in Argentina, but had little experience in Japan, having been to Tokyo only once for a few days to accompany his previous boss. Sodomori had worked as an expatriate in South Korea and Taiwan for two years. In addition, he had done some negotiations with firms in the Netherlands and France. Sodomori spoke native Japanese and good English. Moore spoke English and some Spanish. Since the trade show, the two men have exchanged several e-mails to continue their discussion. They have examined each other's Web sites and exchanged information on production and marketing goals. After several follow-up phone calls, they have decided to meet in Denver. Both Sodomori and Moore want this meeting to go well and wonder how to prepare for it.

Moore is a boisterous, outgoing, and informal person, whereas Sodomori, by nature, is more quiet and reserved. Their international backgrounds have taught them that language alone does not guarantee success, but that cultural understanding is crucial as well. Eric Moore has been reading up on Japanese business culture. He is beginning to realize that formality is important. He also has learned that the Japanese don't jump into business relationships; they take their time and attempt to build a more personal relationship. Hiromitsu Sodomori has talked to several of his friends in Japan who have more experience in dealing with Americans. They have encouraged him to be more outgoing and less formal. Sodomori is quite nervous, but the business opportunity looks good, and he is convinced that cooperation between his and Mr. Moore's businesses would benefit both sides.

Since at this stage they would like to keep any discussions private, they have opted to not use an interpreter and try to communicate in English. When they finally meet, things start out slowly. Both are nervous, but both also recognize that the other has prepared well. Sometimes they have to repeat a point several times, but they are beginning to feel comfortable. Mr. Moore is less boisterous and refrains from calling Mr. Sodomori by his first name. Mr. Sodomori, on the other hand, greets Mr. Moore with a handshake and just a slight bow. He is coming out of his shell, and as they discuss the more technical aspects, they find that they have many similar goals. By the end of the two-hour meeting they feel comfortable with each other. They are not ready to sign an agreement—that will take more time—but they trust each other and are beginning to see the opportunities a cooperative venture might bring. At the end of the visit they have decided to meet again to continue their discussion. The next step will be for Moore to visit Sodomori in Japan.

In the preceding example, the two men have made a conscious decision to try and understand the other side and keep an open mind. Both have realized that their communication needs to take into consideration the language and a knowledge of the other culture.

The Relationship between Language and Culture

In the preceding example, Mr. Moore and Mr. Sodomori speak the same language, although this is not always easy for Mr. Sodomori. After intense discussions in English, he gets tired. However, language is only one of the variables in their interaction. As important as language is the willingness on both sides to understand the other person and adapt to their culture. At the end of the meeting they have developed a sense of trust and a common goal that will help them in their future communication.

As the example shows, culture and language are intertwined and shape each other. It is impossible to separate the two. Language is not a matter of neutral codes and grammatical rules. Each time we select words, form sentences, and send a message, either oral or written, we also make cultural choices. We all agree that language helps in communicating with people from different backgrounds. However, we may be less aware that cultural literacy is necessary to understand the language being used. If we select language without being aware of the cultural implications, we may, at best, not communicate well and, at worst, send the wrong message.

In our own environment we are aware of the implications of these choices. For example, if an American says "How are you?" other Americans register the phrase as *Hello*, the equivalent of *GutenTag, Bonjour*, or *Ohio gozayimasu* rather than the literal meaning. A foreigner in the United States, knowing some English but not familiar with the culture and usage of English, may attribute a very different meaning to the phrase and interpret it much more literally.

Mr. Sodomori, for example, may:

- Consider the phrase too personal and think that it is none of Mr. Moore's business how he is.
- Think that Mr. Moore literally means what he says and proceed to answer the question.
- Consider Mr. Moore insincere because it is obvious that he is not really interested in the answer.

All languages have social questions and information questions. A social question, even though it comes in question form, does not ask for information. It is simply a lubricant to move the conversation forward. In American English, the question "How are you?" is a social question. In many other countries, such as Germany, Russia, and Poland, "How are you?" is an information question. The speaker actually wants to get an answer to the question. In Japan, the question "Where are you going?" is a social question. The same question is an information question in American English. An American may feel that the Japanese question is intrusive and may not know what to answer. However, no answer is expected. A simple "Over there" will do. Similarly, in Korea a typical social question when people first meet is "Did you sleep well last night? " or "Have you had a meal?"[1] It is easy to see that someone not familiar with the conventions of social and information questions may misinterpret the question and the intended meaning.

The point is that words in themselves do not carry the meaning. The meaning comes out of the context, the cultural usage. For example, a German who has lived in the United States for many years will take on, often unknowingly, many American behavioral patterns. She may be more outgoing and enthusiastic, less formal, and more optimistic. When she goes back to Germany, she speaks German, but increasingly with an American frame of reference. At social functions, she will introduce herself by first and last name rather than by last name and professional title: "*Ingrid Zerbe, erfreut Sie kennenzulernen*" (Ingrid Zerbe, pleased to meet you) rather than "*Dr. Zerbe, erfreut Sie kennenzulernen.*" The Germans are at a loss; they don't know how to address her. They could say "*Frau Zerbe*," but if she has a professional title, that would not be correct. In any case, nobody cares about her first name anyway. Ingrid Zerbe finds that those Germans are getting stiffer all the time; with every visit they are becoming more reserved. It is getting more difficult to establish a connection and feel comfortable.

Titah Marseto from Indonesia who has lived in the United States for several years also feels she is losing touch with her native culture. Increasingly, when she talks with other people from Indonesia she will be criticized for being too direct, blunt, and rushed in her communication. To communicate effectively with other Indonesians, she consciously has to place herself into an Indonesian mindset. As time goes on, this adjustment is becoming more difficult. The example illustrates that a person's cultural frame of reference may change over time.

Language as a Reflection of the Environment

Language reflects the environment in which we live. We label the things around us. For example, in the Amazon area, snow is not part of the environment; therefore, people in that region do not have a word for snow. It simply does not exist. In areas where it snows occasionally, people have a word for snow, but it may be just one word without any differentiations. Most Americans, for example, use terms such as *snow, powder, sleet, slush, blizzard,* and *ice.* That's the extent of most people's snow vocabulary. People who live in an environment where it snows most months of the year may have a much more differentiated terminology for snow.[2] If you go to a pub in northern Germany and order wine, you may ask for "*ein Glas Weißwein, bitte*" (a glass of white wine, please). You may specify *Moselwein* or *Rheinwein,* but that's it. The north of Germany is beer country, and the knowledge of wine is much more limited. In Baden, in southwestern Germany, in contrast, a waiter would just stare at you if you asked for a glass of white wine. Here you would specify the type of wine, the vineyard, and the year. Wine is important in this region, and you are expected to know about wine.

The environment influences the development of technology, products, and the appropriate vocabulary. For example, cultures in tropical climates will not develop heating systems and as a result will not have any of the accompanying vocabulary, just as people in cold climates have no need for air-conditioning and its related vocabulary.

Language as a Reflection of Values

In addition to the environment, language reflects cultural values. Hall, for example, points out that the Navajo do not have a word for *late.*[3] Time, he tells us, does not play a role in Navajo life. There is a time to do everything, a natural time rather than the artificial clock time that industrial countries use. As a result, the Navajo do not have the differentiated vocabulary connected with time and clocks that Americans have. Time and the passing of time are things one can't control; therefore, one should not worry about wasting time and setting schedules. In Mandarin Chinese, one word (*qing*) represents various hues of blue and green. What might be called *green* in English is called *qing,* and what might be called *blue* in English also is called *qing.* It isn't that Chinese speakers cannot distinguish the difference in hues; they simply use one word for a range of hues.

One of the problems in dealing with people from other cultures is that we translate concepts from a foreign language and culture with words that fit our priorities and view of reality. For example, businesspeople in the United States typically are frustrated with the *mañana* mentality of Spanish-speaking countries: "They said tomorrow, but they did not mean it." For Americans, *tomorrow* means midnight to midnight, a very precise time period. To Mexicans, in contrast, *mañana* means in the future, soon. A Mexican businessman speaking with an American may use the word *tomorrow* but not be aware of, or not intend, the precise meaning of the word. This vague terminology is not precise enough for the American emphasis on efficiency. The difficulties over the word *mañana* are at least as much an American problem as a Mexican problem. Dictionaries do not help because they typically pretend that there are exact equivalents that have the same meanings. To communicate concepts effectively, cultural knowledge is as important as linguistic knowledge.

The Chinese, for example, do not have a word for *communication* as in the term *business communication*. They use *letter exchange* or *transportation traffic* but not *communication*. The Chinese also do not have a concept of privacy; as a result, there is no corresponding word in the Chinese language. Typically, *privacy* is translated as *reclusiveness,* which brings up very different connotations in English than the word *privacy.* The word *privacy* has a positive connotation for people in the United States. They think of the privacy of their homes, the right to privacy, and the right to private property. The word *reclusiveness,* in contrast, indicates that a person withdraws from society, is a loner, or does not fit in. In the U.S. context, a reclusive person is considered somewhat strange. In China, a reclusive person is viewed much more negatively, and privacy in the American sense is not an accepted value. Equating *privacy* with *reclusiveness* illustrates an uderlying cultral priority of what is and is not acceptable.

The Meaning of Words

Sometimes different cultures use identical words that have rather different meanings. The results can be humorous, annoying, or costly, depending on the circumstances. Let us look at several examples.

An American university and its French partner discussed the possibilities of exchanges for students, professors, and administrators. Both sides agreed that it would be a good idea. The French negotiator spoke fairly good English—at first glance, very good English—while the American spoke good French. In the discussion, they used both French and English. In both languages they used the identical word—*administration*—when they talked about exchanges between the administrations of the two institutions. The surprise came later. For the American, *administration* in the university context meant department chair, dean, or provost. For the French, *administration* meant upper-level clerical staff. What the American considered to be an administrator, the French considered faculty. In New Zealand, Australia, Great Britain, and Argentina, the word *administration* refers to an organizational unit, such as *Faculty of Business,* and teaching personnel are *staff.*

The word *manager* is used worldwide, but it has different levels of importance and meaning in different cultures. The same is true for the title *director.* Many Japanese, for example, have the title *director* on their business cards. In the American context, a director is a person of some importance and power; in Japan, that title may not carry the same level of authority. It may take some time to determine what the meaning of titles is and where a person stands in the hierarchy. The term *director* could be a loan word from English to translate the position for use on a business card; the word is the same, but the meaning may be slightly different. The term also could reflect cross-cultural differences in organizational structure. The word *director* may be the closest translation of the job-level title, which describes a job that does not exist in the U.S. corporate structure. Likewise, the words *office worker* and *staff* often are used for the general administrative workers in a Japanese work group, who tend to have less defined job categories than do their U.S. equivalents. An understanding of the specific title would require a more detailed explanation of the job and its fit in the organizational structure.

The meaning of the word *leader* can create problems as well, as some American researchers found out. In a study on different leadership styles, they collected data from Saudi Arabia and Jordan. When they analyzed the findings, they were puzzled because the results made no sense. Here is what happened. They had asked Arabic-speaking MBA students from Saudi Arabia and Jordan to translate the survey. The translators had used the word *mot* for *leader.* However, *mot* is never used in the context of a business organization; the word is used only in reference to military and political leaders. Since those people are seen as more dictatorial and autocratic, respondents had no reference point for a leader as a facilitator or mentor.

Here is another example of words that look like they should translate as the same thing, but actually have different meanings. In the United States, documents often are notarized. This is not a complex process. One simply goes to a notary public and gets the stamp and signature. Sometimes one pays a fee; sometimes the service is free. The German term, *notarielle Beglaubigung,* often translated as *notarized,* means something quite different. In this case, one would go to a *Notar,* a lawyer. The *Notar* would prepare the document or, at a minimum, sign the document. This service is much more expensive. The meaning of the U.S. concept *notarized* is better reflected in the German term *Beglaubigung,* something any official person can do. The confusing part is the word *notarized* in the American expression. A notary public is not a *Notar.* The same confusion arises in Mexico, where a *notario* is a lawyer with special privileges to perform certain functions that require special qualifications.

Both the French and the Americans use the word *force majeure,* but the phrase carries very different meanings. Literally, the term means superior or irresistible force. In U.S. legal language, it refers generally to forces of nature or possibly war. The implications are that the terms of a contract may be changed because the risk was not allocated in either the expressed or the implied terms of the contract.

In European law, the term has a broader meaning: It includes the changes in economic conditions or other circumstances that were not anticipated when the contract was drawn up. The implication is that when Americans make agreements with Europeans, discuss unforeseen circumstances, and use the term *force majeure,* they need to clarify what they mean and spell out what that term covers.

The preceding examples of language usage illustrate that businesspeople need to examine the context of what is being said and always be aware of the cultural orientation and priorities of their business partners.

Changes in Language

As anyone who has been abroad for any length of time can attest, language lives; it changes over time. Words and phrases that are used commonly at one time may be discontinued or their meaning may change over time. For example, the word *gay* means happy, lighthearted. In recent decades, however, the word has taken on the meaning *homosexual.* As a result, English speakers in countries such as New Zealand, Canada, Australia, the United Kingdom, and the United States don't use the original meaning anymore, and young speakers of English may not even be familiar with the traditional meaning. In other cases, words may take on additional meanings. One must understand the context to understand the meaning. An example is the word *hardware,* which is used to refer to the tools and materials employed in repairing and building houses. Today, the word also refers to computers and components that can be added to a computer, such as a printer or an extra drive.

Foreigners and U.S. citizens who have lived outside the United States for some time may not be familiar with subtle changes in language usage. Twenty years ago, words such as *businessman, chairman, salesman, airline stewardess,* and *fireman* were used regularly. Today, with more women in the workforce and with growing awareness of the way gender and power can be linked to communicate value, gender-neutral terms such as *businesspeople, chairperson* or *chair, sales clerk, flight attendant,* and *firefighter* are common. The old terminology is seen as too restrictive.

Countries such as France and Iceland try to keep their language pure. The French have the *Académie Française* to police the language and ensure that businesses use pure French. But even in France the language changes. The officials may frown on *Franglais,* but people in France eat a *sandwich,* go on a trip for *le weekend,* and go on *le jogging,* all pronounced in the French manner with the accent on the last syllable. To use English is "chic," and somehow the English terms seem to be more precise and descriptive. French Canadians make the *Académie Française* really nervous when they use *char* for car and many other English words in their French. French Canadians do not feel compelled to follow the rules of the *Académie Française.*

The example of Canadian French illustrates that a language, if spoken in different parts of the globe, ultimately will develop differently. The *Académie Francaise* may insist on certain rules, but other French-speaking groups may make their own rules and consider their French just as correct. The same is true for the development of English. What is standard and correct English? Former British colonies such as India and Nigeria increasingly insist that their English is just as correct as Oxford English. The result is the emergence of different "Englishes" used in different parts of the world. Much attention recently has focused on "Singlish"—the English of Singapore that incorporates Malay and the Hokkien dialect of Chinese as well as English words, and follows a syntax like that of other "pidgen" Englishes. The following are three examples of Singlish:

- Eh, this road so narrow, how you going to tombalik your big fat Mareseedeese? You going to do 100-point turn or what? Sekali tombalik into the lang-kau your father kill you then you know! (Oh, this road is so narrow, how are you going to turn around your big fat Mercedes? Are you going to do a 100-point turn, or what? Wait until you turn it into the roadside ditch. Your father will be furious!)

- Eh, Katong sopping sehnta got the "Sah-Leh" you know. Some up to hap-pride ah! (Hey, the Katong Shopping Center has a sale. Some [items] are up to half-price off!)
- Aiyah, you want to chit in your exam tomolloh, har? You tink you can lite the ansir on the table? Cher catch you, lppl (lam pa pak lan) man! (Oh no, you want to cheat on your exam tomorrow? You think you can write the answer on the desk? Teacher will catch you, and it [your plan] will backfire!)[4]

The government of Singapore felt that local television sitcoms were making Singlish too popular with young people at the expense of correct English. Television came under pressure to make the main characters in one show take "proper English" lessons. The rationale was that Singlish was bad for business. However, Singlish remains popular with young people.

You don't have to live in former British colonies in Asia or Africa to experience different Englishes. Business vocabulary in Great Britain and the United States can cause communication problems as well. For example, terminology for automobile parts is quite different. A *hood* is a *bonnet* in British English, and a *trunk* is a *boot.* In British English, the word *corn* refers to wheat, whereas in American English it refers to *maize.* Many of the differences have grown out of different geographic conditions.[5]

Many countries adopt English terms specifically in business and related areas. Some words simply are taken over without changes. For example, Germans frequently use the word *shop* instead of the German word *Geschäft* or *Laden, ticket* instead of *Fahrkarte,* and *Standard* instead of *norm.* They use the words *computer* and *software,* but they do not use the word *calculator.* A calculator is a *Taschenrechner.* In an effort to make the German railway company more modern, the administration introduced a whole new terminology. It talks about *meeting points (Treffpunkt)* in train stations, *bahncard* (a special ticket for discounts), and *service center (Auskunft),* yet most older people have no idea what those terms mean. One of the difficulties is that an outsider cannot be sure whether they will use German or American terminology. An increasing number of Germans are concerned about the use of English in everyday German and advocate the use of German whenever possible. The newly formed *Verein Deutsche Sprache,* for example, is asking to replace English computer terminology with German terms, and there have been some changes. For example, a few years ago Germans would use "download material" and "shut down the computer." Today they say *"runterladen"* and *"runterfahren."*

In some cases, people use foreign words but adapt them to their own language both in grammatical usage and in pronunciation. For example, the Japanese have changed the word salaryman to *sarariman,* homerun to *homurunu,* headhunter to *heddo hantaa,* and the German word *Arbeit* to *arubaito,* meaning a part-time job. After some time, the words are considered Japanese because they have been integrated into the Japanese language and culture. In German, for example, the word *stress* has been integrated. Thirty years ago, nobody used the word. Today, everyone uses it. The pronunciation is German, and when it is used as a verb, it is given a German grammatical form. A German says *"Ich bin gestreßt"* (I am stressed). The word has become part of the language.

The fact that English is used widely in business has convinced some people that English will become THE international language, that there will be a convergence into English. Americans in particular are excited about this because they could imagine the day when they could forget about learning or speaking a foreign language. However, reality is more complex. While English is widely spoken in international business, there is also a divergence of English into Englishes. In a couple of hundred years, English may fragment into several languages that are very different, a development similar to the divergence of Latin into French, Spanish, Portuguese, and Italian.

Acronyms

Acronyms pose special problems because they are based on a particular language. The same institution may have different acronyms in different languages. For example, MITI, the Japanese Ministry of International Trade and Investment, is referred to as MITI by Germans but spelled out as *Ministerium für Industrie und Aussenhandel.* UN stands for the United Nations; the Germans transcribe UN as *Vereinte Nationen.* The World Trade Organization (WTO) is *Welthandelsorganisation* in German; another example where the acronym has no relation to the German word.

Implications of the Language Barrier

As the preceding examples show, communication across cultures and languages is difficult and full of hurdles and pitfalls. Even if two people from different cultures can speak a common language, they may misinterpret the cultural signals. The result is confusion and misunderstanding. Many people have difficulty identifying the root of the problem. For example, American students often complain that they can't understand their foreign professors. In some cases, the professors actually may have a poor command of the English language; however, in most cases the problem is not the language but different intonation patterns and different cultural signals. English-speaking students listen to their instructors with certain expectations. For example, if the instructor's voice drops to a low pitch, the students take that as a signal of a rhetorical topic boundary—"I'm finished with this idea"—whereas the instructor may mean no such thing. Students adjust their interpretation of the lecture according to those intonation signals, thereby misconstruing the instructor's intent. A professor who comes from a culture in which the professor is almighty and is never challenged (Korea or India, for example) may send signals to that effect to his students. If the students are not aware of the cultural issues, in all likelihood they will identify the problem as a language problem rather than a cultural problem.

In this context, the phrase "I don't understand you" can mean any of the following:

- I don't understand the words you use.
- My interpretation of what you say raises a flag and makes me wonder if this is actually what you want to say.
- In my perception, your words and nonverbal behavior do not complement each other, and I am puzzled.

Selection of the Right Language

In other parts of the book, we discuss the importance of cultural literacy in more detail. Here, however, we'll concentrate on linguistic literacy. The United States may be the only country in the world where businesspeople involved in international business do not unanimously advocate fluency in a foreign language. In other countries of the world, it is accepted that one has to learn at least one foreign language if one wants to engage in international business. The arguments Americans use are legion. The following are examples that are used frequently.

- Everyone speaks English.
- You never know where you will wind up, and so you may be learning the wrong language; therefore, it is better to wait until you know what language you will need.
- A good manager is a good manager everywhere (meaning that language is not important).
- I have been successful without learning a foreign language (implying that learning a language is a waste of time).
- You can always hire a translator.
- You probably will not be good enough to negotiate in the foreign language anyway; therefore, don't waste your time.

Misguided research tends to exacerbate the problem. A recent survey, for example, determined that Canadian and U.S. managers of international firms, by an overwhelming margin, did not think that a foreign language is very important in doing business abroad. The conclusion of the study was that language indeed is not that crucial. What the survey did not address was the problem with the approach. Monolingual managers, and the subjects in the survey were monolingual, are probably less likely to advocate fluency in a foreign language than are bi- or trilingual managers. The survey also did not include managers whose native language was not English. In addition, the survey did not examine the implications of monolinguism in a competitive environment.

Another point in the argument that the study of foreign languages may not be necessary in the future is the fact that many European and Asian universities offer an increasing number of courses in English. However, all their students speak at least one other language.

Linguistic Considerations

If you have decided to study a foreign language, the next question is, "Which one?" In light of the number of languages around the world, this decision is not easy and will be influenced by many factors. Experts don't agree on exactly how many languages are spoken; the figure is somewhere between 3,000 and 6,000. Estimates are that within the next 100 years half of those languages will disappear, and with them the diversity of cultures. Since no single language can express all forms of human thought and ideas, this reduction would make all of humanity poorer.[6] One problem is the definition of what constitutes a language. An additional factor is the distinction between a language and a dialect.

At what point does a person speak a language different from ours, and at what point does that person speak a dialect, or a variation of our language? To a German from the north who speaks *Plattdeutsch,* the dialects called *Swabian* and *Bavarian* in the south are in many ways unintelligible and therefore are foreign languages. Officially, however, all three are dialects of German. The Japanese, even though they like to tell us they are a homogeneous culture, have dialects. People from Honshu speak differently than do people from Kyushu. The political, economic, and entertainment centers of Japan are in Tokyo, which is on Honshu. As a result, the speech of people from Honshu carries more clout and people from Honshu tend to look down on the dialect of people from Kyushu. Even within Honshu there are different dialects. A professor from Tokyo commented that one of his colleagues who came from Osaka simply did not fit into the Tokyo culture very well because he continued to speak his Osaka dialect.

India is the prime example of linguistic diversity with about 600 languages, of which 14 are major languages that are spoken by about 90 percent of the population. This diversity causes problems both domestically and internationally. The 14 languages belong to two distinct language families. Languages in the north are Indo-European, and those in the south are Dravidian. To facilitate communication within the country, India recognizes three official languages: Hindi, English, and the local language (for local affairs). Of course, the number of people who actually speak English fluently is small and restricted to the educated upper middle class. Among that group, however, many people speak English even at home. They use the local language for communication with servants. Indians who live abroad find that in most cases the common language among Indians is English. The widespread use of English in India has been a major reason why American companies have located call centers in India. The companies have access to English speakers who are well educated. By Indian standards, the employees in call centers earn good money, but their salaries are much lower than they would be for American employees. Even so, companies have spent a lot of money to train call center employees to be able to use American vocabulary and intonation, and adapt to the cultural dynamics of American telephone communication. Some call centers have gone so far as to have maps of American cities with current weather conditions on the walls so employees can appear knowledgeable and credible when talking to customers in the United States. The managers of these centers have realized that a good accent alone is not sufficient, but that callers want to have the feeling they are talking to someone close by who is familiar with their environment.

China, like India, also has a number of different languages, the two dominant ones being Mandarin and Cantonese. Mandarin is spoken by about two-thirds of the population, and the political power center, Beijing, is Mandarin-speaking. The south and Hong Kong, which are more open to outside influences, speak Cantonese, although Mandarin is the official language everywhere. Mandarin and Cantonese speakers do not understand each other when they communicate orally, but they have no problems when communicating in writing. A businessperson learning Chinese should be aware of the implications of choosing Mandarin or Cantonese. People who speak Mandarin tend to look down on people who speak Cantonese, and vice versa. The Cantonese think northerners are barbarians, and northerners feel superior to Cantonese speakers. This is a clear sign of regional and linguistic snobbery. A quick search on the Internet indicates that the number of Mandarin language schools in Hong Kong has mushroomed during the past few years; however, Cantonese native speakers speak Mandarin with a strong accent, and the Chinese Mandarin speakers don't usually speak Cantonese at all, so the old snobberies persist.

Business Considerations

After weighing linguistic aspects, you also must consider business aspects in deciding which language to learn. Your decision will depend partly on whether you are the buyer or the seller of a product. Many businesspeople argue that one needs to speak the language of the customer. If you want to sell a product, it is in your interest to adapt and learn. However, other economic considerations also will influence your decision. For example, if you are the only manufacturer of a product that is in high demand, you may be able to sell and be very successful without speaking the language of your customer, at least in the short run. However, if you look ahead, you may find that even in these favorable circumstances it is in your long-term interest to adapt to the customer.

After World War II, U.S. businesses dominated the international markets. The production facilities of most other industrial countries lay in ruins. As a result, products made in the United States were in high demand. In the short run, this was very beneficial for American firms. Unfortunately, Americans did not look at the long term. They acted as if that situation would continue forever and as if their products were in demand not because they were the only products around but because they were somehow superior. The United States has paid dearly for its unwillingness to adapt and for the shortsightedness and arrogance of its business-people. For example, Caterpillar Tractor did not consider Komatsu a serious competitor until after Komatsu had established itself in international markets.

If businesses in the United States want to expand their international markets, their people must learn the languages used in the potential markets. The Japanese are learning English, the Koreans are learning English, yet until recently very few native English speakers studied Korean or Japanese. The typical argument was that those languages are too difficult to master and are spoken only in one country. The Japanese have contributed to that sentiment by insisting that their language is very special and that outsiders can never penetrate and master it. In reality, Japanese is not impossible to learn if people are determined. The same is true for Korean and Chinese. Today an increasing number of schools are offering Japanese, Korean, and Chinese. For example, today 13 high schools in Chicago have Chinese language programs. Fifteen years ago, Chinese was not offered.

The language you choose will depend on your goals and purposes. If your native language is not English, you may want to study it since English is the lingua franca of international business. In fact, in many countries English is the most frequently taught foreign language; often it is required in school. Switzerland has three official languages: German, French, and Italian. In the past, schools taught all three and every student was required to learn them. Today, many Swiss learn only one of the other Swiss languages and take English as their first or second foreign language. Chinese university students under present policy must pass a College English Test, level 4 (CET-4) in order to get a bachelor degree, regardless of their performance in other courses. In many cities, like Shanghai, the mandatory test has created a whole new line of business. Students frequently hire someone to take the exam for them. The practice is illegal, but it is tempting if graduation depends on passing the test.[7]

If you live in an English-speaking country and come from a family that considers its ethnic roots very important, you may study that language and decide to do business with that country. For example, if your family is from Iran, you may decide to study Farsi and do business with Iran. You may find that culturally you have some background already and are therefore at an advantage. If it is your life's dream to do business in Brazil, you should study Portuguese and then look for a job in Brazil or with a firm that does business with Brazil.

If you don't have a specific reason to study a particular language, you might want to decide on the basis of political and economic importance in the world, and the importance of the language in business relations with your country. A number of people might argue that if your native language is English, you should choose German or Japanese because those two countries are very strong economically. Others would add Spanish (particularly because of the North American Free Trade Agreement), French, and Chinese. Others might argue that Russian is a good choice, or Arabic because of the oil interests. The point is that you need to think of your goals and then choose the appropriate language. There is no right language, but there is no wrong language if you have good reasons.

What if you study French and then are sent to Japan? This is a realistic possibility. Many U.S. companies still argue that they cannot send someone to a country just because that person is familiar with the culture and language of that country. One major multinational corporation (MNC) actually insisted that business knowledge was the overriding factor in selecting employees for assignments abroad. Language and cultural knowledge were not considered. It is interesting to note that this company has had major problems abroad over the last decade and is facing increasing international competition. It seems strange to think that linguistic and cultural ability are not considered aspects of a business decision.

If you have mastered one foreign language, the second foreign language is easier. Therefore, even if you have the "wrong" language, you may find that it takes less time to gain facility in the second. In many cases, foreign businesspeople react negatively to the fact that an American speaks *no* foreign language rather than the *wrong* language. If the Japanese find out you only know a few words in Japanese but are fluent in English, Spanish, and French, they may be less critical. Although ideally you would speak Japanese, at least you speak other languages; you have worked at languages and made the effort. The sentence "I'm sorry, I do not speak Japanese, but I do speak French and Spanish" can work very well to show that you are not the typical monolingual American.

Political Considerations

If you already work for a firm, your decision about which language to study will be influenced by where your company does business. The political environment of international locations also will play a role. If you will be involved with the government to a large extent and if that communication must be in the native language, you may find it necessary to become at least functional in that language, meaning you can communicate both orally and in writing although you may not have mastered the grammar and fine points of the language. The private sector may be more forgiving than the public sector when it comes to speaking the language. Being able to speak the language also carries symbolic value. If you do business with a firm in Quebec, you may get through with English, but your linguistic insensitivity could have serious negative consequences.

The Appropriate Level of Fluency

Ideally, you should speak several languages fluently; that is, like the natives of the host country, you speak, write, understand, and think in the foreign language. That's the ideal, but most people fall short of that goal. We use all sorts of phrases to describe levels of fluency. Typical labels are *native, near-native, fluent, functional,* and *conversational.* The labels are not very precise, and many speakers have a tendency to overstate their language proficiency. A Midwestern law firm in the United States claims that all of its partners are "fluent" in at least two foreign languages. In light of the typical American attitude toward studying foreign languages, one may wonder what definition of *fluency* the firm uses. Frequently, employees appear to be proficient in speaking a foreign language; however, that appearance may be deceptive. An employee may have mastered the vocabulary in a rather narrow area of business, but outside of that area his or her language ability may be very limited. The employee is said to have mastered the foreign language for *special purposes,* as the following experience illustrates.

In Focus

One of the authors purchased some lace in a lace shop in the city of Antwerp. The shop attendant, a woman of about 60, could communicate without any difficulties in English. She appeared to have a large vocabulary when explaining about the different levels and quality and the origin of the lace. Her accent was excellent, and she was very easy to understand. It was only when the conversation went away from lace to other topics that it became apparent that her communication abilities in English were limited. She was fast to point out that she could talk about lace but very little else. She knew that she was good at selling lace but did not have the linguistic or cultural background to discuss other issues in English. She was very effective in what she did; she had the personality to deal with people from many different backgrounds in a very limited scope. She is a very good example of the intercultural and language competencies required for employees at lower levels. These people must have concrete knowledge in their area and be able to communicate that expertise to people from other cultural backgrounds.

Although linguistic fluency is undoubtedly important and a great advantage in doing business with people from other cultures, it is not the only criterion. Equally important, as was pointed out previously, is cultural fluency. A person who speaks some Spanish but is knowledgeable about the culture of Mexico will be more successful in doing business in Mexico than will a person who speaks Spanish fluently but knows little about Mexican culture. Cultural learning must accompany language learning. Some argue that by learning a foreign language one automatically is exposed to the culture. That is not necessarily true. All too many language courses in the United States, Japan, Thailand, Russia, and many other countries are taught by teachers who have never been to the country or were there only for a short period, possibly quite some time ago. Furthermore, the emphasis in many language classes is on mastering grammar and spelling rather than on understanding the underlying culture. As a result, students studying the Japanese language may learn very little about Japan and the Japanese.

If you plan to live in a foreign country for an extended period, your need to speak the language is greater than it is if you will be there for just a few days. If you want to make that country a major center for your foreign manufacturing, your linguistic needs are greater than they will be if you want to export a product that is in high demand (also see Chapter 10). The need for, and level of, fluency also are connected to the adaptation phase of culture shock (see Chapter 1). Language facility will help with the adjustment process.

If you want to understand why people act the way they do, if you want to get a feel for their way of thinking in order to be better at negotiating, you need a higher level of fluency than you would have if you always use an interpreter. If you rely on an interpreter, however, you should be aware of the limitations you are imposing on your business opportunities.

For most people, it is easier to comprehend than to speak a foreign language. The following lists a few possible reasons for this phenomenon:

- People are intimidated; therefore, they do not try.
- People are worried about using the wrong verb forms and tenses.
- People may be trying to translate a sentence from their own language word for word into the foreign language and realize that this process is not very effective. As a result, they get discouraged.
- People think too long about what they want to say, and so they don't participate in the conversation. By the time they have formulated the words they wish to use, the conversation has moved on.
- People are worried about being judged negatively and about losing face.

Our level of comprehension is influenced by the speed with which the speaker goes through points, by the pronunciation, by the pauses in the conversation, and by colloquialisms and idioms. Speech patterns are affected by a variety of factors, among them ethnic background, geographic differences, and gender. For example, recent research studies have pointed out that men and women have very different speech patterns that greatly influence the perception of communication and the success of communication. Men tend to interrupt a speaker more frequently than women do. Men are more direct, whereas women are more indirect and ambiguous in what they say.[8] If people who are native speakers of the same language have different communication styles that are based on different communication principles, we can understand that the problems are compounded when the speakers come from different cultures.

Perceptions of fluency also are influenced by nonverbal communication. Nonverbal communication plays a major role in all countries; however, the nonverbal is more pronounced in high-context cultures than in low-context cultures. If we are from a low-context background, we may not be consciously aware of the nonverbal and think that the meaning comes out of the spoken word. How much the nonverbal influences our comprehension, specifically if we speak in a foreign language, becomes obvious when we communicate in a foreign language on the telephone.[9] The ring of the telephone in a foreign country can strike terror in the hearts of even courageous people. Even people who are fairly fluent may have problems on the telephone. All of a sudden they are speaking in isolation without nonverbal clues and nonverbal feedback. For example, they cannot see a facial expression signaling approval or doubt. The nonverbal aspects definitely help us in the comprehension process (also see Chapter 6).

The Company Language

Choosing a Company Language

As companies expand their international dealings, the number of languages their employees have to deal with increases. A domestic Korean company does not have to worry about different languages, but as the company expands, the picture changes. When the firm establishes subsidiaries in Thailand and Taiwan, the company must deal in three linguistic markets: Korean, Mandarin, and Thai. In which language should employees communicate with each other? The answer is influenced to some extent by staffing patterns (for a more detailed discussion of the influence of staffing on communication, refer to Chapter 11). If the Korean firm uses **ethnocentric staffing,** filling all managerial positions with Korean personnel in all three locations, all communications with headquarters and among the managers from the three subsidiaries can be in Korean. In ethnocentric staffing, all managers in all subsidiaries are from the home country. In the preceding scenario, the interface between the language of the home country and those of the host countries occurs somewhere in the subsidiaries. The Korean managers either must learn the local language or depend on translators to communicate with the local workforce.

Today, ethnocentric staffing is considered insensitive, exploitative, and outdated. Many firms therefore are using **polycentric staffing** patterns. In polycentric staffing, all managers in all subsidiaries come from the respective subsidiary country. That means that the Korean firm will hire only Taiwanese people for its subsidiary in Taiwan, and only Thais for its subsidiary in Thailand. Polycentric staffing is based on the argument that local managers are better able to communicate in the specific environment. The linguistic interface—the contact between the language of headquarters and the language of the subsidiary—occurs in the communication between headquarters and the subsidiary. Therefore, polycentric staffing makes the communication between subsidiaries more difficult. In which language, for example, do the Thais and the Taiwanese communicate with each other? The communication problem is even more pronounced in **geocentric staffing.** In geocentric staffing, the best person is chosen for a job regardless of linguistic, cultural, and national background. In the previous scenario, the company may have Taiwanese, Thais, and Koreans working at headquarters in Korea. Geocentric staffing brings people from diverse linguistic and cultural backgrounds into the same office where they must work side by side.

In the past few years, companies have started to employ an additional staffing pattern: **the roving assignment.** Under this staffing pattern, employees are sent abroad on an as-needed basis. For example, an information systems specialist may be sent to South Africa for three weeks to repair a system. He may then go to Korea for five months to install new systems. Then he may go back to headquarters for several months. Typically, these roving employees have a technical specialization. While on assignment abroad, they frequently have limited contact with local employees. They are there to solve a particular problem and will be gone within a short time period. Exhibit 2.1 summarizes the characteristics of the various staffing patterns.

As a result of geographic expansion and changes in staffing, more and more companies have designated an official company language. That means that all communication in a company will be conducted in the company language. That sounds easy enough; in practice, however, it is somewhat more complex. A firm that is headquartered in Japan and does business in the United States, France, Germany, Holland, Saudi Arabia, Mexico, Brazil, South Africa, and Nigeria may decide that the company language is Japanese. It is unlikely that all the employees in the various subsidiaries speak Japanese. Speaking Japanese could hardly be made a condition of employment. In this case, the company language refers to communication among managers from a certain level up. In the case of Japanese, given how few non-Japanese people actually speak Japanese, the firm would need a good number of Japanese managers at each subsidiary who would communicate with headquarters.

The firm does not have to choose the language of the home country where headquarters are located for its company language. It could decide that the language of the home country is not spoken by many people around the globe and

EXHIBIT 2.1   Staffing

	Headquarters Managers	Subsidiary Managers
Ethnocentric Staffing	Home country	Home country
Polycentric Staffing	Home country	Host country
Geocentric staffing	Best person regardless of country	Best person regardless of country

therefore a more widely spoken language is a better choice. For example, Philips, a Dutch firm, has chosen English as its company language. Komatsu from Japan has set the goal that all employees, even in the Japanese home office, will communicate in English. The firm provides the appropriate language lessons. Samsung from Korea also has started obligatory English language lessons for all its employees. This clearly represents a recognition of the importance of English in international business. A typical example is the language of aviation. Pilots and flight controllers around the world are expected to communicate in English. For years, French pilots resisted the use of English in French airspace, but then Air France ordered all its pilots to use only English when talking to air-traffic controllers at Charles de Gaulle. It seems that safety considerations favor the change from French to English.

In his book, *Outliers: The Story of Success,* Malcolm Gladwell shows that a foreign language, in this case English, can overcome cultural restrictions of people's native languages. He documents how the Korean language through its emphasis on hierarchy and obedience contributed to the crash of an airplane. In Korean culture, the pilot is the unquestioned ruler of the airplane, and anyone else in the cockpit is expected to follow his orders. This hierarchy is clearly expressed in the language and limits the copilot in questioning decisions made by the pilot. In the example, the copilot and the flight engineer were concerned, but they felt they could not question the authority and ability of the pilot. As a result, many people died. After a long investigation, Korean Air decided to mandate the use of English in all cockpit communication. They were convinced that English would level the playing field because it does not have the linguistic emphasis on hierarchy that Korean does. Therefore, it was hoped that the copilot and flight engineer would feel more comfortable questioning the pilot's decisions.[10]

Business English as a lingua franca (BELF) has been characterized as operating within a domain that provides a specific context for communication, such as in the earlier example with the airline industry. Charles identifies the specific context as "the globalized business community. . . [which] is thus the sociopragmatic backdrop" of BELF.[11] In other words, the globalized business environment is described as very similar to a culture. Common practices exist for members of this global business culture. Corporate organizational hierarchies, roles of speakers and writers, and corporate cultures are some of the elements in the global business sociopragmatic context that affect communication. Communicators in global businesses share expectations about communication protocols for e-mail messages, faxes, memos, and meetings. In the commonly experienced environment of globalized business, differences in employees' cultures and languages are no longer emphasized, but are subsumed by the corporate language and culture. BELF is often the language of organizations with no native speakers of English, and operates among users who negotiate meanings for words in the contexts they share. However, although the sociopragmatic context indeed acts in some ways as a culture, nevertheless, "the speakers *creating* the lingua franca do have a cultural background and, in fact, a diversity of backgrounds."[12] Those speakers—and writers—still retain their languages, values, and culturally based behaviors, and are likely to fall back upon the certainties of their native language and culture in situations where they need to be precise in meaning, rather than the situation-specific lingua franca of the global business environment, in which BELF meanings are negotiated among users.

Modern technology, the Internet, e-commerce, e-mail, and teleconferencing have contributed greatly to the international use of English. What U.S. businesspeople must keep in mind, however, is that *all* these businesspeople are fluent in at least one other language besides English, namely, their respective native languages, and many of them speak at least one additional language. A Korean businessperson fluent in English can do business in both Korean and English; an American businessperson fluent only in English can do business only in English. The Korean market will thus be more difficult to enter for Americans in these circumstances.

Traditionally, the official company language was the language of the home country. That seems to be changing, as the previous examples indicate. If two firms from different countries do business, and the language of neither country is widely spoken, they face a different dilemma. Each may have a company language, but that does not necessarily help in this case. For example, the Polish firm Bechaltow Industries has started a cooperative venture with Tama Corporation in Japan. The two firms have at least three options for communicating with each other, assuming the Poles do not speak Japanese and the Japanese do not speak Polish:

- They can use a Polish-Japanese interpreter; however, the number of Polish-Japanese interpreters is probably quite limited.
- They can use two interpreters, one a Polish-English interpreter and the other a Japanese-English interpreter.
- Both companies may have declared English as the company language; therefore, managers could negotiate directly in English.

Even if both sides speak English, they still face hurdles. For example, do they speak the same English, or does the Polish firm speak British English while the Japanese firm speaks American English? Furthermore, the English the Polish managers speak will have some Polish characteristics, and the English the Japanese managers speak will have some Japanese characteristics. Typically, the cultural references, thought, and language patterns of each side will influence their communication in English. They may have different preferences for organizing material and providing detail.[13]

No matter what the company language is, any international firm experiences the need to adjust to the differences between the company language and the local language(s) of foreign subsidiaries, partners, clients, and suppliers. With a company language that applies to all managers, the interface between languages typically takes place between management and local employees below the managerial level. A U.S. firm that uses English as the company language cannot expect that all its employees in Venezuela will speak English. Employees below the managerial level probably speak Spanish. Therefore, translation will be necessary when the two languages come together.

A company language facilitates communication among subsidiaries and between headquarters and subsidiaries; it can, however, also give headquarters a false sense of security if headquarters personnel think that everyone in the company is fluent in the company language. As many reports attest, businesspeople from English-speaking cultures have difficulties understanding the complications and consequences of limited English.

The following case illustrates some of the issues that arise even if a firm has a company language.

In Focus

A U.S. firm with a subsidiary in Tokyo used English as the company language. The subsidiary had one American employee who spoke some Japanese but was not fluent. He did not read or write Japanese. The president and the two vice presidents spoke native Japanese. The president spoke very good German and, on the surface, good English. The vice president for finance also spoke German and some English, but his English was much more limited. The vice president for sales had very limited English. The marketing manager was Japanese and had a B.A. from a university in the United States. His English was very good but getting rusty. The rest of the employees generally spoke a little English, such as tourist phrases, but not enough to carry on a conversation or do business in English.

Nobody at headquarters spoke Japanese. In this situation, all communication between headquarters and the subsidiaries occurred in English. Headquarters relied on the company language and assumed that communication was no problem. The reality was more complicated. In the Japanese subsidiary, for example, the American employee received all incoming memos from headquarters. He would read many of them and often respond to inquiries and, if asked, help the Japanese managers with their communications with headquarters. In effect, he was an interpreter in the communication between the subsidiary and headquarters. However, he had not been sent to Tokyo for that purpose. He had a specific job to do; he was the operations manager and was in charge of information systems. The interpretation took place "on the side."

Headquarters would send lengthy e-mails with detailed financial figures on a weekly basis to the vice president for finance, whose English was limited. The memos were not adapted to a foreign speaker of English. Headquarters assumed that the vice president for finance read all the material; however, when the correspondence between headquarters and the subsidiary was examined, it became obvious that headquarters had to ask for information a second or third time before the vice president for finance would respond. Initially, the vice president was reluctant to discuss the situation, but after some time he admitted that he was overwhelmed by the sheer volume of the correspondence. He did not read the original memos because it took too much time and because he got frustrated with all the details. He worked under the assumption that if someone *really* needed information from him, that person would get back to him with the specifics. He would have preferred a clear and concise summary of major points adapted to his level of English but was worried about losing face if he explained the problem. What he got was lengthy memos written by native English speakers for native English speakers. The vice president developed his own way of coping with the situation, a solution that was costly and time-consuming.

The vice president for international operations at headquarters in the United States, when first asked about his communication with Japan by one of the authors, said there were no problems: "The Japanese speak English, so there is no language hurdle." Only after lengthy discussions did he admit that he was concerned about his interaction with Japan. He felt that the Japanese president of the subsidiary spoke "social" English but had a limited grasp of English when it came to business concepts and business discussions. The president of the Japanese subsidiary pretended to understand, and on the surface there were no problems, but the vice president at headquarters became increasingly frustrated with the communication process. He somehow did not seem to get through. As a result, communication between headquarters and the subsidiary, although smooth on the surface, was complicated, often redundant, and ineffective.

Using Additional Foreign Language Expertise

How can you use your foreign language expertise if the company language is English? The purpose of the company language is to ensure that everyone in the firm can understand everyone else; therefore, the use of foreign languages may be discouraged or at least limited. This comes back to the assumption that in an English-speaking firm native English speakers do not need a foreign language since everything is written in English and all negotiations within the firm take place in English. As a result, a Japanese subsidiary of a firm headquartered in an English-speaking country may hire not the best person, but the person with the best English.

The point is that in both examples, the Japanese and the French, the company language, although the official language, may not be sufficient for clear and effective communication. An official company language will simplify communication within an international firm, but to assume that the declaration of an official language will eliminate all communication problems, even within the firm, is absurd. There will always be the point of interface between the company language and the local language. Even companies with a definite company language will have to be flexible to some extent and adapt to specific circumstances. Monolingual companies of native speakers have many communication problems; no wonder people from different backgrounds speaking the same company language also have communication problems. Intercultural communication goes beyond the mastery of a foreign language.

In Focus

Patricia, who is French but speaks fluent English, Spanish, and Dutch, works for an American firm in the United States that does business in many countries, one of them being France. The company language is English. She sends a copy of all the memos she prepares to the European subsidiaries to her boss and, if necessary, to other managers. When she corresponds with Arnaud Marchais, who is French and speaks limited English, she must write in English because that is the company language and because the managers at headquarters that she sends copies to speak no French or only limited French. It appears that her language expertise is being wasted.

Patricia has found a way around the dilemma, though. In some cases she will write a memo to Arnaud Marchais in French and then send a copy of the original plus an English translation to the people who need a copy. This, of course, takes extra time, and some managers at headquarters may resent the use of French anyway and be suspicious of secret dealings.

Patricia can use her foreign language expertise more extensively when she talks to Arnaud on the phone or when she visits the subsidiary in France. Arnaud appreciates the fact that he can contact Patricia and talk to her in French about a particular problem and get an answer he can understand. Patricia's ability to communicate with Arnaud in the French language has improved business considerably, and Arnaud feels understood and appreciated.

The Role of the Interpreter

To overcome the communication problems in international business created by the multitude of languages spoken around the world, businesses hire interpreters or translators. Many people use the two terms interchangeably; however, there is a difference.

Translators work with the written word, transferring text from a source language into a target language. This is far more than replacing one word with another. The translator must also convey the style, tone, and intent of the text. The finished document should read as if it had originally been written in the target language for the target audience. Interpreters work with the spoken word, transferring speech from a source language into a target language. This is far more than speaking two languages fluently. The interpreter must also communicate the style and tone of the speaker, while taking into account differences of culture and dialect. The listeners should hear the interpreted message as if it had been originally spoken in their own language.

"Verbatim" translation is not always possible. When the source material includes concepts that are not known in the target language (for example, "snowshoeing" to an Amazonian tribe), word-for-word translation is impossible. Understanding this, translators differentiate between two basic approaches. Formal equivalence generally seeks to preserve the words, their order, and even the grammatical construction of the source material in the target language, rendering it as literally as possible, while dynamic or functional equivalence seeks to communicate the ideas expressed in the source material in a way that is fluent and natural for the target language.

Translators have greater freedom than interpreters do to seek dynamic equivalence. A translator usually has time to think about how to render difficult terms and can consult numerous sources. In contrast, due to the time constraints and immediacy of oral situations (where interpreters translate 120–180 words per minute, and they must be right the first time), it is far more likely that interpreters will, in practice, be more literal in their renderings than translators.[14]

The interpreter facilitates mutual understanding and comprehension. She is a conduit and does not enter the discussion on her own behalf. In successful interpretation, the intended message comes across at the first try. This sounds easy enough, but there are numerous hurdles and problems. Let us look at the process as it is illustrated in Exhibit 2.2.

EXHIBIT 2.2 **Communicating through an Interpreter**

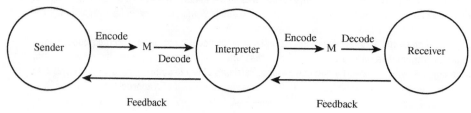

An interpreter must decode what the speaker says and then encode the message for the listener. Businesspeople who are new to international business often assume that the interpreter understands all the signals that are being sent and decodes them as intended. This requires that the interpreter be both linguistically and culturally fluent in both languages and cultures. The interpreter must pick up both the verbal and the nonverbal signs of all the people in the discussion.

As we discussed in Chapter 1, perception plays a huge role in communication. We always communicate with our perception of the receiver rather than with the receiver himself. When we use an interpreter, our message goes through the additional filter of the interpreter, who has her own perception of the sender and the receiver. Narrowing the gap between perception and reality requires an interpreter who understands both sides very well.

Organizations such as the European Union and the United Nations offer excellent examples of the importance of good interpreters. As the following example illustrates, for some languages interpreters are hard to find, and good interpreters are expensive.

In Focus

When the European Union (EU) expanded to 25 countries in May 2004, many people celebrated. However, the people in charge of communication among the member countries worried about finding interpreters to deal with the increased work load. Based on the law of the EU, all written documents are translated into all member languages. All discussions at meetings are translated simultaneously to ensure that every member country gets the information in their own language at the same time—a huge undertaking. When the EU started in 1957, it had six countries and a total of four different languages, resulting in 12 different translation combinations. With 25 members who speak a total of 20 different languages, the possible translation combinations have risen to 380. But the sheer number of options is not the only problem; an even greater issue is the availability of interpreters. For example, there are very few people who speak Estonian and Maltese. In some languages, the modern business vocabulary is nonexistent, raising the issue of either creating the terminology or using foreign vocabulary. Also, given that Malta has about 400,000 inhabitants, some of the other small EU countries have argued that if everything will be translated into Maltese, it would only be fair to translate everything into Gaelic, Basque, or Catalan. So far, only Ireland has succeeded in having Gaelic recognized as an official EU language.

The EU spends about $1.6 billion annually on translation alone. It operates the largest interpretation service in the world, where every day thousands of pages are translated into all the member languages. The sheer size of the operation is overwhelming, and some begin to be concerned about the cost of multilingualism. As the combinations grow, exact translations become more challenging. For example, when a member of the European Parliament described the EU Constitution as gobbledygook, the interpreter for Polish was at a loss, and the discussion stopped until the interpreter found a suitable term.

Yet in spite of all the problems, language in the EU is not merely a linguistic issue. It is, more importantly, a political and cultural issue. If the EU were to declare some languages, such as English, German, French, Italian, and Spanish, as official EU languages, the smaller members would see their role diminished.

Given that the EU membership is scheduled to increase to 29 by the year 2014, the possible translation combinations will then grow to 552.[15]

The Importance of Choosing a Good Interpreter

Interpreters should be chosen with great care. Native speaking ability does not automatically make a person a skilled and effective interpreter. For example, a U.S. transportation company asked a woman from Germany to translate several business letters relating to trucks. The problem was that the woman did not know the terms relating to trucking in either German or English. She was well educated but had no idea what the word *Sattelschlepper* meant in German and therefore could not translate the term correctly as *semi-truck*. When she pointed that out to the American requestor, he was puzzled. His response was, "If you speak German, you can translate this well enough. We just want to know what the letter says."

An interpreter must be fluent in the language of the field in which she translates. A poet may be able to interpret for Japanese and English speakers in the field of literature but be at a loss when asked to interpret in business.

Interpreting is hard work. People study for many years to become effective interpreters. Many businesspeople who don't speak a foreign language are under the assumption that a native speaker can act as an interpreter easily and effectively. They are totally unaware of the work involved in the process. As a result, many U.S. businesspeople hire foreign students or native speakers of the foreign language who live in the United States as interpreters for their companies. The results may be costly, embarrassing, and amusing. Ricks, an international business professor, for example, relates that in one case a student from Indonesia who was not familiar with computer terminology translated *software* as *underwear*.[16] That example goes back several years, and today one might expect that educated people around the globe know basic computer terminology. However, mistranslations and poor translations remain a problem. The economic development committee of a Midwestern city in the United States was interested in attracting foreign businesses to the area. One of the target countries was Germany. The committee developed a brochure in English and then had it translated into German. The brochure looked good but had a number of language mistakes, though no major problems. In the process of preparing the brochure, the names of two members of the council had been omitted. The committee went ahead and prepared a brief statement explaining the omission and providing the names. This statement was translated and attached to all the brochures.

The translation of the supplement was a total disaster. It was almost unintelligible even if the reader knew both English and German. The committee would have done better to leave the names off rather than sending the "correction." Reading the supplement would only confirm all the prejudices Germans have about the low language ability and superficiality of Americans. The disastrous translation also showed that the committee was not very thorough and careful in checking the credentials of the translator.

Interpreters, then, must be chosen with the greatest care. The following guidelines will help you in making a good choice and getting an interpreter whose work you can use.

The Effective Use of an Interpreter—Some Guidelines

Hire Your Own Interpreter

It is amazing how many businesspeople, who are usually very careful about business matters, rely on their foreign business partner to supply an interpreter. You should definitely hire your own interpreter. Most embassies or commercial sections of an embassy have lists of translation and interpretation services you might contact if you don't know anybody. Language institutes such as Berlitz, the Alliance Française, and the Goetheinstitut also may be able to help you find an interpreter.

Why do you need your own interpreter? Because you need an interpreter who understands your side and who is loyal to you.

Whenever Possible, Meet with the Interpreter Beforehand

Before using an interpreter for business needs, you must first feel comfortable with the interpreter and develop a level of trust. Unless you can use the same interpreter each time you do business in Cairo, Taipei, or Seoul, you need to establish some common ground. Meeting them beforehand will also assure you of the interpreter's competency in your language even though you may not be able to check his or her competency in the target language.

Hire Qualified Professionals

Don't ask a colleague from another department to translate for you unless it is that person's job to translate for others. If you use a colleague, you need to set the ground rules very carefully. Do you want translation only, or do you want input from the colleagues? If you want input, the colleague must separate his or her own comments from what the other side says.

Check the Technical Expertise of the Interpreter

Even if you hire the interpreter through a reputable agency, you need to check the technical background of the interpreter. Has she translated in your field before? How much experience does she have? Has she kept up in the field? You may want

In Focus

Midori Ito, a Japanese woman who regularly interprets for Japanese and U.S. businesses, emphasizes this point. She explains that in most cases she is hired and paid by the Japanese side and is asked to translate for both the Japanese and the Americans. Let us assume the Americans are preparing an answer to a question by the Japanese. They discuss the point among themselves before they finalize the answer. Ito says that the Japanese negotiators regularly ask her for a translation or at least a summary of the discussion preceding the official response. The Americans don't know that, and they hardly ever ask for that information on the Japanese side. The translator, for her part, does not volunteer that information. Her argument is that the Japanese pay her; they ask, and the Americans don't. Her loyalty is to the Japanese side, not to the American side. Clearly, the Americans are at a disadvantage in this situation.

to check references from past employers. As was pointed out earlier, technical expertise in your field is very important to ensure correct translations.

Inform the Interpreter of Your Business Plan and Objectives

If the interpreter understands the overall objectives and the purpose of the meeting, she will be more effective than will be the case if she comes into the session uninformed and is asked to translate phrase by phrase. If the interpreter understands the overall goal, she will be able to interpret nuances better and see otherwise isolated statements in the overall context. It is easier to translate in context.

Treat the Interpreter as a Professional

Even though you inform the interpreter of the objectives and provide necessary background information and details, the interpreter is not a member of the negotiation team. She is hired as an outside professional with specific expertise. To ask the interpreter to enter into the actual decision-making process and ask the interpreter for business advice is wrong. It is fair neither to the interpreter nor to your business. Your relationship with the interpreter is professional and at arm's length.

Provide Breaks

Interpreting is hard work. It is both mentally and physically exhausting. If you want good work from an interpreter, you must provide the right environment. Regular breaks for the interpreter are essential even if you feel you can still continue.

Speak Clearly

Even if the interpreter is fluent in your language, you must speak clearly and at a reasonable pace. You should be particularly careful if you speak a dialect, in which case the interpreter may have difficulty understanding you and following your reasoning. Dialects can be difficult for speakers of the same language; with foreign speakers the problems are compounded. The interpreter must feel comfortable asking you to repeat something if he does not understand you the first time. The following example illustrates the difficulties that can arise between two speakers of the same language when one speaks a dialect.

Concentrate on the Business Partner, Not on the Interpreter

Many businesspeople look at the interpreter as they speak and neglect the business partner. To get every bit of nonverbal information you can, you must concentrate on the other side and watch them as you speak. This is even more important if the other side has some knowledge of your language. Maybe they don't speak your language fluently, but they may speak it a little and follow the general trend of what you say as you give your message to your interpreter. In that case, you want to be able to read their reaction to what you say as early as possible. Also, you want them to understand your nonverbal communication; therefore, you need to speak to the audience, not to the interpreter.

When the interpreter translates your message, you must watch the other side for all the nonverbal signals. In some cultures, the nonverbal signals may be obvious;

In Focus

A German MBA student at a university in the United States had an internship with a major German multinational. The student came from the north of Germany, from the area around Dortmund, and had been in the United States for four years. Her English was excellent. The German firm was located in the south of Germany near Stuttgart, where people speak the local dialect, Swabian. This area is also referred to as the German "Silicon Valley," the name used for the area in California where many high-tech computer companies have their headquarters.

Since the area around Stuttgart had been rather prosperous for the last few years, the natives were proud of their dialect and some even argued that the economic success was proof that their language, usually belittled by people from the north, was superior.

The intern had a hard time communicating with her co-workers in German. She spoke German, her manager and supervisor spoke German, but she typically would have to ask them to repeat what they had said. Even after they repeated their messages in what they considered standard German, she might not understand. Pronunciation and word choice were affected by their dialect. A foreign interpreter who learned standard German would face the same problem. International managers need to remember to enunciate as clearly as possible. They don't want to waste time by repeating information needlessly.

in others, such as the Japanese culture, you will have to concentrate and watch more closely. With practice, you will be able to decipher the nonverbal reactions more accurately and use the information in your responses and questions. If, for example, the other side acts surprised at what you say, you may want to find out the reasons for that. You may want to ask about their expectations in more detail.

As the people on the other side discuss your response, again watch closely. You need to ask the interpreter for the specifics of that discussion.

Also watch the other side as the interpreter translates into your language. They will watch for your reaction. In some cases, you may want to ask the interpreter for a word-for-word response and also for the cultural translation of the response.

Find Out about the Role of the Interpreter on the Other Side

The other side may have a professional interpreter or use an employee from the company. Maybe the person is a regular member of the negotiation team. If at all possible, you should find out the status of the interpreter.

A number of businesspeople from the United States, not speaking the language of the partner and not knowing the status of the interpreter, talk to the interpreter. After all, the interpreter speaks English and seems to know what is going on. They feel comfortable with that person. Only too late may they find out that they have just spent time with an outsider or subordinate and neglected the person or persons in charge.

Check the Work of the Interpreter, Especially Numbers

You may argue that the reason you have an interpreter is that you can't speak the language and therefore cannot check the accuracy of the translation. Still, you can do a lot to ensure accuracy. In all written materials you need to check the accuracy of names, dates, and numbers. An interpreter who realizes that you check will be more careful in her work. As numbers can be difficult to translate and as misunderstandings can occur easily, you should always write out numbers to be on the safe side. In Chinese, for example, where 10,000 is a unit of measurement, people should always denote the amount of zeros in the number. Chinese frequently mistranslate as *millions* numbers that are hundreds of thousands. A similar problem occurs between English and German. The Germans use the following sequence: thousand, hundred thousand, million, milliarde, billion. English jumps from million to billion. Whereas Americans say that the damage from a flood in the United States in 1993 was $15 billion (15,000,000,000), in German that would be 15 *milliarden.* If the translator uses the word *billion* in the German context, the damage will be overstated greatly. Even within the English-speaking world, *billion* does not mean the same quantity. In British English, 1,000,000,000 is a thousand million; the British billion is a million million, or a trillion in the United States (1,000,000,000,000).

Communication with Nonnative Speakers

In many situations, you may not be fluent in the other language but cannot have an interpreter, and you must deal directly with a nonnative speaker who is not fluent in your language. The success of the communication will depend to a great extent on how well you adapt to that person. Talking loudly and repeating everything will not necessarily improve the communication. If the other side does not understand you at your regular pitch and volume of speech, they will not understand you any better if you scream. If the other side is not familiar with baseball, they will not understand the statement "This time we are going to be successful; all the bases are loaded, and our heavy hitter is stepping up to the plate," and no amount of repeating will change that. Communicating with nonnative speakers in any language takes skill and experience. The following points may help you be more successful.

Effective Face-to-Face Communication

Enunciate

You must speak clearly so that the person understands the words you use. Contractions are troublesome because they blur individual words.

Speak Slowly

Native speakers in any language seem to speak fast; at least that is the perception of a nonnative speaker. Slowing down helps a nonnative speaker comprehend what you say. You must adjust your speed to the level of the other side. The nonverbal clues your partner sends will help you adjust. If the other person looks puzzled or has to ask you a few times to repeat something, you may be speaking too fast. In that case, you should repeat your idea slowly and, if that does not work, repeat it again using different words.

For example, an Australian who has studied some Arabic wants to show what he has learned. He will appreciate it if his partner from Egypt will slow down and give him a chance to both understand and speak.

Avoid Slang and Colloquialisms

Unless the speaker has lived in your country for some time, you should avoid slang and colloquial expressions. Slang changes; therefore, the other side may not be familiar with the latest terms. For example, a person who speaks English fluently but has not had any contact with the United States over the last few years may not know what a student means when saying "Get a life" or "Awesome." An executive who studied German years ago will not have any idea what *"Ich hab keinen Bock"* means; it is the adolescent expression for "I'm not interested" or "I don't care." French Canadians say *"J'ai mon voyage"* (I have my trip) when an English speaker might say "That's the last straw." They say *"Ce n'est pas un cadeau"* or shorten the phrase to the grammatically incorrect *"C'est pas un cadeau"* (It is no gift) when something is not going well; English speakers might say "It's no joke." In France, these French-Canadian idioms would sound odd and be unclear.

Foreign language instruction in most countries emphasizes correct and formal language rather than colloquial language. Also, in very formal cultures, slang may be offensive and signal a lack of respect. Curse words may also signal disrespect. Although in formal American English cursing is not acceptable, many businesspeople use terms that at one time were considered swear words. *Damn* as in, "I know damn well he is going to be at the meeting," is one of those words. Unless you know the other side very well, avoid any language that could be offensive.

Be Careful about Jokes

Humor does not translate well. What one culture considers funny another may consider not funny, crude, or rude. In addition, humor loses much in translation. Johnny Carson, an American comedian, found that out when his show was aired in Great Britain. His jokes were rooted in American culture and often were based on current events. The British were not familiar with the events and did not share the American sense of humor; the show was canceled after only a short time. To appreciate jokes, the listener must share cultural references with the speaker. In the absence of that common experience, jokes lose their funniness.

In many cases, humor is based on puns and wordplay. Those things seldom translate into another language. And after a lengthy explanation, the situation usually is not considered funny anymore. You may have heard of the speaker who delivers his speech through a translator to his foreign audience. His audience laughs at the appropriate places. What he does not know is that the interpreter supplies his own jokes or asks the audience to laugh because the speaker just told a joke and it would be impolite not to laugh. Just imagine this situation if the speaker speaks to an audience of people from ten different countries who all have their own simultaneous translator. Jokes would be a nightmare in this environment.

At the same time, well-placed and timely humor can connect people from different cultures. For example, when Juergen Schrempp, the chief executive officer

(CEO) of the failed DaimlerChrysler merger, sent Dieter Zetsche to Detroit in 2001 to solve problems at Chrysler, workers at the Detroit plant were very uneasy and afraid that this might be the end of Chrysler and that the Germans would take over. When one reporter asked the question that was on everyone's mind, "How many more Germans are you going to bring to Detroit?" Zetsche answered "Four" with a straight face: "My wife and three kids." The joke broke the ice and made him appear human.[17]

Be Sincere

Although goodwill and sincerity alone do not get the message across, they help create a positive atmosphere. When both sides are sincere and each side recognizes that, both will try harder to communicate verbally. Genuine sincerity can help overcome obstacles. If businesspeople from two different countries sit down to negotiate a deal, one reasonably can assume that both sides are sincere and genuinely interested. One also can assume that they respect each other and don't intend to insult each other. If something sounds strange or even insulting, chances are that the speaker used the wrong words and didn't mean any harm. If both sides assume goodwill, many hurdles can be overcome.

Be Culturally Sensitive

The more you know about the culture of the other side, the easier it will be for you to speak with a foreigner who speaks only a little of your language. For example, a person doing business in Japan will be more successful if he knows the basics of social behavior and etiquette. Even though he speaks no Japanese and the Japanese counterpart speaks only some English, they may communicate if both sides are culturally sensitive. A non-Japanese businessperson who is formal, uses last names, is nonaggressive, and listens carefully may succeed. A Japanese businessperson who in dealing with someone from a more assertive culture is more outgoing and verbal than he normally would be also may be more successful.

Cultural mistakes sometimes drown out the verbal message. That is true both in international business and in domestic firms that employ people with a variety of ethnic and cultural backgrounds. Maria Lopez from Peru has worked for several months as a supervisor in the United States and speaks some English. She comes from a very traditional and formal background and is used to being addressed with her last name by nonfamily. As her fellow supervisor, you think she does good work and want to compliment her. You are outgoing and friendly and say to her, "Maria, you are doing good work." She may be so offended by your using her first name that the rest of the message may be lost.

You may argue that if Maria Lopez wants to get ahead in an American company, she must adapt to American cultural norms. However, you need to ask yourself what your goal is. Is it to Americanize Maria or to build an effective work team? If you want an effective team, you need to consider the values of your employees. Ideally, you would provide training for your nonnative speakers in American language and culture and provide for your American employees at least training in the culture of their foreign co-workers.

Keep a Sense of Humor

Perhaps this should be the guiding rule for communicating in any foreign language. You must be able to laugh at your own mistakes and not be offended by honest mistakes from the other side.

Effective Written Communication

To avoid any confusion on the other side, you must proofread carefully for spelling, punctuation, and grammar. Errors that may not pose a problem for native speakers can be serious hurdles to understanding for a nonnative speaker. The following guidelines will help you be more effective in written communication. They will help you adapt your style where appropriate; they also will help you in interpreting the message of the sender from a foreign company. The goal is not to write like the French or the Japanese but to understand the conventions of formats to facilitate comprehension.

Use Plenty of White Space

A nonnative speaker may need space for comments and translations. Provide that space to facilitate understanding and communication.

Use Correct Titles and Spellings of Names

Accuracy in the spelling of names will show that you care, that you are sincere and have goodwill. Most people get annoyed at the misspelling of their names, so be doubly careful in that area. Ask if necessary.

Understand Patterns of Organization

You will be better able to follow a conversation with your limited language ability if all the other "noise" (any type of distraction) is eliminated. One source of noise is organization. People from different cultures organize information differently (see Chapter 5). People from East Asian cultures organize material on the basis of relationships of elements rather than the linear progression typical of Western thinking. Both groups are convinced that their arguments are logically developed and presented. Within each camp there are differences also. Canadians, for example, like to have recommendations at the beginning of a report. The rest of the report provides a rationale and the necessary background. The emphasis is on the practical use of information. Germans, in comparison, prefer a chronological arrangement and presentation. They give the background first; the recommendation comes at the end. The French, much more than the Germans and the Canadians, delight in the linguistically elegant presentation of the argument. The presentation is of importance for its own sake in addition to the practical considerations.

If the German knows that the Canadian prefers to have the recommendations first, he may decide to arrange his information that way. Since the organization corresponds with his expectations, the Canadian will be able to concentrate on the actual message and not lose patience with the "slower" German presentation (also see Chapter 5). Both the Germans and the Canadians may want to watch more carefully for the style and presentation of the argument when communicating with the French.

The French, Germans, and Canadians, however, are puzzled by the relationship-building arrangement of the presentation of the Japanese. Although rapport is considered important, neither the French, nor the Germans, nor the Canadians consider the building of rapport an integral part of the presentation. The logical argument is what sells, not the establishment of relationships (see Chapter 5).

Use Headings

Headings, important in all business writing, are particularly important in communicating with nonnative speakers. They help the person understand the organization and your line of reasoning.

Be Careful with Numbers

You always need to check the accuracy of numbers and be familiar with the conventions of writing numbers. For example, $5,350.48 becomes $5.350,48 in most European languages. The comma and the decimal point are reversed, and often the punctuation to set off thousands is not used at all. Confusion in the punctuation of numbers creates confusion in the meaning. To be safe, you may want to write out crucial numbers. In addition, in international business it is crucial that writers make clear what they mean by dollars. The United States, Australia, New Zealand, Taiwan, Hong Kong, Singapore, and Canada all call their currency *dollar,* but they are different currencies. To avoid miscommunication, it is important that the writer identify which dollar he or she is citing.

Be Careful with Dates

Dates can become important when two firms disagree on contract conditions, delivery dates, and meeting dates. Different cultures have different ways of writing dates, as the following example illustrates.

> American usage: May 6, 20xx or 05/6/20xx
> British usage: 6 May 20xx
> German usage: 6. Mai 20xx or 6. 5. 20xx
> Increasing international usage: 20xx May, 6 or 20xx, 05, 06
> To avoid confusion, you should always write out the name of the month.

Avoid Abbreviations

Abbreviations hinder the process of comprehension. They may be convenient for the writer but difficult for the reader. The same goes for acronyms, as was pointed out earlier. A reader who does not know that ASAP means as soon as possible will have to pause and think before going on. An abbreviation interrupts the flow of thought. A businessperson from Manila who speaks German may not know that the abbreviation *betr.:* stands for *betreffs* and means *subject.*

Follow the Conventions of Written Communication

You should study the conventions of your counterpart's culture. For example, business letters follow different formats in different countries. In international firms, subsidiaries around the world may use the same format. A letter from a Nigerian subsidiary in France probably uses a French format; Japanese employees of a German firm probably use the German format.

Although business letters from different countries provide information on the sender, the receiver, and the date of the letter, the placement of this information can vary widely. If you cannot read the language of the sender or do not know the placement of the parts, you may get confused. Following are some examples of letters from different cultures. Obviously, within a country there are variations in style and format. The letters presented next are simply samples of formats. Cultural influences on the organization of business letters are discussed in more detail in Chapter 5. The format of letters also is influenced by channel choice. For example, some writers do not follow the conventions for letters when they transmit them by fax. The letters from Iran and Hong Kong (see later Exhibits 2.6 and 2.7) do not provide an inside address.

In most cases, business letters are written on letterhead stationery that provides the address and the telephone and fax numbers. German letters also provide the company's bank numbers.

U.S. Business Letters

In the United States, a business letter has the following parts (Exhibit 2.3): letterhead / return address, date, inside address (address of the receiver), salutation, body of the letter, complimentary close, and signature block with the typed name of the sender below the handwritten signature. After that comes information on enclosures, the initials of the typist, and the names of people who receive a copy of the letter. Increasingly, American business letters are blocked; that means that paragraphs and all the parts of the letter are flush with the left margin. Block style should not be confused with the block format in Word software, which makes both left and right margins line up flush to the margin line. Block format is inappropriate for correspondence and other writing in paragraphs because it introduces spacing errors between words, and is very difficult to read, especially in multipage documents. Business letters are always single spaced.

German Business Letters

The German format is quite different. Most company stationery has a line for annotations. In the example in Exhibit 2.4, this line lists (left to right) the initials of the recipient, the subject of the letter, a filing number for the recipient, the telephone extension of the writer, and the date. Sometimes this line gives the initials of the secretary and the sender. The important difference is that this information comes before the salutation, whereas in the United States most of that information comes at the end, if it is provided at all.

The name of the company appears below the complimentary close. Traditionally, German letters are signed, but the name of the sender is not typed. In this example, it is impossible to decipher the name of the writer. If Frau Boehmer, who received the letter in Exhibit 2.4, wants to send a reply, she must send it to the department rather than to a particular individual. In contrast to the practice in the

EXHIBIT 2.3   U.S. Format for Business Letters

COMMUNICATION CONSULTANTS INTERNATIONAL

CCI

3829 Willow Road
Normal, Illinois 61761
Tel: (309) 452-1111
Fax: (309) 452-2222

February 29, 20xx

Mr. Abraham Monroe
Director of Marketing
Leisure Wheels, Inc.
501 Grant Street
Kansas City, MO 64141

Dear Mr. Monroe:

Thank you for the background information on marketing training at Leisure Wheels, Inc. This material will be very helpful in preparing training sessions that will meet the particular needs of your people.

At your request, the two-day seminar will pay special attention to intercultural communication issues to enhance the skills of the marketing team as Leisure Wheels, Inc., expands internationally. The attached seminar schedule reflects the changes we discussed on the phone yesterday.

For the seminar I will need the following equipment:

- overhead projector
- flip chart
- video equipment
- slide projector

Communication Consultants, Inc., appreciates the opportunity to provide the training for your employees. I look forward to being in Kansas City on March 20 and 21, 20xx.

Sincerely,

Maxwell Hamill
IV

United States, the German style emphasizes the company rather than the identity of the individual sender. The writer is an agent of the firm. Frequently, German business letters are signed by two people, particularly if a letter deals with financial information.[18] The conventions for the signature block are beginning to change. Several companies, particularly in international correspondence, do type the name of the sender; however, the name usually is typed in a smaller font.

EXHIBIT 2.4A   A German Business Letter

Bayer AG

Personalabteilung
Auszubildende

5090 Leverkusen, Bayerwerk
Telefon: (02 14) 30-1 (Vermittlung)
Telex: 85 103-0 by d
Telefax; (02 14) 3066328 und 3066411
Telegramme: Bayerpersonal Leverkusen
Konten: Postgirokonto Köln 37 82-501
Landeszentralbank Leverkusen 37
508001

Frau
Christina Boehmer
401 Walker Hall

USA-Normal, Illinois 61761

Ihre Zeichen	Ihre Nachricht	Bewerber-Nr.	Telefon-Durchwahl (0214) 30	Leverkusen
		nk	81477	29.09.04

Sehr geehrte Frau Boehmer,
Sie haben sich bei uns um ein Praktikum beworben.
Leider können wir Ihre Bewerbung nicht berücksichtigen, da im angegebenen Zeitraum alle Praktikantenplätze in der von Ihnen benötigten Fachrichtung bereits vergeben sind.
Wir bedauern, Ihnen diesen Bescheid geben zu müssen und senden Ihnen Ihre Bewerbungsunterlagen zurück.
Mit freundlichen Grüßen
BAYER AG

Anlage

(*continued*)

EXHIBIT 2.4B **A German Business Letter (Translation)**

Very honored Mrs. Boehmer,

You have applied for an internship.

Unfortunately, we cannot consider your application because during the time you requested all internship slots have already been filled.

We regret to have to give you this decision and send back your application materials.

With best wishes

BAYER AG

Encl.

The name of the company in both the old style and the new style always appears before the name of the sender in the signature block, thereby emphasizing the point that the writer is writing in the name of the company.

French Business Letters

French letters (see Exhibit 2.5) typically use an indented style; the block style is rarely used. The date can follow or precede the inside address. The inside address in French letters appears on the right-hand side. As in German letters, the zip code precedes the name of the city, and the name of the city is set off by a double space. The format of the address is governed by postal regulations.

French business letters always have a subject line. Initials and reference numbers, if they are given at all, appear after the inside address, before the subject line and salutation.

In French business letters, the complimentary close may be followed by the signature of the writer and the typed name or just the typed name.[19]

Iranian Business Letter

The letter in Exhibit 2.6 is from Iran. Unless you can read Farsi, you will not be able to understand anything in the letter, not even the date, the name of the sender, or the name of the company. The letter is written from right to left. The English translation appears in the Western style, left to right. In the upper right-hand corner of the original appears the reference number of the letter by which it is filed. Below that number comes the date, October 2, 1360. The date is based on the Islamic calendar, which starts in 632 A.D. of the Western calendar. The signature at the bottom comes after the typed name of the sender and the company.

EXHIBIT 2.5A   A French Business Letter

ETABLISSEMENT MAZET

15, rue de Verdun
44000 Nantes

Tél.: 605 90 22   TELEX 340722
Adresse Télegraphique EDUREX   CCP PARIS 23650
                                                            Banque Société Générale

IRAF COMMUNICATION
23, avenue Gaston

33100 BORDEAUX

Nantes, le 26 mars 20xx

Réf. JL
Objet: LAKISRA ESAL

A l'attention de Messieurs Frédéric et Michel Ruselary

Messieurs,
    Faisant suite à nos divers entretiens, je vous confirme, par la présente, que je détiens actuellement 50% des parts de la LAKISRA ESAL dont le siège est situé à Paris, 78 rue de Richelieu et dont le gérant est Monsieur Attregab.

    Je m'engage irrévocablement par la présente à vous en céder le nombre correspondant à 50% des parts totales de la dite LAKISRA ESAL.

    Cette opération sera réalisée dans les meilleurs délais, et selon des modalités conformes aux pratiques professionelles. En particulier, la valeur de cession des dites parts sera établie en fonction de la situation comptable de la LAKISRA ESAL au jour de la cession.

    Par ailleurs, je vous confirme que le capital de cette société est en majeure partie constitué par l'apport du scénario du projet du film "Hotel Godin" dont je suis l'auteur intégral et exclusif.

    Dans l'attente, veuillez recevoir, Messieurs, nos meilleures salutations.

Jaques Lagose

EXHIBIT 2.5B   A French Business Letter (Translation)

Gentlemen,

   To follow up on our many meetings, I am confirming to you by this letter that I am actually holding 50 percent of the shares of LAKISRA ESAL whose headquarters is located in Paris, 78 rue de Richelieu, and of which the general manager is Mr. Attregab.

   I am engaging myself irrevocably by this letter to transfer over to you the amount corresponding to 50 percent of the total shares of said LAKISRA ESAL.

   This operation will be carried out without delay, and according to modalities that conform to professional practices. In particular, the value of the transfer of said shares will be established within the accounting regulations of LAKISRA ESAL for the day of the transfer.

   Herewith I am confirming to you that the assets of this corporation for the greater part consist of the revenues of the script of the film project "Godin Hotel" of which I am the main and only author.

In the meantime, please receive, gentlemen, our best salutations.

Jaques Lagose

Chinese Business Letter from Hong Kong

The letter from Hong Kong in Exhibit 2.7 is written by hand, although new computer programs now enable the Chinese to key in words. The letter is written from left to right although traditionally Chinese is written from right to left and top to bottom. In this letter, the date appears last after the signature. Since the letterhead is in English, a non-Chinese reader can read the name and address of the company.

The Impact of Technology on Oral and Written Communication

The technological revolution during the last decade has had a tremendous impact on intercultural communication practices. We will address the influence of technology throughout this book.

   As telephone service has improved around the world and as prices have dropped, more and more businesses are using the telephone for discussions that would have required formal letters or a personal visit in the past. For example, a call from Germany to most parts of the world costs around two cents per minute. However, costs have not dropped from, or to, all countries. A phone call from the United States to Uzbekistan, for example, costs about U.S.$2.50 per minute.

Clearly, a manager at Procter & Gamble in Cincinnati would not call the manager at the sales office in Uzbekistan unless there was a good reason to do so. A phone call from New Zealand to the United States can cost $0.78 NZ per minute. Costs also depend on which provider one contracts with.

The immediacy of contact has advantages and disadvantages. In the past, Cheetan Shah from India could take some time and contemplate the business relationship with Mario Escalante from Chile. He might think about the relationship for several days, discuss it with some business colleagues, and ultimately send a letter to Mario Escalante. Today, it is very likely that Cheetan Shah gets on the phone

EXHIBIT 2.6A   An Iranian Business Letter

شـماره ۱۲۲۷
تاریخ ۱۰/۲/۱۳۶۰

شرکت سهامی تکش ـ تولید کننده انواع نان ـ کیک ـ شیرینی
نشانی ـ تهران ـ خیابان برادر شماره ۱۲۰ ـ صندوق پستی ۴۹۳
شماره تلفن ۷۴۷۹۶ ـ شماره فکسی ۴۱۵۷۱۱

شرکت نادا ـ تولید کننده مواد غذائی

آقای احمدی ـ مدیر عامل شرکت نادا

پیرو مذاکره تلفنی باطلاع جنابعالی میرساند که در تاریخ اول خرداد ماه ۱۳۶۰
شعبه این شرکت در شهر اصفهان افتتاح گردیده وآقای ناصرخزانه بسمت
نماینده و سرپرست شعبه تعین شده است. اینک باسرفی نامبرده خواهشمند
است به نمایندگی آن شرکت در اصفهان دستور مقتضی صادر فرمایند که نسبت
به تأمین و تحویل سفارشات مربوط به شعبه شرکت تکش در شهر اصفهان اقدام
نمایند. ضمناً یک نسخه از صورت حساب سفارشات تحویل شده را جهت پرداخت
باین شرکت ارسال فرمائید.

با احترام

مدیر عامل شرکت تکش ـ جواد ابراهیم زاده

(continued)

EXHIBIT 2.6B **An Iranian Business Letter (Translation)**

No. 1327
Date: 10/2/1360

        Takesh Corporation—Producer of Various Breads, Cakes, and Pastries
        Address—Tehran-Bahar Street No. 120-mailbox # 293
        Telephone 247960   Fax 415711

Fada Corporation—Food Supplier
    Mr. Ahmadi—President of Fada Corporation

Since our previous telephone conversation, I have to inform you that as of date March 1st 1360 Takesh Corporation opened a new branch at the city of Esfahan and Mr. Nasar Kaha has been placed as the branch manager. With the introduction of the new branch, you can order your pastry supplies directly from Esfahan. In addition, please send a copy of your receipt indicating that you have paid for the pastries back to our home office in Tehran.

        Sincerely
        President of Takesh Corporation—Jawadeh Ebrahimzade

to discuss the issues at hand. That means that Mario Escalante must react immediately; it also means that both sides are confronted directly with language issues.

Videoconferencing is used by more and more businesses in an effort to cut down on travel costs. People can have a virtual meeting and be in the "same room." They can see each other and get all the verbal and nonverbal feedback. For this medium to be successful, participants should get training. Even if everyone who is participating speaks the same language, a videoconference may be intimidating, particularly for people from more quiet and reserved cultures. An Italian manager, for example, may come across as domineering, while a manager from Vietnam may come across to the Italian as not interested. In addition, hooking people up from ten different locations around the world may present a logistical problem. In addition, time differences and holiday schedules may make a global videoconference challenging. For example, if you want to set up a teleconference between your offices in Tokyo and Chicago, the time difference is a real issue. Japan is 14 hours ahead of Chicago. That means people in the Chicago office will have to be there at 6 p.m. on a Tuesday evening to meet the employees in Tokyo for a conference at 9 a.m. Tokyo time on Wednesday morning. If the videoconference also is to include managers from Belgium, the Belgians need to be at work at 1 a.m. Furthermore, Belgium and the United States switch to daylight savings time on different dates, and Japan does not use daylight savings time. Scheduling this conference will not be easy.

Managers also need to be aware of technical problems. Frequently the sound is delayed by a fraction of a second, resulting in a lack of synchronization of picture

EXHIBIT 2.7A   **A Letter from Hong Kong**

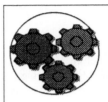

EFI-TECH INTERNATIONAL
ROOM 1200
16 CHATER ROAD
HONG KONG
Tel: 63124   Fax: 64144

李文山先生：

　　您好，我們雖然不相認識，但我曾通過萬年塑膠廠的何廠長介紹，對貴公司產品很感興趣，何廠長自上月到貴廠參觀後，事後感觸很深，特別是對您們所用的科技以及產品的質素，更是讚不絕口。

　　本公司是經營出入口生意，已有廿多年經驗，產品多從內地入口，再轉消到世界各地，尤以美國為主，從何廠長口中得知貴公司最近有意找出口商把產品轉消到美國，我相信本公司有絕對的能力和經驗給您提供服務。

　　所以，我希望李先生能在百忙之中，安排一個時間讓本人親自與您介紹本公司，我十分希望能早日收到您的回音。

祝　　商安

張 元 欽 敬上

2004 - 4 - 20

(continued)

EXHIBIT 2.7B **A Letter from Hong Kong (Translation)**

Dear Mr. Lee:

How do you do? Even though we have never met before, I have heard a lot about your company from Mr. Ho, the plant manager of Men-Nan Manufacturing Company. Mr. Ho visited your factory last month, and he is impressed by the kind of technology you use in your factory and the high quality of your product.

We have twenty years of experience in the importing and exporting business. Most of the merchandise comes from mainland China and then is resold to the United States. According to Mr. Ho, your company is looking for an exporter to help expand the U.S. market for your products. We truly believe that our company has the ability and experience to serve your needs.

I hope that we can arrange to meet sometime in the future. I am looking forward to introducing our company to you.

Wishing you prosperity in business,

Truly,

Yuen-Yam Cheung
General Manager

20th April, 20xx

---

and sound. Although a fraction of a second does not sound like much, the communication can lose spontaneity and nonverbal signals can become more difficult to read.

Videoconferencing also has gained in popularity because of concerns about terrorism and diseases, such as severe acute respiratory syndrome (SARS), avian flu, and swine flu. In a videoconference, people can see each other as if they were sitting around the same table without facing the dangers and the cost of travel. Yet videoconferencing does not have the personal touch, and people may not feel comfortable speaking, particularly if their native language is different from the conference language.

Skype is a form of videoconferencing. The necessary software can be downloaded for free, and computer-to-computer communication is free in many countries. Skype calls to landlines cost something, but compared to telephone, the price is low. In addition, a camera can convert the call into a videoconference. It is possible to have several people participate in a Skype conference. What was a dream just a few years ago has become an affordable reality. Videoconferencing and Skype have added to the communication options. They are useful tools, but they do not totally replace a face-to-face meeting.

E-mail, texting, and twitters have become channels of choice for communication. Phones, such as BlackBerrys, have added communication options that weren't avaliable just a short time ago. As a result, modern communication is fast and is not restricted by differences in time zones. The new technology allows both for synchronous and asynchronous communication. The people communicating may be on the computer simultaneously and use instant messaging (synchronous), or they can read the incoming e-mail whenever they wish and respond when they are ready (asynchronous). It allows for some thinking time. However, there are other issues. E-mail lends itself to an informal and personal writing style that may turn off someone with a more formal cultural background. Given that the nonverbal feedback is missing, the sender of the message does not get any signals that would help in gauging the level of the tone and the salutation and complimentary close. E-mail seems to invite a more chatty approach; it feels more like talking, and as a result the writer may use an informal approach where a formal one would be more appropriate. In addition, many writers send copies of a message to too many people, regardless of whether the receivers actually need the information. As a result, e-mails clutter inboxes and can slow down work or interrupt it.

Easy accessibility by e-mail also increases concerns about virus infections and the confidentiality and security of company information. Companies have developed guidelines and rules to deal with some of these concerns; however, open systems are vulnerable. Lichtwehr PharmaAG, a German pharmaceutical company, includes the following statement in all confidential e-mails in case the message was sent accidentally to the "wrong" person:

> This e-mail contains confidential or legally protected information. If you are not the correct addressee or should you have received this e-mail in error, you are not permitted to read, copy, re-send or make other use of it. Please inform the sender of the transmission error and delete this e-mail. The content of this e-mail is legally binding only when confirmed by us in a letter sent by mail. You requested that our firm correspond with you via Internet per e-mail. We call to your attention that e-mail correspondence can be lost, altered, or falsified, with or without third-party intervention. We therefore accept no responsibility for the intactness of e-mails after they have left our control and cannot provide compensation for any consequential damages. Should a virus enter your systems through an e-mail sent by us, despite our use of virus protection programmes, we are not liable for any damages resulting therefrom. This exclusion of liability is applicable to the extent permitted by law.

Instant messaging and cell phones have added to the channel choices for intercultural communication. Cell phones in particular can create an intercultural communication minefield. In cultures that value family life and personal time, it may be inappropriate to call a business partner at home in the evening or on the weekend. The explosion of communication technology has made instant communication anywhere and anytime possible, but a culturally astute manager will have to decide when and where it is appropriate to communicate. These days one can rent or buy a cell phone (*mobile* in Great Britain, Australia, and New Zealand; *handy* in Germany) at most international airports. Sim cards and special chips allow a traveler to use a cell phone around the globe. Buying a local cell phone may be a good investment.

Potential business partners and clients may see a local phone as a sign that the user is serious about doing business. For example, a team of students went to China to explore export opportunities for a medium-sized business in the United States. They bought a cell phone and had their business cards translated into Mandarin. They were convinced that the local touch helped them in getting appointments.

Compatibility of technology has become less of an issue, but even now it can play a role. Lynn Robertson sent an e-mail with an attachment to Brian Eldridge in Moldova. She wanted to make sure that the format of her message was retained. The e-mail message was a short cover note. The problem was that Brian had a hard time opening the attachment. Even worse, once the technical issue of downloading had been overcome, it turned out that the downloading process took almost 45 minutes. In a country where telephone lines are not reliable and the cost of Internet use is based on the length of the connection, this became a very expensive message.

Some Guidelines for Communicating with Businesspeople from Different Cultures

Every language has unique speech patterns, idioms, and metaphors that are difficult to translate, and the dictionary, as was pointed out earlier, does not always help. For example, businesspeople from the United States use many words and idioms from the military and from sports. Businesses have strategies, they plan the attack, they dig in, they have price wars, they destroy the enemy (the competition), they rally the troops, they are on the offensive or defensive, they have intelligence-gathering systems, and so forth. Most Americans use this terminology without being aware of its military origin. To people from a more reserved and peaceful culture, businesspeople from the United States may come across as very combative and aggressive. Therefore, U.S. businesspeople may want to tone down the fight symbols and take a more cooperative approach in their language.

Sports provides U.S. businesspeople with countless metaphors. Again, most businesspeople use the terminology without being aware of the consequences. Baseball and football are important sports in the United States, and both men and women have integrated sports terminology into their business vocabulary. They assume that everyone understands what it means even though in many cases they themselves do not know or care much about sports.

Some typical phrases are listed next.

- The bases are loaded.
- He hit a homerun.
- He got to first base.
- Send him down to the minors.
- He struck out.
- He is out in left field.
- He has a good batting average.
- We want a level playing field.

- All the bases are covered.
- Monday-morning quarterbacking.
- Third down and nine to go.
- Touchdown.

Unless people from other cultures are familiar with baseball and football as they are played in the United States, they will not understand these phrases no matter how good their English is. A professor of English business communication in Belgium, for example, had read a book by Lee Iacocca, past president of the former U.S.-based Chrysler Corporation. However, he admitted that he did not understand much of the terminology. For example, Iacocca used U.S. sports terminology, and the Belgian, not being familiar with baseball and football, had a hard time understanding the meaning. He found reading the book a frustrating experience.

A dictionary, unless it is specialized in sports or colloquial expressions, will not help in all cases. For example, *Langenscheidt New College German Dictionary* translates homerun as *Baseball: Lauf um sämtliche male auf einen schlag* (run around all bases with one hit).[20] This means absolutely nothing to a German who does not understand baseball. The German will not understand the meaning of a homerun in baseball, let alone the meaning the term takes on in business. *The New Cassel's French Dictionary* does not even list *homerun.* As with military terminology, an American English speaker must avoid sports terminology when speaking to nonnative speakers of English.

You may understand that non-English-speaking countries have difficulties with American sports terminology; however, it is important to recognize that even in English-speaking countries, sports metaphors make no sense. For example, an American professor teaching in New Zealand realized after she used terms such as *hit one out of the park* that her students were totally lost. They had no idea what she meant. She might as well have spoken a foreign language. Her students could relate to metaphors from rugby—a *game with two halves*—but non-Rugby English speakers have no clue what that phrase imparts to Kiwis and other rugby-playing cultures.

If you know some of the characteristics of a foreign language, even if you don't speak it fluently, you may be able to adapt your English better to speakers of the other language. Many English words have either a Germanic or a French/Latin root. You can communicate with a native speaker of French who has limited English better if you choose English words based on French or Latin. The French person will find it easier to understand *descend* rather than *going down,* and *ascend* rather than *going up.* The German, in contrast, will understand you better if you say *going down* rather than *descending,* and *going up* rather than *ascending,* because these words are closer to German.

You must, however, be careful that you don't use words that appear to be similar but have very different meanings. You may know that the word *gift* also is used in German and decide to use it when talking with a German. In that case, you need to know that *gift* in German means *poison.* The word is exactly the same, but the meaning is radically different. A gift shop in northern Michigan in the United States whose owner was trying to give the establishment an ethnic flavor was called the *German Gifthaus,* literally the *German House of Poisoning,* hardly what the owners intended to communicate.

Clearly, the more you know about another culture and language, the easier it will be for you to communicate. For any country you do business in you need to learn at least the basic phrases for greeting, asking directions, making an apology, and showing appreciation. This does not make you fluent, but it can show your sincerity, especially if you improve your language proficiency over time.

Communication with a Multicultural Workforce

Since World War II, the world has seen an unprecedented migration of people. The United States has had an increasing number of immigrants from India, Pakistan, Arabic countries, Mexico, China, and Southeast Asia. European countries recently have had to cope with an influx of people from Russia, Poland, Turkey, Bosnia, Algeria, and Vietnam. Many of these people come in hopes of a better economic future. Even Japan, which prides itself on having a homogeneous population, faces a growing foreign workforce, though it is very small by American and European standards. Oil-rich Arabic countries employ a number of foreigners from the Philippines, India, Pakistan, and Indonesia.

As a result, businesses in all industrial countries are confronted with an increasingly diverse workforce, and business must deal with the issues of diverse languages and cultures on an everyday basis. Intercultural communication is an important topic not just for international business but for domestic business as well. The question is what businesses need to do to build a team with common goals, which is not always an easy task. The old attitude that immigrants should adapt to the culture of the host country and learn the language may be unrealistic. Some immigrant groups cling to their native language; others don't want to give up their culture. They may perceive a materialistic obsession in industrial countries and resent it even though they may come to an industrial country to improve their economic situation.

A business that manufactures high-precision instruments must make sure that all the employees understand the importance of accuracy and tolerances. The business must see to it that all nonnative speakers understand instructions clearly and follow them. Social issues aside, it is in the best interest of the business to educate the foreign workforce in the goals of the business. For the process of education to be successful, managers need to understand the backgrounds of the workforce.

If the workforce has a mixed cultural and linguistic background, the business must see to it that people from different backgrounds get along with each other. Management should provide intercultural training to all employees from the top down to facilitate the work toward a common goal.

Companies may have to prepare instructions and policies in the major languages spoken by the employees and establish groups and teams to help overcome cultural hurdles. This process takes time and resources. It is important that all employees receive training, not just the ones from the "foreign" culture. Although one can argue that it is the responsibility of immigrants to adapt both culturally and linguistically, one must look at the broader context and the nature of the business. A business may very well decide that adaptation to the immigrants' culture pays off.

In Focus

A woman from China who sells insurance in central Illinois has developed the Asian community as her major clientele. She has been extremely successful with that group and ascribes her success to the cultural and linguistic adaptation of American insurance practices to the values of the Asian clientele. She has business cards and brochures printed in Japanese, Chinese, and Korean, her major client groups. She wants to sell insurance; therefore, she works very hard at pleasing her clientele. This saleswoman has adapted to the culture of the United States in many ways; she is assertive and outgoing, and she has a good grasp of the concept of profit. She also knows, given her own background, that she must be more indirect and willing to enter into long-term relationships with her clients that in many cases go beyond a typical American business relationship. A number of her clients ask her to give marital advice for their children, act as a go-between in marriage arrangements, and help with other personal matters.

The insurance saleswoman in the previous example could argue that the people she deals with are in the United States and therefore should adapt to American practices; however, with that attitude she would not reach her customers, who are from East Asian countries. As a result, she would restrict her business success severely. Her ability to communicate in a foreign language and at the same time understand the cultural background of her clientele makes her successful.

Summary

In this chapter, we examined some of the major issues related to the use of language in intercultural business communication. The focus has been on five issues:

The language barrier and its consequences, real and perceived:

- Language and culture are intertwined and shape each other.
- Our environment influences our language and the development of linguistic concepts.
- Language reflects our priorities and values.
- Different cultures may give different meanings to identical or similar words.
- Language changes over time.
- Acronyms present special challenges in communicating.
- The language barrier makes intercultural communication more difficult.

Selection of the right language:

- When selecting a language for intercultural communication, managers need to be aware of
  - *Linguistic considerations.* Out of the thousands of languages around the world, which one would be most appropriate?
  - *Business considerations.* Are you the buyer or the seller? Which language do your partners speak? What are the implications of the role of English as the lingua franca of business?

- *Political considerations.* Governments frequently determine which language is acceptable for official use with the government.
- *Appropriate level of fluency.* To be effective, linguistic fluency must go along with cultural fluency.

The company language:

- *Choosing a company language.* Many companies use one official language for their worldwide operations.
- *Using additional foreign language expertise.* Even if a company selects an official company language, not everyone in the firm will be fluent in that language. Expertise in the local language will still be an asset.

The role of the interpreter:

- *The importance of choosing a good interpreter.* A good interpreter has linguistic, cultural, and technical fluency.
- *The effective use of an interpreter.* You need to prepare the interpreter before a session. You need to provide breaks and determine what role the interpreter should play in any discussions.

Communication with nonnative speakers:

- *Effective face-to-face communication.* You must speak clearly and be able to read the nonverbal and cultural signals your partner sends.
- *Effective written communication.* Knowledge of different business formats, organizational patterns, and conventions will help you become more effective.
- *The impact of technology on oral and written communication.* The development of communication technology, such as e-mail and teleconferencing, has changed the communication patterns in international business by allowing instant messaging.
- *Guidelines for communicating with businesspeople from different cultures.* People from other cultures, even if they speak your language, may not be familiar with metaphors and idioms that are used frequently in your culture, which can present a communication barrier.
- *Communication with a multicultural workforce.* Intercultural communication has become an important issue not just for international businesses but also for domestic businesses.

Notes

1. Yong-Jin Song, Claudia L. Hale, and Nagesh Rao, "The South Korean Chief Negotiator," *International Journal of Cross Cultural Management,* 5, no. 3 (2005), pp. 313–328.
2. Richard Mead, *Cross-Cultural Management Communication* (New York: John Wiley & Sons, 1990).
3. Edward T. Hall, *The Silent Language* (New York: Doubleday and Co., 1959).
4. http://www.geocities.com/SiliconValley/Heights/4766/shumor.html.

5. James Calvert Scott, "Differences in American and British Vocabulary: Implications for International Business Communication," *Business Communication Quarterly* 36, no. 4 (2000), pp. 27–39.

6. "Death Sentence," *The Guardian,* October 25, 1999.

7. www.chinadaily.com.cn/english/doc/2005-01/11/content_407916.htm.

8. Deborah Tannen, *Communicating from 9 to 5* (New York: William Morrow and Company, 1994).

9. Richard D. Babcock and Bertha Du-Babcock, "Language-Based Communication Zones in International Business Communication," *Journal of Business Communication* 38, NJ (2001), pp. 372–412.

10. Malcolm Gladwell, *Outliers: The Story of Success* (New York: Little Brown and Company, 2008).

11. Mirjaliisa Charles, "Language Matters in Global Communication," *Journal of Business Communication* 44, no. 3 (2007), pp. 260–282.

12. Leena Louhiala-Salminen, Mirjaliisa Charles, and Anne Kankanraanta, "English as a Lingua Franca in Nordic Corporate Mergers: Two Case Companies,"*English for Specific Purposes 24* (2005), pp. 401–421.

13. Janet Frank, "Miscommunication across Cultures: The Case of Marketing in Indian English," *World Englishes* 7, no. 1 (1988), pp. 25–36.

14. The American Translators Association Web site, http://www.atanet.org/careers/index.php.

15. Aexei Barrionuevo, "Land of Babble: As Europe Seeks a Stronger Voice, Words Get in the Way," *The Wall Street Journal,* January 5, 2005, p. A1; James Owen, "With 20 Official Languages, Is the EU Lost in Translation?" *National Geographic News,* February 22, 2005.

16. David Ricks, *Big Business Blunders: Mistakes in Multinational Marketing* (Homewood, IL: Dow Jones-Irwin, 1983).

17. J. Muller and C. Tierny, "Can this Man Save Chrysler?" *BusinessWeek,* September 17, 2001, pp. 86, 93.

18. Iris Varner, "Cultural Aspects of German and American Business Letters," *Journal of Language for International Business* III, no. 1 (1988), pp. 1–11.

19. Iris Varner, "A Comparison of American and French Business Correspondence," *Journal of Business Communication* 25, no. 4 (1988), pp. 5–16.

20. *New College German Dictionary, German–English, English–German* (Berlin: Langenscheidt, 1973).

CHAPTER THREE

Getting to Know Another Culture

Juan Marin is meeting with Lei Peng about a business deal. Marin wants to open a Chinese restaurant in Mexico City and is working out a joint-venture agreement with Lei who has several successful restaurants in Hong Kong and Los Angeles, California. But Marin is discovering a number of things that surprise him about his would-be partner as they negotiate the details, meeting face to face at last in Los Angeles.

Lei has just mentioned that Juan should construct a fish tank in the entrance to his restaurant. "Why?" Juan asks. "We're not just serving fish, apart from a few dishes. But people will see the fish and think it's a fish restaurant."

"You need fish," Lei asserts. "You need that because it means good profit!" He explains that in Chinese the phrase "to have fish" (pronounced *yo yu*) sounds like the phrase "to have profit after expenses," and for that reason Juan must have a fish tank. Juan is amazed that the Chinese man thinks he should go to the expense of placing a large fish tank at the front door of his restaurant simply on the basis of the sound of the Chinese word for *fish*.

While he and Lei continue their discussion, Juan notices several times that people are interrupting them to bring Lei a telephone, provide tea, or ask for answers to quick questions. Juan doesn't really mind; he understands that these are signs of how important and busy Lei is.

Juan is a little hungry, though, since it's three o'clock in the afternoon and time for his large meal of the day. Lei seems unaware of the hour, and although someone provides tea for them, there is no mention of dinner. Juan thinks he'd better clarify the hours during which the restaurant will operate in Mexico. Lei simply says, "No problem. The Chinese staff I'll get for you will work whenever you tell them." Juan wonders about that. What if a relative needs some help at home? After all, Juan himself arrived at their meeting just before 2 p.m., although he had meant to come at 1 p.m. as agreed. His son had asked him to bring a special video game back from the United States to Mexico, and the traffic between the store and the meeting was heavy, causing Juan to be late. Lei didn't show any emotion, so Juan couldn't tell if he was angry. Family matters always take priority, as the Chinese must agree. But maybe the Chinese restaurant isn't such a good idea for his family business interests. How will he explain the fish tank?

For his part, Lei Peng is surprised at Juan Marin's behavior in person. How serious is he about this restaurant venture? He was an hour late for their first meeting! And although it's the middle of the afternoon, he keeps suggesting they go out for a meal to a nice Mexican restaurant he knows. As if Lei weren't an owner of restaurants in Los Angeles! How odd his associate is. Is it a good idea to open a restaurant in Mexico City?

Understanding another culture is an ongoing experience that can last a lifetime. However, sometimes businesspeople have only a short time to prepare to do business in another country. How can a brief amount of time best be spent to yield the greatest understanding?

Ways to Study Culture

We have said that understanding a culture opens the door to understanding how people see and make sense of their world. Now we examine more closely how scholars and researchers study culture.

Traders for centuries have wanted to understand the motivations of buyers from different cultures, and to master some of their language. Language experts have been curious about the countries where foreign languages were spoken, especially the root languages of current languages. Historians studied records about other societies in other times. In the 19th century, European scholars in the new academic discipline of anthropology actually began to travel to foreign lands to study their cultures.

In the 20th century, scholars began to be interested in the daily lives of ordinary people, in order to understand culture. They examined television advertisements, for example, and popular music, among other daily expressions of a culture. They expanded the way culture is studied. The new discipline in European universities is called "cultural studies." Cultural studies also forms part of the study of culture and communication.

Studies of culture today are expanding, because people in many areas are interested. Businesspeople, of course, want to know how culture affects their international and domestic aims. Governments around the world want to know how culture affects the way people settle down in new countries. World leaders want to know how culture affects their efforts to establish peace among countries. Individuals surfing the Internet or connecting with people in other countries by Facebook and other electronic means want to know how to interact and how to interpret the impact of culture on their interaction. Thoughtful people everywhere want to understand how culture is related to ethical behavior. Studies about culture are multiplying.

Research Approaches to Studying Cultures

We can begin an overview of how cultures are studied by considering two general approaches: studies that focus on a culture as a whole, and studies that focus on the individual.

Studying Whole Cultures

Cultures are social groups. Sometimes they coincide with the geopolitical boundaries of countries, but often they comprise people who live in more than one country, although that geographical region may be associated with the culture. For example, Portuguese culture came from the part of the European continent called the

Iberian Peninsula, and is an important contributor to the culture of Brazil, which was a colony of Portugal, and where Portuguese is the language spoken. Portuguese culture also affected a part of western India that was ruled by Portugal. In fact, Portuguese sailors left the mark of their culture on places as far apart as Oman in the Arabian Peninsula, Taiwan in East Asia, and Hawai'i in the United States. Scholars can study the Portuguese influence on the cultures of these very different lands.

When studying a whole culture, researchers can use *emic* and *etic* approaches. These terms were introduced in an In Focus section on page 35.

Emic Studies

Studies that concentrate on one culture alone are called *emic* studies. They focus on one culture and describe it from within the culture. *Emic* studies consider the characteristics of a particular culture that are meaningful to people within that culture. The factors they reveal may not occur in other cultures. For example, a study of Brazilian culture today will involve a number of contributing cultures, including Portuguese.

Etic Studies

Studies that look for factors that exist in more than one culture are called *etic* studies. They examine how characteristics are shared with other cultures. A researcher who looks at the culture of Hawai'i and the culture of Brazil can examine the Portuguese influences as a shared characteristic. *Etic* studies usually involve comparisons to find similarities and differences.

Cultural Generalizations

Studies about whole cultures give us conclusions that are generalizations about the culture. For example, from culture-based research we learn that Chinese culture has these values:

- Face (public esteem)
- A reciprocal network of connections with others
- Lasting membership in groups

The high value placed on face means that losing face is a negative experience that people try to avoid for themselves and for others. Certain behavior follows. Members of this culture may give face to others by praising them in front of others. They will try to minimize face-threatening situations such as a criticism, perhaps by laughing to show it isn't important. They will often communicate using words and phrases that do not give offense, so as not to cause any pain.

For example, when being offered hospitality—tea or food—the Chinese cultural practice is that a guest should refuse at least once, and probably twice. This act of politeness involves a desire to show how generous the host is, and how humble the guest is.

Politeness in communication brings harmony to social situations. The host and guest both follow rules for hosts and guests that allow the host to be generous and the guest to be served well. This situation of hospitality means that in the future the guest will return the favor, perhaps by being the host. The changing about of roles from host to guest illustrates the reciprocity—exchange of favors back and forth—that is an important glue for holding relationships together in Chinese culture. Networks of relationships are called *guanxi* (pronounced gwan-shee) in Chinese, and they are important in Chinese culture.

The value of group membership suggests that family is very important in Chinese culture, and within the family, the links are durable. Chinese networks of connections also exist in the neighborhood and in the workplace. Because membership is lasting, people in Chinese culture identify themselves with the groups to which they belong.

Studies that give us these insights into Chinese culture are based on large amounts of data collected from many respondents. Means or averages of questionnaire responses allow researchers to make general statements about the population that is Chinese culture. In other words, studies about whole cultures often use a positivist approach.

Hofstede's Research and Other Studies

Perhaps the most important researcher to collect data about characteristics of whole cultures is Geert Hofstede (pronounced *hoff*-ste-duh), a Dutch social psychologist. His definition of culture was introduced in the first chapter.

Here is some more information about Hofstede's research. At the request of the international firm IBM, Hofstede conducted a huge study into corporate climate. He gathered data in 1966 and 1967 from managers in IBM offices in 44 countries around the world. He collected 116,000 completed questionnaires. When he began to analyze his data, he realized he could identify characteristics that could be the basis of comparisons from culture to culture. He called the characteristics *cultural dimensions*.

The result of his study, published in 1980, was four cultural dimensions:

- Individualism versus collectivism
- Power distance
- Uncertainty-avoidance versus uncertainty-tolerance
- Masculinity versus femininity

Among these dimensions, the first one is the most widely researched. Individualistic cultures are those that emphasize individual achievements and rights, including the individual's right to make decisions for himself or herself; collectivistic cultures emphasize the group's achievements and rights, including the group's right to make decisions for the individual.

Power distance is the degree to which less-powerful members of an organization tolerate unequal distribution of power, say, between managers and employees. Uncertainty avoidance is the tendency to behave so as to arrange things in a way that minimizes unforeseen consequences; uncertainty tolerance results in behavior that is less concerned with unforeseen consequences. Masculinity, according to Hofstede, is a way to characterize cultures that value assertiveness, competitiveness, and material success, while femininity characterizes cultural preferences for collaboration, nurturing, and harmony.

Hofstede's work often is cited by international business and intercultural communication scholars. Later, Michael Bond, a Canadian working and living in Hong Kong, developed a way to assess cultural values based on a survey instrument written by Asians, not Westerners. This resulted in a fifth cultural dimension reported by Bond and Hofstede as long-term orientation.[1] It includes values that can be called "future-looking," such as perseverance, thrift, observing a hierarchy of status in relationships, and having a sense of shame. Short-term orientation, looking more to the past, includes protecting one's own "face," respecting tradition, maintaining personal steadiness, and reciprocating favors and gifts.

Hofstede's study, which remains the largest social science project ever carried out, resulted in generalizations about cultures that are still important to scholars today. It is also a good example of positivist research.

Another Dutch interculturalist, Fons Trompenaars, developed seven cultural dimensions.[2] They include universalism versus particularism, individualism versus collectivism (from Hofstede's and other scholars' influence), neutral versus emotional, specific versus diffuse, and achievement versus ascription. To these dimensions Trompenaars added attitudes toward time and the environment.

Meanwhile, other scholars were developing cultural values by which to compare cultures. André Laurent looked at European managers and came up with four parameters for understanding how culture affects relationships of power: the perception of organizations as political systems, authority systems, role formulation systems, and hierarchical relationship systems.[3] Shalom Schwartz developed a values survey in the 1990s based on theories that tried to account for some of the biases that may have affected earlier studies, notably Hofstede's.[4]

The GLOBE Study

Other large-scale studies have also resulted in generalizations about whole cultures. The GLOBE study came out in a volume entitled *Culture, Leadership, and Organizations*, published in 2004.[5] The study used data collected by 170 researchers in 62 countries. Data came from 17,300 managers in 951 organizations. The focus of the study is culture's effect on leadership in organizations around the globe. The project was the idea of Robert House, a professor at the Wharton Business School of the University of Pennsylvania. He gathered an international team to develop the research design, so it would not have a United States bias.

Many other researchers study whole cultures. Areas of study that focus on cultures include, among others:

- Adaptation and acculturation
- Marginal and minority groups
- Networks and theories of communication contacts
- Culture as a theoretical construct (more about this later)

Studying Individuals

Another way to study culture is to focus on individual members of a culture. Individuals carry the values and attitudes of their culture within them, and they may behave according to expectations—in other words, according to predictions made from large positivist studies. But often individuals don't have the values, attitudes, and behaviors predicted by the generalizations.

Individual people have multiple influences in their thinking and acting, of which the general culture is one. Individuals may have any number of experiences, personal insights, personal goals, interests, and expectations that are part of their identities. Not every individual in a cultural group will be identical to every other individual.

Here is an example. Think back to the host and guest situation in Chinese culture, where the host's duty is to provide food and serve the guest, and the guest's duty is to say it is too much, and the host shouldn't have gone to such a lot of trouble, and the guest is not worthy of this honor.

Now picture a young Chinese nurse from Beijing who was invited to dinner by a Canadian couple in Toronto, Canada. She arrived with the words, "I hope you cooked a lot of food, because I'm really hungry!"

The Canadian hosts were expecting the young woman to act with typical Chinese politeness, refusing offers of food at least once, or taking only a little bit. They told each other to be sure to press more than one offer of helpings, so the guest didn't go home hungry. But the young Chinese woman announced right away that she was hungry for the Chinese food that had been cooked by the Canadians. She also looked upon her hosts as like her parents, of the same generation. So she let her host know right away she was looking forward to eating.

However, although the Canadian hosts were surprised by the atypical communication, they also realized that the young Chinese woman was speaking as if she were among her family, rather than among strangers, and they took that as a great compliment.

Individual-based studies examine the way culture affects individual perception, individual cognition (or thinking), and individual behavior.

Areas of scholarship that focus on the individual include:

- Interpersonal communication
- Conflict communication between individuals
- Coaching communication
- Facework and issues of face
- Cultural identity of individuals

Culture as a Theoretical Construct

Culture itself, as a concept representing a particular group of people, can operate as the basis for generating theories. In this book, we look at culture as a recognizable collection of behaviors, values, attitudes, and beliefs that people share. People themselves identify with those values, attitudes, and behaviors. They recognize the processes and relationships among themselves.

Culture is a dependent variable in this approach. In other words, a researcher views a particular culture as stable and consistent. Then the independent variable is a particular cultural dimension or some other construct about culture. A study can examine how big an impact the same cultural variable has in more than one culture.

This approach means that we can generalize about a culture. We can identify behavioral practices and say, "That is typically Pakistani" (a young woman's female relatives and friends color her hands with a henna pattern before a wedding) or "That is typically Polish" (a bride's female relatives and friends put her hair into two braids, not the one she has worn until now). Then we can compare Pakistani and Polish culture in relation to the behavioral practice. Although Polish brides do not use henna, and Pakistani brides do not have their hair in two braids, we can say that both cultures have traditions about making the bride beautiful, showing her new status, and wishing her good luck in her marriage. And in both Pakistani and Polish cultures, the female relatives, especially the bride's mother, play an important part in her wedding appearance.

We can compare cultures not only by using a behavior, but by using an identified value or cultural dimension. For example, we can take *collectivism,* which refers to the preference in a culture for identifying oneself as a member of the group, rather than as an individual apart from a group, and compare that from culture to culture. We can look at group membership in two or more cultures, and compare how long a period of time people remain members of a group. Some memberships last longer than a person's life, and children carry on with the membership in a group (such as a craft or profession). Some memberships are short, only weeks or months, as people move around a lot and live in different places. We can look at how important group celebrations are in each culture, and how important individual celebrations are. We can consider how people live with family members—in large extended families that stay close to each other, or in small families of parents and children only, perhaps far away from other family members.

Generalizations and Stereotypes

In order to compare cultures, we use generalizations about them. Making generalizations leaves us open to the charge of *stereotyping.*

Stereotyping means using oversimplified generalizations to understand people.

To explain *stereotype,* we begin with how the word *stereotype* came into being. It was first used in 1725 to refer to a historical development in printing and described a new way of setting type. Type—individual letters of the alphabet—formerly had to be put into a frame, one at a time, to make up the words and sentences to be printed. The metal type or letters were slightly raised. They were covered in ink, then paper, and then a press or weight came down and squeezed the ink into the paper. The frame holding the type had to be very firm so the type wouldn't move around when the press came down upon them. The movable type was taken apart when the printing was done. But later, instead of each line of alphabet type having to be laid down and the printing done directly from it, a plate was made. It exactly reflected the type that had been set, and printing was done from it. It was called "stereotype" because it was a hard inflexible image of the type: *stereo* is from a Greek word meaning hard, firm.

So what does this have to do with stereotypes of people? The answer is that stereotypes are fixed, firm, inflexible mental categories. As the historical origin of the term suggests, they are rigid and unchanging, so when new information is received, they are unable to contain it. Therefore, the problem with stereotypes is that they are incomplete information about people, and using them, rather than seeking more information, means that the picture is limited. Stereotypes are painted with only a few colors, so they do not capture shadings and multiple hues or tones.

Instead of calling mental categories *stereotypes*, we might call them *prototypes*. Prototypes are the original concepts or models for something. Mental representations are created as prototypes when we are confronted with something unfamiliar or complex. We categorize data to make sense out of it. If we couldn't make generalizations and put similar items together into categories, we couldn't make sense of any unfamiliar subject.

Nor are all stereotypes bad. Some are positive. For instance, one stereotype about people who live in the oil-producing countries of the Middle East is that they are all wealthy. A positive stereotype about Japanese is that they are sensitive to human feelings. A positive stereotype about Americans is they are generous.

We need to have mental categories so we can quickly understand all the information coming at us in our world. As discussed in Chapter 1, when learning about something new, we put new information into old categories or create new ones. When people do not bother to examine new information and add it to the categories, or are not mentally open and flexible, their understanding of people is limited to their stereotypes.

We need to be careful to avoid cultural determinism as a consequence of generalizations. Cultural generalizations can be used to make *predictions* about how a culture in general thinks, acts, and believes. Because of this, it is tempting to treat culture as an influence that ***determines*** the values, attitudes, and behaviors of individual members of a culture. In other words, individuals in a culture are treated like robots, and are assumed to think and act a certain way simply because they are members of that culture. It is easy, and also useful, to generalize about a culture. However, generalizations hide many individual variations. We can identify typical values or the typical behaviors of the whole culture, while recognizing that on an individual level, many individuals in the culture will not fit the "typical" description.

High-context Communication and Low-context Communication

Researchers can explain communication differences by taking a variable in communication behavior and tracking how it differs in different cultures. One researcher who has contributed valuably to research into the relationship of culture

In Focus

A very distinguished 75-year-old Chinese scholar and statesman was being honored by a university in the eastern United States. He and his wife had just made the 21-hour flight from Beijing, and they were met at the airport by some friends who exclaimed, "You must be very tired!" His response was *keyi,* "It's possible" or "Perhaps." Of course he was tired! He was an old man who had sat on airplanes or in airports for 24 hours straight. But the context—the meeting in an airport at night, the fact of his long journey, his age, his slightly glazed eyes—communicated the obvious. He did not think it was necessary to put it into words.

Consider a person from a Western culture, traveling to Beijing and getting off the plane after 24 hours of continuous travel. His or her response to the same comment, "You must be tired!" could be, "Tired! I've never been so tired in my life! I've been sitting on planes or in waiting rooms for 24 hours and wondered if my legs would work again! My eyes are so gritty with sleep, they feel like the Gobi desert was in that plane!" and so forth. What the Westerner is *not* likely to say is "Perhaps."

and communication, Edward Hall, used this approach. He examined the role of *communication context* in exchanges, and theorized about cultures, terming them high-context and low-context.[6]

High-context cultures rely on the context, either the actual physical environment of communication or an internalized social context, or both, to convey a large part or even all of a message's meaning. In cultures in which context is referred to implicitly in communication, the messages can be elliptical, indirect, and allusive. In cultures in which context is not assumed to be understood, messages are explicit, direct, and completely encoded in words. This describes low-context cultures, in which the meaning is entrusted almost entirely to words.

Hall drew a continuum reaching from the extreme of low-context cultures to the opposite extreme of high-context cultures and then plotted national cultures along the continuum. He identified German Swiss as a very low-context culture in which messages are spelled out fully, clearly, and precisely. He identified Japan as a high-context culture in which messages are ambiguous and meanings are implied by the context. He put the United States on the low-context side of middle. High-context cultures, in which the context of the message is well understood by both sender and receiver, use the context to communicate the message.

Members of low-context cultures put their thoughts into words. They tend to think that if thoughts are not in words, the thoughts will not be understood correctly or completely. When messages are in explicit words, the other side can act on them. But high-context cultures have less tendency to trust words to communicate. They rely on context to help clarify and complete the message.

In Focus

A Turkish male graduate student in the United States lived in a residence hall where he shared a room with an American. One day his roommate went into the bathroom and completely shaved his head. The Turkish student discovered this fact when he visited the bathroom and saw the hair everywhere. He returned to his room and said to his roommate, "You've shaved your head." The American replied, "Yeah, I did."

The Turkish student waited a little and then said, "I discovered you'd shaved your head when I went into the bathroom and saw the hair." "Yeah," the American confirmed.

The Turk was at a loss. He believed he had communicated in the strongest possible language his wish that the American would clean up the mess he'd made in the bathroom. But no such meaning was attributed to his words by his roommate.

Later, he discussed the surprising episode with Turkish friends, who told him, "Listen, with Americans you actually have to say 'Clean up the bathroom'!" The Turkish student believed his message had been very clear. He was relying on the context of the communication for the message to be understood: Hair was recently and widely scattered all over the bathroom, and his roommate suddenly had no hair.

The differences between high-context communication and low-context communication can lead to unintentional problems in the workplace. In China, when people feel they have been disrespected or treated badly, they are as angry as any other people in the world, but do not usually express their anger and hurt in words to those who offend them. In the following true situation, a Chinese doctor took the unusual step of putting her feelings into words—with fortunate results, since the high- and low-context communication had gone awry.

In Focus

A female neurologist from Beijing was working on a research project in a Toronto hospital. She shared a small office with a young Canadian man who loved peanut butter. He was so fond of peanut butter, he kept a jar in the office. One day, he came into the office and exclaimed, "Who took my peanut butter?" (He really meant, "Where is my peanut butter? I can't find it.") But the Chinese woman immediately felt accused. After all, there were only two of them in the office.

She was deeply distressed, but true to her learned cultural behavior of never showing anger in public, she said nothing. Later that day, she was working in a room where a physiotherapist was treating a patient who had suffered paralysis of his legs and arms from a motorcycle accident. The physiotherapist moved one of the patient's legs in a way that caused him pain.

"Ouch!" he cried. "Oh, I didn't do that," said the physiotherapist, mischievously. "It was that doctor over there," and she pointed to the Chinese woman.

"How could she have done it since she's on the other side of the room?" the patient asked. "Ah, she has three hands," the physiotherapist replied.

At these words, the Chinese doctor became even more upset. She was so disturbed that she behaved in a way uncharacteristic of her culture. She waited until the patient had gone and then said to the physiotherapist, "I'm very upset by what you said." The physiotherapist was taken aback. What had she said? "You said I had three hands," the doctor finally choked out. "You think I took the peanut butter."

What was going on in this exchange? The physiotherapist was making a joke when she said the doctor had "three hands." She expected the patient to be amused by her suggestion that the doctor on the other side of the room could have reached an imaginary third hand out to touch him.

The Chinese woman came from a culture where the question "Who did this?" means that someone is to blame. Her culture furthermore prohibits direct accusation unless a person has been targeted for shame. Shame is a terrible ordeal, since it means punishment for not being a cooperative member of the group.

Finally, in Chinese a "three-handed person" is slang for a thief.

The physiotherapist didn't know that, nor did she know anything about a missing jar of peanut butter. The therapist explained to the doctor that she said "three hands" only because it was so obvious that the doctor was not responsible for causing the pain to the patient.

The Cultural Dimensions Approach in This Book

The brief descriptions of well-known studies on pages 96-7 indicate that there are many ways to approach understanding a culture. We synthesize these studies into the following five categories of questions that focus on values in a culture, allowing you to compare cultures by assessing how each of the questions can be answered for different cultures. Questions about a culture that need to be asked for business fall into these five categories:

- Thinking and Knowing
- Doing and Achieving
- The Big Picture
- The Self
- Social Organization

The first three categories are discussed in this chapter, and the last two in Chapter 4. These categories cover the **cultural dimensions** that motivate people to behave in certain ways. They reveal cultural priorities. *Priority* is a useful term because it implies relative importance along a sliding scale. Our questions ask about relative values: For example, does a culture value youth or age more? Does it look upon change as positive or negative? Are results more important than relationships, or are relationships more important than results?

Finally, each of the questions to pose of a culture—24 in all—should be thought of as a continuum, with opposite characteristics at each pole and the continuum as a line stretched between the poles. (Think of a clothesline and cultural priorities as the hanging laundry. See Exhibit 3.1.) You can position the culture you are considering at any point between the two poles, wherever it seems appropriate in light of your level of knowledge of that culture. For example, consider the question "Are results important or are relationships important?" If you are asked to locate United States culture somewhere between those two poles, where would you put it? Right

EXHIBIT 3.1
Cultural
Dimension of
Individualism–
Collectivism along
a Continuum
Clothesline

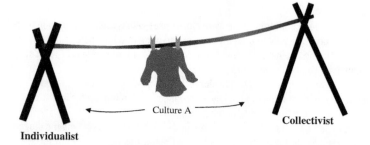

Culture A

Individualist   Collectivist

in the middle? Slightly toward the results end? Strongly toward the relationships end? You can draw on your own experience and understanding to formulate an answer. This is the way to consider each question in the five categories. Then, as you learn more about a culture, you can continue to ask and continue to adjust where you would locate the dimensions and priorities of the culture. In this and the next chapter, you will encounter 24 cultural dimensions for your clothesline.

Where Can Information about Cultures Be Found?

Anyone can ask the questions that follow in this chapter and the next, but of whom? The obvious place to start is to ask people who are members of the culture you want to understand. A logical source is someone who comes from a background similar to yours (economic, educational, family), or someone who has had similar experiences or holds the same kind of job. For instance, if someone asked you whether members of your culture learn by asking questions or by memorizing information, you probably could give an answer like others in your culture.

But some of the questions are not easy for people to discuss because they have never considered them. For instance, most people don't know whether they think in a linear pattern or in a cluster pattern. In fact, *the members of a culture are not necessarily the best authorities on that culture.*

That may surprise you, but culture is embedded deep in the unconscious part of the mind. As Edward Hall pointed out in *Beyond Culture,* the closer something is to seeming true, the less aware we probably are of its cultural origin.[7] People's own culture seems normal to them; it seems just the way things are.

Another good source may be someone who has spent considerable time in that culture but is not a native member of it. Someone who has lived in the other culture has had exposure to the differences between his or her own culture and the culture you want to understand. You may be able to learn from a nonnative about cultural priorities that a native of that culture simply takes for granted.

You can inquire into a culture by reading fiction from that culture. By reading how characters act and why, you can learn about what is important to that culture, and what is appropriate behavior. For example, you can learn how Japanese culture views the public expression of emotion, the relative status of older people compared with younger people, the importance of not causing someone to lose face, and the difference between outward public action and private opinion by reading modern short stories in translation. You also can watch Japanese movies and see what people's behavior looks like—their nonverbal communication—when they behave in Japanese ways, and how they sound when they speak the Japanese language.

Another approach is to find out what people of a culture say about themselves. Countries publish books in translation that describe their institutions, history, beliefs, practices, and goals for the future. Even travel guides contain insights.

Cultures also define themselves less directly in communications that are nevertheless revealing. For example, television commercials offer insights into cultural priorities—not so much in the products they advertise as in the values implied by the appeals the commercials make to the viewers. Whereas convenience is the central appeal in certain breakfast cereal advertisements to young single working people in the United States, family membership is the central appeal in advertisements for the same breakfast cereal in Mexico.

A Japanese television commercial offers a contrast.

In Focus

One particular television commercial [for a Lexus] several years ago showed the car being driven down a country lane. It stopped, and a woman in *kimono* and a man in a suit emerged. As they walked around the car, the camera showed a close-up shot of a green leaf that had fallen on the windshield. There were drops of moisture on the leaf and the window. The only sound was the singing of birds. The man and the woman walked up next to a potter who was holding a recently fired bowl. The three gazed in silence at the bowl. The potter threw the bowl to the ground and it broke into pieces. Nobody spoke. The couple got back in the car and drove away.[8]

The message is that only perfection is good enough for the master craftsman (the product's slogan in English is "The pursuit of perfection"). It is communicated without words in the Japanese ad.

Print ads also reflect values, so they can offer insights into backstage culture and also into the differences between cultures. One Southeast Asian country has advertised its airlines for years by showing attractive young women attentively serving male customers. In North America and Europe, this approach has offended some who see the women as having a limited role as serving men. In some Islamic cultures, the Asian women in the commercials display an availability to male strangers that devout Muslim women are taught to reject. As the case that opens this chapter shows, visual images convey cultural values.

Information about cultures also comes from studies by anthropologists who research cultures in the field, going to live among the members of the culture they want to understand. They are trained to observe and report their observations. As a result, their accounts are more objective and less anecdotal than are those of other visitors. But even the casual anecdotal tales of travelers often can add to your understanding.

General insights you form about a culture from asking about cultural priorities will continue to need revision and reexamination in specific contexts. Finding answers to questions about cultural priorities in the cultural dimensions we examine is an ongoing process. You can continue to learn about other cultures and your own culture for as long as you continue to pose questions.

Category 1: Thinking and Knowing

Does Knowing Come from Concepts or Experience?

How do people know things? The answers vary from culture to culture. Some people know because they have experienced for themselves what a thing means. Few of us would argue that knowing how to bargain prices for cold-rolled steel is acquired by anything other than experience. However, since few of us have done that, we know *about* doing it from reading about bargaining and the market and past prices. Our information is secondhand, but in English-speaking cultures most people accept the validity (if still second best) of knowledge that is acquired from a reliable source—books, training programs on bargaining—rather than from first-hand experience (see Chapter 8 for a discussion of validity).

In some cultures, however, firsthand experience alone legitimately constitutes what is known. All else is hearsay. This is particularly true in cultures that have no written language, but it also can be identified in cultures that emphasize personal vision. The vision of the individual prophet or priest or shaman constitutes knowledge that is truth to the visionary. Followers believe also that the visionary knows what they cannot know. Reading or hearing about a vision is not the same as experiencing it. Visionaries play powerful roles and enjoy high status in many cultures. Corporations cannot assume that all their employees, associates, partners, and subsidiaries share the same definition of *to know.*

In many cultures, knowing and being wise come with age. In Thailand, for instance, elders are presumed to know what is necessary and true, even though they may not be on top of cutting-edge technological research. In cultures in which age and status go together, younger members don't challenge the truth of what seniors say.

Knowing by intuition is another kind of experience. Intuition is a kind of instinctive knowledge that does not require deliberate consideration. Or consider meditation, which isn't the same as intuition. In cultures in which Daoism, Buddhism, and Hinduism are the dominant religions, knowledge of the true nature of things comes from meditation, the intense focusing of the mind on one thing, including emptying the mind of all thoughts. Buddha taught that each person has truth within; meditation is a way to reach that inner knowing and allow it to be recognized. Accordingly, Buddhists believe that knowledge gained from study or listening isn't as valuable as knowledge that comes from meditation. Only by emptying the mind of sensory stimuli and concerns and finally of thought, can one experience true understanding.

The notion of *knowledge* in European cultures often calls to mind a traditional body of abstract concepts, philosophies, and arguments reaching back in history. Knowledge sometimes seems rather solemn, dusty, and remote. Perhaps that is why we have a number of other terms for the activity *to know,* including to *grasp, comprehend, understand,* and *perceive.* There are even more terms for a person who knows, or is *in the know: smart, knowledgeable, savvy, perceptive, clever, astute.* Another key term is *learned.* This leads to the next question we can ask of a culture.

Does Learning Come from Asking Questions or Mastering Received Wisdom?

What does it mean to learn? Cultures have a variety of answers. People learn how to learn when they are very young, first at home before they go to school and then later at school. Those early learning patterns continue with little change throughout people's lives. In Canada and the United States, learning is a process that involves asking questions. This book is by one United States–Canadian citizen who is a New Zealand resident and one United States resident originally from Germany. Asking questions opens the door to understanding in these cultures. Therefore, the process we present for learning about cultures is one that involves asking questions.

In the United States, from kindergarten through seminars in graduate school, students who ask questions are rewarded. They earn their teachers' approval and often receive higher grades than students who simply listen. U.S. teachers tend to think question-askers are intelligent. In commerce, industry, and medicine, stories are told about innovators who asked, "What if we do it this way?" and "Why not?" Stephen Wozniak and Steve Jobs, the computer whiz kids who began their company in a garage, asked *Why not make computers fun to use by someone who had no technical background?* and they thereby created the Apple Computer Corporation. The heroes in your own organization asked questions that led to new learning. Many leaders in U.S. businesses believe—with a fervor that the 18th-century Age of Enlightenment would have approved—in the candlepower of question-asking. They believe that when they have answers to their questions, they *know.*

In many cultures, knowing involves laying something open and examining its components minutely. Other cultures have quite the opposite approach. To them, knowing involves seeing the connections and links between everything. Knowing something means being able to fit it into the scheme of things. A prominent Chinese scientist once described the difference between Western and Chinese approaches to knowing, using the disease AIDS as an example. He pointed out that in the West, medical researchers were diligently trying to isolate the virus that causes the disease. But in China, researchers were trying to find ways to strengthen the body's immune system. One method looks at the most elemental unit of the disease, while the other looks at its place in the context of what the disease does.

In many cultures in Asia, Latin America, the Middle East, and Southern Europe, learning does not come from asking questions. Learning means receiving and taking in what is given by teachers. Some teachers may speak through written texts. Teachers *know.* Their role is to pass knowledge on to learners, so that the learners also will know. In China, Japan, Korea, Thailand, Hong Kong, Vietnam, Malaysia, Cambodia, and Indonesia—among other places—the teacher in the classroom is an absolute authority. The textbook and the teacher do not disagree. What a teacher delivers to the students is true knowledge and is not to be doubted. Although sometimes students ask questions for clarification, they do not question the authenticity or reliability of the knowledge they are given. Their role is to master it.

Frequently that means committing knowledge to memory so they can reconstruct it when called upon to do so, as in an exam. Reproducing exactly what was delivered is the best possible demonstration a student can give of really having learned.

Culture defines what it means to know and to learn. This basic fact is important for any organization, since today organizations must operate with personnel from many cultures.

Does Knowledge Have Limits?

Can everything be known eventually? In cultures with highly developed research economies, some people assume that with enough science, the right theories, and the best equipment, eventually the physical world will be known. Probes into space, into the seas, into the atom, into human behavior—all these will yield final answers one day. This is a view often held by nonscientists who have faith in what science can achieve.

But many people who aren't engaged in science hold a different view, believing that scientific inquiry into the physical world will never reveal everything. They think some things are unknowable. In Western Christian cultures, following a separation between the sacred and the secular that began hundreds of years ago, the spiritual truths generally have been held to be knowable through *faith:* If you believe, you can know. When scientific findings and faith are in conflict, science has little effect on the beliefs of the faithful. Scientific analyses of the Shroud of Turin, for example, which some Christians believe bears the imprint of Christ's body, have had little effect on belief or unbelief.[9] For those Christians, knowing in spiritual terms involves a different approach from knowing in material terms.

Other cultures find this approach to knowing very strange and schizophrenic; for them there is no separation between sacred and secular. For many Hindus in India, for example, all human undertakings and all things in nature are embraced by the spiritual. Believers visit temples daily, sometimes three or four times a day. Businesspeople obtain blessings for ventures, and new work premises are blessed before they are occupied. No separation is made between material life and spiritual life; all life is seamlessly part of the real, unseen but felt, realm of the divine. All of life is sacred. Any foreign organization that wishes to do business in India has to accept this view of knowing.

For many cultures, some things are too ineffable—too sacred and inexpressible—to be known by any means. The ineffable may be delineated to a greater extent by the persons who are assigned that role—priests, shamans, wise women—than by ordinary businesspeople. When this is true in cultures in which such knowledge is valued, these people enjoy a high status.

How Do People Reason?

How people know is closely related to how people reason. Reasoning varies from culture to culture. This is not always evident, since people tend to assume everyone reasons the same way.

Western Logic. Perhaps the most typical way of reasoning for members of Western cultures involves cause and effect. To speak of *reasons* in English is to speak of causes, of reasons why. In fact, a *reasonable* person is one who sees relationships of cause and effect between things. *Why* questions in Western cultures inevitably invoke explanations of causes: Why has the market share shrunk for widgets in Malaysia? Why are productivity figures up for March? Why is the chief accountant not at work today? (Because our widget competitor launched a marketing campaign last month. Because the new equipment was running without problems in March. Because her husband is in surgery.)

Cause-and-effect thinking is linear. We could draw a straight line from cause to effect, with an arrowhead at the results end. Many sentences in English employ this pattern. Consider that last one: The subject is *sentences,* and it has some descriptors around it (*many, in English*); *employ* is what the sentences do; *this pattern* is the outcome, or the result of the activity of the verb. The subject does the activity. That's how the sentence unfolds, and that's the linear pattern of what actually happens, not just what the sentence describes.

Westerners think that cause-and-effect patterns are logical and that *logical* means cause and effect, the pattern Westerners call Aristotelian syllogism. So deeply embedded is this notion that it is assumed to be universal. But it isn't.

> The syllogistic reasoning of Aristotle . . . is not a universal phenomenon; it has been a part of the Anglo-European tradition for such a long time that speakers of English tend to assume that it is a natural phenomenon of the human mind, rather than an invention of the human mind.[10]

Western logic also holds another Aristotelian principle: that two opposite things cannot both be true. This is called *the principle of non-contradiction*. It forces one to choose which is true and which is not. The result of this principle is that Westerners tend to think in terms of a binary choice between true and untrue, black and white, good and bad. It is the reason Westerners often seem to oversimplify issues.

Asian Logic. *Logical* means something very different to non-Western people. For example, Chinese people often use a pattern of logic that contrasts elements: An A must have an opposite B, hot implies cold, summer pairs with winter, and so forth. However, the opposites co-exist, and seem to hold each other together in a balanced state. This balance of opposites is represented symbolically by the yin-yang (pronounced *een-yahng*) image (see Exhibit 3.2). This pattern of thinking results in communication that contrasts opposite items in equal terms. Items may be in a sequence of opposites or antitheses. Reasoning structured by complementary opposites is common in East Asian logic.

EXHIBIT 3.2
The Yin-Yang Symbol

In Focus

The Chinese *yin-yang* symbol used in many Asian countries and displayed on the Korean flag (see Exhibit 3.2) expresses the way opposites contain something of each other.

Yin is negative, cold, downward and inward, dark, and night; it is also feminine. *Yang* is positive, hot, upward and outward, light, and day; it is also masculine. The *yin* and the *yang* interact. Where one grows, the other contracts, but they make up a whole. Neither can exist without the other.

Furthermore, each has an element of the other within it. As the *yin* grows larger, so does the *yang* element within it, and vice versa.

Yin and *yang* can offer a perspective for understanding technological growth and development in Asia. Urban development, telecommunications, and fast transportation systems bring people into contact: This is a *yang* aspect of technology. Family structure is threatened by urban growth as people leave their villages and migrate to urban centers: This is a *yin* aspect of development and technology.

The key in Asian patterns of thinking is linkage. Links are always being sought to show the wholeness of life, even when that whole embraces contradiction. The importance of the fish tank to Lei Peng in the case that opens this chapter shows a linkage of ideas because of the sounds of the words that represent those ideas: fish and profit. Events are likened to other, larger events that occurred in the past. Businesses in China use this linkage pattern in negotiations. For example, a meeting between negotiating companies is related to momentous encounters between nations in distant historical accounts. This kind of historical reference often figures in the early informal stages of negotiation: the toast by a Chinese host to the foreign guests.[11] Toasts often sail past Western guests, who do not recognize in a historical reference any substantive link to the business at hand. The unity of human experience with the whole of life is the fundamental philosophical basis for the thinking patterns that can be identified in Chinese business communication.

The point for business communication is that Asian businesspeople tend to look at the links between things and the relationships that give things meaning by providing a context. Western businesspeople, however, tend to consider issues in isolation. For example, a Westerner trying to establish joint-venture guidelines in

Japan may look at professional credentials only in relation to hiring personnel. The Japanese look at credentials, but also at the character of employees, their seniority, their past service, perhaps their family members' service, and certainly who the candidates' contacts are—a large tissue of interrelated factors that form a context for hiring and wages.

Roderick McLeod, an entrepreneur in China more than 20 years ago, made this prediction:

> I believe that the subject of patterns of thinking, explored in all its daunting depths and complexities, holds a promise of a "quantum leap" in cross-cultural understanding and communication.[12]

His projection still holds true today. Richard Nisbett engaged in an exploration of the differences in the ways Westerners and Asians reason. Westerners, according to Nisbett, going back to the classical Greeks, consider the perceivable world as made up of objects. The reasoning method by which objects are grouped into categories entails identifying attributes that objects have in common. Individuals that have fur, for instance, can be classed together into a group.

East Asians, in contrast, reason that objects that *influence* one another belong in a group. For example, a group could include "spring," "east," "wood," "wind," and "green," all of which influence each other. Both Westerners and Asians focus on the relationships of things, but Westerners look at the relationship of an individual item to the group, whereas Asians look at the relationship of part to whole.[13]

Arab Logic.   Reasoning in Arabic cultures is different again. Arabic reasoning differs from East Asian reasoning in that it does not try to reconcile opposites. Arabic reasoning is more like Western reasoning, holding that two opposites cannot both be true. The historical development of reasoning in Arabic-speaking cultures has origins that predate Islam but were focused in a particular way by Islam.

In Arabic-speaking cultures, *presentation* is the conveying of true meaning. Presentation is the way communication is enacted. It involves three key elements:

- Language and word choice
- Ability to raise emotion
- An authoritative voice

Arabic reasoning often begins with an assertion that then is restated and repeated so that the accumulated weight of repetition demonstrates its truth.[14]

We can look at the way people reason as a cultural dimension that can be examined in any culture. For example, in Russia, as in Asian countries, thinking patterns embrace opposites, rather than oppose them. Extremes and contradictions delight Russians, who do not seek to reconcile them but to see them exist together in a pattern.[15] We will return to reasoning as an independent variable in the study of culture when we examine how culture affects persuasive communication (Chapter 5).

Category 2: Doing and Achieving

The next six value dimensions have to do with how people view work and the ways they create meaning out of work. They are presented, just as with Category 1 dimensions, as situated between opposite poles.

Is Doing Important or Is Being Important?

The existential view of some cultures calls for valuing the present moment and celebrating being. One worker expressed an existential view by saying that he regards work as a blessing; you work hard at whatever your work is. But you don't continue to set yourself new challenges or imagine new activity beyond the blessing you have been given. This is hard for the activity-oriented to understand. To them, it looks like shirking.

In contrast, to the celebrators of being, a great deal of activity in *doing* cultures looks pointless. Where are people going in such a hurry? What have they left behind? What is the meaning of so much activity? *Being* cultures value stillness, collectedness, and serenity. Many visitors to Western cultures are amazed by the pace of life, especially in cities: so many activities crammed into a short time, requiring so much speed to fit them all in. Such crowded agendas seem to leave little room for simply being.

According to Condon and Yousef, Clifford Clarke (as foreign student adviser at Stanford) first observed the correlation between cultures in which activity is valued—almost for its own sake at times—and in which silence is of little value.[16] Members of *doing* cultures view silence as a waste, a time when "nothing is doing." Members of cultures that value *being* also often value silence. In silence the present moment can best be appreciated and experienced. A foreign businessperson in Japan who is unaware of the importance of silence in that culture may rush to fill silence with words. Silence is discussed in more detail in Chapters 6 and 9.

Obviously, great potential for conflict exists when co-workers have opposing views about doing versus being.

Are Tasks Done Sequentially or Simultaneously?

Even when many cultures value activity, they may regard *doing* differently. In some cultures, performing tasks one-by-one in a sequence is considered normal behavior, whereas in others, performing multiple tasks simultaneously is normal.

People may have personal styles and preferences for getting work done apart from the norms of their cultures. That is, within a sequential-task culture, individuals may prefer a flexibility that allows them to do more than one thing at a time. (They may be called "disorganized" by others in that culture.) In general, however, workers in sequential-task cultures know at the start of the day what they will do during the segments of the day: morning, lunch hour, afternoon, and evening. When unexpected tasks arise, others that had been scheduled are rescheduled. The essence of *time management* is organizing and sequencing tasks, a notion that seems peculiar to members of cultures where things take as long as they take.

In Focus

Rosemary Andrews, a Canadian sales representative from British Columbia to Venezuela, goes to the office of a shipping company to arrange for the ongoing shipment of an order in transit from Quebec to another country. She is on time for her appointment but has to wait while Juan Caldrón, the shipping agent, serves a number of customers who are already in the office. When Rosemary's turn finally comes, she explains what she needs, and Juan begins filling out the documentation for the shipment and discussing prices. At the same time he takes a phone call, responds to a question from a co-worker about schedules, and directs the faxing of a message about something else—in effect working on three other projects besides the Canadian's. Juan is efficient in the Venezuelan culture.

To Rosemary, however, this is unfocused activity that is not nearly as efficient as it would be—particularly from her point of view—if Juan simply dealt exclusively with her during her scheduled appointment.

In Canada, as in many industrialized countries, businesspeople typically write appointments and activities into the day's agenda every day. They then work sequentially through the agenda until they have completed each task, or until the day is over.

In contrast, although a simultaneous-task performer knows in general what the tasks in a given day will be, the day has a fluidity that allows for more and less important tasks that take more or less time, and the performer assumes that many tasks will be attacked simultaneously. (The question of time and how it is valued is discussed in detail later in this chapter under the heading "The Big Picture.")

Simultaneity is extremely useful when people and relationships between people are valued highly: You can spend all the time you want or need with a person when you are at the same time giving some attention to other (valued) persons. This leads to the next question to pose of a culture concerning doing and achieving, a key question in comparing cultures.

Do Results or Relationships Take Priority?

Results cultures regard ends as more significant than the means used to achieve those ends. The United States is where Management by Objectives (MBO) had its origin; that isn't surprising when one considers the dominance of cause-and-effect thinking in United States culture. The basis of MBO is that you identify your goals and then work out a strategy to achieve them. Along the way, you measure how close you have come. That's how you know you're making progress.

Goals-oriented societies place a very high value on making progress, which naturally leads to methods by which to measure progress. Measurements that seem logical to Americans may not seem so logical to others, however. The French (among others) often marvel at the American penchant for statistics and measurements of qualities they consider intangible. ("How satisfied are you with your present superior: 10 percent, 25 percent, 50 percent, 75 percent, or 90 percent?" "On a score from one to five, how well do you think you are performing in your job?")

Not all cultures feel the need to identify goals and work toward them. One reason is that an important goal in many cultures is nurturing close relationships with co-workers. Even if the proposed sale falls through, relationships have been strengthened by the effort to close a sale.

In countries where power is concentrated at the top levels of organizations and is wielded according to personal favor, a healthy and strong relationship with the powerful ones is a primary goal of every endeavor.

Relationships are the basis for much of the business conducted in Asia and the Arab world. In places where relationships are highly valued, business is done only with people who have entered into a relationship with you and whose organization has connections to your organization. In fact, in relationship-oriented cultures, business preferably is transacted face-to-face.

In China, for the last half of the 20th century and beyond, every government-based work unit had a travel allocation in its budget from the government so that representatives could travel and meet with suppliers, buyers, associates, and related organizations (those reporting to the same ministry in Beijing). Many work units had hotels on the premises to receive visitors from within and outside China. Business correspondence was minimal; business was transacted face-to-face. The preference for face-to-face communication is still strong today. Relationship building is a key activity.

When there is a strong relationship, specific outcomes can be planned. Contracts can be written and signed because relationships exist that will ensure their performance. The outcomes flow from the relationships. No wonder relationship-oriented cultures value the relationships as a means to an end more than the end itself. Furthermore, if success is elusive, the parties can always try again, if the relationship is intact.

Finally, people don't necessarily agree about what signifies an achievement. You may assume that all businesspeople equate achievement with profit, but that assumption is not always correct. Furthermore, even when people agree that making money is their goal, they may have very different ideas about what it means to have money—what it is worth.

For instance, in Brazil wealth is important because it can buy an elite car, a spacious apartment in a desirable area, servants, memberships in private clubs, travel, exclusive brands of liquor, clothing, personal entertainment equipment, and entertainment for friends.

When graduate students in Shanghai were asked in 1985 to describe *wealth,* they all agreed that it meant having money in your own pocket; they also agreed with the statement "If you have 10,000 yuan in your pocket, you're rich because you can buy the best banquet for all your friends!" Today, the same people may indeed be buying banquets *along with* homes, cars, and consumer goods. Economic growth of an average 8.5 percent in China since the mid-1980s has fueled huge leaps in prosperity for many. Consumerism is rampant in China today, driven in large part by the willingness and ability of parents to spend money on their one child. Still, people value being able to buy banquets for family and friends.

This dimension, results versus relationships, corresponds in part to Hofstede's dimension of individualism versus collectivism. Individualist cultures are performance-oriented and emphasize personal achievement and winning the competition. Collectivist cultures are relationship-oriented and emphasize supportive networks and collaboration.

Is Uncertainty Avoided or Tolerated?

Uncertainty—the inability to be sure about exactly what the future will hold for oneself and one's business environment—exists in all cultures and, Hofstede points out, in all organizations as well. Some people react to uncertainty with greater levels of anxiety than others. An employee who is averse to uncertainty will want to know what the prospects are for job advancement, based on what criteria, at the recommendation of whom, at which times of the year. Employees who calculate carefully and minutely what the effect is on a retirement income of working an extra month before retiring and base their decision to retire on that information are probably uncertainty-averse. They strive to protect themselves from the unknown. By comparison, an employee who tolerates uncertainty may be willing to transfer to a different geographic location at short notice or leave a place of employment before lining up the next job. Such employees are more open to accepting the unexpected. What Hofstede showed is that like some individuals, some cultures react with greater anxiety than others. As a broad generalization, *being* cultures tend to be more uncertainty-tolerant, while goal-oriented *doing* cultures tend to be more uncertainty-averse. Doing cultures have a Plan A, and then a backup Plan B, and often even a Plan C "just in case" the first two fall through.

Two members of an organization who come from different cultures and have to work together—say, a production manager and a supervisor—who do not agree about whether to avoid or tolerate uncertainty may have a hard time understanding each other. If the person from the avoiding culture wants more guidelines about how to deal with uncertainty, and if that person is a subordinate, then the subordinate's relationship with the boss may suffer from distrust and diminished respect. The uncertainty avoider may not understand that a different attitude toward uncertainty lies behind what appears to be simply an irresponsible approach on the part of a superior who is supposed to be responsible. The one tolerating uncertainty, the boss, may identify the subordinate as anxious for no good reason—simply a worrier—rather than someone with a different attitude toward uncertainty.

Uncertainty is not the same thing as risk. Risk involves a specific potential loss, but uncertainty does not involve a specifically identifiable loss. Risk in business is an everyday fact; risk in business that involves multicultural and multinational contact is even more inevitable. The risk may be social rejection, economic loss, or a legal liability. Businesses must consider risks in all business transactions. Businesspeople from various cultures approach risk differently, but all organizations want to minimize risk.

Is Luck an Essential Factor or an Irrelevance?

Luck is one way to deal with one's anxiety about the unknown. Cultures vary in the importance they attach to the influence of an unseen power over events. Is luck (fortune, fate) responsible for success? Or is success the responsibility of the human engineers of it? Not surprisingly, in cultures that think in cause-and-effect patterns and that value results, *planning*—not luck—is the key to success. Westerners are fond of sayings that present this view: "We are the architects of our own destiny."

Planning appears to equal control. If you plan carefully and omit no detail, you may ensure the outcome. Control means calculating the variables so that nothing unexpected can intervene between cause (means) and effect (ends). Attending carefully to the details resembles an orientation toward rules, as is discussed in the next section; they are both attempts to shape outcomes by controlling variables.

As anyone who has carefully laid plans knows, however, the unexpected has a way of ambushing you. Even some Westerners think that Western rationalism, which is our heritage from Aristotle through Voltaire to modern technocrats, has traveled too far from human experience. The discounting of fate and the belief in human planning and engineering seem foolish to some Western thinkers.

Western cultures, which have tended to discount the role of fate since the Enlightenment of the 18th century, nevertheless number millions of horoscope readers. This perhaps is because, in spite of technology and planning and control mechanisms, life frequently persists in not being orderly. People whose cultures acknowledge the role of luck in human affairs view the attempt to control life through planning as merely an illusory and pointless activity.

In Focus

Hong Kong may be the place where practices to ensure good luck and avoid bad luck are most often observed. For example, a desk in a business office may display a jade carving of a stylized bat (the flying rodent); the word for bat sounds like the word for prosperity, and the jade carving is a conscious invocation of luck that brings prosperity. (Luck means material wealth to the pragmatic Hong Kongese.) Fortune-tellers abound, and businesses consult them about making business decisions. *Feng shui* (literally "wind water") is the ancient practice of geomancy—aligning sites and buildings in harmony with the earth's energy forces so that locations will be propitious. Its expert interpreters typically are called in when buildings are oriented on construction sites. Owners of restaurants, hotels, and retail businesses also call in *feng shui* experts when trade slumps. The experts' recommendations often include repositioning the manager's desk or hanging mirrors to deflect the flow of disharmonious influences into the building or partially screening the entrance to prevent money from running out the door. *Feng shui* is not always a guarantee of luck, however. A Chinese-American–owned business in California was poised to purchase a property adjacent to it when the property came up for sale and the business had an investor willing to loan the $1.2 million price. However, when a *feng shui* master expressed strong negative opinions about the purchase, the company did not complete the purchase. Instead, an Armenian businessman bought the land. Within 18 months the value had soared to $3 million, and the hapless Chinese-American business owners were deeply chagrined. They needed the property but now lacked the funds to buy it.

Some numbers are lucky in Hong Kong, such as eight (which sounds like the word for prosperity), seven, and three. The government raises extra money by auctioning off auspicious-number license plates, and in recent years one man paid $5 million HK (USD $645,000) for a car license plate with a string of lucky number eights. By contrast, the number four is unlucky since it is pronounced like the word for death. Hotels and office buildings do not have a number four, and observers say subway passengers are reluctant to pass through gate 44 even during rush hour. Phone numbers and street addresses with a four in them are also regarded as unlucky by many.

In Taiwan, the Ghost month (the seventh in the lunar calendar) is traditionally not a time of good luck for making an important decision such as a new business venture. Rather than risk a business loss, some people figure they might as well wait until the (lucky) eighth month to make decisions. Good luck comes, according to the Chinese, when invoked by homonyms, such as the fish in the opening case of this chapter. To "have fish" sounds exactly like "to have prosperity."

Filipino fatalism is summed up in the phrase *bahala na,* which in Tagalog roughly means "accept what comes and bear it with hope and patience"; success in a business venture may well be attributed to fate rather than effort.[17] In Thailand, *mai pen rai* means "Never mind; it's fate, and you are not responsible." In Chinese, *mei guanxi* has a similar meaning. It literally translates as "no connection" and suggests that a person isn't responsible for the whims of fate.

In India, fate is widely credited for events. It is preordained and can be known by studying the stars and the procession of the planets. Many companies in India have their own astrologers who practice the 5,000-year-old *jyotish,* or astrology. Businesses consult with astrologers when they recruit new employees to ascertain whether they are lucky. After all, if employees have no luck as individuals, how can they be lucky for the organization?

Wearing specific precious and semiprecious stones can counteract the planetary influence and mediate fate somewhat; many Indians wear specific stones for the purpose of just such intervention. In Turkey, people, including those engaged in business, often wear a blue-bead amulet for good luck and more specifically, for warding off bad luck. It looks like an eye, and is for protection against the "evil eye."

In Mexico, the unexpected working of fate is well known. A supplier may promise delivery on Thursday, for example, knowing all the indications are that Thursday will not be possible since he has a full agenda of promised orders for Thursday. But the supplier may consider that perhaps one of the previously scheduled orders will be canceled, or perhaps the driver of the delivery truck won't come to work that day, making all deliveries impossible, or perhaps it will rain too heavily for delivery, or perhaps the company placing the new order will change it, which could alter the delivery day. Fate is always a possible factor. A Mexican student sighed over a failed exam, "It was my fate, I guess."

It's important to recognize that an attitude of "Oh, well, might as well play it safe . . . you never know" in one culture can be an earnest belief in another culture. In cultures in which luck is acknowledged to play a role in business, people who discount luck may not only insult the luck seekers but can also risk being thought negligent or even threatening to the business.

In Focus

In the United States, observances to ward off bad luck also affect business. Office buildings frequently do not have a 13th floor, for example, and some airplanes have no aisle numbered 13. Then there are the pyramid letters that supposedly bring good luck to the person who doesn't break the chain (throw the letter away) and bad luck to the scoffer who fails to send the letter on to more people. (While few executives admit to playing along, nevertheless their names often crop up on the lists of senders of the chain letters, with comments about not needing any more bad luck.)[18]

Although most people in the United States (and in other English-speaking cultures as well as Europe) are aware of "unlucky 13," not many know it comes from the Last Supper in Christian teaching, at which 13 were present, including Jesus' betrayer. Jesus was crucified on Friday, and so combining the two, "Friday the 13th" was thought to be especially unlucky in Europe in past centuries.

Are Rules to Be Followed or Bent?

This cultural dimension is closely related to uncertainty avoidance versus uncertainty tolerance and to luck. Having rules and following them—and making sure others follow them too—is a way of diminishing anxiety about the uncertain. However, whether rules are followed also has to do with what is important in a society: Is neat, predictable behavior by everyone preferable? Or is having the flexibility to meet human needs preferable? In all societies, conflicts arise between what the rules state ought to be done and what is convenient or helpful to individuals.

For example, take the simple act of crossing the street. In strongly rules-adhering societies, pedestrians may not cross anywhere they like. They must use crosswalks that are marked; they must wait until a signal indicates they may walk (perhaps a white-lit figure walking, a traffic sign used throughout the world). When the signal changes to a blinking red hand, they must hurry to finish crossing and must not begin to cross at this point. When the red hand is unblinking, they must remain on the side of the street. In London, the corners of some intersections have railings so that pedestrians cannot cross exactly at the corner but must use a designated crosswalk several feet away. In Canadian cities, pedestrians are ticketed for jaywalking. But in rules-bending societies—Mexico is one—people cross whenever they perceive a break in motor (or bicycle) traffic and wherever it is convenient for them to cross. Although they have been told that the rule is to cross at a designated crosswalk only when the signal indicates they may, they cross where and when it suits them. Rules-oriented cultures are puzzled by this seemingly cavalier attitude toward safety.

Category 3: The Big Picture

This category of cultural priorities encompasses the big things cultures deal with: the questions every society tries to answer. Why are we here? What is the significance of life? Where did we come from? Where do we go after this life?

The ways in which cultures answer these questions correspond to many of the beliefs and attitudes we can identify with a particular culture. The answers to these questions also enable us to understand the motivations for behaviors that belong to a specific culture.

Religion is a *belief system* that informs the attitudes and behaviors of members of a culture, even of those members who do not actively practice the religion. As a way of learning about an unfamiliar culture, studying the religion(s) is a lengthy and demanding undertaking. It's like studying Russian so you can read the street signs—a worthwhile endeavor but not the first thing you need to know to begin doing business in Russia. Religions or belief systems come from cultural values and also contribute to cultural values.

Do Humans Dominate Nature or Does Nature Dominate Humans?

Nature is the natural environment and natural phenomena that envelop human endeavors. At one extreme, humans view nature as an inexhaustible resource. The assumption is—or, at any rate, was— that the land is there to sustain life, especially human life. The Book of Genesis in the Bible proclaims that after God made man:

> God said, "Behold, I have given you every plant yielding seed which is upon the face of all the earth, and every tree with seed in its fruit; you shall have them for food. And to every beast of the earth, and to every bird of the air, and to everything that creeps upon the earth, everything that has the breath of life, I have given every green plant for food." And it was so.[19]

However, archaeologists have shown that ancient cultures, for example those around the Mediterranean and Aegean seas, cultivated land for crops in ways that ultimately exhausted the soil, and deforestation caused its erosion. Nevertheless, the assumption that the earth and all that flourishes in it is for us to use as a God-given right has persisted into this century. Only in the last several decades has the argument for environmental protection been put forward seriously as public policy. Simultaneously, the assumption that the earth is an inexhaustible source of sustenance is part of the historical traditions of Judaism, Christianity, and Islam.

In religions such as Hinduism, Daoism, and Buddhism, as well as earlier animistic religions—religions that honor the spirits of certain trees, rocks, rivers, and mountains—nature plays a different role. But what role? Japanese culture, which reflects the value orientations of Buddhism and Shintoism more than other religions, views nature as a source of aesthetic appreciation. Nature is observed; it is contemplated and meditated upon just like a painting or an object of sculptural art, and it is shaped into art in forms such as *bonsai*—trees that have been carefully pruned to grow in miniature. Wilderness, actual unadulterated nature, plays virtually no role in modern Japan. For example, boatloads of Japanese citizens organized protests against a dam in the Nagara River, but not to protect the river. Rather, it was to protest the intrusion of a large concrete structure in the carefully cultivated scenery. (It was also to protest the impact on the fishing industry since the dam would prevent trout from spawning.) However, Japan has pledged the largest amount of money of any nation for environmental protection worldwide. The Kyoto Treaty of protocols called on the nations of the world to agree to protect the global environment, and it was presented to the world in Japan.

In India, some Hindu sects, such as the Bishois, do not allow the cutting down of any trees or the slaughter of animals. This is extreme reverence for nature, which has precedence over human activities. However, piety does not always mean protection of the environment in that country. The pollution of India's rivers has been an enormous problem for the environmental protection ministry. It is particularly tricky when the river is the sacred Ganges with its freight of untreated waste, including the ashes and remains of cremated people from the funeral pyres of the devout.

The Daoists in traditional China held that the Way, the *dao,* meant becoming one with nature and its life energy. Chinese gardens represent mountains, streams, and caves, all places where spirits dwell that are sources of meditative serenity in escaping from the pressures of the world. Nature dominates human activity in that view. But in modern China, traditional gardens are state-owned and constantly crowded with Chinese visitors who litter. One of the most renowned natural beauty spots in China, the Three Gorges of the Yangzi River, has been flooded by a great dam built to provide electricity for the major cities downriver from it, including the enormous city of Shanghai. Over a million people have been relocated from their homes along the river, and the project has been decried by the international community. The traditional value of nature has given way to the need for hydro-electric power.

Among cultures whose priority is dominating nature, technology often is invoked. Technology is concerned with the relationship of people to their natural environment. All cultures develop tools for survival in their immediate environment. Very old and very new cultures share this human endeavor; creating tools is something all cultures have always done and will do. It has been called a particularly human activity; certainly only humans can create tools by pondering imaginatively upon other tools.

Members of cultures with advanced tool-making capabilities often assume their culture is superior to others with less advanced technology. This is not a basis on which to assess a whole culture; it is only one priority. Present-day technology is not necessarily the most sophisticated ever known; some processes used by ancient civilizations, like mummification of corpses in the Egypt of the pharaohs, and the firing of certain ceramic glazes in China, cannot be reproduced exactly today. Technology, the relationship of people to their natural environment, is often tempered and influenced by other cultural priorities.

In places where nature is endowed with spiritual life, such as certain mountains or rivers, human activity appears to believers to be too insignificant to have a lasting impact on transcendental nature. At the same time, scientists in all parts of the world warn of the damage to the earth from global warming, and propose changes in behavior to protect the earth. Thus, most cultures have a plurality of complex attitudes from different value orientations toward nature. That means that businesses have to contend with complex attitudes toward nature. A foreign firm may identify an ideal site for a joint-venture manufacturing plant on a river, but the site may be revered by local citizens as a spot of natural beauty or spiritual significance. Who wins—the sacred or the secular—will depend on the priorities of the culture. That brings us to the next question to ask of a culture.

Are Divine Powers or Humans at the Center of Events?

Who controls the outcomes of activity? Of business? Of life and death? In many cultures today, deities exist in a sphere of influence that is apart from the secular world.

Businesspeople may pray regularly to a God they revere but base their business decisions on factors that appear not to be divinely inspired. Devout individuals may indeed act on private divine guidance but probably will not publicly explain their actions that way. This is generally the case in societies that follow a stated policy of separation of public affairs and private belief. Religious spokespersons in those cultures are respected but not relied on for decisions. Questions of ethics may be referred to them, but the decisions rest with those whose responsibility it is to make the decision: organizations' chief executive officers (CEOs) or managing directors, union presidents, newspaper publishers, directors of government programs, and so forth. Even in societies in which human activity is accountable for outcomes, such as Great Britain, Poland, Hungary, Austria, and Greece, to name a few, public reference to a deity in the carrying on of human activity varies greatly. Canadians, for example, are bemused by the frequency with which leaders in the United States refer to God.

Some cultures see little or no separation between secular life and sacred life. All human activity, including business, comes within the all-embracing circle of the divine. A deity is at the center of every occurrence. In Madras, India, a businessman goes to the temple several times a day and has his company truck blessed each morning before work begins. In Bangkok, Thailand, a businesswoman offers food to Buddhist monks early in the morning before opening up her shop, and she may stop at a street shrine later in the day to pray. In Ankara, Turkey, the day begins with prayers to Allah, and prayers follow at intervals throughout the day in response to the muezzin's call. India, Thailand, and Turkey are all secular states and guarantee freedom of religion for all, but the practices of the faith of the majority have an impact on all affairs.

Of course, some nations historically have been theocracies whose governments followed the principles and regulations of a religion in conducting their activities. A modern example is Iran. Yet the tendency to see divine power at the center of human endeavor is widespread.

Let's examine some of the major world religions.

Hinduism

Hinduism arose in India, which is where most believers are today. It is one of the world's oldest religions. Today, around 900 million people follow Hinduism. It includes the idea of the world as a great system of hierarchies, with the purest at the top. Living things are reborn in cycle after cycle of death and rebirth until at last they reach *nirvana,* a state of eternal peace and bliss. In hierarchies of people, called *castes,* the purest are the *Brahmin* priests. They are not necessarily also the most powerful, and this can confuse businesspeople from Western cultures. Each caste carries its own *dharma,* or duties, and members of each caste are encoded with aptitudes for certain work.

Traditions are changing in modern India. The caste system means people spend their lives at one level of society, but in modern India people are seeking upward mobility. The caste system cannot legally be used any longer in India for hiring and promoting decisions.

Hinduism has many gods, although the most abstract supreme being includes them all. The many gods and goddesses help to describe certain aspects of the supreme being. Different regions of India worship different gods, or perhaps the same aspects with different names. Tantric Hinduism is a mystical tradition.

Most Hindus do not eat beef because cows are considered to be holy. Cows are revered as important symbols of the gifts and nurturing of the supreme Divinity. Some Hindus link cows to Lord Krishna, an important figure in worship and tradition. Injuring a cow can get you in trouble with the law in India, although the many cows in the streets of crowded cities are a hazard. Many Hindus prefer not to eat any animal meat, because killing animals involves violence. However, there is no teaching in Hinduism that says Hindus should not eat meat.

Hinduism has a dynamism that is the result of its embracing many ancient beliefs and rituals and also embracing newer religions such as Buddhism. This means that Hinduism has remarkable diversity. Hindus in western India do not worship the same god or observe the same holy days as do Hindus in eastern India. Basic beliefs in one part of the country are rejected in another part. Hinduism has been called the most accommodating of religions and also has been charged with resisting change.

Hinduism as practiced by many believers covers all aspects of daily life. No separation exists between worship and work. Millions of Hindus begin the day with prayer. Often in a family the women draw a symbol on the house doorstep at dawn. Family members will go to a temple or stop at a shrine for prayer or perform rites at home every day. Bus drivers have their buses blessed before going to work in the morning; they stop for blessing at night when they finish work.

The important basis for religious ritual is the distinction between purity and pollution. Avoiding the impure means performing certain behaviors. Purification usually involves water, and perhaps a sacrifice, in a ritual. Leading a pure life and gaining merit through good works and charity are valued.

Hinduism has five basic principles:

- God exists: One absolute divinity that includes one Trinity of the gods Brahma, Vishnu (Krishna is one form of this god), and Maheshwara (Shiva) in their several divine forms.
- All human beings are divine.
- Unity of existence is through love.
- Religious harmony underlies Hinduism.
- Three Gs—Ganga (or Ganges, the sacred river), Gita (the sacred script), Gayatri (sacred mantra) are important.

Hinduism has a number of values that underlie the way Indians and other Hindus view life. These values include truth, non-violence, celibacy and non-adultery, no desire to possess or steal, no corruption, cleanliness, contentment, reading of scriptures, austerity and penance, and regular prayers.

Although for many Hindus, the belief system embraces all of life, educated Indians are likely to separate work and the rest of life, often as a result of Western influence. A businessperson who is a foreigner will have to learn what people's beliefs are in the specific area of India. Gentle questioning will reveal how willing an Indian is to speak about religious issues and the impact of caste on professional life.

Buddhism

Buddhism, whose principal figure is the Buddha, began in India in the 6th century B.C. A rich prince named Siddhartha Gautama led a sheltered life of luxury and wealth. One day he met a beggar and one who was dead. He began to understand the pain and suffering of life, and he left his home to think about suffering and its meaning. He fasted until near death, and finally he sat down under a bodhi (or boda) tree. That night he was *enlightened*—that is, he understood the meaning of life and suffering. He stayed another seven nights under the tree without moving, according to the story, meditating upon what he had learned. Following his enlightenment, he was called the Buddha, which means the Enlightened One.

His Four Noble Truths are as follows:

• To exist is to suffer.
• Suffering is caused by desire, which is never satisfied completely.
• Suffering stops when desire ceases.
• The Noble Eight-fold Path is the way to end desire and thus suffering.

The Eight-fold path dictates ethical behavior. It teaches that one should avoid evil and violence, and think about the temporary nature of the body and its physical life. Meditation is the complete concentration of the mind on a single thought in order to be free from desire and ultimately from all feeling.

Buddhism began as a way to reform the religion of Hinduism, since Siddhartha was born a Hindu. Some similar concepts exist in both. For example, the concept of *karma* is important to Hinduism and Buddhism. In Buddhism, karma is the inevitable result of one's ethical behavior. This cause-and-effect idea means that doing good toward others in life will result in good karma; good will come back to you, in this life and in the next life. Similarly, doing bad things will result in bad karma, and bad things will happen to you in this life and in the next.

Buddhists believe in a cycle of life-death-rebirth, and the Buddha taught that the end of this cycle of rebirths is *nibbana*. Nibbana is similar to the Hindu concept of nirvana, except that it is a state of nothingness. Individuals finally reach a state of nonbeing. This is the ultimate end of suffering.

Buddhism, with 376 million believers, has two main traditions: Theravada and Mahayana. Theravada (which means "the teaching of the elders") is the Buddhist tradition based on scripture. Believers do not mix beliefs from any other religions with this tradition, which has written teachings to keep believers clear about what is and what is not Buddhist. Theravada Buddhism is strong in these countries: Sri Lanka, Cambodia, Myanmar, Thailand, Laos, and Vietnam.

Mahayana Buddhism is strong in East Asia. Mahayana means "the greater vehicle" or the broader and more eclectic teaching. (*Eclectic* means made up of parts from many sources.) Mahayana Buddhists believe the Buddha intended his teachings to be combined with other teachings as well. In China, Nepal, Mongolia, Korea, and Japan, Buddhism combines teachings from other religions such as Daoism in China. In Korea, Confucian priests share temples with Buddhist priests. (However, Confucianism is not actually a religion. It is a set of principles for living in harmony with others in a society. Confucius is the English name for a teacher who lived in the 5th century B.C. He taught ethical behavior. He never claimed any divine status or spiritual insights as a prophet.) In Japan, most people worship in Buddhist temples *and* in Shinto shrines. Shintoism is a different religion; however, Buddhism in Japan is generally not opposed to Shintoism, but instead is in harmony with it.

Mahayana Buddhists pray to, and ask for blessings from, various representations of the Buddha or supernatural beings. To many (mainly Theravada) Buddhists, however, the Buddha, the Enlightened One, is not a god. In fact, Buddhist scripture does not teach anything about a god. Buddhist philosophers and scholars do not support the idea of a creator-god or a personal god. Nibbana, the final deliverance or liberation of the human soul into nothingness, is not the same as passing into the presence of a divine being. Nothingness (*anatta*) is non-self and non-substantiality.

In some Buddhist cultures, such as Thailand's Theravada Buddhism, strict observances have an impact on business life. Men become monks for some period of their lives, usually before entering the workforce. Women must never come in physical contact with monks or their robes but daily offer rice and other food to gain merit. Monks may be influential in decisions that affect local businesses in areas such as labor and wages, locations for new businesses, and markets. Theravada Buddhism emphasizes learning not to desire things, and this can be contrary to a market economy. Yet many countries with Buddhist followers—Thailand, Taiwan, Japan, and South Korea—became economic dynamos in the early 1990s.

Hinduism is a polytheistic religion—that is, more than one god is worshipped—and Buddhism has many representations of the enlightened ones, although they are not gods. In contrast, three other major world religions are monotheistic—meaning worshippers pray to only one god.

Judaism

Judaism, the religion of the Jews, has fewer followers (14 million) than the others we are reviewing in this section. It is older than the others, except Hinduism, since it began before 1200 B.C. Judaism thus precedes both Christianity and Islam, which make reference to Judaism. Judaism has a strong influence today partly because it forms a background for both Christianity and Islam, and is one of the three religions of "the book."

Judaism is rooted in the Torah, five "books" that make up the first five sections of the Old Testament in the Christian Holy Bible. Another important Jewish book is the Talmud, which is made up of the Mishna—the legal teachings handed down orally about what is right behavior and what is not—and the Gemara, which is a commentary and interpretations of the Mishna by scholars over centuries. The Talmud and the Torah form the basis of the practice of Judaism. Practice means following holy rules.

Differences of opinion exist in Judaism about who exactly is a Jew. Nevertheless, people who identify themselves as Jews recognize a tradition that is the history of the Jewish people.

Most Jews share certain beliefs. Among these are beliefs in:

- One God
- God's concern for humans
- The concern that one person should show for another
- The *covenant,* an agreement between God and the people of Israel expressed through God's laws for the proper use of the universe
- Belief in the world to come or in the Messiah or the Messianic Age.

Jews who participate in religious observances also share

- Jewish practices
- Jewish holy days and the Jewish calendar

Judaism today is divided into four modern religious movements represented by synagogue membership: Orthodox, Reform, Conservative, and Reconstructionist. A small percentage of Jews identify with more conservative movements (such as Hasidism) that had their origins in 18th-century Europe. A large percentage of Jews worldwide identify themselves as secular, with no connection to a synagogue or movement. Some Jews center their Jewish identity on Zionism, the political movement to create and sustain a Jewish nation in Israel.

No matter what beliefs a Jew subscribes to, there is a sense of solidarity among Jews that is born of the recognition that Jews share a common history, heritage, language, and culture. They also feel themselves to be a community. The Talmud expressed its recognition of this commonality in a positive statement, "All Jews are responsible one for another." This captures the Jewish value called *Klal Yisrael,* the "Community of Israel."

Christianity

Christianity has 2.1 billion followers, which makes it the largest religion in the world today. Christians are divided into several main branches: Catholicism, Protestantism, and Orthodoxism. However, Protestants are fragmented into many *denominations* (groups with teachings that are different from each other). Catholicism also has subgroups, but the largest by far is the Roman Catholic church, which is rooted in Western Europe. Roman Catholics are the largest body of Christian believers. They emphasize the authority of the Roman Catholic Church in a centralized, hierarchical system. Orthodox Christians have geographical roots in Eastern Europe and Russia, and they also emphasize the authority of the hierarchical Orthodox Church.

Christians believe in one all-powerful God who is creator and sustainer of life, and in Jesus, whom Christians believe is a historical figure who lived about 2000 years ago. Jesus is claimed by believers to have been God incarnate in the historical person, Jesus, who was an itinerant teacher in Judea, Samaria, and Galilee (all present-day Israel). He spoke about God as Father and about himself as the Son of

God. Jesus lived in Palestine, in what is now modern Israel. His spoken words were written down from memory 45 to 100 years after his death, and the four written versions or books are called, in English, the Gospel. The word comes from the Old English term *gōd spell,* meaning "good news." Jesus was born during the Roman occupation of the area, and he was put to death by the Roman powers, who saw him as a political threat, with the cooperation of the local governor and religious leaders. His death was not the end, however; after three days in a tomb, according to Biblical accounts, Jesus appeared and walked among people who knew him. He claimed to have eternal life and furthermore to be the way to eternal life for believers in him as the agent who connects them to God.

The resurrection of Jesus is what Christians celebrate at Easter, the holiest event of the Christian year. His followers believe that his resurrection means they also can, after death, gain entry to God's eternal presence in the next life. Christianity is based on the teachings of Jesus. Christians also believe that Jesus will come again to judge humans, although many variations exist about the details of that second coming. Christians also believe in the Holy Spirit, called the "giver of life," who with God and Jesus forms the Holy Trinity that is worshipped by Christians.

Stories of the life of Jesus include people like his mother, Mary, and his disciples who traveled with him. In the Catholic and Orthodox traditions, they are saints and have special relationships with God, so they can bring individual Christians closer to God. In the first century A.D., Paul, later called a saint, was the author of 14 letters, called "books" of the New Testament, in the Christian Bible. His letters form the basis of much Christian doctrine.

The Catholic Church centered in Rome historically had large economic interests, but discouraged its priests from involvement in business. Individuals in religious orders usually renounce personal economic and business endeavors. The Protestant movement broke away from the Roman Catholic church in the 16th century. Protestants were protesting against

- The hierarchy of the Roman Catholic church
- The idea that only priests could have direct contact with God or read the Holy Bible
- The wealth and size of the organization
- The teaching that only through the sacred rites of the church and the go-betweens of Jesus or his mother, could individuals have salvation from eternal hell—the opposite of heaven and God's kingdom

The Protestant Reformation emphasized the lack of distinction between religious and secular life, and thus the way was opened for the merging of the pursuit of financial goals with spiritual goals. Catholics had kept the sacred quite separate from secular life. Men and women who dedicated their lives to devotion to God were—and are today—in communities where they typically give up personal economic and business activities. In monasteries and convents even today, days are spent in prayer, worship services, and meditation.

The concept of predestination, which is prominent in some Protestant denominations, holds that the elect or chosen individuals are the ones who receive the gift of grace. Some historians see the linkage of material prosperity to the elect as a visible sign of God's blessing, as the linkage that made the development of capitalism possible and even pious. Wealth came to be taken as a sign of God's approval and blessing. Wealth wasn't to be spent on self-indulgence, however. Along with the notion of gaining riches went the notion of not spending wealth but rather saving and investing it—in other words, creating capital. Capitalism grew in that environment.

Orthodox Christianity refers to the movements that developed in modern-day Turkey and Greece, and in Eastern Europe and Russia. The church in Rome and the church in Constantinople (Istanbul) split in the 11th century, and the split is called the Great Schism. The Orthodox church rejects the political organization of the Roman church, which has a Pope whose formal statements are "infallible"—unable to be wrong. Cultural, political, and geographical differences between the Eastern and Western churches kept them apart. Until the Great Schism, there were five recognized centers of Christianity: Rome, Constantinople, Alexandria, Antioch, and Jerusalem. The last four—Constantinople, Alexandria, Antioch, and Jerusalem—belonged to the Orthodox or Eastern church. That continued until the centers were dominated by Islam.

The Orthodox church believes it is the original true church, created by Jesus and his apostles (or followers). They keep the teachings of the original church and compare new ideas to the traditional ideas, rejecting what does not relate to the original teachings. The Orthodox faith, taught by Jesus and his apostles, is called the Holy Tradition. It is the same Christian religion of the Catholic and Protestant churches in the West, with some variations in interpretations and practices.

The Orthodox church, like the Roman church, has hierarchies of priests. Bishops are in charge of the priests in a geographical area. Every bishop in the Orthodox church traces his lineage back to one of the original 12 apostles or followers of Jesus. Sacraments in the Orthodox church are called Mysteries. The Orthodox church also has monasteries and convents for people who choose a life without marriage and who live in a community that prays, fasts, and performs as many as nine worship services daily.

Orthodox worship is highly formalized, meaning the same prayers and teachings follow in the same order in worship services. The most important service is the Divine Liturgy. Worship focuses less on the believer and more on God who is worshipped with awe, repentance, thanks, and praise.

Islam

Islam is the second-largest religion in the world today, with 1.5 billion believers, and it is the fastest-growing religion. It has more members than Hinduism, Buddhism, and Judaism combined. Muslims live in countries all over the world, but Islam is the dominant religion in 19 nations.

In the year 610 in the Western calendar, a trader who worked with caravans began to receive revelations from God, called Allah in Arabic, through the Archangel Gabriel. The teachings were in turn delivered orally to Arabs in Mecca and later in Medina. The withdrawal to Medina in 622 A.D. is called the *hegira*, and it marks the beginning of Islam. This was not, according to Muslim belief, the start of a new religion, but rather the restoration of the original faith of Abraham, Moses, and the prophets. Mohammed was a descendant from Abraham, and became the final Prophet.

Many of the revelations or *suras* transmitted by Archangel Gabriel were memorized by professional reciters. That way the revelations were preserved without changes. The Prophet Mohammed was illiterate, but the suras eventually were written down in the words he had received. The language was Arabic of the 7th century in the Arabian Peninsula. The collection of the written revelations is the Qur'an, the holy book of the revealed word of God. Islam spread rapidly through military conquest in the next two centuries to Africa and the Middle East.

Islam means "to submit" or "to obey." A believer submits to the word of God transmitted through the Prophet. A central belief in Islam is that everything, good or bad, comes from the will of God. A phrase heard throughout the Muslim world in daily conversation is *Inshallah*, meaning "let it be according to God's will."

God's will extends to all aspects of life; God is the one creator who is just, omnipotent, and merciful. Muslims also believe in Satan, who drives people to sin, and they believe that all unbelievers and sinners will spend eternity in Hell. However, Muslims who sincerely repent and submit to God will return to a state of sinlessness and go to Paradise—a place of joy and bliss—after death. The Qur'an speaks of resurrection of the body.

Muslims everywhere subscribe to the Five Pillars of Islam.

* *Shahadah*, or profession of faith, summed up in the belief: "There is no god but Allah, and Mohammed is His Prophet."
* *Salah*, or worship: Five times a day a muezzin or mosque official calls Muslims to prayer. They face Mecca and pray in Arabic, the sacred language. Around noon on Friday, men are expected to go to the mosque for public prayer.
* *Zakat*, or giving alms. Muslims are especially taught to give to the poor, widows, and orphans; the Prophet Mohammed himself was an orphan, at the age of 6. The *zakat* is a charity tax, at 2.5 percent of income, but additional donations are also given.
* *Sawm*, or fasting. The month of Ramadan, the ninth month of the Muslim calendar, entails 30 days of fasting during daylight hours. Fasting offers the opportunity for contemplating Islamic teachings and the deep values of Islam.
* *Haj*, or pilgrimage. Every Muslim is asked to make the pilgrimage to Mecca, the holy city, at least once in his or her lifetime, during the 12th month of the Muslim calendar. Specific rites take place in and around Mecca, that have spiritual meanings. One is to circle the Kaaba, the sacred black stone. Tradition says it was originally white, but turned black because of the sins of the world.

Islam offers many specific teachings about how to behave. Alcohol, drugs, and gambling should be avoided, as should racism. Part of the appeal of Islam today as in past centuries is that members of all races and beliefs are welcome if they accept the teachings of Islam. Islam affects all aspects of daily life through *Sharia,* the laws and rules for religious, social, political, domestic, and private life. Today, Iran and Libya are two countries that follow Sharia in their national courts of law.

Islam is practiced differently in different countries. Muslims in Indonesia, Egypt, Saudi Arabia, and Tunisia differ from one another in some behaviors while remaining obedient to the precepts of the *Qur'an.* For example, a difference that is easily observed is the degree to which Muslim women cover themselves in public. In some cases, such as in Malaysia or Turkey, Muslim women may not even wear a scarf or *hijab* over their heads. In Saudi Arabia, Iran, and Afghanistan, women outside the home are covered entirely by a burqa or chador.

Some international business practices are at odds with Islamic codes of behavior, so Muslims in some countries have made adjustments to maintain both Islamic teachings and successful international businesses. For example, Muslims are not supposed to charge interest or pay interest on loans. By receiving guaranteed interest, an individual gets a reward without working for it, and that is prohibited. A return on the deposit is acceptable only if the individual works for the return, or if the profit or loss is shared with all depositors. This has given rise to Islamic banking, in which profit and loss sharing replaces interest earning and speculation. Another different business practice concerns insurance. Since the will of Allah is omnipotent, Muslims who carry insurance policies risk being accused of lack of devotion or even defiance of Allah's will. In Western countries, Muslims' daily prayers may be at odds with business schedules; in Muslim countries, Westerners are often out of step with the prayer schedules.

Like other religions we have discussed, Islam has two major branches in the world today: Sunni and Shia. They differ based on whom they regard as the Prophet Mohammed's rightful heirs to his power. Sunnis—who won a majority of followers—claim the Prophet's disciples are the ones who should carry on the Islamic faith. Shiites claim a nephew (actually, a very young cousin) of Mohammed's, called Ali ibn Abi Talib, carried on the true teachings of the Prophet. In general, Shiites—who dominate in Iran, eastern Iraq, and are a powerful minority in other countries—are more conservative than Sunnis in that they say Islam should return to its fundamental teachings and not compromise with the modern world. Other smaller branches of Islam exist, such as Ibadism in Oman.

Other Religions

After Christianity and Islam, the third-largest group of people in the world identify themselves as *non-religious.* Sixteen percent claim not to belong to any one religion, although half of those say they do believe in a god. People who say they do not belong to any one religion exist in every part of the world.

Other religious groups with many members include the worshippers of spirits of certain landscape features (mountains, rivers, trees, rocks, springs, and pools). These groups are primarily in Africa, Asia, and the South Pacific. This form of belief is called *animism* from the Latin word, *anima,* meaning "spirit." Chinese traditional religion is Daoism (or Taoism), which is based on the belief in an abstract life force that people can connect with through following the correct "way" of thinking and acting (*dao* means "way" or "path"). Other belief systems we haven't discussed here continue to be meaningful for people. They are part of the answer to the question: "Are divine powers or humans at the center of events?"

The role of religion in people's lives is something businesspeople need to know about. Most cultures have some procedure for young people to learn about their family's religion. Children in Roman Catholic homes have their first Communion at about seven years of age. Protestant children in mainline denominations are accepted as members into a church as teenagers (in some Protestant churches adult members are received upon Baptism). Jewish offspring have bar mitzvahs and bat mitzvahs at the age of religious responsibility, usually 13. In Thailand, every male is expected to spend some time as a Buddhist monk, usually for six months to two years, after completing his education and before getting married and establishing a family.

One way religion affects people's lives is in the special days of observance or celebration. Business travelers need to be aware of religious holidays in other cultures. Friday is Muslims' holy day, Saturday is the Sabbath of Jews, and Sunday is the holy day of Christians. That may mean that stores and places of business are closed on the relevant holy day. Ramadan, the ninth month of the Islamic year, is a month of fasting from sunrise to sunset—thus it's not the time to invite a business colleague to lunch.

The new year begins for Buddhists on the first new moon of the lunar year, any time from late January to mid-February, and usually involves several days' closure of businesses. (But Thailand, the most Buddhist nation in the world, also celebrates the new year in April.) In China, the Buddhist lunar new year has been replaced by Spring Festival, which takes place at the same time: the first new moon of the first month of the lunar calendar. The festival in China is a national holiday that usually lasts a week, when many factories close down and the transportation systems are overloaded with travelers. Obviously, a business visitor to another country needs to find out when that nation's holidays are and when people will be available to meet in order to plan an effective visit.

Businesspeople also need to be very careful not to make assumptions about other religions based on stereotypes. Whether welcoming a new employee or investigating the possibility of a business operation abroad, businesspeople need to keep their minds open and their inquiries gentle.

How Is Time Understood, Measured, and Kept?

Another value orientation that has to do with *big* questions concerns a culture's view of time. Traditional cultures think of time as cyclical. The rhythms of nature and the cosmos dictate this view: Day yields to night, which in turn yields to day again; rain follows dry periods that come after rain; the time to plant leads to the time to nurture, then the time to harvest and the time plants die. Everything follows a pattern of birth, life, death, and renewal—even daily activity, after which the weary body sleeps and wakes refreshed. Within the cyclical framework, events that occur take as long as they take; their duration is dictated by their essential nature. This view is common among agrarian cultures whose members are closely attuned to the rhythms of cultivation. The corn will be ripe when it has finished ripening, in its own time. It is also persistent in cultures that value human interaction and relationships.

Monastic life in the Middle Ages often is credited with the development of a notion of time as modern European and American cultures know it. The monks needed to regulate their prayers as a community. If everyone woke up later one day and earlier the next, the community's prayer life would be undisciplined and other activities would be erratic. Monasteries began ringing bells to maintain a scheduled, ordered life. An idea took shape: to measure something abstract, intangible, and defined however you wanted to define it, called *time*. Time could be given an identity and then segmented into component parts. Monks gave the segments names, such as *none* (noon, the fifth canonical hour and mid-afternoon prayer) and *compline* (the seventh and last of the canonical hours and evening prayer).

European monks weren't the only ones to try to measure time; Mayan priests had been doing it in Mexico, Guatemala, and Belize for a thousand years. Measuring instruments became more precise as navigational needs grew in Europe and as astronomy developed. By the 18th century, the instruments used to measure time and the movement of planets seemed able to reveal the secrets of the clockwork universe, and time became a commodity.

What does it mean to be "on time"? The definition of punctuality varies from culture to culture. The cultural priority of time has close links to another priority: relationships versus results. When people are important and the nurturing of relationships matters, the time necessary for nurturing activities is flexible.

You may have an appointment in Puerto Rico for 10:30 in the morning; you may be the second appointment on the other person's agenda, and you can still be waiting at 11:30. Everybody is so important that no meeting can be rushed for the sake of a schedule that is imposed arbitrarily. In São Paulo, Brazil, traffic snarls often delay people from arriving on time at meetings, and although an apology is expected, lateness is not considered an insult. Both Puerto Rico and Brazil have strong orientations toward building relationships to do business effectively.

In results-oriented cultures, adherence to schedules is much more important. In Israel, for example, promptness is a basic courtesy as well as an indication of seriousness about work. In Russia, time is not related to cost or profits, and punctuality— being "on time"—is an alien concept: "Russians are notoriously not on time, and they think nothing of arriving long after the appointed hour, which is not considered as being late."[20]

What does effective use of time mean? As we discussed earlier, results-oriented cultures tend to use a cause-and-effect pattern to understand something and use planning to control uncertainty. These cultures also have a linear view of time; after all, a cause-and-effect sequence unfolds in time from the generation of something to its results. People who view time as a highway progressing from the past into the future also tend to believe that the past is background and preparation for the present. They think the present will be the basis for the future. Time is used effectively when goals can be accomplished speedily. They are very different from people who see cyclical patterns that repeat themselves.

In Focus

"Time is money." "Save time." "Spend time." "Use time wisely; don't waste time." "Make time." "Take your time." These are some of the phrases we commonly use that underscore the value of time as something to be bought and sold. Employees sell their time to an organization and are paid for their time. Lawyers and consultants of all stripes bill clients for their time. Workers talk about doing something on the company's time versus doing it on one's own "free" time. Telecommuting employees who work at home using a computer modem say "my time is my own," suggesting that they "own" their work schedules and can work when they please, not only when the organization's doors are open to the public. The opposite case is an employee whose hours are "owned" by the organization.

People who view time as linear, and as divisible into chunks that have a market value, measure time in relatively short periods: minutes, hours, and days. In cultures in which time is expansive, measurements are in weeks and months, as in Russia, where patience has a high priority.

Time can be monochronic (one-dimensional time) or polychronic (multidimensional time). Monochronic time is linear. People are expected to arrive at work on time and work for a certain number of hours at certain activities. Then, after resting for an appointed period, they are expected to resume work activities. In some monochronic organizations, being even a few minutes off schedule is not acceptable.

In polychronic cultures, time is an open-ended resource that is not to be constrained. Context sets the pace and rhythm, not the clock. Events take as long as they need to take; communication does not have to conclude according to the clock or arrive at a closure of the business at hand. Different activities have different clocks. The idea of monochronic or polychronic time can be related to a previously examined cultural dimension: whether tasks are done serially or sequentially. Monochronic cultures do one thing at a time. Polychronic cultures have several time-schemes running simultaneously; people in these cultures can be observed doing more than one thing at a time to accommodate more than one clock. Modern multitasking is also doing several things simultaneously, and is talked about primarily in monochronic cultures. It occurs because of the value of efficiency and timesaving—the idea of being able to manage time effectively. This isn't the same as a polychronic approach, where doing more than one thing at a time occurs because that is how activities unfold. Polychronicity isn't planned and managed.

Is Change Positive or Negative?

The culture of the United States thinks of change as desirable and positive. At the nation's founding, the *new* was thought to be better than the old. In advertising slogans today, new means *better* products and services. Change means moving forward in linear time toward ever more desirable achievements. The business culture of the United States puts a high priority on the accomplishment of goals, the accumulation of wealth, the efficient use of time to do this, and a positivism that claims that tomorrow will be better than today just as today is better than yester-day. When change has a high priority, the members of a culture express optimism about the future.

Traditionally, agrarian cultures typically view change in the opposite way. Since people who live on the land cannot move away and take their land with them, they tend to develop stable, static communities. They see the cycles of planting and harvest, rain and sun, day and night at a very close view. They also think of change as negative. It means disruption to the established patterns of life. They believe that yesterday was better than today and tomorrow will be worse than today. Products that call themselves *new* are not to be trusted.

Russians, for example, view change as negative. They expect things to be bad in the present and worse in the future, and in part this is a posture that enables them to face change and uncertainty stoically. There is justification for pessimism. After all, historically the "best and brightest have traditionally been banished. In Old Russia, independent thinkers were exiled to Siberia . . . Stalin's purges of the 1930s further decimated the intelligentsia, and today many of Russia's best are being lost through emigration."[21] Endurance is one of Russian culture's top priorities.

Clearly, the priority involving change has a close connection with an earlier one: uncertainty avoidance. Change always involves uncertainty about what will result, and cultures that view change negatively are typically keen to avoid uncertainty. The old ways are best; the familiar is trustworthy even when it is known to have faults. Yesterday is often endowed with a golden glow and thought of as superior to today; the past may come again one day if things stabilize, and we may even return to the old ways. Cyclical views of time are consistent with anti-change cultures.

Cultures that are conscious of their long histories cannot easily understand severing connections to the past or wanting to do so. Businesspeople from younger cultures such as the United States or Australia are often impatient with the clinging to old ways that they observe in other cultures. They operate with cause-and-effect logic and see that to accomplish a particular goal (an orientation they value highly) new ways (or products or procedures) are helpful. They cannot understand why others balk at adopting something new.

Is Death the End of Life or Part of Life?

The last priority we'll consider in this chapter for posing questions of a culture involves final things. Some cultures view death as the end of life, a quenching of the light. It is dreaded. Some cultures view death as another phase in life, a necessary step in the pattern of life. It is accepted.

Hindus believe in reincarnation, and in India's burning *ghats*, bodies are cremated and sent on their journey toward another birth. People are reincarnated over and over in a cycle that can't be numbered. Your status in life is the result of how you lived a former life, and your present life will affect the next life. When a loved one dies, the loss is mourned just as it would be in Copenhagen or Cairo, but the mourners know the soul will be born again. In Russia, death is familiar; it is fought and welcomed, in a contradictory attitude. A former American foreign service officer quotes a modern Russian poet's response to his question about what Americans should know to understand Russians better:

> In our cold winter each opening of the door is a repetition of dying. Russians do not fear death because every day is a struggle. It is a pity to die, and a pity not to die.

> —Mark Davydov[22]

Death is not such an enemy as it is in the West.

In Holland, death is sometimes embraced by appointment, since doctors may legally assist terminally ill patients in dying. This enables patients to die with dignity rather than dying in slow stages with increased discomfort and perceived humiliation. There is a relationship between this death by appointment and control over the unknown; uncertainty avoidance and a preference for planning and doing correlate with this approach to death.

Many cultures have religious beliefs that teach death is the only way to join the gods or God. In Islam, life after death is freedom from obstacles to the enjoyment of God's gifts. A Muslim's heaven is experienced through the senses. A Christian also looks forward to heaven after death, to joy and an absence of pain, but the Christian heaven is less clearly defined than is the Islamic heaven. Attitudes toward dying vary widely among members of Christian cultures and among members of Islamic cultures.

Funerals also mean different things in different cultures. In Nigeria funerals are very important. Unless you are dying yourself, you are expected to attend. It is thought that the deceased will reward you for your presence. In the Māori culture of New Zealand, funerals typically involve a three-day observance (*tangi*), although for royalty and other important figures, the *tangi* can last a week. Employers recognize the need for relatives to be absent from work for this occasion. Family members sit around the departed loved one and receive visits of condolence from relatives and friends in the community. People tell stories, pray, and sing while shedding tears together. After three days the body is buried, and the community has had its relationship bonds affirmed by the experience of shared grieving.

Funerals are dreaded in Asian cultures, where even the suggestion of death or funerals is considered rude. That's why you should never give a clock or watch to a Taiwanese as a gift (a reminder of the inevitable end of one's life span) or a bell (rung in funeral ceremonies) or white flowers (white is the color of mourning). You must even avoid using the word *death*. In Hong Kong recently, many people were upset when clairvoyants charged that ghosts of dead children had appeared in TV commercials. Reminders of death are impolite at best and unlucky at worst. In Japan, it is intolerably rude to stick your chopsticks straight up in a bowl because then they resemble the incense sticks burned in urns at funerals.

Some take a proactive position toward death, however. In Singapore, as in other Chinese cultures, funeral objects such as televisions, cars, and money, all made of paper, are burned to accompany the deceased into the world of the dead and to ensure a comfortable existence in the next life. In China, expensive tombs have been created, some for living people who have not yet been able to use them.

Businesspeople need to be aware of the cultural priority put on death and the observances that attend it. Chapter 1 gave several examples of different expectations work colleagues may have toward a co-worker who has lost a family member. The expectations for how the mourning friends and relatives will act differ from culture to culture.

In many cultures, mourners wear a black armband or black clothing to signal to others that they are grieving the loss of someone and should be treated with respect. The traditional color of mourning in China is white, however, as it is in India. (Brides in those cultures traditionally wear red.) Mourning is signaled with a white armband or rosette in some countries, and with white flowers.

Special observances besides the funeral service may include a wake or a special feast where mourners come together to solidify new social relationships without the departed one. This is true in such divergent cultures as Catholic Ireland, with its wakes, and Buddhist Taiwan. These two different cultures share characteristics common to high-context cultures, however, where the meaning of the individual is derived from the network of relationships into which an individual life is woven. The next chapter deals with cultural priorities concerning relationships, and discusses the two remaining categories of questions you can ask to learn what you need to know about a culture. It concerns the self and the self in relation to others.

Summary

This chapter introduced the approach of asking questions in order to understand cultures.

Asking questions involves identifying where information can be found. Answers may be general, and to be useful, they need to be generalized. Questions can be posed in five categories; the first three are Thinking and Knowing, Doing and Achieving, and the Big Picture.

The first category of questions is Thinking and Knowing, which covers the following dimensions:

- *Does knowing come from concepts or experience?* Some people truly know something only when experience has taught them; without experience, they merely know *about* something. For others, knowing comes from conceptual understanding.

- *Does learning come from asking questions or mastering received wisdom?* In many cultures, the acknowledged authority gives knowledge, and one knows when one has mastered what the textbook or teacher says. In other cultures, going beyond what one has been given is how one truly knows something.

- *Does knowledge have limits?* In some cultures, not everything is knowable. Other cultures have the idea that everything can be known if the key is found.

- *How do people reason?* Western cultures use a cause-and-effect pattern of thinking. Other cultures use different patterns. The balance of complementary opposites, as illustrated in the *yin-yang* symbol, is one example.

The second category of questions covers Doing and Achieving—how people understand their actions at work.

- *Is doing important or is being important?*

- *Are tasks done sequentially or simultaneously?* Some cultures view one who works efficiently as one who accomplishes several things at once. Other cultures value a one-thing-at-a-time approach as the most efficient.

- *Do results or relationships take priority?* Relationship-oriented cultures tend to be collectivistic. The relationships that connect people in networks are more significant than the tasks people accomplish. Results-oriented cultures value the outcomes of actions, especially measurable outcomes, as what matters at work and in life.

- *Is uncertainty avoided or tolerated?* People who are uncomfortable with uncertainty tend to stay with their employers and follow established procedures at work. People who are able to tolerate uncertainty with lower levels of anxiety may attempt new things in their professional lives.

- *Is luck an essential factor or an irrelevance?* Luck or fate or destiny plays a large role in cultures in which people recognize that their role in achieving success has less effect than do forces outside themselves. In other cultures, outcomes are not left to luck but are considered to be largely controllable by human effort.

- *Are rules to be followed or bent?* In places where relationships are primary and power distances are great, rules may be bent to serve those more important values. In places where results matter, rules are viewed as important to facilitate results.

The last category in this chapter is The Big Picture. This section deals with the "big" questions cultures answer:

- *Do humans dominate nature or does nature dominate humans?*
- *Are divine powers or humans at the center of events?* Belief in divine beings underlies the values, behaviors, and attitudes of many people of different cultures. Two major polytheistic religions are Hinduism and Buddhism. Three other major world religions—Judaism, Christianity, and Islam—share roots and a belief in one deity.
- *How is time understood, measured, and kept?* Cultures differ in attitudes toward time and how it should be observed. Some view time as cyclical, whereas others view it as an unrolling continuous line. Some cultures treasure time as a commodity; others use it as the flexible medium in which activities take place.
- *Is change positive or negative? New* may not be positively received in traditional cultures. *Old* may not be a word of approval in cultures that embrace change.
- *Is death the end of life or part of life?* How death is viewed and how that view affects business varies from culture to culture.

The last two categories of questions to pose of an unfamiliar culture follow in Chapter 4: "The Self and Social Organization."

Notes

1. Geert Hofstede, *Cultures and Organizations* (New York: McGraw-Hill, 1991).
2. Fons Trompenaars, *Riding the Waves of Culture* (Burr Ridge, IL: Irwin, 1994).
3. Andre Laurent, "The Cultural Diversity of Western Conceptions of Management," *International Studies of Management and Organization* 13, no. 1–2 (1983), pp. 75–96.
4. Shalom H. Schwartz, "A Theory of Cultural Values and Some Implications for Work," *Applied Psychology: An International Review* 48, no. 1 (1999), pp. 23–47.
5. Robert J. House, Dr. Paul J. Hanges, Dr. Mansour Javidan, and Peter Dorfman, *Culture, Leadership, and Organizations* (Thousand Oaks, CA: Sage, 2004).
6. Edward Hall, *Beyond Culture* (New York: Anchor Press/Doubleday, 1976), pp. 85–128.
7. Edward Hall, *Beyond Culture*.
8. Sheila Ramsay, "To Hear One and Understand Ten: Nonverbal Behavior in Japan." In *Intercultural Communication: A Reader,* 4th ed., Larry A. Samovar and Richard E. Porter, eds. (Belmont, CA: Wadsworth, 1985), p. 311.
9. Ed Schwortz, www.shroud.com, retrieved on July 24, 2006.
10. Robert B. Kaplan, "Writing in a Multilingual/Multicultural Context: What's Contrastive about Contrastive Rhetoric?" *The Writing Instructor,* 10, no. 7 (1990), p. 10.
11. Linda Beamer, "Toasts: Rhetoric and Ritual in Business Negotiation in Confucian Cultures," *Business Forum* (Winter 1994), pp. 22–25.
12. Roderick McLeod, *China Inc.: How to Do Business with the Chinese* (New York: Bantam Books, 1988), p. 72.
13. Richard Nisbett, *The Geography of Thought* (New York: Free Press, 2003).
14. Barbara Johnstone, *Repetition in Arabic Discourse* (Philadelphia: John Benjamins, 1991).
15. Yale Richmond, *From Nyet to Da: Understanding the Russians* (Yarmouth, ME: Intercultural Press, 1992), p. 45.
16. John C. Condon and Fathi Yousef, *An Introduction to Intercultural Communication* (New York: Macmillan, 1975) p. 137.
17. *Culturgrams,* Vol. II (Provo, UT: Brigham Young University, 1984).
18. Mike Clowes, "Superstition Extends Yet to Top Levels," *Pensions & Investments,* 15 (April 1991), p. 14.
19. Genesis 1:29–30, rev. ed.
20. Richmond, p. 122.
21. Ibid., p. 43.
22. Ibid., p. 40.

CHAPTER FOUR

The Self and Groups

Sheila Graham is a businesswoman from New Zealand whose work in sales requires her to travel. Her company makes quality stainless steel food-processing equipment. Today her marketing effort has brought her to Warsaw, Poland. She is meeting at 1:30 p.m. with Jan Zamoyski, the vice president of a firm with which she has been corresponding about the possible purchase of several mixers. Sheila wants to make the most of her visit, which is expensive for her company, so she's learned what she can about the market in Poland for food-processing equipment and even something about the financial picture and how international transactions are usually carried out. She doesn't know much about Jan Zamoyski except that he is in his fifties, is at least 15 years older than she is, and speaks English.

She is a little unsure how to take his behavior when she introduces herself, and he takes her proffered hand and kisses it instead of shaking it. Is this an attempt at humor? Should she laugh or take it seriously? Then he compliments her on her appearance. This is unexpected too; after all, she arrived early that morning and knows she could look better. She doesn't want to be perceived as unprofessional because she is a woman, so her manner becomes a bit more distant. Jan uses formal address, last name and not first name. Sheila uses Jan's first name, the way she would in New Zealand, and that makes her feel she has things under control as an equal—a professional woman. Jan has an odd, almost comic, way of asking if she'd like a coffee: "Would the lady drink a coffee?" For a second she wonders what lady he means, and then she realizes he's addressing her.

After a little conversation about her flight and the weather, Zamoyski begins to tell her about Warsaw and makes references to various historical events that are obviously vivid to him. Sheila wants to talk about their business together but isn't sure how to introduce it into the conversation. He seems to want her to respond in sympathy to his rather emotional statements about Poland's history and heroes. She doesn't know anything about Polish heroes, apart from the fact that a Polish cardinal became the former Pope John Paul, and since she isn't Roman Catholic, she doesn't feel comfortable entering into a discussion about him. Instead, she replies that the language is very unusual to her ears. He promptly asks her to repeat a series of sounds she knows she can't imitate ("W Szczebrzeszynie chrzaszcz brzmi w trzcinie") and tells her that being able to say that was once a test of true Polish identity.[1] Again, she can't decide if this is a joke or if it's completely serious and some kind of test of her.

Zamoyski next produces a small gift for her, and Sheila experiences new doubts. Should she have prepared a gift, too? Should she accept this gift, not knowing exactly what it means? She doesn't want to be rude, but doesn't want to look like she can easily be bribed either. She takes the small object but doesn't unwrap it. Now she decides to try to introduce the subject of the purchase and sale of equipment. "I've brought a breakdown of our offer for you to look at," she says, taking papers out of her briefcase.

But Zamoyski's response is to talk instead about the lunch he proposes they now enjoy. Sheila ate before she came to the meeting, assuming Jan would have already had lunch by 1:30 p.m. She puts her papers back in her case. He escorts her to a new dining room on the company grounds, where he introduces her to six other people, and they sit down to an enormous meal. Sheila protests that she can't eat, but her host keeps offering her food. He also offers her vodka, along with a toast to the relationship they are starting. Sheila doesn't like straight vodka but sips a little of the cold alcoholic beverage from her glass to be polite while the others all down their glasses in one gulp. The glasses are refilled immediately. She picks at the abundant food and tries to ask questions of appropriate persons at the table to facilitate the sale of her company's equipment. She doesn't have much time in Warsaw and needs to make the most of this contact opportunity.

Sheila finally manages to give specific details about the sale to the young man on her left. He listens attentively. The meal finally ends, and Zamoyski has another engagement, so she goes back to her hotel. When she phones Zamoyski the next day, she learns he cannot meet with her and regrets that the sale will have to be postponed indefinitely. She knows the price and quality of her company's products are good; she knows the Polish company is looking to buy. What went wrong?

In Chapter 3, we considered question categories of Thinking and Knowing, Doing and Achieving, and The Big Picture. Now we consider how people view themselves and how their cultural priorities affect the way they interact for business purposes.

Category 4: The Self and Self-identity

In the Western world, awareness of the self comes out in language use. For example, in English (the same is true in German and French) if a person refers to himself/herself, she or he uses *I*. Obviously, we adapt our language to circumstances and the person or groups we are talking with. However, it seems that regardless of circumstances, we use the first-person pronoun *I* to refer to ourselves. An exception to that is a parent who tells a child: "Mother told you . . ." In that instance, the parent pulls rank. In Japan, the situation is very different. The specific first-person pronoun (*I* word) depends on the person one is talking with. There are many different words for the first-person speaker. This would indicate that the identity depends on circumstances and linguistically adapts to the environment. Culture shapes how people think of themselves and their self-identity.

One way to understand identity is as something formed in part by the self and in part by group membership. This approach to understanding identity recognizes that the self has many identities—daughter, wife, mother, nurse, member of a specific family—and so on. These identities are important according to values in the culture. People communicate as a result of their sense of self—in other words, their self-concept. The idea of self-concept is important to the discussion of who we are in terms of our culture. Self-concept can be formed in three general ways.

Self-identity—A *Social Psychology* Approach

One way we can think about self-concept is that we build up our sense of self from childhood, based on experiences we have had that contribute to our sense of self. These experiences are, for example, when we find out we are good at doing something, or when our sense of who we are is challenged, or when we recognize ourselves in other people's words and actions. We learn about our own identities in the context of group membership. Other people encourage, criticize, and comfort us. We try out ideas about ourselves, and see what reactions we get. We test different interests—some we develop for a lifetime and some last only a short while. We ponder different values. We develop a variety of abilities. Our sense of self grows in jumps, not in a continuous smooth curve. When we compare ourselves to others and the identities which they present to the world, we refine our self-concept.

Various contexts—home, family, religious gatherings, work environments, and so on—give us a chance to develop multiple identities.

Self-identity—A *Communication* Approach

Another way to understand self-identity is through communication. The communication approach builds on the self-concept and multiple-identity base of the social psychology approach just discussed. The difference is that the communication approach includes the important principle that identities are expressed in communication. A self-concept is co-created through communication. For example, think of the way you communicate with various people in your life. Do your teachers, friends, younger siblings, or merchants all see you as the same? Probably not. Do they all see you as you see yourself? Probably not. Some scholars see communication with different people in different contexts as the process of the self creating different identities.

Identities are communicated in core symbols, labels, and norms. For example, a core symbol of a culture may be hospitality in the form of a hot coffee. Arab cultures have this symbol. Labels are the terms for categories of core symbols, and the way we talk about groups of people: *Arab* is a label. Norms of behavior are the expectations for how people express their identity. For example, in many Arab cultures, the offer of coffee should be recognized as an offer of welcome and hospitality, and the coffee should be accepted by a visitor who does not want to give offense. Arabs are expressing an identity through a normative behavior that communicates who they are.

Self-identity—A *Critical* Approach

The critical approach to self-identity uses history, economics, politics, and public discourse. That is, the critical approach holds that self-concept is formed against the background of large social contexts. Power relationships are important in these contexts. Some of the labels that we apply to ourselves (and others) come from large social contexts. For example, we may call ourselves *minority* or *dominant* culture members or *natives* of a particular culture.

Sometimes members of other cultures use negative language we do not like in order to identify who we are. Racial and ethnic slurs are an example. The point about the critical approach is that many of the ways we are identified by others become part of our self-identity, both positive and negative. And many of the labels from these social contexts have to do with power and its distribution in a society and in the world.

The critical approach recognizes that forces in societies are always changing. In other words, social forces are dynamic. Therefore, the critical approach to self-identity says that identities are always changing. For example, since the formation of the European Union, the label "European" has changed its meaning. Today it means a member of a multinational society that has a common currency—the Euro—and common laws, and has a European identity. Before the European Union, being European merely meant living in the geographical area called Europe.

Self-identity and Cultural Value Dimensions

We now consider culture's impact on self-identity in more detail, using the social psychological approach. That is, we take a look at a number of ways a culture's values affect the development of the self-concept. The value dimensions or priorities in a culture may appear to be static, but we can keep in mind the dynamic and continuous creation of self-identity in communication acts. We can also keep in mind that self-identity is changing as social forces change.

Self-construal: Independent and Interdependent

Self-construal is how we see ourselves in relation to others, with regard to feelings, thoughts, and behavior. We construe or structure an image of ourselves that influences how we relate to others. The term came from scholars' comparison of Western and Eastern views of self,[2] and how culture affects how we see ourselves in relation to others. In general, Western cultures have an **independent** self-construal, and Eastern cultures have an **interdependent** self-construal.

In cultures that value *independence,* the idea of the self includes making decisions for one's own life, taking care of oneself and not relying on others, and taking responsibility for one's own actions. The individual sees himself or herself as unique. Heroes in independent-self cultures are individuals. "I can do it myself" is a statement from a self that values independence.

For example, in the dominant culture of the United States, members have independent ideas of self. Images of this independent self are everywhere. An example exists in the cowboy heroes of the historical "wild west" who are strong and independent, who ride their horses where and when they choose, and who fight alone against independent enemies—and of course, win. The image of the independent cowboy is very strong in U.S. culture, even though the historical period in which cowboys might have acted this way lasted only about 20 years.

The idea of the independent self predominates in individualist cultures. At the same time, members of these cultures also *have interdependent self-concepts*, but the independent self is in the majority of images.

In contrast, many cultures see the self as *interdependent*. In cultures that value interdependence, the self consults with others before making decisions; one relies on others for one's sense of well-being, and one takes responsibility for meeting the needs of the group before satisfying one's own needs. The individual sees himself or herself as part of a large network of social relationships, and others in that network take responsibility for the individual. The heroes of interdependent-self cultures are group members. "I will do it for all of you" is a statement from an interdependent self.

Japanese culture gives a good example. In Japanese history, the heroes who were most like the American cowboy were *samurai*. Samurai were a highly trained social class of superb swordsmen who served a lord by fighting his enemies. Above all, they were loyal to their lord (called *daimyo*). According to the Japanese image of samurai, they lived by a strict code of behavior (as did the cowboy, according to the American image). They fought together with honor for their daimyo. If the daimyo lost his life, the samurai became non-persons, and were called *ronin*. In a famous account called *The 47 Ronin*, a lord lost his life because he attacked a court official and for honor's sake had to commit suicide. His ronin then killed the court official in revenge for their lord's life. Then the ronin themselves had to commit suicide to satisfy the honor of their lord.

The idea of the interdependent self predominates in collectivist cultures, although of course the independent-self idea also exists in collectivist cultures.

Culture also shapes the way the self communicates. A person who has an independent self-construal uses communication to present the self and further the self's goals. A person who has an interdependent self-construal uses communication to further the harmony of the group and the relationships among its members.

The following cultural priorities explore the way culture affects the idea of self in business interactions.

The Basic Unit of Society: The Individual or the Collective?

In cultures in which the individual is a unit of society, a single person can earn credit or blame for the outcome of an organizational project. **Individualism** values individual achievements, failures, and rights over the collective. In cultures in which the collective is important, credit or blame goes to a group. **Collectivism** values the group above the individual, and individuals have a responsibility to the group that supersedes individual needs or rights. As has already been suggested, the United States and Japan are among the least similar cultures in the individualism–collectivism cultural dimension.

When businesses in the United States first began exploring the reasons for Japanese success and ways to market products in Japan, they encountered these differences. In Japan, an individual is a fraction of a unit; the group is the fundamental unit of society. An oft-quoted proverb in Japan is "the nail that sticks up will be pounded down." Any assertion of individualism—valuing the individual over the group—is regarded as a negative threat to the group and will result in punishment by the group.

Individualism in Japan is tantamount to selfishness. Japanese collectivism means that Japanese managers are closely knit to the departments they manage, which are also highly cooperative and closely knit. Organizations can count on the loyalty and wholehearted commitment of their employees. Organizations have their own songs, uniforms, and retreats for building loyalty and groupness.

Companies in the United States motivate employees by offering individual rewards. They cannot count as much on employees' loyalty to the organization or the work group as Japanese companies can because competition in the United States job market means that employees will go where they feel they will have the best personal success. Individuals in other Western cultures (Canadian, Dutch, French, English, and German, to name a few) also make career choices on the basis of *personal* needs and goals. If a job offers insufficient opportunities for advancement, for example, or a personality conflict arises with a superior, or the tasks become boring, or the employee's lifestyle changes, then an ambitious individual probably will move to another job.

In Japan, however, these situations may not be reasons for a move. Changing employers is still an admission of failure and brings loss of face, both to the one who could not cooperate in harmony with the organization, and to the organization for spawning such an antisocial misfit. In Japan, if personal goals are not met by work, the employee is often persuaded to change goals. When lifestyle changes create new needs, the superior expects to be told and to share the concerns, because the boss is owed the information and is expected to take an interest in the family life of the employee. When the organization demands overtime, employees respond eagerly. In many organizations in Japan, employees come in for overtime work even when they have little actual work to do just to show their solidarity with other members of the corporate group.[3]

Throughout Asia, in varying degrees, collectivism is celebrated. This is not surprising, considering the high value given to relationships in those cultures. What matters is the close-knit interlocked human network. Individual recognition is less important, particularly if it means a penalty or some kind of ostracization. Harmony among the interdependent group members is the key, and it takes priority over nearly all other values. In collectivist cultures in which interdependence is valued, individuals do not seek recognition and are uncomfortable if it is given. The reluctance to be singled out, even for praise, can present obstacles to a manager who is trained to motivate subordinates by offering personal rewards. A study of joint ventures in Shanghai in 1997 revealed that the Chinese are motivated by a sense of belonging. That sense is especially motivating when it is combined with prospects of long-term employment. "Relationships facilitate results" is the way one interviewee put it.[4] The motivational power of belonging is also strong in many Latin American cultures. One way a sense of commitment to long-term relationships is cultivated in Mexican companies is through company functions, such as family picnics, in which everybody is included. Employees feel they are valuable to the company when they and their families are invited to socialize together.

In Focus

In individualist cultures, people make decisions on their own, without consulting others. An example is the decision a student makes about what to study at university, and where to apply to study. Here is an example: A student—let's call him Mel—has been thinking about what to study and has been gathering information. He makes his decision and announces to his parents that he will study history or maybe law (that would be at the graduate level in the United States). He also has decided where to go to study, and tells his parents. If Mel (short for Melvin or Melville, perhaps) lives in Canada, his parents are glad to hear what he has decided, and ask what he will need to do to achieve his goals. They may ask about how much it will cost, and what sort of job he plans to get to help pay for his education. Canada's culture is individualist.

If Mel (short for Melek, perhaps) lives in Qatar, the story is different. Melek and his parents and older brothers and uncles and especially his grandfathers will discuss his education choices and will make a decision. Mel may or may not be present during the discussions. His father will tell him what the family has decided. If extra money must be found for his education, his family will provide it. Qatar's culture is collectivist.

A characteristic of individualist cultures is competitiveness; the corresponding value in collectivist cultures is cooperation. In the United States, where individualism is valued, competition is the means for determining the best. When individuals compete against one another, inevitably there are many more losers than winners, but the competitiveness principle asserts that as long as you can enter into the competition again and again, you too may win one day. In other words, consolation for losing lies in having a chance to compete. The United States has passed legislation for equal opportunity that is based in part on the value of having a chance to compete.

Surveys of large samples in national cultures, both by Hofstede and more recently by the GLOBE project, have shown that Japanese rank high on a competitiveness dimension (called "masculinity" in Hofstede's research and "assertiveness" in the GLOBE project).[5] At first, this is hard to understand. After all, Japanese are strongly collectivist. How can they also be competitive?

The answer may lie in the willingness of Japanese *groups* to compete. A drive for excellence is an evident characteristic of Japanese culture. Where achievement can reflect well on the group, or on the Japanese as a nation, Japanese individuals focus and work very hard.

Collectivist cultures in general tend to include everyone in the collective when a success is achieved, rather than singling out winners. At Sony, for example, departments form teams whose members are in a closely bonded relationship. Exclusivity comes at the team level, where other Sony departments are not part of the collective. Some loyalties, of course, are divisional or organizationwide. Foreign managers of branch operations need to look at motivation issues carefully in terms of whether individualism or collectivism is more important in an organization's host culture. Managers of multicultural workforces also need to consider what motivates employees of different cultural backgrounds. So far, this discussion of individualism–collectivism has contrasted United States and Japanese cultures to illustrate the concepts related to individualism–collectivism as a dimension of culture.

In both Hofstede's (1981) and the GLOBE (2004) studies, the surveys result in mean scores that represent the way the culture in general reports its attitudes. They are studies of whole cultures. Behavior by individual members of a culture and the values they hold are not necessarily identical to the findings of whole-culture studies. Furthermore, people in all cultures may be individualist in some contexts and collectivist in others. It's important to remember that the research looks at averages from data to draw generalizations about a national culture. The way individuals actually behave does not reflect the generalizations in every instance.

In Focus

New Zealand scores very high on Geert Hofstede's individualism scale—nearly 75 compared with a world average of about 40.[6] Other scholars, along with Hofstede, have explained what individualism means for communication: low-context communication—direct, unambiguous, explicit—is preferred in individualist cultures while high-context communication—indirect, implicit—is preferred in collectivist cultures.

New Zealand's history of colonists from Great Britain (the majority) and Europe furnishes some reasons why it is individualist. Early settlers in the mid-19th century worked on the land and sea as farmers, miners, foresters, and fishermen. They needed to be self-reliant, since the journey "home" to Britain was six months by sea. Traits such as resourcefulness, hardiness, common sense, and discipline helped them achieve success.

But there is a great complexity in Kiwi culture. The British and Europeans were not the first settlers; 800 years earlier the (Polynesian) Māori established societies on the islands of New Zealand. Māori culture has chiefs (*rangatira*) who have authority over tribes (*iwi*) and subtribes (*hapu*) that are made up of people related to one another. Māori today identify themselves by *hapu* and *iwi*; identity is based on the extended family. When making a formal introduction of oneself, called a *mihi*, Māori refer to their ancestors in a recitation of a family tree or *whakapapa,* and some can go back more than 40 generations. These examples alone can serve as evidence that the Māori culture is highly collectivist. Besides Māori, New Zealand is also home to many other ethnic groups. The main city, Auckland, has the largest population of Pacific Islanders in the world.

Here is some more complexity: the non-Māori, New Zealand's European settlers (called *Pākehā* in the Māori language) prefer an indirect communication style. On the other hand, when Māori are among themselves, in informal communication they prefer directness. These are the opposite of what one might expect of individualist and collectivist cultures. Why do *Pākehā* use an indirect communication style, when the British and European cultures they came from prefer a more direct communication style?

Pākehā settlers, while needing a degree of self-reliance and independence, also needed to be able to call upon their neighbors. Cooperation was vital to survival, and even today New Zealand has only 4.2 million people. People are connected to one another through others in a network of friendships and family relationships, and have to take care not to rupture relationships that might turn out to be needed. As in collectivist cultures, *Pākehā* communicate with a view to maintaining harmony in the group. These are some of the reasons for *Pākehā* New Zealanders' communication preferences.

As for Māori, they have a tradition of respect and esteem for articulate, polished speakers. They have a strong oral tradition that was established before the *Pākehā* came. Being able to say what you mean is highly valued, and in an in-group that means not holding back, but rather coming straight out with it.

How New Zealanders appear in the surveys of values does not necessarily match how they behave. This difference has been identified in the GLOBE study completed in 2004. Compared with the other 62 countries in the study, New Zealand scores *third-highest on collectivist in-group values*, and in a remarkable contrast, *third-lowest on collectivist in-group practices.*[7] In other words, Kiwis value collectivism but behave as individualists. As we have already noted, behavior and values of members of a culture are not necessarily congruent in all situations.

Obligation and Indebtedness: Burdens or Benefits?

Individualist–collectivist priorities mean that cultures interpret differently what obligation means. Everyone has had an experience in which someone came to the rescue and offered help just when it was needed. Maybe it was a stranger who offered the last coin you required for the bus fare. Maybe it was a friend who agreed to drive you to an important event when your own arrangements for transportation failed. Maybe it was a colleague who agreed to represent you at a meeting so you could attend another important function. In English-speaking societies, a slang expression sums up the feeling that accompanies gratitude: "I really owe you." It means that one feels indebted to the favor-grantor. But obligation has rules that are determined by different cultural priorities, and that can cause problems in intercultural encounters.

In Focus

A young Chinese girl, Song Mei, moved away from her village and her family to work in a large, far-away city. She sent nearly all her money home every month. But because she was so far away, coming home to visit was difficult and expensive to arrange. After more than two years away, she finally came home to celebrate the Chinese New Year with her family.

She arrived after a long journey, and everyone was very joyful. Her parents and aunts and uncles had cooked a special meal to celebrate her return. It was a happy time, but then one by one her family members began to look uneasy. Her mother was frowning slightly and her cousins several times drew their breath in sharply. Finally, with a pained voice her father said, "Why are you treating us like strangers? We are your family!"

She had been saying "thank you" when her relatives served her various dishes. She had learned that behavior when she and her co-workers ate special meals with strangers. In her native culture, saying *thank you* and *please* is for people who are **not** in a relationship of ongoing reciprocal favors.

To consider the issue, we'll turn to a situation that generates obligation. Person A must meet a visitor at the airport but finds that the means of transportation relied on to get there is currently unavailable. Person A thus asks Person B to make a trip to the airport, carrying Person A. In India, friendship means having a willingness to be indebted. In fact, in some languages in India no word exists for "thanks"; if one is in a relationship, one eventually incurs indebtedness, and one is expected to repay the debt owed. No words are necessary. Nor does one hesitate to request a favor of a friend; that's what friendship means.

Compare this with obligation in the United States, where someone may preface a request with "I really hate to ask you, but . . ." or "I wouldn't dream of asking you, only . . ." This opening usually is followed by a detailed explanation as to why the asker has no alternative but to become indebted. The request may finish with elaborate thanks: "Thanks a million! I'm so grateful!" In a culture that values individual achievement, independence, and control over events through personal action, a request that puts someone in another's debt is almost an admission of failure. Sheila Graham in the Warsaw sales situation, in the case that opens this chapter, regarded accepting a gift as acknowledging indebtedness, which made her uncomfortable. She wanted the sale to go through on an impersonal business basis, not on the basis of a sense of obligation. The Poles, in contrast, wanted to build a relationship before entering into a business agreement.

People in cultures like Sheila's are not happy about being indebted and often try to repay, and thus erase, a debt as quickly as possible. Perhaps too many obligations make people feel that their personal freedom is threatened and that they have lost some control over choices they could have made. Some independent individuals may go to great lengths to avoid putting themselves in someone else's debt and avoid making others indebted to them. For example, in an individualist culture, Person A, who wants to go to the airport but doesn't have transportation, might hire a taxi rather than ask someone to make a special trip on A's behalf. Similarly, rarely are gifts given for no apparent reason in individualist cultures. On occasions when they are, their importance is downplayed by a casual giving style. The reason: The giver does not want to make the receiver feel too heavily obligated.

Scholars observe that these characteristics are true of the dominant culture in the United States. They observe that African-Americans differ, however; this group is much more likely to enter into relationships of obligation (by someone or to someone).[8] Latino-Americans also are more comfortable with reciprocal obligation—two neighboring households may share a garbage-collection contract, for example, with each household paying every second month instead of every month, and the two households pooling their garbage. Their non-Hispanic neighbors, however, may not like sharing the cost because of concerns about who creates more garbage and therefore who should pay more.

The dominant culture in the United States, with its value of individual responsibility, invented the "no-host" cocktail reception where each person pays her or his own tab, the potluck dinner where everyone brings a dish and thus nobody is host and nobody is indebted, and "going Dutch" (people who go to a restaurant or entertainment together and pay their own bills). Asians, Europeans, and Middle Easterners are appalled; their values of hospitality and indebtedness as the mark of a relationship are offended. This is discussed in depth in Chapter 7.

In fact, in most cultures of the world, significant relationships are those that involve webs of obligation. Relationships between two or more individuals—or groups—can last for decades and even generations. In China, Japan, and other Asian countries, a first act that places someone's family under an obligation leads to a reciprocal act, and so on through the years, and the responsibilities to repay the obligation are passed down to succeeding generations. The obligations are the responsibility of everyone in the group, not only the individual who first became indebted. **To clear the ledger so that neither side owes anything to the other is to end the relationship.** This is serious. In fact, ending a relationship is an event of such magnitude that usually every measure is taken to avoid it. The webs that bind a group together and the whole network of connections between groups are threatened when one connection is severed.

In Filipino culture, indebtedness because someone has done you a favor is called *utang no loob*. This generally refers to indebtedness outside the family. The repayment may be in a different form from the favor received and may be spread out over several occasions, according to the wishes of the original grantor of the favor.[9] The obligation is shared by the whole group.

In modern Japan, a wedding invitation may be greeted with horror and dismay because it means that the guest family must present the bride's family with a very large gift. The choice is either to give a large sum of money or to lose a close relationship. Indeed, some Japanese deliberately cool relationships with families that have daughters of marriageable age. Once the daughters are safely married, the relationships are resumed.

Japanese culture distinguishes between two kinds of indebtedness: *giri* and *on*. An example of *on* is the indebtedness a new employee incurs. He spends the rest of his life working to repay the debt he owes for being hired through looking after new employees.[10] *On* is the obligation a child owes to its parents for the nurturing they gave through the years the child was growing up. Because of this obligation, the child will take care of the parents when they are old to repay the debt. Or in an organization when a senior looks after a junior, this means the junior incurs *on*. But the junior shows loyalty to the senior, which repays the *on* or reverses the debt.

Giri is also obligation. It implies that self-discipline is necessary to overcome personal feelings and fulfill the debt owed to others. For example, *giri* requires an employee to agree with a superior, not argue.

Obligation and indebtedness are taken for granted as part of business relationships in most of the world's cultures. A business organization may incur indebtedness by asking a favor, say, extended terms of payment. In return, that business will continue to buy from the organization to which it owes a debt of a favor. Similarly, individuals in business organizations often ask special favors of individuals in cooperating business organizations, based on the ongoing relationship between their two employers.

Obligation can involve issues of ethics when cultures disagree about how far obligation can go.

In Focus

A foreign company offered an information systems manager in a firm in the United States a regular monthly payment into a bank account in his name in a third country in return for informing the company whenever his firm had a contract to fill. The foreign company then knew when to submit a bid. The information systems manager didn't have to lobby his employer on behalf of the foreign company; he only had to transmit the information that his firm was in

(continued)

the market for products or services. It was up to the foreign company to compete successfully. Of course, the manager's firm didn't know he was taking money from the foreign company. The foreign company earned over $12 million simply because it knew about the potential for selling to the manager's firm. The manager did well, too; he received enough extra money to send his children to expensive universities. The foreign firm was happy to be obligated to him and pay him well. But what of his obligation to his own company? This case raises legal and ethical questions.

Where do one's obligations lie? Would the obligations of the manager have been different if the information-seeking company had not been from a different country? What if the foreign company were owned by a relative of the manager? Perhaps being paid (obligated) to supply information seems acceptable; after all, the information systems manager did not try to influence the purchase decision. But then, why didn't he want his employer to know he was taking money from the foreign firm? In fact, the employee in this case subsequently found he couldn't carry on with divided loyalties; his obligation to his employer won, and he ended his deal with the foreign firm. One may speculate why he did so.

Age: Is Seniority Valued or Discounted?

In cultures that value age, the older a businessperson is the more credibility he or she has. Seniority in an organization is directly linked to seniority in years. Organizations send senior members to negotiate with other senior members when business transactions are held. Elders are treated respectfully, which means that nobody disagrees openly with what a senior person says. Meetings are never occasions in which the younger members challenge the positions or opinions of the senior members, and the result is a harmonious unit.

When a senior person seems to be in error, quiet behind-the-scenes discussions take place in which the senior is shown alternative ways the position can be carried out or is given several possibilities, both positive and negative, to allow a reinterpretation of the position. Never is anything done or said that could cause loss of face to a senior person. On the contrary, extraordinary measures sometimes are taken to ensure that face is saved and even gained.

This is true in Asia, where old members of organizations enjoy great freedom and power. They can make choices for themselves and others in a way that is not open to younger people. Since others must listen to them and be directed by them, they have a degree of freedom from the need to conform that only comes with age. They have the most impressive job titles and often the most responsible jobs.

When U.S. organizations send executives to Asia, they often risk not being taken seriously unless their representatives look appropriately senior. In a delegation to a Vietnamese trading corporation, for example, the oldest-looking person usually will be assumed by the Vietnamese to be the leader of the group. In cultures that equate youthfulness with vigor, some individuals may change their white hair to more youthful colors; in Asia, white hair earns respect. In a delegation of three people, one of whom has white hair, that person will be first to be seated, first to be greeted, first through doors, and so forth. Young executives puzzle Asian hosts, since in Asia one becomes high-ranking only with age.

By contrast, in youth-oriented cultures being young seems to mean having more choices, more power, more energy, and more freedom. Advertisements for consumer products in the West—cars, liquor, clothing, watches, fitness equipment, cell phones—appeal to the desire to be vigorous, healthy, and powerful, and these are related to looking young. Young corporate heroes are profiled in weekend newspaper supplements because they are young. Middle-aged people appear at times to take lessons from their children on how to dress, what activities to pursue, how to wear their hair, and what slang to use in an attitude of respect for youth that baffles members of seniority-oriented cultures. The word *old* has bad connotations: It means loss of power—physical, mental, political, and sexual—and with it loss of respect, loss of capability, loss of status, and loss of position. Old employees are "kicked upstairs," "put out to pasture," "waiting for retirement."

Businesspeople need to understand the great differences in how age is valued. If your employees include a number of Asians, you may not be prepared for their dismay when older workers are laid off. Asian managers who retain older workers out of respect for their age when younger workers are more productive and more adaptable risk the scorn of employees from youth-oriented cultures.

Manufacturers, distributors, and retail sellers of products designed to help mature adults look younger may not have the market they seek in age-respecting cultures.

Gender: Are Women Equals or Subordinates?

Images of women differ around the globe. Two facts provide a starting point for looking at women in different cultures. The first is about women in society: Although women make up half the population in every culture, women have fewer high-level positions in organizations outside the home. The second fact has to do with biology: Women, unlike men, bear children and nurture them.

In traditional cultures, the two facts are related. Child-bearing and child-nurturing are the main roles of women. In traditional cultures, women have less time or opportunity to compete outside the family home for high positions in chosen careers, until their children are old enough to look after themselves or unless someone takes care of them while they are young. While many poorer women have some work for income in traditional cultures, such as selling handiwork or food from a family garden in a market, others do not. Roles such as chief surgeon, university president, managing director of a company, government minister, or market (*souk*) administrator require many years of preparation to achieve.

Furthermore, in traditional cultures around the globe, men take the responsibility for supporting and providing for women. They go outside the home and bring back what the family needs, so women do not have to go outside the home. In the traditional Chinese culture, the word for husband was "outside person" and the word for wife was "inside person," referring to the role differences.

Men in traditional cultures not only have the role of bread-winner, bringing food and money for food to the family and providing shelter. Men also have the role of protector of their women and children. Women then are free to focus on their roles of homemaker, food-preparer, and child-nurturer. All cultures have had these separate roles for men and women, historically. Traditional cultures continue the same way today; *traditional* is a positive term in those cultures, since it reflects the values that have been maintained through many generations.

Non-traditional cultures are sometimes called *modern* cultures; *modern* is a positive term for them, since it reflects a positive value toward change. Often these non-traditional cultures are individualist cultures that value equality of opportunity and equality of treatment for all people. For example, in Britain, equality of treatment was an important value that the practice of slavery challenged, in the late 1700s. Slaves were not equal to free men. In 1833, after years of disagreement, Britain made slavery illegal. Former slaves were free, and began to claim the same treatment as people who had never been slaves. Then women wanted equal treatment and challenged the government by asking for the same voting rights as men. In 1928, after years of disagreement, women got the equal right to vote. Women then began asking for other equal treatment. In Britain today, women are considered to be valued equally with men in the workplace.

However, women in Britain today generally earn less money and have lower positions than men, even when they have the same education or training, and when they do the same work. Women continue to point out that this is not equal treatment. Full economic equality has not yet been achieved.

Economic equality is only one way to examine the roles of women. Not all women everywhere want to be considered equal to men in all situations. In traditional cultures, where men's and women's roles are clearly different, many women would not want to give up their special status and have to take on the same responsibilities as men. In modern cultures, too, many women want to spend time with their children and feel privileged when their husbands make enough money to allow them to stay at home and not work for income for the family.

We can consider what it means to be female in a culture by referring back to *self-concept.* A woman's self-concept is formed not only by the political history of her country (the critical approach to self-identity), but primarily by the expectations and assumptions her culture has for her, learned through her experiences and through the teaching of others. Whatever the self-concept is, when women successfully perform their culture's roles for women, they enjoy esteem and respect.

In some cultures, women's high status comes primarily from bearing children. Being a mother gives a woman a special status in Saudi Arabia, for example, where she has a new name, "Mother of ____" [blank to be filled in with the name of a child, usually the first son]. In China, a woman who is not a mother is pitied because she cannot claim the status of having a child. In Italy, a mother is honored. In Mexico, adult children view their mothers as models, to be treated with great devotion. These are just a few examples of the high esteem women enjoy in many traditional cultures because of motherhood.

In other cultures, women enjoy high status primarily from achieving personal and organizational goals and receiving recognition. They compete and succeed; often men are their competitors. Their private lives as wives, mothers, daughters, and sisters may not even be mentioned.

Women communicate according to their culture's expectations for gender and communication. In their communication, they present their identities and fulfill their roles. Traditional cultures have rules about women's communication when greeting someone (rules are different for inside the home or outside the home, among relatives or strangers, communicating with men or other women only). Non-traditional cultures have rules about asking a job applicant to identify herself as a woman (for instance, in the United States it is not legal to ask, because it is not legal to make a hiring decision based on the gender of the applicant).

In most cultures of the world, women do not achieve key business positions in equal numbers with men. The priorities of cultures in which women do not earn executive titles cannot simply be dismissed, however; members of those cultures do not necessarily regard women as lesser beings, unworthy of power. There are complex power dynamics within the workplace even in societies in which men are clearly dominant.

In the United States, Canada, New Zealand, Australia, and Great Britain, where equal opportunity is an official policy and where women can perform in every area of employment, the view is that women and men are equally capable of achieving organizational goals. Women and men are equally intelligent, equally competent, and equally worthy of recognition for jobs well done. The fact that women in organizations do not have equal status or equal pay with men is often deplored, although it is tolerated. A majority of single and married women in these and similar cultures work outside the home, and most two-parent households rely on two incomes to meet the basic costs of housing, food, utilities, transportation, and personal needs.

Studies of gender show that men and women select priorities differently from the general culture. For example, women are reported to be more consultative in their management style and less directive than men. They are said to have more interest in the emotional well-being of subordinates and co-workers than men and to listen better and cultivate personal relationships with co-workers more than men. Men who exhibit these behaviors are said to have "feminine" characteristics, and women who lack them are called "masculine"; their behavior sometimes is explained as being more masculine because they have had to learn to compete in a man's world. Managers—male or female—who have so-called feminine qualities (cooperativeness, intuitiveness) are looked upon more favorably by so-called feminine cultures, whereas managers who are masculine—again, male or female—and have masculine characteristics (assertiveness, decisiveness, competitiveness, and aggressiveness) are valued primarily in masculine cultures.[11]

In Focus

A male student in his mid-twenties recently approached one of the authors to discuss a concern he had with his wife and the Muslim practice of covering her head. It was not that she wouldn't follow his demand for her to wear the head-scarf. Rather, she was a devout Muslim and had always covered her head and hair in public as an outward sign of her

(continued)

devotion, in the same way that members of other religions show their faith publicly (Christians wear crosses; Sikhs wear turbans around their heads; conservative Jewish men wear yarmulkes or *kippah*—skullcaps—on their heads).

But she and her husband had emigrated from North Africa to New Zealand where only a small minority of women wear a headscarf that covers hair and shoulders. Her husband was anxious for her because he believed she was hurting her chances of employment by wearing the headscarf, and she was eager to find a good job. However, she had discussed the issue with women at the local mosque and had decided to be covered when out in public. He tried to talk her out of it, but she was determined, and he respected her right to make that decision.

His classmates were intrigued by this issue, since most had had limited contact with Muslim women and had assumed they only wore modest covering because their husbands insisted upon it as an exercise of power over their women. Husbands in many cultures have powers of decision-making over their wives' lives, but an observer cannot always interpret visible, onstage behavior accurately using the norms in one's own life. Not all women who wear headscarves are doing so because their husbands insist on it. Not all wives (Muslim and non-Muslim) who have uncovered heads in public have the power to make decisions for themselves.

Muslim women, especially women who wear a modest covering in public, may be viewed by non-Muslims as powerless and lacking knowledge and ability to compete in the workplace. (Being covered does not mean a woman is not present. It means she is showing her devotion. Consider the Muslims in the Tuareg tribe of Mali and nearby West African countries: Women do not cover their faces in that culture, but men do.) She may not shake hands with men in business meetings. However, Muslim women in many cultures fill a wide range of business and professional roles. In Malaysia, Singapore, Indonesia, Turkey, and Pakistan, for example, Muslim women hold high corporate and government positions. In Iran, nearly half of all medical doctors are women. Also, in countries where Islam is one of several widely practiced religions, such as India and England, Muslim women achieve high positions in business organizations and in professions from engineering to education to university lecturers.

In currently and formerly communist countries, women enjoy high status in the work world. Chairman Mao's famous statement "Women hold up half the sky" is often quoted as evidence that women in China are not excluded from any professional achievement. As a matter of record, however, few women rise to the top ranks of the party or government. Nevertheless, they can have considerable professional status. Women are expected to be employed outside the home. They are also expected by most families to do most of the domestic work in spite of working full-time. (Similarly, in modern Russia, a familiar image in fiction is an overworked mother who has to be committed to a sanatorium. Luxury means staying at home with the children and not having to go out to work.) The extended family pattern in many cultures, in which grandparents live with or near their children and grandchildren, means that child care for working women is usually built in, within the family unit.

In Japan, some women hold professional jobs. Women work in business organizations also, but often in low-status jobs; as OLs (office ladies) they perform clerical and even hostess duties. Many choose to work so they can find husbands, and large organizations encourage marriage between employees since wives will then understand their husbands' loyalty to the company. Employees are acceptable wives (having already been screened for employment) and should get along with the wives of other employees; this is an important consideration, since the couple's socializing will be almost exclusively with other employee-and-wife couples. Young married women may continue to work until the arrival of their first child, but then they usually do not remain employed.

As mothers, Japanese women enjoy high status in society; the bond between mother and child, called *amae,* is regarded as the most important bond in life. Japanese sociologists describe it as a basic dependence upon uncritical acceptance, such as mothers give children, which in turn fosters a desire for the security of acceptance. They attribute the Japanese drive toward conformism to *amae.* The desire for acceptance and the dependence upon others to provide acceptance are apparent in the polite Japanese greeting at a first meeting. It translates "Please take care of me." But women generally have lower status in Japanese society than men. An indicator of this is that women in Japan use a different vocabulary from men in referring to self and others. Women bow lower than men to show their status is not as high (although their relative power may be greater).

Yet women typically hold the purse strings of Japanese homes, which gives them some power. In fact, women often enjoy economic power that is greater than the power of male family members in a number of cultures ranging from West Africa to Ethiopia to Thailand and the Philippines. Women often are responsible for taking food grown by the family to market, and market stalls operated by women abound; you can find them everywhere, such as in Peru, Ghana, and Indonesia. Temporary market stalls can lead to more permanent locations and ultimately to women-owned retail and service businesses. In Mali, West Africa, for example, many women are involved in business, primarily at the micro level.

In Focus

Many Malian women belong to the West Africa Businesswomen's Network (WABNET), along with women from Ghana, Guinea, Niger, and Burkina Faso. A major export for these countries is shea butter, a component in cosmetic and body creams. It comes from the shea nut, which is produced by the large flowering shea-butter tree, called *karité* in French. The shea butter is produced in a traditional manner, based on centuries of experience, by women in the villages. They soak the fruit and remove the soft pulp manually to obtain the five-centimeter (two-inch) seed or nut. The *karité*, or shea butter, is extracted from the nut.[12]

In Burkina Faso, an estimated 80 percent of the shea butter is produced by women in the traditional way. The demand for shea butter is rising for products marketed by Body Shop and other international cosmetic firms.

However, the legal status of women in West African countries such as Burkina Faso means that they still cannot inherit land or the right to the fruit from the trees. A woman's right to the means of production is therefore not secure. Disputes have occurred between men and women over control of shea nuts and shea trees. To remedy the problem, the United Nations Development Fund for Women (UNIFEM) is currently helping women develop strategies to attain security and rights in the shea butter industry.[13]

Cultures in which women's status and power come from traditional roles rather than from management roles in business organizations may be viewed by people from modern gender-equity cultures as morally wrong in their unequal treatment of women.

In these cases, it is important to recognize that "wrong" is a culturally based attitude. Certainly, professional women in the United States and Europe find inequity on the basis of gender unacceptable. Some groups, such as the repressive Taliban in Afghanistan, view women's roles as traditional in a narrow definition, refusing to educate them or allow them to go out to work (although wider Afghan society does have many schools for girls, a number of whom go on to university). Globally, women make up more than half the workforce. They also make up more than half the world market for food and household goods. And 33 percent of households in the world are headed by women (45–50 percent in some countries of Africa and Latin America).[14]

Our responsibility as students of culture is to keep from *evaluating* cultures according to the roles women play in them. What is worth considering is how attitudes toward women differ, and how communication by and with women differs from culture to culture.

Category 5: Social Organization

The way society is organized has great impact on how members of that society interact and how they treat outsiders to their culture. Members of multicultural workforces, managers in foreign subsidiaries staffed by native employees—and, conversely, employees with managers from foreign cultures—and workers in global organizations who deal with people around the world all carry with them expectations about business behavior that are based on the social organization they learned in their native society. Like attitudes toward gender, age, and relationships, these notions about how people ought to interact are learned when one is young and are thought of as normal.

Group Membership: Temporary or Permanent?

Individuals in the United States are members of many groups simultaneously. Work associates generally are not all social friends. Friendships develop from a variety of contacts: school, neighborhood, place of worship, clubs, and community service organizations.

Furthermore, group membership is impermanent. If an individual loses interest in an activity, she or he drops out of the club and may lose contact with the friends with whom that activity once was shared. If one moves to a new neighborhood or changes one's religious affiliation or gets a new job, one's friendships can wane. If personal goals are no longer being met by a group, an individual moves on and probably looks to new associates for the benefits previously received from the former group.

In fact, even membership in families is subject to personal choice. Spouses often choose not to remain married, children occasionally decide not to continue in relationships with siblings or parents, and even parents occasionally decide not to relate to their offspring. The breakdown of family groups is regularly deplored in the United States, but nevertheless it is tolerated. A majority of members in the dominant culture of the United States agree that the individual's needs come first. When one's own needs are met to an acceptable degree, then one can fulfill one's responsibilities to others.

In other cultures, the responsibilities of membership come before rights. Individuals cannot expect that their individual needs will be met as a first order of priority. For example, the notion of choosing to loosen family ties simply never occurs to members of collectivist cultures. In cultures where group membership is permanent, belonging starts with the family.

Social organization in Chinese culture has been described by a famous Chinese sociologist, Fei Xiaotong, who studied the culture of the Midwest United States in the 1930s.[15] He characterized Chinese culture as a series of concentric circles with the family at the center along with *I*, the ego.

The individual's parents, grandparents, spouse, siblings, and offspring are all in the center of the pattern. The next circle may include spouses of siblings, aunts and uncles, cousins, and children's in-laws. The next circle is for one's dearest friends, perhaps from one's earliest school days; subsequent circles include work colleagues (who may also be neighbors in China today) who are especially trusted. Then come those who are familiar but not so close, and so on, until everyone has been placed in a circle—everyone, that is, to whom one might possibly be under obligation because of a relationship. Everyone else in the geographic area or nation or world is on the outside of the concentric circles; thus, one has no obligation to respond to their needs. While the circle inside which someone is located may change, with a person becoming nearer to or farther from the center, the circles themselves do not.

Social organization in China is relatively stable because everyone understands the pattern of concentric circles and knows the key: If you want to enter into a relationship with someone and therefore be able to incur reciprocal obligation (which is the essence of a relationship), you must locate yourself somewhere inside a circle. You need to present yourself as the friend of a friend of a relative, the classmate of a former colleague, or at the very least a co-worker of someone who was in a relationship with a co-worker of the other person. Once you can identify yourself as having some place in the social structure of another person's circles, that person has a responsibility to enter into a relationship with you. The Chinese word for relationship, *guanxi,* also means *connection.* The way business gets done in China is through connections.

In contrast, Fei described American culture as *contractual.* Instead of a network of responsibilities ranging from most to least important, he said people in the United States regard all relationships as contracts. They can be broken whenever one party chooses. Even close friendships and family relationships can be severed when they threaten the individual's personal goals. Work relationships, club memberships, and ties with schools and former classmates tend to wither if an individual moves away. Americans do move away a lot; it is rare nowadays for an individual to live a whole life in one place. This makes social organization loose and impermanent. You can get lost in the United States. You can even move to a new location and change your identity.

China and the United States offer an interesting basis for comparison because they are so far apart on the question of the duration of group membership. Many collectivist cultures value permanent group membership, such as the countries of Latin America, the Middle East, Africa, the Pacific Islands, and Southern Europe.

Communication, especially within permanent groups, has specific functions. We'll now consider three functions of group communication.

Communicating to Give and Save Face

The permanent nature of relationships affects communication in collectivist cultures. Members of groups in collectivist cultures do not seek to speak up, to set the record straight, or even to express a contradictory point of view; instead, social harmony is a hidden goal of every communication.

This is very different from the tendency in individualist cultures to verbalize—that is, to put things in words, whether written or oral. Westerners may seek to express a different point of view so as to be recognized or to triumph in presenting a point of view that carries the majority with it. In collectivist cultures, being right isn't as important as being in concord with the group.

In cultures throughout Asia, the Middle East, and Africa, *losing face* is a terrible thing to suffer. Besides expressing agreement, various other ways of communicating diminish potential loss of face also, such as laughing to discount the significance of some word or act and therefore discount its ability to cause loss of face. Simply choosing not to hear is another ploy.

The profound desire not to be the cause of someone's losing face results in many cultures in a great reluctance to say *no* or bear bad news. Where the unspoken objective of every transaction is to create and nurture harmony so the relationship can thrive, bad news is a serious threat to that objective. Or to be precise, the *communication* of bad news is a serious threat. The news itself may or may not turn out to have disastrous consequences; maybe the context can be changed and the party need never know the actual bad news. But uttering bad news has to be—well, bad news. Delivering criticism to someone who might lose face because of it becomes tricky. Indirectness is the usual policy when one must point out weaknesses or make criticisms of another, in order to *save face.*

Face is not only individual, but also collective. Children are taught not to lose the family's face. If an employee makes an error that causes the company problems, the company loses face. Often, the blame for an error is diffused so no one individual is responsible, but the group loses face.

Similarly, the importance of *giving face* in collectivist cultures is often overlooked by members of individualist cultures. Giving face means making someone look good in front of others of the same collective, particularly (but not exclusively)

In Focus

Some of the communication differences discussed here emerged in a cross-cultural training program delivered by Canadians for Chinese participants. The trainers had invited guest speakers for the Chinese to hear, but the Chinese trainees repeatedly came late to afternoon sessions and inconvenienced the guest speakers. The Canadian trainers became angry and scolded the trainees. The trainees' response was bewilderment and shame, but it wasn't shame for being late to hear the guest speakers. It was shame on behalf of the trainers for having let themselves behave so emotionally!

So the trainers asked how the Chinese would behave if, say, a friend repeatedly arrived late for a movie date, so late that it wasn't possible to see the film. The appropriate way to deal with such a person, the trainees agreed, would be to go see films with someone else and to become cooler toward, and more distant from, the person who behaved so irresponsibly. They said they would feel angry but it was not appropriate to show anger. The other person would certainly lose face if anger were directed toward him or her, and the angry person would look foolish and childish and therefore would also lose face. Social harmony would be disrupted twice. (The trainers apologized the next day for their angry words.)

superiors. Using titles, recognizing special achievement or expertise, praising a job well done, acknowledging an obligation—these are all ways of giving face. Not disagreeing publicly with superiors is also a way to give face.

Face can also be borrowed. That is, when someone is at risk of losing face, that person can claim a connection with someone who has face, thereby "borrowing" face. A young person in an unfamiliar business situation who mentions an older, experienced, and known businessman is borrowing his face. A company that is initiating a business association with a foreign company may borrow face from another company with a long-term relationship with the foreign firm.

According to more metaphors, face can be "stretched" to embrace more and more, and even can be "beaten" (to make it swell up to larger than normal size) when someone goes so far as to appear to have a lot of face that it causes some difficulty ("pain"). This might describe going into debt in order to live up to the terms of a contract that was difficult to land.

Communicating to Display Emotion

Showing emotion in nonverbal and verbal communication varies in degree along the lines of high-context and low-context cultures. In China, Japan, Korea, Thailand, Vietnam, and other collectivist Asian countries, culture socializes people from an early age not to show emotion publicly. No doubt this is because a display of emotion could have potential consequences of disrupting the harmony that is so important to collectivist cultures. In Iraq, Dubai, Jordan, Kuwait, and other collectivist Middle Eastern countries, culture teaches people from an early age to show emotion and how to do it.

Obviously, the level of emotion shown can have consequences in work environments where an emotion-expressive culture is in contact with an emotion-repressive culture. When someone from an emotion-expressive culture—say Polish—carries on a communication transaction about a perceived wrong with someone from an emotion-repressive culture—say Thai—each can be sending messages the other has trouble decoding correctly because of the communication style. The Pole may be perceived to be immature, out of control, and egocentric. The Thai may be perceived to be remote, unsympathetic, and uptight. These perceptions then form the context for the worded message, which is subject to distortion and misinterpretation, or in other words, faulty decoding.

Egyptians display socially acceptable emotion. The emotion of anger is not socially acceptable, but not to show emotion in the face of another's grief, or jubilation, or disappointment is self-centered and egoistic—that is, to be impassive is to deny group membership.

Communicating about Shame or Guilt

Cultures can be categorized into those that communicate to cause shame in order to make people behave according to cultural rules and those that cause guilt. Both emotions can be powerful elements in cross-cultural business interactions. Shame is an emotion of embarrassment experienced by a group, or member on behalf of the group, when the honor of the group is called into doubt. It is in public view, and is the result of (alleged) misconduct.

Guilt is an emotion of self-reproach experienced internally and privately at the recognition of misconduct. (This is not the same meaning of guilt as being responsible for wrongdoing, the opposite of innocent.) Some cultures use the painful emotion of guilt to punish members. The guilt-ridden suffer in private until their guilt is admitted in public, and then the behavior about which they feel guilt is forgiven or punished or dealt with in some way. The guilt may or may not go away as a result of getting its cause out in the open. In individualistic cultures, where individual responsibility, results, and privacy are valued, guilt is a potent way for a culture to enforce rules of behavior.

In collectivist cultures where group membership, relationships, and public knowledge of one's life are important, shame enforces the rules of conduct. Group members suffer the disgrace of belonging to a dishonored group. Shame is not the same thing as *face*, which involves status. A group may be shamed but still not lose face. For instance, if the oldest son of a family incurs a debt and creditors are known to be pursuing him, the family is publicly shamed. But if the debt is paid, there is no loss of face.

Members of shame cultures may not be able to give answers to questions from foreigners without losing the collective's face—questions about their business organization's technological capability, or expertise, or manufacturing experience, or ecological progress, or human rights achievements. Persistent questioning can cause shame if it implies wrongdoing. Similarly, any public comment—even in a joke—that refers to a person's, or company's, or nation's failings causes shame for the group (family, employer, country).

In Focus

It is quite possible for people who are not members of a shame culture to cause shame without realizing it. Dr. Wong, one of a group from China working temporarily in an Australian hospital, reported to a Malaysian surgeon. The surgeon's secretary was Australian. The surgeon and the doctor happened to meet and pause for a brief conversation at the secretary's desk. The secretary interrupted, saying, "Dr. Wong, where were you yesterday? I looked all over the hospital for you!" The doctor had been in a lab elsewhere in the hospital—a perfectly reasonable place to be—but hadn't informed the secretary. He felt shamed, on behalf of all the visiting Chinese medical staff in the hospital, by the secretary's question in that situation. He thought she was trying to make him look bad in the eyes of the surgeon, his superior in the organization. He felt accused of misconduct that reflected on the Chinese group as a whole. But the secretary had no intention of causing him shame. She was simply saying what occurred to her when she saw him and remembered she hadn't been able to reach him the previous day.

Form: Important or Untrustworthy?

Form means protocol: the rules of etiquette and manners for doing something. It is related to communication issues for permanent versus temporary group membership, and is usually more important in cultures where preservation of harmony in permanent groups is critical. **Behaving according to form means behaving correctly**. Cultures that consider form important ensure that everyone can operate by the same knowable rules, and following rules reduces the risk of losing face through some unintentional mistake. Everyone is more comfortable because the rules are well established and comprehensive. Trustworthy people follow form. In some cultures, doing things by the book is an essential mark of maturity, adulthood, and responsibility.

Form is the reason why Thais do not show anger in public words or actions. Form is what requires Indians to greet one another with *namaste,* which is a gesture that accompanies the greeting, putting the palms of the hands together with fingers pointing toward the chin and slightly bowing the head. Form requires you to offer your right cheek for a token kiss to every social or business contact you meet in Argentina. Form is why Jan Zamoyski addressed Sheila Graham by her last name and "Ms.," kissed her hand in greeting, and used formal language to offer her coffee in the case that opened this chapter. The deliberate setting aside of form—which could be called a form in itself—accounts for Sheila's using Jan's first name right away. Form is what dictates that overcoats must be checked at the door in Russia.[16] Form may even determine when it is acceptable to talk business (at dinner? on a train ride? at meetings only?). Some cultures seem to follow form when the substance itself is not significant: form for the sake of form.

In negotiations, correct form dictates that only designated speakers speak; others are silent unless invited specifically to participate. One correct form for saying "no"—which Japanese people employ reluctantly—is to draw in the breath through the teeth with a hiss and then expel it—"Sahh!"—while looking sadly at the table.

In Focus

Japanese have a very high regard for form. A specific Japanese word exists for it: *kata*. It means form, and comes from the word *shikata,* which translates as "the way of doing things." (*Shikata ga nai* is a Japanese expression that means "no way!")[17]

Everything has *kata* in Japanese culture, and following the *kata* ensures harmony. For instance, there is a *shikata* for wearing *kimono,* the traditional clothing of Japanese. Traditional performances such as a Japanese tea ceremony, sumo wrestling, samurai swordsmanship, and Kabuki theater are wrapped in *kata*.

In everyday life, one encounters many *kata*. The bow, for example, with which everyone greets everyone has *kata*. If a neighbor is behind the wheel of her car when you first exchange glances, she will bow over her steering wheel. Women bow lower than men; older persons bow less than younger persons. On a university campus, professors bow to one another in passing with the senior persons bowing less than the juniors. Students bow to professors they know; professors nod back.

In the special event of finding a spouse, Japanese also have various *kata*. Some families in Japan still have a Family Registry, which is a family tree of past and current generations. If an adult child contemplates bringing a life-partner into the family, the parents and grandparents must first consider if this potential family member is worthy of being entered into the Family Registry. If the parents say no, then the marriage cannot take place. The consequence of ignoring this decision is that the child of the family is stricken from the Family Registry, and the record no longer shows that person's birth. Form minimizes uncertainty and contributes to the preservation of the status quo in society.

In Focus

One Japanese business researcher commented about the odd use of given names when the prime minister of Japan, Yasuhiro Nakasone, met with President Ronald Reagan several decades ago, but the same practice is used today.

It made an interesting news item in Japan when then Prime Minister Nakasone reportedly mentioned that he dealt with President Reagan on a first-name basis and termed the two men's relationship as the "Ron-Yaso Relationship.". . . The fact remains, however, that no one, including his cabinet ministers, ever called him by his first name in Japan.[18]

Using titles is another aspect of form practiced in many countries. The proper form for addressing someone in Argentina is by title (Vice President, Engineer, Professor) and family name. In Samoa, the Minister of Education is also a high chief of her clan and is always addressed by the title for chief, along with the title "Minister." In many countries, the equivalent of "Mr." or "Mrs./Ms./Miss" is the form that expresses the minimum level of politeness. In Britain, given names are only used in close relationships with friends, rarely by business associates. Similarly in European cultures, which have many differences but share a respect for form, business contacts almost never address one another by their given names, even when they work together for long periods and see one another regularly.

In written messages, correct form means the use of certain phrases and formulas. French business letters invariably include subjunctive verbs to show politeness, and close with an expression of much warmer compliments to the reader than British and American letters. In Mexico, business letters use elaborate language and also tend to be extremely courteous (check the examples in Chapters 2 and 5).

In contrast, some cultures mistrust form. *Standing on ceremony* is perceived as giving oneself airs and substituting etiquette for sincerity. In the recently invented culture of the United States, emphasis on form looks mannered. It is dangerous sophistry, even deceit. Businesspeople from the United States are known around the world for their preference for addressing business colleagues by given names rather than family names. In New Zealand, an even younger culture, emphasis on form is called "poncing around"—assuming a false sophistication to impress others ("ponce" is slang for a person, usually male, who is showy in appearance and manner). *Pākehā* New Zealanders mostly address people by their given names only, to emphasize the egalitarianism of the culture and to make people feel they are all accepted. But what may be intended as an attempt at genuineness, at leaving behind stuffiness and formality, can come across as presumptuous intimacy. In some instances, use of first names can sound comical. An example is a public speaker who displays a quotation from the very well-known scientist Dr. Albert Einstein and says, "Let's consider what Albert has to say." The goodwill gesture of putting an arm across another's shoulders can translate as boorish bonhomie. To the venerable cultures of Asia, Africa, and Europe, lack of form looks unmannerly. It is dangerous naiveté, even ignorance. By the same token, members of other cultures may find the behavior of United States businesspeople to be a "form" of informality with rules about informality that have to be learned in much the same way as rules of formal protocol have to be learned.

To communicate effectively, businesspeople need to be aware of the different attitudes toward form and to adjust their reactions to other cultures' communication messages.

Personal Matters: Private or Public?

The degree to which possessions, programs, and organizations are private or public varies with the culture and can affect how business is carried out. This is a cultural priority, not a description of how companies are structured. We aren't talking about privately held shares versus stock traded on an open market. We're discussing the degree to which people believe work and private life are separate.

This is another of the priorities that people the world over take for granted, assuming theirs is universal, until they are confronted with another view. In Europe, as in Britain, Canada, the United States, Australia, and New Zealand, a person's work life is kept fairly separate from private life. As a rule, workers are not expected to bring private concerns with them to work; employees do not bring children to the office to play at their feet while they work; personal phone calls and visitors are not appropriate. Hours that the organization pays for belong to the organization and its concerns.

However, lunch breaks and even coffee breaks are not paid time in many jobs and therefore are the employee's personal time. This is when an employee receives and makes personal phone calls, keeps personal appointments, and so forth. In some offices, considerable effort is expended to keep employees from discussing personal issues as they work. Organizational policy usually implies, if not directs, that workers should not even be *thinking* about personal issues on company time if such thoughts may affect work adversely.

Not surprisingly, cultures that emphasize relationships, view group membership as long term, and value harmony have a blurred distinction between what is private and what is public (or at least what is "group"). As illustrated by the Japanese worker with the hangover in Chapter 1, superiors in Japan are expected to be paternalistic counselors in matters to do with private lives of employees. The same is true in China, where an employee would appear secretive and deliberately destructive of group harmony who did not share the particulars of personal problems—serious ones that might interfere with work—with a superior. (Nothing is actually secret, and the superior would find out from someone else anyway in that collectivist culture.) In China, where the work unit provides so many of the commodities of personal life, the line is even more blurred. In Argentina, which is strongly influenced by European values, employees are expected to put work priorities first, but family and private concerns are treated with a somewhat flexible attitude.

In much of Latin America, the summer weather is very hot and humid; workers typically have a long break in the middle of the day during which many go home and sleep. The hot and humid nights mean workers don't get enough sleep between dark and dawn. Workers who live too far away to go home frequently have their siestas at their desks.

In Great Britain, by contrast, an employee who comes back to work from lunch and sprawls over the desk for a nap will be under fire from the employer. The employee is expected to sleep in private, on personal time. And even if it is the employee's time, sleeping at work looks bad for the organization in a culture that values achievement and activity.

Finally, differences about public and private touch the question of ownership of intellectual property. In a socialist country, ideas and intellectual products belong to the people along with everything else. Individuals may be recognized for their books or inventions or other creative acts, but their products belong to the people. The creators ought not to seek to get rich at the expense of the people from whom they themselves have come. This is a problem for exporting countries, where intellectual products are commodities just like manufactured goods. Creativity is valued and deserves recompense.

This can be a critical difference where a company's proprietary information is concerned. Some organizations have experienced problems with trainees and even employees from China and from formerly communist Eastern Europe sharing technological information such as patented processes with colleagues back home. Since costs for research are theoretically shared by everyone in socialist states, the results of research can be argued to belong to everyone. In Western countries, where research costs are borne by a specific organization in order to compete, there is a need to protect that investment. Each viewpoint is understandable within its own context, but it's important to recognize the cultural variations in the line between private and public.

Social Organizational Patterns: Horizontal or Hierarchical?

Social organization in cultures tends toward one of two extremes: at one extreme are rigid vertical levels in society, and movement between them is very limited; at the other extreme, society is horizontal and operates with few levels. In modern history, hierarchical (vertical) social organization is associated with monarchies, and horizontal organization with democracies. Of course, most cultures are somewhere between those extremes.

As we saw in Chapter 3, India has a system of classes based on the old system called *castes.* In most business encounters between Indians and non-Indians, however, these classifications play a small role. That is partly because foreign businesspeople have limited contact with them in the course of doing business. It is also because the caste system has been officially ended by law and therefore is not easily visible to a non-Indian. The stratification of society by class still exists, however, and is of sufficient importance in Indian life that non-Indians should be careful how they ask questions about it.

Monarchies today vary in the mobility between levels of society. In Holland and Denmark, for example, the distance between monarch and subjects seems small. Queen Beatrix of Holland frequently stops her car and gets out to shop at town stores, in the midst of her subjects, who have great affection for her. In Thailand, however, the royal family is regarded with deep awe and reverence; the lives of all the king's family members are recorded and followed by subjects who think of them not as familiar but as vastly superior, almost divine. In Japan, the Emperor was, until 1945, actually viewed as divine by his subjects. When Emperor Hirohito broadcast his announcement of surrender to the allied forces at the end of World War II, most of his subjects had never heard his voice. (Since the imperial court used classical Japanese, not the common language, most of the country didn't understand his broadcast.) At his funeral in 1991, many mourners confessed his renunciation of divine status had not persuaded them; they still believed he was the direct descendent of Japan's divine female founder.

Japan is conscious of hierarchy in all things. This is fitting for a country that has had only one dynasty in its entire history. One uses different words to say the same thing, depending upon one's status compared with the status of the person to whom one is speaking. There are degrees of depth of bow, degrees of elegance in dress, degrees of restaurants, degrees of gifts, degrees of social occasions, degrees of status of universities, and degrees of manufacturers, banks, and other businesses. Japan also derives some of its levels of hierarchy from Confucian ideas imported from China.

In Focus

What is *Confucianism?* Confucius lived about 2,500 years ago, and his teachings affirmed an existing social order that reached from the Emperor (the "Son of Heaven") down to the lowest levels of Chinese society.

Confucianism is often mistakenly called a religion by people in the West, but it is not. Confucius' precepts were ethical guidelines for behavior to which a true gentleman (*junzi,* pronounced *jooin-zuh*) should aspire. The ideas were preserved, challenged, and revisited over the centuries. Neo-Confucianism, a synthesis in the Song dynasty (960–1279) of Daoism, Buddhism, and the commentaries on the works attributed to Confucius written over the 1,300 to 1,400 years since his death, was exported to Korea, Vietnam, Taiwan, and later Hong Kong and Singapore. Those cultures still preserve the orientation toward a hierarchical organization.

In the Five Relationships described in literature attributed to Confucius, a husband is superior to his wife, who owes obedience to the man. Parents are superior to children, who owe parents respect, obedience, and reverence—the famous teaching of "filial piety." The emperor is above his subjects; the servant is below his master, and only one relationship, friend to friend, is equal. Unequal relationships characterize Asian cultures, and probably existed a long time before Confucius' life.

The highest status in society, according to traditional Chinese thought, belonged to the scholar. Only scholars were trusted with the task of administrating the country and carrying out the emperor's justice. Next highest were the farmers whose labor provided sustenance for everyone. After farmers came soldiers and artisans, and at the bottom of the ladder were those engaged in commerce. Strange as it may seem in view of the rapid economic growth and dynamic businesses in Asia in the past half-century, businesspeople were traditionally held in contempt. They were thought of as parasites who would seek financial gain from merely brokering commodity exchanges; they were merchants and traders who created nothing by their labor. Even today in villages of western China and Tibet, merchants do not sell to their own family members. If the entire village is related in some way, nobody lives by commerce. (As we noted earlier, Confucianism is not a religion. Nor is it a systematic basis for a nation's economic behavior, although many popular business writers have treated it so. Most Asians do not learn Confucianism in formal settings. Much of what is called "Confucian" by authors writing in English is actually traditional Chinese culture.)

The difference between horizontal cultures and hierarchical cultures lies in what birth means. In a hierarchical society, you are born into a level that you cannot leave no matter what your education or income. In a horizontal society, you are able to rise to a higher level than you were born to, with more status, more power, or more wealth, based on merit.

People of the United States value social mobility because historically most immigrants to the United States were escaping a more rigid system that worked to their disadvantage. The United States proudly calls itself "the land of opportunity," and its people—for example, Arnold Schwarzenegger—tell stories about individuals of humble birth who began with nothing and became known and powerful and rich. Schwarzenegger first became a well-known body-builder, then a movie star, and then a governor of the state of California. Horatio Alger wrote in the early 1900s for a young male audience about boys who worked hard and single-handedly changed their level in society. His stories became widely accepted as a true type for citizens of the United States.

Generations in the United States were raised on the twin ideas that everyone ought to be able to rise in society through hard work and achievement, and that rising to the top is unquestionably desirable. For them, the hierarchical social organization common to other cultures has been baffling. Why would anyone embrace a system that keeps you at one level all your life? (However, as young people face the prospect of not rising and even of not attaining the level of their parents, the permanence of class membership has an appeal that may have been previously unrecognized.)

Both Australia and New Zealand have proudly let it be known that they have had prime ministers whose education ended with high school but who have nevertheless not been held back from rising to the highest level of political achievement. New Zealand is a highly egalitarian, flexible, horizontal society in which birth alone does not determine what level an individual may attain in the society. (This is true in the general society for both *Māori* and *Pākehā*.) This attitude toward mobility is very different from Great Britain, from which a large number of the European people of New Zealand trace their roots.

In England in the 1940s, servicemen from the United States had a hard time grasping the fact that the English had ideas about who could eat appropriately at which restaurants or vacation in which hotels, according to membership in a class. The attitude held by the majority in England has been that everyone has a place or station in society and that is where one is most comfortable. To try to rise above one's station is to ask for discomfort or even pain. To lower oneself is equally wrong and brings about disastrous consequences. These attitudes are not as strongly held as they once were in England. Nevertheless, although highly regarded entertainers and sports heroes blur class distinctions today, traditional attitudes still exist.

The majority of people in hierarchical societies don't seek a change in status out of their birth level. They are comfortable knowing what the levels are and where they fit. In Central America, for instance, millions of people of humble birth seek not to move to another level of society but rather to carry out their lives taking responsibility for the things within their scope.

Business organizations in hierarchical societies reflect the same hierarchical structure. People have no desire to lose the security of knowing who is where in relation to everyone else. They do not wish to exchange that security for a wide-open, unstructured system in which everyone is on an equal footing. In Indonesia, businesspeople were alarmed by the familiarity with which an Australian joint-venture representative treated them, asking them to call him by his given name, for example. Where was his sense of self-respect? Didn't he have a high regard for his subordinates? If he did, surely he wouldn't insult them by treating inferiors the same way he treated their betters. An intention to appear friendly and egalitarian on the part of an Australian can come across as foolish and dangerous to his subordinates.

Approach to Authority: Direct or Mediated?

Authority means different things in different cultures.

In Focus

A Pakistani-based Canadian manager was approached during office hours by a cousin of one of his employees, complaining that a neighbor had cheated him over a land deal. The cousin himself was not an employee, and the Canadian manager didn't know him. Nevertheless, he wanted his cousin's Canadian boss to come and sort out the claims and counterclaims. This role as a kind of arbiter or judge for local disputes would normally be carried out by the highest-ranking (Pakistani) person in the area. The Canadian, by virtue of his status as a manager, was expected to fill the role. It was a vital social function of social leadership that went far beyond his position in his company.[19]

The relative importance of hierarchy and the priority assigned to form both relate to another factor: How does one approach an authority figure? Is it by simply and directly appealing to that person? Or is access more appropriate if done through mediators, representatives, or lobbyists?

In many cultures, the approach to authority is indirect. Only certain avenues lead to the seat of power; only approved escorts can take you to their leader. In Latin-American cultures, a mediator is typically the way to reach authority. Often this is also one's patron.

The *patron–client* relationship is a reciprocal one in which the patron looks after the interests of the client and helps smooth difficulties and further the client's career. The client is loyal to the patron and supports the patron without swerving; the client helps build up the patron's power base through this loyalty. The patron–client relationship functions when the authority to be approached is high above the client in a hierarchical structure.

In Mexican organizations where a patron–client relationship often applies, the manager is owed respect because it has taken some effort (good performance) to reach the position of manager, or it is a result of birth, or both. The power distance between manager and workers is large, so the manager is somewhat remote from workers. Often intermediaries open doors so the worker can approach the manager, or perhaps intermediaries even carry the message for the worker.

The patron–client relationship also was typical of business organizations in pre-communist China, where the senior would *ti ba* (pull up) his junior person through mediation on his behalf (it was always men) as well as create opportunities for the junior. In return, the junior gave the senior man absolute loyalty and assiduous work. In the patron–client relationship, the client moves upward with the patron's promotions. The patron–client relationship is one of tyro and protégé, master and disciple, but it exists within the larger context of a hierarchy, at the top of which is the great power.

Another common hierarchical pattern requires an individual to approach authority only through the established *channel of superiors;* one's superior goes to his or her superior, who then goes to his or her superior. There is no formal patron–client relationship, and usually the hierarchy operates by status and job title as much as by inherent individual status. The position—the rung on the ladder—is more significant than the individual who holds the position. This is particularly true in organizations and cultures where there is job mobility. In a German organization, for example, the manager of a department may move to a different department, or a higher position, or a new employer. Regardless of whether the superior is the same person or not, a subordinate nevertheless will go first to the manager, whoever that is, who will then go to a superior, and so forth.

In hierarchical cultures where the approach to authority is through mediators, low-level employees rarely have any communication with high-level employees. Communication tends to be mostly downward, occasionally lateral. Messages are often directive, or a combination of directive and informative. Sending a message from the many at the bottom upward to one of the few at the top is difficult because there are many roadblocks to unsolicited upward messages. When messages from below *are* solicited, there are constraints upon the content; Those at the top do not favorably receive messages that are contrary to what they want to hear.

In New Zealand, in which horizontality has priority, the approach to authority is direct. Everyone calls former Prime Minister Dame Helen Clark by her first name, even to her face. People like the idea they can "go straight to the top" and like to think that an individual who wants to get a message to the boss simply walks into the boss's office and speaks to him or her face to face. In spite of a fondness for this image of easy access to authority in New Zealand—and in the United States, too, in fact—in large New Zealand and U.S. organizations the hierarchy can be rigid, and access to authority can be restricted. Small organizations lend themselves more easily to lateral power and communication structures, while large organizations often have levels of authority and mediated access.

What does this have to do with intercultural interaction for business? Here is an example. A consulting engineer from the United States on a hydroelectric dam joint-venture project in Brazil may assume equality with a Brazilian who is also a consulting engineer and may assume direct access to that person. But in fact the Brazilian may think that the correct channel for official communication is from the consulting engineer to a superior—say the project manager—and then to the highest-level person from the United States partner of the joint venture, who communicates with the highest-level Brazilian, who will communicate down to a Brazilian project manager, who will communicate to a Brazilian engineer. Getting the communication right, with the right person, can make the difference between success and failure in a joint-venture project.

This tooth-pattern communication often seems ridiculous, time-consuming, and inefficient to United States businesspeople. But then, they are not as concerned with hierarchy and status; they place a high cultural priority on direct access to authority.

Conclusion

This chapter, together with the one preceding it, has given 24 questions to pose of cultures in order to gain an understanding of business priorities. Whether you know a lot or nothing about a culture, you can use these categories in order to discover the *why:* why they act that way or think that way or have that belief.

These categories of questions can help you come to terms with aspects of an unfamiliar culture in a way that will enable you to make good guesses about how people will behave in situations you have not foreseen. No list of do's and don'ts can do that for you. The five categories give you a framework for creating, in an ongoing process, your understanding about what things matter in business with another culture.

Some dimensions cluster together, as we have pointed out. For example, cultures that prefer individual achievement and activity also often tend toward a direct approach to authority, toward a view that humans can prevail over nature toward a view that change is positive, and toward a view that planning instead of luck determines success.

Cultures that are collectivist have long-lasting group memberships, tend to prefer form, are hierarchical, use mediated access to authority, tend to be less averse to uncertainty, may wish to keep things the way they are and avoid change, and often bend the rules to accommodate relationship needs.

To repeat what we said at the beginning of Chapter 3, learning about a culture is an ongoing experience. You may never feel you know a culture completely. In fact, after reading this chapter you may feel you have learned things about your own culture you didn't recognize before. However, the more cultures you understand, even with a little insight, the more you'll know your own. And now you have a five-pronged tool for learning about any culture.

Summary

This chapter first discussed questions in the category of Self.

- *Is the basic unit of society the individual or the collective?* This is perhaps the most researched dimension of culture. It forms a good starting point for clustering a number of cultural dimensions.

- *Is obligation a burden or a benefit?* Collectivist cultures tend to see it as a benefit to nurturing relationships. Individualist cultures tend to see it as a burden to independence.

- *Is seniority valued or discounted?* In hierarchical, collectivist cultures, age often places people at the top of the ladder. Youth is valued by horizontal, individualist cultures.

- *Are women equals or subordinates?* The answer to this question may involve finding out how roles and status are attributed to women in a particular culture. Women make up more than 50 percent of the world's employees.

The chapter then looked at the category of Social Organization. This is one of the most important categories for intercultural business interactions, since it helps explain the cultural context of businesses.

- *Is group membership temporary or permanent?* An insight into this cultural dimension comes from attitudes toward family membership. Collectivist cultures treat group membership as permanent, serving the group's needs, while individualist cultures treat group membership as temporary, serving the individual's rights.

- *Is form important or untrustworthy?* Form, or protocol, tends to be highly valued in cultures that are hierarchical, where face can be lost by not conforming to etiquette, where harmony in the group is important, and where relationships matter. It is distrusted in cultures that associate emphasis on etiquette with phoniness and superficiality; often these are cultures where individual results matter.

- *Are personal matters private or public?* Employees in some cultures assume personal circumstances should be shared with everyone. These tend to be relationship-oriented collectivist cultures. In individualist cultures, an employee may wish to keep some personal facts private and not even tell the boss.

- *Is social organization horizontal or hierarchical?* The general pattern in society also is reflected in companies. Where hierarchy characterizes the national or social culture, companies also will have a clearly defined corporate ladder. The levels are generally agreed upon by members of the collective. In horizontal cultures, people can move from their birth level up (or down) as their individual achievements and desires warrant. Mobility depends on the accomplishments of individuals, although their families may partake of the new status.

- *Is approach to authority direct or mediated?* This is related to how hierarchical an organization is and how much weight an individual has. In collectivist and hierarchical cultures, business organizations tend to be hierarchical, and authorities are remote, making one or more intermediaries necessary. In individualistic and horizontal cultures, organizations tend to be more horizontal, with authorities more directly accessible.

You can ask these questions of a culture, assign that culture a place along the continuum represented by the question, and see how a culture's profile takes shape. Once you have plotted a culture somewhere on the dimension between individualism or collectivism, for example, you can slide the marker of the culture one way or another based on new information you receive. Your placement of a culture along a dimension can shift with your growing knowledge.

Notes

1. Yale Richmond, *From Da to Yes: Understanding the East Europeans* (Yarmouth, ME: Intercultural Press, 1995), pp. 51–62.
2. Hazel Rose Markus and Shinobu Kitayama, "Culture and the Self: Implications for Cognition, Emotion, and Motivation," *Psychological Review,* 98 (1991), pp. 224–253.
3. Gary Katzenstein, *Funny Business: An Outsider's Year in Japan* (New York: Prentice-Hall, 1989), pp. 74–75.
4. Linda Beamer, "Bridging Cultural Barriers," *China Business Review,* 5–6 (1998), pp. 54–58.

5. Robert J. House, Paul J. Hanges, Mansour Javidian, Peter W. Dorfman, and Vipin Gupta, eds. *Culture, Leadership, and Organizations: The GLOBE Study of 62 Societies* (Thousand Oaks, CA: Sage, 2004).

6. Geert Hofstede, http://www.geert-hofstede.com/hofstede_new_zealand.shtml. Retrieved August 3, 2009.

7. House, et al., *Culture, Leadership, and Organizations,* pp. 468–469.

8. Edward C. Stewart and Milton J. Bennett, *American Cultural Patterns: A Cross-Cultural Perspective,* rev. ed. (Yarmouth, ME: Intercultural Press, 1991), p. 96.

9. Larry A. Samovar and Richard E. Porter, *Communication between Cultures* (Belmont, CA: Wadsworth, 1991), p. 131.

10. Dolores Cathcart and Robert Cathcart, "Japanese Social Experience and Concept of Group." In *Intercultural Communication: A Reader,* 4th ed., Larry A. Samovar and Richard E. Porter, eds. (Belmont, CA: Wadsworth, 1985), p. 193.

11. Geert Hofstede, *Cultures and Organizations: Software of the Mind* (Berkshire, UK: McGraw-Hill, 1991), p. 94.

12. Wild Shea Tree Benifitting Burkina Faso: Women Engaged In Shea Sector Gain From Trade In 'Shea Butter' http://genderandtrade.org/gtinformation/164419/164962/168885/shea_butter/. Retrieved January 7, 2010.

13. "Women's Economic Capacity—Building in the Sheanut Sector," Financial Times Information, *Accra Mail,* March 3, 2003. Retrieved from Lexis-Nexis, May 26, 2003; "Burkina-Faso: Women's Economic Capacity—Building in the Sheanut Sector," *Africa News,* March 3, 2003. Retrieved from Lexis-Nexis May 26, 2003.

14. http://www.un.org/Conferences/habitat/unchs/press/women.htm. Retrieved on August 4, 2009.

15. Fei Xiaotong, *Shi Hui Diao Cha Zi Bai [Statement about Social Investigation],* unpublished trans. by David Tsow (Shanghai: Zhi Shi Chuban Shi, 1985), Chapter 4.

16. Yale Richmond, *From Nyet to Da: Understanding the Russians* (Yarmouth, ME: Intercultural Press, 1992), p. 120.

17. Boyé Lafayette De Mente, *Kata: The Key to Understanding and Dealing with the Japanese* (Boston: Tuttle Publishing, 2003).

18. Hiroki Kato, "From FOBs to SOBs: Japanese Vary Too," *Newsaction* (Northwestern University, IL), 36 (1988), p. 30.

19. Richard Mead, *Cross-Cultural Management Communication* (New York: John Wiley & Sons, 1990), p. 73.

CHAPTER FIVE

Organizing Messages to Other Cultures

When American Express writes to potential customers for its credit card in the United States, the letter begins with mention of milestones on the road to individual success. Results-oriented cultures value measurements of success, like the carved stones on English highways that told travelers how far they were from London, the presumed goal of every journey. American Express tells letter readers that only those who have already achieved a certain "measure of financial success" merit their credit card, along with the benefits American Express offers. One of the benefits it offers, to those who have already proven by their results that they merit it, is no set spending limit in advance. Another benefit is the ease of application: Just complete the short form and sign. People who are busy obtaining results want simple steps to getting the credit card. The letter uses a symbol, a centurion that is recognized as a logo of American Express. His helmeted profile signals responsibility, fearlessness, and strength.

When American Express writes to potential customers in Mexico, however, the emphasis is on membership in the society of cardholders. Not everyone can appreciate the card's true worth, the letter says. Members are only those who *can* appreciate it—and by implication the receiver of the letter is one of that select group. "Now you, like [equal to] those" can count on the incomparable services and benefits of the card. The reader is invited to take a few minutes to look at how the credit card can help in various situations. The letter urges the reader to "ask anyone" about the wide acceptance of this card in fine establishments. The message is that anyone in the know recognizes the membership that this credit card confers.

The letter goes on to say "you have seen" that cardholders don't need to worry at the moment of paying, when taking family or friends out, because there is no credit limit. In Mexico, the bill for dining or entertainment is never shared; one person hosts the rest. Avoiding embarrassment from not being able to pick up the tab because the credit card is maxed out is a selling point in Mexican culture. (Ads in the United States also mention "no spending limit," however.)

"Surely anyone knows . . ." that the medical and legal assistance you can obtain when traveling is worthwhile, says the letter. With a few phrases, the letter sketches a host of knowing people who form an in-group of cardholders. A nonverbal symbol, the image of the card itself—a badge of membership—appears, but no rugged individualistic centurion. The appeal is to Mexican collectivism.

Furthermore, although both are direct-mail sales letters, the U.S. letter underlines specific phrases for emphasis so as to make the main points stand out. The Mexican letter is gracious in tone and has no underlined points or bullets to grab the reader's attention. The reader instead is guided through various scenarios in which she or he will benefit from being a cardholder.[1]

This chapter examines the way culture impacts business correspondence and other documents. After a review of the communication process, the chapter looks at how communication is organized for routine, persuasive, unwelcome, and problem-solving messages. It then considers the force and role of words in various cultures, the channels of business messages, and finally cultural factors in writing style.

Review of the Communication Model

How does communication take place between organizations? As with communication between individuals from different cultures, when organizations communicate from different cultures, the potential for failed communication is multiplied.

Meaning and the Communication Model

Communication is usually modeled as a process. That is, although the model itself is a static, two-dimensional diagram on the page, it in fact represents constant movement. The basis for most communication models is that an **Idea** travels from **Sender** through **Channel** to **Receiver.** To these four basic components are added (1) the notions of *encoding and decoding* the idea into a message in verbal and non-verbal vocabularies, (2) the idea of *noise* as interference with the transmission, and (3) *feedback* from the receiver to the sender. The process of communication thus has come to be thought of as circular and simultaneous. The communicators understand meaning from the messages they exchange based on their culture. When they operate within different cultures, their meanings are likely to be different, too.

This model shows the receiver as the sender and the sender as the receiver (see Exhibit 5.1). The process operates in double circles, each starting with and returning to each communicator.

But where does culture go in this model? Culture is not really visible in this process model, yet it is absolutely critical.

A few sentences ago you read that an idea travels from sender to receiver. English communication is often perceived as a stream or continuous flow of coded elements. "Bits" and "bites" of information are sent "like so many billiard balls— from a sender to a receiver."[2] This image isn't really the best way to think of communication, though. In fact:

> The idea itself does not really travel, only the code; the words, the patterns of sound or print. The meaning that a person attaches to the words received will come from his own mind. His interpretation is determined by his own frame of reference, his ideas, interests, past experiences, etc.—just as the meaning of the original message is fundamentally determined by the sender's mind, his frame of reference.[3]

The meanings do not move from sender to receiver. They remain in the data banks of the sender and of the receiver, and the reception of the message triggers a decoding into meanings stored in the receiver's mind. This describes communication

EXHIBIT 5.1   **The Process Model of Communication**

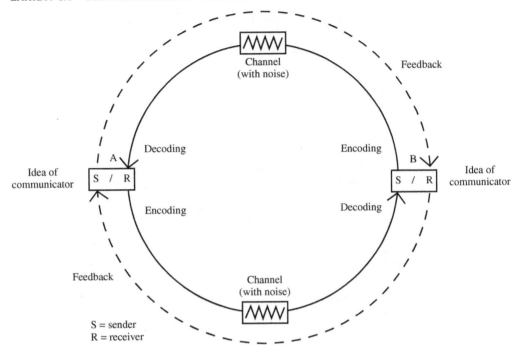

S = sender
R = receiver

between individuals, and the same is true for organizations. When the organization that receives a message has a similar frame of reference as the organization sending it, then likely both organizations assign similar meanings to the message. The more different the stored experiences, categories, attitudes, values, beliefs, and behaviors are—that is, the more different the cultures—the more likely it is the members of the organizations will assign different meanings to the encoded message. The message will not be understood. This is what happened to the company that sent a message in English that it would like an order filled "right away"; its Korean receiver anxiously responded, saying it would be happy to fill the order but asking what *was* the "right way"?

So, while communicators operate from a set of culturally determined meanings that may not exist in the receiving organization, at the same time we *have* to assume some similarity in meanings or else we can't begin to do business. Simply put, the intercultural business communicator has to try to get the assumptions right. One way to improve your chances of understanding the meanings of the other communicator is to use a matrix of intercultural dimensions such as those we have just seen in the five categories of questions to pose of cultures, discussed in Chapters 3 and 4. When you understand where a culture's priorities lie along certain dimensions, you can begin to make informed guesses about *what* messages mean.

Besides meaning, how does culture affect the way organizations structure and encode-decode messages both as senders and receivers? This chapter is about process more than meaning. In other words, it considers the *how* of intercultural business communication using examples to illustrate. The chapter also examines the *why, who, where,* and *when* of the process.

Why: The Purpose and Factors of Communication

Business functions require communication. In other words, business communicators send messages because they want to perform certain functions for the organization. A basic fact about business communication is that it is *purposeful*. Senders of business messages have the following purposes:

- Instructing
- Directing
- Informing
- Reporting
- Eliciting information, opinions, authorization
- Generating enthusiasm
- Resolving conflicts
- Analyzing situations and problems
- Motivating
- Negotiating
- Selling
- Reprimanding
- Refusing
- Evaluating
- Persuading
- Agreeing
- Granting requests
- Proposing
- Transmitting other messages (documents)

These are largely goal-oriented purposes. Purposes that contribute specifically to nurturing relationships are also important. They include:

- Praising
- Expressing concern or sympathy
- Encouraging
- Coaching and mentoring
- Thanking
- Rejoicing with the receiver
- Warning about possible problems
- Guiding around pitfalls
- Apologizing
- Expressing acceptance of an apology
- Reconciling
- Expressing hope
- Congratulating

In Focus

The earliest written business communication we know of comes from Sumeria—present-day Iraq. The messages were about trade and labor, which are subjects of modern business communication, too. Even earlier, scribes keeping commercial accounts would make miniatures of objects being sold, and by 3400 B.C. they would scratch pictures of the objects in damp clay. Later they came to use symbols to represent the pictures, since that was faster. They used reeds to write with, pressing the end of a reed into wet clay tablets to produce wedge-shaped images that are called cuneiform, from the Latin words meaning "wedge form." When by 2100 B.C. they used specific patterns of wedges to represent sounds, the Sumerian scribes had developed a system of writing that could serve business needs.[4]

Exhibit 5.2 shows a record of payment for five cows. The translation is line by line.

EXHIBIT 5.2
**A Sumerian Record
of Payment for Five
Cows**

Line one: Five full-grown cows
Line two: From Ludingira, son of Irhula,
Line three: Shulgi-ayamu accepted;
Line four: Month, the 28th day has passed,
Line one: (blank)
Line two: Month "piglet meal,"
Line three: Year: ìAmar-Suen destroyed Urbilum."[5]

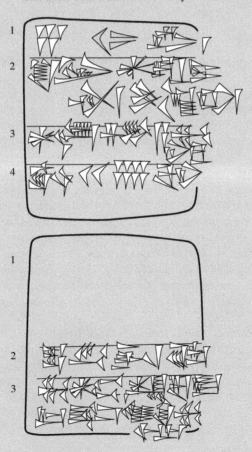

(*Continued*)

Another example of a cuneiform business text dates from about 2036 B.C. It is the year's account by a foreman called Lu-Šara of the work done by 33 laborers, whose names are all recorded, along with the kind of work they did and how much time each worked. The agents of the household set the tasks, and foreman Lu-Šara used the actual time the laborers worked, verified by receipts, along with the time that had been established, in this planned Babylonian economy, that they should have worked. The foreman calculated an annual total of worker days, which is how production was expressed. The record shows a deficit of 1,700 worker days for the year. "It is difficult to overstate the seriousness of these deficit workdays for the foremen involved, since a capricious central administration at the level of the province governors, or the crown in Ur, views them as effective loan debts that can be called in at will."[6]

The workers harvested grain and maintained or dug new canals. For example, 150 worker days were counted for harvesting grain and piling the sheaves up in the "*Oxen boot* field, in the field *Constructed wall,* in the field *Cattle herder of Nin-Arali* and (in the field) across from the new field."[7] They plastered silos and threshed grain to store in them. They also did irrigation work, excavating to put water in fields. Workers also are recorded as transporting products, including oil, cheese, and fish, by barges along the canals. The scribe carefully concludes that all the work took place in the year "the boat of Enki was caulked."

In these Sumerian examples from more than 4000 years ago, the purpose of communication was meticulous record keeping, made possible by the cuneiform system. The writing was an important tool for a hierarchical culture that controlled economic resources carefully.

Communication skills are highly valued by organizations. The functions of planning and implementing strategies for achieving goals are important. People who do these jobs are valued when their communications are successful. Measuring progress toward goals is also important to these organizations. People who can communicate their estimating, monitoring, and justifying of costs are valued. Identifying obstacles and communicating speedy methods for removing obstacles are valued. Finding ways to motivate workers to achieve goals is important, and managers who can motivate employees are valued. Timing of steps is important, and of course money to pay for them is important; employees who communicate about scheduling and costing are valued. Selling a product or service to the largest or best market is important, so communicating to promote and sell is valued by the organization. Since the organization needs to know when goals have been reached, people who can quantify and assess productivity and employees' performances are valued. The development of the double-entry bookkeeping system in Europe at the end of the Middle Ages meant that businesses could accurately show financial transactions. Some argue that the new financial communication tool sped up the development of "modern" business.

Organizations value employees' knowledge and try to capture that knowledge for the benefit of others who serve the organization. The methods employees use for communicating what they have learned vary, but the goal is to have effective communication in place so what employees know about working in a specific position is not lost when they move from that position.

*Purposes are the **why** of business communication.* All cultures value the functions previously listed. However, agreement across cultures about *how* the purposes are accomplished is rare. ***How*** *involves the way messages are organized and encoded* and will be our subject for the rest of this chapter. But before we turn to it, we'll look briefly at the other process aspects of communication.

Who in Business Communication

When organizations agree about the purpose(s) of a message, they are likely to assign similar meanings to it. When they agree about **who** is involved, they also lower the risk of an unintentional message—say, about status—interfering with the meaning. They can agree whether communication is one-way, as from a superior to a subordinate organization—perhaps a head office to a subsidiary in another country—or two-way, as between subsidiaries of similar status. This is related to the notion of access: If one organization makes its access open (open means several levels can communicate with the other organization), then the other organization can agree to be open. Closed access means the messages have to go through one person or one job function.

Who *within an organization is the appropriate person to receive or send a message?* Questions of status are tricky. In organizations that value hierarchy, the status of the communicator is important. But in organizations that are horizontal, the role (the job function) of a person may be more important than status (the job title).

As we saw in Chapter 4, **who** definitions may come down to family relationships. You may be the son of the company's chief executive officer (CEO) and therefore able to speak for her, which will make your message different from someone who is a junior employee and not a family member. Similarly, you may want to know that the receiver of your message is the son of the CEO.

Where: Channels of Communication

Organizations can also agree on the *channel of communication, or* **where** *it will take place.* Channel choice involves the issue of what should be put in writing and what should be communicated orally. Will messages be communicated by fax? Telephone? E-mail? Facebook post? Face-to-face exchange? When communicators agree about the channel, they can avoid misunderstandings on that score. Such misunderstandings may seem trivial but can be significant.

Individuals and organizations are always running up against problems that could have been avoided if the channel had been agreed upon. Americans are contract makers and usually don't think any agreement exists unless a contract has been written and signed. But in other parts of the world an oral statement is as good as a contract, if it is within the context of a relationship. A member of a United States organization can innocently say, "Oh, I'd really be interested in that new product," meaning at some future time it sounds like it could (conditional) be worth looking into more closely. But a member of an Asian culture, in which relationships make contracts possible, may understand such a comment as "I *will* be looking forward eagerly to receiving that product." If an oral channel, like the telephone, is used for making agreements by one communicator, and a written channel, like a contract, is used by the other, misunderstanding can result. Agreeing on the appropriate channel can save companies trouble.

When is it appropriate to leave a voicemail message rather than speak with the person? In Latin America, a voicemail message may be fine for making contact but not for giving substantive information. In cultures where relationships come before results, doing business with a voice message appears heartless and impersonal. In England, leaving information on the voice message system may seem an efficient way to move forward toward a business goal.

In Focus

Chinese users of technology are notably reluctant to respond to telephone voicemail. Before mobile phone technology became more widespread than landline telephones, it was the telephone itself that Chinese had a distaste for answering. One of the protocols, as a manager in Shanghai reported, was "Never tell your name!" If the intended receiver of the phone call was out, a caller was usually told "Not here!" followed by a disconnection click. Often phones in offices would simply ring and ring without being answered. Phone calls were rarely returned.

But now nearly everyone has a mobile phone and It seems nobody ever turns it off, not during meetings or at the movies or even at funerals. Text messaging is popular, too. However, Chinese do not pick up voicemail messages and rarely leave them. One businessperson was sent to China seven years ago with the instruction to get a good phone with long-distance capability and voicemail. He did, but never received a voicemail message on a landline. One cultural reason Chinese reject voicemail is senior-status persons feel they lose face by leaving a message for a junior who can pick it up at his or her convenience instead of being instantly responsive to the caller. Because personal relationships are so important in doing business, Chinese also have a cultural preference for face-to-face meetings, which is the way most transactions are conducted. Often a face-to-face meeting has to take place first, before a Chinese business contact will give out a mobile phone number. Another Chinese behavior with telephone technology involves using cell phones in meetings. Before mobile phones were in wide use, Chinese meetings included interruptions from subordinates bringing messages, subordinates pouring tea for everyone, and entrances from latecomers. Today the tolerance for interruptions includes taking calls from cell phones. Could this be connected to status? Public evidence that one is important and in demand enhances one's face. Perhaps it is also connected to a polychronic approach to tasks. Or perhaps the primary explanation for the Chinese behavior of answering and sending mobile messages during meetings is their reluctance to use the more impersonal voicemail and their preference for direct personal contact.

In some U.S. and European companies, voicemail is used much more than e-mail because busy executives who travel frequently can't stop to read and write e-mails. Foreign businesspeople are often frustrated by their inability to reach Chinese through voicemail, although no documentation exists that business has been hurt because of it.

Nevertheless, China remains a "voicemail-free zone."[8]

The same general rule may apply to the use of text messages: Results cultures rate efficiency highly, whereas relationships cultures rate personal contact highly. Cellular text messages are typically short and use an encoding system of phonetic abbreviations that depart from standard language usage. "R U OK mtg 2day—C U @ 3?" looks very informal compared with a standard written request: "Would it be convenient for you to meet with me today at 3 p.m.?" In organizations where form is an important part of the culture, distortions of language and format in business communication may not be productive.

A further discussion of communication channels appears later in this chapter.

When: Time and Timing of Communication

When *to communicate* is more complex than simply keeping time zones in mind, although that can be complex enough in a worldwide organization. Global business means having to stay up late in Germany to communicate with Hong Kong or having to rise early in Mexico to communicate with Israel.

Cellular telephone technology has made it possible for people to reach across continents and time zones to speak to one another. John in Australia can take a phone call from Aziz in Dubai about the latest news from the Foster's Brewing International Ltd. company branch—even when it is 10 p.m. in Sydney and John has just left a concert—if Aziz has his mobile phone number. Worldwide satellite transmission of mobile phone messages has increased communication efficiency for international firms. It has also extended the workday for employees, eroding the distinction between work time and private time. Future research no doubt will track the ways cultures view and react to this blurring of work and private life.

Knowing when to communicate also means choosing the right moment for a particular message. Can you raise a business issue during lunch with someone from another culture? (Sheila Graham, in the opening case to Chapter 4, made that mistake.) When riding in a host's car? During a casual moment? Or only in a formal environment? Often this is related to the question: "Who is communicating?" You may choose a formal moment to discuss sales figures with the executive vice president, but an informal moment with the manager of accounting.

The question of who goes first in negotiation is in part a **when** question. North Americans often assume that every culture wants to go first and get their position out on the table because frequently *they* do. Teams in Japan or China usually want to be last so they can hold back their own position until they've heard the other side.

When to communicate also involves being "on time," something discussed in Chapter 3, as well as the issue of a simultaneous versus sequential approach to tasks. If you are expecting exclusive attention from someone whose typical method of operating is to carry on several communication tasks at the same time, you may be disappointed. Someone who expects you to be carrying on simultaneous tasks may be uncomfortable with exclusive attention.

Organizing Routine Messages

The Direct Plan

Business communication books come mainly from Western cultures, particularly the United States. Accordingly, their authors tend to emphasize the things that are important in business communication in the United States.

For example, they urge writers to avoid ambiguity, get the message across clearly, and be concise. Choosing words with care for exact and precise meanings and eliminating unnecessary words and phrases are keys to a successful business writing style in the United States. Sentences are short and use a subject–verb–object pattern in preference to complex structures. Active-voice verbs signify doing and achieving; passive-voice verbs are passive, so a culture that values doing and achieving prefers active voice. Concrete nouns have shape, weight, and mass. What's more, you can experience them, if only in imagination, with your senses. Abstract nouns are shapeless, weightless, and amorphous. You can't see or smell or touch them. They are very hard to measure. Achieving, goals-oriented, can-do cultures prefer concrete nouns. Such cultures often express abstract ideas in metaphors that are more concrete, such as the sports metaphors discussed in Chapter 2. "Success," an abstract word, is a less compelling term to results-oriented cultures than "hitting a homerun" or "scoring a goal."

Business communication books also often urge directness in delivering the message. Cultural priorities in the United States include sincerity and openness; going straight to the point displays both. Beating around the bush, on the other hand, suggests you have something to hide. (This can be useful when the point of the message is one you'd rather conceal.) When the message involves a straightforward request, or good news, or information the receiver has been waiting for, indirectness seems unnecessarily complicated, even devious, and at the very least it seems to waste the reader's time. Directness shows consideration for the receiver of the message, since he or she probably values time too much to waste it on unnecessary paragraphs or speech.

These reasons may explain why business communication texts from the United States instruct writers to put the main message in the opening paragraph of correspondence unless there is a particular reason not to do so. If you put the main message at the end of the document, the busy reader may never get to it. Direct-plan reports, written and oral, relay the conclusion and recommendations *first,* before the slower information about how and why the report is being made, and what it covers.

After the main message comes the explanation. In correspondence, this may be one or more paragraphs. In reports and proposals it includes several sections: purpose, scope, methodology, facts, analyses, and interpretation. The tendency among low-context cultures is to explain in a linear—often chronological—sequence. Background information can help make the main message clearer, but the direct plan stipulates that background information comes *after* the main message.

Here is a direct-plan letter from Jordan, translated from the original that is handwritten in Arabic. The direct plan gets down to business immediately and is the very best way to organize routine business messages for most American, Canadian, Australian, British, New Zealand, and Northern European readers. As Exhibit 5.3 shows, the direct plan is also used by some businessmen in the Middle East for certain messages.

The main message is given before the specific detail. But it isn't necessarily the best way for members of other cultures to structure correspondence. For example, the French can find the direct approach insulting. To high-context communicators, a direct-plan message may seem rude and abrupt. The writer may be perceived as unfriendly or unwilling to be in a relationship with the reader, "just wanting to do business, not wanting to get to know us."

The Indirect Plan

The indirect plan does not put the main message in the first sentence. This plan has other priorities than the quick delivery of ideas, such as nurturing a relationship or developing some other context for the message. Japanese business messages often

EXHIBIT 5.3
Sample Letter #1

AMMAN CIGARETTE TRADING COMPANY
Jabal Amman, 6th Circle, Al-Basra Street 12, 2nd Floor
Amman, Jordan P.O. Box 123456, Amman 11182
Tel. +962 6 7654321

Date: 28/3/2002
Reference FC/W/221

Respected Filterona Company, Jordan
Attention/ Respected Mr. Mohammad Abu Umman

Subject: Request for Filters

Salutations,

   We request your courtesy in supplying us with 357 cartons of Cigarette filters, each carton to contain 22350 filters; therefore the total will be 7978950 filters, with the same specifications that you have supplied us before, requesting the delivery as soon as possible, using this information in the Iraqi manifest:

Sender   :   Amman Cigarette Trading Company/Amman
Receiver :   Iraqi company for cigarette production
                   Mr. Samaani Utthman Makhmoud/Baghdad
                   Customs broker: Sa'ad al Jaff—Office (3) Tel: 5115115/7711717

Also, please supply us with a copy of the Iraqi manifest after it is issued.

We thank you for your good help,

Accept our utmost respect,

                                        For: Khalid al Assel

                                        Saif Khalil

---

begin with a reference to the season: "Now it is autumn and the red leaves are covering the ground with color." In Muslim countries, the opening paragraph of a business letter frequently invokes Allah's blessing on the reader and the reader's family members, particularly when the business is family-operated.

   Indirectness can achieve at least five results for the writer:

- Diffusing responsibility
- Revealing the subtlety of the writer
- Digressing to embellish the message
- Elaborating to show courtesy
- Developing a communication context

Indirectness is often accompanied by deliberate ambiguity. Indirectness can *diffuse responsibility*. Even in routine situations, such as a request for information, indirectness saves face in case the request is denied or ignored. Indirectness signals the writer's intention to take care over things, including care not to make the reader lose face. Ambiguity means that words are chosen for their ability to mean more than one thing, and patterns of words can have more than one interpretation.

Ambiguity has another function: It reveals the subtlety and *sophistication* of the writer. What is not said may be as important as, or more important than, what is said. Indirectness and ambiguity mean a writing style that favors circumlocution rather than straightforwardness. Sentences may seem to ramble because ideas are developed in relation to each other. Metaphors are preferred because they infer a context of concepts and principles. They suggest unfolding possibilities.

Indirectness may also mean *digression,* or what may be termed side conversations and ramblings by results-oriented cultures. These added bits of circumstance and situational description help develop a context for business communication for members of relationship-oriented cultures. Edward C. Stewart writes:

> Particularly in some African communication styles, excursions into related subjects are normative, and listeners are expected to embellish the theme rather than to prod for the main point or the problem. In the words of one African student, "I know I have been understood when the other person makes statements that express the same idea as mine."[9]

Specific wording showing *consideration for the reader* often appears in indirect-plan letters. Expressions of courtesy can become quite elaborate. Even the standard French complimentary close, for example, for someone who is not a close associate contains far more elaborate courtesy than English letters:

> Veuillez agréer, Monsieur, l'expression de mes sentiments dévoués [Would you please accept, Sir, the expression of my devoted feelings].[10]

Developing a *context for communicating* information is very important to members of Asian cultures. This is based on the conviction that context is what gives meaning to information, and without the context, the information cannot be properly understood. In a study of Chinese-authored letters in the 19th century written to the Jardine-Matheson Company, a British-owned trading company in South China, indirectness correlates with the writer's desire to establish a context.[11] For instance, one writer named Kean Wo Cheong, inquiring about the status of a shipment of silk in 1874, begins "It is now about six months, no information has been given us, for that two cases of Silk which was sent to Europe for sale through your Company on our behalf." Only after establishing this context in this sentence does the writer continue with his main message: "We beg that we may be informed the amount realized from the sale of the silk . . ." Establishing the context is perceived to be a way of ensuring the main message is not misunderstood. By contrast, a direct-plan request would simply begin, "Please inform us of the price obtained in the sale of our silk." It would then go on to give the details: the consignment made six months ago, the lack of information to date, and so forth. What remains unsaid in the indirectly organized message is the writer's concern that the ship carrying the silk has encountered some mishap and the silk has been lost at sea or been pirated away. Direct-plan users often are low-context communicators who may put such worries into words.

To members of low-context cultures, indirect-plan communication can seem tedious, slow, and unfocused. To them, it may seem that the writer is not able to come to terms with the communication task. The reader may question the writer's thinking ability as well as writing ability (see Exhibit 5.4).

This is an example of an indirect-plan letter, translated from the original that was handwritten in Chinese. The letter is a request for help from a third party in collecting a debt. The main message comes in the next-to-last phrase. The person to whom the message was written, Mr. Guo, has added a message in his handwriting at the bottom and forwarded the message. Note that Mr. Guo's message is also indirect.

EXHIBIT 5.4 **Sample Letter #2**

Attn: CEO Mr. Guo

How are you!

For a long time we have not had any connection; how's your business been recently?

There is something I really ask you to concern yourself with, which is: Before the Spring Festival our factory helped Xu Xuefong, supplying several hundred clothing samples to him. The goods were already sent to him some time ago, [but] to date the payment has not been sent to my factory. We have waited a long time [probably 90 days] as accounting requires before we can close the account.
The international department also knows about this. I looked for him several times and he mentioned payment, but up to now we still have not received payment. Would you please help us speed up this matter?

Thank you so much.

Yang Zhiyan

Li Jianxin,
How are you!
This is regarding Manager Yan, who gave me this letter.
Xu Xuefong still has not given payment for the samples
he ordered. This will not do for confidence! Please
connect with Mr. Xu and get him to pay for the samples.

Guo Qingshang
5-20-2003

Organizing Persuasive Messages and Argumentation

Persuasion often uses an indirect approach in low-context cultures as well as high-context cultures. This is when "beating around the bush" is preferable to directness, even in cultures that value directness for most kinds of communication. You give the explanation first and then work your way to the main message. The rationale for using this organization is that a reader will be persuaded by *reasons*. If you marshal your reasons in a logical sequence and support them with facts, you can persuade. This works in a culture where persuasive arguments are based on objective facts. But not all cultures give facts high priority, and persuasion may depend on who the persuader is rather than on the reasons.

EXHIBIT 5.5A Sample Letter #3

7.3.1997

Saksbeh. Mona glosli
AutoPark A.S.
Postboks 30 Stovner
0913 Oslo

Vedr.:   Klage på kontrollavgift 0011031

Deres ref: 0011031

Jeg takker for brev datert 6.mars 1997, og ønsker å opplyse om følgende:

1. Jeg har en nesten ny bil og husket derfor ikke skilt nummeret.
2. Det regnet ganske kraftig og det var defor ikke spesielt hyggelig å løpe ut for å sjekke om nummeret på bilen var riktig.
3. Resepsjonsdamene sa at det ikke var nødvendig å skrive hele bil nummer ned, hvis jeg skrev hvilken biltype jeg hadde. De sa videre at jeg bare kunne understreke numrene og sette enn "?" tegn ved siden av. Jeg fulgte deres råd og gjorde som jeg ble bedt om.
4. At dine parkeringsfolk ikke forstår at ett "?" tegn betyr at vedkommende ikke var sikker på nummeret, kan ikke jeg belastes for. Heller ikke at dine parkeringsfolk ikke skjønner hvorfor en understreker nummerene samtidig som en skriver ned hvilken bilmerke det er, kan jeg heller ikke belastes for.
5. **Jeg kan ikke akseptere at jeg skal betale for denne boten etter at jeg fikk godkjennesle i resepsjonen for hva jeg gjorde. Denne må være en sak mellom dere og resepsjonen I Nixdorf.**

Med vennlig hilsen,

B. A. Smith
Church Road 100
361 Oslo

(continued)

EXHIBIT 5.5B Sample Letter #3 (Translation)

7.3.1997

Saksbeh. Mona glosli
AutoPark A.S.
Postboks 30 Stovner
0913 Oslo

Re: Complaint on Registration Fee 0011031

Your reference: 0011031

I thank you for the letter dated March 6, 1997 and wish to inform you of the following:

1. I have an almost new car, and therefore do not remember the license plate number.
2. It rained quite heavily and it was therefore not particularly comfortable to run out to check whether the number on the car was correct.
3. The receptionist said that it was not necessary to write down the whole vehicle number, if I wrote which type of car I had. She further said that I could just underline and put a question mark "?" sign by the page. I followed her advice and did what I was asked.
4. [The fact] that your [formal pronoun] parking staff does not understand that the question-mark sign means that the individual was not sure about the number, cannot be blamed on me. Furthermore, the fact that the parking staff does not wonder why one underlines "number" while simultaneously writing down the make of the car, I cannot be held responsible for.
5. **I cannot accept that I should be required to pay this fine after I got approval in the reception area for what I did. This must be a matter between you and the reception function.**

With friendly regards, [formal closing]

B.A. Smith
Church Road 100
361 Oslo

Argumentation and Logic

In low-context cultures, objective facts reside outside the communicator or the organization. They have an independent existence. Facts often can be quantified and measured. (Chapter 8 develops this notion in relation to the collection of information, its reliability, and its validity in different cultures.) Since emotion is slightly suspect, you are better off basing your argument on facts. After all, you can go to court—an ultimate kind of persuasion—based on facts. You can count on them.

Exhibit 5.5 shows a persuasive letter that argues by marshaling facts. This letter argues by carefully organizing facts into a logical sequence. The writer puts key items in boldface type: the addressee (inside address) and the "therefore" conclusion of his argument at the end of the letter. The writer of this letter is unwilling to pay a parking fine incurred for not filling in the car registration form completely for a parking lot. He appears to present information objectively. He uses a numbered list and takes an objective position about the "facts": His car is new, it was raining, he followed the receptionist's instructions, and therefore he cannot be held responsible for the error and the fine. His argument is constructed like a syllogism: The facts lead to a conclusion that the writer puts in boldface type for emphasis.

This letter also uses sarcasm, something that may not always achieve the writer's objective and persuade the reader, even in a low-context culture. The writer says he cannot be held responsible for the *fact* that parking staff do not understand the question-mark symbol. Nor can he be blamed for the parking staff failing to consider why the word *number* is underlined on the form while at the same time the make of the car is entered on the form—showing he knows the make but not the number. This kind of sarcasm is common in Norwegian culture and is a customary way for someone to proceed in a complaint. Another sarcastic dig comes from the use of the informal *you* singular pronoun throughout, except for the formal *you* in point number 4. (The reader is an ombudsman or *Skasbeh*; her job is to hear complaints and attempt to give individuals with relatively little power some assistance in dealing with the organization.)

In high-context cultures, facts are not objective or impersonal. Words and arguments are not separate from the writer or speaker who expresses them. Facts come with a person wrapped around them. If you argue against those facts, you are arguing against the person who uttered them. Even in a court of law, you can't count on facts to help you achieve your goals in cultures that do not put a high priority on litigation; you have to count on people. Relationships are how things get done.

Since status is usually important in high-context cultures, the person is always a key factor in how a message is understood. Words cannot be distinguished from their source, and influential people can influence and persuade by virtue of their status. Furthermore, in high-context cultures the web or context of relationships and obligations is ever present. A tug on one side of the web sends vibrations throughout the web. How can a receiver refuse to be persuaded when the entire network—other people—know about the attempt at persuasion?

Western Persuasive Logic

The Norwegian letter is one example of European reasoning in order to persuade. Greek philosophers 2,500 years ago presented the concept that each individual thing has a unique core that is the basis of its identity. "Each thing" includes the physical world of objects and the metaphysical world of abstract concepts. Once you take away everything that an object or concept has in common with others, what is left is the core. It is unchanging, and constitutes the basis of a unique identity.

Furthermore, the Greek philosophers thought that the individual identity—or truth—of something can be discovered by looking for it. In other words, intellectual inquiry is the way to find the essence or truth about something. This is an important key to understanding the European and also North American emphasis on truth and the emphasis on facts. It also explains the conviction in Western cultures generally that it is possible to find out facts and learn the truth.

Another key to understanding Western logic is the *principle of non-contradiction,* which also comes from classical Greek thinkers. We first encountered this principle in Chapter 3. The principle says that *two opposite things cannot both be true.* (When two opposites both claim to be true, that is a contradiction.) Since knowing the truth is important to Western reasoning, when two opposites each claim to be true, members of Western cultures become agitated and feel they are being deceived.

Because of the focus on facts and the truth, persuasiveness in Western cultures involves presenting facts clearly and in a logical sequence. It also means distinguishing between true and untrue since opposites cannot both be true, and urging the other person to accept the truth.

East Asian Persuasive Logic

Persuasive reasoning in East Asia has roots that go back more than 2,500 years. Ancient philosophers in China, such as Laozi (pronounced laow-dzuh), considered the world and everything in it to be in a state of constant change. The way to understand something, they believed, is to recognize how it is connected to other things. Everything must be understood as a part of an interrelated context. Everything belongs in a network or web of linkages, and the relationships and linkages are what give meanings to things. This is quite different from the Greek-based approach, that holds each item has a true core, and knowing the truth means finding that unique core.

The emphasis on connectedness, when applied to humans, results in a primary concern for managing human relationships. Correct behavior, not truth, is the focus of reasoning.

East Asians observe that because of constant change, contradictions occur often. Two opposite things often co-exist. Because of change and contradiction, one single individual item cannot be isolated and examined independently. This leads to an approach that can be called *dialecticism.* Dialecticism suggests that an object, an idea, a value—almost anything—can be considered in relationship to its opposite, and that in view of its opposite, the meaning of a thing can be discovered. Daoism is an ancient Chinese approach for understanding the meaning that exists in contradiction. *Dao* (pronounced dow) means "the way" in Chinese. (In older writings it is spelled *Tao*.) Paradox contains core meaning, and paradox requires at least two opposite points of view.

An important principle in East Asian reasoning is balance. In life, which is dynamic and fluid, where contradictions and oppositions exist, the key is to find a balance. As we saw in Chapter 3, page 110, a symbol that represents the ideal of balance is the *yin-yang* (pronounced een-yahng). Contradiction is embraced within a whole. Balance is perfectly achieved within a paradox.

Because of the importance of balance and harmony in human relationships in East Asian cultures, persuasiveness comes from describing and urging patterns of behavior that lead to balance in relationships.

Arabic Persuasive Logic

Arabic reasoning differs from East Asian reasoning in that it does not try to reconcile opposites. Arabic reasoning is more like Western reasoning, in that two opposites cannot both be true. The historical development of reasoning in Arabic-speaking cultures has origins that predate Islam but were focused in a particular way by Islam.

In Arabic-speaking cultures, *presentation* is the conveyance of true meaning. Dialog is especially important, because it gives speakers the chance to engage in the activity of presentation. Arabic cultures have a long history of argumentation, which means the construction of logical arguments or well-developed positions (it doesn't mean arguing as in a quarrel).

Presentation is the way communication is enacted. It involves three key elements:

- Language and word choice
- Ability to raise emotion
- An authoritative voice

Presentation first involves language. The Arabic language, with the tri-radical basis of words (three consonants as the root of words), lends itself to repetition of sounds. Phrases are easily constructed with echoing, repeated syllables. The language lends itself to many parallel constructions in wordings, so plays on words are common. Parallel syllables and consonants produce repeated vowel sounds, repeated consonant sounds, and rhymes. See also the discussion of Arabic language on page 200 later in this chapter in the section titled "The Role and Force of Words."

The Arabic language itself has great persuasive power for its listeners. An Arab historian, Philip K. Hitti, writes:

> No people in the world, perhaps, manifest such enthusiastic admiration for literary expression and are so moved by the word, spoken or written, as the Arabs. Hardly any language seems capable of exercising over the minds of its users such irresistible influence as Arabic.[12]

The emphasis on Arabic language dominated scholarship in the 7th to 9th centuries, especially the language of the Qur'an, since that historical Arabic is held by Muslims to be the language chosen by Allah in which to reveal and communicate truth to believers.

Presentation also involves emotion. The emotion of the speaker signals a sincere belief and commitment to what is being said. Even more important is the speaker's ability to create emotion in the listeners or readers. Historically, during the *Jahiliyya,* or period of pagan ignorance, orators were storytellers. They told stories in poetry, and by telling the stories they urged Bedouin tribal lords to act with courage, loyalty, generosity to guests, ferocity in war, and honor in nomadic journeys and hostile raids upon enemy tribes. The storytellers' persuasive force came from their ability to arouse emotions that linked the listeners to the actors in the stories. The strong oral tradition continued into the 9th and 10th centuries with public debates among scholars that encouraged development of debate techniques.[13]

However, presentation ultimately comes from having an authoritative voice. One way to give authority to a presentation is to repeat an idea, perhaps more than once. Repetition comes from the language itself and also from the familiar use of a line of poetry or a line of *saj,* which is the verse of the Qur'an. Of course, the Qur'an itself is the ultimate authoritative voice. Intellectual curiosity, a desire to know, means to have knowledge of the Qur'an, the authoritative source of all knowledge since it is directly from Allah. This is a fundamentally different view from the Greeks' curiosity to find out the nature of things, or the Chinese desire to reconcile conflicting elements in a harmonious worldview.

Because of the emphasis on language, emotion, and above all authoritative voice, persuasiveness in Arabic cultures comes from presentation aspects of communication, such as word choice and repetition.

The three general modes of persuasion—European, East Asian, and Arabic—have key differences. However, they all share the same goal: to move the mind of the reader. When the different modes of presentation clash, the result is not only miscommunication but often also mistrust. Westerners can view Asians as unprincipled, because of their need for the truth in situations where Asians see the truth as dependent on context. Asians can see Westerners as rigid and unsophisticated. Arabs can see Westerners as untrustworthy because their communication is low in emotional expression and therefore seems insincere. Westerners can view Arabs as emotionally volatile and therefore undependable. These are only a few of the possible failures to persuade across cultures.

Persuasion Tactics

People and organizations in relationships adopt certain roles in order to persuade. One role is to *take the moral high ground.* For example, business organizations in India have played the role of the Morally Superior in negotiations with the United States and Japan.[14] India is an old and venerable culture with well-established regulations for social behavior and deep-rooted expectations for business behavior. In 1984, a pesticide manufacturing company in the city of Bhopal, India, experienced a disastrous leak of toxic gas. Thousands died, and thousands more suffered terrible injuries. The episode was viewed as morally wrong by the Indians (and others around the world), who felt the company had failed to behave responsibly. The company was a joint venture, 50.9 percent owned by Union Carbide, a U.S. chemical company, and 49.1 percent owned by Indian investors and the government. Some Indians called for the extradition of the American president of Union Carbide at the time. The morally outraged victims who survived continue more than 20 years later to charge that the company did not release information about the gas and about possible treatment, and to ask for more compensation.

The United States, which assigns a high priority to equality, was not persuaded by India's moral posture in this case, although Union Carbide awarded $470 million in a settlement. The U.S. company claimed that (1) no Americans were present in India at the plant when the disaster occurred, (2) the plant was Indian-built and operated, and (3) an investigation showed the reason for the gas leakage: deliberate sabotage by a disgruntled Indian employee. According to the facts collected by Union Carbide, it was not at fault.

Japan is another country toward which India takes the moral high ground, such as for some World War II atrocities committed by the Japanese. (Japan has not been persuaded by this tactic.) However, many cultures use the tactic of taking the moral high ground to persuade, and they do succeed in many cases.

Another tactic for persuasion may come from organizations in cultures that feel they have been *the disadvantaged party in international relations.* Acting in this role, some may adopt a dependent posture with a country like the United States or Germany and the corporations that represent them. Mexican organizations, for example, may suggest they are owed favorable treatment by the United States—and make persuasive requests based on this notion—because the company from the United States is bigger or has more capital or is gaining a great concession with access to Mexican markets.

Persuasion also comes from emotions, as mentioned earlier with Arab communicators. To people of many cultures who view emotional involvement as a sign of sincerity, facts alone seem cold and impersonal and therefore unpersuasive. Thus, the very characteristic that is suspect in low-context cultures—emotion—is what moves people in other cultures (such as Arabic cultures). Leaving out emotions will have the opposite effect of what is intended. One emotion that can motivate in Asian cultures is pity. A tactic is for the persuader to generate pity by describing the pain and misfortune that have been experienced. For instance, a small supplier may run into problems with delivery schedules and wish to persuade the customer to accept delayed delivery. The argument may run as follows: "We are so small a company, we have little power to force our agents to deliver promptly. Please consider how small we are." The company being persuaded is supposed to respond with pity. In some cultures, this works well. In a U.S. context, such persuasion tactics may not be so effective, since the company may simply seem pathetic.

Persuasion is important because in a sense *every communication task a manager performs involves persuasion.* Even when the manager communicates information, the purpose is usually partly persuasion: "giving away purposeless information is a symptom of irrational behavior."[15] You could argue that even small talk has a persuasive undercurrent: "Trust me, I'm on your side. Be my supporter." Making an oral presentation also has a persuasive element: "Believe me to be a credible speaker. Take my message seriously. Trust me." Persuasion in intercultural business negotiation is discussed in Chapter 9.

Persuasion begins with establishing the credibility of the party doing the persuading. As we have seen, this can be accomplished in different ways, such as using facts, taking the moral high road, and needing special consideration. The next step is for the party doing the persuading to *establish common ground,* so the party being persuaded feels there is something to be gained for them also. Successful business persuasion usually involves *the revelation of some benefit for the party being persuaded.* How much the benefit is valued is, of course, dependent on the culture. Subsequently, *the persuading side must make its case* and engage the appropriate emotions of the other side.

Organizing Unwelcome Messages

Communicating about Problems

Talking about what's wrong is not easy for people in any culture, but people in high-context cultures like China put a high priority on keeping harmony, preventing anyone important from losing face, and nurturing the relationship. That is why letters and meetings often include references to past solidarity. Historical references to episodes between organizations and nations may be frequent.

In low-context cultures where information typically is encoded in explicit wording, the tendency is just to "spit it out," to get it into words and worry about the result later. Americans want a clear apology: "I am sorry." Senders of unwelcome messages use objective facts, assuming, as with persuasion, that facts are neutral, instrumental, and impersonal. You can say, "The order arrived with 30 percent of the contents damaged" and not point fingers of blame in low-context cultures. Business communication textbooks suggest a direct plan for talking about a problem that is the other party's responsibility: "Your overdue balance is still outstanding."

In Focus

When Ron Kelly, a visiting management professor from St. Lawrence College, experienced conflict with his Chinese hosts in Sichuan about the number of courses they wanted him to teach or the number of students per class, he would arrange to meet with them. He would begin with expressions of gratitude for their assistance in making his experience of teaching in China so rich. He would praise their work, their students, and their institute. He would mention the comfortable accommodations and good food and the excellent sights within an easy bicycle ride of the institute. Near the end of their meeting he would mention "just one little thing" that was a cloud on his horizon, and he would express confidence they would be able to help him sort it out, for the sake of the good relationship they all enjoyed. Rather than press for immediate action, Ron would indicate he'd ask again in a few days. He would usually "forget" a packet of cigarettes, or leave behind a bottle of spirits, and depart with warm smiles all around. He had few lasting difficulties in China.

Ron Kelly had to learn a different organization of the message when he was in China. At home in Canada he would have been polite and professional and would have gone directly to the point. But in China, as in other high-context cultures, going directly to the problem carries a piggyback message that is even stronger: "You have failed to live up to your responsibility; the honor of your organization is in question; the very relationship between us is in doubt." In high-context cultures such a message is serious and damaging.

Occasions do arise when a direct message is appropriate in high-context cultures, but they are not always the situations a member of a low-context culture would identify for directness. For example, a manager might issue a command to a subordinate with a directness that could seem harsh: "Fill the following orders and ship them before noon."

Indirectness is the way members of high-context cultures communicate about a problem (also see Chapter 8). Stewart reports that a Japanese husband would suspect his wife was upset if "a flower was askew in the entryway arrangement, but he would be sure of it if his teacup were only partially filled with lukewarm tea."[16]

The Japanese whom Stewart consulted said they would take special pains to be attentive in such circumstances, but would avoid bringing up actual incidents. Asking "What's wrong?" would cause unnecessary disruption of harmony and potential loss of face. (In Holland, a husband might suspect his wife was upset if she clattered the knives and forks unnecessarily loudly when setting the table or banged down the plates with more force than necessary. Signals vary, and so does the response to them.)

In Focus

Two Canadian visiting professors to a university in China encountered some difficulties when the bad news was simply never communicated at all. The bad news was that the boiler for the guest house they lived in would be out of service for at least two weeks. That meant no hot water and no heat during November, when the weather is cold. They only found out the bad news indirectly, from someone unconnected to the *wai ban* (office for dealing with affairs outside the university) that was designated to communicate with them. Once they heard about the boiler, they went to see a person from the *wai ban* and began a conversation, telling the *wai ban* person about an invitation they had received to go to another institution for a visit of about two weeks. The visit was discussed, and dates were proposed for the visit (which, not surprisingly, happened to coincide with the dates of the boiler repair). The host officer agreed, the Canadians agreed, and everyone was happy. Nobody ever mentioned the boiler until after the visit had taken place. By then, the professors were back and the hot water was on.

Bad news may not be communicated at all, or may be communicated indirectly. In the example in China, the discussion was about the visit to the other organization for the very two weeks the boiler would not be operating. The boiler was an unspoken item; the context for that item was the conversation about the visit elsewhere.

When an unwelcome message must be delivered in a high-context culture, and context alone cannot deliver it, the message will probably be organized indirectly, in circumlocutory words. Often, nonverbal signals will carry the message (see the Japanese steel company example on page 209). Smiling, certain hand and head gestures, and other nonverbal behavior may signal an apology that is hard for low-context communicators to read. In worded messages in which someone from a low-context culture would probably begin the correspondence with a request for a refund because the order arrived too late to be used, someone from a high-context culture might give an entire history of the relationship between the organizations before asking for a refund.

Saying No

Saying no is done with delay and indirectness in low-context cultures, as most U.S. business communication textbooks agree. They advise writers to "say no slowly." The rationale is to explain *why* first, and since facts persuade readers, by the time the reader gets to the *no,* he or she has been persuaded to accept it. Not all businesses in the United States have caught on to this practice, however, which argues that it isn't a priority everywhere in the culture.

Asian cultures are renowned for saying yes. In fact, in Japan, Westerners have heard *yes* and gone home happy when the Japanese really meant *no.* It is much easier for Japanese and other high-context cultures to say yes. It is "yes, I'm listening," or "yes, you have a good point," or "yes, I see (but don't agree)." Often, it has the function of the American "uh-huh" to encourage someone to keep talking (this unworded communication is similar to the meaningless sounds that indicate social involvement with the speaker's act of speaking, like "mmhmm"). Sometimes, of course, *yes* means "I agree; I will carry out your request." The problem for low-context communicators is they can't always tell which meaning is meant. When people from a high-context culture receive a yes response, they often seek to verify it so they can tell which meaning to give it. A Korean manager in a U.S. firm was given the opportunity for a new and more prestigious job. He responded, "I will be willing to do it if nobody else will." He was saying, "Yes! I accept!"

Saying *no* is more difficult for high-context cultures. As when they communicate about problems, they would rather not actually have to put a refusal into words. In Chinese, a *no* may reside in the words "That may be difficult." The Japanese equivalent to that would be a drawn-out hissing breath and drawn-out words: "Sssaaaah . . . muzukashii naaaaaaa." (Also see Chapter 4.)

In cultures that put a high priority on face, a refusal is a potential loss of face for both the refusal makers and those being refused. The refusal-makers lose face because they have failed to perform according to the expectations of the party they have a relationship with—a web of obligations and favors often related to the roles of host and guest. They are shamed. The refused lose face because they have been turned down by the very party with whom they have a relationship, and they go away empty-handed. They too are shamed. The balance of obligations is askew. The relationship itself is momentarily at stake.

No in high-context cultures is frequently couched in an expression that turns the situation around. For example, a person who has to refuse an invitation to dine out with a business associate may say by way of refusal, "You must be very tired and want to have a quiet evening." This way, the refused person does not lose face, although the refusal is clearly understood in a high-context culture.

Organizing Problem-Solving Messages

Storytelling

One way to communicate about a solution to a problem is through narrative. An ethnographic study in the 1980s involved the problem-solving communication of photocopy machine repairmen in the United States.[17] The repairmen would be sent out on jobs, where customers would greet them with relief and high expectations. They would start to take the machines apart and try to identify the problems. If the problems persisted, they often would attract other men who would stand around and offer suggestions. Then, according to the study, if the problems still were not solved, the men would start telling war stories. Many repairmen had been mechanics in the army, and they had had experiences trying to fix equipment with little more than their ingenuity.

Pretty soon, after a number of stories, the solution would be found and the equipment would be fixed. The stories offered guidelines when there wasn't enough information in the manuals. Stories are a way for results-oriented cultures that like to rely on facts to discuss situations in which facts are available only from anecdotes and personal experience.

Stories circulate throughout organizations. They often tell about "heroes" who didn't take no for an answer or succeeded against steep odds or who performed amazingly well. Stories also circulate about those whose failures are lessons to others. Through the Internet, in blogs, on Facebook, on YouTube, and in e-mailings, stories are circulated to illustrate lessons about working life. The following is an example:

In Focus

A sales representative, an administrative clerk, and a manager are walking to lunch when they find an antique oil lamp. They rub it and a Genie comes out in a puff of smoke.

The Genie says, "I usually only grant three wishes, so I'll give each of you just one."

"Me first! Me first!" says the clerk. "I want to be in the Bahamas, driving a speedboat, without a care in the world." Poof! She's gone.

In astonishment, the sales rep says, "Me next! Me next! I want to be in Hawaii, relaxing on the beach with an endless supply of piña coladas and the love of my life." Poof! He's gone.

"Okay, your turn," the Genie says to the manager. The manager says, "I want those two back in the office right after lunch."

Moral of the story: Always let your boss have the first say.

Storytelling is a way of making meaning for organizations. Stories often can be interpreted variously to reinforce common values and can be used to talk about solutions to management problems, too. When management wants to introduce change, for example, a story can help employees understand and accept the change. An international firm's CEO told a story to 300 managers about Willie B., a silverback gorilla, who after 27 years in a small bunker was moved to a new spacious habitat designed specifically for him. Even though the change was a positive one for Willie B., he spent the first few days taking cautious little steps to get to know his new home. A photograph that hung on the wall of the executive's office showed Willie B. testing the grass with his toe. The executive's point to the managers was: Remember that change takes time and courage, even when it is for the better.[18]

In Focus

Martin Woolnough, manager for Nestlé in Uzbekistan, uses stories frequently. He says, "I like stories . . . they help people understand complex problems or totally new concepts." When he needed to get across concepts that were unfamiliar about the structure of the financial relationship of the factory to the Nestlé parent company, he told the following story.

Let's pretend we are young and want to buy our first car. We don't have enough money but we have one uncle who is very, very rich. [Woolnough said he used this analogy since staff and local authorities and traders were "taking us for granted" as a rich company with deep pockets.] So, we ask our rich uncle if he would lend us the money so we can buy a car. Would he just give us the money? Probably not . . . he would want to know when or how we were going to pay it back, wouldn't he? So, let's say we told our uncle that the reason we wanted to buy a car was so that we could make some extra money by having a taxi service. We agree that for every three passengers we will keep two fares for ourselves to live on and give the third one to our uncle to repay the car. After five years, we estimate that the loan will be repaid.

Our uncle likes this proposal. Not only does he get to help out one of his family, but he also sees that we are going to learn about business. So, he lends us the money and we go out and buy a brand new shiny car. Fantastic! Now we own a car . . . but . . . does this make us rich? Of course not! In fact, we are even poorer than before since we now OWE money. What about our very rich uncle—just because he is a millionaire, does that make us one? Of course not! Well, Nestlé Uzbekistan LLC is like this. Our "rich uncle" in this case is our company Nestlé S.A., which has "lent us" the money to build this fantastic factory.[19]

Here is another example of using storytelling to bring home a problem.

In Focus

The town of Guryev on the Ural River in Kazakhstan is perhaps the world's best source of caviar from the beluga sturgeon. In 1991, Kazakhstan achieved independent status as a state, with a government in the capital of Almaty instead of in Moscow and the right to sell openly to the West. But unfortunately, the sturgeon are in dwindling supply. A major reason is that they are being appropriated by the officials in the new government—who were the Communist party officials in the old government—before they can reach the factories. In autumn, there is a "mad beluga season" when the black market does a roaring business.

Communication about the problem in this high-context culture is diffused through narrative. Kazakhis do not point fingers at specifically named people. Instead, they tell humorous stories and use proverbs—methods of indirectness typical of high-context cultures—to illustrate the "crazy history" of caviar in Guryev. Here is one example.

The ghosts of Stalin, Khrushchev, and Brezhnev pay a visit to Yeltsin, who naturally has to offer his guests some food and drink. He pours out four glasses of vodka and then hands around a meager plate of caviar sandwiches.

Brezhnev says, "Mr. Yeltsin, when I was in charge, I would put a whole kilo of caviar on the table."

Krushchev says, "When I was in charge, I gave my friends caviar by the ton."

Finally, Stalin says, "When I was in power, I had so much caviar that my people went abroad and force-fed foreigners with it."

The Russians have a proverb: "Don't count your caviar until you've caught your sturgeon."[20]

Analogy

Analogy—drawing an extended comparison—is another way of talking about solutions to problems. Sometimes the analogy is in a narrative, but not necessarily. Māori teachers formally and informally use extended analogies in their storytelling to advise or caution or make sense out of a situation for their listeners.

Military language offers rich material for analogies in corporate problem solving in the United States: *operation, briefing, debriefing, offensive, attack, troops, maneuver, ammunition*. This language also reflects the action orientation of the business culture in the United States.

Sports analogies often describe solutions to problems, especially when teamwork is important. Ricardo Vasquez uses baseball analogies—"we need to hit one out of the park"—with his contacts in Puerto Rico when extra effort is needed to make a sales goal. Game analogies work well to communicate business strategy to solve problems. For example, negotiation between Asian and Western teams has been compared with the games of Go (in Japanese, or *Wei qi* in Chinese) and chess.[21] When Piet Kreft from the Dutch company Unilever wanted to stop theft from the warehouse in Azerbaijan where Lipton tea was being stored, he brought all the employees together and told them, "I want us to become a club where *we*, the honest staff, consider it inappropriate for anyone to steal from our 'family.'" By appealing to the Azerbaijani sense of family and clan, he wanted to implant the ideas that as employees looking for long-term stability for their families, he and they were the beneficiaries of having a profitable company, and stealing detracted from their profit and directly from their own personal success.

Syllogistic and Inductive Reasoning

Narrative and analogy are examples of nonsyllogistic reasoning. But for low-context cultures, reasoning means deductive syllogisms and inductive logic. Syllogistic thinking is deductive, moving from a generalization to a specific instance. Induction works from examples to a generalization. Inductive logic:

> reflects Western intellectual traditions of precise, scientific detachment, and appeals to an abstract sense of reason existing outside the relationship between speaker and hearer. Thus it has the effect of establishing the distance between them.[22]

The problem and the reasoning both exist apart from the speaker and the hearer, which creates a sense of objectivity about the problem-solving discourse. Individuals' feelings appear not to be involved. In low-context cultures, problem-solving finds expression most often in *reasons why*, leading to *therefore*.

Deductive reasoning is used by French, Spanish, and Italian communicators, who prefer to argue from abstract concepts and principles. They tend to dislike an approach like that of the United States, finding it too pragmatic and too quick to rush to application before the theoretical framework is in place.

High-context cultures do not see reasons as outside and apart from the relationship between communicating parties. Any problem-solving discourse must take the relationship into consideration. If a solution ignores or jeopardizes the relationship, it cannot be a good solution. Reasons by themselves alone do not have the power to convince; it is the context of the relationship that gives significance to reasons. So, for example, inductive organization may be used in talking about a problem out of deference to the relationship, because it moves from specifics to a generalization. That may be less likely to cause loss of face or wound someone, whereas an accusation could do both.

Bargaining Discourse

Problem-solving discourse in some cultures, such as Arabic-speaking cultures, may follow the model of the Arab *souq* (market). This discourse is a kind of bargaining that begins with an opening bid from each side that is far beyond what each expects to settle for. After haggling, the two sides finally arrive at a point of convergence in their bids. Although it resembles negotiating a compromise, this bargaining discourse is not confined to purchase situations; the marketplace is an analogy. Each side presents a position and then argues for a solution to the problem that fits that position. Then both sides bargain to modify each other's position and their own until a solution to the problem is reached. This is communication exchange that involves two or more parties. It cannot be carried out by only one party, unlike narrative or analogy or syllogistic reasoning, which can be within one's own head or from one to another person or from one to many. Bargaining takes at least two. It is a problem-solving approach favored by many collectivist cultures where the process of reaching a solution is a collective one, rather than a task for one individual.

The Role and Force of Words

The Relative Importance of Encoding Messages in Words

Words are inventive tools for communication, and the enjoyment of using this toolbox of symbols varies from culture to culture. In low context-cultures, the role of words is informational; in those cultures, "Subtlety and allusiveness in speech, if grasped at all, serve little purpose."[23]

Meaning is encoded explicitly in low-context cultures. Not to encode messages explicitly is to risk being misunderstood in Britain, Germany, and Switzerland. Good communication is saying clearly what you mean. Saying something other than what you mean is a waste of time, if not downright deceptive. The self-deprecation that is appropriate in Chinese culture, where boasting or putting one's self forward disturbs social harmony, is inappropriate in the United States or Canada, where people are often taken at their word about their worth—say, in a job interview. From early childhood, quickness in verbalizing perceptions about the world is rewarded in the culture of the United States.

Communication can also be achieved without words, of course, but *actions instead of* words are employed fairly frequently in high-context cultures.

In the following Chinese trainees' tea episode, communication occurred in the behavior (serving boiled water) that followed the invitation to drink tea. Later, after prompting, communication occurred in the worded messages that contained consideration for the teacher's situation, and the unworded message about unclear understanding of possible obligation on the trainees' part. Communication was taking place on several levels at once. Encoding messages in words often has low priority. In this case, the behavior was the loudest communication.

In Focus

In a training session to orient mainland Chinese to North American work practices, one of the authors delivered a half-day session about "putting messages into words." The theme was that in North American business environments, if you have a problem, you should articulate it to someone rather than struggle along trying to cope in silence.

At midday, the trainer and trainees sat together around their conference table to eat lunches they had brought. The room had a kettle along with a box of Chinese tea so the trainees could enjoy a cup of tea with their lunch and throughout the day. The trainees were not accustomed to having trainers eat lunch with them, but nevertheless they graciously asked her if she would like some tea. She said yes, thank you very much, she would like tea.

A few minutes later, she was politely presented with a cup of boiled water. "Where is the tea?" she asked. "All gone," she was told. "When?" "A few days ago." "Why," she asked, "didn't anyone say anything sooner?"

After some exploratory discussion, several reasons emerged. One trainee volunteered that they weren't sure the trainer, a teacher who automatically had high status in their eyes, was the right person to ask about something like tea. They didn't want to insult her. Another trainee said they didn't want to mention the exhausted tea supply to the trainer in case she felt personally obliged to buy tea with her own money. They weren't certain the program had funds for additional tea for her to be reimbursed if she did buy them tea. Also, they felt perhaps they should not have drunk up the tea so soon or should have replaced the tea themselves, although that meant the risk of an expenditure that might turn out to be unnecessary.

No doubt the unannounced presence of a trainer at their lunch table raised another uneasy question in their minds: Were they supposed to have reserved some tea in case a trainer decided to have some? Finally, a young man offered the opinion that in China the person who identified a problem was then identified *with* the problem and in his words, "became the problem." It was better not to draw attention to a problem, he said, and the others agreed that this could be true.

This episode says a number of things about expectations by the trainer and different expectations by the trainees about communication. The Chinese were conscious of the social impact of their words and therefore chose to communicate in actions rather than risk a consequence that was difficult for them to calculate accurately. The act of offering a cup of boiled water in a context where tea was expected was as eloquent as any specifically worded message.

In high-context cultures, the purpose of communication is often socially lubricative. That is, communication between organizations and their representatives has a responsibility first to sustain relationships, and only within the context of a relationship does it then have a responsibility to transmit information.

In general, people from Latin cultures enjoy talk as one of the great pleasures of life. Mexicans love to spend time talking with friends. Italians claim talk with friends is a sign of a good life. Not all that is verbalized is taken literally, but enjoyment comes from the act of verbal—and nonverbal—connection with others. Lots of noise characterizes conversation, and often two or more people talk at one time. Mediterranean and Hispanic cultures are relatively high-context, and that means relationships and connections between people are important.

The Role of Words in Arabic Cultures

Arabic speakers enjoy verbalization, as the following proverbs attest.

- Your tongue is your horse; if you take care of it, it'll take care of you, and if you offend it, it will offend you.

- Kissing hands is fooling beards. [Inflated, indirect methods, not going straight to the point, can succeed with the elders.]
- Humming in one's ear [making incessant complaints] is more [effective] than magic.
- Kiss the dog on his mouth [sweet-talk him] until you get what you need out of him.
- [You might as well] Blow in a torn bagpipe [when no one is listening].
- Don't argue with a stupid person; don't allow him to argue with you.
- Raise your voice; otherwise their arguments will beat you.[24]

Arabic is the language of the *Qur'an,* the language Allah chose to reveal His truth to Mohammad, and that makes it a holy language. Muslims believe it is precise and unchanging in meaning, and that a critical response to the language is inappropriate. "The reader is not trained to interact with the text as in [English-speaking] cultures, mentally editing and disputing points. He or she does not easily distinguish more or less significant points."[25] Furthermore, the structure of Arabic lends itself to combinations of ideas, strung together. In English, this would be something like compound phrases joined by *and.* This can make Arabic writing or speech seem unfocused when translated into a language that encodes separate ideas efficiently. Arabic is superb for elaborations, however, and Arabic speakers value the ability to embellish utterances.

Arabic was used by nomadic Bedouin tribes long before it was written down. The *Qur'an* was the first "book" in Arabic, and it was only written down after the revelations to the Prophet Mohammed had been transmitted orally. Classical Arabic lends itself to memory and oral transmission because it uses repetition: of sounds and of phrases. Related words repeat the same syllables. Arabic words (like Hebrew) have three-consonant roots with vowels around the consonants. Cognates (related words) thus have the same syllables/sounds. The consonants *k-t-b* for instance are the roots that mean *write* and produce *kitâb* (*book*), *kâtib* (*writer*), *kâtaba* (*he wrote*), *kutiba* (*it was written*), *yaktubu* (*he writes*), *maktûb* (*written*), *kutub* (*books,* plural), *mukâtaba* (*correspondence*), *takâtaba* (*he corresponded with someone*), *maktaba* (*library*), and *maktabun* (*office*).[26]

Exaggeration, figures of speech, and repetition are some of the ways Arabic lends itself to the exuberant use of words. Arabic-speaking cultures generally admire the artistry of accomplished writers and speakers. In fact, the language itself has a power over listeners and readers; the words can have more impact and more reality than what they describe. So words can be used for their own sake, not for the meaning they convey.

It isn't surprising that self-congratulation and self-praise are part of the exaggeration of Arabic speakers. Describing one's own accomplishments, the high status of one's friends, or the superiority of one's abilities in exaggerated terms is usual. It shows one's place in the hierarchy through one's connections. Lavish language also protects one's face, and losing face is a terrible thing in Arabic cultures. All this inflation of language means that Arabic statements may use 100 words when English would use ten.[27] Arabic cultures are relatively high-context cultures;

members share experiences and memories of famous users of language. When speakers communicate informally, one may speak before another has finished, and it isn't unusual for speakers to interrupt and overlap each other's speech.

Writers of business documents in Arabic use many of the flourishes and embellishments of speech.

The Role of Words in Japanese Culture

Perhaps at the other end of the spectrum is Japanese culture. In Japan, words are not trusted. Many Japanese proverbs emphasize this point:

- Those who know do not speak; those who speak do not know.
- To say nothing is a flower.
- With your mouth you can build Osaka castle.
- Sounds like paradise; looks like hell.[28]

Putting thoughts into words has a low value in Japan, where harmony and contemplation are highly valued and members of the culture learn "to hear one and understand ten" as they listen to what has not been said. There seems little need for speaking, and when someone does speak, the preference is for understatement. Boasting about one's own powers or achievements is very bad taste. It is putting oneself above others, which is shameful in Japanese culture. This use of language is very different from Arabic speakers' use of language, even though Japanese culture is very high-context.

The Japanese also value indirect expression. Bluntness is regarded as unsophisticated or even rude. To challenge directly what someone has said is also extremely rude. Since people are not separable from their words, an attack on what someone has said is an attack on that person.

Listeners wait until a speaker is finished before speaking themselves. A moment of silence after someone speaks is respectful; it suggests thoughtful contemplation of what has been said. Conversely, interrupting someone is rude. Japanese listeners pay as much attention to what is *not* said as to what is said. They are "listening" to the unspoken context of the worded message.

The Japanese way of encoding messages sparely but understanding messages on many levels is *enryo-sasshi* communication. The image created by these words is a gateway which transmits messages through a small exit (*enryo*) and receives messages through a wide entrance (*sasshi*). To accomplish this, Japanese communicators use a number of speech patterns such as hesitancy, unfinished sentences, and incomplete expressions of thought.[29] Japanese thought patterns are clusters or webs; language patterns also move from one idea or cluster to another and another, but the idea clusters may not have an obvious relationship. They are related more by association than by cause and effect, like stepping stones that lead to a destination but are spaced out from each other and not in a straight line.[30]

Japanese communication is extremely polite. Attention is carefully paid to doing things in the proper way or *kata,* according to the rules of etiquette. In other words, form is very important. Communicators encode messages with form because that is the way they can show respect and concern for the face of the other person, and the way they can feel satisfied they are meeting the cultural expectations for communicating in the right way. Relationships that are nurtured with careful attention to the proper way of doing things are likely to be lasting relationships.

The Role of Words in English-Speaking Cultures

English speakers, in contrast, tend to use language in a bridge pattern that goes more or less in a straight line from the first idea to the next and so on to the conclusion. Unlike Japanese culture, English-speaking cultures value verbalization highly, and there seems a great need for using language. Above all, using the *right* word, the *best* word to communicate meaning is especially admired. Consider these English proverbs:

- A word fitly spoken is like apples of gold in pictures of silver.
- There is as much difference between the right word and the nearly right word as there is between lightning and a lightning bug.
- A man is as good as his word.

The general preference in the English-speaking world is for the most appropriate word. This corresponds to the legalistic weight words carry in the U.S. culture. Contracts are worded with great care; in business correspondence one is held responsible for whatever one has written down. In oral communication, however, slang, exaggeration, and overstatement are ways to flout that preference, and such vocabulary is associated with being young and hip. Words in colloquial (conversational) speech like *brilliant, great, catastrophe,* and *tragedy* refer to things that are not so tremendous after all. British speakers of English find that speakers in the United States tend toward overstatement. Choosing words carefully in English-language cultures has pragmatic value. It shows confidence in one's own powers to control and order things—a can-do mentality.

In English-speaking cultures generally, something exists when it is put into words; if it is not spoken or written, it isn't possible to *listen* to it the way Japanese communicators do. Words are taken literally, at their face value, in most situations. Bluntness is admired in many situations; speaking frankly about potential problems, for example, can be viewed as sincerely caring about the welfare of an organization. In meetings, being able to express your opinion clearly and perhaps persuasively when others disagree often results in praise or reward. Speakers often interrupt each other, especially in informal situations, or begin speaking before another person has completely finished, in a rush to get their thoughts into words and thus gain the attention of others.

The Effect of Language's Structure

In the 1950s, scholars began to explore the relationship between language structure and thinking. Benjamin Whorf wrote:

> We dissect nature along lines laid down by our native languages. The categories
> and types that we isolate from the world of phenomena we do not find there

because they stare every observer in the face; on the contrary, the world is presented in a kaleidoscopic flux of impressions which has to be organized by our minds—and this means largely by the linguistic systems in our minds.[31]

Now, over 50 years later, Whorf's hypothesis that language organizes reality has been largely discredited. Perception is viewed as a habit that can be learned and changed, not something programmed. Perception constructs reality, but the extent to which language limits perception is not clear. We understand our world by categorizing it, and the categories are influenced by our language.

We can see differences in thinking, in a simplified illustration, by comparing an English and a Chinese sentence. In English: "The interpreter who arrived yesterday has already visited the factory." The subject is "interpreter" and the verb is "has visited" in this simple sentence. The nonrestrictive clause "who arrived yesterday" merely says something specific about the "interpreter." We could leave it out and the sentence would still communicate correctly and meaningfully. The main message is in the last words: "the factory." The adverb "already" places the visit in time. The entire sentence moves in a linear sequence from the subject through the action of the verb to the object. It unravels syntactically the same way it happens in time: First the interpreter arrives, then he visits, and specifically he visits the factory. As he moves in time, so does the sentence reveal its meaning. The structure of English cause-and-effect sentences is sequential and linear.[32]

Chronology is the structuring principle. The English sentence can be shown as a simple movement through time, from left to right (see Exhibit 5.6).

The same sentence in Chinese would be structured differently, as a series of spatially related frames or levels. It begins with the word and concept that establish the largest possible context in the sentence: "yesterday." This frames the whole sentence. The next largest context identifies the interpreter as an *arriving* interpreter, as compared with any other kind of interpreter. The next more-specific frame identifies the interpreter, as opposed to anybody else who arrived yesterday. Next, the event is placed in a timeframe by the word "already," which signals a completed action. The next frame is the specific place where the action occurred: "to the factory." Finally, the most specific information of all is reached: the main message, as in English, is the activity that occurred: "visited." A literal translation of the sentence would be "Yesterday-arriving('s) interpreter already to the factory visited" (*Zuotian daozherde fanyiyuan yijing dao gongchan fangwen qu guole*).

EXHIBIT 5.6
Sequential Relationship of Syntactical Elements in an English Sentence

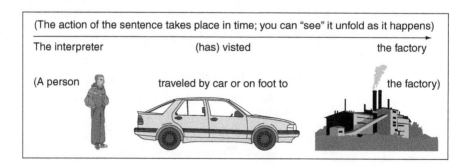

(The action of the sentence takes place in time; you can "see" it unfold as it happens)

The interpreter   (has) visted   the factory

(A person   traveled by car or on foot to   the factory)

The organization of this sentence is not based on a temporal relationship, but on the spatial relationship of items to each other. The sentence is a sequence of evermore-specific levels, like concentric circles, until the heart is reached. Exhibit 5.7 illustrates the concentric circles.

The result of this cultural preference for different ways of structuring thinking is that when Chinese speakers approach communication tasks that require more than routine attention, they tend to follow a general-to-specific sequence.

The indirectness typical of Chinese discourse is understandable, and even predictable, in view of the logic of the sentence structure. Similarly, English-speaking cultures' preference for linear directness and logic that reveals cause-and-effect relationships (usually inductive, arguing from reasons to conclusions) can be predicted from the way the language is structured.

Here's another example of how language patterns affect business communication. In a culture that has a rich oral tradition but not a long history of writing business documents, the written discourse will have characteristics of oral communication. Repetition, rhyme, alliteration, imagery, and hyperbole are important in oral communication to help the listener remember. Chronological sequence is easier to remember than another sequence; chronological sequence is what storytellers use.

These preferences, and others not discussed here, are deeply rooted in the mind and have a strong relationship with cognition—thinking, knowing, understanding. When we are confronted with new experiences and new languages, we tend to structure them according to our perceptions and previous experiences. When you communicate with

EXHIBIT 5.7   **The Spatial Relationship of Syntactical Elements**

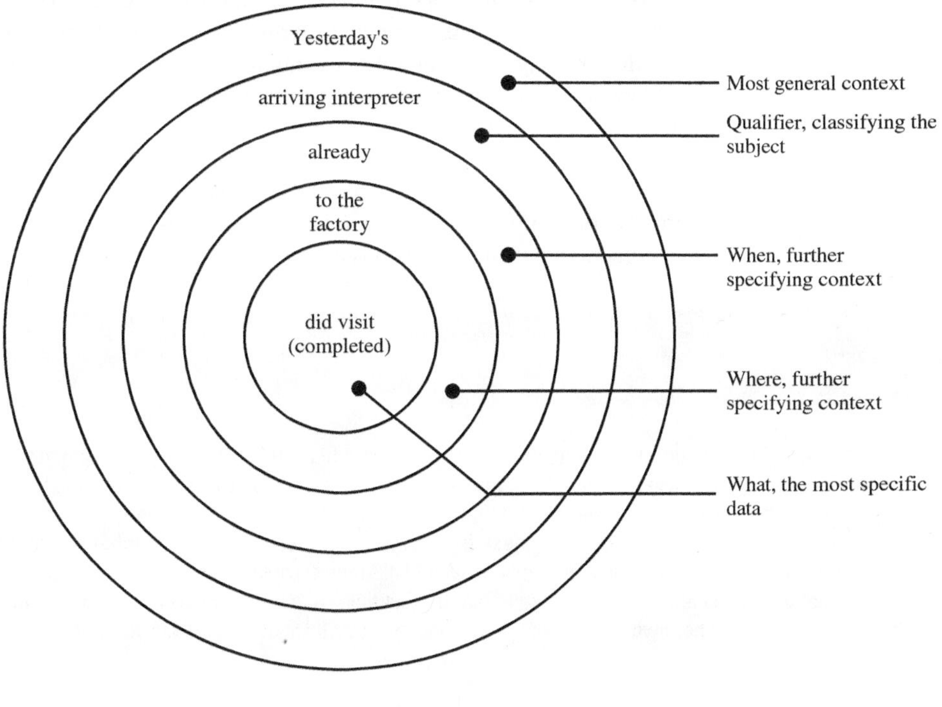

someone from another culture, you experience these differences. You may feel you understand the words and the message, but you may also feel some uncertainty about the communication because it is organized in an unfamiliar way.

Channels of Business Messages

Choosing the right channel and the appropriate form for business messages is a communication skill. When the communication is between cultures as well as organizations, the skill is even more important. In the United States, according to business communication guides, efficiency, clarity, conciseness, accuracy, and accountability are the keys to making the choice. A telephone call may be the fastest way to get clarification, but you may need something in writing before you can act.

Other considerations to keep in mind when communicating with a high-context culture are harmony, face-giving and face-saving, status, and ambiguity to allow flexibility. We've seen that these factors affect how messages are encoded. They also affect the choice of channel or medium through which to send the message.

This section considers channels of written internal communication, such as from a subsidiary to a head office (memos, e-mail, and faxes); written external communication that goes outside the organization (faxes, e-mail, letters, press releases, and customer communication); and oral communication (telephone, voice messages, teleconferences, and meetings).

Internal Channels for Written Messages

Memos, e-mail, networked intranet bulletin boards, printed reports, and other written documents are channels of written communication within companies.

Memos play different roles in different cultures and organizations. In North American businesses, memos are the standard channel of communication from superiors to subordinates, subordinates to superiors, and employees at the same level. (Memos can also be written to file or as reminders to oneself.) They can be formal or informal in tone. When informal, a memo is a convenient way of communicating information in writing—so there is a record of it—without the weight of a formal document. Increasingly, memos are sent by e-mail.

In Focus

Judith, a New Zealand consultant, thought memos would provide an accurate record of information without too much formality. So she wrote memos to her client, the owner of a family business in Taiwan. She put her comments in writing in order to reduce misunderstanding. But the owner never acknowledged the memos. So she wrote more. Still no mention of them. Finally, she asked Taiwanese friends what this meant. She learned that her status with the owner meant she could have face-to-face discussions with him. Memos are impersonal, and he thought she didn't want to have to get to know him. That made him reluctant to trust her.[33] She was responsibly using an effective communication channel as far as her own culture was concerned, but it was counterproductive in Taiwan.

As a means for sending feedback from employees to management, memos (especially e-mail) excel—at least in cultures where feedback is expected by managers. Feedback is not easy for managers to gather if subordinates are not used to giving it. Managers who don't solicit feedback will not receive as much as those who do. Memos may not be the best channel in these situations. Face-to-face exchanges, in which a wide range of nonverbal signals can be sent along with the worded message, may be a better choice.

E-mail and hard-copy memos are also, perhaps primarily, channels for managerial communication downward. What they signify varies within different cultures. In explicit, low-context contract cultures, a memo may have the force of a written agreement. It can be counteracted with another memo, but once it goes out, it is official.

In Focus

A Thai civil servant was told about an interoffice memo announcing his posting to a regional office. He had not been consulted, had not seen the memo, and had strong personal reasons for not making the move. He tracked the progress of the memo to its final recipient, the director general of his department. He explained his objections and was given permission to destroy the memo and thus cancel the posting.[34]

Apart from the priorities in the Thai culture that allow an employee to be transferred without being consulted and the authority of the superior to unmake the decision, a third point can be made. The memo lacked the legal force that the same memo would have had in a low-context culture. Its contents could simply be reversed by crumpling up and throwing away the memo. All those who had already read it would presumably simply erase it from their minds.

Electronic mail (e-mail) has made an impact on interoffice communication in format, tone, and content. It can be printed out, thereby providing a hard copy for records. E-mail is a less formal channel than hard-copy memos and letters, without established rules for format, and the tone tends to be informal as well. The content is often less well organized because writers are more spontaneous in creating messages. Sending them requires merely the click of a mouse, and rarely involves proofreading. As a result, follow-up messages are often necessary to cover information that was left out of the original message. Study needs to be done on the effect of e-mail on organization patterns: Does the ease of message creation lead to more direct organization? Anecdotal evidence suggests not; writers who wish to open a message by paying attention to relationship building do so with e-mail messages just as they do with hard-copy messages. The culture affects the way technology is used, just as the technology affects the channel. E-mail is not private, however; managers can read messages presumed confidential by their senders.

Employees have been embarrassed by seeing their supposedly private gossip about co-workers reproduced on company letterhead. It is always possible to send a "recall message" e-mail, but that can arouse curiosity and send more readers to open the message than if it is not highlighted by a "recall" message!

Instant Messaging (IM) is used by businesses for connecting employees and offering customer service. IM allows people to have a written conversation in real time. A line of text appears as soon as the next line is begun or a final punctuation ends a sentence.

Networked bulletin boards allow employees to communicate through an expanded informal grapevine, but these have been replaced by blogs in some cases. Fax—facsimile transmission of a document electronically—also is still used widely in organizations, especially when people need to see original documents. However, both fax and telephone voicemail can be delivered to a receiver's mobile phone, BlackBerry, or computer.

As mentioned earlier in this chapter, texting using an electronic handheld device such as a mobile phone or a PDA or BlackBerry is a way to send a written message that can be stored. Most text message writers use abbreviations, symbols, and numbers to communicate. English texting is a phonetic code in which words are spelled according to their sounds. Texting also employs keyboard symbols to create smileys—faces such as :o) (clown)—and emoticons—faces that suggest an emotion such as :`-((crying).

2 txt U transl8 swNdz in2 sht wrds, w few vowLz. L%kz llk hIrOglifs; itz mob fone cmUnik8shn. If U cant rEd dis, hlp is at www.transl8it.com:-). (To text, you translate sounds into short words with few vowels. [It] looks like hieroglyphs; it's mobile phone communication. If you can't read this, help is at www.transl8it.com. ☺)

Some teachers have voiced concerns that the phonetic spellings in text messages will spill over into other written messages. Text message spellings and symbols such as emoticons are used in e-mails, but mainly by young users. Texting is extremely popular in countries where telephone charges are relatively higher. The United States has been slow to catch up to the rest of the texting world, since telephone calls are relatively lower in cost in the United States.

External Channels for Written Messages

External channels communicate outside an organization. External channels include all the internal channels discussed earlier as well as Web sites, blogs, public announcements in press releases, news stories, contracts, marketing promotions, user manuals, and social network sites such as Facebook and Twitter, among a host.

E-mail networks enable businesses and private individuals to hook up to the Internet through service providers. Databases allow access to thousands of publications, making it possible to retrieve information without leaving one's desk. Google Scholar is making whole libraries increasingly available online. Web sites give companies a public face unlike any they have had before, and give customers access to products. The company story is available to anybody who logs on to the corporate Web site. Companies are now able to track individual customers through electronic databases so customers get the feeling they are individually recognized by the company. New meanings attached to "relationship marketing" and "customer service" and new terms such as data mining are corporate activities. New companies continue to pop onto the scene, and new technology is enabling entrepreneurs to move in new directions.

Structured Behavior Channels

You've already read two examples of deliberately structured behavior to communicate, particularly in Asia: the Japanese husband whose wife communicated annoyance through a flower arrangement and the Chinese trainees who served boiled water to announce the fact the tea was gone. Here is a third example.

In Focus

An American lawyer working in a Japanese steel company was part of a group that welcomed a visiting American delegation. But he found himself shut out from the company group deliberations he had been a part of before the visitors arrived. He had lived in Japan long enough to feel this exclusion deeply. After the Americans went home, however, senior members of his company invited him to Tokyo for a lavish dinner: the cost for eight people was over $5,000. Although the company behavior toward him during the Americans' visit was never mentioned, he understood that the lavish entertainment was the company's way of apologizing and reassuring him that they still valued him.

These acts of communication are carefully planned, with a beginning and an end, as an alternative to written or oral channels. This behavior occurs frequently in cultures in which discussing the situation would cause potential loss of face. But behavioral communication exists in all cultures and can be eloquent in getting a message across. A subordinate may signal unhappiness about an assignment in the way he or she dresses for work or participates in the social life of the office. A manager may signal pleasure with an employee by an invitation to lunch or a gift for the employee's workplace.

This structured activity is a communication channel that replaces worded messages. Thus, it is different from nonverbal codes in communication: facial expression, tone of voice, gesture, and physical distance are familiar examples of nonverbal codes. They are discussed in Chapter 6.

Oral Channels

When do you prefer oral channels in your job? When do you phone, drop into someone's office, or catch someone at the elevator or in the parking lot in order to communicate a message? Chances are it's when you put a higher priority on keeping things running smoothly than on the information itself. In low- and high-context cultures, voice communication has a more lubricative function, smoothing relationships, than written messages. In cultures where relationships are more important than results, word-of-mouth and face-to-face channels are more frequently used. You may choose business partners because of oral recommendations; you may come to a decision after talking it over with others; you may deliver unwelcome messages orally so you can establish a personal tone at the same time. As we saw earlier in the discussion on memos, written messages can seem impersonal and unfriendly to some recipients.

Managers in low-context cultures need to keep in mind that employees from cultures with strong oral traditions probably prefer oral channels to putting things in writing. Members of oral cultures place high priority on their word and will follow through no less willingly than if it were in writing.

On the other hand, in some cultures some kinds of oral communication presume too much familiarity for some situations. A follow-up telephone call from a Western salesperson in Tokyo who sends a mailing to prospective buyers will seem too aggressive. The proper contact is through a go-between or reference who makes an appointment and is present at the face-to-face meeting. That is an appropriate oral channel.

Voicemail is another oral channel, although the line between voicemail and written messages is blurring with technology that translates voicemail onto a computer screen and e-mail to voicemail (see the discussion under the section "*Where: Channels of Communication*" earlier in the chapter). Voicemail allows the caller to leave his or her voice in the receiver's electronic mailbox. Unlike a message written down by a third party (or no message at all), voicemail transmits some of the nonverbal characteristics of the message directly from the speaker. The listener hears it later in time but hears it complete, with the nonverbal qualities such as pitch and volume, pronunciation, pace, and pauses.

Teleconferencing transmits many nonverbal communication cues that other oral channels such as voicemail and telephone calls cut out. When it is too costly for a company to send people thousands of miles to meet face to face, teleconferencing can be a good alternative. However, certain restrictions exist: It is not always possible to see the nonverbal behavior clearly; of course, both locations must have the appropriate equipment; time differences can mean that one party is up in the middle of the night (as was discussed earlier); and only one person can speak at a time. This may entail having to learn a new set of rules for turn-taking in oral communication for some participants.

Still, individuals who are equipped with Skype and other video/voice software on computers and smartphone devices can communicate visually and orally with one another. Tiny cameras that sit on computer screens transmit live images of the sender to the receiver and can send images of objects such as models as well. People see and hear each other using a range of technology, and can send graphics and written words in the same transmission. To what extent is this communication a substitute for being face to face in the same room together? Some cultures have more flexibility than others in bending traditional conventions.

This leads to our final consideration: the formality or informality of communication style.

Communication Style

Formal or Informal: Hierarchical or Horizontal

In some cultures, a manager has reached that position through hard work, and the achieved status is important. Therefore, managers employ a formal writing style that emphasizes power distance and authority. Formality stresses the hierarchy of the organization and the manager's superior status in that hierarchy. Paradoxically, the hierarchy reinforces social harmony by reducing uncertainty about status. Subordinates expect managers to use a formal style; not to do so is to risk losing the respect of the lower ranks. The subordinates want to be confident their manager is indeed firmly fixed above them, being accountable on their behalf and looking out for their best interests. This style lends itself to quick decisions, since subordinates are not likely to question them.

Memos written from managers in these hierarchical cultures—Arab, African, Asian—sound authoritarian to members of horizontal cultures that emphasize equality. Horizontal cultures—English-speaking cultures and cultures from Northern Europe—give more priority to the equal status of employees. Their style is inclusive, and they play down the power distance between manager and subordinate. Indeed, the power distance may be slight, and the manager's authority may rest on the willingness of the subordinates to acknowledge it. This style tends to be less efficient than the authoritative style. If everyone has a valid voice and can contribute feedback in two-way communication, issues can take a long time to discuss.

Business communication textbooks from the United States instruct memo writers to adopt a friendly tone and an informal style in order to get the most cooperation from readers. They urge the writer to write from the point of view of the reader. When an issue is serious, formality indicates a writer's commitment to the issue rather than to friendly relations.

Managers who want feedback from subordinates may have difficulties, however, when subordinates are accustomed to treating managers as authorities who do not make decisions based on subordinates' wishes. The notion of two-way communication—up as well as down—may be unfamiliar and uncomfortable. Employees may wonder why managers ask them for information; they may suspect managers have hidden purposes for it.

When communication is structured with little flexibility for feedback or another response, or for other channels of communication in other directions, a grapevine communication system develops. In contrast to the official formal system, the grapevine is informal. The more rigid the structured system, the more the informal system flourishes. Studies indicate that the grapevine has more credibility than the official communication network and is often more accurate (see also Chapter 8).

You can see a flourishing informal network in organizations that have a hierarchical culture; the informal network usually involves someone in the office of the most powerful person and also involves people who have access to more than one department or location in the organization. The same is true in a general culture where the system is naturally more complex. Chapter 8 deals with the nature of information in detail, but here it is appropriate to point out that the informal information network may be the one you need to pay attention to in an unfamiliar culture.

Framed Messages

"Framing" is explaining the context of a message before delivering it. It lets the receiver know how to interpret the message. Is it a serious criticism? Is it a joke? The frame, like a picture frame, can be nonverbal, but here we'll consider verbal frames. The opening of a letter that transmits a proposal—"Here is the proposal as you requested . . ."—is a frame for what follows. Frames are widely used in English-speaking cultures in oral communication: "I hate to bother you, but the courier will be here in five minutes. Could you please . . .?" They pay attention to the status of the other party and the grooming of the relationship: "The temperature seems to have gone down, and I didn't bring a jacket. Would you please close the window?" Frames are particularly useful with requests to soften the authoritative tone. Even the context (frame) must be verbalized in low-context cultures so nothing is left ambiguous or open to misinterpretation.

Because frames attend to the relationship, they seem appropriate for high-context receivers. But be careful. They can make the sender—if a superior—sound too anxious and can make the power distance between superior and subordinate seem too small. A high-context receiver may prefer the ring of authority in the request: "Have the report on my desk by 5 p.m. today." Authority is a piggyback message on the worded message; it says, "I make this request because I am your superior, and since you are my subordinate, your role is to fulfill this request." A frame that suggests the roles of superior and subordinate are fluid and may make a high-context receiver uncomfortable: "I have a meeting at 8:30 tomorrow morning when I'll be presenting our ideas on the information you have been gathering, so could you please share your findings with me later this afternoon?"

As is evident in that last example, framing is adding explanatory detail to a message. Detail is an aspect of style, and the question of how much detail to use has its answer in the culture of the receiver. Detail, or volume of information, in a request suggests equal status between sender and receiver and common goals. However, detail in response to a request shows concern for cooperating, building trust, and entering into a relationship.

Summary

This chapter looked at the way culture affects how messages are organized, as demonstrated by the following points:

- The model shows that communication, whether interpersonal or interorganizational, is a *simultaneously reciprocal process*. Senders of messages are at the same time receivers of messages. However, the meaning of the message depends on culture and context. Organizations from different cultures experience greater potential for miscommunication.

- *Business communication is purposeful.* All business functions require communication.

- *Why, how, who, when,* and *where* are critical factors in understanding communication differences in organizations. When these factors can be agreed on, miscommunication is minimized.

The chapter then discussed ways messages are organized:

- *The direct plan is favored largely by results-oriented cultures* such as the United States.

- *The indirect plan is favored by relationship-oriented cultures* such as Asia, Latin America, Africa, and the Middle East.

- Persuasive arguments are based on different approaches in different cultures; logical arguments persuade some, whereas adopting the moral high ground, taking a dependent posture, or making emotional appeals persuades others.

- Reasoning in Asia is dialectical and inclusive of contradiction, whereas logic in Western cultures follows syllogistic rules that exclude contradiction.
- Reasoning in Arab cultures uses careful presentation of communication, through language, emotion, and authoritative voice.
- Unwelcome news is generally presented indirectly, or may not be said at all in cultures where harmony and saving face are important.
- Problem-solving messages may be organized in stories (narrative), in analogies, in syllogistic or inductive reasoning, or in bargaining discourse.

Cultures vary in the role they assign to words, as well as the impact words have. This was shown by pointing out the following:

- Low-context cultures encode meaning in words, while high-context cultures rely more on nonverbal communication.
- Arabic-speaking cultures enjoy the use of words in repetitions, elaborations, exaggerations, self-congratulations, and other creative patterns.
- Japanese speakers place little confidence in words and rely more on implied meanings.
- English speakers in Britain use less exaggeration than speakers in the United States, but nevertheless both tend to encode meaning explicitly in words; something has reality when it is worded.
- Language structure is related to the way meaning is structured and understood.

The organization of business messages also is connected to the channels those messages take:

- *Internal channels* (within an organization) of written communication include e-mail, networked bulletin boards, memos, voicemail, texting and IM messages, printed reports and other written documents, and fax.
- *External channels* of written communication include all the internal channels, as well as Internet Web pages, public announcements in press releases, news stories, marketing promotions, and manuals.
- *Structured behavior* refers to carefully planned nonverbal communication acts that have a beginning, middle, and end and are used instead of worded messages.
- *Oral channels* include face-to-face encounters, telephone calls, and teleconference exchanges.

Finally, the chapter looked at the formality of messages and the framing of messages, making the following points:

- Formality emphasizes status; informality emphasizes equality. In hierarchical cultures, formality prevails. In horizontal cultures, the messages managers write do not call attention to their status.
- Framing is explaining the context of the message before delivering it so the receiver knows how to interpret it. "I really hate to impose, but . . ." is a frame that suggests an awareness of the obligation the request-maker is about to incur.

Notes

1. Linda Beamer, "The Cultural Basis of Persuasion: Case Studies of Mexican and United States Correspondence for Sales," *International Business Practices: Contemporary Readings:* Proceedings of the 1995 International Meeting of the Academy of Business Administration, pp. 126–133.

2. Raymond Cohen, *Negotiating Across Cultures,* rev. ed., p. 20 (Washington, DC: United States Institute of Peace, 1997).

3. Lorand B. Szalay, "Intercultural Communication—A Process Model," *International Journal for Intercultural Research* 5, no. 2 (1981), p. 135.

4. Jim Mann, "Social Evolution," http://www.social-evolution.org/about.html (retrieved April 24, 2006).

5. Robert K. Englund, "The Year: 'Nissen Returns Joyous from a Distant Island,'" *Cuneiform Digital Library Journal,* vol. 1 (2003), §8, http://cdli.ucla.edu/Pubs/CDLJ/2003/CDLJ2003_001.html (retrieved May 30, 2003).

6. Ibid.

7. Ibid.

8. Rebecca Buckman, "Why the Chinese Hate to Use Voice Mail," *The Wall Street Journal,* December 1, 2005, Section B, p. 1. http://www.careerjournal.com/myc/workabroad/20060112-buckman.html. Retrieved 25 April 2006.

9. Edward C. Stewart and Milton J. Bennett, *American Cultural Patterns: A Cross-Cultural Perspective* (Yarmouth, ME: Intercultural Press, 1991), p. 156.

10. Based on Iris I. Varner, "A Comparison of American and French Business Correspondence," *Journal of Business Communication* 25, no. 4 (1988), p. 59.

11. Linda Beamer, "Directness in Chinese Business Correspondence of the Nineteenth Century," *Journal of Business and Technical Communication* 17, no. 2 (2003), pp. 201–237.

12. Philip K. Hitti, *History of the Arabs* (New York: Palgrave MacMillan, 2002), p. 90.

13. Robert Irwin, *Night & Horses & the Desert: An Anthology of Classical Arabic Literature* (New York: Anchor Random House, 2001).

14. This discussion is developed from Cohen, pp. 73–74.

15. Richard Mead, *Cross-Cultural Management Communication* (New York: John Wiley & Sons, 1990), p. 62.

16. Stewart and Bennett, p. 153.

17. Marietta Baba, "Decoding Native Paradigms: An Anthropological Approach to Intercultural Communication in Industry." Presented at the ABC Midwest-Canada Regional Conference, Luncheon program, April 27, 1990.

18. Nancy K. Austin, "Story Time," *Incentive,* December 1995, p. 2.

19. Martin Woolnough, personal e-mail correspondence with one of the authors, June 2003.

20. Aurea Carpenter, "What Comes First," *London Times,* Features Section, February 22, 1992.

21. Linda Beamer, paper entitled "Chess and Go as Metaphors for American–Chinese Business Negotiations," presented at the conference on East–West Communication: Challenges for the New Century. Hong Kong Baptist University, Hong Kong, November 1997.

22. Mead, p. 115.

23. Cohen, p. 27.

24. "Arabic Proverbs," http://www.arabji.com/proverb (retrieved June 25, 2003).

25. Mead, p. 87.

26. Kees Versteegh, *Landmarks in Linguistic Thought III: The Arabic Linguistic Tradition* (New York: Routledge, 1997), p. 26; Barbara Johnstone, *Repetition in Arabic Discourse* (Philadelphia: John Benjamins, 1991), p. 54.

27. Larry A. Samovar and Richard E. Porter, *Communication Between Cultures.*

28. Sheila Ramsey, "To Hear One and Understand Ten." In *Intercultural Communication: A Reader,* 4th ed. Larry A. Samovar and Richard E. Porter, eds. (Belmont, CA: Wadsworth, 1985), p. 312.

29. Satoshi Ishii, "Enryo-Sasshi Communication: A Key to Understanding Japanese Interpersonal Relations," *Cross Currents,* 11 (1984), pp. 49–58.

30. Satoshi Ishii, "Thought Patterns as Modes of Rhetoric: The United States and Japan." In *Intercultural Communication: A Reader,* p. 100.

31. Benjamin L. Whorf, *Language, Thought, and Reality: Selected Writings of B. L. Whorf,* ed. by J. B. Carroll (New York: John Wiley & Sons, 1956), p. 213.

32. Linda Beamer, "Teaching English Business Writing to Chinese-Speaking Business Students," *Bulletin,* LVII, no. 1 (1994), pp. 12–18.

33. Mead, pp. 89–90.

34. Ibid.

Nonverbal Language in Intercultural Communication

Rana Zarvi from Lebanon has been working for a Swedish firm for several months. When she arrived in January, she did not think she would last very long; the short days and the cold winter made her wonder how anyone could live in such an environment. But now that summer has arrived, she is getting used to the climate and her surroundings. She likes her work, and her colleagues are friendly, but she has no real feel for them. What do they think? How do they live? What do they do in their free time? What are their hobbies? In her previous job in Beirut, for example, she would socialize with her co-workers after hours. She knew about their families, and in the office there was an easygoing camaraderie. Rana misses the enthusiastic greetings with co-workers and the hugs with the other female employees. In Stockholm, her co-workers are friendly but more distant. Rana is used to speaking with her whole body, using her arms to emphasize her points, and showing her emotions through her facial expressions. Increasingly, she is wondering how she is doing. Her boss, Arne Gustafson, seems to appreciate her work, but sometimes she has doubts. He never just comes out and says, "Great job!" Yesterday he called her into his office to set the agenda of an upcoming negotiation session with managers from Malaysia. Rana knows that the firm faces tough competition and a joint venture with the Malaysian firm would help open the Asian market. Arne discussed the negotiation strategy and gave her several assignments for the negotiation. He was all business, correct but without emotion. Rana is wondering: Is he confident that this Malaysian negotiation will go well? Does he have any doubts? What does he think is going to happen? Is she doing her part? His words sound confident, but during her time in Sweden she has found that she has not been very successful at reading the thoughts and emotions of her co-workers.

How often have we listened to someone speak and wondered what the speaker really was saying? We may agree intuitively with the words, but in the back of our minds we feel that there is more to the message than the words. We may even come to the conclusion that the speaker means the opposite of what she says. We may base our judgment on an evaluation of tone, intonation, emphasis, facial expressions, gestures and hand movements, distance, and eye contact—in short, on nonverbal signals, or the silent language.[1]

Although nonverbal signals tend to enhance and support language, they can minimize or even contradict a verbal message. For example, the phrase "I would love to meet with you and discuss this issue in more detail" can take on different meanings depending on the nonverbal signals accompanying the words, such as the following:

- A smile while pulling out a calendar will support the words.
- Going on to the next topic without pausing after the statement may indicate that the speaker is not serious and is not interested in meeting, at least not now.
- A frown and a search for something on the desk while uttering the words may contradict the message altogether.

Some researchers maintain that in face-to-face communication up to 93 percent of an oral message is communicated nonverbally and that the nonverbal elements are a much better indicator of the true meaning than the actual words are.

Yet the true meaning and the interpretation depend on a variety of factors. As we will see in this chapter, people from different cultures attach different meanings to nonverbal signals. As one example, in Western cultures eye contact can signify honesty, whereas in Asian cultures it may indicate rudeness.

The interpretation of nonverbal signals is complicated further by the fact that within a culture not all people use the same signals. Men and women often use different nonverbal language. Men in Western cultures tend to be more outspoken than women are; however, with women asserting their rights more, women's communication is changing.[2] People from different social classes within a culture also may use nonverbal signals differently. People from the upper classes or people in leading positions may be more assertive and outspoken in many cultures when they are communicating with people from lower classes and in lower positions.[3]

Nonverbal communication is influenced by a number of factors, including:

- Cultural background
- Socioeconomic background
- Education
- Gender
- Age
- Personal preferences and idiosyncrasies

All these factors complicate the interpretation of the nonverbal aspects of communication.

Needless to say, valid generalizations are difficult to make and always must be reevaluated and seen in the context of the situation. For example, in a Western cultural setting crossing one's arms may be interpreted as being defensive, rejecting the other person, or being closed-minded. However, it is also possible that the nonverbal signal simply means that the speaker is cold. The isolated symbol may not carry any deeper meaning. It is only one contributor to communication. To get the whole meaning, one must look at all the signals together.

Other nonverbal symbols may be interesting but not carry a deeper meaning. For example, when Europeans use their fingers in counting to five, they start with the thumb and go in sequence to the little finger. Americans, in contrast, start with the index finger, go on to the little finger, and count the thumb last. The Japanese start with the little finger and go to the thumb.[4] Although these differences are interesting, they do not influence the meaning of what is being said. A German manager who works in Dallas or Osaka needs to sort out which signals are important and which ones are not.

You may wonder why we are concerned at all with nonverbal communication if its interpretation is so difficult. The point is that nonverbal communication, because it varies so much and because it carries so much meaning, needs close attention so we can decode and get our messages across more effectively. In this chapter, we examine nonverbal language in several cultures, but bear in mind that these are generalizations; although the descriptions are true generally for a culture, there are many variations within a culture. As you learn more about a culture and meet more people from that culture, you need to adapt and adjust your interpretation of nonverbal language signals.

What exactly is nonverbal language? Although researchers agree that nonverbal communication refers to nonworded language, they use a variety of definitions that can be divided into two major categories:

- Nonverbal or nonworded communication includes *all* communication beyond the spoken or written word. It includes aspects such as the language of friendship and material possessions, as well as the nonverbal aspects of written communication, like weight and color of paper, format, typeface, and binding.
- Nonverbal communication consisting only of nonverbal language using the body, including paralanguage.

In this chapter, we will specifically examine:

- Paralanguage
- Vocal qualifiers
- Vocalization
- Nonverbal conventions in face-to-face communication
- Eye contact
- Facial expressions
- Gestures
- Timing in spoken exchange
- Touching
- Language of space
- Appearance
- Silence

Paralanguage

Paralanguage lies between verbal and nonverbal communication. It involves sounds but not words. The *uhs, ahas,* and *uhms* we use in our conversation are examples of paralanguage. Researchers divide paralanguage into three categories: voice quality, vocal qualifiers, and vocalization.[5] Voice quality seems to be more of an individual than a cultural characteristic, and so we will examine vocal qualifiers and vocalization.

Vocal Qualifiers

The term *vocal qualifiers* refers to volume, pitch, and the overall intonation or "melody" of the spoken word. For example, does the speaker raise or lower his voice at the end of a sentence? Does the speaker vary the speed of what she says, or does she speak very evenly? Does the speaker vary the volume between loud and soft; in other words, does he speak softly or does he shout? Vocal qualifiers differ from culture to culture. For example, a non-Japanese person listening to a Japanese man can get the impression that the Japanese speaker "spits" words out in clusters. A cluster comes very fast, followed by a slight pause before the next cluster emerges. Japanese women, by comparison, may seem to speak more evenly.

In English as it is spoken in the United States, a speaker raises the pitch at the end of a question, signifying a nonverbal question mark. If the rise in pitch is accompanied by a pause, the listener interprets this to mean that the speaker is waiting for an answer. However, if the speaker asks a question without the pitch going up, he may not expect or want an answer. The speaker may be asking a rhetorical question and then be ready to make the next point. A speaker who has finished expressing an idea typically lowers her pitch, signifying she is done. The pause indicates that someone else can speak now.

Vocal qualifiers provide important signals in turn taking in a conversation. If everyone in the group is used to the same signals, the conversation can flow and speakers seem to take their turns almost automatically. The rhythm of the conversation feels natural. In contrast, if people use different intonation patterns, interlocutors may feel that the conversation is strained, that one side is trying to dominate or is not contributing to the discussion.

Ending sentences with a high pitch in American English may indicate self-doubt and uncertainty. In French, in contrast, sentences tend to end on a higher pitch than they do in German or English. A French speaker may be very certain of what she is saying, yet given the cultural background of the United States or Germany, a listener may have a different impression and misinterpret the meaning based on different intonation patterns.

Vocalization

All cultures use nonword noises such as "ahem," "um," "er," sucking in one's breath, and clicking one's tongue. These noises may be used as connectors between ideas; they also may be used to indicate that someone is ready to say something or that more time is needed to think things over. Generally, the interpretation of these noises does not present a major hurdle in intercultural communication. The frequency of their use, however, varies from culture to culture.[6]

Related to the nonword vocalizers are fillers. For example, in English, "okay," "like," and "you know" often are used as fillers. The words have a meaning, but a speaker who uses them does not attach that specific meaning to them. The words simply build a bridge to what the speaker says next. The use of *hai* (literally translated *yes*) in Japanese serves the same function. Most Japanese use *hai* as a filler without a particular meaning. Germans tend to use "*na,*" "*mann,*" and others to similar effect. Fillers serve as a lubricant for the flow of the speech. In intercultural communication, people must be aware of the appropriate frequency and meaning of fillers. If these words serve as fillers, they lose their dictionary meaning.

Nonverbal Business Conventions in Face-to-Face Encounters

Nonverbal messages can be broken down into subcategories. Although this makes the discussion easier, we must be careful not to assume that speakers use nonverbal signals in isolation. In most cases, speakers use many different signals at the same time. We may move our hands, nod with our heads, smile, and keep close eye contact, all at the same time. The nonverbal messages that give listeners the most trouble are those which accompany words. It's the tone of voice, the look on someone's face, or the lack of eye contact that makes you wonder if you are understood. As we discuss nonverbal conventions in face-to-face encounters, we will start with the nonverbal signals that most closely accompany the verbal message and go on to those that are not connected with words, such as the use of space, appearance, and silence.

To some extent, we are able to manipulate the signals consciously: We may smile because that is expected of us even though we may not feel like smiling. In many cases, however, we send nonverbal signals without being aware of doing so. Those signals, the experts agree, are a reflection of our true feelings and reactions. One of the goals in intercultural communication is to interpret *all* nonverbal signals.

Eye Contact

In most cultures, superiors are freer to look at subordinates than the other way around. Eye contact, therefore, also is related to power and perceived power. If Alberto looks directly at his employee John, he indicates that he has a right to do so. If John lowers his eyes when Alberto looks at him, he may be indicating that he accepts his subordinate position. Of course, eye contact is only one aspect of showing power. Traditionally, men can look more at women than women can look at men. In the United States, for example, "ogling," looking at the other sex, may be interpreted as a form of sexual harassment and may even have legal consequences. Eye contact, as a result, is becoming complicated in that culture. European women sometimes comment that men from the United States are cold and don't know how to flirt, the innocent game of looking and establishing eye contact. At the same time, women from the United States who visit Southern European countries are often uncomfortable when men look at them. The looking is interpreted as offensive staring.

Rules governing eye contact are different in different cultures, and that difference can make people feel uncomfortable without being aware of why they are uncomfortable. In the United States, it is customary to look at the speaker's mouth when listening but make intermittent eye contact with the eyes of a listener when speaking. In China, it is the opposite: A speaker rivets the listener with sustained, unbroken eye contact, but a listener does not make eye contact or look at the speaker's face consistently.

In Focus

Two professors from the United States went to a university in South Korea to negotiate an exchange program between the U.S. and the Korean university. One of the professors was a native of Korea, but he had lived in the United States for a long time. The other professor was a woman who had originally come from Norway. They had known each other for many years but had not worked together closely. Before the first meeting with their colleagues from the Korean university they met for lunch in the hotel restaurant to discuss how to best present their proposal. They sat across the table from each other and talked about the business at hand but also about their personal experiences and backgrounds. During the conversation, the woman professor noticed that her colleague did not sit facing her directly but rather sat at an angle. When he talked with her, he did not look at her directly and did not speak to her directly. He seemed to focus on a spot on her side. She began to feel awkward but did not know what to do. She felt uncomfortable asking him what was going on, and she began to wonder whether there were cultural reasons for this behavior.

Since several cultures consider the eye to be "the window of the soul," eye contact or its lack is interpreted to have special meaning. In these cultures, eye contact is related to honesty. In other cultures, eye contact is seen as an invasion of privacy.

Eye Contact as a Sign of Honesty

"He couldn't even look me in the eye" is a common phrase that in Western cultures indicates that the speaker had something to hide. In North American and Northern European cultures, eye contact shows openness, trustworthiness, and integrity. One doesn't have anything to hide. If a woman from the United States looks directly at someone, she allows that person to see her eyes and decide whether she is trustworthy. Someone who does not make eye contact is considered shifty and makes the listener suspicious. In that case, the defenses go up and one becomes more careful. People from all cultures carry their cultural attitudes toward eye contact with them, and like most aspects of nonverbal behavior, eye contact does not travel easily across cultural boundaries. In most cases, we don't consciously think of eye contact; we do it subconsciously. As a result, habits relating to eye contact are difficult to change.

Arab cultures, even more than Western cultures, use very intense eye contact and concentrate on eye movement to read real intentions. The feeling is that the eye does not lie. To see the eye more clearly, Arabs move closer, and that makes non-Arabs uncomfortable. This links eye contact to the use of space. As we will see throughout this chapter, nonverbal communication signals are linked.

A person from Japan, for example, would feel uncomfortable both with the intense eye contact and with the close physical proximity. That person will feel even more uncomfortable if the Arab, in addition to making close eye contact and standing very close to the listener, touches the listener. In this case, the Arab is sending three very strong nonverbal signals, all of which run counter to what is acceptable nonverbal behavior in Japan.

In many cases an Arab speaker may not want to disclose his innermost feelings, yet because of the culture, he cannot refuse eye contact. Therefore, he may look for other means to protect his feelings and intentions. Some people say that the former Palestinian leader Yasser Arafat, for example, always used to wear sunglasses so that the people he was talking to could not follow the movement of his eyes. They argued that the sunglasses were an attempt to hide his true intentions and motives.

Eye Contact as a Sign of Invasion of Privacy

To look someone in the eye in Japan is to invade that person's space. It is rude. When samurai held power, a strict code of behavior was enforced regarding who could look at whom and for how long one could look, and one violated those codes at one's peril.[7] This has carried over into modern society. The Japanese may sit close together in an office, but they seldom look each other in the eye.

The Japanese feel uncomfortable with direct eye contact, and they want to avoid it. In addition, not looking someone in the eye preserves that person's private space or bubble. In a crowded country, the preservation of privacy by any means is considered important. When greeting someone, one bows and looks past the other person. If you do not want to acknowledge a person at all—for example, if you are concentrating on something important and don't want to lose your focus—you may simply look down as you walk past the other person. What could be seen as a slight or insult in Western countries would simply be a signal that you do not want to be interrupted. The degree of American eye contact would be considered staring and rude in the Japanese environment. Even on the crowded subways and trains, nobody makes eye contact. People look past each other. As we will discuss in greater detail later in the chapter, during negotiation the Japanese may look down past their counterparts. In fact, they may even close their eyes, which can be very disconcerting to American negotiators who are used to looking at the people across the negotiation table.

Facial Expressions

Words often are accompanied by distinct facial expressions. In many cultures, when people are surprised, they may open their eyes widely and also open their mouths. When they like something, their eyes may beam and they may smile.

When they are angry, they may frown and narrow their eyes. Although many facial expressions carry similar meanings in a variety of cultures, the frequency and intensity of their use may vary. Latin and Arab cultures use more intense facial expressions, whereas East Asian cultures use more subdued facial expressions.

Smiling

People in all cultures smile at times; however, the meaning of a smile may vary. Depending on the culture, it can indicate joy and amusement, but it also can indicate embarrassment.

In an attempt to appear open and friendly, people in the United States smile a lot. Everyone smiles at everyone. To those in other cultures, the American smile often appears insincere and frozen. Why, for example, should a waitress smile? Restaurants in the United States go to great lengths in training to ensure that all employees use the appropriate smile. Americans are surprised and puzzled that the rest of the world does not seem to share the American emphasis on the smile. McDonald's, for example, had a hard time teaching waitresses in Moscow the importance of the smile and the proper type of smile.

In Japan, people don't smile the way people from the United States do. One does not show feelings freely and force one's emotions on anybody else. Men don't smile in public, and women are not supposed to show their teeth when they smile. To guarantee that the teeth are hidden, Japanese women tend to put a hand in front of their mouths when laughing. The women who greet customers in banks and stores with a deep bow do not really smile by U.S. standards. They look pleasant, but they don't really smile at the customer the way an American would.

Germans smile, but not nearly as much as people in the United States do. They will say bluntly, "Life is severe, and there is very little to smile about." Germans are very reserved, but for reasons different from those of the Japanese. The Japanese don't want to intrude; the Germans recognize that the world is not necessarily a pleasant place. Life is doing one's duty, and duty does not necessarily lend itself to smiling. Walmart wanted to lighten up the poor service in German stores (Germans frequently say that Germany is a *Service Wüste,* literally meaning a desert as far as service is concerned) by insisting that personnel greet shoppers and smile at them. The Germans, while moaning about unfriendly service, were not impressed by the efforts. They saw the smiling employees as manipulative and insincere.

Koreans consider it inappropriate for adults to smile in public. Smiling at strangers is something the mentally retarded do or children do before they are trained properly. In addition, for Koreans, as for the members of many other cultures in East Asia, a smile often is an expression not of pleasure but of embarrassment. When a person from the United States or Europe might blush with embarrassment or become defensive, an Asian might smile. To avoid serious misunderstandings, people who engage in intercultural communication should be able to interpret a smile appropriately.

Related to the smile is the laugh. Americans can have a very deeply felt belly laugh that comes from the deepest emotions. In Arabic and Latin cultures, the laugh often is accompanied by expressive gestures such as arm waving and touching. The Japanese seldom laugh that way except among intimates. A laugh is not necessarily an expression of joy and happiness. Like a smile, a laugh often is an expression of being uncomfortable, nervous, and embarrassed.

Showing Anger

The expression of anger also varies from culture to culture in terms of both intensity and type of expression. In addition, cultural values dictate who can show anger. For example, negotiators from Korea are expected to behave with dignity and maintain face so as not to violate the emphasis on formality and courtesy. As Korean society has become more industrialized, younger businesspeople may behave less traditionally, but the influence of tradition is still strong.[8] Generally, older people, men, and people in authority may show anger more readily than do younger people, women, and subordinates. The boss may get angry at the subordinate, but the subordinate is well advised not to react in kind. The result is that the interpretation and the display of anger are influenced by culture.

One of the milder forms of showing anger in Western cultures, for example, is frowning. Depending on the context, frowning can indicate anger, doubt, questioning of authority, suspicion, or disagreement. In cultures in which the open expression of one's feeling is not appreciated, frowning may be much more subdued. The Japanese, for example, avert the gaze to hide anger; showing anger openly even through frowning is considered inappropriate in business contexts and may result in loss of face.

Another way to show anger is to shout and gesture. As we mentioned earlier, nonverbal communication signals often are combined. Germans, Canadians, Arabs, and Latins often raise their voices when angry. The Japanese seldom raise their voices when angry. Instead, anger may be shown by sucking in one's breath rather than letting it out with a scream. When Germans are angry, their faces may get red and they may shout, but typically they are still fairly correct in the way they address the opponent. Many would still call the opponent "*Sie*" (the formal address for "you") even if they throw all sorts of epithets at him.

Some cultures use intense and expressive gesturing to show anger. People from the Middle East accompany their verbal tirades with big gestures. The whole body is involved in showing anger and outrage as if to illustrate that the entire person is affected. Showing anger means not just a battle of words but a battle of one's entire existence.

Research in Korean companies has revealed the surprising fact that Korean managers often show anger toward subordinates not only with verbal criticism but also with nonverbal acts of violence—even throwing coffee on a subordinate or causing physical injury![9] This is surprising behavior because it is so different from what is known of Asian attention to face and harmony. It also shows that people in cultures in the same geographic area may act very differently.

Asian cultures tend to restrict the range of facial expressions by Western standards. As a result, anger is not expressed openly in work environments in many Asian cultures. People from Asian cultures are able to read the message of the subdued nonverbal facial communication of anger, but people from Western cultures tend to have a hard time deciphering the code. Compared with Japanese culture, facial expressions in Arabic cultures tend to overstate feelings such as anger. From the facial expression, an outsider may find it hard to determine how angry a person from the Middle East really is. Nonverbal and verbal communication in Arabic cultures tends toward greater expressiveness and emotion. Eloquence is valued in Arabic cultures, and how one says something is as important as what one says. Arabic speakers repeat ideas, phrases, and words to show sincerity about what they are saying, and sometimes to show authenticity of authority. Outsiders may easily interpret the show of emotion as anger.[10] The point is that people from the same culture have no trouble reading the message. The problem comes when people cross cultural boundaries and enter a different system of communicating through facial expressions and gestures.

Gestures

Head Movements

In most cultures, nodding one's head is seen as agreeing. Shaking one's head is seen as rejecting, although Bulgarians do the opposite—they shake their heads when agreeing. In southern India, moving one's head from side to side is not a negation. Even in this area where most cultures agree, there is some disagreement.

A speaker may nod her head to affirm what she is saying and emphasize the verbal message. The listener may nod to signal understanding and approval. Nodding can be a signal that the listener understands and that the speaker can continue with the discussion.

A lowered head in Western culture can signify defeat or uncertainty. In Asian cultures, lowering one's head may represent accepting one's place in the hierarchy, but it also may be an indication of intent listening. Japanese managers, for example, frequently lower their heads and close their eyes during negotiations. Americans see this as a lack of interest or even disrespect; for the Japanese, this may merely be natural listening behavior. In contrast, tilting the head upward in Western cultures is interpreted as being arrogant, as is illustrated in the expression "His nose was in the air."

Arm Movements

Arm movements take up space and thus enlarge the size of the speaker. A speaker who uses big arm movements can intimidate the listener and appear more powerful. In most cultures, men tend to use larger gestures than women do.

When a businessman from the United States wants to emphasize a point in a discussion, he may pound his fist on the table and underline his statements with staccato drumming of the table. Businesswomen in the United States in the same situation use far fewer arm and hand movements. However, compared with Japanese women, American women use very expressive arm movements.

Japanese men use far fewer arm movements than do both men and women from the United States. Personal space in Japan is limited, and big arm movements could invade someone's private space. In addition, big gestures draw attention to the speaker and single him out from the group, thereby threatening the harmony of the group. Someone from a more openly expressive culture may interpret the subdued arm and body movements of a Japanese person as submissive or timid. A non-Japanese negotiator may even think that the Japanese businessperson is not interested and does not care about the discussion. Yet by Japanese standards this person may be quite expressive. People who are used to expressive gestures often have difficulty recognizing and interpreting subdued gestures. They may be so busy talking with their arms that they don't hear the body language of the other person. The person from the subdued culture, however, may be overwhelmed by the gestures that he too has difficulty understanding. The gestures seem to scream at him.

Arab men use their arms even more than men from the United States do. Gestures and waving of the arms accompany almost every spoken word and seem to embrace a wide space. Arm movements can signal happiness but also anger (see the earlier discussion in the "Showing Anger" section of this chapter). The expansive gestures run parallel to the hyperbole in the spoken language. The exaggeration and repetition help establish credibility and seriousness. In the process of waving his arms, an Arab may touch the listener occasionally. For Arabs, words do not seem to be sufficient to express thoughts. The nonverbal signals do not just accompany the spoken word; they are an integral part of the verbal message.[11]

In Focus

One of the authors videotaped students making oral presentations in English and in their native languages to see if the nonverbal codes differed in the same speaker. These presentations seemed to indicate that nonverbal codes learned with a specific language did not transfer to another language. For example, an Iranian student, when speaking Farsi, put his hands behind his back in a gesture of respect, straightened his back, and spoke with his chin up, making eye contact only with the professor, the authority figure. When the same student gave his presentation in English, he looked like an ordinary American student, keeping one hand in his pocket, occasionally shifting his weight from one foot to the other, and maintaining eye contact with everyone in the room.

It would be interesting to see the extent to which the change in body movements was a conscious effort to fit into American culture and the extent to which it was a subconscious connection of English with a certain set of nonverbal signals.

As we discussed in Chapter 2, English is used frequently in international business, but many businesspeople speak English as a foreign language. Do those businesspeople synchronize their nonverbal communication with English nonverbals or with nonverbals from their native culture? If they synchronize it with English nonverbal signals, which nonverbal patterns do they use? Those of Great Britain, the United States, Australia, New Zealand, or India? Unless a businessperson is fluent linguistically and culturally, she probably will combine English with nonverbals from her own culture.

Posture

The way we sit, stand, and walk sends a nonverbal message. In Western culture, standing tall conveys confidence. A confident person stands erect with the shoulders back and the head up. The posture signals, "I am not afraid of anything." The appropriate posture is related to a person's status in society. For example, a manager may stand erect when talking to subordinates, but the subordinates may drop their shoulders when talking to the manager. In traditional societies, the person lower in the hierarchy may be expected to prostrate himself in front of the tribal chief or village elder to show respect. Although this form of showing respect and submission is not practiced in intercultural business communication, an international manager needs to know what is acceptable posture in a given culture.

Although in most business situations people sit on chairs, in many Arab cultures men conduct business while sitting on the floor. In traditional Japanese businesses, people also may sit on the floor. The Japanese style of sitting with the legs tucked under can be very taxing for outsiders who are not used to that posture. In after-hours entertaining, the Japanese like to challenge Westerners to sit in the Japanese pose. However, young people frequently prefer a Western arrangement and increasingly find the traditional seating patterns uncomfortable and difficult. Typically, multinational companies tend to use Western conventions. Smaller companies and domestic companies are more likely to preserve local traditions. A business person, therefore, needs to be aware of the entire context of the situation.

In many cultures, women with middle-class and upper-class backgrounds are supposed to sit with their legs and ankles together and their arms close to their bodies. Women are to be modest and take up little space. When women sit in an easy chair, they seem to "borrow" the space; men, in contrast, seem to "own" the space. In Western cultures, this has changed quite an extent over the last two decades, and young women often are as relaxed as men are while sitting. When Western women do business in more traditional societies, such as Japan and India, they need to adapt the way they sit and stand to avoid giving offense.

The way we use our bodies when communicating indicates how we perceive our power, authority, and position in relation to the person with whom we are communicating. If the other person comes from the same culture, she can read the signals fairly accurately. If the other person is from another culture, she may have difficulties. She may interpret the lack of body language as rejection or the expressive body language as threatening when the speaker was simply using his or her own cultural style.

Timing in Spoken Exchanges

A conversation is a verbal exchange between people. Although the words are obviously important, the timing of the exchange also carries a significant nonverbal message. To examine the timing of nonverbal communication, we must answer several questions:

- Who initiates the communication?
- What are the patterns of frequency of exchange?
- What is acceptable behavior for interrupting the speaker?
- What are the patterns for terminating the exchange?

In their own culture, people know what the typical patterns for verbal interaction are. For an outsider, the timing issue becomes more complex because it is related closely to issues of gender, status, and hierarchy. In many cultures, men initiate verbal exchanges more frequently than women do, older people are more likely to start the exchange than younger people are, people with authority are more likely to initiate communication than are subordinates, and this behavior is carried into the office.

Questions 2 and 3 are connected. Whoever interrupts also controls the exchange. Again, in most cultures the patterns are similar, but Japan is an exception: Interrupting others is not acceptable. In cultures in which interrupting the speaker is acceptable, businessmen tend to interrupt businesswomen more often than the other way around. Older people interrupt younger people more often, and people in power positions interrupt subordinates. Although anyone can end the communication, frequently men, older people, and people in positions of authority are the ones who control the termination.

The roles that gender, age, and authority play in the timing of communication in all cultures might suggest that culture-based differences in timing are small, yet the differences are significant. For example, even though research has shown that in the United States men tend to dominate the timing of communication,[12] American women are much more assertive and outspoken in business and in public than Saudi and Japanese women are.

The following examples illustrate the timing behavior in three different environments:

- An environment that emphasizes equality
- An environment that emphasizes seniority and hierarchy
- An environment that emphasizes the role of men

These areas overlap; the Japanese, for example, value seniority, but life is dominated by men. In Saudi Arabia, women are almost banished from public life but seniority plays a role in the lives of both men and women.

Emphasis on Equal Status

For most people in the United States, a discussion is a give-and-take procedure in which people take turns speaking. The speaker gives clues indicating when he expects the other side to come in, when to wait, and when to be silent. The listener also sends signals indicating when he wants to get in. These signals are internalized, and most people don't think much about them unless the reality clashes with their expectations. One of the signals an American may use to indicate readiness for a reply is to lower the voice, pause at the end of a phrase or sentence, gesture for a response, or look expectantly at the other person. A person from another culture who is used to different rules for turn-taking may misinterpret the signals or even miss the signals that it is appropriate to enter the conversation.

Women and young people in the United States have become more assertive and outspoken over the last few years and increasingly influence and even control the timing of communication. Many companies proclaim open-door policies and strive to empower employees in an effort to tap the creativity of their workers.

They encourage subordinates to initiate communication with supervisors and express their ideas more openly. As a result, employees have gained some control over the timing of both verbal and nonverbal communication.

The millennium generation in the United States, the "Little Emperors" of China, young Japanese, and well-educated young people from Latin America, all seem to have a feeling of entitlement that typically does not go well with traditional values. It will be interesting to see in the coming years whether these young people will truly change the culture or whether they will go back to the more traditional cultural orientations as they grow older.

Emphasis on Seniority and Hierarchy

The timing in a Japanese conversation is dominated by the person with seniority, who also typically is higher in the hierarchy. A younger person will wait to be addressed and avoid eye contact while being addressed and while speaking. For a non-Japanese person, the timing of a Japanese interchange is difficult to follow because much of the conversation is nonverbal and the nonverbal signals are difficult for outsiders to decipher. The timing signals are more subtle than those in the United States, almost imperceptible. The verbal duel, common in Western culture, is frowned upon.

Emphasis on the Role of Men

In contrast to Japan, Arabic cultures are more verbally oriented. People enjoy the lively exchange of ideas. At first glance, one may get the impression that everyone can interrupt everyone and jump into the conversation. Yet older men clearly dominate the exchange and timing. Although many people, including younger ones, may speak, a few older men control the process. Women in many Arab countries do not speak in public, and in business settings women are seldom participants. The timing of communication typically is controlled by men. Women appear to be more reactive than proactive participants.

Touching

In many international business settings, the handshake has become an accepted touch, a "lingua franca," between businesspeople when they first meet, replacing or complementing traditional greeting rituals. But the type of handshake varies widely (see Exhibit 6.1). Germans and Americans prefer a firm handshake, which is seen as a symbol of strength and character.

EXHIBIT 6.1   The Handshake

Country or Region	Type of Handshake
United States	Firm handshake
France	Soft handshake
Germany	Firm handshake, for men, traditionally accompanied by a slight bow
Japan	Handshake with arm firmly extended, accompanied by bow
Middle East	Handshake and free hand placed on forearm of other person

The French generally have a much softer handshake. They may feel uncomfortable with the grip of a German, and a German may wonder about the limp handshake of a French person. Middle Easterners and men from many Latin cultures may put the free hand on the forearm of the person with whom they are shaking hands. As a result, the distance to the other person diminishes. The Japanese, who are used to bowing, may shake hands with foreign business partners but keep the arm firmly extended to maintain a greater distance. In addition, they may bow slightly and thereby combine the Japanese and Western greeting rituals. German men traditionally also bow when shaking someone's hand. The German bow, however, differs significantly from the Japanese bow.

The handshake with the bow illustrates that greeting rituals in many cases combine different types of nonverbal communication. As was mentioned earlier, the German and Japanese bows differ (see Exhibit 6.2). The Japanese bow from the hip with a straight back. Men keep their arms at their sides with the hands extended at the sides of the upper legs. Japanese women when bowing put their hands on the front of their thighs. During the bowing the neck remains straight. In German bowing, by comparison, the hips remain straight; the bow comes out of a lowering of the head. The German bow is called a *Diener.* This means it is a bow to, and a recognition of, authority. The word *Diener* means "servant," and so with the bow the German says "at your service." Older Germans may still do a *Diener,* but most people today just give a slight nod of the head. The bow does not fit with notions of democracy and equality. Former Chancellor Helmut Kohl was criticized by a

EXHIBIT 6.2
Greetings

Japanese bow

Men

Women

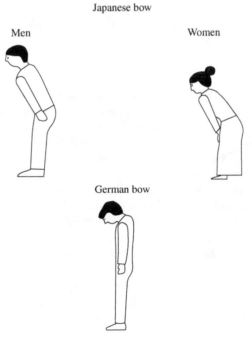

German bow

number of people and magazines because he did a *Diener* when greeting the first President Bush. The gesture was seen by many Germans as unacceptably servile.

In Argentina, when women meet work associates or friends, they stretch forward so that their right cheek is touching the other person's right cheek and perhaps kiss the air below the other person's right ear. Women do this when meeting men or women; men do this only when meeting women. Not to perform this greeting ritual is to appear cold, unfriendly, and even angry. In Lebanon, men typically kiss the right cheek, the left cheek, and perhaps the right cheek again of other men. In Estonia, however, cheek kissing is not approved of. Estonians expect a firm handshake upon meeting and again when taking leave of someone.

The German culture uses the handshake more frequently than does almost any other culture. In fact, this form of touch is the acceptable and expected form of touch in virtually every situation, whether meeting a stranger or greeting a family member. Not following the custom is viewed negatively.

In Focus

Ulrike Schumacher, a German student, worked as an au pair girl with an English family for a summer. She had a very good experience and improved her English tremendously. The host family welcomed her and was rather generous. In many ways, she was part of the family. However, she thought it strange that throughout her stay she never once shook hands with the family, neither at the beginning nor at the end of her stay. She became accustomed to the lack of touch, though, and did not think much about it; she adapted. When she returned to Germany, her family members were gathered and eager to hear about her experiences. As Ulrike entered the living room where everyone was congregated, she said, "*Guten Abend, schön wieder daheim zu sein*" (Good evening, nice to be back home again) and nodded to the group. Afterward, her parents criticized Ulrike for being distant and uppity in not going around the room and shaking everyone's hand.

In Germany, shaking hands is an accepted and expected greeting ritual; however, Germans seldom embrace. Hugging, even among family members, is rarer than it is in France and in Latin cultures. The handshake establishes touch, but at arm's length, whereas an embrace represents too much invasion of the personal bubble.

Increasingly, German managers who are working internationally go through training programs to become familiar and comfortable with different greeting rituals. At first glance, a German manager may expect a manager from Slovakia, a country in central Europe, to exhibit similar behavior patterns. After all, the countries are very close. Yet, managers from Slovakia, while formal during the first meeting, typically become less formal in the second meeting. They touch each other and even embrace. In their view, the German formality is considered cold and impersonal.[13]

The Māori of New Zealand, in contrast, expect touching as part of the greeting ritual. Māori businesspeople may feel left out of business meetings if the traditional greeting, the *hongi,* or pressing of noses, and the *karanga,* or formal cry of welcome, are not performed. They serve a similar function to handshaking in German society, setting everyone at ease. It would be unthinkable for a Māori function not to begin with both *hongi* and *karanga,* however many non-Māori are present.

People from low-context cultures tend to feel crowded by people from high-context cultures, and people from high-context cultures feel left out and rejected by people from low-context cultures. People come with certain expectations that frame their behavior, and when those expectations are not met, they feel confused, resentful, or excluded. All people from all cultures bring their unique cultural baggage with them. However, as people learn more about another culture, they adjust their expectations. They become more sophisticated and adjust their behavior according to the context and their degree of awareness of that context.

A Bolivian and a Dutchman who meet for the first time to do business will both be dissatisfied unless they understand each other's touching behavior. The Bolivian comes from a culture that is close, where people touch each other frequently while speaking. He will approach his Dutch counterpart with this background and act accordingly. The Dutchman comes from a much more reserved culture where people are more distant and cold. He too will bring his background to the meeting and act accordingly. If they want to work together, they need to come to terms with these differences.

How do we know what the "right" distance is and what acceptable touch is? As in childhood, we learn by observation in individual situations. Books can help, but lists of dos and don'ts, while providing some initial guidelines, do not give the underlying reasons for individual differences, variations, and changes.

Touching behavior can, and does, change as people adapt to new cultural environments. Sometimes they very consciously decide to change to fit in. When Vittorio Sanchez goes to Chicago on business, he refrains from touching the businessmen he meets because he knows that businesspeople in the United States touch each other less frequently than Latins do. In other cases, the adaptation occurs more at the intuitive level, at which people are not necessarily consciously aware of changes in their touching behavior. Urs Luder, a businessman from Switzerland, has noticed that his past few visits to Abu Dhabi have been much more pleasant. He is not as tense and nervous as before, and the atmosphere is more relaxed. His hosts seem more pleasant. What Urs may not be aware of is that his nonverbal behavior has changed. He does not avoid being touched by the people he talks to, and he approaches people more openly and feels comfortable putting his hand on someone's arm.

If we understand that touching is natural to some cultures, we will be less offended if someone touches us. By the same token, if the other person knows that we need our space, he or she will allow us more room and breathing space.

Above all, we need to keep things in perspective and not get offended each time we deal with someone who has a different relationship to space. Men in Africa hold hands with other men while walking down the street. Men in the Middle East kiss the cheeks of other men in greeting. Russian men embrace in a bear hug. Doing business with people from other cultures may mean setting aside ideas about touching learned in one's culture. During a television interview, the late Egyptian president Anwar Sadat, in the excitement of the discussion, slapped the former British prime minister, Margaret Thatcher, on the knee. Most people think of Mrs. Thatcher as properly British and fairly distant, but she was not offended. She correctly interpreted the gesture as acceptable in the Egyptian culture.

The Language of Space

The language of space is powerful. How close can we get to people? How distant should we be? Most of us never think about space. We intuitively know what the right distance is. Our use of space in communication is an excellent illustration that culture is learned and not inborn. Though our parents may have given us some verbal instruction on space, we have learned most of our behavior by means of observation. We simply do what is "right."

Arabs learn the same way, and so do Japanese, Mexicans, Russians, and the members of all other cultures. The problem is that the acceptable use of space varies widely among cultures. What feels right for us may be totally offensive to someone else. Space in many ways becomes an extension of us, and we feel uncomfortable with people who play by different rules.

Private Space

In many cultures, the private space is sacred, and people feel violated if someone invades that personal bubble. In the United States, that bubble is about the length of an arm, and we talk about arm's-length relationships, meaning that we keep someone at a distance and don't allow that person into our personal sphere. That bubble is a little bit smaller in France, but larger in the Netherlands and Germany. It is even larger in Japan, but much smaller in Latin countries and the Middle East (see Exhibit 6.3). The size of the private space also is influenced by social status, gender, age, and level of authority, further complicating the interpretation of space in communication. Our attitude toward space reflects our attitude toward privacy. If we understand how people arrange their personal space at home, we will gain insight into the way they communicate through space at work.

EXHIBIT 6.3
Personal Space in Several Cultures

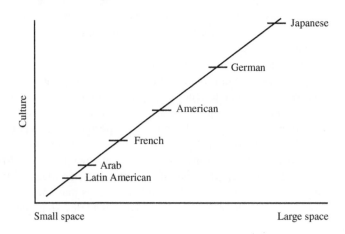

Northern Europeans cherish their privacy and arrange their dwellings accordingly. Property boundaries are marked carefully, and everyone ensures they are not violated. Fences and hedges separate gardens. Traditionally, a German house had a fence around the front yard with a gate that was closed and in many cases locked. Over the last two decades, the front gate increasingly has been left open, and today it usually is removed altogether. As more and more Germans acquired automobiles, dealing with the gate became inconvenient.

In Germany, elaborate laws detail rules on the use of the garden. Fences must be on the property line, and their height is regulated. In a country that is crowded and where sunlight is cherished, the fence must be low enough that it does not hinder the growth of vegetables in the neighbor's garden. Trees must be planted at a prescribed distance from the lot line so they don't shade the neighbor's property. Germans send a strong signal that they don't want anyone to invade their space. If necessary, legal regulations will enforce the cultural predisposition toward privacy.

In Focus

When Mr. Schubert came home from work, he would have to get out of the car, unlock the gate and open it, unlock the garage door and open it, get back into the car, and drive the car into the garage. Then he would have to lock both the garage door and the front gate. This process became too inconvenient; hence, the changing custom. Today, gates in the front are rare, but hedges and low fences around the front yard are still common, signaling that there is a sphere of privacy.

In a German house, the emphasis on privacy also is obvious. For example, all rooms have doors with locks, and the doors are closed and often locked. It would be inconsiderate to enter someone's room without first knocking on the door and waiting for an invitation to come in. In the common areas, one may enter without knocking, but the doors are still closed. As more and more houses have gotten central heat, the doors to the common living area now tend to remain open, but bedroom and bathroom doors are always closed.

In contrast to Germany, houses in the United States may have fences or hedges surrounding the backyard, but the front yards are wide open and inviting. Doors tend to be open, an invitation to come in. If someone wants to be alone, the door may be closed.

In Japan, privacy is defined altogether differently than it is in the United States and Germany. Japan is a crowded country, and space is costly; therefore, houses and apartments are smaller. Yet within this crowdedness the Japanese are able to create a private sphere. The private bubble and the personal space are more a creation of the mind than an actual entity. Americans connect privacy with physical space, whereas Japanese people connect privacy with mental space.

The Swiss deal with lack of space and the desire for privacy by creating elaborate rules. Many apartment complexes in big Swiss cities, for example, prescribe how late one can take a bath, flush the toilet, or use the washing machine.

Middle Eastern and Latin cultures also reflect their attitudes toward privacy and personal space in the way they arrange their houses. A house in the Middle East traditionally has few or no windows to the street; all the windows open into an inner courtyard. The family is protected from the outside world by walling itself off in a realm of privacy. Within the house, however, personal space for the individual is often limited; family togetherness is emphasized. To remove oneself physically and insist on one's own space is not acceptable and is not easily tolerated. Individuals are first and foremost part of a family, and the living arrangement emphasizes that concept. Within the family space, men's and women's areas are separated in Islamic homes. In many ways, men and women dwell in the same compound but live separate lives in separate quarters. Uzbeks emphasize family as well. When an Uzbek man marries, his parents traditionally add a room to the compound. The couple has one private room; the rest of life is shared with the family.

An interesting use of private space that blurs into business space comes from Arab cultures whose members traditionally do business with people whom they know. The men develop relationships that can be business contacts when they visit the *dewaniah,* the room for social gatherings near the front entrance of a house. The *dewaniah* is a kind of open house salon, where friends, neighbors, relatives, and business associates come to chat once a week or more often. Everyone sits in a circle, either on couches or on carpets on the floor, having first removed their shoes at the door.

Office Space

Our attitudes toward private space also are carried over into our attitudes toward office space. Generally, cultures that value a big personal space value large and private offices. In cultures in which personal distance is smaller, the size of the office is not as crucial. Japan does not quite fit into this pattern. The Japanese prefer a larger interpersonal distance, yet they seldom have private offices. We must keep in mind, however, that the Japanese, as was mentioned earlier, do not so much emphasize actual physical distance to attain privacy as they emphasize mental distance. In addition, the emphasis on group orientation in Japan carries more weight than does any consideration for privacy. The whole issue of office space in the case of Japan is influenced by other cultural values and considerations.

The following examples illustrate the idea that the arrangement of office space is a reflection of underlying cultural values.

In the United States, the size of an office and its location are indicative of a businessperson's success, importance, power, and status within the hierarchy. In a country where many offices do not have windows, windows are a status symbol. Top managers have their offices on top floors with plenty of windows. In a Midwestern university, for example, offices are assigned by seniority, and a goal of every professor is ultimately to have one of the rare outside offices with a window.

In addition to size and location, the furnishings signify the level of importance. A Midwestern insurance firm in the United States has three grades of wastebaskets.

The kinds of desks, desk lamps, artwork, and plants employees can have in their workspaces are dictated by status and level of importance.

The French are horrified when they look at typical American offices with their artificial light because both in France and in Germany every employee is entitled to a workplace with natural light. They are puzzled how human beings can work and concentrate in offices without natural light. Schools in Germany, by law, must have windows large enough that the square footage of the windows equals at least two-thirds of the square footage of the room. American schools without windows look like prisons to Europeans.

Office size and furnishings are important in Europe also. A manager who has a private office with a *Vorzimmer* (outer office) and a secretary is important, and everyone knows it. As in private houses, German office doors are closed. It would be unthinkable to barge into an office without first knocking at the doors, both the boss's and the secretary's, and waiting for *"Herein"* (come in). An office is a private workplace that one does not enter uninvited.

French offices tend to reflect the cultural value of centralization. Just as France is centralized, with every major road converging on Paris, offices are spatially organized around the manager who is at the center. The manager is the controller and observer of everything going on in the office. Currently, most companies are headquartered in Paris. The top managers control all activities at headquarters, and headquarters in Paris controls all company activities across France. Most French people agree that anyone who wants to get ahead in this environment must move to Paris. Ambitious people are petrified at the idea of being "banished" to the provinces. The centralized office arrangement reflects the historical developments and realities of France.

Office space in the Middle East and in Latin America can be quite different. Big multinationals in the Middle East and high-technology oil firms have a more Western approach to office space, but the attitude in smaller and midsize Arab firms is quite different.

The office is a meeting place. A businessperson thinks nothing of having several different persons in the office at the same time and doing business with them simultaneously. Westerners, who may be offended by the informality and lack of privacy and total attention, may have a hard time coping, but an Arab businessman sees nothing wrong with the arrangement.

Offices in the Middle East tend to be crowded. Importance is not necessarily reflected in the size and location of the office, and the typical American status perks may be meaningless. That does not mean, however, that there are no symbols to indicate the level of importance. Since in many ways status is conveyed by the importance and number of connections one has, a manager who has many visitors and receives many phone calls during your visit may show his importance that way. Where an American manager may ask her assistant to hold all calls while she is meeting with a potential client, a manager in Saudi Arabia may make sure that a lot of calls come in while he meets with a future business partner. Foreign businesspeople may be invited to the *diwaniah,* as described earlier.

In Focus

Two German women living with an Iraqi family for a summer had to see a doctor; one had an ear infection, and the other suffered from laryngitis. The family contacted a specialist, and the son of the host family accompanied the two women to interpret for them. The doctor had a long line of patients waiting outside the office, all of whom had applied for work at the Baghdad airport and needed vision and hearing examinations. The Germans and their friend were whisked past the line of people and taken directly into the office. The doctor, who had studied in Europe, was delighted to see them and interrupted the examination of a patient to serve tea to the new arrivals. He invited them to sit down and then finished the examination of the man. Next he examined the German women and gave them each a shot of penicillin. He asked them to stay longer and visit with him. During that time he continued his examination of the other patients, and nobody seemed offended (also see Chapter 3 on the simultaneous performance of tasks).

This scene would be unthinkable in North America or Europe. It is important to keep in mind that the patients were there for a routine check of vision and hearing and did not have to undress or discuss personal matters; even so, a Western patient would expect total attention from the doctor and resent having other people sitting in the examination room. Yet this is acceptable behavior in the Middle East.

In Focus

Fred Brunell, a French manager, is visiting Ayub Rabah in his office in Amman, Jordan. They intend to discuss possible joint-venture opportunities. They are still in the beginning stages and are trying to get to know each other and determine relative status, position, and power to negotiate. While Fred Brunell sits in the office, Ayub Rabah receives several phone calls, including one from a friend in the government office for foreign investment to arrange an evening together and another from an old school friend who is a banker. The banker is discussing some financial arrangement. The phone conversations are personal and illustrate that Ayub Rabah is well connected and has clout. Fred Brunell is impressed by the prospect of working with someone who can get things moving. In a culture in which connections are important, Ayub Rabah has shown that he is somebody. He has sent important signals to Fred Brunell, but it is up to Fred to interpret those signals in the context of doing business in Jordan.

Japanese offices also reflect cultural values. In Japan, the individual is expected to fit into the group and respect group goals and norms. Harmony is an overriding principle. As a result, private offices in Japan are rare and are reserved for upper managers; even then, depending on the firm, managers may sit or work in the same area with their employees. A typical office arrangement has file cabinets along the outside walls of the office. The employees sit in groups at large tables in the center of the room (see Exhibit 6.4). In many cases, regular tables are used rather than desks with drawers, and everything is out in the open. The employees are facing each other, with the leader of the group seated at the head of the table. Unless the nature of the business requires a phone, individual employees typically do not have phones at their workstations. Although Japanese businesses have undergone a number of changes, the traditional office arrangement has remained the same.

EXHIBIT 6.4 **Japanese Office Layout**

The Japanese believe that this arrangement emphasizes the importance of the group and the need to work together. When an employee needs to discuss something with a co-worker from the same table or from another table in the room, he or she goes to one of the tables near the file cabinets to avoid disturbing the rest of the group.

From the Western viewpoint, with its emphasis on individuality and privacy, this arrangement seems oppressive. With everyone watching, one can't even use the phone without the rest of the group listening. And of course private phone conversations, such as calling the children when they get home from school and making social arrangements with friends, are out of the question. Many Westerners would resent this arrangement, seeing it as a lack of trust (also see Chapter 3).

Another typical arrangement in a Japanese office is to have everyone sit at individual tables or desks facing in the same direction. Sometimes the manager sits in the front of the room, facing the employees, but in many cases the manager sits in the back, behind the employees (see Exhibit 6.5). Again, businesspeople from the United States or Canada would be uncomfortable with this arrangement and would feel as though someone were looking over their shoulders the whole time they were working. The Japanese, who are accustomed to the group watching and to being expected to follow norms, have far fewer problems with this arrangement. At work, the employee is first and foremost a member of the team rather than an individual with individual rights to privacy and territory.

If a Japanese manager has a private office, it often has windows to the large common work area, where the manager can look out at the employees but the employees also can look into the manager's office.

The Japanese office layout sends a strong symbolic message: "We are in this together." The welfare of the whole is more important than are the concerns of individuals. Although behind the scenes there may be quite a bit of maneuvering for individual recognition, on the surface harmony rules and everyone works for the common good.

EXHIBIT 6.5 Japanese Office Layout

Manager →

As a result, the furnishings in Japanese offices are not as important as they are in U.S. offices. Even in big companies the office decor usually looks rather modest by Western standards. Businesspeople from the United States, used to more lavish furnishings, may misinterpret the signals and question the importance or profitability of the Japanese business they are dealing with.

Furnishings also may signal political clout. A private business school in Tashkent, Uzbekistan, has rundown facilities. The school, an offshoot of a public university, is housed on two floors of the university. The two floors are in terrible shape. Holes in the walls, lack of paint, dingy lighting, and a broken heating system are all the result of years of neglect. Yet this business school is the most innovative in the country. Politicians send their children there because they know they will get a Western education. Employers in Uzbekistan and foreign firms like to hire the graduates. The manager of the Eurasia Foundation in Uzbekistan offered to provide the money for an updating of the facility, but the director of the school declined. She would have liked a better facility, but she figured it was not worth the price. She was convinced that as soon as the two floors were renovated, the university would all of a sudden find that it really needed that space. However, it would happily provide space on other floors, which of course were in bad shape as well. Because furnishings in Uzbekistan indicate power, the university probably would claim the two floors for itself if they were to be refurbished. In this case, furnishings and surroundings show power, but the power structure makes it dangerous to show the power through better facilities.

Public Space

The way people arrange and use public spaces also reflects their cultural attitude toward space and privacy. Businesspeople from the United States who go to Japan or China often comment on how crowded the cities are and state there just is not enough breathing space. That may be true by U.S. standards, but the Japanese and Chinese may interpret the conditions differently. Two people from different cultures may look at the same space yet come to different conclusions, as the following example illustrates.

In Focus

Aki Hayashi, a Japanese visiting professor at a university in Illinois, was going to a convention in New Orleans, about 800 miles (1,200 kilometers) away. His American colleagues were all flying, but he was going to take the train. He wanted to see something of the country. Brian Ober, one of his American friends, warned him that the train would be very crowded and that he would not like it at all. Mr. Ober was very surprised when Professor Hayashi told him that his compartment on the train had been very nice and spacious.

Numerous articles have illustrated the prime example of crowdedness in Japan: rush hour on the subway in Tokyo. They usually show a picture of a person whose job it is to push people into the train so that the doors can close. This phenomenon has been exaggerated greatly in the American press, however. In 2003, it seems there were still some pushers at Shinjuku station, but only during rush hour.[14]

When looking at these pictures one wonders how the throngs of people fit the cultural emphasis on personal distance and private space. How do the Japanese cope with that? Many Japanese do not like the crowded conditions, and increasingly people are moving from Tokyo back to their hometowns to have more space.

Most Japanese people have found a way to cope with the overcrowded public space of the subway system. In this environment, filled with people pushing and shoving one another, the Japanese riders become islands. Each is alone as long as he does not acknowledge any of the other people; the others do not really exist in his space. As was pointed out earlier, space becomes a psychological phenomenon. The use of cell phones in Japan is interesting in this context. In public places, the Japanese do not use cell phones because that would mean forcing oneself on other people. On the subway and trains, people text but they do not talk. The Chinese, on the other hand, talk on the cell phone in public and even make and take calls in the middle of meetings.

People from the United States carry their idea of individuality over into public spaces. Cell phones are everywhere, and they are used. Anyone who has taken public transportation or waited at an airport can attest that American cell phone users discuss their most private concerns in public without thought for the people around them.

Public places become an extension of private domains. For example, Americans consider it their right to walk and play on the grass in the park. After all, it is their park; their taxes paid for it. Government buildings in the United States are open to the public. Anyone can go into the Capitol in Washington or the various state capitols. In no other country is the residence of the president open to the public. Access has become tighter since the September 11, 2001, terrorist attacks, but Americans still see it as their right to have access to public buildings. A manager from Poland recently had the opportunity to visit President Abraham Lincoln's mid–19th-century house and the new Lincoln museum in Springfield, Illinois. He was quite impressed and appreciated the building's historical significance. However, it was the visit to the United States Capitol in Washington that really excited him. The fact he could go to the galleries of the Senate and House of Representatives, and that he could observe the Senate in action was absolutely amazing to him. In the United States, the right to access is considered important. In contrast, Schloss Bellevue in Berlin, 10 Downing Street in London, and the Elysee Palace in Paris are all closed to the public. Ordinary citizens are not allowed entry into the new Shanghai city hall. It is where the mayor and vice mayors, as well as all the key officials for the city, work. Ordinary people have no business there and are turned away by security officers.

The Germans organize their public spaces in the same way they organize their private lives. *Alles muss seine Ordnung haben* (Everything must have its order). Order is an overriding concern, and detailed provisions are made to guarantee that order. Germans tend to not have problems with this control because they grew up with an emphasis on order. As a result, parks tend to be clean and neat; the grass is not trampled down. This order is achieved through the use of numerous signs; *Betreten des Rasens verboten* (It is forbidden to step on the grass) is typical and is enforced strictly. For most Germans, there is nothing wrong with the content or tone of the rules, most of which are issued as clear orders in a negative tone. The emphasis is on clarity rather than friendliness. However, during the last decade the universal acceptance of the tight regulation of public spaces has been breaking down. One of the side effects has been more litter in parks and plazas. This change in behavior indicates that the nonverbal language of space can change over time. The study of nonverbal communication therefore must be an ongoing activity.

Germans tend to be very aggressive in crowds. The British queue (line up) at the bus stop, in stores, and at theaters. Theatergoers in London, for example, follow strict unwritten rules on queuing to get tickets; it is expected that everyone will follow the unwritten honor system. Germans, in contrast, form throngs and push and shove without any order at all, and they are surprised at the voluntary order of the British. One evening during rush hour, two friends—a German and an Englishman—wanted to take the Tube (subway) in London. As they approached the station, they encountered a long line of people waiting to buy tickets. As the Englishman turned toward the end of the line, the German said, "Waiting in line is going to take forever; let's just get to the front." The Englishman was horrified and explained that such a move was absolutely unthinkable and could not be done. The German, in turn, was amazed at how fast the orderly line moved; waiting in line did not take so long after all.

The Japanese tend to be even more disciplined than the British. The Japanese wait in marked spaces on the train platform in rows of three. People who want to wait for their next train because they figure that the current one is too crowded will wait in the same formation in a line right next to the people who want to take the immediate train. Everyone understands the two-line system. Once that train has departed, they will move over into the space in which passengers wait for the immediate train.

Generally, people from Northern Europe prefer a larger physical space and therefore stand farther apart in waiting lines. People from Latin countries, in contrast, prefer tighter physical space and stand closer. Seeing spaces in lines at EuroDisney, Latin visitors frequently try to fill in the spaces left by people from Northern Europe. This annoys the Northern Europeans.[15]

In public spaces, Germans also emphasize their rights. Individuals are expected to protect and insist on their rights. Children must be prepared for a rough and cruel world; therefore, they must practice insisting on their rights from an early age.

In Focus

A German woman who had lived in the United States for many years was visiting her hometown and took her two young children to a *Schulfest,* a school carnival. When her children wanted to ride the merry-go-round, they waited on the side till the merry-go-round came to a stop. Even though they had been in front of the other children, they were swept aside and did not get on. The same scene repeated itself several times. German parents were saving places for other children or were pushing their own children on. Finally, the visitor used her elbows, too, and got her children on the ride.

In the United States, this scenario would have been entirely different. First of all, all the children would have waited in an orderly line. Everyone would have taken one turn and would have been expected to get off after one ride. If a child wanted another ride, he would have had to go to the end of the line again. Everyone would have understood that the procedure had to be fair to everyone and not be based on bullying.

As conditions in big cities become more crowded, traditional etiquette and rules of acceptable verbal and nonverbal communication behavior may face major challenges. The pushing and shoving on Japanese subways, as was pointed out earlier, does not fit the traditional value of personal distance and harmony. Japan is not the only country that must deal with a breakdown of traditional behaviors. In Mexico City, for example, the subways are overcrowded with commuters on weekdays during rush hour and with families on weekends. Traditionally, unrelated Mexican men and women do not mix in public. In particular, unmarried women are protected by their families to preserve their virtue. In this traditional environment, men are seen as protectors of women, and women are expected to behave modestly and shy away from public places.

In modern Mexico, many women (young and old, married and single) have jobs. They must get to and from work on their own without any chaperon or male protector. In the past, young women moving about on their own were suspected of dishonorable behavior. Men knew that such women did not require the same courteous treatment they extended to their own sisters. Today, the lines are blurred, and many men do not know how to behave. In this case, the changing social environment has had a profound influence on nonverbal communication. During rush hour, many female riders were being molested by men in overcrowded subway cars. The solution was to separate women and men on the subway during rush hour. Now men are not allowed into cars reserved for women, and women who go into the men's cars do so at their own risk. The crowded conditions encouraged nonverbal behavior that was not acceptable in normal circumstances. As the environment of a culture changes, society must reevaluate its standards of nonverbal communication and develop safeguards to protect those standards.

Behavior in public spaces is carried over into offices and business practices. One cannot separate general cultural behavior from business behavior. The two go together. The way we approach people and the way we deal with space and issues of privacy have deep cultural roots. We may not agree with or like what others do. That is not the issue; the point is that we must understand what the others are doing and why they are doing it.

Appearance

The way we dress also communicates. Dressing according to custom and expectations shows respect for form and establishes a foundation for future dealings. Subtle aspects of dress can let people know where one is from.

In Focus

Two professors from the United States were sitting in the office for foreign trade in Poland, waiting for an appointment. A businessman entered and sat down, obviously also waiting for an appointment. Without having spoken to the newcomer or having heard him speak, the two professors looked at each other and agreed: another American. How did they know? The button-down collar, the style of the suit, and the wing-tip shoes were clear signals. They were right; he was American.

When one is examining appearance in intercultural communication, one must ask a number of questions, such as:

- What is appropriate business dress for men and women in a particular culture?
- What is the difference in attire when doing business in one's own culture and doing business with another culture?
- What degree of importance is attached to one's attire?
- What are the penalties for inappropriate attire?

In some ways, business dress for men is universal around the world, yet there are differences. The suit, the dress shirt, and the tie are generally acceptable, but the styles may vary widely. Europeans tend to wear suits that are more tailored and youthful looking than those worn by businessmen in the United States. The severe business suit, sometimes described as the IBM look, is rare in Europe today. The Japanese, in contrast, remain conservative. They tend to wear either gray or dark blue suits with white shirts. Japanese young people tend to wear T-shirts and jeans. They may have long hair in a variety of colors. On the outside, they look very similar to young people in North America or Europe. Yet, when interviewing season starts, these very same people become conservative overnight. They dye their hair black, get traditional haircuts and wear the traditional interview uniform. Arabs may wear Western suits, but when doing business in Arab countries, they usually wear traditional dress, the white flowing robe called a *thawb,* or in some places a *dishdasha,* over pants and shirt, along with a headdress.

In Southeast Asia, the European business suit, with its origin in cool and cloudy England, is giving way to a new uniform: slacks and a short-sleeve shirt worn outside the pants with a collar and an attached belt. However, when a businessman from that part of the world travels to the United States or Japan for business, he will wear a conservative business suit.

For women, dress is more complicated. Businesswomen from the United States tend to wear suits. Even though the suits have softer lines and are less masculine, and even though dresses have become more acceptable, business dress for American women in managerial positions is still more severe than it is in Western Europe.

A German student, after finishing her MBA in the United States and looking for a job in her native country, discovered very quickly that her American business suit was totally inappropriate for interviews. It was too severe and too conservative. No young businesswomen were wearing that kind of suit. A short skirt with a stylish blouse was the norm.

French female students who return to France from the United States make the same comment. They too find that French businesswomen dress more femininely than their American counterparts. These returning students feel uncomfortable in the typical American business dress; however, they also point out that although women in French or German businesses tend to dress more fashionably, very few are in managerial positions. That, of course, is another question, a matter of tactics, perhaps. If women want to succeed in business, they have to dress and look the part.

In Japan, women often work as office ladies who serve tea and greet customers. They do not have to worry about what to wear; the company provides them with a uniform, usually a conservative suit with a blouse, white gloves, and a hat (also see Chapter 1). However, as more women enter management training programs at Japanese firms, they may change their appearance to indicate the different status.

In Muslim countries, some businesswomen wear the *hijāb*, which means *cover* in Arabic, when they are in public. The Qur'an says both men and women should wear modest dress in the company of strangers of the other sex, although it does not use the term *hijāb*. Wearing the *hijāb* signifies Muslim devoutness today, and contrary to Western suppositions, women who wear it do so most often because they prefer it. In many places, women wear *khimār*, a headscarf, which is mentioned in the Qur'an. A black rectangle of cloth that covers the clothes and falls from the shoulders to the ankles, covering everything but face and hands, is called *abaya* in the Arabian Peninsula and Gulf states, *chador* in Iran, and *burqa* in Afghanistan, where it is often blue as well as black. When women are in a private place, or with other women they know, they do not cover.

In most cultures, dress also identifies a person as belonging to a specific group and having a certain status. Dress can offend, but it also can protect. With the growing number of assaults on foreigners in Germany, the Japanese issued a dress code for after-business hours for all Japanese employees in that country. Immediately, all Japanese had to wear dark conservative suits with white shirts, ties, and dress shoes at *all* times to establish them as businesspeople and distinguish them from other Asians who might be in the country illegally and involved in illegal dealings. The business dress, it was assumed, would identify a person as doing business in Germany rather than wanting to immigrate illegally.

With the growing emphasis on comfort and leisure-time activities, attitudes toward appearance and dress are changing in many cultures. In many cases, young people around the world have more in common with young people from other cultures than with the older generation of their own culture when it comes to dress. Jeans, tennis shoes, and sweatshirts are taking the place of formal business attire.

A few years ago, Germans were very conservative in their dress both in business and in their private lives. It was expected that one would dress up for the office and on Sundays. Every German man, from age 14 on, owned a black suit to be worn at weddings, funerals, and other important occasions. During final examinations in the *Gymnasium* (high school) and the university, both men and women were expected to wear black suits to acknowledge the importance of the occasion. Much of that has changed. The young people are very informal, and many go to interviews in casual dress. Although older Germans may bemoan casual dress as a sign of lack of respect and the general decline and downfall of behavioral norms, young people are enjoying the more relaxed attire.

If a person from a more casual culture with an emphasis on comfort does business with someone older from a conservative and formal culture, dress can become a serious issue. After all, dress signifies seriousness, credibility, and importance. In and of itself it may not be important, but it sends a powerful message.

In Focus

A group of professors from the United States attending a four-week seminar in Taipei were moaning about the heat and the lack of air-conditioning. The seminar leader, a Chinese woman professor, at first did not say anything; she simply assumed that everyone agreed on what appropriate dress was for the seminar lectures and company visits. When some of the professors started showing up in shorts and T-shirts, she asked them to dress up, meaning suit, shirt, and tie. The Americans immediately tried to negotiate down the expected level of formality. As a Chinese woman, she felt very uncomfortable telling the mostly male group what to do, but finally she had to be direct. The group was to visit Chiang Kai-shek's tomb, and there could be no compromise. She ordered suit, dress shirt, and tie, and the Americans finally gave in.

Silence

Many people connect communicating with doing something verbally, nonverbally, or both. Communication means action such as encoding a message, decoding a message, sending a message, and sending feedback. At first glance, silence does not indicate action, yet communication through silence plays an important role in all cultures. The importance of silence as a communication tool, and the interpretation of silence varies from culture to culture, but all cultures use silence at times to get a point across.

Differences in the use of silence can be best examined by looking at high-context and low-context cultures.

Silence in Low-Context Cultures

In low-context cultures in which ideas are encoded explicitly into words, silence often is interpreted as the absence of communication. It is *downtime.* Silence means that the act of actively worded communication has stopped.

Yet even in low-context cultures, silence is not necessarily without meaning. When someone is silent after being asked a question, the silence is an answer. The English phrase "The silence was deafening" describes this interpretation. When someone falls silent in conversation, another person may ask, "What's wrong?" The silence communicates a message. It may indicate that the receiver of the message did not hear the message, is angry at the message, needs time to think, or is embarrassed. Usually, low-context cultures view silence as communication gone wrong. To them it indicates that a rupture has occurred in the communication process.

Phrases such as *Reden ist Silber; Schweigen ist Gold* (speaking is silver; being silent is gold) seem to contradict the view of silence as being negative; however, when given a choice, people in low-context cultures tend to choose speaking over being silent. Silence is ambiguous; it must be interpreted, and the interpretation of silence is more difficult than the interpretation of words. Silence does not fit with a low-context culture's emphasis on precision and clarity.

For this reason, people in low-context cultures generally are uncomfortable with silence. They often feel responsible for starting a conversation or keeping it going, even with strangers. Passengers on a train that makes an unscheduled stop in the countryside, for example, may start a conversation because they feel uncomfortable just sitting there.

Silence in High-Context Cultures

High-context cultures have a different attitude toward the use of silence. Perhaps the most obvious example is Japan, although other Asian countries share the Japanese attitude about silence. The Japanese believe that silence is preferable to conversation. It is through silence that one can discover the truth inside oneself. Contemplation and meditation take place in silence. Buddha taught that words make truth untrue, and there is a view in Japanese society that words contaminate understanding. Reading another person's inner core, a kind of communication without words, can take place only in silence. Speech distracts people from true understanding. This attitude toward, and the use of, silence can become a serious stumbling block in the progress of negotiations between businesspeople from Japan and the United States. Most of the discussion in Japanese negotiations is in groups, and much is said through silence, facial expressions, and body gestures among the Japanese team.

Silence to the Japanese is not empty. Whereas Westerners typically view silence as gaps in conversation, the Japanese believe that silence is part of conversation. In a crowded country, silence evokes space; a person can be in his or her own realm through silence even when surrounded by others. Japanese speakers are comfortable with silence in communication and do not hurry to fill it up with speech. In fact, they may use silence as a very powerful communication tool.

Summary

This chapter examined the major aspects of nonverbal signals in intercultural communication. Much of what people say in all cultures is said without words or in addition to words. In many cases, the nonverbal symbols support the spoken word, but they also can contradict what is being said.

Paralanguage lies between verbal and nonverbal communication, as in the following:

- *Vocal qualifiers.* The term refers to volume, pitch, and intonation. Different cultures use different vocal qualifiers.
- *Nonverbal business conventions* in face-to-face encounters.
- *Eye contact.* Conventions relating to eye contact are related to position in the hierarchy. Eye contact has implications for perceptions of honesty and the importance of privacy.
- *Facial expressions.* Facial expressions have different meanings in different cultures. A smile can express friendliness or embarrassment. A frown can be an indication of anger or doubt.

- *Gestures.* Head movements, arm movements, and posture communicate a message to the other side.
- *Timing in spoken exchanges.* Timing behavior reflects the importance of equality, hierarchy, and gender relationships.
- *Touching.* Cultures have different conventions for touching in social and business situations. Touching typically is related to status, gender, and seniority.
- *The language of space.* We communicate through our use of private, office, and public space.
- *Appearance.* Dress sends signals relating to respect.
- *Silence.* High-context and low-context cultures differ in their interpretation of silence. In high-context cultures, silence frequently is seen as an absence of communication, whereas in high-context cultures silence is an important communication channel.

The interpretation of the nonverbal language is complicated by the fact that different groups within a culture often use different nonverbal signals. To be successful in interpreting the nonverbal language of a culture, you need to go beyond memorizing the dos and don'ts of touching, using space, making eye contact, and using facial expressions and gestures. To be successful in reading the nonverbal symbols, you must understand the cultural values that give rise to a specific nonverbal language.

Notes

1. Edward T. Hall, "The Silent Language in Overseas Business," *Harvard Business Review* 38, no. 3 (1960), pp. 87–95.
2. Deborah Tannen, *Communicating from 9 to 5* (New York: William Morrow and Company, 1994).
3. Kate Fox, *Watching the English: The Hidden Rules of English Behavior* (London: Hodder & Stroughton, 2004).
4. David Victor, *International Business Communication* (New York: Harper-Collins, 1992).
5. Ibid.
6. Ibid.
7. Ruth Benedikt, *The Chrysanthemum and the Sword* (Cleveland: Meridian Books, 1967).
8. Yong-Jin Song, Claudia L. Hale, and Nagesh Rao, "The South Korean Chief Negotiator: Balancing Traditional Values and Contemporary Business Practices," *International Journal of Cross Cultural Management* 5, no. 3 (2005), pp. 313–328.
9. In-ah Ha, unpublished paper presented at the IAIR inaugural conference, Kent State University, April 1999.

10. For a more detailed discussion see: Margaret K. Omar Nydell, *Understanding Arabs,* 3rd ed. (Yarmouth, ME: Intercultural Press, 2002); K. Versteegh, *Landmarks in Linguistic Thought III.*

11. Nydell, 2002.

12. Deborah Tannen, *You Just Don't Understand* (New York: Ballantine Books, 1992).

13. Andreas Unger, "Auf Tuchfuehlung Gehen," *Die Zeit,* no. 48 (November 24, 2005), p. 86.

14. http://home.comcast.net/~subwaymark/trips/Japan/Trip2003-5.htm.

15. Susan C. Schneider and Jean-Louis Barsoux, *Managing Across Cultures* (Harlow, UK: Pearson Education Limited, 1997).

CHAPTER SEVEN

Cultural Rules for Establishing Relationships

The U.S. company Homecrafts was in the process of buying the Swiss firm Alpine Treasures. The talks had been going on for some time, and David Goldstein was getting frustrated. Several months ago it had looked as if the deal could be signed within days, but then things just slowed down.

When they first met, the owner of Alpine Treasures, Louis Semar, seemed surprised that someone as young as David would be in charge of negotiating a transaction of such magnitude. Mr. Semar was used to working with people about his age who had proved themselves for a number of years. David thought that Louis was a bit stuffy and old-fashioned. The use of last names and the formality of the interaction made him feel uneasy. But in spite of the differences, they informally agreed to conclude the deal. David e-mailed headquarters to announce that the deal would go through shortly. He was excited and figured that the conclusion of this purchase would be a step toward his next promotion.

When they met to work out the details, David assumed they knew each other well enough to do away with last names. But when he opened the discussion with "Well, Louis, what do you think?" he could not understand why Mr. Semar addressed him as Mr. Goldstein. What was his problem? He had invited Mr. Semar to eat with him on numerous occasions and had inquired about his family and hobbies, but Mr. Semar remained distant. He answered all the questions politely but never gave more personal information than necessary. David considered himself a friendly guy who took pride in his ability to make people feel at ease, but in this case nothing seemed to work.

At the same time, Mr. Semar got rather frustrated with this pushy American kid. Why was he always inquiring into his private life? And the young man kept up the pressure to sell, to persuade him to take the money and retire. David Goldstein was young enough to be his son, and here he was acting as if he were a close friend.

After another round of discussions, when David thought things surely would work out, Louis Semar withdrew even more. He had built this company. The offer was good financially; he stood to make a lot of money. But that was only part of it. His heart was in that firm, and to sell out, and to Americans at that, did not seem right. In addition, he was disturbed by talk of reorganization and changes in employment practices. The firm employed about 100 people, mostly from the little town where the company was located. He knew those people; he had gone to school with them. He relied on them, and they trusted him. What would happen once the Americans took over?

David could not understand these concerns. Mr. Semar would be very well off; he could re-tire in comfort and do whatever he wanted to do. In his opinion, this indecision on Mr. Semar's part was simply ridiculous. After all, this was a business, not a family affair. And from a busi-ness viewpoint this was the right thing to do.

David was willing to offer more money. He carefully laid out his approach; he prepared charts detailing the financial benefits. He pulled all the arguments together showing why this was an excellent business deal that would benefit both sides.

Mr. Semar listened politely. He did not disagree with anything David said, but he asked for more time to consider the offer. Several weeks went by, and David did not hear from Louis again. As he began to realize that Louis Semar would never sell, he started to think what he might have done differently to make it easier for the Swiss owner to sell his stake in the company.

In previous chapters, we examined how various cultures communicate verbally and nonverbally, and how they organize their messages. In this chapter, we will examine how people establish relationships. As the opening scenario illustrates, people from different cultures have different ideas about what is important and who is important. They have different ideas about who has the authority to make decisions. As a result, the rules for establishing relationships and working together differ as well.

Respect for Authority and the Structuring of Messages

Different cultures use different symbols to show respect toward authority. As was pointed out before, those signs are neither correct nor incorrect; they are different. They are learned, and they may change over time.

Signals of Respect

Nonverbal signals of respect can be obvious or subtle. For example, as was dis-cussed earlier, consider the Japanese bow. The depth of the bow clearly indicates who ranks higher. The subordinate must bow lower, and if the wrong person bows lower, the ritual will be repeated until everything is done right. It can be an amusing scene with both sides continuing to bow when one party is a Westerner who does not understand the rules of the game.

In some cultures, people of lower status kneel in front of superiors and author-ity figures, or even prostrate themselves in front of rulers. People from the United States with their notions of equality may have trouble with those types of rituals. A man from the United States who worked in the Peace Corps in Nigeria married a Nigerian woman. As part of the ritual for seeking to marry the woman, he was expected to prostrate himself in front of the woman's grandfather, who was the village chief. Although in cities and urban centers those traditional signs of respect for authority may have vanished, it helps to be aware of expected behaviors toward authority in both social and business relationships.

In most Western cultures, younger people hold doors open for older people, subordinates open doors for superiors, and men open doors for women. Letting a person go through the door first indicates respect. Similarly, younger people stand up when an older person enters a room. In the United States, the tradition of holding doors open and standing up to show respect is changing. The cultural rules are not quite as clear anymore. For example, Jim, who has just entered the management training program, has received mixed signals when he opens doors. Brian, his immediate boss, frowns when Jim opens doors for him. Brian is energetic and athletic. He does not want to be seen as older or incapable. Mark, who is Brian's superior, appreciates the gesture of recognition. And then there is Gloria, a co-worker, who told him directly that she can open her own doors. As traditions change, it may be more difficult to gauge what is acceptable and appropriate behavior.

Guests are treated with respect in all cultures. In Europe and North America, the honored guest typically sits on the right side of the host. Middle Eastern traditions of hospitality dictate that a host will serve the guest and keep him safe. In Japan, the honored guest is the first one to take a bath, before anyone else in the household. In turn, the guest usually shows respect for the host by bringing presents for the host (also see the section titled "Gift Giving" later in this chapter).

Signals of respect can be different from culture to culture, and it may take some time to learn what is expected behavior.

If a person expects certain signs of respect, he or she may be upset if those expectations are not met. At best, the situation may be awkward; at worst, it may lead to tension or even open hostility. The following examples, involving Queen Elizabeth of Great Britain, did not result in an international crisis, but they illustrate the point.

In Focus

When Queen Elizabeth II visited the United States, people who were to meet her were given detailed and careful instructions on how to behave on the occasion. Protocol prescribes how to address royalty, and how to walk and talk in the presence of royalty. This carefully choreographed ritual was rudely shattered when a woman in Washington, DC pushed protocol aside and hugged the queen. The queen was gracious, but it was an obvious breach of etiquette that only "barbarian" foreigners would commit. The American woman was not being disrespectful, but clearly her way of showing respect and welcome was different from the ancient tradition of keeping physical distance from superiors.

When Queen Elizabeth visited Sydney, Australia, in 1991 as the honored guest for that country's 150-year celebration, the prime minister, Paul Keating, put his hand under her elbow when ushering her into a room. The gesture was seen around the world on television. Mr. Keating had publicly stated previously that he believed Australia should be a republic and no longer accept the queen as head of state. Throughout Great Britain, Australia, and New Zealand the gesture was discussed widely in the context of Keating's viewpoint. The British tabloids saw it as unforgivable rudeness, but many Australians saw it as the behavior of a strong, independent leader. The controversy continued long after the event.

In both examples, the people who "violated" the expected ritual of showing respect came from egalitarian societies that believe in individual achievement rather than the inherited power of a monarchy, and both in their way expressed the notion that they considered themselves equal as human beings.

In Focus

In another example, Suzuki of Japan and General Motors built a joint-venture plant in Ontario, Canada, to manufacture a car called the Cami. During the construction of Japanese-style apartments for some Japanese engineers, the Japanese project manager went to the surrounding farms to apologize in advance for any inconvenience the neighbors might experience from the construction noise and heavy equipment. He knocked at the door of a farmhouse across the road, carrying a large box, beautifully wrapped, that contained a cake. He introduced himself with a bow and explained to the farmer's wife what his visit was about. Then he presented the package. This was all within his cultural tradition. The farmer's wife was Hungarian. She responded from *her* cultural tradition—she threw her arms around the surprised Japanese man and hugged him.

Positions of Authority

In all cultures, certain positions and professions enjoy a high level of authority. In many societies, medical doctors have prestige because they can help the sick. In some cultures, poets and scholars demand respect. In Asian societies, teachers carry authority. They are considered wise, and their teachings are not questioned. A Korean student would not think of questioning his professor. The professor is older and more experienced and therefore must know. These attitudes are also true for China, Japan, and most of Southeast Asia. Teachers are persons who command respect, as is illustrated in the following example.

In Focus

A professor from the United States had attended a four-week seminar on Chinese business culture in Taiwan some years ago. At the airport, things got hectic, and she was worried about missing her plane. The line for the security check was long and moved very slowly. On her jacket she carried a Chinese badge identifying her as a professor and a member of a special group. When she asked whether the X-rays were safe for film in her carry-on luggage and voiced concern about missing her plane, the official looked at her, saw the badge, and passed her carry-on luggage around the checking system. He said to her as she passed, "Good-bye, Teacher." She did not receive such treatment upon arrival in San Francisco!

When doing business with people from other cultures you need to find out what kinds of people and what professions are accorded special respect. Those people's views may carry more weight, and their opinions may be asked before decisions are made. A senior manager in Japan, for example, is not considered just a manager by a new recruit. The new recruit looks up to the senior manager as his *sensei* (teacher).

You may get a glimpse of what commands respect in a culture by looking at who the heroes in the culture are. In American culture, for example, the popular heroes are sports figures and Hollywood stars. Until the business scandals surrounding Enron, AIG, and Bernard Madoff became headlines in the first decade of 2000, businesspeople were heroes as well. For example, Lee Iacocca was seen as a hero who could save companies and bring prosperity. Warren Buffet, Bill Gates, and Steve Jobs are still revered businesspeople known for their drive and success.

Hindu culture has very different heroes. Gandhi is a hero because he focused on the liberty of India and the spiritual health of the individual. Germans look to philosophers and poets as their heroes, and Germany therefore is frequently called the country of *"Dichter und Denker"* (thinkers and poets). Frequently Arab culture looks to religious leaders as heroes. In traditional Korean culture, the Confucian scholar was the guiding figure. By learning who the heroes are, you may find out what a culture values and where its priorities are.

In many cultures, authority figures are not to be interrupted when speaking, and their opinions carry a lot of weight. For example, in China the senior member of the family is the absolute authority, and children would not even think of questioning that person's authority or presenting their own viewpoints. The conditioning starts very early. Businesspeople must be aware of the implications of this cultural value for business decisions. A Thai job applicant who seems quiet is not necessarily wrong for the job. He may simply be reflecting his culture's acceptable behavior toward someone who is in charge. Asking many questions or speaking a lot during an interview may be interpreted as arrogance and egotism and disqualify a candidate with a Thai firm in Thailand. An interviewer from Canada, in contrast, may interpret the behavior as lack of drive and ambition. Unless the job applicant is familiar with employment communication in Canada, he is at a disadvantage. At the same time, unless the interviewer is familiar with the behavioral patterns of the applicant's cultural background, the interviewer may miss a good employee.

In contrast to Asians, businesspeople in the United States are expected to be assertive. Although authority figures in the United States carry more clout and typically set the tone and speed of an interchange, employees can interrupt and give their opinions and comments. Children are raised to be assertive and to discuss options freely. Likewise, employees are encouraged to speak their minds. In the interview process for a job in the United States, for example, individuals are conscious of their accomplishments and will emphasize their possible contributions to the firm. In fact, job applicants are expected to pitch themselves to the employer and highlight their potential contributions to the success of the firm. The behavioral interview underlines this characteristic even more. In this type of interview, the interviewee is given a situation and asked how she or he would solve a specific problem. In fact, she is asked not what she might do in the abstract, but how she would proceed in this specific situation.

A business professor from New Zealand commented that American business communication texts about job searches are not usable in New Zealand. The letters come across as too assertive and egotistic. New Zealanders—and Canadians—prefer a less pushy approach. A job applicant states his or her accomplishments and skills and lets them speak for themselves. "To sell yourself" is traditionally inappropriate in these cultures. In the future, it will be interesting to see how the growing globalization of business will affect traditional cultural communication patterns. For example, business students from Indonesia point out that they tend to use an American approach when they apply for jobs with an American multinational and a more traditional Indonesian approach when applying for a job with an Indonesian firm.

On the surface, German résumés today are very similar to U.S. résumés, but there are some significant differences. The German applicant always provides more contextual information. Germans tend to indicate where and when they received a high school degree. Date of birth, family status, and information on health tend to be included when Germans apply to German companies.

When Japanese people look for jobs with Japanese companies, information on family, health, high school, and even elementary school is included. Typically, Japanese students do not even prepare a Western-style résumé. Rather than having one résumé that they will send out to many companies, they will fill in company-specific sheets, also called the information sheet. It is not so much the students who present their accomplishments, but rather the companies that through their particular forms let the students know what information they want and in which order they want that information. When Japanese graduates apply for jobs with American firms, applicants tend to adapt the résumé to American practices.

These developments also illustrate the fact that international businesspeople need to distinguish traditional cultural behavior from "international" business behavior, which is influenced by traditional culture but also by international business culture. In short, an international businessperson needs a deeper understanding of underlying reasons for the information presented on a résumé.

Dress as a Symbol of Authority

As we have said elsewhere, the standard business dress around the world is the suit, shirt, and tie for men, and some sort of suit or dress for women. That sounds easy, yet there are enough variations indicating authority that businesspeople must be aware of local customs and traditions.

In Focus

Tom Sides is flying to Tokyo for a business meeting. He will meet a potential joint-venture partner for the first time. The flight from Chicago is about 13 hours long, and exhausting. Tom has packed several suits, shirts, and ties in his luggage. But for such a long flight he wants to be comfortable, and so he wears jeans and a sweatshirt and tennis shoes. He knows that someone from the Japanese firm will meet him at Narita airport, but surely that person will understand the need to relax on a long flight. Kyuofumi Katsuki, who meets him, does not comment on Tom's dress, but Tom is beginning to wonder whether he has done the right thing when he sees Katsuki wearing formal business attire even though it is the weekend. Tom is getting a sense that his casual dress may have eroded his authority and credibility as a business partner.

When traveling, businesspeople from the United States tend to emphasize comfort and practical clothes. Their Japanese partners may, however, wonder how to read someone who is so set on personal comfort that business etiquette is put second. The formality of dress is also crucial in South East Asia and Latin America. Not to dress appropriately, which is to say conservatively, is easily interpreted as lack of interest in, and disrespect for, the *person with whom you are meeting* and your own authority (also see Chapter 4 on business form).

You show respect and sincerity by the way you dress and by respecting certain rules of appearance of the host culture. That does not mean you have to adopt the local dress, but it does mean you should adapt your clothes to the customs of the host culture. This can present a particular issue for women in positions of authority because rules for appropriate dress for women can vary widely across cultures. In Arab countries, even the less fundamentalist ones, women are expected to dress modestly. Miniskirts, sleeveless blouses, sleeveless dresses, tight skirts, and tight dresses are not considered appropriate. A woman who wants to do business in the Middle East must be aware of the basic rules and make sure she does not undermine her credibility and authority, not to mention insult her business partner. Offensive dress easily can lead to embarrassment and loss of status; therefore, she may want to cover her head with a scarf or hat.

In Focus

A university official in Malaysia invited a visiting professor from Sweden and her teenage daughter to a formal lunch. The arrangement was for the daughter to meet the host, the host's wife, and her mother at the restaurant. The daughter arrived wearing a modest but sleeveless dress. The host was extremely gracious, ushered his guests to seats, sat with the group until everyone had ordered, arranged for the payment, and then departed and sat elsewhere. Even though his wife was there, he could not eat lunch in the company of an undressed woman. Eating with the guests in these circumstances not only would have embarrassed him but also would have undermined his professional standing and authority.

In a sense, it is easier for women to choose appropriate dress in stricter countries than in more liberal countries such as Italy because the dress rules in stricter countries like Iran are spelled out clearly. Arms, legs, and hair should be covered in public. There is no room for variations. The rules in other countries may be much vaguer and less official. In Taiwan, for example, women may wear slacks but should stay away from sleeveless blouses. There is no law, but it simply is not done by people in positions of authority. Two women professors from the United States who attended a seminar there felt very uncomfortable wearing their sundresses and decided on their own that this was not appropriate attire for sight-seeing and definitely unacceptable for visiting businesses and government offices.

In Focus

In order to be properly dressed for a job interview in Japan, Japanese female job-seekers nearing the end of their university education must wear a black, dark charcoal, or very dark navy suit (jacket with skirt at the knee), with a white blouse. Today pant suits are also acceptable. Students interview in March–June in their penultimate year of study, to land jobs that will begin in April of the following year. They go to department stores, to the "recruit suit" department, to get advice about (and purchase) the suit that is right for their prospective employer. The suits are all very much alike, with variations in small details such as buttons (made of metal or that match the fabric color), buttonhole type, presence or absence of pockets, collar style, cut of the blouse collar, and depth of the blouse sleeve cuff. Companies aggressively distribute brochures on campuses; one example is the "Perfect Prejudice" brand of recruit suit. Students also seek advice about the right shoes and handbag to accessorize the recruit suit. They wear stockings of skin color, and no jewelry apart from small earrings. Finally, although university students often experiment with different hair colors and degrees of curl, for their interviews females' hair must be black, below the ear in length, and straight. For male students, the code is similar: black suits, white shirts, black shoes, and black hair worn straight and short.

The emphasis on dress is not new. In feudal Japan, all levels of society from the royal court, the Shogun's court, the merchant class, and down through the commoners had prescribed dress codes. Everyone changed from winter clothes to summer clothes, and vice versa, on the same day, which was announced by the Emperor. Wearing the wrong clothes was a serious offense and could be punished.

By wearing the proper recruit suit for the interview, a job candidate shows her preparedness for *shigoto no shikata*, "the way of working." This "way of working" involves a number of cultural values in the Japanese workplace: harmony within the work group, integrity, trust and trustworthiness, and doing one's best to achieve an ever-higher standard of work.[1] The recruit suit communicates her earnestness, subordination of self to the group, and willingness to give all she can to the company. She is saying, in the nonverbal vocabulary of clothing, that she is of the same cloth as the other interviewees, and will be of the same cultural cloth as the others in her hiring group and in the company.[2]

Businesspeople must be particularly sensitive to dress in other cultures because of the often negative image tourists have created. For example, Westerners often assume that their leisure dress is appropriate everywhere. Many come in shorts to visit churches and museums. Hordes of tourists flock to the beaches of Greece, Sri Lanka, and Morocco and promptly go topless or entirely nude. After all, the tourists have money, which they suppose gives them the right to do whatever they want to do, including disregarding local customs and norms of behavior. At best, that kind of behavior shows insensitivity, and at worst, it shows cultural imperialism. In no case does it foster mutual respect and understanding. In fact, it may undermine the credibility of a businessperson even if that person is sensitive to cultural attitudes toward dress. As a result, businesspeople, in addition to doing the business at hand, also may have to overcome negative cultural images created by mass tourism.

Power Distance and Symbols of Power and Authority

According to the work of the Dutch researcher Geert Hofstede, power distance in the United States is comparatively small. That means that, true to a democratic society, Americans are less accepting of inequalities in power than are people from cultures with high power distance. Cultures with a smaller power distance are more horizontal, less hierarchical, and less authoritarian than are cultures with a high power distance. Understanding where a culture ranks on the power distance scale can be helpful when one is dealing with a businessperson from another culture. For example, based on Hofstede's research on cultural priorities in 40 countries, Austria has the lowest power distance index at 11 points, whereas Malaysia has the highest at 104 points. The English-speaking and Northern European countries all have a power distance index of less than 40 points.[3] Differences in power are expressed in many different ways, some obvious and some more hidden.

Tone and Behavior of Power and Authority

In spite of claims to democracy and equality, symbols of power are everywhere in U.S. businesses. The size and location of an office and the type of furniture indicate power. An employee entering the office of a powerful manager will read the nonverbal signals and act accordingly. Plants, real wood furniture, and original artwork all spell a higher position in the U.S. context.

Although the person in power in many ways controls the interaction, the position of power also brings with it an obligation to be gracious. In many cultures, the subordinate is expected to remain standing when entering the office of a superior as a sign of respect; the gracious host is expected to offer a seat. Letting the subordinate stand during the discussion while the superior is seated indicates that the superior is busy and would not like to be disturbed or that he might not consider the matter or the person important enough to engage in a discussion. Any particular meaning depends on the context. If a boss you have known for many years does not invite you to sit as you enter, you know how to read the signal. The unfamiliar is more difficult to read, particularly in dealing with someone from a different culture.

At the end of a meeting in the Netherlands, the superior will send the message that the discussion is over by standing up. The subordinate will get up and leave after the appropriate leave-taking ritual. In cultures in which hospitality is important, it may be impolite for the host to send signals that a get-together is over. In that case, it may be the guest's duty to announce that he or she is leaving. The host then will press the guest to stay, but a guest who knows what is expected will politely decline. This is a typical ritual in Arab countries. The difficulty for a foreigner is to know what the right time is and how to read the invitation to stay a little longer.

Businesspeople in the United States, who are used to a more egalitarian society, prefer a collegial to an authoritarian tone in business dealings. This is made easier by the fact that modern English, in contrast to many other languages, does not distinguish between a familiar form and a formal form of address and that most people after a short time call each other by their first name. For example, the informal address in German uses *Du,* and the formal one uses *Sie.* In French, the distinction is expressed by *tu* for informal address and *vous* for formal address. In Spanish, *tu* is informal and *usted* is formal. The formal address is used with the last name, whereas the informal address typically is used with the first name.

A friendly and considerate tone is important in business communication in the United States, but clarity is the overriding goal. If there is any concern that a pleasant tone might cloud the meaning, U.S. businesspeople opt for clarity. The major goal is to get the meaning across. The purpose of Western communication is the transfer of meaning and the establishment of rational and logical relationships between ideas. To ensure that the message is clear, businesspeople from the United States may use many words and lots of examples, typical characteristics of a low-context culture. Ideas are encoded explicitly.

Germans have a tendency to establish their authority by giving very clear, precise, and often blunt directions. Germans tend to spell everything out; nothing is left to chance, and the language is very precise and definitive.

In Focus

A gymnastics school in southern Germany ran summer programs for teachers from other European countries. Most of the participants came from England, and all the participants stayed in the residence hall. In the opening session the director of the school welcomed everyone and then proceeded to announce the rules that everyone would be expected to follow. She asserted her authority by the tone and words she used. She gave strict guidelines on expected behavior in the residence hall: which kinds of linens were acceptable, when to use the showers, what to wear for the gymnastics sessions, and so on. Her comments were packed with *verboten, nicht erlaubt,* and *Sie müssen* (forbidden, not allowed, and you must). The leader of the English group had to translate the comments for the English participants. It was remarkable to see what she did. In her translation, the *must* and *don't* and *forbidden* became *it would be nice if, you might want to,* and *please consider.* She never once commented on the tone, but she certainly changed the tone of the message for her audience. The regulations were made palatable to people who were not used to being ordered around by an authority figure.

In German businesses, managers have a remarkable degree of authority. They are in charge of their departments, and interference from outsiders is not common and not easily accepted. Employees generally accept the authority of managers and don't argue. As long as the law is followed, Germans often are very willing to do as they are told.[4]

Titles are important and are used. Two American professors checked into a hotel in the city of the partner school. The partner school had made the initial reservation and provided the names of the two professors. In typical American fashion, the two professors went to the front desk and gave their first and last names. The clerk then said, "Yes, Herr Professor Dr. Lust and Frau Professor Dr. Guenther." The two professors delighted in the esteem they felt these titles implied but also realized that at home nobody would address them that way.

As was pointed out earlier, the distinction between *Du* and *Sie,* the familiar and formal words for *you,* and the use of last names further position people much more clearly in the hierarchy than is the case in the United States. People know their place, and they want to find out what someone else's place is in business and in society at large. Degrees and titles are the typical indicators of a person's status.

The Japanese like to point out that theirs is a society without class distinctions; however, they also emphasize that ranks and levels of society are very important. The individual is clearly subordinated to the common goals of the group. Indeed, Japanese use the word *harmony* whenever possible when describing their relationships. Clarity, which is so important to Westerners, is not the overriding goal. If clarity may cause loss of face or weaken harmony, harmony is considered more important. A superior will not criticize a subordinate openly, will not emphasize his superior status, and will not issue directives with *must, will,* or *shall* because doing so might result in loss of face for both the subordinate and the boss. The subordinate is supposed to understand the situation and accept his or her place in the hierarchy. This, of course, requires tuning in to the fine points of cultural discourse and being sensitive to nonverbal messages. The power distance is definitely present, but it seldom is verbalized. A manager will not sit down with a subordinate who is not performing well and clearly lay out what the employee will have to do to improve. Any criticism in front of a group is unthinkable, but even clear and constructive criticism in the privacy of the manager's office is usually considered inappropriate. In all likelihood, the manager will ask the employee to go out for a drink after work. In the social atmosphere of a bar and after a few drinks the manager will gently and indirectly raise the issue of performance, probably couched in a story. An American would probably never get the intended message; yet the Japanese employee will understand exactly what the manager is trying to say.

As is typical in high-context cultures, Japanese businesses assume that people know their place and will act accordingly, but the reality may be somewhat more complicated. First of all, there is a tremendous difference between smaller and larger firms. Small, family-owned firms can be very authoritarian. There is no question in anyone's mind who is in charge. The owner tends to make decisions and expects that they will be carried out. The system of consensus, typically known as *the* Japanese decision-making model, is practiced more in larger firms. But even in large firms someone is in charge, the hierarchy is enforced, and the final decision is often the boss's. It is the discussion process that leads up to the announced decision that gives the impression of equal participation. Everyone gets an equal chance to express his opinion, but the discussion often is aimed at bringing everyone around to the boss's opinion in the end.

The communication process is influenced by the history of the firm. If the firm is bureaucratic and run by managers, the power of groups is greater. In a firm such as Sony, which has a distinct individual founder, the imprint of the founder is stronger. Although groups are important and harmony is important, the original founder has a much more active role and more say in all company decisions. People at all levels listen to what Mr. Sony has to say.

In typical Japanese fashion, power and respect are a part of *amae* and reciprocity. *Amae* means that managers and employees know that they depend on each other and are willing to accept the dependency. The relationship is very similar to a parent–child relationship. The child needs the parent, but at the same time the parent needs the child in order to fulfill the role of parent. The relationship is a complex web of obligations that is central to Japanese interpersonal relations, including business relationships. The firm guarantees a job and decent wages; the employee promises top performance. Each knows that the other has a certain amount of power, but as long as both sides subscribe to the same set of values, they will get along. If that common bond begins to break, the situation changes. If employees no longer commit themselves to the firm and keep their eyes open for better opportunities, companies will decrease their commitment also and move away from lifetime employment.

In reality, the touted lifetime employment system has never covered more than 30 percent of the employees. It is practiced only by large firms and applies only to men. Women are not part of the system, and neither men nor women in small businesses are guaranteed lifetime employment. Furthermore, even in large firms lifetime employment is only for regular employees, not for part-timers and temporaries, who account for an ever-growing proportion of the workforce. During the last few years the lifetime employment system has come under additional attack. A number of Japanese firms have concluded that to be competitive in the global market, they need to focus on performance and merit rather than longevity with the firm. As more foreign companies have bought Japanese firms, the practice of lifetime employment has declined, but Japanese still consider it the ideal. Foreign firms are interested in efficiency and profitability. To achieve that goal, they feel they have to reduce the workforce. DaimlerChrysler, for example, bought a controlling share of Mitsubishi Motors because the automaker felt it could make Mitsubishi profitable by reducing the number of workers and increasing quality. The economic problems over the last few years have resulted in further inroads into the lifetime employment practice. In companies where lifetime employment is still practiced, increasingly women are included. For example, Mitsui Trading Company hires women into its management training program. The changing employment patterns will bring with them a new power structure and a new relationship between employees and employers. Foreign firms also have introduced a Western style of employee evaluations that is direct and has personnel consequences. For example, Procter & Gamble, the U.S. firm based in Cincinnati, Ohio, in the United States has introduced a very American evaluation process for its managers. Only a certain number of managers may receive an evaluation of outstanding or acceptable. Managers who do not meet the criteria are let go and need to look for employment elsewhere. Other Western firms are using similar approaches to human resource management. Clearly, the emphasis has shifted from harmony and group orientation to efficiency and performance.

Although people in a firm know very well who has power, the issue is not discussed openly. To people on the outside, the façade of harmony must be maintained at all costs, and saving face becomes an overriding issue. Companies go to great lengths to present an image of harmony.

In Focus

Kazuo Ota, an employee in a Japanese subsidiary of a U.S. firm, gave notice that he wanted to leave the company. That seemingly simple act started a flurry of activity. Mr. Ota's boss, Masataka Abe, refused to accept the resignation because Mr. Ota did not have "valid" reasons for leaving. As it turned out, Mr. Abe was glad to get rid of Mr. Ota, but as he explained, this was Japan, and appearances were important. He said that he would talk to Mr. Ota in a few days, and they then would agree that they would part with mutual respect and satisfaction. That way nobody was to blame; there would be no fault on any side. To Mr. Abe, this saving of reputation was extremely important.

Japanese firms have tremendous power over suppliers. The big firms buy exclusively from the supplier, and the suppliers depend on the firms for their business and economic well-being. The suppliers are the ones expected to absorb excess workers in hard times; they are the ones that must absorb fluctuations in business. In return, they know they have a customer for their goods and know they will receive help with development costs and technical changes. As a result, however, they are totally dependent on one manufacturer. Traditionally, in Japan the buyer has been in a considerably more powerful position than the seller, and the seller tends to accept the power position of the buyer, as the following example illustrates. In this context it is interesting to observe a change in how Western researchers look at Japanese management. In the 1980s, Japanese culture with its emphasis on harmony and lifetime employment was seen as the driver for Japanese business success. Today, Japanese culture is often cited as the reason for Japanese business problems.

In Focus

Two Norwegian businessmen were visiting a kimono wholesaler in Nagoya. On the day of their visit several suppliers were in the offices of the wholesaler, who was in the market for luxurious and very expensive kimonos. The layout of the offices and the atmosphere were very traditional; all the floors were covered with tatami mats, and everyone had taken off his or her shoes at the entrance of the building. People were sitting on the floor in the traditional style.

The Norwegians discussed several aspects of the business with the wholesaler. While they were talking, a Japanese man approached, but the owner of the business barely acknowledged him. After a deep bow, the "intruder" stayed at a respectable distance. When the Norwegians asked a question about the production of kimono belts, however, the owner waved to the person and asked him to come closer. It turned out that the "intruder" was a kimono belt maker who manufactured exclusively for this wholesaler. The supplier bowed several times and answered the questions asked of him. When the discussion went on to other areas, he was waved away and quietly withdrew. To someone watching the scene, the more powerful partner was easily identifiable.

Japanese firms frequently take the emphasis on harmony into their foreign subsidiaries. An American working for a Japanese firm in Chicago faced the following situation.

In Focus

Brent Weber, a recent graduate with a degree in international business, was excited about his job offer from a Japanese firm in Chicago. He had heard about the excellent training Japanese companies provide for their employees and was looking forward to a promising future with the firm.

After some time with the firm, however, Brent became disillusioned. He felt he just did not get the training to move ahead, and he started looking for another job.

Somehow his Japanese manager found out; he called Brent in and made it clear to him that he was expected to leave. Before Brent left the firm, however, the Japanese manager met with him once more. He went to great pains to point out that even though Brent's actions had been disloyal to the firm, they were parting on good terms: Brent was not fired, but they had come to a mutual understanding that parting was best for both sides. The appearance of harmony and agreement was important.

The buyer sometimes is compared to the father who has authority over the supplier, the son. The father has the authority, but because he loves his son, he will not harm him. That means the buyer has the power, but he will see to it that the supplier is treated fairly. Nevertheless, they are not equal in stature and status, and both sides are keenly aware of their respective levels of authority and power.

Guanxi relationships fill a similar purpose in China. Business is done on the foundation of relationships that are ongoing. They take a long time to establish and they have to be nurtured. *Guanxi* cannot be rushed. It is a web of social connections that are almost impossible to untangle. *Guanxi* brings certain privileges, but it also brings obligations. It binds business partners to help each other. In today's business environment in China, people may use the word *guanxi,* but the traditional time-consuming ritual of relationship building has been frequently supplanted by paying bribes and asking for favors. Not all relationships in business are *guanxi* relationships. *Guanxi* relationships are characterized by (1) a warmth of feeling that can sustain a sense of connection, (2) instrumentality, (3) reciprocity, (4) cultivation, and (5) trust. The warmth of feeling is often expressed by the Chinese word *renqing.*[5] Instrumentality refers to the outcomes of the *guanxi* relationship; benefits come from being in a *guanxi* relationship. Benefits offered as favors may be intangible, such as contacts with others in a network, or they may be tangible, such as gifts. Reciprocity is the giving and receiving of favors that knits together parties in a relationship. These favors often involve face: giving face and avoiding loss of face to the other party are the key facework behaviors. Sometimes favors are gifts, or putting someone forward for a beneficial outcome, or making a connection on behalf of someone.[6] *Guanxi* relationships need to be cultivated and nurtured, primarily by the exchange of favors. Once a *guanxi* relationship exists and has fostered exchanges of significant favors, it can endure over generations with only occasional exchanges. In the business environment of China today, trust is especially hard to come by and therefore is especially prized as a characteristic of *guanxi.* The term *guanxi* has been invoked by businesspeople who do not always follow through with trust and reciprocity in modern China, and that has cast some suspicion on those who use the term glibly.

In cultures where business relies on relationships and trust, agreements take time and cannot be rushed. The relationship may be helped along with some small gifts, but the gifts are not the major contributors. What really counts is the connection with people and a willingness to be indebted to each other over time. The tangible gift is but a very small part in the process.

Language as an Indicator of Power and Authority

In addition to tone and behavior, language is an indicator of authority in most cultures. Japan provides a good example of the way language is used to establish authority.

In Japan, power becomes obvious through nonverbal symbols such as bowing, as was pointed out earlier, but vocabulary is also an indicator of power. The Japanese society is a hierarchical society. The language subordinates use differs from the language superiors use. The vocabulary can be quite different, and everyone is aware of the connotations of words. For example, when a manager addresses subordinate men, he will add the suffix *kun* to the name rather than the respectful *san* (the equivalent to Mr.). The subordinate will address the superior with the last name and title, or use the title and *san.* For example, the boss will call the employee *Nakasone-kun,* but Mr. Nakasone will call the boss *Abe-kacho* (Abe being the name of the boss and *kacho* meaning section chief).

Address reflects one's standing in the group. This is emphasized even more by using a person's title or position plus *san* rather than the name plus the title. In this situation, the boss is not *Abe-kacho* but *kacho-san,* not *Tanaka-bucho* (department head) but *bucho-san.* This practice is carried over into family relationships. A boy will call his older brother *anisan,* older brother, rather than Wako, and call his older sister *oni-san,* rather than Noriko. In a way, the person loses his or her individual identity and takes on an identity in relation to his or her position in the group.

Lately, several Japanese companies have started to move against extreme status consciousness in addressing people. They are promoting the use of the suffix *san* for everyone regardless of position. *Nakasone-kun* would become *Nakasone-san,* and *Abe-kacho* would become *Abe-san.* It is interesting to note that the Japanese, who have emphasized group membership by pointing out that everyone from president to storeroom clerk wears the same uniform, are now talking about the need to equalize the language. The United States is cited as a positive example in this effort.

The preceding examples indicate that to use correct language one needs to know where one stands in the hierarchy. Different groups use different vocabulary. For an outsider, it may be difficult to notice the variations, as the following example shows.

In Focus

Thomas Reed had been a missionary in Japan for almost six months. He had taken some Japanese courses before going to Japan and had continued his language training after his arrival in Japan. As a missionary, he would go from door to door to talk with people about his religion. In that context, he met a lot of people and practiced his Japanese. Typically, the people who answered the door were housewives. One day, however, one of his male friends took him aside and told him that he spoke Japanese like a woman and had to learn to speak like a Japanese man.

The hierarchical thinking of Japanese society also is apparent verbally in the way people refer to themselves. In Western cultures, people refer to themselves as *I.* This identity stays with them and does not change. It does not matter whether a man talks to his parents, spouse, friends, co-workers, or boss. When he refers to himself, he uses the pronoun *I.* That is different from the practice in Japanese culture. First of all, it is considered egotistic and impolite to refer to oneself because that draws too much attention to oneself. If at all possible, one should avoid any reference to *I*. The subject *I* will become clear in the context. If the speaker does use the personal pronoun, the pronoun will change depending on the people the speaker is addressing. The Japanese have many words for *I*. Each depends on the relationship of the speaker to the listener, and each indicates the hierarchy of the group. The particular word that is used depends on status, gender, age, and familiarity. Boys, for example, will use *boku* for *I* when talking to each other. A man will use *temae* for *I* when talking to his boss. Young men talking to each other will refer to themselves as *ore*.

A discussion of groups in Japan must take into account the fact that group membership is permanent (see Chapter 4). Groups are important because they help define one's identity and role and establish authority relationships that last for a lifetime. This helps explain the importance of university clubs. All Japanese universities have a variety of student clubs, from soccer to martial arts, fencing, rock climbing, theater, and politics. Seminars also have a special place in Japanese universities. A professor will handpick the students for his seminar. Each student is interviewed personally. Once the students are accepted, they will become members of the seminar for life. At the beginning of the seminar, the professor will go on a retreat with the new seminar students. During the duration of the seminar, the professor and the students frequently go out together in the evenings. Once the seminar is over, the professor will invite his seminar students from all the years he has taught for a get-together once a year.[7]

The Japanese take these clubs and seminars very seriously. Joining is not casual or temporary but for a lifetime. When graduates go their separate way after graduation, they stay in touch. They belonged to the same club or seminar; they had the same experiences. If one works for MITI and the other for Mitsubishi, they know they can count on each other. Westerners often complain about the close ties between Japanese business and industry. What they may not understand is that this is not necessarily an official tie but an unofficial tie based on group identity and personal relationships that have grown over many years (also see Chapter 4). These relationships are often the basis for power in Japan. For example, one large conglomerate, Tokyu Corporation, formerly required new hires, who all begin work for the company at the same time (the beginning of April), to live together in a dormitory in order to be formed into a unit.

The Koreans also establish life-long relationships and a complex web of connections while they are still in school. As they advance in their careers in business and government, these connections play an important role. One Korean professor who had emigrated to the United States to work on his doctorate in finance explained that he went back to Korea regularly to visit his parents; however, he no longer had the close connection to his network. He had become an outsider without access to the old network.

What appears harmonious on the surface is not necessarily harmonious beneath the surface, however. There is an amazing amount of shuffling for power and position, but all behind a façade of harmony. Employees know very well where they stand and what their chances of success are in a firm. Whereas the older generation still emphasizes seniority and promotion based on seniority, younger people are increasingly disillusioned with this approach. Japanese who have studied abroad or worked abroad are rebelling against the seniority system. They want more power based on knowledge and experience rather than number of years with the firm. With growing global competition, the Japanese elite is beginning to review the issues of merit and group harmony. Any changes will have far-reaching consequences in traditional business culture and behavioral norms.

Family and Societal Structures as Indicators of Power

So far, we have discussed the tone and language of power, but in most cultures power also is conveyed by the social groupings and structures of groups (see also Chapter 4).

Although Islam stresses the equality of all believers, in reality there is an emphasis on hierarchy and authority. The symbol for the underlying power structure is the extended family or clan that is tightly ruled by the senior male member. For younger people who may have studied abroad and have gotten used to questioning authority, the return home can be a tremendous culture shock. No matter how much they know, they will be expected to bow to seniority. The head of the group officially has the say.

Most Arabs are used to this structure and accept the authority of a person as long as it is clear that that person is officially in charge. However, Arabs have a hard time dealing with people when there is no clear indication who the leaders are. Free-flowing discussion in the Western sense is difficult in Arab culture. The give-and-take approach to discussions is furthermore complicated by the fact that in Arabic there is no equivalent word for *compromise.* Clearly, if the concept is not there, negotiations will be rather different from the American approach where negotiators talk about *dividing the difference.* In the severity of the desert environment, only the strong survive, and therefore one constantly has to protect one's position. In this context, give-and-take is seen as a sign of weakness. As a result, Arabs stick to small talk when lines of authority are not clear to avoid confrontations and arguments.[8] Group decision making using the Japanese approach probably would not work because the Japanese approach does not have an obvious leader who is in charge.

Western businesspeople doing business in the Middle East will be much more successful if lines of authority, power, and responsibilities are spelled out clearly. They also can help discussions move along if the Arab businessperson realizes that the Westerners have the full support and confidence of their companies back home. Arabs respect clearly identified authority, but any sign of insecurity will be interpreted as weakness and ineffectiveness and will be attacked relentlessly.

Similar to the Arab tradition, the Latin American tradition is male-oriented and based on a strong authoritarian leader. The tradition evolved from the strict hierarchical organization of the Catholic Church in Europe and the system of large haciendas in Latin America.[9] Traditionally, the hacienda is run by a *patron,* a father figure who takes care of the people living on the hacienda. It is a very paternalistic model based on reciprocity and loyalty. The employees owe duty and obligation.

Their loyalty is a personal loyalty to the owner rather than to a group, as in Japan. Loyalty is not abstract but real and shows up in the carrying out of orders. In this system, both sides accept their place: the owner/manager who makes the decisions and the subordinate who carries them out. The patron clearly is the authority figure, and he also is expected to take care of the employees; however, the employees have some power also, even though it is more indirect. They control important information that they will pass on only in return for certain favors.

Because the patron as the authority figure is supposed to know what to do, he culturally cannot ask for information. Asking would be interpreted as weakness. As a result of the traditional communication pattern, communication, particularly horizontal communication, in Latin American organizations even today is not very effective. People try to protect their reputations and positions; people do not work together freely to achieve common goals. In such an environment, teamwork will have to be prepared and nurtured much more carefully.

Decision making by consensus, or setting common goals in a group, is difficult in Latin American cultures because managerial practices do not take the cultural realities and constraints into account.[10] Many a North American management consultant has failed in Latin America when preaching the advantages of an open communication system in which the boss asks for input from the employees and the employees freely share their opinions. Communication patterns are culturally conditioned. The one higher in the hierarchy takes care of the lower one, who in turn owes obedience and carries out orders. The lower one does not interrupt and ask questions. That is not his place. If the superior asks for input, the subordinate may legitimately question the ability of the superior to run the firm.

Assertiveness vs. Harmony

Standing Up for One's Rights

U.S. businesspeople believe in assertiveness training. Assertiveness is seen as a positive value, and the emphasis on assertiveness highlights individual rights over obligations to groups and society. If in doubt, Americans often push for truth rather than peace and harmony. They believe it is better to know the truth. "The truth will set you free" symbolizes their faith in asserting what is true and right.

Germans, even more than people in the United States, emphasize the importance of standing up for their rights, of consciously asserting their rights. In many cases, outsiders can see those characteristics much more clearly than insiders can.

Germans tend to see life as tough and not always fair; therefore, children must learn to fight early (also see Chapter 6). A German mother once said that it was important that children learn to cheat on tests because life is hard and often cruel. Everyone cheats; therefore, it is important to learn how to do it for self-protection. Although not all Germans may agree with the attitude of the mother, it is a common attitude that illustrates our point.

This need for assertiveness can be humorous, but it also can be more severe. In the extreme, it leads to the person who is an expert on everything. Germans find

In Focus

An Iranian doctor who had lived in Germany for many years commented on the German need to assert oneself. From childhood on, she noted, German children are taught to defend their rights as people and their right to property. *Was recht ist muß recht bleiben* (right must remain right) indicates this attitude. One should never give up one's right or give in. The Iranian formed the opinion that, in Germany, doing this stamps a person as weak and incompetent. As a result, life is regulated and rules govern the most minute details of life. The Germans may have their possessions, but in the process, according to the Iranian doctor, they miss the interpersonal warmth that comes with sharing.

This example illustrates the fact that people approach other cultures with their own set of values and priorities. The Iranian doctor evaluated the German culture on the basis of her own background, which firmly places the individual in a hierarchical group that emphasizes interdependence rather than an insistence on personal rights.

it difficult to say that they don't know or admit that they were wrong. When a person in the United States might say, "I'm sorry, I guess I was wrong," a German would be quiet or explain why he was right. Insecurity frequently leads to exaggerated assertiveness.

In Focus

A group of German and U.S. students discussed the construction of houses in both Germany and the United States. The Germans were horrified by how thin the walls of American houses are. Because of the temperature extremes of the Midwest's continental climate, they thought that the walls should be thicker to conserve energy. The U.S. students pointed out that thickness of walls does not automatically mean better insulation. They explained the significance of the R-value of insulation and discussed how thick a stone wall would have to be to reach the equivalent insulating value of a six-inch fiberglass pad. The Germans listened until the Americans had finished, and then one of them simply said: "This is wrong. Thicker walls are better." He probably knew nothing about R-values and insulation values, but he "knew," and he asserted his knowledge.

This behavior also can be observed in business. The German subsidiary of a U.S. pharmaceutical company regularly sent reports and requests for additional funds to headquarters. The manager at headquarters in Chicago repeatedly told them that they needed to justify their requests, that to say they needed the funds for effectiveness and competitiveness was not enough. The Germans continued to send requests without the justifications. If they said they needed the funds, they needed the funds. They were right. The U.S. manager, in exasperation, suggested some training in American-style business report writing. The Germans were furious; how dare he suggest that they needed to change!

In another case, the German manager of a German subsidiary of a U.S. firm refused to go to European regional meetings. He knew his job; why should he waste his time going to France or Great Britain? If they needed help, they could come to him. In contrast to Americans, Germans tend to be more production-oriented; public relations is often a distant last concern. German advertisements typically assert product superiority in a technical sense. Companies, like individuals, seem to say, "We know we are right, so why bother about appearing nice?"

For example, a German manufacturer of high-quality steel products was unsuccessful at selling its products in Shanghai. The firm could not even sell its products through a joint-venture company. On sales calls, the Germans would simply state the superiority of their products and give the price. The Chinese, however, were looking for an advantage, a special favor, a sign of some consideration due to them because they were entering into a buyer–seller relationship, and always looking for a better price than another buyer would pay. The Germans reputedly stated, "You can't have a Mercedes at a Volkswagen price," packed up their brochures and specifications, and walked out. The Chinese had thought they were negotiating and had only just begun the process. The Germans had no time to waste: They knew their product was of high quality and said so and named their price. Nothing further remained to be said as far as they were concerned. Although the focus on production and quality is laudable, it has resulted in rigidity. The lack of flexibility has become a hurdle in an era with an emphasis on globalization.

Preserving Harmony

In contrast to Western assertiveness stands the concept of peace and harmony in Asian cultures. The Japanese proverb "the pheasant would have lived but for its cry" is symbolic of that concept. One is quiet and fits in. To tout one's rights or superiority is not acceptable. The emphasis is on duty, obligation, and loyalty rather than on rights. Both Confucianism and Buddhism emphasize duty over rights. The verbal assertiveness of Western cultures is alien to Eastern cultures. However, younger people may follow a more assertive course and begin to question authority.

Assertiveness implies that I assert my rights because I am right; therefore, I must maintain and defend my view of what is right. In cultures whose members believe that circumstances define what is right and wrong, the insistence on absolutes becomes hollow and makes no sense. Businesspeople from Eastern cultures may consider the Western emphasis on absolute principles unrealistic and pushy, and Western businesspeople may view the Eastern emphasis on circumstances as an attempt to avoid commitment.

The different cultural backgrounds influence how people approach each other and present their ideas. A businessperson from Western cultures is likely to push assertively and openly for acceptance of a proposal. East Asian businesspeople also fight for their proposals, but typically the fight is more subtle, more quietly persuasive than openly assertive. Unless both sides understand the reasons for their behavior, they may not be able to communicate effectively and may miss business opportunities.

Recognition of Performance as a Signal of Authority

Recognition of performance can be divided into two major types: monetary recognition and nonmonetary rewards.

Monetary Recognition

Cultures that emphasize relationships over individual achievement and material possessions tend to play down the role of money in recognizing performance. Cultures that admire individual performance tend to connect salaries with recognition. In the United States, for example, recognition of achievement is reflected in one's salary. Surveys over the last few years have shown that American executives are the highest paid in the world not just in terms of absolute dollars of compensation but also in terms of what other people in business make, even though surveys show that interesting work rather than salary is the prime motivator.[11] The differentials between pay for manufacturing employees and chief executive officers (CEOs) is highest in the United States and lowest in Japan and Germany. The scandals at Enron, WorldCom, Tyco, and other companies have brought to light what CEOs and top executives at some American companies make. Although the public may accept huge salaries for CEOs whose companies are profitable, they certainly were aghast to find out that in many cases CEOs received huge salaries even if their companies lost money.[12]

However, the gap between U.S. chief executives and their foreign counterparts is closing fast as foreign firms have started to make stock options part of executive pay. Many Germans were convinced that Juergen Schrempp, the CEO of DaimlerChrysler, hoped for the merger of the two companies only because he wanted the salary of an American CEO. Today, executives of multinational firms in many countries, among them Argentina, Germany, and Japan, include stock options in the pay package. In the United States, these packages have to be transparent, and regulators require that the facts are clearly laid out. In Germany and Japan, on the other hand, executive pay is considered a private matter. Executive pay is reported in one total of all executive pay in the firm. Only recently, with growing scandals, are these countries requiring American-style transparency. This development is another example of the impact of globalization. In an era when business seeks talent globally, compensation packages are competitive at a global level.

As European firms are hit by "merger mania," more and more executives are receiving golden parachutes—that is, special payments, special retirement bonuses, or special stock options if they are let go as a result of the merger. German, French, and British CEOs made international headlines when their severance agreements were disclosed. Traditionally, those CEOs might have received a cash payment for the loss of compensation in a takeover, along with a nice pension, but multimillion-dollar parachutes were virtually unknown. This definitely is changing.[13] Golden parachutes for American CEOs have made headlines as well. Jack Welch, who was an icon of American industry, lost much of his stature after his retirement deals became public.

The big pay differences between lower-level employees and executives have become an issue in several countries. In the United States, for example, employees and stockholders are more and more disillusioned and complain about managers taking rewards but avoiding punishment.[14] Managers are accused of giving themselves huge salaries, bonuses, and stock options regardless of performance. Even the Securities and Exchange Commission (SEC) has entered the discussion. Increasingly, American critics argue that the system needs to be more participative and consensus-oriented.

In many developing countries, pay differentials between managers and lower-level employees are tremendous and are an expression of traditional hierarchical class structures. Since class membership often is attained by birth rather than by individual accomplishments, the salary structures reinforce the existing system.

Nonmonetary Rewards

Appropriate recognition must be based on cultural motivators and culturally acceptable norms. In a culture that considers individuality positive, singling individuals out for praise is positive. U.S. firms, for example, may recognize the salesperson of the month or the employee of the month. Singling out an individual both praises the individual and provides an incentive for the others to do well so they too may be recognized. A successful saleswoman at Mary Kay Cosmetics gets to drive a Cadillac. The whole world can see that she is a top performer. Local newspapers in the United States regularly run columns on who has been promoted in the community. A brief description and a recent picture recognize the individual achievement. Americans want others to see what they have done. For example, McDonald's and other service companies post the Employee of the Month with a picture and brief biography in each franchise. In contrast, at Beijing Jeep some workers actually turned down a pay increase because the apprehension they felt about the resentment of less-productive workers outweighed the benefit of getting more money.

Some U.S. companies organize special trips and retreats for successful employees. Company-paid trips to Hawaii or Florida, particularly in January—if the firm is in the northern part of the United States—indicate appreciation and success.

In cultures that do not put a high value on individuality, the open recognition of individual achievement may not be desirable. Singling out one salesperson as the top performer in a Taiwanese firm could be embarrassing for the employee and not endear him to his co-workers. What he achieved was a result of group interaction and cooperation. Nobody alone can reach the top. As a result, companies tend to reward everyone. Everyone gets a bonus; everyone gets to go on a trip. A small firm in Taipei, for example, sent all 54 employees to Hong Kong for three days. They went in two groups so that the business could remain open, but everyone down to the lowest clerical employee went. Another Japanese firm paid for all employees to travel to Italy together. Any other arrangement would have been unthinkable. Similarly, a software company in California that was owned by several Taiwanese made headlines in 1998 when it awarded a Christmas bonus of nearly $60,000 to each employee! This was a monetary reward but also a collective one.

In a Japanese firm, one of the women was asked whether she was willing to accept a position as a manager in training. She would have been the first and only woman in that position in the firm. Most businesswomen in the United States or Western Europe would have jumped at the opportunity. She declined, saying she did not think it appropriate to be singled out from among all the other women. For the sake of maintaining harmony and not being the object of criticism by others, she felt it more important to remain a member of the group of women. She was willing to forgo personal advancement in the interest of remaining a member of her group. The Japanese emphasis on fitting in does not mean there are no personal ambitions and maneuvering for positions. The difficulty for Westerners is that the surface seems to be so harmonious and smooth that it is difficult to recognize and interpret any undercurrents. They are there, however. A Japanese businessman described the Japanese approach thus: "Like a duck—serene above and paddling like hell below."

Pay differentials in formerly communist countries were small; however, much of the compensation in those societies came in the form of privileges rather than salaries. A Russian manager might not make much more money than a first-line supervisor, but the manager might have access to special stores, vacation spots, inexpensive and heavily subsidized theater tickets, and travel within the communist bloc countries. In this kind of environment, salaries alone do not give a clear picture of actual power and authority.

In developing countries, recognition may come in the form of products that are difficult to get. For example, an employee may be much happier with a VCR, cell or mobile phone, or television set than with the equivalent in the local currency if those products are not readily available. Having them may indicate prestige and connections. Sometimes better apartments, houses, vacations, and automobiles may be coveted possessions, and employees may go to great lengths to get them.

Any firm employing people with diverse cultural backgrounds needs to be aware that people with different backgrounds look at rewards differently. What may be a dream come true for one person may be disappointing to the next. Some companies have tried to avoid problems abroad by implementing the same policy for recognition worldwide only to find out that this does not work. Just as with the other aspects of communication, the reward process must be adapted to the cultural norms of the people with whom one is dealing. Any policy must be soundly based on a study of what is culturally appropriate and acceptable. In addition, the firm must be fair to all subsidiaries. If individual recognition is not appropriate, a more group-oriented approach may solve the problem. However, it would not be appropriate to give no recognition at all.

Increasing globalization has made recognition of performance more complex. Small and medium-sized firms may continue to follow traditional patterns for recognizing performance, but many large multinational firms may need to combine approaches from several cultures. If an Australian firm practices polycentric staffing and employs Australians at its headquarters in Brisbane, and Japanese people in its subsidiary in Osaka, the firm can design a reward structure that fits the Australian culture at its headquarters and the Japanese culture at the subsidiary. If, however, the Australian firm uses a staffing pattern in which Japanese and Australian employees work at headquarters and at the subsidiary, both locations must take both cultures into account. Developing an award structure that corresponds to cultural priorities requires sensitivity and careful study of the culture.

The Role of Social Contacts in Intercultural Business

As we pointed out in Chapter 3, the importance of form is related to cultural priorities. In this section, we will explore some of the key factors that influence success in the social settings of international business because much intercultural business communication takes place through social gatherings and gift giving. Appropriate behavior in the social setting is crucial for success; however, the definition of appropriate behavior varies from culture to culture.

Conventions for Extending Invitations

Business relationships, especially in international dealings, often involve entertaining businesspeople from other cultures. Whom does one invite, when does one invite people, and how well does one have to know people to invite them? These can be complicated points in business relationships across cultures. In the United States, people are fairly open and invite people easily into their homes. Even if they have not known the other person very long, many extend an invitation. The invitation is a gesture of welcome and goodwill and does not necessarily mean that the person issuing the invitation wants to become a close friend. In many ways the invitation is similar to the social question "How are you?" which does not require an answer other than "Thank you." Foreigners who come from cultures where one invites only close friends to one's home, however, typically use this goodwill gesture as proof of the insincerity of Americans.

Open hospitality is not universal. At an elementary school picnic in the United States, two American parents met the parents of a Japanese student. The Japanese father was a visiting professor at the local university. They were new in town and didn't know anyone. The Americans, to make them feel welcome, invited them for Sunday afternoon. The couple came with their son, and the afternoon was very pleasant. In the course of the conversation, the Japanese expressed their surprise at having been invited after just having met the host. In Japan that would not happen, they pointed out. Indeed, it is much more difficult to receive an invitation into a Japanese home. Socializing takes place outside the private home either in a public place or at the place of work.

The Japanese are expected to fit in the group, to share, and not to insist on private space, but families are kept very separate from work life. The work team may be a second family for the employee, but the private family and the company family in many cases do not mix. This separation may be partly a result of crowded living conditions because with small apartments it is difficult to entertain at home, but the reasons for the separation of work and family seem to go deeper.

It is a nightmare for the Japanese if a foreign businessman announces that his wife will accompany him on the next trip. The Japanese do not know how to deal with this situation because wives typically are not included in business functions. Asking a Japanese wife to take care of the visitor's wife also poses problems. The foreign woman may feel uncomfortable, and the Japanese woman may resent having to be involved in her husband's business affairs, not to mention having to overcome language problems.

Guests in Japanese homes must follow certain customs. At the entrance one takes off one's shoes. Perhaps this goes back to the time when the entire floor was covered with tatami mats. These mats are delicate and difficult to clean; therefore, to prolong their lives, people would take off their shoes when entering the house. Even though today most people in Japan have carpeting or wooden floors and usually just one tatami room, if any, the custom has survived. All guests are expected to take off their shoes.

Many families provide slippers for guests. For this purpose, most houses have a set of shelves at the entrance filled with a number of pairs of slippers. Men find out very fast that the best shoes to wear are slip-on loafers rather than shoes with laces. For the use of the toilet, a separate pair of slippers is provided. The slippers that are worn in the rest of the house must never be worn in the bathroom, and especially vice versa! Exchange students typically infuriate their hosts before they catch on and change slippers intuitively.

The ritual of taking off one's shoes and putting on slippers provided by the host is perfectly natural to the Japanese. The host shows hospitality by providing slippers; the guest shows respect by taking off the shoes. People from other cultures may view the ritual somewhat differently, especially if they want to present a certain image.

In Focus

A group of businesspeople from the United States was invited for a Fourth of July party to Mitsubishi in Nagoya. At the entrance, everyone took off his or her shoes and put on the provided slippers, which were olive green. In the eyes of the Americans, the slippers looked odd with the business suits the men were wearing, and they ruined any ensemble and color coordination the women were trying to achieve. The businesspeople from the United States felt as if they had lost their professional dignity when putting on the slippers. The Japanese, in contrast, did not even seem to notice. To them it was quite natural—what else would one do?

Arabs may invite outsiders into their homes more easily than the Japanese do, but an outsider will only be permitted in the official or public places of the house, and typically the public part of the house, the *dewaniah*, is accessible directly from the outside. That means a visitor enters the public areas without ever being anywhere close to the private areas of the house. Women are typically not present and will not appear while an outsider is in the house. An Arab may entertain at home but separates the public and private aspects of his life. In Northern Europe, business entertainment at home is rare. People are more protective of the private sphere and separate work life from private life. Clearly, to avoid misunderstandings and hurt feelings, international businesspeople need to learn how to read the signals of hospitality in different cultures.

Mixing Social Engagements and Business

Typically, the host sets the agenda and guides the visitor through the course of engagement. The host will determine whether to meet for dinner at a bar, at a nightclub, or in his or her home. The host also will invite the appropriate persons. These arrangements may be fairly easy. More complicated is the question of how fast to proceed to business. Businesspeople from cultures that consider time a perishable commodity want to move fast; after all, time is money. They may invite the potential partner into their house for dinner but then proceed to talk business most of the evening.

In cultures in which business is based on trust, the personal relationship must be established before any business discussions can begin. Businesspeople from these cultures use the social gathering as a way to get to know the other person and avoid business discussions during that time.

No culture is right or wrong; cultures are different and approach business differently. They develop different norms and expectations. For example, Americans are used to the business breakfast, the business lunch, and the business dinner.

If a manager invites people for a working breakfast, it is understood that the participants should arrive on time and focus on business. If a business breakfast is not the custom, the participants may not know what to expect and what to do. Uzbeks, for example, do not do business breakfasts. When an American invited people for a business breakfast for 8 a.m., two other Americans were there. The Uzbeks came gradually. The last one arrived an hour and a half late. The Uzbeks felt uncomfortable and did not know what the rules for such an occasion were.

Businesspeople should learn how the other side approaches business and what the principles of hospitality are. Then they can make the necessary adjustments or openly talk about the differences and come to a mutual understanding. Generally, however, the rules of the host culture carry more weight. If you are doing business in another culture, you may have to be the one who makes most of the adjustments.

Appropriate Behavior for Hosts and Guests

If you follow the conventions of hospitality in a particular culture, your foreign business partners will look at you as sensitive and respectful, and appropriate behavior in social settings will open doors; however, although attention to form is beneficial, we believe that it is ultimately more important to look beyond the *what* and focus on the *why* of the appropriate behavior. Throughout this book, we have discussed the reasons underlying cultural priorities and behavior, and we encourage you to use this knowledge when you are interacting with businesspeople in social settings. For example, cultures that do not like uncertainty tend to develop clearer rules for behavior. Hierarchical societies pay particular attention to the relationship between host and guest and are more sensitive to who can invite whom. If you are hosting a party in a male-dominated society, you need to pay attention to whether it is appropriate to invite women and how to seat your guests at the dinner table.

A typical U.S. symbol of hospitality is the cocktail party. A manager may invite employees, clients, and customers so they can get to know one another. The goal at a cocktail party is to meet as many people as possible. Nobody expects to get into deep discussions. In fact, it would be rude to monopolize any one person. One makes small talk and "works the room," exchanging business cards and phone numbers so one can get into contact later and establish future business relationships.

To Europeans, the cocktail party is a curious phenomenon. In Austria, for example, one invites only as many people as one has chairs for. To invite crowds and expect them to stand would not be hospitable and thus is not acceptable. The art of small talk is not a forte of most Northern Europeans either. They tend to view the U.S. style of entertaining as superficial and lacking sincerity, and they do not understand the American conventions for meeting people, exchanging business cards, and engaging in small talk.

A U.S. firm that hosts a cocktail party in Japan creates all sorts of problems because the cocktail party is based on the premise that one can walk up to anyone in the room and introduce oneself. In Japan, with its hierarchy and protocol for addressing others, it is almost impossible to introduce oneself without knowing the age and status of the other person. What is intended as a friendly gesture by the manager from the United States may cause discomfort and embarrassment for the Japanese guests.

In cultures in which the development of personal relationships is important in doing business, the offering and acceptance of an invitation imply that both host and guest devote themselves exclusively to that particular engagement. In cultures that look at entertaining simply as a prelude to business, the implication may be quite different. For example, invitations in the United States may announce: "Cocktail party 5–7:00 p.m." This is unthinkable in cultures where hospitality is supposed to be unlimited. To invite someone for a set time period is rude. Americans, in contrast, find this arrangement very considerate and efficient. The guests know that they don't have to reserve the entire evening for the event; they can make other plans for the rest of the evening. In some English-speaking cultures, invitations are issued that read, for example, "7:15 for 7:30" which can be initially puzzling to the foreigner. They indicate that the real business of the evening (perhaps dinner or a business presentation) will be at the later time, and the preceding interval is for socializing, perhaps with drinks and small appetizers to be eaten while standing.

In Focus

A couple of Dutch businesspeople who were visiting the United States were troubled after their second day. They finally approached their American friends and asked for help. They had been to a party arranged by their U.S. client the night before. Somehow, they felt they had done something wrong. They also felt that they should have left earlier than they did, but they did not know the appropriate length of stay. In the discussion, it came out that in the Netherlands guests show appreciation by staying until the end. Since the guests from the United States dropped in and left, not all the guests were there at any one time, and the Dutch did not know what to do and how to get away. They did not know what the expected social behavior was in that setting.

In their own cultures, people know when to arrive for business meetings and business-related social functions. In the United States, for cocktail parties one is expected to be not too punctual and can leave after a short stay. For a dinner party, in contrast, one is supposed to be on time for dinner, which is usually later than the stated hour in the invitation, and then stay for the evening. In cultures that don't live as much by the clock, an invitation for seven o'clock does not mean one must be there at seven o'clock. In fact, nobody in Spain or India would expect the guests to come at seven. An hour later or even two is common, and nobody thinks anything of it. Filipino guests will arrive up to two hours later. Dinner typically is served late in the evening. A hostess from Canada or Northern Europe would be very upset by this behavior and vow never to invite those people again. After all, if the invitation is for seven, dinner probably will be served at seven-thirty or eight at the latest since the hostess probably has a sequential or monochronic view of time—discussed in Chapter 3. The evening is much more programmed, and the hostess will do everything to make things "run smoothly." Her reputation as a hostess will depend on the smooth functioning of the event.

In Canada and the United States, guests may linger after the dinner, whereas in Japan and China the host and the guests will get up shortly after the meal is over and say their good-byes. The ending to social functions in Japan and China strikes Europeans and Americans as abrupt. They often feel the evening has barely started and wonder what to do with the rest of it.

As with most other aspects of intercultural communication, one needs to be aware of the customs in the other culture. For an Australian to be insulted at not being invited to a Japanese partner's house, even though the Japanese was in the Australian's home, is petty. A businessperson from New York who insists on inviting a client from Saudi Arabia (a culture in which business and families are kept separate) to his home may not foster his business interests. However, in Brazil it is normal for a person who is about to go on vacation to give a little party with drinks and hors d'oeuvres for his friends from the workplace, usually on Friday evening. Not to do so is unthinkable. Thus, the issue of *when* to invite is also a cultural mine field. In many cases you can overcome problems by saying something like "In my culture it is the custom. . . . It is appropriate, therefore. . ." Similarly, it is acceptable to ask what is appropriate behavior for a visitor. Most people will praise you for your sensitivity and intention not to offend and be much more forgiving of mistakes if they know that you want to do what is right.

Gift Giving

Many companies have specific rules for gift giving in a business context. They may have items on hand that managers can use for gifts; calendars, pens, and golf balls are popular items. In giving business gifts, businesspeople from the United States also must be aware of legal restrictions based on the Foreign Corrupt Practices Act, which outlaws bribery and strictly limits the value of gifts one can give and accept. The official company rules on gift giving may not specify what to do if an employee is invited to attend a social event such as a dinner party.

In many cultures, it is appropriate to take small gifts when one is invited to enjoy hospitality. In Northern Europe, a fitting gift is flowers or chocolates for the hostess. A bottle of wine, especially in France, could, however, be viewed by the host as an insult, indicating that he or she does not serve good wine. In Germany, roses and chrysanthemums are not considered appropriate. Roses are for lovers, and chrysanthemums are for funerals. Flowers also must be in uneven numbers and are taken out of the paper before being presented, unlike the custom in Great Britain.

In Japan, gifts are important. Twice a year, at New Year's and in July, people present gifts to work associates, friends, and family members. These two times coincide with the payment of the twice-annual bonus.

An unwritten protocol dictates what is appropriate. Levels of hierarchy are observed closely. People know what to give to a subordinate or a boss. Importance is attached not only to what one gives but also to where the present was bought. A present from a prestigious and expensive department store counts for a lot more than does the same present bought at a small neighborhood store. However, the Japanese are beginning to change their behavior somewhat and are becoming more price-conscious, increasingly buying gifts at discount stores. Elaborate wrapping of the gift in special paper is declining somewhat as well, since the wrapping paper is increasingly seen as contributing to pollution. Nevertheless, the paper bag that shows the name of the store where the gift was bought is still an important part of the whole gift. A gift bought at Mitsukoshi in the Ginza, for example, in the store's paper wrapping, still carries a certain degree of prestige. A Japanese business professor presented a visiting professor from Belgium with several gifts: books, teacups, and a fan, all nicely gift wrapped. As he gave the presents, he pointed out that they came from the best department store in town.

Purchasing gifts for co-workers can become a financial burden; therefore, several companies have started to set rules that abolish gift giving in the office. A few years ago, such a rule would have been unthinkable because gift giving was part of life. However, times have changed, and increasingly people are reluctant to spend money on gifts for people to whom they don't feel close.

The problem for an outsider is to determine what is appropriate. If one is not familiar with the ritual, one is at a loss about what to select. Japanese businessmen appreciate gifts of whiskey. Given the price of whiskey in Japan, however, a foreign visitor may want to secure the gift outside Japan. Nicely packaged food items, such as fruit and meat, are welcome gifts, too. Personal items are taboo; gifts should be neutral unless you know the recipient fairly well. Packaging also is an issue. Elaborate wrapping is considered very important in Japan, less so in the United States and Canada, and even less so in Great Britain. Because of packaging laws in Germany, for example, wrappings may disappear completely. The law requires stores to take back any packaging that is considered superfluous. Under this provision, a store must keep the toothpaste carton and cartons for six-packs of soft drinks and beer. Germany, which already restricts the amount of household garbage, is contemplating charging garbage collection fees by the pound of garbage. In this situation, a host may not appreciate elaborate wrapping of presents.

In the United States, the recipient of a gift is expected to open the gift immediately upon receipt. Doing otherwise would show a lack of interest and appreciation; it would be rude. Children are taught early on to open gifts and acknowledge them with elaborate praise: "How wonderful; just what I always wanted!" Germans open presents too but are more reserved in their comments. The Japanese and Chinese, in contrast, never open presents while the giver is around. This would be very rude because of the potential loss of face for the giver and even the receiver. Parents take great care to emphasize appropriate behavior with their children. One Chinese mother explained that it was hard at times to ensure that her daughter would not jump to open the present. It was difficult, but for obvious reasons it was necessary. Chinese or Japanese who are familiar with the custom in the United States may go ahead and open presents from foreigners. If you are not certain, the best approach is to explain the custom of your culture and ask if it is acceptable to open the present. Most people understand that customs are different in different countries. They may find it strange, but they will appreciate the fact that the foreigner asks.

In the United States, it is typical to ask whether one can bring anything when being invited. The hostess will say "no" unless she knows the guest very well. It all follows a ritual in which the actors know their roles. The institution of potluck dinners where everyone brings a dish is unheard of in Europe. If one invites, the assumption is that one can prepare the food and generally handle the work associated with entertaining. In China, it is unthinkable to bring something for dinner. The host is gaining face by offering hospitality to guests and is storing obligation debts to his credit.

The way people from different cultures express appreciation for hospitality varies. In the United States, a businessperson who is invited for dinner to the private home of a business contact is expected to write a thank-you note shortly after the event. The Japanese tend to not write thank-you notes. Giving and showing hospitality are part of reciprocity that characterizes a relationship. It is an ongoing process that never ends. To thank someone with a thank-you note could be interpreted as a signal that the writer wants to settle the "debt" and close the relationship. Germans hardly ever write thank-you notes. They say "thank you" at the end of a visit. They are sincere in their appreciation, but they don't send notes.

Dealing with Controversy in Social Settings

In other parts of the book, we have discussed how people from different cultures deal with controversy in business settings. In social settings, behavior is very strongly influenced by attitudes toward hospitality. In Arab countries, hospitality is a sacred duty. One must be polite and considerate to visitors. Open disagreement is not acceptable. That does not mean that Arabs cannot loudly argue and disagree among themselves, but with a guest in the house, the rules are different. Both sides should avoid controversial subjects.

The French, in contrast, love to introduce controversial topics and are eager to make their points clear and disagree with each other. They take great pleasure in the elegance of an intellectual argument. Open disagreement is a sign of a successful evening, and everyone enjoys the verbal game. The Japanese are much more careful, and disagreements are avoided. One does not argue at social functions, and as a host it would be impolite to disagree with the guests; therefore, controversial topics are taboo.

Businesspeople in the United States, who often pride themselves on being outspoken, avoid controversial topics at social functions. The other side, they feel, is entitled to its opinion, but increasingly businesspeople also worry about being accused of insensitivity to people who hold different views. It therefore is considered best to avoid discussing certain topics.

Hospitality in the United States is important and shows openness and friendliness, but it does not include the same far-reaching obligations it may have in other cultures. Opening one's house does not mean unlimited hospitality. Americans look at hospitality more pragmatically: It facilitates social intercourse and establishes pleasant relationships that make it easier to conduct business. Americans generally are more concerned about creating a pleasant atmosphere even if only for a specifically prescribed time and a specific purpose.

Holiday Greetings

Many firms in Western countries send Christmas cards or season's greetings to their suppliers, customers, business associates, and government contacts. The Japanese send New Year's cards; the Taiwanese send Lunar New Year's cards. When a firm starts doing business in a different culture, it must ask when, and if, it is appropriate to send greetings and who should receive a card.

You may wonder whether it is appropriate to send cards that celebrate a holiday in your culture to business associates in cultures that do not celebrate that holiday. This becomes an issue particularly if the holiday has religious significance and the other culture does not practice your religion. The answer depends on how well you know the country and the individual. In most cultures, it would be appropriate to send best wishes for the new year or season's greetings for the holidays. Japanese firms often send their best wishes for the new year to their Japanese business partners, but many also send Christmas cards to their Western business associates and friends. The mainland Chinese, most of whom are non-Christian, also send Christmas cards. Even Chinese organizations send them, although for most Chinese people Christmas has no spiritual significance. The sending of the greeting and best wishes is seen as respect for the other person's traditions and cultures. Therefore, they want to honor their foreign business partners by acknowledging their special holidays.

If you add your foreign partners to the list for your own culture's holidays, they may feel honored that you have included them, but they also may be offended. You need to find out what is acceptable. For example, Saudi Arabia does not allow any Christian symbols, such as the cross and the Bible, into the country. Even secular symbols of Christmas such as Christmas trees, Christmas cards, and Santa Claus are banned. An American businessman reported that the rubber Santa Claus he had taken to Saudi Arabia for his son was confiscated at the airport. Iran appears to be less strict these days. Islam prohibits eating pork; in predominantly Islamic countries, pork is not sold or consumed. In the United Arab Emirates, a visiting professor from the United States who brought her cat, Porky, had to rename him Perky, which was less offensive, on the official documents to bring him into the country. The popular assumption is that Iran is the most fundamentalist Islamic society, but a Western woman doing business in Iran explained recently that there was a Christmas market in Teheran, and that one could buy Christmas trees in the streets. People also were free to gather for Christian worship regularly, although for practical reasons on Fridays rather than Sundays.

The timing of greetings also is important. Holiday greetings in most countries are expected to arrive on time, preferably before the holiday. In France, however, season's greetings can be sent until the end of January.

Ethical Considerations in Intercultural Engagements

As we have discussed the various ways people from different cultures establish business relationships, you may have started to wonder what the right or ethical foundations of these relationships are. What do businesspeople around the world consider ethical behavior? What is considered ethical depends on the cultural background of the partners involved.

For some this may be difficult to accept. After all, many of us assume that ethical standards are universal. We may define ethical behavior as being honest, being fair, telling the truth, and being considerate and caring, and we may think that these values are culture-neutral. Yet as we have seen throughout this book, none of these terms exist in a vacuum; they are influenced and shaped by the cultural priorities of the people who use them.

The philosophical foundations of ethics in various cultures help illustrate this point. For example, Aristotle, a Greek philosopher, argues that a person can find the "good." In fact, the virtuous person will see it as his or her highest goal, or *summum bonum,* to find and do what is good or virtuous. Furthermore, Aristotle maintains that people can be taught to do what is good and that they will gain happiness from doing the virtuous or the ethical.

Kant, a German philosopher, held that a person is not only capable of knowing the good or the right but also has an obligation to do what is right. This is known as the categorical imperative. Like Aristotle, Kant saw the good and the bad, the ethical and the unethical, as opposites.

Much of Western thought has been shaped by the conviction that knowledge to do the good will lead to the good and that there is a rational way of getting there. Therefore, people from those cultures have strong opinions about what is right and wrong. As a result, they have a tendency to look at ethics as an either-or concept. They know that there is a gray area, but generally ethical standards are seen as absolute and objective. This view holds that ethics can be legislated, as the United States has done with the Foreign Corrupt Practices Act (also see Chapter 10). Not all Western countries accept this view; they may look at bribes as unethical but a necessary evil. For example, in Denmark a company can claim a tax deduction for monetary payments to foreign companies in countries where such a practice is common. The pragmatic Danes recognize that their ability to compete internationally will be compromised severely if they cannot offer the under-the-table incentives their competitors can. Typically, these bribes are labeled "entertainment" rather than bribes, but everyone is aware of the practice. Recently, however, the European Union moved toward disallowing bribes as a legitimate business expense for both ethical and pragmatic reasons. It decided that bribes ultimately were too expensive and were distorting the market.

If there is a universal ethical standard, a universal standard of right and wrong, it should be possible to clarify standards through rules and laws and thus ensure that everyone understands and accepts the standards (also see Chapter 3). An Aristotelian human resources (HR) manager recognizes that there is a "good" that is knowable. At the same time, the manager tries to ensure that employees are acting in accordance with company rules and guidelines. The HR manager will attempt to inculcate good or virtuous habits in the employees to carry the company to the good.

Philosophers in East Asia have taken a different view. Daoism, for example, sees reality not as an either-or proposition but rather as a holistic unity that encompasses all aspects of reality. In Daoism, as in Western philosophy, people have an obligation to do the virtuous; however, the virtuous is not absolute. It is impossible to have the absolute good or the right because reality consists of both opposites. Daoists therefore are concerned about an appropriate balance in the universe, and that balance always depends on specific circumstances that require a careful weighing of options. Westerners, not understanding this background, frequently refer to this view of ethics as situational ethics or opportunism. The argument is that if the circumstances dictate what is ethical, there are no standards for ethical behavior. People from East Asia, in contrast, view Westerners as narrow-minded and unrealistic. In this system, the HR manager will weigh what are the best or most virtuous practices in the particular circumstances. The Chinese philosopher Confucius taught 2,500 years ago that one should not do to someone else what one wouldn't like to be done to oneself—a version of the Christian "Golden Rule": Do unto others as you would have them do unto you.

Islamic culture draws on yet another source for determining what is ethical and unethical, right or wrong: religion. Islamic ethics ultimately are based on revealed truth. Allah provides appropriate guidance for all actions. The virtuous HR manager will act on the basis of religious principles. In the increasingly secular Western world, this is easily interpreted as old-fashioned and fundamentalist. However, to understand Islamic views on ethics, it is necessary to recognize the role of religion in the shaping of ethical thought. The philosophy of ethical behavior also is influenced by other cultural variables, such as group orientation versus individualism.

Businesspeople from relationship-oriented cultures may have a view of what is ethical that is very different from that of people from results-oriented cultures. They may use the same terms but assign radically different meanings to those terms. Honesty may not be an absolute term but instead may be seen in the context of the group from which a businessperson comes. For example, fairness does not signify some abstract ideal but means that one is willing to fulfill one's obligations to one's group or family. Thus, in a results-oriented society, fairness may dictate that a manager hire the person with the best credentials for the job, an almost clinical decision that is separate from the person. In a high-context society, in comparison, fairness would dictate that a manager hire a family member, the child of a friend, or someone who has special connections. Honesty is dependent on the context as well. Honesty may be what it takes to establish the relationship to do business together.[15]

One of the challenges is that all businesspeople from all cultures judge ethical behavior by their own self-reference criteria. It is tempting to apply one's own definition of ethics to what a partner from another culture does and conclude that the partner is unethical on the basis of those standards. Not understanding the ethical framework of the people one is dealing with can lead to misunderstandings and frustrations.

For example, firms from the United States frequently try to avoid nepotism, the hiring of relatives of employees, because this is seen as bad and an unfair advantage. These views are related to the value placed on social equality in the United States. To hire someone on the basis of his or her family relationship to an employee seems to be unequal treatment, favoring people who have employed relatives and disfavoring those who do not. Managers are afraid that the relatives may stick together and that the resulting cliquishness may hurt the morale of the work unit.

In Focus

When a U.S. company went into Mexico, the managers took that standard with them and made it a point not to hire relatives; it seemed to be the ethical decision. However, the firm found out that the Mexican view of nepotism was very different. Employees had an ethical obligation to help relatives obtain a high-paying job in the U.S. firm. Everyone accepted that obligation. In fact, it would have been unethical not to try to help one's family. In return, family members understood and accepted the obligation that they had to work hard to avoid bringing shame to the family member who helped them get the job. What originally had been seen as an ethical dilemma, giving an unfair advantage by hiring relatives, turned out to be a motivator to do good work. The company changed its standards and accepted a practice that made sense in that environment.

Businesspeople with results-oriented backgrounds typically separate the business deal from the relationship with the other side. The goal is the business connection, the contract, the sale. The relationship is superficial, just enough to do business. It is a connection with a very specialized purpose. They may consciously avoid any personal connections to avoid muddying the waters. This strikes people from high-context cultures as odd. Each side may attach the label *unethical* to the behavior of the other side and strain the relationship further.

Although Americans groan about high taxes, most accept the idea that it would be unethical not to pay the taxes one owes. After all, taxes are needed to run the government and carry out programs that help society as a whole. The Chinese have a somewhat different opinion about those kinds of societal obligations, and many feel they can do more good by helping their families directly than by paying taxes whose results they cannot observe directly.

The way people from different cultures handle obligations also sheds light on attitudes toward ethics. In places where the building of relationships is crucial to doing business, obligations typically are seen as ongoing. By not repaying a debt immediately, the partner signifies that he or she is interested in a continuation of the relationship. In Japan, for example, the willingness to accept an obligation is a positive sign. In fact, the concept of *amae* refers to both the willingness to take care of someone and the willingness to be dependent on someone. In this view, the individual is clearly tied into a relationship. Repaying the debt would end the relationship because it would signal that the person no longer was willing to accept the obligation. This attitude stands in great contrast to the American ideal of self-reliance, where the goal is not to be a burden on anyone. It is expected that one will repay one's debts promptly (also see Chapter 4).

Pacific Island cultures are collectivist. They live within extended families, and their values mean anyone with resources shares them with the family. Samoans joke that the best way to manage their finances is to have a bank balance in the red, since anyone with a bit extra will be asked by relatives to share it. The value of sharing resources comes from the Polynesian Islanders' historical traditions to ensure survival of the community. The largest Polynesian city is Auckland, New Zealand, since more Pacific Islanders live there than in any one island town. The traditions are outside the norms for New Zealand culture, which has a European-descended majority population. The family member who has an income never has any extra money because relatives expect a share. By the same token, when that member is in need, relatives contribute and fill it.

As we will discuss in greater detail in Chapter 10, HR issues, including rules on hiring, promotion, and safety, are tied to specific laws, but there is also an ethical element involved. Most industrialized countries have outlawed child labor, and condoning any type of child labor would be seen as a violation of ethical norms. Not all cultures share this viewpoint. In industrialized countries, childhood has been extended to an age group that a century ago would have been considered young adults. In developing countries, children grow up faster and are considered adults at an earlier age, frequently around age 14; therefore, it is acceptable and expected that they contribute to the family income. (We are not talking about young children working in sweatshops many hours every day.) The idea that young adults should be allowed to play when they could contribute to the well-being of the family would be considered irresponsible.

In group-oriented societies, seniority plays a major role in establishing ranking and order. It gives belonging and clarifies one's status in the group. With industrialization, merit and individualism tend to gain in importance.[16] As a result, the basis for promotions may change from seniority to merit, and with that change, what is considered ethical may change as well.

As businesspeople engage in relationships with partners from other cultures, they need to be aware of the cultural foundation of what is considered ethical behavior. One of the most crucial steps is to examine why a culture has certain ethical standards and what they mean in that particular context. As the following story illustrates, different views of what is ethical can lead to problems for everyone involved.

In Focus

David was conducting a seminar in Los Angeles for a delegation of midlevel civil servants from China.

One evening David's associate received a phone call from an office of the state's department of motor vehicles (DMV). The department had one of the delegates, a woman, in its office. They wanted to go home and did not know what to do about her. The woman spoke no English but was very distraught. Here is what she told them after they found an interpreter.

She had read an ad in a Los Angeles Chinese-language newspaper by an organization that said it could get people documentation papers to enable them to stay in the United States. She phoned the number and was told that someone would come to the hotel and meet her. She waited, and in about an hour two men came. They asked her to bring all her documentation papers—her Chinese passport and her visas, both the Chinese exit visa and the U.S. entry visa for a visitor—and then took her by car to an impressive office. It was a DMV office, but apparently the men told her that it was the office of the organization that would help her stay in the United States. The woman could not read English. The two men sat her in the outer office and took all her identification documents saying they needed to make copies and would be right back. Apparently they left the building through a back door. The woman sat for hours waiting for the men to return. Finally she called the hotel, and the hotel informed the delegation organizer.

She was the victim of some Chinese scam artists, but she also was trying to circumvent the U.S. immigration system by using unofficial channels. This willingness to circumvent, to do things by making one's own arrangements, is often a strategy used by Chinese and can lead to trouble, especially in an environment where following the legal route is considered normative behavior.

This example shows legal standards that were not observed by the woman and ethical standards that were not observed by the fly-by-night operators who took advantage of her—and crossed the legal line when they stole her passport. Similarly, Chinese companies negotiating joint ventures with U.S. firms often expect a U.S. company to use its "influence" to enable the joint venture to circumvent U.S. import–export law. They believe influence exists, when in U.S. law it does not.

We all behave according to our own code until we bump up against somebody else's code. At that point, we need some way to reconcile differences and point to a code we can use. Businesspeople have to make decisions regarding ethics all the time. Richard Mead suggests there are two approaches to ethical issues across cultures:[17]

- *Ethical universalism*—a single ethical code everybody should follow. Hofstede connects this to individualism. The United States seems to be the key proponent of this view, since U.S. culture is a legalistic, individualistic culture that assumes that one system can operate everywhere (universalistic). The Foreign Corrupt Practices Act is an example of this view. The problem is that this approach neglects the fact that other cultures, such as the Danish culture, may have a different definition of ethical behavior in business.

- *Ethical empiricism*—behavior is related to the group and your responsibilities to it, and so you maintain a higher standard of ethical behavior with in-group members. You have different standards for the different groups with which you interact. This also extends to different cultures. This view easily comes across as patronizing, unprincipled, and ethically suspect.

Mead also suggests some practical ways an international manager can identify ethical norms in another culture, such as:

- Comparative analysis of ethical norms.
- Reference to institutional norms, such as a national legal system, religious leaders' teachings, professional associations, and family.
- Informal behavior guides, such as "face" in Asian cultures.
- So-called tests (the "secrecy" test—if your partner insists the deal be kept secret, it may not be ethical; the TV test—would you want your deal on TV?; how would the people you admire view it?; and so forth). These tests aren't very useful, however, because they do not come to terms with underlying ethical issues and definitions of ethical behavior.

Summary

This chapter illustrated that appropriate social and business behavior is dependent on cultural orientation.

- *Respect for authority and structuring of messages.* Businesspeople will be well served to understand the symbols of authority and power. Nonverbal behavior, position, and appearance signal level of authority and power.
- *Power distance and symbols of power and authority.* Understanding where a culture ranks on the power distance scale can be helpful when one is working with a businessperson from another culture. The use of language is an indicator of authority in most cultures.
- *Assertiveness versus peacekeeping.* Businesspeople from assertive cultures may lose out on contracts and alienate partners who come from cultures that emphasize harmony. At the same time, businesspeople from cultures that value harmony and peace may come across as weak and indecisive to people from assertive backgrounds.
- *Recognition of performance.* Rewards for performance are based on cultural priorities. In some cultures, the major sign of success is a monetary reward, such as a salary. In other cultures, nonmonetary rewards, such as recognition by powerful people, may be a more significant recognition of performance.
- *Hospitality.* Businesspeople meet in both work and social settings. Each culture has its own unique rules and customs regarding what is acceptable social behavior. For example, is it acceptable to mix social life and business life? What gifts are appropriate and when?
- *Ethical considerations.* Different cultures have different views of what is ethical. What is considered ethical behavior depends at least to some extent on cultural priorities and philosophical viewpoints.

Notes

1. Boye Lafayette De Mente, *Kata: The Key to Understanding and Dealing with the Japanese* (Tokyo: Tuttle Publishing, 2003).

2. Ibid., p. 103.

3. Geert Hofstede, *Culture's Consequences*, 2nd ed. (Thousand Oaks, CA: Sage Publications, 2001).

4. Susan Schneider and Jean-Louis Barsoux, *Managing Across Cultures*, 2nd ed. (London: Prentice-Hall, 2003).

5. Ge Gao and Stella Ting-Toomey, *Communicating Effectively with the Chinese* (Thousand Oaks: Sage, 1998).

6. Y. Luo, "*Guanxi* and Performance of Foreign-Invested Enterprises in China: An Empirical Inquiry," *Management International Review*, 37 (1997), pp. 51–70; Y. Peng, "Kinship Networks and Entrepreneurs in China's Transitional Economy," *The American Journal of Sociology*, 109:5 (2004), pp. 1047–1074.

7. Interview with H. Koga and H. Hayashida, alumni of Kanagawa University, June 2002.

8. C. Pezeshkpur, "Challenges to Management in the Arab World," *Business Horizons*, 21 (1978), pp. 47–55.

9. W. Woodworth and R. Nelson, "Information in Latin American Organizations: Some Cautions," *Management International Review*, Winter 1980, pp. 6–69.

10. Ibid.

11. K. A. Kovach, "What Motivates Employees: Workers and Supervisors Give Different Answers," *Business Horizons*, September–October 1986, pp. 58–65.

12. *Fortune Magazine*, May 2003.

13. A. Ragharen and G. T. Sims, "Golden Parachutes Emerge in European Deals," *The Wall Street Journal*, February 14, 2000, pp. A17, A18.

14. Daniel Kadlec, "Where Did My Raise Go?" *Time*, May 26, 2003, pp. 444–454.

15. For a detailed discussion on merit versus status see F. Trompenaars, *Riding the Waves of Culture: Understanding Diversity in Global Business* (London: Economist Books, 1993).

16. Martha Maznevski, Joseph DiStefano, Carolina Gomez, Niels Noorderhaven, and Pei-Chuan Wu, "Cultural Dimensions at the Individual Level of Analysis: The Cultural Orientations Framework," *International Journal of Cross Cultural Management* 2, no. 3 (2002), pp. 275–296.

17. Richard Mead, *International Management*, 2nd ed. (Malden, MA: Blackwell, 1998), p. 196.

CHAPTER EIGHT

Information, Decisions, and Solutions

In 1768, three Scottish printers cooperated to produce a compendium of knowledge that would bring into one set of books all the basic information on all the topics they could think of. The result of that massive undertaking was the *Encyclopaedia Britannica*. For the next 200 years, all over the English-speaking world, the *Encyclopaedia Britannica* became the most trusted source of information for schools and libraries. After being revised 14 times, it was still considered the most comprehensive of all its imitators worldwide, and its scholarship was widely admired. In the early 20th century, its ownership passed to businessmen in the United States, and by 1990 global sales had reached USD 650 million. But then at the end of the 20th century, sales fell a catastrophic 80 percent.

Why? Information was no less valuable—in fact, in what has sometimes been called the Information Age, people consulted more and more sources of information than ever before. The answer, of course, is *access*. Technology made information easily available right on personal computers. The first Microsoft Encarta CD-ROM—an encyclopedia that came already loaded on computers—appeared in 1993, and over the next five years it dealt the venerable hard-copy *Encylopaedia Britannica* a crippling blow. In early 2000, the company announced it would no longer publish its multivolume set of books, citing high costs (the company employed 4,000 authors who wrote the articles) and lower sales.

Britannica's last 20th-century edition sold for between US $1,500 and US $2,200 per set. In contrast, the Microsoft-licensed Encarta was free with the purchase of a personal computer. In past generations, people had bought an encyclopedia set because they believed they were doing something to help their children excel in their homework assignments. The encyclopedia gave readers a single-source access to high-quality information. By the end of the 20th century, parents were buying their children a computer for the same reason. (Computers cost less than a set of the *Encyclopaedia Britannica*.) The Britannica story to this point was about how evolving access to information turned the print-encyclopedia world upside down and nearly killed the Britannica company.

But Britannica did not die, and that wasn't the end of the story. In 1996, Swiss financier Jaqui (Jacob) Safra bought the ailing company at a bargain price and made two important decisions in order to regain sales and reassert *Encyclopaedia Britannica*'s position as the premier information source: to make the entire encyclopedia accessible on the Internet, for a fee, at www.britannica.com, and to continue to print hard-bound volumes.

Then 2005 brought another challenge to the encyclopedia world: Wikipedia, the free online encyclopedia that can be edited by anyone. Now Britannica had two competitors, Encarta—free with the purchase of a computer—and Wikipedia. In its 2008 version, Encarta had 62,000 articles. Wikipedia is high on the list of search returns because it has over one million articles. In many ways, it is the realization of the ideal of the World Wide Web originators: free, open to any contributor, easy to access, and without profit-making middlemen. Britannica looked like it would go under this time.

But the next twist in the Britannica story is that as a direct result of the Wikipedia challenge, Microsoft made the decision in 2009 to get out of the Encarta business, and no longer sells the product. The changing nature of information access—the very same challenge Encarta had presented to Britannica 15 years earlier and which almost killed Britannica—killed Encarta. Britannica had outlasted the giant Microsoft in the encyclopedia business.

That left Wikipedia and its imitators, which offer faster access to broader information. However, Britannica still survives, and still sells sets of hardbound volumes.

What can explain Britannica's survival? One key reason is that users of encyclopedias want accurate information and need to be able to trust their sources. Accurate information has always been Britannica's stock-in-trade, and customers have trusted it as a reliable source for over 240 years. Britannica remains committed to high-quality information and to making it available to the widest possible audience.

Excellence in providing quality information is expensive. The Britannica board includes Nobel Prize winners and Pulitzer Prize winners—thinkers and researchers whose work has achieved the highest possible recognition. Their authors are respected for their care and accuracy, although critics have found some targets. Whereas online encyclopedias are free, users have to pay to use Britannica. The company believes, however, that information must be of a high quality to be useful, and that the market is willing to pay to access it.

Access to Britannica has evolved as well. Britannica Mobile is an application for iPhone and BlackBerry users who can download a 28,000-entry encyclopedia to their device. Consumers now can get one million pages of quality *Encyclopaedia Britannica* information wherever they are.

The Britannica story is about how a company that published reference books held to two key principles: the enduring value of reliable and high-quality information, and meeting the changing nature of access to it. Both are important to students, of course. Both are also important to decision-makers in the world of work.

It is a mistake to assume that because technology can transport information across oceans and national boundaries that information has the same definition everywhere in the world. As we have seen in previous chapters, businesses have different priorities because of the cultures in which they operate. That means they define information differently, and they place different priorities on information and on processes they need information to accomplish, such as making decisions. Even the need for a decision is not perceived the same way.

This chapter examines the nature of information and differences in how information is gathered, assessed, and valued by managers and their organizations. Next, since information is used for making decisions, various decision-making processes are discussed. Then the chapter looks at problem solving and at resolving conflicts across cultures.

The Nature of Business Information

Business information is goal-oriented. Businesses gather information for business purposes, not simply for the sake of general education or for collecting statistics. They want the information in order to do something. But as we'll see, different cultures look for different kinds of information for different reasons to reach different goals.

The Impact of Culture on What Constitutes Information

What constitutes information? It differs along the continuum between high-context and low-context cultures.

High-context cultures value relationships, teamwork, and long-term group membership. People in these collectivist environments seek information about groups in order to make business decisions. Of course, they also look at costs, benefits, processes, suppliers, markets, and management structure. But knowing *who* is involved is critical.

Furthermore, high-context cultures rely on subjective information that is internalized; that is, it is information that forms people's personal views of their world. It is made up of opinions, attitudes, deductions, and insights based on *personal experience*. Most importantly, information in high-context cultures is always viewed with reference to the context: the relationships within the group, the history of the group, the long-range goals for the group, and so forth.

Low-context cultures value independent decisions, activity that achieves goals, and individual accountability. They rely on objective information that is externalized; that is, it consists of data that exist independently of the person who gathers it. It is made up of opinions, attitudes, deductions, and insights based on *measurable units*. Tests of reliability and validity assess the value of data.

The U.S. business culture is more low-context than high-context, and it devotes effort to considering the nature of business information. It is a culture whose members like to define terms and pin down explicitly what they mean. Information in the United States is explicit and often it is quantifiable.

The Assessment of Information

Information used for specific communication objectives is usually assessed as to its reliability and validity. Both high-context and low-context cultures look for reliability and validity of data, although ways of defining those characteristics vary.

Reliable generally means that the information is consistent, timely, and stable. The same information could be gathered again at another date from the same people, using the same means, provided the factors in the situation are the same. It doesn't depend on the emotions of the information-gatherer or the people involved. Reliable sales figures for the month of March are not subject to variation depending upon whether the sales manager is angry with the production manager.

Valid means that the information is about what it purports to be about. Information from a parts supplier about the availability of a part for an assembly job is valid when it refers to that specific part, not to another part. Unless the information is indeed about *what* it claims to be about, it is not valid even if the measure (say, the quantity of that part manufactured per month) is reliable.

People who make decisions value information. Managers want lots of information, and they want it to be useful in the decision-making process. Managers often ask subordinates to supply information so they can make good decisions.

In many contexts, effective managers give their subordinates lots of information when they explain an upcoming decision so that their subordinates understand the direction of the decision. When subordinates have information about the larger objectives and goals, they are more likely to feel a commitment to them. Their commitment can grow if they are informed about the background to a decision: the history, the reasons, the long-term objectives. Managers also feed information to subordinates to generate feedback of information.

As discussed in Chapter 5, the logic businesspeople use to assign meaning to information is determined by culture. Western logic tends to look for rules, such as the rules of syllogisms. East Asians tend to look for syntheses, including over-arching concepts that embrace contradictions. Westerners see objects with attributes that don't change. East Asians see relationships and contexts that constantly change. Businesspeople cannot assume things add up the same way in all cultures.

The Possession of Information

Information is a useful resource in competitive situations. A person or group that knows what another does not know has an advantage. Let's say you are one of two candidates for a position, and your interview with the hiring team is next week. You'll want to find out everything you can in order to strengthen your candidacy. If you are working within a low-context, results-oriented culture, you'll want to know the job description, the qualifications the team is looking for, and the things it values in an employee in that position. You'll also want to know what strengths and weaknesses your competitor has, if possible. This will give you some power in the interview to respond and perhaps even direct the conversation.

If you are working within a high-context, relationship-oriented culture, you'll also want to empower yourself for the interview, but you may want different kinds of information. You'll want to know who the people are on the hiring team and who will have the greatest say. You'll want to find out what links (connections between people) you might have with the hiring team—common interests, acquaintances, experiences—and others you'll be working among if you are hired. You'll also want to know what links your competitor has with the hiring team and the organization. Of course, there are many other factors you'll want information about as well, but the point is that in both high- and low-context cultures, information is power and confers an advantage—even when the nature of the information varies.

In organizations in high-context cultures, in which the career path of an individual is closely tied to the team or group of which the individual is a part, information is "owned" by the group. Individuals share information. This is related to the cultural priority discussed in Chapter 4 about what is private versus what is public, as well as to the cultural priority about permanent group membership. In a high-context culture like China, for example, little is *not* shared. Information belongs to the group, not the individual. That way, individuals are linked together into a collective.

In Focus

In China, one of the authors was a visiting professor and she discovered a different attitude toward confidentiality, to her chagrin. She had written a personal assessment of each student at the end of a course. She had given each student a personal copy and had given the whole document, labeled "Confidential," to two people only: the chair of the department in which she taught and the president of the university. She was amazed when she saw her confidential evaluations *published* in a university-wide periodical, complete with the "Confidential" heading duly translated! As a Westerner, she had not understood the collective ownership of information.

Human resources management implications come out of this different attitude toward information about people. In New Zealand, people zealously keep personnel data private. Teachers go through elaborate procedures to ensure that students do not have access to each other's grades. In business, it is the same. Evaluations are confidential. The right to privacy, like many other rights in low-context cultures, comes from an individualistic cultural dimension.

Ingroups   Information is a link that joins people in a collective or group. For example, Thais seeking employment include not only university education on their résumés but also high school education.[1] That's because they may have gone to a school that a member of the royal family or some other aristocrat attended. That links the candidate to a high social status and would link future co-workers as well. Shared information creates an in-group in both high-context and low-context cultures. It is a community of the knowing, the knowledgeable, the ones in the know.

From secret handshakes and codes in social organizations to vacation experiences in specific locations to membership on boards or committees, information that is shared by the group but not by those outside the group defines membership. In group-oriented cultures, what is known by one member of a group may well be known by all members of the group. In individualist cultures, what is known by one individual is not automatically the property of the group. One who knows has a power others do not have, and when one chooses to share the information, a link is forged and a group is formed.

In individualist cultures, in which the career of the individual is to a greater extent the individual's own responsibility, information is owned by the individual and shared judiciously when the individual will benefit. In Australia, for example, individuals value the confidentiality of information and do not share it. If a job candidate has had a link with a prestigious person, the candidate might use that to enhance his or her status, but co-workers would not expect to be included in the linkage or to benefit from it.

Information Gathering   Imagine a culture that views change as negative, that values being rather than doing, that considers the group a basic unit of society and individuals as fractions of the whole basic unit, and that looks upon its own cultural priorities as the only ones worth holding. Then imagine someone—probably a foreigner—coming in to ask questions and gather information about behavior, preferences for products, prices paid for goods, and other market data. Such inquiries will almost certainly be treated with suspicion, resentment, and hostility. The way business information is defined and gathered has to be put in the context of a specific culture.

The collection of information in a carefully designed research study is determined by the researcher's paradigm, as discussed in Chapter 1. Positivists believe the researcher stands outside what is being investigated, is objective, and has no impact on what is being researched. Conclusions about what the findings mean are generalized to apply to other situations. Interpretivists, on the other hand, believe the researcher is interrelated with what is being researched, and that the research impacts it and therefore cannot be absolutely objective. The information collected is rich in detail, but cannot be generalized widely. These two research paradigms are the conceptualization of Western minds, which tend toward dichotomies and mutually exclusive alternatives. In reality, most research is a combination of paradigms.

Information Is Power

> In all cultures, information creates and reflects power, depending on who has it, how it is used, and to whom it is transmitted or not transmitted. It distinguishes the "ins" from the "outs;" thus, whether or not you share the secret reflects your social standing. And so vice versa, any information restricted to an elite is perceived to be important, perhaps even when it has little instrumental value.[2]

Businesspeople speak of the importance of "getting all your ducks in a row"— an image from a fairground shooting gallery—to refer to the need to have all the pieces of information possible and understand how they fit together before revealing one's intentions to others. That is a way to minimize the risk that a powerful person with more information could come between you and your objective.

A young Thai executive in a finance company came up against a boss who refused to tell her what was involved in his job and refused to train her. After all, status came from what he knew that nobody else did. She reported the following:

> He will not tell anybody what he is doing, even me. He is frightened that we are going to take his job. He's old, he has to retire in four years. Everyone respects him because he's old and he's the only one who has the information. He just likes to give orders and nobody can say anything because we don't properly understand. Even [*sic*] he won't help me although our managing director told him to. . . . When he goes, the company can easily go bankrupt because we don't have his knowledge. So I have to go abroad for training and then come back and train other people.[3]

Formal and Informal Information

Information can be characterized as **formal** and **informal.**

Formal Information

Formal information comes from four sources:

- Publications and public information from radio and TV
- Observation
- Interviews and surveys
- Experimentation

The methods for accessing information from these sources are the same across cultures. For example, experiments must follow certain procedures to yield valid results, such as control of variables, selection of subjects, and explicitly identified equipment. Then another researcher can repeat the experiment exactly. The use of published information involves documenting the sources carefully so that another researcher could consult the same sources. Similarly, observation has to be described so another researcher can duplicate the observation and get the same results. Interviews and surveys involve questionnaires that should be designed carefully and be pre-tested before data are gathered. They also should be open to scrutiny by other researchers.

The information yielded by these four methods is thus presumed to be untouched by the researcher's personal and subjective bias. In other words, it is considered *objective* data. *Low-context managers think that objectivity ensures a greater degree of accuracy.*

Informal Information

Informal information that is *subjective* often comes through a "grapevine" or another informal network inside or outside an organization. Subjective data can also be useful because the emotional bias as well as the data are useful information for the gatherer that can affect a decision. If the informal talk about the implementation of a training program carries emotional messages of suspicion and fear, a manager can respond to that emotion, allay fears and suspicions, and thereby possibly increase the likelihood of success of the program.

One reason talk-with-contacts information may be more valuable than formal information is that it is always within a context. The source and the information gatherer assign meaning within a context. *High-context managers think understanding the context and the people ensures a greater degree of accuracy.*

Informal information from the Internet is easily available—so available, in fact, that it is often mistaken for formal information. Informal communication channels such as online chat, social networking sites like Facebook, and blogs, give people who have never been introduced to each other an opportunity to discuss pretty much anything. This is a greatly expanded "grapevine" that provides access to a breathtakingly broad range of informal information. For example, you can find out what's happening at a company by chatting online or reading a blog or exchanging e-mails with an employee, even if you never learn that person's real name. You can learn what people really think about someone they work for before that person is hired by your company. You can find out what people who bought a product really think of it. Chatting online involves participants engaged in an immediate personal dialog carried in an authentic "voice." People communicate in an unmediated and direct onscreen conversation that seems to give more trustworthy information than does an official company press release or memo. Electronically facilitated conversations also go on among employees of companies, often through an intranet, or a network that serves specific users.

But the unfiltered information also introduces a whole host of new problems. Verification of information may be more difficult. Anyone can put information on the Internet, regardless of its accuracy. Just because something appears on a Web site that looks impressive doesn't make it true. Publicly edited information sites such as Wikipedia, to which anyone can provide information (although Wikipedia has announced that it will have all new entries reviewed by a board for accuracy), don't distinguish between majority and minority views, and that is both the great virtue of this most democratic of electronic media and its greatest drawback. Web sources' authenticity, trustworthiness, and credibility need to be verified.

Employees increasingly communicate by using their natural voices through company weblogs, or blogs. Blogs, electronically published and frequently updated logs or diaries of what people are thinking and working on, have exploded all over the Internet. They are also the material people tweet using Twitter and similar sites that allow communication from an individual to many recipients at once. Today, millions of people engage in personal electronic communication that is public. People air their views on a wide range of topics, from company products, to specific experiences, to political opinions. It is word-of-mouth on a global scale. And just as marketers plant their representatives to spread word-of-mouth marketing campaigns, political messages are being transmitted through social networking sites in countries around the world. Thanks to smartphone technology, the messages are not only text but include audio and video as well.

The line between employee communication and personal social networking communication is blurred, as more organizations are turning to Facebook and its like to facilitate employee communication. Employees using personal handheld devices can send out e-mails, photographs, meeting minutes, ideas generated by informal conversations, ideas that result from individual pondering, general advice, specific solutions to problems, and all the other content that makes up a company's knowledge base. The communication is horizontal, not top-down directives or bottom-up reports. Communication is direct unmediated discourse in an authentic voice. It doesn't sound like the official language of business, which conforms to norms of business discourse. Customers and employees alike are increasingly engaged in a conversation through informal communication channels like blogs and Q&A sites in the "real" voice of everyday people. As a result, the voice companies used in the 20th century has had to change. The distant paternal tone that said the company knew best what people needed is not so persuasive today.

With the increase in online employee activity, an increase in employee-monitoring software has developed. Companies can track what computer applications an employee uses and what keystrokes an employee makes. Software can monitor and store e-mails and their content. Sites accessed by employees can also be monitored. Although these "eyes over the shoulder" of employees make some uncomfortable, monitoring software has helped companies recover productivity that had been lost to hours spent online. In the United States, monitoring software also helps ensure that companies are in compliance with the Right to Privacy Act, which regulates what information can be published. In other countries, monitoring may be done to ensure that only approved Web sites are accessed.

In Focus

The authors of *We Blog* predicted in 2002:

To date, there hasn't been a lot of discussion of intranet weblog use because there's little opportunity to examine what's happening behind corporate firewalls with weblogs. If weblogs were icebergs, what you've seen online are only the tips. Business weblogging's potential is the vast expanse hidden from view beneath the surface. Just because you can't see intranet weblogs in action isn't reason to believe they don't exist, or to overlook the tremendous potential of intranet blogging. From meeting notes to project or task-based weblogs, the ease of use of weblogging software and the chronological format of the weblog can transform an intranet site into a vibrant, engaging, and useful online resource.[4]

Today that blog prediction has become standard practice for many organizations.

Soft vs. Hard Data

Another characteristic of information that varies with cultures involves what is known in English as "soft" and "hard" data. Hard data are often numerical. Of course, as you know, statistics can be used to mean anything. Numbers are valued because they appear to be objective and verifiable. Numbers supposedly could be duplicated by another statistician looking for the same information in the same places.

Figures that show quarterly earnings, for example, seem to be incontrovertible. But in fact they may not measure the same things in different organizations. Market share figures can include or exclude factors, and so they can vary from company to company and product to product.

Relevance and appropriateness of data are culturally defined. High-context cultures with market economies like Japan may identify "relevant" data differently from low-context cultures such as Europe and the United States. For example, issues involving family or obligations may count more than hard data. A Korean father who founded a family noodle shop may not be the fastest worker (the most productive), but it is important to him to make noodles, and the loss of face he would suffer if his children were to decide to replace him would make such a decision impossible.

Soft data are estimates, non-numerical projected trends, guesses, and suppositions. Businesspeople sometimes talk about "flavor" when discussing imprecise characteristics of a product or market or partnership, or they talk about "feel." For example, a Middle Eastern company that wants to import cotton fabric may order more patterns with green because of a guess that consumers will prefer the color green, since it is identified with Islam.

Much information is *not* quantifiable but nevertheless is important. For example, employees may report they enjoy working in a particular department within an organization, but they may not be able to say exactly why.

Criteria for Business Information

A number of criteria exist for assessing business information, regardless of its source:

- Verifiability
- Trustworthiness
- Accuracy
- Credibility

We'll consider each of these criteria.

Information gatherers often wonder whether data **can be verified.** That means confirming the information with another unrelated source. When Lexus receives information about the success of its North American advertising campaign for the IS250 car from its advertising agency, it will ask its sales department for confirmation. When Dow Chemical Company receives information from a construction contractor about the scheduled completion date for a plant in Kuwait, it will ask for information from other divisions with previous experience for confirmation.

Another criterion is **trustworthiness.** This is related to the source of information. If the source has proven correct in the past, the source is probably trustworthy now. Newspaper articles frequently quote a "reliable source"; the author of the article has had some reason to believe the source's information is correct and has probably confirmed it with another independent source. Sources are trustworthy if they are accountable—that is, if they can be called on to verify their information. Nationally known publications and news media that are shown to be untrustworthy lose credibility (and therefore market). Trustworthiness also applies to the information itself—the degree to which one can count on or have confidence in it.

Is the information **accurate?** This is a key criterion for the usefulness of information. A businessperson who asks about the market for cellular telephones in Nairobi wants data that are as accurate as possible. Obviously, the answer depends to some extent on the source and the verifiability of the information. In some cultures, accuracy is not verifiable and businesspeople have to make do with the best information they can get. If they wait for what they believe is accurate information, they may never make the decision.

Another criterion is **credibility.** Can the consumer of information believe it? If information seems too good to be true, it probably is. When production turnaround, construction schedules, costs, or potential market figures are much more favorable than you had believed they would be, they probably are not believable, and you are right not to believe in them. Information that looks odd may *be* odd.

These four criteria—verifiability, accuracy, trustworthiness, and credibility—have been discussed from the point of view of the authors of this book. That point of view is low-context, with a priority on hard data and information sources that meet the criteria discussed here. But the criteria are culturally defined. They mean different things in different cultures.

In the absence of shared definitions of the criteria for business information, business decision-makers need to be flexible. They need to adopt new definitions about information. For example, they may need to look at the connections (people) of their sources or the validity of contextual signals.

Information, like everything else in business communication, is culturally defined.

Sources of Business Information

Managing the information tidal waves that threaten to drown gatherers is a big job in itself. In fact, an industry exists to offer information about how to manage information.

Formal Sources

It is assumed in the United States that the collection of personal information about people is acceptable in many situations. Europeans have a rather different attitude. For example, the United States keeps detailed cancer statistics, including follow-ups and the effectiveness of treatment. Patients are not identified by name, but the information is collected and managed. In Germany, no such research bank exists because hospitals are not allowed to collect that information. It is considered a violation of privacy. This has ramifications for determining the effectiveness of treatment options.

Information is gathered by a wide range of information services and made available in libraries, newspapers and other publications, nonprint media like radio and television, and online sources. Information is gathered by private companies that sell it, such as J.D. Power and Associates, which does analyses of automobiles. Information is gathered by independent researchers who make their findings public and who are often funded by public sources. Journalists gather information for publication. Academics gather information for publication. And information is gathered by governments and published in documents available in libraries. Organizations and individuals publish information on the Web.

Online information is proliferating at an astounding rate. In August 2008, there were over 8.05 billion pages on the World Wide Web.[5] Access to Internet information is increasing by great leaps: In 2003, the number of Internet users was over 700 million worldwide. By 2009, the number of worldwide Internet users exceeded 1.668 billion, with more than 700 million users in Asia alone.[6]

Gathering information is taken for granted as a valid business activity in Western cultures. It is necessary and reasonable for businesses to gather and use information. In non-Western cultures, however, especially in societies with governments or research institutions that look upon their information as exclusively theirs,

Information she has just received about the size of the market in Malaysia for Fisher-Paykel kitchen appliances looks odd to New Zealander Naomi King, a marketing manager. The information lacks verifiability and accuracy, and she is unsure about the degree to which it can be trusted. However, it seems it is the only information available. Her Malay informant, to whom the context of the information is well understood and the implications for its use are obvious, thinks the information is extremely helpful. He gathered the information from people whose judgment he trusts and whose experience he knows to be extensive. Importantly, even if the information is not as accurate as Naomi would like, it is considered trustworthy by the contacts who supply it to her because *their* Malay sources will put their reputations at risk to stand by it.

gathering information can be dangerous. It threatens the sources that control information. Since information is power, holders of information don't like any dissipation of that power. In addition, the act of gathering information can seem threatening to people who have had information about themselves used against them. In different cultures, people who gather information about others and hold it secretly, from secret police in dictatorships to powerful military rebels, generate fear.

Informal Sources

The grapevine—the informal information network—flourishes where formal official information is limited. The secretary to the president, someone in the mail room, a good friend of a relative of the chairperson, a confidant of the director—these are the kinds of sources with the greatest credibility in an informal network. Informal Internet sources also have greater credibility when they are known persons or entities.

People from open-information cultures who are used to formal sources that offer reliable and accurate information tend not to place much value on factual information that comes from informal sources. But informal sources of information may be much better at revealing the context than formal sources are, and *informal information may be more accurate than the official version.*

In some cultural environments, unofficial spokespersons, unsigned newspaper articles, and references in an organization's internal documents can be reliable sources. They not only provide data but also interpret the data, and interpretation means putting the information in context.

Businesspeople unaccustomed to reading contextual signs are at a disadvantage in high-context cultures. Those with cultural interpreters who are able to decipher the context get information earlier than their competitors who rely on "hard" facts and published sources.

Internet sources and informal personal contacts have made informal information much more important than it was only a decade ago. However, issues of verifiability, trustworthiness, and accuracy are still important. Some critics of participative information sources like YouTube are skeptical about their merit, seeing

In Focus

For example, in Bangladesh, a couple of American businessmen met with the Minister of Textiles. They were seeking a favorable garment quota allocation. The Americans had been told that a competitor from abroad had been turned down on a similar request just recently.

The meeting took place on a typically hot and humid day in Dhaka. The Minister's office was equipped with an air conditioner, but it apparently wasn't working. The Americans made small talk while they suffered and sweated in the hot dark business suits their consultant had told them to wear. The Minister was cool and dry in his tropical linen.

After almost 90 minutes of conversation that seemed to the Americans to be going nowhere, the Minister stood up smiling and told them he would grant their request. The Americans were happy, if a bit puzzled. The next day their consultant told them he had had a conversation with a contact in the government. He had learned through that informal source that the Minister had deliberately turned off his air conditioner to subject the Americans to a kind of test.[7]

them not only as "soft" information sources but also as biased, opinionated, unmonitored, and unfactual. Proponents see them as calling forth the knowledge, experience, creativity, and imagination of the unnamed masses of people who use them. Most people have a story about some information learned from someone through the Internet that solved a problem.

Some people find these myriad ongoing conversations a kind of exploitation of people as unpaid sources of work and expertise. Others find these multiplying connections between people an expression of democracy that was the original vision of the World Wide Web, allowing people to access an expanding sea of information.

In Focus

After Britannica and Wikipedia became involved in a public mud-slinging over which encyclopedia had more errors of accuracy, the former editor-in-chief of Britannica, Robert McHenry, made an unflattering analogy. He likened Wikipedia to a public toilet facility. He said that you may find it isn't altogether clean, so you are very careful, or you may find it is quite presentable, so your anxieties are lessened, but the bottom line is that you never know who was there before you.[8]

Information and Knowledge Management

In recent years, the availability of information has transformed not only the way businesses operate but the very economic environment in which businesses exist. Information technology or IT has changed the way information can become knowledge. Electronically available information converts to useful business knowledge.

Small businesses can compete with big companies in terms of business information. Employees have access to more information and, as a result, express greater satisfaction with their work.

What is "knowledge" *within* a company? The example from Thailand on page 294 illustrates what this means: the accumulated experience, understanding, contacts, and information that exist within the minds of employees. Companies are right to view this intangible resource as valuable. Capturing what employees know so that knowledge can be accessed in the future can give a company a competitive edge. To take one example, an employee who has experienced a posting overseas has gathered considerable knowledge that she can pass on to the person who replaces her.

In Focus

Anupama Joshi has worked for Hinduja TMT, a large Indian conglomerate with a strong IT services sector, for 12 years. Recently she has been working with a client in Belgium, KredietBank. While there, she helped secure other clients for HTMT in Luxembourg and Switzerland. During her time in Brussels she learned a great deal about how to communicate effectively with Flemish-speaking Belgians as well as other Europeans. She can save HTMT a great deal of money if she can communicate what she has learned to the person who will follow her. She has worked with Ms. Arathi Vedantham, the Manager of Corporate Communications, to devise ways to capture her knowledge so that her replacement can quickly step into her shoes when she returns to Bangalore, India.

To capture and capitalize on this knowledge, companies must come up with a way to manage information. When managing information involves technology, it is an IT function by which knowledge is stored in databases so others can access it.

In developing economies, companies leapfrog into up-to-date IT much more quickly than observers in developed economies may realize. They have a "latecomer advantage" in not having to invest in the development of technology, but just adapting what has been developed elsewhere. In older economies, the availability of more timely information in recent years has enabled business management to reduce inventory and eliminate unproductive workers. The extraordinary surge in technological innovation, particularly in information access, has given companies worldwide a new awareness of the need to manage information.

Of course, the huge gaps that have existed between people with technology and world citizens without it is closing. The global population is over 6.83 billion.[9] Although many people in the world have never seen a computer, let alone used one, the number of computer owners is estimated to be 1.3 billion, or one in five.[10] Ten years ago, Manhattan had more telephone lines than all of Africa; today Africa has more phone lines than both the United States and Canada combined.[11]

Technology is spreading fast. As long ago as 2000, on a visit to India, former President Clinton was amazed to see in a small poor village a computer, operating in both Hindi and English, that a person with basic literacy skills could operate. A young mother demonstrated that she could access a Web site complete with good graphics from the health department in India to get information about what a mother should do during her child's first six months. She printed out the information and took it home. In another village, a dairy cooperative tracked its output by computer and satellite-delivered information. In Bangladesh, the Grameen Bank launched a project to finance a cell phone in every village. That way, poor villagers were connected to the rest of the world. The International Telecommunications Union (ITU) of the United Nations published a report in 2009 that stated six in ten people in the world pay for mobile phone technology, and two-thirds of the payers come from developing countries.[12]

In Focus

A World Bank representative went to Ethiopia to determine how the World Bank could assist in the development of e-business. He thought he was going to deal with people who had no experience or understanding of e-business, and he said to a group of local businesspeople, "Does anybody here know what a Web site is?" Someone raised a hand and said, "I do; I have a Web site." The World Bank employee asked how he could have a Web site in Addis Ababa, since there were no household connections and few computers.

The Ethiopian said, "It's very easy. In the United States, cab drivers in Chicago, New York, and Washington are Ethiopian. And what they want to do is send goats to their families in Ethiopia. So I've opened a Web site in New York. I go to my cyber café here every day, and I collect the orders from the cab drivers in the United States to send goats to their families in Ethiopia."[13]

In organizations, people gather information primarily for making decisions. Business information and business decision making are closely linked. We began this chapter talking about information and what it means in different cultures. Now we will turn to the subject of decision making.

Decision Making

The ways people in different cultures make decisions is an important factor in cross-cultural encounters. The principles governing decision making differ and are culturally based. Take the decision 12 people who serve on a trial jury must make. They may have 12 different ways of arriving at a judgment about the defendant. Some might draw up complex charts of pros and cons, "guilty" and "not guilty" indicators. Others might add some kind of weighting factor and add up the numbers. Still others could lock on to a key piece of evidence and take that as the deciding factor. One or two may go by something more intuitive.

Within a culture, people use a variety of decision-making strategies. Business decisions are usually based on hard data, although decisions are sometimes based on feelings or luck. The variations in decision-making practices come from cultural priorities.

Making Decisions Based on Ends

Companies in low-context cultures make decisions by focusing on results, or ends. The Ford Motor Company decides to lay off thousands of workers because that will enable the end-of-year profits to be higher. Philip Morris, an international tobacco company, decides to lower the price of its cigarettes in order to increase the volume of sales and stop erosion of the market share to generic brands. Mövenpick, a Swiss-based company, decides to open a new café in Madras and close a café in Montréal because the shift in the economic levels of those populations means the market has changed.

The cause-and-effect thinking of low-context cultures means they argue from causes to effects and back. They measure profits or market share or number of clients and look for reasons; then they identify other reasons that they believe will result in better profit figures, bigger market share, or larger numbers of clients. For instance, people who make staffing decisions with ends in mind often have to lay off employees who cannot contribute to the achievement of the organization's goals and hire other employees who can. These decision-makers are valued by the organization.

Decisions also are driven by *personal* goals. That is, personal decisions also are based on an assessment of results in low-context cultures. An employee will decide to work here for five years to accomplish a specific personal goal, and then he or she will be prepared to move over there with the purpose of accomplishing a different goal.

Employees at many levels get to make decisions in organizations in ends-oriented cultures like the United States and Canada. True, at the lower levels they may only be small decisions that are easy to make. But the employees can be held accountable for their decisions, and that helps the organization measure and evaluate their employees—and employee evaluation is another of the organization's goals.

Making business decisions in English-speaking business cultures usually involves subdividing points and issues and dealing with the subsections in a specific order until everything has been addressed. Clarification of detail is important so that the relationship of subsections to the larger issues can be understood. Cause-and-effect relationships are established. "What if?" questions are posed, and potential answers are offered.

In Europe (France, Germany, and Holland, to name a few countries), organizational decisions are based on results, but not so many people in an organization make them. In France and Germany, a very few at the top of an organizational pyramid make decisions. In Holland, the few may be a slightly wider circle, but people in the lower levels do not participate. This is a meaningful difference from Canada and the United States. One cannot expect someone in a middle-level position in an organization in Europe to influence a decision of any magnitude. Canadian and United States companies often delegate authority to make decisions to their representatives, even midlevel ones.

Finally, in low-context cultures that value achieving goals, making decisions can be a goal. There is a tendency to consider a decision as an end in itself. Management practices often involve making decisions as a form of action. A matter has been dealt with when a decision has been made.

Making Decisions Based on Means

Companies in high-context cultures make decisions based on means. That means the possible effects of the decision on people, processes, organizations, and outcomes are all considered. Means cultures are people cultures in which relationships matter more than results.

In Focus

Juan Carlos Aguilar has decided to use Luis Calderon's firm as a supplier for his graphic arts company because he has met Calderon several times in social situations, and over a long breakfast last week Calderon assured him of his firm's ability to supply what Aguilar's organization needs. This decision has been made in spite of the fact that Calderon's firm is known in the industry as having a hard time shipping promptly and shipping correct orders.

Another firm has sent Aguilar a promotional mailing with impressive figures, but Aguilar knows nobody in that firm. It also sent a representative, but Aguilar wasn't impressed when they met briefly in his office. He will go with someone he feels he can trust personally.

When Aguilar wants to promote his ability to produce printed materials using a new color process to a government official, he has a third party arrange a lunch with someone close to that official, say a lower-level official. In this case, the third party happens to be the lower official's brother-in-law, whom Aguilar knows. The friend and brother-in-law is a go-between.

He and Juan Carlos and the lower official will meet, have drinks and order a meal, and talk about family and other things. Then Juan Carlos will inquire about the lower official's responsibilities so that Juan Carlos, in response to what the lower official and the go-between say, can appear very impressed with the lower official's position, responsibilities, cleverness, and so forth. Then he will ask the lower official—who has thus been established as wise and well connected—to recommend a higher-level official Juan Carlos could talk to about his new color process and printing ability.

If possible, Juan Carlos will get a card from the lower official. Then he will approach the person recommended and use the lower official's name. The higher official will usually be in a position to make decisions or influence them. That person may be impressed that Juan Carlos knows the lower official (Juan Carlos will say, "Oh, yes; in fact we had lunch the other day"). Because of the chain of contacts between people from Juan Carlos, through his friend the brother-in-law of the lower official, to the lower official, and then to the ultimate target, a decision may be made in Juan Carlos's favor, to use his company's services. Juan Carlos will owe his friend a favor for his work as a go-between.

Where decisions are based on means, trust is a key issue. Hard information, statistics, and measurements are not as important as trusting a relationship.

Chains of relationships linking people in networks of favors owed and granted exist in most high-context, or means, cultures. In Hong Kong, for example, the connection of people by the reciprocity of exchanged favors, called *guanxi,* is an important factor in decision making

Another key issue is solidarity within one's group. In the early 1980s, an internationally renowned steel company in Japan entered into a contract to supply steel to another Asian government when it was not feasible to do so. The company could not meet the deadline at the agreed price. But the honor of the company and the honor of the country were at stake. The company performed the contract to the last letter but suffered a great financial loss doing it. The contract wasn't so important in itself, but not losing face as an organization, and as an organization representative of the Japanese nation, was very important. It outweighed the cost in money of fulfilling the contract.

Managers take personal responsibility for decisions in Western, low-context cultures. A manager's power comes in part from this role, and when decisions have good results, the manager wants to take credit for them. But managers in non-Western cultures are the opposite. As Victor writes,

> In Asian cultures, the powerful eschew decision-making . . . In the West, power is demonstrated by the ability to override the dictates of social pressure. By contrast, in Asia, the social order is seen as designed for those in power, and thus power is enhanced as it adheres to—rather than overrides—that social power.[14]

China's culture diffuses decisions and ultimately spares the powerful from having to take responsibility for them.[15] In China, decisions are made with reference to relationships. The process involves gathering opinions and arriving at a consensus among the group in an informal way. If a group cannot be consulted, historical precedents are. In other words, the group is expanded to include people who made well-known decisions in the past. Mao Zedong, Chairman of the Chinese Communist Party and the leader of China until his death in 1976, used historical precedent for some of his decisions, quoting events that had taken place over 2,000 years earlier. Although he had extraordinary powers as the head of the party that ran the country, he needed to present his decisions as the result of consensus between himself and a group—in this case, a group of famous heroes from China's long past. Decisions thus are linked to former decisions, and decision-makers join the company of renowned heroes in Chinese history. Relationships are how business gets done. Results-based issues that occupy decision-makers in low-context cultures are unimportant compared to fostering and nurturing relationships, especially relationships between greater and smaller political entities.

In Focus

In Ceqikou, a village outside a suburb of Chongqing in Sichuan province, a fine wide highway crosses a creek that swells in the rainy season—and comes to an abrupt halt on the bank on the other side of the creek. Trucks that bring goods to the village have to turn around and be unloaded onto handcarts, since the village lanes are narrow and paved with cobblestones, and thus the trucks can't use them. The Chinese built the road because someone who wanted to display his connections got someone in Beijing to authorize it. But to continue the road into the village would have meant the demolition of the majority of homes along the narrow lanes.

In the West, a feasibility study would have been done, and factors like the need to demolish houses to widen the lane would have been calculated into the final decision about building the new road. The goal of providing a road would have been weighed against the cost of relocating the villagers into new homes. But the decision to build in Sichuan was made in Beijing, based on relationships, and other considerations were not important compared with keeping relations good between the village, the district, the province, and Beijing.

Where relationships are important, the consensus of the group is also important. The Japanese *ringi-seido* method of organizational decision making emphasizes consensus. This method has been misunderstood by some in the West who apparently think that decisions are made by top management only when low-level groups approve or even initiate decisions. In fact, Japanese corporate decisions do not originate in the mail room.

In Focus

The *ringi-seido* works like this.[16] A manager introduces an issue for discussion and proposes a decision. He goes to each department that is affected and discusses it with each department manager, and he goes to his vice president for approval also. If someone has a concern about the proposal, he discusses it with the proposer after work in informal and formal meetings. These informal soundings and exchanges are called *nemawashi,* which in Japanese means "root-binding." The word describes how a plant's roots are gently and carefully shaped to produce the desired plant. Thus are the deep concerns, emotions, principles, and goals of employees gently handled. Next, the proposer has to get agreement from other department managers who will be involved in any way. This also means after-hours discussions: *nemawashi.*

Once the proposal maker has talked to everybody individually and resolved any concerns anyone has, he presents the proposal (which may be very different from the original) at a meeting of all department managers and produces a form called a *ringi-sho.* After this form has been issued, the proposal maker presents his proposal at a vice-presidential meeting. Each vice president has been briefed about the issue by his department managers before the meeting. There is no unresolved reservation in anyone's mind by this time. In essence, the decision has been made. The document, the *ringi-sho,* is circulated to the department managers, the vice presidents, and perhaps the president for signatures of approval.

Approval doesn't take long in Japanese companies once the document for signatures has been circulated. What takes a long time is the *nemawashi* that the proposal maker undertakes with any manager or vice president who has a problem with the original proposal. But it means everyone from a manager up to the president has had a chance to present concerns to the sponsor of the proposal, and those concerns can alter the original proposal. After official authorization seals the proposal, everyone is in agreement about carrying it out. Nobody has reservations or anxieties that have not been discussed. Nobody is excluded from the decision making; everybody is a member of the ingroup. (Actually, not quite everybody. Lower-level employees, which usually means all women and some young men, traditionally do not participate.)

Final authority for decision making in most Japanese organizations rests with one man, the president. But it is unusual for him to authorize a decision without first assuring himself of the agreement of others. The lower-level representatives of an organization do not have the authority to make decisions. When pressed, for instance in negotiations, they cannot commit the organization.

Other Asian cultures have less formalized methods than Japan's *ringi-seido* for obtaining consensus; nevertheless, unanimity is important throughout Asia. Harmony matters more than putting oneself forward or having a more powerful voice in decision making than one's colleagues.

Two points need to be emphasized. First, as you probably have already realized, the values of harmony and consensus are most important in cultures that are hierarchical. This may seem paradoxical, but in places where people have the least chance to change their social status and where those in power take it for granted that their position won't change, harmony is the method of operating.

But consider this: Consensus doesn't threaten the hierarchical structure. Those in power do not risk losing power and those with little power do not stand to gain power, so both can agree and present a unified face. In Asia, saving and giving face to individual group members and holding up the group's face are more important than any specific outcome or end.

Second, the discussion we have just had about decision making broadly contrasts an *Asian* style with a *North American* style, and an *English-speaking* style with a *Hispanic* style. But in reality, all the decision-making methods discussed here can be found in all cultures. Every day in some organization in the United States, a lot of informal discussion is taking place at various levels, and problems are solved and consensus is reached before any formal decision is made in a meeting. Every day in some Chinese organization, a situation is arising that requires an immediate decision, with no opportunity to consult a group, and so the decision is made on the basis of what the desired results are. Every day some Canadian, United States, and Australian businesspeople are following Juan Carlos Aguilar's strategy for getting access to a target person by using a friend as a go-between and getting a business card or permission to use the name of someone who already is known to the target person. And every day in a Latin American organization, someone makes a decision without regard to personal relationships.

Nevertheless, *in general,* decision making does come from the values of a culture. If a culture values results, encourages individual competition among workers, and quantifies and measures goals, decisions will usually be made on the basis of goals, or *ends.* If a culture values relationships, encourages harmony among workers, and emphasizes trust, then decisions will usually be made on the basis of *means.*

Among the decisions managers have to make, within groups or alone, are decisions about solving problems and resolving conflicts. We next look at how culture affects the way problems and conflicts are identified and managed. The issue is especially important when people from different cultures encounter problems and conflicts between them.

Problem Solving and Conflict Resolution

When people from different cultures engage in business, they often have different expectations about what to do when problems and conflicts arise. Ways of defining problems, ways of handling them, and goals for resolution are all likely to vary, depending upon cultural priorities. Ways of handling conflict vary also.

Some authors discuss conflict along with negotiation, but we see conflict and negotiation as separate. Negotiation across cultures is a specific communication task, but it doesn't have to be called "conflict." On the other hand, conflict is an inevitable part of doing business. It occurs regularly, and it is unavoidable. It is even more present and unavoidable in business between members of more than one culture. It crops up in day-to-day activities and isn't limited to negotiations. Therefore, conflict communication is discussed here, along with problem solving. At the same time, a problem and a conflict are not exactly the same thing. Problems arise over people and also over things: events, equipment, resources, plans, and solutions. Conflicts arise between people.

Defining Problems and Dealing with Them

People in different cultures see problems differently and talk about them differently, as we have seen. What constitutes a problem? And whose problem is it, anyway? *In general, a problem is an obstacle that gets in the way of individuals and groups reaching their goals.*

In *individualist* cultures, where people are responsible for the consequences of their own individual actions, problem-solving skills are learned at an early age. Western societies praise and reward the person who solves a problem; some valued employees have the title "troubleshooter" and the responsibility for finding solutions to problems. School exercises in individualist cultures involve getting students to compete to see who can reach a solution first.

In low-context cultures, problems are objectified and externalized. They lie outside the plan for accomplishing the goal. They are extraneous to the cause-and-effect pattern of Western thinking. English speakers talk about "bugs" that have to be worked out or "wrinkles" that need to be ironed away. Problems need solutions, so they can be erased. Individuals who achieve solutions to problems are valued. Individuals take responsibility for solutions as well as blame for failure to solve problems. Individuals who cause problems also are blamed.

But in *collectivist* cultures, problems are not an individual responsibility. Blame is usually generalized to the group, and the group members work together to find a solution. In process-oriented cultures that emphasize the group acting together, that very cooperation itself is worthwhile. Problems are not externalized or considered nuisances that interrupt and interfere with the accomplishment of a goal. Rather, they are part of the context and process in which the group operates. Working on the problem is as important as solving it. Quality circles in Japan are an example of this approach. The line between what is *problem* and what is simply the situation is not as clear in collectivist cultures as in individualist cultures that place the problem somehow outside the normal situation. Thus, the way a problem is defined is different.

Problems can be things like a devaluation of the Mexican peso that makes it harder for a gallery owner in Guadalajara to buy art from Canadian Inuit sculptors. When the peso goes down, her costs go up, since the Canadian dollar is now more expensive to buy with pesos, and Canadian products are also more expensive to buy. Problems can include unusual weather that disrupts the movement of people or goods. Problems are obstacles to business objectives that do not directly result from disagreements between people. Problems can also be people, of course.

Managing Conflicts

When problems involve disagreements among people, they are called conflicts. *Conflict is a clash between people or between ideas that engages people in a struggle against each other.* The whole idea of managing conflicts comes from results-oriented, individualist, low-context communication cultures.

In individualist cultures, conflict is accepted as an integral part of life. Borden writes that although the negative results of conflict are widely acknowledged, nevertheless "some feel that a relationship without conflict is no relationship at all."[17] It seems that in results-oriented cultures, conflicts are looked upon not only as inevitable but sometimes as necessary and even healthy.

In results-oriented cultures, there is a fear that if everyone simply agrees with a viewpoint someone offers, and nobody disagrees, the lack of disagreement allows people to settle for mediocrity, not necessarily the best result. They call the lack of disagreement *groupthink*.

Groupthink is a made-up word first used by the American writer William H. Whyte, whose book *The Organisation Man* was a best-seller in 1956. He defines groupthink as a drive among group members toward conformity in their thinking, without critical assessment. Groupthink replaces a reasoning process. In the United States, some treat groupthink as a more dangerous behavior than conflict. That is because they see groupthink as threatening the successful accomplishment of goals. Conflict, they believe, may actually lead to better ways to accomplish goals.

Of course, conflict also can cause damage. Even in results-oriented cultures, people value relationships. The closer the relationship, the more damage conflict can cause. As a way of controlling outcomes of conflict that may be destructive, members of low-context cultures often verbalize their feelings and discuss conflicts as if they exist apart from people.

Results cultures value objectifying, depersonalizing, and analyzing issues apart from the people involved. Disagreement makes discussion possible in these cultures. Israeli culture is an example; in a sense, the entire tradition of the *Mishna* is a matter of ongoing debate or argumentation based on disagreements. The debaters may have the greatest respect for one another and still disagree. In fact, the attitude is that conflict can *only* be resolved when it is brought out into the open and explicitly discussed.

In the culture of the United States, conflict generally is said to arise from five areas:

- Disagreement over tasks (what)
- Disagreement over processes (how)
- Disagreement over allocation of resources (with what)
- Disagreement over goals (why)
- Disagreement over power (who)

In Focus

Let's try to see how these work out in an example. Say that you are working for a Public Relations organization, and your job is to find ways your client—a sports team—can get support from the public for games they play. The team needs to sell more tickets to events. You have come up with the idea that the team can host a public event where youngsters who play the sport receive awards for their public service. Public service means the young people have worked on projects to help people in their society. Maybe they have offered to carry shopping for elderly people. Maybe they have cleaned up a beach, or have taught people to use a computer who never had a chance to learn before. Your plan is that your client, the sports team, will honor the young people with a public celebration of their service, and will give out awards to them.

However, your client does not want to do this celebration. First, the sports team does not agree that because they participate in giving the awards to young people that they will sell more tickets. They disagree with the **goal** of your plan. Second, they do not want to spend the money on the awards, or pay the costs for making society aware of the celebration. Nor do they want to take the time away from their training and practice at their game. They disagree about **resources**: that is, money and time.

Furthermore, the team members want the team's manager and his assistant manager to come to the award celebration instead of the team. They disagree with you about **roles**. They also disagree about the **process** you have created. You want the team members to take turns giving awards to young people, and as a team, to show their approval for the projects the young people did. But the team members want *you* to give out the awards. In fact, they don't want to be connected to this award celebration at all, because they are worried that people will think they had something to do with the choice of projects or how the young people carried them out.

Finally, they disagree about the **power** you have to make them look socially responsible or irresponsible. They see you as putting them in a difficult position. They do not agree that your idea should represent them.

These disagreements, in results-oriented cultures, are called conflicts.

Here is another example. Let's say a product such as a new microwave snack food is losing market share. Perhaps this is due in part to a competitor's new product. But it may be due in part to conflicts between people over resources, processes, goals, and power. Production employees may not feel they were consulted when the marketing department decided to launch the new snack, while the marketing employees may feel they are being held back by the production staff who are cautious about letting a product go (disagreement over process). The production manager may feel she should be the one to stand in front of the microphones and announce the new product, not the marketing manager, who did not participate in its creation (disagreement about power). Marketing may wish they could move faster, while production may want more time to test the product (disagreement about the resource of time). The aim of the production people is to develop a product that will not be flawed; the aim of the marketing people is to sell the product in as great a quantity as possible (disagreement about goals). This simple illustration shows how conflicts arise when people are doing their jobs within one cultural environment. When groups from different cultures disagree, the conflict is more complex.

In collectivist cultures, on the other hand, conflict is usually viewed as just one dimension of the ongoing relationships among group members, not something outside those relationships. Conflicts are part of collective life. But conflict that is openly identified threatens the harmony of the group. Indeed, when conflict is out in the open, it is almost always destructive in collectivist cultures. Instead of verbalizing conflict, high-context-communication cultures use actions to compensate, show goodwill, and restore harmony to the group. Apologies are not asked for or given because they are a recognition of conflict. "Talking it out" may make a high-context person feel the open admission of conflict has caused an irreparable rupture in the relationship.

In collectivist cultures, disagreements are called conflicts when they have grown beyond the power of members of the group to diffuse them. In these cultures, *disagreements* and *opposite viewpoints* do not fit the definition of conflict as "a clash between people" who "struggle against each other." People don't have to spend conscious time and effort on conflict resolution—it's simply part of the culture to deal with conflict without calling attention to it.

In relationship-oriented cultures, if something as serious as conflict occurs between people who have a close relationship, the relationship itself is threatened. In other words, the value of relationships, which is probably the most important value in the culture, is at risk. Members of these cultures go to great lengths to uphold relationships.

Conflict Management Modes

Managing conflict is culture-specific, just as the definition of conflict is. In results-oriented cultures, conflict management involves maintaining one's own viewpoint, arguing convincingly, and persisting until the opposing side agrees. In relationship-oriented cultures, conflict management means trying every tactic to diffuse the conflict. People develop conflict management skills from an early age. They learn what works to resolve conflict in their culture.

Results-oriented cultures and relationships-oriented cultures are very different in how they manage, so let's look at a results-oriented culture—Australia—and a relationship-oriented culture—Mexico—to illustrate. To help explain the cultural differences, let's use three cultural dimensions from Hofstede: individualism, power distance, and uncertainty-avoidance. You can see Hofstede's rankings of Australia and Mexico at www.geert-hofstede.com.

In Australian culture, the individualism ranking is very high, over 90. It is the second-highest of all the 74 countries Hofstede has studied. The Power Distance index is low (36), meaning that Australians feel people should have about the same power, rather than some having a lot of power and others very little. Put another way, people have about the same power, so every voice has equal weight. That makes people willing to listen to diverse viewpoints.

Australia's uncertainty-avoidance index is 38, well below the world average of about 60. That means Australians in general are open to different opinions and other people's ways of doing things. They are not as anxious about finding the one right way of doing things as high uncertainty-avoiding cultures are. Individualist, horizontal, uncertainty-*tolerant* cultures lead to a conflict-management strategy of bringing the conflict out into the open and discussing it.

In many other similar individualistic, low power-distance, uncertainty-tolerant cultures, putting conflicts and feelings into words is the way to handle conflict. They think that even when the outcome of conflict can possibly be damaging, if everybody talks about the conflict, and everyone has a chance to explain his or her opinion, the threat of damage is less. Typically, a conflict leads to a meeting where people express their needs, wants, and goals in a conflict. In sum, the way to handle conflict in these cultures is to discuss it explicitly.

In Australia and cultures like it, conflicts exist objectively, outside the people who experience them. In discussion, conflicts are depersonalized. They are objectified, that is, turned into positions held *by* people but *separate from* people. Of course, that separation only works to a certain extent. If someone's idea about your promotion conflicts with your idea, and especially if you do not get the promotion, your conflict may be with that *person* and not just that person's idea.

The Australians' way of handling conflict—bringing it out into open discussion—leads to explicit conflict communication. More about that later.

In Mexican culture, the individualism dimension is very low, just over 30. That means Mexico is a *highly collectivist* culture. The Power Distance, on the other hand, is very high (81), indicating that Mexicans prefer some in their culture to have a lot of power, while most others have very little. Uncertainty-avoidance is also very high (82). That means Mexicans are not so open to new viewpoints. They look for right answers to issues, and once they have found the right answers, they do not like to have to change.

The Mexican way of handling conflict is to diffuse it before it actually reaches the level of conflict and everyone has to recognize it as conflict. Mexicans keep conflict from becoming obvious. Only when conflict is out in the open does someone have to do something about it. The best management means neutralizing it, and keeping conflict from erupting.

Mexican culture has rules against talking about conflict. Typically in low power-distance, high-collectivist, and high uncertainty-avoiding cultures, people do not openly recognize conflict unless they have no other alternative.

In addition to not talking about the conflict, Mexicans will use deflection to handle conflict. For example, if one person in a group wants to perform a role, such as speaking at a meeting, but another person does it, the first person may feel disappointed and angry over a perceived conflict of roles. In a Mexican environment, a leader may offer the disappointed person an alternative role (since the leader's role is to be sensitive to the feelings of the group members). The focus of the disappointed member in the group moves, or is *deflected,* from the first role to the second. This is a familiar way of handling conflicts in everyday issues. A mother might use it to manage a conflict between two young brothers over who gets to carry a package for mother. When the one who is disappointed protests, the mother gives him an alternative role; she might ask him to be the door-opener for them, and successfully direct his attention away from the package-carrying role.

When two colleagues clash over a goal, or resources, or roles, or a process, or power, in Mexico they try to cooperate in finding agreement. They may focus on areas where they have no conflict, as a way to compensate for their disagreement. They will emphasize common ground.

In relationship-oriented cultures, the sports team's differences with the PR firm's viewpoints may never be called conflicts. The disagreements can simply be treated as disagreements, by deflection, but not conflicts. The client may express the opinion that, "the award celebration for the young people is a fine idea, and should be seriously discussed at a future time, but in the meantime, could the PR firm please think of a way to raise ticket sales?" Before a conflict develops about goals, the conversation has been changed toward finding some PR means to increase sales. Changing the subject, turning attention to something else, is a way relationship-oriented cultures diffuse (spread out and cause to disappear) the reasons for a dispute.

The Japanese, for example, don't talk about conflict as the result of five areas of disagreement or create narratives about it. They prefer not to mention conflict directly at all. The perception may exist that marketing, in the microwave snack example, did not consult fully with production about the new snack or that production is not supporting marketing adequately. But high-context cultures such as Japan and China look for ways to *cooperate* and build consensus rather than focus on what has fallen short of expectations.

To understand ways of managing conflict, we will begin with five modes, which are related to concern for one's own goals and concern for the other side's goals:

- Competing (insisting your goals rank above those of others)
- Collaborating (showing high concern for others' goals while being assertive about one's own)
- Compromising (settling for less and making others do so, too)
- Avoiding (not pursuing your goals or others' openly)
- Accommodating (allowing others' goals to take precedence)[18]

(See Exhibit 8.1) Which mode a person or an organization chooses depends on the specific goals, circumstances, priorities, and, of course, culture. This list offers a description of each of the options.

Competing is openly encouraged in individualist cultures. Salespeople are challenged to outdo each other, for example. The salesperson of the year is singled out for an award in many companies. But collectivist cultures do not encourage open competition. Individual goals are not to be placed above the goals of the group.

Collaboration is also encouraged in many individualist-culture companies. Being able to work with others, being a team player, is important for success in most organizations. Many corporations that use collaboration to resolve conflict urge conflicting sides to establish a common goal and get away from the focus on one's own interest. Some organizations' definition of collaboration is very individualist: One continues to keep one's own goals firmly in view while accommodating others' goals. This is not the approach used in collectivist organizations; they encourage commitment by teams and groups to common goals. Individual goals are not worthy of the effort that common goals merit. If individual goals conflict with the group's goals, the individual goals fade or are postponed.

Compromising involves giving up something voluntarily. Both or all parties are expected to do so until finally a resolution is reached. The implication is that when goals, roles, or processes conflict, different sides give up some things while managing to retain other aspects of their goals. So although the conflicting parties all yield something, they also all gain something. Cultural attitudes toward compromise vary, and this will be discussed more fully in Chapter 9. **Bargaining** and negotiating may be necessary to reach this partial-loss/partial-gain position.

When the parties themselves cannot reach agreement, a *third party* may be asked to intervene. When the third party is a go-between, an information conduit, **mediation** takes place. When the third party is asked to make a judgment and impose a solution to the conflict, the process is called **arbitration.**

These third-party roles can exist in a culture that places a high priority on the explicit encoding of messages and the achievement of goals as markers of success. In cultures accustomed to authoritarian behavior and hierarchical power structures, the use of a third party may move quickly to an arbitrator. This is the case, for example, in India, where conflicting brothers will appeal to the president of a family-owned company for a ruling rather than sit and discuss their conflict on their own or with a go-between. The resolution of the conflict, rather than conflict management, is the goal.

Avoiding conflict is another way of resolving it. In results cultures, it is rarely a satisfactory, long-term solution. The parties simply agree to stop disagreeing openly. Perhaps they get tired of conflict. Perhaps the parties feel no meaningful goal can be achieved if they have to give up anything. In collectivist organizations, avoidance is the most common method of handling conflict. When disagreements arise, parties hold back from openly pursuing their goals in the face of opposition. They may continue to work toward goals, but they will do nothing openly that might disrupt the harmony of the larger group.

Accommodating the other party's goals and abandoning one's own is not a common process for the resolution of conflict in individualist cultures. In collectivist cultures, however, such a move may be taken more often because it results in an indebtedness. At a later date, the party that gave up its goals can remind the party that was assisted in reaching its goals of the favor. Such a move is not unknown in individualist cultures. But in collectivist cultures, accommodation of the other is a way to build the network of obligation discussed in Chapter 4.

An employee from an individualistic culture and an employee from a collectivistic culture who disagree thus may find themselves in disagreement also over how to handle their conflict. If a collectivistic person's secret and concealed activity is discovered, the individualistic person will make accusations of underhanded and sneaky behavior. If the individualistic person insists on bringing the conflict

EXHIBIT 8.1 Five Conflict Management Modes (based on Rahim and Bonama, 1979)

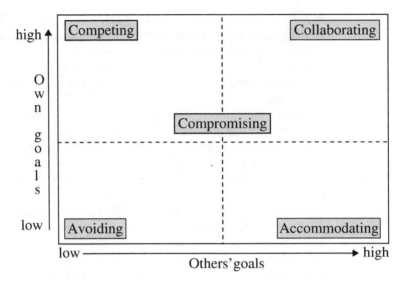

out into the open through bargaining or mediation or arbitration, the collectivistic person may feel threatened with a loss of face and may be shamed by the rupture to the outward harmony of their relations.

Conflict Communication Modes

Results cultures like the United States consciously spend time and effort on conflict resolution. Conflict is brought out into the open and is specifically addressed with procedures that comprise *conflict communication*. The goal of the communication is to resolve the conflict.

The different styles of managing conflict that we have just discussed correspond to communication styles. These styles are based on the communicator's concern for self and concern for others. They are dominating, integrating, bargaining, avoiding, and obliging.[19]

Obliging conflict communication style   Obliging is the communication style of the conflict management mode that is called *accommodating*. *Obliging* suggests a communication approach that uses an obliging tone of voice, to put the other side's goals first. Obliging communication is strongly you-attitude communication. One's own goals are not mentioned. The other's goals are the focus of communication.

In individualist, low power-distance cultures, the obliging conflict communication style has a negative meaning. It suggests placating the other side in the conflict. Placating means saying what will please the other side in order to resolve the conflict. It implies a lack of sincerity—just saying what the other side wants to hear but not meaning it, or lacking commitment to one's own position in a conflict.

For some collectivist cultures also, ones where winning is a matter of honor, such as Japan, South Korea, and Russia, communicating without commitment to one's own position is strongly negative. Commitment is a combination of dedication and steadfastness. Commitment is never losing sight of the goal, and working constantly to achieve it. Commitment in a communication style is talking about the goal in a consistent way. It means that in a conflict, a side argues forcefully for an outcome that leads to winning the goal, and does not change to a different argument. Obliging communication is the opposite. It is communication that leads to the other side winning their goals. On the other hand, the obliging conflict communication style is gentle, not forceful.

In many collectivist cultures, however, obliging communication has a positive meaning. Because it is gentle communication, no great display of emotion is involved. Emotion can be risky since it can lead to the loss of face, so an effort is made to keep emotion out of conflict.

For example, in East Asian cultures, displays of anger make one lose face because showing anger is immature behavior, and adults should have more self-control. Collectivist cultures avoid loss of face, as a rule.

Obliging communication is considered to be a strategy for *giving face* in collectivist cultures. It seeks to please the other side because it is agreement about the importance of the other side's goals. Obliging communication also gives the obliging side face, because they are doing so much for the other side's face. The side that reaches its goals wins the conflict, but the obliging side also wins, in esteem and face. This strategy has positive value in collectivist cultures.

Integrating conflict communication style   Integrating means expressing one's own goals and one's interest in winning the dispute *and also* expressing the other's goals and the other's interest in winning. This style of communication matches the collaborative mode of conflict management. An integrating statement might repeat a goal that the other side has put into words, along with a goal of one's own side. This is a communication style that is viewed as positive by both individualist cultures and collectivist cultures.

So why isn't integrating communication always the norm, in both individualist and collectivist cultures? Because the factors involved in conflicts can be complex. When two individualist-culture sides are in conflict, integrating may be the style for talking about goals, but when it comes to processes, the style is more dominating and assertive. In collectivist cultures, integrating may be the style for talking about who gets resources, but obliging is the style for talking about goals.

Bargaining conflict communication style   Bargaining communication style is what happens in a compromising mode for managing conflict. It is a back-and-forth dialog or discussion. This conflict communication style is a bit like bargaining in the marketplace. When a merchant offers a platter at a certain price, the buyer suggests a much lower price. The merchant and the buyer both know each will have to move from their first position. The game of bargaining involves small moves on both sides, so agreement can be reached. The agreement in bargaining is that the merchant gets money and the buyer gets the platter. The agreement in resolving a conflict is that one side gets something they really want and so does the other side.

The bargain can be expressed explicitly or implicitly. Explicit bargaining is when one side actually says, "We want x and you want y, so we will give up a if you will agree that we get x, and if you give up b, we will agree that you get y."

This explicit communication is more likely to describe what happens in individualist, low-context communication cultures. Implicit bargaining is when one side says, "We are very interested in x, and know you are interested in y. We could offer to make some agreement about a, in order to have your agreement about x." The other, reciprocal half of the agreement is not spelled out in so many words, but is implied.

Bargaining style works when both sides have some concern for the other's interest as well as their own interest. Neither is as strong as in the integrating style.

Avoiding conflict communication style   The avoiding communication style means not communicating about the conflict. Avoiding is also the mode of conflict management. Communication in this style is not about the conflict, but rather is about something else. Conflict parties simply turn away from mentioning conflict.

In individualist cultures, as with the obliging communication style, this style is usually negative. It shows a lack of commitment to the goal. Where commitment is important and winning is important, avoiding communication is a failure to pursue the goal. Of course, some conflicts are not worth the time and effort—the commitment—to win. If the issues are not so important, neither is the commitment to winning the conflict. In such cases, avoiding communication about the conflict is a good strategy, even in results-oriented cultures.

In collectivist cultures, as with the obliging style, the avoiding style is often positive. Although it does not show a strong concern for the other side's interest, it does protect the other's face.

Dominating conflict communication style   Dominating communication corresponds to a competing mode of conflict management. Dominating communication pushes for winning the conflict. A side using dominating communication stresses the desire to achieve what they see as a winning outcome. They express their needs and wants strongly.

This communication style shows a great concern for one's own interests and very little or no concern for the other's goals. Therefore, it does not give the other side face, or protect the other side's face. Instead, it emphasizes the face of the dominating communicator.

In individualist cultures, the dominating style is frequently seen as showing power. In oral communication, the dominating style is often loud. Communicators seek to display strength and might, and by doing so hope to achieve their goals. They want to overpower the other side, by showing them to be weaker.

Dominating communication therefore is a style that is rarely used by collectivists in conflict management. However, it can be seen as positive in individualist cultures, where two sides, both using dominating communication style and taking care only of their own interests and their own face, can be parties in a conflict.

In summary, the five communication styles are dominating, integrating, bargaining, avoiding, and obliging. They correspond to the five modes of conflict management—competing, collaborating, compromising, avoiding, and accommodating—five modes that are the way a Western mind sees conflict management. However, in Eastern cultures (Asia and Pacific Islands) and Middle-Eastern cultures as well as African cultures, other ways of managing conflict exist.

Three additional communication styles have been suggested for conflicts.[20]

Emotion-expressing conflict communication style   The dominating communication style is often related to another style to resolve conflict, and that is using *emotional expression*. Exhibiting powerful emotions can be effective in helping a person achieve his or her goal in the dispute. Communicators using this style may employ nonverbal signals to reinforce the worded messages about what they need and want, such as facial expression, thumping the table, and making other forceful hand gestures. This style may also use volume in oral communication or capital letters and exclamation marks in written communication. The tone is insistent.

Emotion-expressing communication style, with its emphasis on winning, is one that individualist cultures use. In some collectivist cultures, showing emotion can lead to loss of face. Emotional expression is risky, and in high uncertainty-avoiding cultures, risk of loss of face is too uncomfortable. The less risky behavior is not to show emotion. However, sometimes displays of dismay and even tearfulness may be used in this conflict communication style by members of collectivist cultures.

Third-party intervention conflict communication style   A primary way of managing conflict in collectivist, high power-distance, high uncertainty-avoidance cultures is to *turn to a third party* who has power. That person, in high power-distance cultures, can mediate in the conflict, telling each side how to act to resolve the conflict. The third party mediator is from outside—and above—the conflict. The person of power is also a person of authority in an organization or in a government.

When the third party determines who wins the dispute, the issue is settled. Both sides recognize the authority of the mediator (high power-distance) and accept the mediator's decision. The parties involved in the conflict may not want to talk about it to each other, but each will talk to the person of power, because they are willing (power distance) for that third party to have the authority to solve the dispute (high uncertainty-avoidance).

In individualist cultures, turning to a third party to help resolve the conflict means the two sides have failed to reach a solution. Such a failure is negatively viewed in results-oriented cultures because it shows the parties in the conflict could not achieve a result.

Neglecting conflict communication style   Our final style of communication for managing conflict is *neglect*. This is different from avoiding, which is walking away from the conflict. Neglect is acknowledging the conflict, but refusing to do anything about it, and by refusing, forcing the other side to make some resolution of the conflict.

It is passive-aggressive behavior, and forces the other side to have a concern for your goals. The communicator agrees that conflict exists, but refuses to participate in a discussion about either side's goals, needs, or wants. Worded communication is minimal. Instead of stating what he or she wants, the communicator speaks few words but uses nonverbal signals to show unhappiness. The burden of the resolution

EXHIBIT 8.2 **Eight Conflict Communication Styles (based on Ting-Toomey & Oetel 2001)**

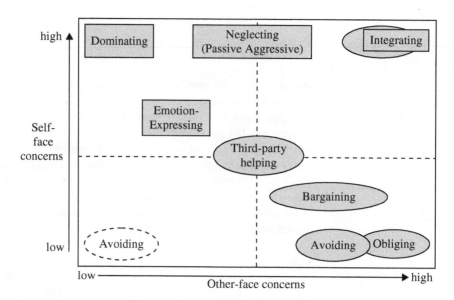

of the dispute rests with the other side completely, and the other side is forced to consider the interests of the neglecting communicator.

In summary, the three additional styles of communicating about conflict bring the total to eight.

In Exhibit 8.2. the grid of the eight styles of conflict communication, with individualist self-concerns in square boxes, and collectivist other-concerns in ovals, gives a picture of how culture affects conflict management.

The upper left corner of the grid shows behavior that is typical of strongly individualist, results-oriented, low power-distance cultures. The lower right quadrant shows behavior that is typical of strongly collectivist, relationship-oriented, high power-distance cultures.

Communicating about Conflicts between Members of Different Cultures

What happens when conflict exists across cultures? Now that we have seen how results-oriented cultures differ from relationships-oriented cultures in the ways they manage and communicate about conflict, we can begin to appreciate how difficult communication about conflict is when one side is from a results culture and the other side is from a relationship culture.

Not only does conflict itself put the two sides into a struggle against each other. They also have to struggle against different conflict management modes and different communication styles.

Conflicts involving sides from different cultures are common. Not only are people likely to disagree over power, process, resources, tasks, and goals, they can also be in conflict over ways to manage and communicate about conflict. When people go about the management of conflict differently, their first suspicion is that the others are not playing fair, and cannot be trusted. Then the conflict, which is defined as a clash between people that engages them in a struggle against each other, is amplified.

In Focus

Let's look at what might happen between two people of different cultures in a conflict.

Imagine a conflict between an individualist-culture member and a collectivist-culture member over money. In a contract for service they agreed on a fee, but because the service became more complex than expected, one side now wants more money. The person who wants more money is from an individualist culture. He—let's call him Indy—communicates explicitly and in a dominating style about what he wants, and why his goal is justified.

The person who does not want to pay more than the originally agreed amount represents a group from a collectivist culture. She—let's call her Colly—would prefer not to have any communication about this subject, but now that the group has been engaged in a struggle with Indy, Colly speaks about the need and desire Indy has for more money, and Colly's group's own need and desire to pay no more. Colly's conflict communication style is integrating.

What does Indy hear when Colly validates her group's own goals *and* Indy's goals? Chances are Indy hears that he is winning the struggle. He believes he will get more money. Colly is yielding.

What does Colly hear, when Indy insists on more money? She hears that Indy is not interested at all in Colly's or her group's face. He is demanding that he get his goal. He has no concern about the needs of Colly's group.

Because Indy thinks he is winning, he presses harder. Because Colly thinks their concerns are being overlooked, she either tries harder to show consideration for Indy, hoping for a reciprocal consideration, or she uses obliging communication, hoping if Indy sees she is taking his concerns seriously then he will have some concern for her group. Or Colly might use bargaining communication to reduce the amount Indy wants and so protect both her face and Indy's face. Or she finally may use avoiding style to abandon the conflict communication. In any case, she has lost her confidence that Indy will collaborate, putting her group's interests as high as his own.

Perhaps Indy will win—this time. But he probably will not win a second time. In winning, he will have forced Colly and her group to lose.

Indy, in this scenario, is following normal conflict communication behavior for someone from a results-oriented, individualist, low power-distance culture. He uses a dominating communication style in order to win. He probably is not aware that Colly is adopting a different mode of conflict management and a different conflict communication style. He may just think Colly is not as good at managing conflict as he is.

Colly thinks Indy is narrowly focused on his own goals and refusing to cooperate with her to arrive at both their goals. She and her group will avoid interacting with Indy again.

The sad result is that the management of this conflict has contributed to making the original conflict worse. It also has set the two sides, Indy and Colly, on a path of distrust. Furthermore, when Colly encounters a conflict again with people from an individualist culture, they will have to work harder to gain her trust. When Indy encounters a conflict the next time with people from a collectivist culture, he will assume they are not able to prevail against him successfully, and that he will win. Furthermore, collectivist stereotypes of arrogant individualists will be reinforced, and individualist stereotypes of weak unreliable collectivists will be reinforced, because neither understands the other's conflict communication style.

Certain communication strategies can enable you to handle conflict: to talk about it or talk around it and use communication strategies to resolve it. But remember that in some cultures, actions are the best communication. There are five recommended strategies:

- Listen sincerely.
- Express agreement where you can.

- Identify common goals.
- Explain your position.
- Identify resolutions that accommodate cultural priorities.

Listening Sincerely

Listening sincerely is an important strategy for conflict communication when only one culture is involved; it is even more important when the conflict is intercultural. We often assume we understand the other's point of view and don't need to listen to it being presented. Assuming you understand someone else's perceptions, reasons, and values because they are probably like yours is called **projected cognitive similarity.** This concept was introduced in Chapter 1. When you acknowledge another set of perceptions, reasons, and values, you may be assuming you understand them. But this assumption is especially likely to be wrong when you don't have the same priorities as someone from another culture.

In his book on intercultural communication for managers, Richard Mead offers suggestions for *how* to listen.[21]

First, *listen with an attitude of interest* in what the other party is saying.

The interest may be apparent rather than real, but an appearance of interest will encourage the other side to speak about the conflict. This is important, because as we have seen, in many high-context cultures a public acknowledgment of disagreement is not acceptable. If the other party comes from such a culture and you come from a low-context culture, you may have a hard time getting any discussion about the conflict out in the open. An attitude of interest in the other's concerns can help. If you are one who prefers to deal with the conflict indirectly and your counterpart wants open and frank discussion of the conflict, you still need to listen with interest. Then you can say you appreciate the statement and appear sincere to the other side rather than indifferent, even if you go on to ask for a postponement of the discussion.

Sometimes the opportunity to express a position is all that is necessary for a party to drop a conflicting position. This is true when one grievance in the conflict is a feeling of not being heard. Writing about United States–Russian conflicts, Yale Richmond advises:

> Confrontations over differences of views can often be avoided by letting Russians talk themselves out. After they have unburdened themselves and expressed their righteousness and indignation, their opposition may moderate and the differences may turn out to be not as great as originally believed. In fact, after talking themselves out, Russians and Americans may even find that they have a unanimity of views.[22]

Second, *assess the meaning of what you are hearing.* Don't rush to judgment but pay attention to the unspoken cultural priorities behind the words. Ask questions for clarification, being careful to avoid making the other side feel defensive. The other party may use a communication style that is ambiguous and indirect on purpose, so listen for style as well as content.

Finally, *think before you respond,* which may mean taking time. Results-oriented cultures tend to encourage quick responses for quick resolutions to problems: Get it fixed! Get over it! Move on! These are attitudes that easily find expression in results cultures. Relationship-oriented cultures are the opposite. Taking time allows one to think carefully about all the ramifications of a response for the lives of the others. There is also the hope that if enough time passes, the conflict will fade and be resolved without having to be managed.

Expressing Agreement Where You Can

Expressing agreement where you can means letting the other party know you find the other position understandable and legitimate. Note these words in this advice: *where you can.* The agreement should be genuine on your part. Usually, people have reasonable concerns, and if you put yourself in the other person's position, you can agree with his or her view of the issues. Your agreement at this stage is with the other person's concerns but probably not with his or her solution—otherwise, you don't have a conflict. It may be sufficient to express agreement on items that you can agree upon for the areas of disagreement to recede in importance.

Identifying Common Goals

Identifying common goals is the key to an agreement that is usually labeled "win–win" (discussed in more detail in Chapter 9). It is what happens when the sides collaborate to reach some agreement. It may be through recognizing the other's goals, or through bargaining or mediation. When both parties can identify common goals, both can work to reach them. Terpstra and David describe a family-owned business in India that entered into a joint venture with a firm from the United States. An organizational specialist from the United States suggested tightening the loose Indian business structure. He drew up an organizational chart that placed a younger brother, who had an MBA, in a higher position than two older brothers who did not have MBAs. Conflict immediately arose among the brothers, and the two brothers in the older generation became involved. "They both said, 'What is the business good for if it breaks up the family?'"[23] The conflict could only be resolved when the common goal—the family united in an ongoing business—was clear to all parties, Indian and American. If the business itself threatened the family, the business could go.

Explaining Your Position

Explaining your position means stating your concerns. It is not the same thing as persuasion or argumentation. At this stage, you are setting out your position clearly and neutrally. If the conflict has arisen because of a misunderstanding, this is where it will come to light and can be resolved. Some conflicts do arise simply from misunderstanding.

For members of low-context cultures, messages are typically encoded explicitly, and delicacy is not as important as accuracy. If you are a low-context culture member communicating about conflict with someone from a high-context culture, explaining your position can be a step that needs special attention. You want to get your position across clearly, but you do not want to risk losing the goodwill of the other party. Knowing where to draw the line is tricky.

If you are a high-context culture member, your efforts at explaining your position may need to focus on explicit and factual presentation. Appeals to the other party's allegiance to the organization may not be helpful.

In addition to explaining your position, you also need to make clear what outcome you desire. Making your wishes clear is *not* necessarily the same thing as explicitly stating them, however. As we have seen in Chapter 5, actions can communicate. Behavior can call attention to issues and reveal feelings without explicit encoding in words.

In Focus

A manager in an IT company was having difficulty dealing with a conflict between a young ambitious French-Canadian male and his co-worker, an older Chinese woman who was on a special visa from China. She had recently become uncooperative and had made it clear to the manager that she would not be willing to travel to the capital, Ottawa, with her co-worker to hold discussions with legislators about a new product. Yet she had worked on the development of the product with great enthusiasm.

When the manager asked her what the problem was, he received no clear explanation. When he asked her co-worker, the young man had no insights to offer. The young French Canadian was clearly annoyed, however, that the Chinese woman was refusing to share her data with him. That meant he couldn't make the presentation to the legislators, because she had all the key data on her flash drive.

The manager's repeated questions to her about her "problem" got nowhere, so he changed his approach. He began explaining his concerns, as a manager and as a spokesperson for the company, about the upcoming meeting with legislators. His explanation of his position was unemotional. In that climate, she then felt that she could explain her position. She revealed that she felt as an older—and in her mind more senior—person she should not be sent to the capital with a younger employee who would do the presentation of material she had worked hard to develop. That would diminish her status, she felt, and diminish her face.

This was obviously a conflict about power and, more particularly, about roles. Because the manager explained his position without blame or emotion, the woman was able to respond with an explanation of hers. Once the manager understood her position, he could take steps to resolve the conflict. He announced through a general memo that the woman was the senior consultant on this project and her name would be first on the documents. The young man would do most of the presentation because he was a native English speaker. This satisfied her and allowed the project to continue.

The Meaning of "a Resolution" According to Culture

As we have seen, for low-context cultures, *resolution* means a termination of the conflict.[24] This may mean that individual goals are met; it may mean organizational goals are met. Another possibility is that the conflict itself ceases without goals being met; parties simply stop being in conflict. Disagreement may exist about the means to reach the end of the conflict, in other words, but the end is recognized by all.

In high-context cultures, however, resolution has a very different meaning or perhaps has little meaning. Conflict is simply seen as an ongoing part of the relationship. It may take one form or another and may involve certain issues at one point and other issues at another point, but the conflict doesn't "end." It simply is not overt and does not disrupt the functioning of the group.

This is implied by Lucien Pye, for example, in his discussion about the tendency of Chinese negotiators to see any agreement as simply part of a context of ongoing discussion, not an end.[25] The goal of conflict resolution may be to diffuse the conflict through ambiguity.[26]

Much of the research on conflict resolution comes out of Western thought and paradigms. Western researchers assume that conflict can be managed and that people can take charge and shape resolutions to suit them. Not all cultures share this view.

Summary

Business information is culturally defined. Information is valued by businesses because it is used to attain business goals.

- *Possession of information means power.* Being "in the know" makes one a member of an in-group, compared with out-group members who are not in the know.
- *Information is usually valued when it is reliable and valid,* but of course these are also culturally defined terms.
- *Formal information* comes from publications and publicly available sources, including the Internet, observation, surveys and interviews, and experimentation. Results-oriented cultures look on it as objective and therefore more accurate than informal information.
- *Informal information* comes from the grapevine, IM, blogs, chat rooms, and bulletin boards. It always comes with a context and a personal bias.
- Individualist low-context cultures value "hard" information, often numerical measurements. Such information is not always available in collectivist high-context cultures.
- Business information is assessed on the basis of *verifiability, trustworthiness, accuracy,* and *credibility.*

Business information sources are formal and informal. In some cultures, gathering information is regarded as inappropriately invasive.

- Information technology (IT) has opened access to information.
- Information management—the capture and storage of employees' knowledge for future access—is practiced by more and more companies.

Businesspeople use information for making decisions. Individualist cultures generally make decisions based on ends, while collectivist cultures generally make decisions based on means. Conflicts are perceived differently, problems are defined differently, and solutions are arrived at differently in different cultures.

- *Cultures define "what is a problem?" differently.*
- *Conflict usually occurs in one or more of five areas:* tasks, processes, allocation of resources, goals, and power.

- *Five ways to manage conflicts* are competing, collaborating, compromising, avoiding, and accommodating.
- *Eight styles of conflict communication* are dominating, integrating, bargaining, avoiding, and obliging, plus third-party intervening, emotion-expressing, and neglecting.
- To communicate about conflict, whether with high-context or low-context cultures, the following guidelines may help: listen sincerely, express agreement where you can, identify common goals, explain your position, and identify resolutions that accommodate cultural positions.
- For some high-context cultures, resolution may mean simply diffusing the conflict through non-conflict-oriented communication and absorbing the conflict into the ongoing relationship.

Notes

1. Richard Mead, *Cross-Cultural Management Communication* (New York: John Wiley & Sons, 1990), p. 74.
2. Ibid., pp. 66–67.
3. Ibid., p. 67.
4. Paul Bausch, Matthew Haughey, and Meg Hourihan, *We Blog: Publishing Online with Weblogs* (New York: Hungry Minds Inc., 2002), Chapter 8.
5. http://www.worldwidewebsize.com/.
6. http://www.internetworldstats.com/stats.htm.
7. Richard R. Gesteland, *Cross-Cultural Business Behavior* (Copenhagen: Copenhagen Business School Press, 2002), pp. 50–51.
8. "The Wiki Principle: A Survey of New Media," *The Economist*, April 22, 2006, p. 11.
9. http://www.census.gov/ipc/www/popclockworld.html.
10. http://www.geeknewscentral.com/2004/12/15/computer-ownership-to-double-by-2010/.
11. http://ict4dblog.files.wordpress.com/2009/01/m4d-policy-priorities-to-connect-africa-v1-0.pdf.
12. http://www.guardian.co.uk/business/2009/mar/02/mobile-phone-internet-developing-world.
13. James Wolfensohn, "Transcript of Remarks at Afternoon Session of White House Conference on the New Economy" (5/9), National Desk, *US Newswire*, April 5, 2000, http://web.lexis-nexis.com/ universe (retrieved May 29, 2000).
14. David A. Victor, *International Business Communication* (New York: HarperCollins, 1992), p. 174.
15. Lucien Pye, *Chinese Commercial Negotiating Style* (Cambridge, MA: Oelgeschlager, Gunn & Hain, 1982), p. 17.

16. Robert T. Moran, *Getting Your Yen's Worth: How to Negotiate with Japan* (Houston: Gulf, 1985), p. 15.

17. George A. Borden, *Cultural Orientation: An Approach to Understanding Intercultural Communication* (Englewood Cliffs, NJ: Prentice-Hall, 1991), p. 111.

18. K. W. Thomas, "Introduction." California Management Review, 21 (1978), p. 66.

19. M. Afzalur Rahim and Thomas V. Bonoma, "Managing Organizational Conflict: A Model for Diagnosis and Intervention." *Psychological Reports, 44* (1979), pp. 1323–1344.

20. Stella Ting-Toomey and John G. Oetzel, "Intercultural Conflict: A Culture-based Situational Model," *Managing Intercultural Conflict Effectively* (Thousand Oaks, CA: Sage, 2001) pp. 27–62.

21. Mead, p. 118.

22. Yale Richmond, *From Nyet to Da: Understanding the Russians* (Yarmouth, ME: Intercultural Press, 1992), p. 130.

23. Vern Terpstra and Kenneth David, *The Cultural Environment of International Business*, 3rd ed. (Cincinnati: South-Western, 1991), pp. 187–188.

24. Lawrence B. Nadler, Marjorie Keeshan Nadler, and Benjamin J. Broome, "Culture and the Management of Conflict Situations." In *Communication, Culture, and Organizational Processes*, International and Intercultural Communication Annual, vol. IX, William B. Gudykunst, Lea P. Stewart, and Stella Ting-Toomey, eds. (Newbury Park, CA: Sage, 1985), p. 95.

25. Pye, p. xi.

26. Ting-Toomey, p. 81.

CHAPTER NINE

Intercultural Negotiation Teams

Two Canadians representing Canwall, a manufacturer of wallpaper printing equipment, went to a town north of Shanghai in the province of Jiangsu, China, to negotiate a sale to a new wallpaper production company. Charlie Burton, the president of Canwall, was traveling with his Marketing Director, Phil Raines. The company had never before sold its equipment outside Canada, and the two Canadians were delighted with the warm reception they enjoyed in China.

This wasn't the first meeting between the Canadian company and the Chinese wallpaper factory. The manager of the Chinese company, Mr. Li, had been a member of a delegation to Canada. He had met with one of Canwall's senior salespersons and the director of manufacturing. Subsequently, a trade representative from Canada had been in China representing Canwall's interests to the Chinese manager. After those meetings and numerous letters and faxes, Canwall's top people were now ready to negotiate the sale.

The day they arrived they were met at the airport in Shanghai by Manager Li himself and transported in a chauffer-driven car 125 kilometers to the town. Their accommodation was in a newly built hotel. A few hours after their arrival they were treated to a 12-course banquet given by their host, with several high-level municipal officials present. This red-carpet treatment made them feel optimistic about the sale.

The next day, they were taken to see the sights nearby: a large port for container ships and several factories that indicated the prosperity of the region. They were eager to begin discussing the sale, but after lunch they were given time to rest. In the late afternoon, one of the manager's English-speaking employees came by with news that they would be taken to see a local dance company's performance that night.

On the third day, they finally sat down to meetings. Progress seemed very slow, with each side giving generalizations about itself that seemed to the Canadians to be unrelated to the sale. They used an interpreter supplied by the Chinese, who was eager to please them, so the Canadians felt comfortable with her, but translation slowed down communication.

The Chinese also spent a lot of time talking about the Canadian trade agent who had been in their town earlier and asking about him. Burton wasn't able to tell them much about that person since he had never met him.

When the Canadians at last were able to make the presentation they had prepared, they were surprised at the number of people who showed up: Ten Chinese faced them across the table. The Canadians were a bit disconcerted when several people at different times answered mobile phone calls, without leaving the room and without apologies. Still, the Chinese frequently nodded and smiled and said "yes." Burton and Raines had prepared sales data and showed, effectively they thought, that within five years the factory could double its current production. At the end of the day, the jubilant Canadians returned to their hotel rooms confident they had sold the equipment.

The next day they were asked to explain once again things they thought had been covered already to a Chinese team with four new faces on it. They were confused about who their negotiating counterparts really were. Their jubilation began to evaporate. They were asked to explain the technology in minute detail. Neither Burton nor Raines had been involved in the engineering of the high-tech component that was the heart of the equipment. After doing the best they could, they returned to the hotel exhausted.

Their interpreter also seemed to be unfamiliar with technological terms since she and the interpreter for the factory spent some time discussing the terms between themselves. Because the Canadians' interpreter was a woman, they had to meet with her in the hotel lobby to discuss their plan for the next day. The two tired men would have preferred to sit in their room while they talked with her, rather than in the noisy lobby where they were the object of curiosity, but she requested they remain in a public place because as a woman she could not meet with them in their room.

The following day a member of the first-day Chinese team pointed out discrepancies between what they had said and what the manufacturing director, an engineer, had told them in Canada. Burton and Raines were chagrined. The Chinese were reproachful about the discrepancies, as if the Canadians had been caught trying to deceive them. The two Canadians quickly texted Canada for specifications and explanations, but it was nighttime in Canada. The afternoon session was uncomfortable, although everyone was polite. Burton and Raines were a bit unsettled when a middle-aged woman suddenly burst into the negotiating room and whispered in the ear of one of the key Chinese speakers, who immediately got up and left the room. The Canadians expected some explanation for the emergency, but none ever came.

The Canadians didn't receive some of the documentation they needed until the following day because of the time difference. Discussions resumed with the same questions being asked, yet again. It all went very slowly. The Chinese appreciated the high quality of the Canadian product but worried they wouldn't be able to fix the equipment if it broke down. They suggested—delicately, to avoid implying that they *expected* breakdowns—that perhaps the Canadians could give them some help with maintenance training. The Canadians pointed out the expense and difficulty of keeping someone in their city for several weeks or months and expressed confidence that there wouldn't be any problems the manual didn't cover. They confidently asserted that Chinese would be able to look after the equipment just fine.

Finally, the technical discussions gave way to the issue central to most business negotiations: price. This proved to be the most difficult of all. The Chinese began by asking for a 20-percent price discount. The Canadians thought this was simply an outrageous negotiating ploy; they stuck to their price, which they knew to be fair, and offered a 3-percent discount on the printing cylinders.

Although Burton and Raines had heard that negotiations took time in China, they had thought a week would be ample. Now time was running out, and they were due in Beijing in two days. The Canadians began to ask pointed questions about what the Chinese were unhappy with and where they needed to go over issues again. During the last two sessions, the Canadians tried to get the Chinese to focus on the unresolved points, but the Chinese seemed reluctant to do so.

Things were still unresolved when the farewell banquet was held the following noon. The question of price seemed near a solution, but not the method of payment, which was the final hurdle. The Chinese couldn't guarantee the payment schedule; it seemed that payment was tied to deadlines and requirements of the municipal officials. Nevertheless, Manager Li smiled and spoke of mutual cooperation for the future, past Chinese–Canadian relations, and the great amount he and his factory could learn from the Canadians. They signed an expanded version of the letter of intent that had been signed nine months earlier in Canada. The Canadians left disappointed but with expressions on both sides of willingness to continue to discuss the sale by mail and fax.

The Canadians were stunned to learn two weeks later that the factory had decided to buy from a Japanese equipment manufacturer. They knew their product was good and their price was fair. What had happened to derail their sale?

Intercultural Negotiation

Negotiating is a special communication task. It occurs when two or more parties have common interests and therefore have a reason to work together, but who also have conflicts about their goals and how to accomplish them. Negotiation is the communication that takes place in order to reach agreement about how to handle both common and conflicting interests between two or more parties. Negotiation always has an element of persuasion in it.

Negotiating "how-to" books abound. Some authorities on negotiation claim cultural difference is only one of many factors and may boil down to being "simply differences in style and language."[1] But this view assumes that negotiating *skills* are value-free and are the same around the world, like the rules of chess for opening moves, middle game, and endgame.

One interculturalist has this to say about negotiation:

> In the USA several books have appeared on the art of negotiation; it is a popular theme for training courses. Negotiations have even been simulated in computer programs, which use a mathematical theory of games to calculate the optimal choice in a negotiation situation. These approaches are largely irrelevant.[2]

This critical view comes from the author's observation that the books and simulation games are based on the assumption that both sides have the values of the United States. Raymond Cohen refers to the "instrumental and manipulative" style of negotiators from the United States.[3]

Not only does this view mistakenly discount the role of culture in framing the priorities of negotiators, it also overlooks what happens when people from different cultures interact. The *interaction* produces an intercultural communication situation that is the product of both cultures and of the personalities of both teams, which in Chapter 1 we called *transactional culture.*

Culture tells negotiators what is important, and enables them to assign meaning to the other side's communication and guess at their motives. Cultural Intelligence (CQ) enables negotiators to behave appropriately to the members of the other culture (see Chapter 1). Therefore, to negotiate effectively, intercultural negotiators not only need special communication skills, they also need to understand both their own and the other team's culture. They need to be able to switch from behavior they use in their own culture to the behavior that will be most appropriate for another culture.

What *Really* Happened with Canwall in China?

What happened with Canwall in China was a combination of cultural factors that worked against the Canadians, some within their control and some outside their control. Here are a few of the reasons for the outcome of this episode.

Chinese Emphasis on Relationships

First, the Chinese felt they had already formed a relationship with the Canadian firm because they earlier had formed a relationship with the trade representative. But Burton and Raines, who came to negotiate the sale, were new to them and didn't seem to know the trade agent very well. The trade representative had actually been an agent who represented a number of Canadian light industry manufacturers, not a Canwall employee. The Chinese also had developed a relationship with a salesperson and the director of manufacturing of Canwall, neither of whom was on this visit. They were disconcerted by having to develop new relationships from the beginning, all over again. But the Canadians typically used lower-level people for preliminary discussions where technical details were ironed out and then sent in their top-level people to sign the contract.

Canadian Expectations about Time and Efficiency

The two Canadians had expected a much faster pace of negotiating and had not expected to spend so much time eating, resting, and sight-seeing. After all, their product was familiar to the Chinese, and it was a good product, fairly priced. They had looked forward to ironing out any wrinkles about payment and schedules and concluding the sale in three or four days. In fact, Charlie Burton had worried they'd have time on their hands after the contract was signed. The Chinese, however, wanted to get to know these two men they hadn't previously met. Also, Manager Li had to make sure the political officials of the municipality would support his purchase from overseas; the party secretary and other government party officials had to be kept informed and also had to get to know these new Canwall people.

Differences in Negotiating Style

The Chinese began with generalities about their factory and the local government's successes. This was done to create a context for the negotiation at hand, but it seemed inconsequential to Burton and Raines. On the other hand, the Canadian presentation of specific data, moving to generalized projections, seemed rushed and incomplete to the Chinese.

The Chinese spent a long time on the technical specifications of the equipment partly because they wanted to learn how it was made and partly because they wanted to be sure they were being given accurate information. When Burton fudged a bit on the details (with which he was unfamiliar), the Chinese suspected he was trying to deceive them. It took a lot of time to undo the loss of trust and to verify the true information with the faxed documents. The Chinese were painfully conscious of being perceived to be lagging behind in the latest technology, and their sense of national honor made them determined to show China's technological savvy.

Once the negotiations were well under way, the Canadians focused on points of contention that remained unresolved; the Chinese preferred to focus on what had already been agreed. The Canadians found the Chinese slow and unwilling to be specific about the outstanding problems; the Chinese found the Canadians assertive and too absorbed with the negative unresolved conflicts.

Differences in Ranking Issues to Be Negotiated

Price   The Chinese had determined that sensible price negotiations meant getting a good price. Negotiations between Chinese and foreign companies routinely involve asking for price concessions and getting them. Li's purchase costs were market-driven, not state-determined as in earlier decades, but Li was not very experienced at costing out his expenses or profit. He was not able to rely absolutely on the stability of his financing arrangements. So his inflated opening price gave him a comfortable margin.

During negotiations, the Chinese had also reminded the Canadians that other manufacturers—notably the Japanese—could undercut the Canadian price; however, the Canadians responded, with some chagrin, that their industry was not subsidized by their government in the way Japanese industries were. They were touchy about that fact (and their bargaining position as a consequence of it) within the global field of competitors.

Payment Schedule   The issue of the payment schedule was thorny. The Chinese manager wanted some leeway so he could make the most of his capital. He was wary about being taken advantage of.

Attitudes toward the Relationship   The Chinese also welcomed a chance to form a relationship they could pursue further. For them, the relationship was still "on" even if in a dormant period. They were well aware of the high quality of the Canadian equipment but were happy to do business with the lowest-priced supplier. The Canadians, for their part, felt that when they lost the sale, they had lost their chance in China, after spending considerable time and money to chase it. For them the deal was dead.

Factors that Determined the Deal

The week after the Canadians left, a Japanese manufacturer's representative made his third visit to Manager Li's operation. He was authorized to offer a lower price on the equipment than the Canadians; his price on pattern-printing cylinders was higher, however. He also offered to have a company employee stay in the town for four months and train Chinese employees in the maintenance of the equipment. The Chinese manager felt this was a better deal, although he also looked forward to future negotiations with the Canadians. The Chinese party secretary, who also had his own personal agenda to consider, sent up to the provincial government a report on the manager's decision to buy the Japanese equipment at the lower price. This enhanced his personal standing as a shrewd negotiator. He didn't mention the higher price of the pattern cylinders.

Pattern cylinders were the costliest part of the equipment. Since Li wanted his firm to produce more than one pattern, his expense in the end was no lower than it would have been with the Canadian product. (Subsequently, Li felt he had not negotiated well with the Japanese because the pattern cylinders had to be replaced more frequently than originally planned.)

As for the maintenance issue, the Japanese firm was happy to supply someone to teach the Chinese how to maintain and troubleshoot the equipment. They planned to keep this trainer in China in order to learn about other market possibilities. Of course, the distance from Jiangsu to Japan is about one-fifteenth the distance to the Canwall head office. The Japanese employee could go home frequently, whereas for a Canadian such travel would be very costly.

How Knowledge of Culture Can Help

This case illustrates a number of negotiation strategy differences and expectations at work. All interactions with other cultures are more likely to succeed when you know something about the other culture's differences in values and expectations. The negotiation communication task requires knowledge about the company and the industry, about the culture, about processes for decision making, and about communication preferences. Negotiation also requires a commitment and confidence in being able to succeed, and the ability to enact this knowledge. In other words, good negotiators are people with high CQs.

For instance, the Canadians could have kept in mind that the Chinese value **relationships** as much as results. They are disconcerted when people they have entered into relationships with suddenly disappear, like the agent they mistakenly had thought was closely tied to Canwall. The Chinese expect to spend **time** developing the links that knit individuals into webs of relationships. Guests are treated to sight-seeing jaunts and special dinners and entertainment in order to give the Chinese a chance to share some experiences with them and chat informally. They want to cultivate a sense of friendship and, with it, **obligation.** Then they will pursue their goals by appealing to the obligation of friendship.

Relationships need a context in which to flourish, so the Chinese spent time giving background information and reminding the Canadians of historical China–Canada ties. Their value of **harmony** in group interactions means they prefer to focus on the things that already have been agreed upon rather than on conflicts that remain unresolved. They are careful to **avoid displays of anger** or express criticism that might cause **loss of face** for the other side. However, they are masterful at using **shame,** which only works when one side feels it has let down its members and the others from the organization it represents. Pointing out the inconsistencies in the specifications was a way of causing the Canadians shame and thereby moving the Canadians to a weaker negotiating position. (The Canadians, however, missed this maneuver, so it didn't produce shame or concessions.)

In negotiations, the Chinese often dwell at length on technical details. They want to understand the technology; they also want to be sure they are being told the same thing each time. Since in general the Chinese do **not use question asking as a primary learning method** the way Westerners do, they often ask questions in order to verify the accuracy of what they have been told, as much as to find out something they have not understood. Asking questions is also a way to get to know someone, to develop an understanding of someone, and build a relationship.

The Chinese **perform tasks simultaneously;** a mobile telephone call may be taken by someone on the negotiating team (since Chinese mobile phones are rarely turned off) who disappears and then reappears without explanation. The Canadians viewed this as a most unusual interruption—either a sign of their low status in the eyes of the Chinese or, more probably, an indication of an emergency of grave importance—but that is because Canadians tend to do tasks sequentially, devoting their entire attention to only one thing at a time.

The Chinese have a **preference for form** in negotiations or, in other words, for following a specific protocol. This usually means that the opening discussion will be very formally conducted. The host side will first describe themselves—who they are and what they do—with many statistics. Then they will expect the guests (in this case, the Canadians) to do the same. None of this has any real relevance to the issue being negotiated, but this form is important. The preference for form and correct manner—which preserves the harmony mentioned earlier—provides the context within which the negotiations will take place.

The most important person on the negotiating team from the Chinese perspective is the one who is most **senior in age;** this is a key, along with membership in the Chinese Communist party, to the **hierarchy** of the Chinese workplace. The key persons on the Chinese team may not be much in evidence during the negotiations. It will also be how the Chinese view your negotiating team.

Since **access to authority is mediated** in Chinese culture, the real decision-swaying power may not be identifiable to a foreigner. The company doing the negotiating with Canwall was government-operated, and the municipal party officials, while not determining the purchase of the wallpaper printing equipment, nevertheless were involved because their goodwill could be crucial to Manager Li. The people with the authority to make decisions—the manager, the powerful municipal officials, and the most powerful people in the factory—were Communist party members. Their network of obligations would also have played a role. When a company is privately operated, there are also stakeholders whose approvals count.

Interdependence characterizes Chinese social organization, and the members of the Chinese team are conscious of representing a larger collective. The employees of the company, from the manager down, could spend their entire working lives in that factory. The county officials may never change jobs either. Their work colleagues are also their neighbors; many are even relatives. Even after retirement, employees are still associated with their workplace, which may provide housing, access to food and other products, health care, and many other services.

Since the Chinese value relationships and can accept failure in specific undertakings as long as the relationships are intact, they can **tolerate uncertainty** about outcomes. If success doesn't come this time, it may come the next. As long as the relationship has not been ruptured, there is always a chance for future cooperation. The Canadians viewed the loss of the sale as the end of their dealings with this factory.

Awareness of these cultural priorities can help Burton and Raines prepare for their next Chinese sale. Neither side is right or wrong; just different. But as sellers in this case, the Canadians probably need to develop more understanding of cultural priorities than the Chinese.

This chapter will now address negotiation teams. After that is a discussion of the factors in negotiations. They include expectations for outcomes, the orientation of the team, the physical context of the negotiation, communication, and style of negotiating. A discussion of the phases of negotiation follows the factors.

Teams in the Workplace

Teams are groups with common purposes, but not all groups are teams. Workplace teams are assembled in order to achieve a goal for the organization, such as negotiation. They are unlike social groups that are formed by people who want to spend time together. Teams have leaders and members have a range of specific roles, so that by interacting, the teams can be productive units for larger organizations.

Daft and Lane offer a good definition of a workplace team: **A team is composed of two or more people who interact and coordinate their work to achieve a shared goal.**[4] Most teams have fewer than 15 people, and they work together regularly. They may meet face-to-face or virtually; they may communicate by e-mail, in hallways and elevators, or by video teleconferencing.

Teams often have specific tasks or functions within an organization. Negotiation is one such task. Often, but not always, teams have the responsibility of making decisions or solving problems. Organizations have increased the number of teams over the past several decades in a response to spreading globalization and the competition it brings. More and more organizations are using teams instead of individual managers to deal with complex issues organizations face.

Organizational Goals for Teams in the Workplace

Organizations form teams in order to have better results for their strategies and goals than they would get from individuals. According to recent studies, teams bring benefits to organizations, such as:

• Increased productivity
• Effectiveness in decision making
• Improvement of quality

- Increased innovation
- Enhanced employee satisfaction

Team members often see different benefits to teamwork, including:

- Satisfaction in working with fellow employees
- Accomplishing more than individuals alone can
- Developing a record of cooperative achievement

The three individual-level ways to evaluate teamwork are (a) *personal* effectiveness, (b) *task* effectiveness, and (c) *relational* effectiveness.

Because teams can be assembled quickly, set a task, and be dissembled quickly, they are flexible and responsive when organizations need tasks done.

In this chapter on negotiation we discuss teams as if a team's members are all from the same culture. That provides an opportunity to examine later in this chapter what happens when teams from one culture communicate with teams from other cultures.

Of course, not all communication between teams of different cultures involves formal negotiation tasks. Some intercultural team communication occurs on task forces between two organizations, such as when a company merges with another firm from a different culture, or when two or more companies share a contract. However, negotiation gives us a chance to look at intercultural communication between teams in detail. We begin with the roles of team members.

Team members play different roles within the team. However, roles vary according to culture, so team roles in individualist cultures are compared with team roles in collectivist cultures.

Roles of Team Members in Individualist Cultures

Team members in Western cultures fill a number of roles, from five to nine, according to various American scholars:

- Leader
- Idea person
- Skeptic
- Recorder
- Gatekeeper
- Finisher
- Implementer
- Negotiator
- Specialist

Leader   The first role is **leader.** The leader is responsible for setting the agenda and informing the team members about what their purpose is. The leader stresses the shared goal. In addition, the leader's job is to try to make sure the team has what it needs in order to achieve their purpose. This might include information, or a location in which to meet, or connections for virtual meetings and communicating.

The leader monitors progress. The leader often has the responsibility of enabling team members to act together, and is a facilitator or coordinator for getting members to communicate with each other.

Team leadership may rotate among team members. This is especially true in organizations that believe any member can be the leader, and do not see the same people as the leaders in every team.

Idea Person   Another role is **idea person,** or **suggestion-maker.** This role involves coming up with ideas for the team to discuss. Many members may play this role at the same time. Their role is to share knowledge and expertise and not withhold information. They also stimulate creative thinking from others. They ask questions, even seemingly "dumb" ones. Often their new viewpoint can help the team members reach new understandings.

Skeptic   Some teams have at least one member whose role is a **skeptic,** to analyze ideas. This member's job is to respond thoughtfully to others' ideas. A skeptic often has special expertise. If the skeptic sees value in an idea, and supports it, the team may agree. When the skeptic sees little value in an idea and is negative about it, the team may also agree. The role of skeptic can therefore be very influential.

When the skeptic sees his or her role as finding flaws in every idea, the result can be conflict. Other team members look upon such a person as negative. In equalizer teams, everyone else may disagree with the skeptic, setting up division in the team. In destroyer teams, negativity contributes to members taking sides.

A useful critic shows respect for every idea and each team member. Such a role can prevent the team from groupthink, and becoming an equalizer team where no critical thinking at all applies to any idea.

Recorder   The **recorder** is the team member who keeps careful notes about the team meetings and the team's work. The recorder captures the discussion among members, ideas raised, and votes taken. Decisions are recorded.

The record is very important in individualist cultures, where results are the way team effectiveness is measured. Sometimes team members are absent from meetings, or do not accurately remember what was decided in past discussions. The record is the official account of what happened, what people said, and what was decided. Although team members may have a different memory or understanding of what is happening with the team, what is in the record is the reality.

The record makes up part of what the team presents to the organization's management, to show progress toward goals and to show process. Assessment of the team depends in some part on the record.

Gatekeeper   The **gatekeeper** has the role of encouraging participation from everyone. Sometimes the leader also performs this role, but the gatekeeper can be any team member. This person keeps track of people's opinions and contributions to discussion. If someone seems to want to participate but does not, the gatekeeper can turn the team's attention to listen to that person. If one team member dominates the discussion, the gatekeeper can ask that person to let others speak.

The gatekeeper role implies fairness and a lack of personal bias. If the gatekeeper only encourages team members to speak with whom the gatekeeper agrees, and shuts out other voices, then the gatekeeper is building a destroyer team.

Finisher   A **finisher** is a team member who urges the team members to finish their work according to the schedule. This role may by played by the leader, or another team member. The finisher worries about deadlines, and reminds the others about what remains to be done.

Finishers also pay attention to detail. They want the finished work to be without errors.

Implementer   Finishers are also often implementers. The **implementer** role may be taken by several people at once. Implementers look for ways to put the team's ideas to practical use. They make plans. They are well organized, and other team members rely on their help to get things done. These team members are disciplined in the way they approach their work.

Negotiator   The **negotiator** role is often taken by more than one team member. Negotiators work to develop relationships of mutual respect among team members. They negotiate agreements when conflicts arise. They are committed to helping the team work cooperatively. For negotiators, the process is as important as, or more important than, the actual work of the team.

In successful teams, most members are negotiators.

Specialist   A final role is the **specialist.** These members have expertise to help the team accomplish its aims better. Some teams are made up of many specialists, and other teams have only one or two. Besides special knowledge, a specialist may have particular skills. For example, often teams need information that is new to many members. A specialist may be someone who can get information so the team can continue its work.

Roles of Team Members in Collectivist Cultures

Collectivist cultures have fewer roles, but the responsibilities of several are greater.

- Leader
- Leader surrogate
- Suggestion maker
- Consultant
- Specialist
- Implementer

Leader   In collectivist cultures that are also hierarchical, such as East Asian cultures, Arab cultures, Latin American cultures, and African cultures, the leader is the most important member of the team. Leadership rarely rotates. Instead, the most senior person on the team, and the one with the most responsibility granted by the top levels of the organization, retains the position of team leader. The leader's role is to set the agenda, articulate the goal, make sure the team has resources to do its job, monitor and direct members, and be aware of possible conflict areas among members in order to resolve them before they appear.

The leader usually takes on the role of finisher, encouraging the team to meet deadlines and reminding the team of work that is still to be done.

Because the leader has greater face to lose than any other member of the team, the leader may not engage in much communication during team meetings. The leader's contributions may be communication through close subordinates who are also members of the team.

Surrogate for the Leader   One or more team members may be communicators with team members on behalf of the leader, and serve as conduits for team members to communicate with the leader. In other words, they are mediators between team members and the authority who is the leader.

Suggestion Maker   More than one member may take the role of offering ideas or suggestions, and stimulating discussion. Knowledge and expertise is shared with the team in order to make the team's work successful.

The suggestion maker also takes over the role of the *skeptic* in individualist cultures. Rather than openly critique an idea, the suggestion maker usually offers another alternative idea as a way of avoiding the possible negative consequences from another team member's idea. This behavior preserves harmony among the team members, which is as important in collectivist cultures as working out a solution to a problem or arriving at a decision. For this reason, suggestion makers are highly valued team members. They may use humor with team members to communicate ideas outside the hierarchical communication structure that makes communication formal.

Consultant   Multiple members of the team may take on a consulting role. This role involves conferring with members outside the scheduled meetings, to uncover unspoken concerns and find ways to reconcile them. Because the goal is to arrive at a consensus, this consultation practice outside the actual meetings leads more quickly to agreement when the team meets.

Consultants take on similar tasks to *negotiators* in individualist cultures, but their communication is largely outside the team meetings.

Consultants also perform the role of *gatekeeper* in individualist cultures, insofar as they keep track of members' concerns and reactions to what is being said at meetings. However, consultants do not encourage open disagreement at meetings, since that could cause loss of face for the member who has a different view, whereas gatekeepers in individualist cultures may urge members to speak openly about divergent opinions.

Consultants may be especially aware of nonverbal behavior of team members, and read unspoken messages, which can later be the basis for personal communication outside the meetings.

Specialist As with teams in individualist cultures, specialists have knowledge and skills that help the team accomplish its goals. They are sometimes chosen as team members because of the specialized help they can offer.

One specialist role may be to generate a written or oral report to the organization's managers.

Implementer More than one team member may perform this role. Usually at the direction of the leader, in a communication before all the team, a member will take responsibility for some aspect of the team's overall task. Implementers report progress back to the team and leader.

Note-taking and record-keeping of all that has been communicated between team members during the work on a task is not as important as the final communication, which is with one voice, from the team. For that reason, the role of record keeper at meetings is usually not important.

Communication Effectiveness in Teams

As mentioned earlier, a team's effectiveness comes from three areas: *personal effectiveness* (the individual's sense of satisfaction), *task effectiveness* (the product or outcome of the team's work), and *relational effectiveness* (the ability of the group members to work together in the future).[5] Let's look at how culture affects these three areas of team effectiveness and communication.

In teams whose members come from collectivist cultures, the relational effectiveness of the group is the most important area in teamwork. Collectivist cultures form teams that have cooperation and collaboration as high priorities. Although they may be in danger of agreeing too easily, and thereby missing the depth of analysis of ideas that may diverge from or contradict what is being discussed, collectivist cultures' teams understand the importance of common goals. They are usually eager to work together as a team.

Team members from collectivist cultures have interdependent self-construals. That is, each individual sees himself or herself as part of a network or group. Consequently, the individual's personal satisfaction with the team derives from the individual's interdependent self-construal. The individual's sense of personal effectiveness as a team member is directly related to the individual's sense of belonging to—and being valued by—the team.

Collectivism and interdependent self-construal affect team communication in the following ways:

- Communication styles are related to group goals.
- Other-face concerns predominate in the choice of topics of communication.
- Others'-goals concerns prevail in conflict communication.

Collectivist teams with interdependent self-construal communicate in ways that will lead to good team relationships, not merely the completion of tasks. Collectivist teams communicate using indirectness. Members may use metaphor and storytelling in order to make a point, and may use jokes and humorous references to comment upon the formal discussion. Indirect communication comes from other-face concerns. The team's aim is to complete its tasks with unity of mind, and to communicate its outcomes with one voice.

In teams whose members come from individualist cultures, recognition for the commendable performance of tasks is the most important aspect of effective teamwork. Personal satisfaction comes from knowing one's work is valued. Relational effectiveness is valued, but not as highly as recognition of the excellence of the work.

Team members from individualist cultures have independent self-construals. That is, each individual sees himself or herself as independent from the other members, a unique human with his or her own emotions and values concerning the tasks and the other members.

Individualism and independent self-construal affect team communication in several ways:

- Communication styles reflect individual goals, rather than group goals.
- Self-face concerns predominate in the choice of topics of communication.
- Own-goal concerns prevail in conflict communication.

Individualist teams communicate using directness. Members get to the point, use evidence to back up their ideas and challenge others' ideas, and express disagreement openly. The team's aim is to get to the best possible outcome as efficiently and effectively as possible.

The more similar the members of a team are, the more likely they will communicate similarly with each other. Their norms for communication may make it hard for them to imagine what the communication norms are for a team that is different from them. For example, a collectivist negotiating team may not foresee the individual, independent communication of an individualist negotiating team. The individualist team leader may not be evident, when everybody is talking and when each team member is saying something different. The collectivist team may seem "programmed" to the individualist team, who can be puzzled by hearing the same message from one or two team members, and nothing from anyone else.

Culture affects team communication as it does other kinds of workplace communication. Because teams are used widely in organizations, not only for negotiation purposes, it is important for you to know how teams communicate, how to assess their effectiveness, and how culture influences team communication.

For a detailed discussion on multicultural teams and how they fit into the overall business strategy and the achievement of corporate goals, see Chapter 12.

Factors in the Negotiation Task

The next section of the chapter discusses the special communication task of negotiation, which involves four factors:

- Expectations for negotiation outcomes
- Team composition and motivation
- Physical factors
- Communication and negotiating style

The aim of this discussion is to show how culture affects negotiations. A number of books on *how to* negotiate exist in your own culture. Primarily, since this is a book about communication, we'll concentrate on the fourth item. But we'll examine all four aspects of negotiating, beginning with expectations for what the negotiations will accomplish.

Expectations for Outcomes

Different Goals

Different sides of the negotiating table often seem to be after very different things. This may appear to be the result of shrewd negotiating tactics—and maybe it is—in which a side doesn't disclose openly what its goals are. You may decide the other team is craftily hiding what it wants behind some other, seemingly unimportant aims. But another reason for this obliqueness may simply be that they want something different from what you think they want. People from different cultures often are looking for different outcomes. As far as possible, you need to identify ahead of time what the probable goals of the other side are.

For example, in the case of the Chinese–Canadian negotiation, the Chinese had four goals: (1) to buy the best quality they could find at the very best world price, (2) to develop an ongoing relationship with Canwall, and (3) to learn as much as they could about Canwall's new technology. Had the contract been signed, the Chinese also would have expected (4) exclusive access to the Canadian equipment. The Canadians understood only the first of the Chinese negotiation goals. The second goal may drive the opening encounters with high-context cultures.

As high-context negotiators, the Chinese were concerned with getting a sense of the people they were dealing with.

Fairness and Advantage

As the case shows, the Chinese were interested in developing a relationship. Negotiating teams from other Asian cultures—as well as teams from African, Middle Eastern, Latin American, and southern European cultures—usually are, too. A relationship, as was discussed in Chapter 4, implies a willingness to incur indebtedness. This may help explain the tendency among countries on the lower end of the technology scale, as illustrated in the opening case, to believe the wealthier, more advanced side should give proportionately *more* than the less advanced, less wealthy country. The less advanced team will thus be indebted to the other party in the relationship. The payback date, however, may be far into the future, since the collectivist view of relationships is that they extend for generations. The Philippines and Indonesia are among the countries today that are looking to bridge the digital divide.

North Americans and Europeans are not usually happy with an agreement that gives one side greater advantage than the other. They are accustomed to thinking of a "fair" settlement as one that evenhandedly splits advantage between the two parties. But obviously the 50–50 ideal is not shared among all cultures. As some researchers point out, the use of the English term *fair play* does not seem to be translatable into some other languages; if the term does not exist, it is likely the identical concept does not exist either.[6]

Negotiation Outcomes: Winning, Losing, and Reaching a Stalemate

Competition cultures, especially those that put a strong priority on achievement, doing, accomplishing goals through planning and taking control, and national or family honor (powerful in Middle Eastern and Korean companies, for example), look upon negotiations as situations to *win.*

Winning means not having to make concessions beyond the reserve point—the bargaining limit established by a negotiating team before the negotiations begin—but still gaining the team's objectives.

In order to "win," a team may have to give up some wished-for things. *Compromise* is a standard expectation in bargaining and negotiation in many Western countries, and a mode for resolving conflict as we have seen in Chapter 8. The notion of fairness in results-oriented cultures means that in compromise, both sides have to give a bit, and the bits are equal. A good end is achieved when the compromises made by each side are about the same size. However, you may need to be careful about using the word *compromise:*

> In some cultures, such as Iran, the term *compromise* has moral connotations and implies a corrupt betrayal of principle. So it has to be kept out of your vocabulary.[7]

Russians do not view compromise as a fair and equitable conceding of position by each side:

> Russians regard compromise as a sign of weakness, a retreat from a correct and morally justified position. Russians, therefore, are great "sitters," prepared to wait out their opposite numbers in the expectation that time and Russian patience will produce more concessions from the impatient Americans.[8]

Win–Lose

Winning can also mean you have achieved an agreement in which the other side gives up more than you do. To some negotiators, however, winning means more than getting everything; it means beating down the other party so it has to go past its reserve point. This may involve price or schedule or marketing terms, or any of a host of issues. Or winning may mean making a small compromise but demanding a large compromise from the other side. In other words, in this outcome winning means that the other side also has to *lose.* This is sometimes called *zero-sum* negotiation.

Win–Win

Collectivist cultures that value ongoing relationships between organizations often prefer outcomes that emphasize the advantages gained by both sides. In other words, the objectives are win–win or *non-zero-sum.* When both sides win, nobody loses face or is shamed.

The difference between a win–win outcome and compromise lies in a negotiator's focus. If the negotiator primarily thinks of his or her own team's outcome, the attitude will probably be to expect compromise: what we will gain in return for what we will have to give up. The focus is on our loss as well as our gain. If the negotiator looks at *both* his or her own team and the other team, then the attitude will probably be to expect each side to gain. The focus is on mutual gain. One of these three modes is usually what a negotiator expects: compromise, win–lose, or win–win.

Stalemate

However, negotiators sometimes have to accept a stalemate when no agreement can be reached. In this outcome, the negotiating parties walk away from the table without any agreement. Nobody enters into trade negotiations with this goal in mind. It represents a failure of the negotiation. Occasionally, one side gains everything without giving up anything, and the other side simply agrees. In this case, rather than a failed negotiation, no negotiation has taken place. This is a simple agreement without conflicting interests. The two fundamental characteristics of all negotiation are (1) agreement about a goal and, at the same time, (2) disagreement about how to reach it:

> "Without common interests there is nothing to negotiate for, and without conflict there is nothing to negotiate about."[9]

Finally, fundamental advice about expectations for the outcomes of negotiation is to make sure what you are negotiating is negotiable. It may *not* be negotiable because the party negotiating with you doesn't have the power or access to grant what you want, or because it doesn't exist, or because what you want simply cannot be obtained.

Orientation of the Negotiating Team

Negotiators fit one of two basic descriptors: strategic or synergistic.[10] A **strategic negotiator** is out to win and sees the process as something to be won through cleverness, competitiveness, and even deceit. This negotiator is suspicious of, and hostile toward, the other side. The style is confrontational. A **synergistic negotiator** wants to avoid confrontation and is cooperative rather than competitive. This negotiator focuses on common interests but allows opposing interests to exist even beyond the point at which agreement is possible. The style is trusting and friendly.

Members with High Status

Negotiators frequently are chosen because they are high-status members of the organization or society. Their presence on the team indicates the organization is serious about concluding negotiations successfully. In the case example, Canwall's president—the highest-status person in that company—led the negotiating team to China. Many firms follow the practice of having lower-level negotiators do the groundwork and then sending in top-level people to close the deal. Considerable "face" can be gained by the top-level people when a negotiation reaches a successful conclusion, but having the lower-level workers involved is also useful. A manager of a Japanese–Chinese joint venture in Shanghai told one of the authors that high-level executives and politicians had initiated that joint venture, following the successful outcome of negotiations, with great fanfare. But it was low-level employees who had to make it work. He said their valuable contributions were not solicited during the negotiation process, at a time when potential problems and conflicts could have been addressed. Nor were pictures of the lower-level employees in the newspapers!

The presence of a high-level person on the team also signals the authority to make a binding agreement. Some companies delegate that authority to other team members when a high-status person is not part of the team. Negotiators from some results-oriented cultures value efficiency—achieving goals with the smallest expenditure of time and money—more than status. Consequently, they view as wasteful the practice of sending a team to negotiate that has to keep going back to higher authorities at home for decisions. They want their negotiating team to be able to conclude an agreement on the spot. Koreans, with their value of respect for seniority, want their older and higher-status authorities to exercise their judgment about agreements. If the senior person is in Korea and the negotiations take place in another country, time must be allowed for the senior person to be reached and the progress of the talks discussed.

Members with Special Expertise

As has been noted earlier, one of the roles of team members is *specialist*. Some negotiators become members of a team because of their specialized expertise. For example, a person with technical or technological knowledge may be very important, or an expert in financing with accurate cost figures may be able to make the difference between success and failure. Someone with marketing expertise in a specialized product or legal experience in a particular country can make or break negotiations. For example, one person's experience with Japan's import regulations governing agricultural products and health inspections enabled a German company to negotiate an agreement for the sale of sausages to Japan. The expertise may consist of knowledge of the culture and values of the other side. Richard Welzel, a German-Canadian broker of food-processing equipment, was able to negotiate a purchase of secondhand German-made stainless steel machinery in Bulgaria because his expertise meant he understood the quality of the machinery.

The Translator

One of the most important people on the team is the translator. This role is discussed also in Chapter 2, and although language skill means it is a specialist role, it is of such importance in international negotiation, it deserves separate recognition.

Many negotiating teams choose not to take their own translator, but rather depend on the host country to supply a translator. This is usually a mistake. Obviously, a translator's first loyalty is to his or her employer. The Chinese who supplied the translator to the Canadians in the Canwall case could have asked their translator for daily reports on what the Canadians said when they were alone with her. This would have given the Chinese a great advantage in the negotiations. Similarly, a Chinese team in another country would be wise to bring its own translator.

Having your own translator means you have an ear to hear what the other team says in side conversations and comments among themselves. English-speaking teams frequently rely on the widespread use of English around the globe. They assume it is possible to negotiate in English—and cheaper—if they don't have to take a translator with them. But they miss out. They don't understand what the other team is saying when its members converse in their own language. When the English-speaking team has a side conversation, however, the other team's translator and English-speaking members can understand what is being said.

Another benefit of having your own translator is that the translations by the other side's translator can be heard and understood by yours. This means errors or omissions—which are frequently unintentional—can be corrected immediately. Translation is extremely hard work and doesn't stop just because the formal session is over. At social gatherings, the translators work just as hard as they do at the meeting table. It is understandable that a tired translator may misunderstand or mistranslate. A second translator offers a check against errors.

Translation errors are mines waiting to explode around unsuspecting negotiators. Simple mistakes in translation can cause days of delay while a misunderstanding is identified and cleared up. One key to preventing errors is not only to have your own translator but also to have a translator who is familiar with the vocabulary of the business. Someone with a degree in language studies may have read bookshelves of literature in the other language but lack technical vocabulary. In fact, the translator needs to have a technical vocabulary in *both* languages.

Another factor in the selection of a translator is *specific* language skills. Many foreign firms negotiating in China take with them a Chinese person who lives in the firm's country and works for the firm. This can be excellent, provided the language spoken by the Chinese employee is the language spoken in the area of China where negotiations will take place. The Chinese also, like people in many countries around the world, practice regional snobbery about accents.

Like India and many other countries, China is a land of multiple dialects. The regional language in the case study example would have been Shanghai dialect, but in addition, the factory town has its own dialect. That means even if the Canadians from Canwall had brought their own Mandarin-speaking translator—even if they had found one who also spoke Shanghai dialect—the opposite team could possibly have exchanged comments in its local dialect that would not have been understood by the Canadian translator. Similarly, in India the regional dialect (and there are over 600 of them) may not be known to your translator. This means the microphone—your translator—for eavesdropping on the other team's side conversations is closed off.

You can make your translator's job easier, as mentioned in Chapter 2, if you speak in very straightforward language. Consider, for example, the difficulty a translator would have translating the warning uttered by a spokesperson for a non-government international aid organization who said the United States should continue its involvement in rebuilding a country that had been at war "or else the line will not be drawn in the sand and we'll be back in the soup again."[11]

Analysis of the Other Side's Team

Analysis of the other team is very important. With a bit of application of what you have learned about a culture from the questions you have posed, you can see the cultural priorities that generate communication behavior at the negotiating table.

Take a Kuwaiti negotiator, for example. Posing the questions from Chapters 3 and 4 results in the following information. Kuwaiti culture encourages competitiveness among organizations. Women are not usually part of negotiating teams. Achieving goals for the sake of the group's honor—often the royal al-Sabah family's honor—is very important, although the will of Allah may intervene. Goals may be long-term, and Kuwaitis are patient. The society is hierarchical, with members of the ruling family in key positions. Access to authority is mediated. Form and protocol are important, and negotiations may have a ceremonial aspect. Courtesy and patience are characteristic of Kuwaiti interaction with others, since acceptance in the group is an important part of their Bedouin heritage. Language may be used flamboyantly and with an eloquence that is valued for its own sake, beyond or beside the meaning of the words. The way the Kuwaiti understand and think about issues is to take several factors into account rather than move in a mental linear path. The chess-playing characteristic of some negotiations is renowned. A display of emotion is typical.

Once you have gathered responses to the culture questions and have considered typical behavior, a picture of the Kuwaiti negotiator emerges. He is educated and skilled, a member of the ruling family or valued by it, with a strong expectation that negotiation will involve a need for cleverness on his part in order to win. Suspicion and hostility will probably not be evident because he will display Kuwaiti politeness and Bedouin hospitality. His love of verbal play and the importance of emotion in communication may make the Kuwaiti negotiator's wording of messages seem theatrical to a low-context communicator who shuns ambiguity and trusts in directness and simplicity. He will probably possess technological expertise and expect to be given accurate and complete information. His religion, Islam, will frame his thinking and communication, and he may quote the *Qur'an* as a guide for his behavior. He will be patient and will be ready to spend months negotiating. Finally, he will value a personal relationship with the negotiator on the other side of the table.

This analysis is what a negotiator should do for any team member he or she faces from another culture.

Members' Decision-Making Authority

You will want to consider as far as possible the question of how much authority rests with the negotiating team to conclude an agreement. In hierarchical cultures, the ultimate authority may lie with someone who is never present at the negotiating table. Where hierarchy and consensus both characterize a culture, the most influential person may be present at some meetings but may not be introduced in a way that suggests the power that person wields.

In Japanese negotiations, for example, the senior member of the group may not appear at all—or even any—meetings. He (nearly always it's a man) will receive regular and detailed reports, however, of all that is said during the negotiations, and he will direct his team members to proceed in a certain way. No agreement will be reached without his approval. No hint will be given by team members that an agreement could exist until they have had a chance to discuss things with him. If the senior authority is not physically present as a member of the negotiating team, he may be in a hotel room or office nearby. Or he may be in another city or country. In that case, obviously consultation with him will take more time than if he were present. On the other hand, the team members you are negotiating with may have full power to commit their organization to an agreement.

Team Members' Status

Members of the other team, like yours, may be chosen because of their status. In addition to high status within the organization, sometimes being in a special relationship to someone in power is a reason for inclusion on a team. The relatively young and inexperienced nephew of the president, for example, may have a place on a negotiating team mainly because his uncle owns the company. But this may not simply be nepotism. This may make good business sense: It may be that a family member can be trusted best to look after the interests of the family in reaching a certain agreement. If the family rules the country, as in some Middle Eastern nations, then the family's interests coincide with national interests, and family members play key roles in foreign negotiations.

We've already seen that family loyalties can motivate negotiators, and so can company loyalties or national loyalties. The desire to win through the use of clever strategies can motivate negotiators. The wish to develop a relationship that will continue and will allow for indebtedness and favors is a motivator. The value of harmony in human interactions, along with avoidance of confrontation, can motivate negotiators to reach agreement rather than continue to hold discussions.

The Physical Context of the Negotiation

Where the negotiation takes place—the physical context for the communication—has an impact on the outcomes. For example, if the negotiation takes place by telephone or fax, the nonverbal messages have a diminished impact compared with face-to-face negotiation. Indeed, most negotiation involves meetings between parties. The host team for the negotiations has an advantage because the environment is under its control. The guest team doesn't have the same degree of control.

Site and Space

The hosts can determine what city and what building will hold the meetings. If it's the boardroom of the building where the host organization members work, all the resources of that organization are at the disposal of the host team—from photocopiers to telecommunications and from files to assistants. Therefore, the hosts have an advantage of *convenience*. Mobile electronic telecommunication devices such as BlackBerrys are increasing the convenience of access to one's own office for the visitors but there are still advantages to being in one's own setting.

The home negotiators' workspace will be familiar to them. It will not be familiar to the visitors. The visitors will be getting used to an unexpected environment, and this can distract them from their negotiating goals. The visiting team may experience some *culture shock* (see Chapter 1) that could increase the longer they stay.

Schedule and Agenda

Jet lag can make the visiting team unable to perform well on the hosts' schedule. People whose internal clock says it's midnight find it difficult to stay alert even if the clock on the wall says it's 11 a.m. Some teams have been known to conduct very long sessions at a time that is uncomfortable for a visiting team suffering from jet lag.

Control of the schedule also often carries over to control of the negotiating agenda. For example, hosts may suggest postponing certain discussions until guests are more rested, with the result that the hosts control the order in which issues are addressed while giving the appearance of concern for the guests' comfort.

The order of the items discussed on the agenda can have an impact on the outcome. If the two sides agree to one principle or goal, then subsequent points may be presented as simply subsidiary to what has already been agreed.

In Focus

Dr. Jehad al-Omari, a consultant with the British firm Canning, says that for him, an Arab, an agenda is a very Western thing that is an effort by Westerners to compensate for their short and limited memories. Agendas seem to him to be impersonal, linear, and rigid. They may lead to confrontations. He prefers the flexibility of being able to take things off the table if the time doesn't seem right and to avoid potential confrontations. He likes to be able to surprise his counterpart and to spend time getting to know him.

"As a high-context person, I do not like the Western reductionist approach that tries to do one thing at a time, it is all so monochronic. . . . What I like is to be able to approach the meeting in a holistic way, to spend some time discussing everything and nothing, to get the feel of my counterpart, his mood and temperament, his eagerness and readiness, before I launch into business."[12]

The power of the keeper of the agenda is considerable, since the agenda determines when meetings take place and what amount of time is allotted to discuss which issues. An issue that isn't on the agenda may never be discussed. The visiting team has to be alert to its responsibility to participate in setting the agenda.

Negotiators often also operate from a "hidden agenda" that is not shared with the other side. The "open agenda" contains the agreed items for discussion, while the "hidden agenda" is the priorities a team has agreed upon privately.

Arab negotiators may have different ideas about how much sharing of priorities they are willing to do compared with, say, British negotiators.

Use of Time

The use of time is related to the agenda. Monochronic cultures see time as moving through the agenda in a linear pattern and excluding whatever is not scheduled. Polychronic cultures see time as allowing simultaneous activities that take as long as they need to, even if that means bending the schedule, and including whatever needs attention. (These concepts were introduced in Chapter 3.) When negotiators from monochronic cultures face polychronic negotiators, the guests have the greater responsibility to accommodate to the hosts.

Russians often use time to their advantage as part of the nonverbal communication in negotiations. For instance, they may delay negotiations in order to make the other side anxious. This behavior toward North Americans, for instance, is based on two assumptions: Americans "regard compromise as both desirable and inevitable, and . . . Americans feel frustration and failure when agreements are not reached promptly."[13]

Negotiators from the United States are well known for their impatience. Timothy Bennett, a former United States trade negotiator to Mexico, characterizes his countrymen and countrywomen as thinking that some solution is better than no solution, which leads them to compromise more than their Mexican counterparts.[14] Decades of negotiations have taught the Japanese that Westerners, especially delegates from the United States, are not patient. If the Japanese prolong the negotiations sufficiently, the Westerners will probably agree to whatever the Japanese want. In Japan, however, to take time is to show maturity and wisdom. Haste shows poor judgment and lack of genuine commitment. Foreign negotiators who go to the Middle East often complain that they don't get meetings. Foreign negotiators who go to Latin America complain that they have to wait. In Asia, foreign negotiators complain they do too much sight-seeing and not enough negotiating. In the United States, foreign negotiators often feel rushed.

Host Hospitality

> "[In Hungary] we drink *palinka,* a plum or cherry brandy. It's 200 proof. When we start, the Americans are already drunk. The Hungarians aren't. We're seasoned. In Hungary, the Hungarians use this. They try to influence Americans with good drink to sign a favorable contract. It's an instrument to oil the wheels." . . . A foreign man who can't hold his liquor is probably discarded as a potential business associate. . . . [It is] reason to break off negotiations.[15]

Most negotiating involves some socializing (discussed in some detail in Chapter 7). This may be a way to initiate the negotiations and establish some advantage for the host. Sometimes when negotiations are stuck, a meal together or an evening out can be a good strategy for refocusing the agenda. Socializing is often done at the end, after negotiations have been concluded favorably. The Canwall team was treated to a farewell banquet; in China, as in other Asian countries such as Korea and Vietnam, the toasts that are made at welcome banquets carry messages about what items are particularly important to those negotiators.[16] In all cultures, socializing provides an opportunity to get to know the other party better and build relationships with its members. However, the food, beverages, and beds in which visitors sleep may be unfamiliar. With jet lag and unfamiliar food may come digestive and sleep disorders, and the visiting team may suffer a loss of *physical well-being.*

Communication and Style of Negotiating

Negotiation is a special communication task that uses special verbal and nonverbal skills.

In Focus

A recent study of negotiation between companies in New Zealand and Argentina asked businesspeople to rate the importance of four factors in negotiation: communication, dependability (of the other party), customer orientation, and cultural sensitivity.[17] Cultural sensitivity was rated as *least* important by the respondents. Communication was the most important factor.

At first glance, this seems to contradict what this book is saying: that culture matters. However, the study goes on to report that the researchers broke down communication into four dimensions: friendliness, congeniality, keeping to time, and punctuality. Yet all these dimensions are *determined by* culture. What defines "friendliness" varies by culture, especially friendliness on first face-to-face contact. Is it friendly to shake hands or not? To greet visitors standing or to go to the street door to escort them in? What constitutes "congeniality"? Smiling, maintaining harmony and avoiding confrontations, emphasizing the positives, trying to cooperate—all are driven by culture, and all play a part in the enactment of culturally appropriate behavior. Issues of time have already been discussed here (and in Chapters 3 and 7) as culturally defined. So in this study, "communication" was another way of talking about culture's influence on negotiation.

We will now look at specific factors in negotiation communication.

Differences in Focus

Focus may be positive or negative, explicit or implicit, general or specific. Cultures that emphasize communication as a tool for articulating specific goals in order to accomplish them tend to look upon negotiations as a series of points to "settle." Their language in negotiations is explicit and zeros in on what has yet to be agreed. These explicit statements may in fact be questions and emphasize negative points of disagreement, such as, "What do you still not like about this detail of product design?" Americans prefer this direct approach because their aim is to clarify and resolve an issue.

But cultures that use communication to encourage harmony, preserve face, and develop long-term relationships are not comfortable with direct and explicit talk. In Japan, for instance, getting straight to some point about which agreement has yet to be reached may result in confrontation and emotions—even anger. Someone may lose face. The Japanese, like negotiators from other Asian cultures, prefer to emphasize the positive points of agreement. They begin with general terms and seek agreement from the other side about general goals. Then regardless of the remaining details, the general agreement holds the two sides together in a relationship. They do not ask—and do not enjoy being asked—pointed questions. They want to develop relationships because once a relationship exists, each side has an obligation to consider the needs of the other, so the issue resolves itself.

The Chinese military strategist and philosopher, Sun Tzu (pronounced "swin zuh"), writing in the third century B.C.E., described the inexhaustibility of indirect tactics as being as unending as the rivers and as recurring as the seasons.[18]

Potential conflicts can be diffused by indirectness. In more modern times, indirect "many-layered" negotiation with the Chinese has been compared to

> courtyards in the Forbidden City, each leading to a deeper recess distinguished from the others only by slight changes in proportion, with ultimate meaning residing in a totality that only long reflection can grasp.[19]

The metaphor of many-layered courtyards is an apt one to describe the way the negotiations proceed.

The approach that focuses on particulars, especially unresolved ones, is typically Western. Negotiators look at the unsettled issues and one by one address them. That approach is logical for the Western problem-solving mind. But it isn't shared by all cultures. In Asia, unresolved issues are part of the whole web of the relationship being woven by the negotiation process. A simultaneous, not sequential, approach means the negotiators look at unresolved issues as potentially resolved because of the developing relationship between the two sides.

Businesspeople from Western cultures need to remember that Japanese, Chinese, and most other Asians dislike confrontation and will not argue when they feel they are right. Attacks on statements are the same as attacks on the people making the statements. Japanese and Chinese and other Asians need to remember that businesspeople in Western cultures prefer directness and the airing of different opinions, and to a large degree consider words apart from the people who produce them. When words are attacked, persons are not necessarily attacked also.

Honor

Group membership, when it is highly valued, can affect negotiations in a number of ways. Negotiators whose allegiance is to a family group, such as the ruling household of some Arab countries, or to a nation, such as Korea, may be motivated to gain the best advantage for the honor of their group. The fact that something bigger than the individual seems to be at stake can make a negotiating team less flexible.

On the other hand, negotiators who are motivated by a desire to uphold their individual reputations and records can also be inflexible about backing down. The key is to understand what motivates your counterparts. Then you can accommodate the needs of the other side. If your counterparts are motivated to succeed for the honor of the group, then you need to send messages that show you understand. Your own group membership will be important to emphasize. In either case, words that provoke a defense of honor can be the wrong words to use.

Not backing down is related to a team's decision-making process. If it is a consensus-based process, then the team's position will have been determined by lengthy discussions in the group before the negotiations take place. This makes the team less able to change its position spontaneously. The team members have to go back and consult the others in the group before they can agree to changes in their initial position. If individuals have authority to make decisions, the team's position may be flexible and open to change.

Verbal Communication Style

Verbal (worded) communication styles vary across cultures, as discussed in Chapters 5 and 8. Some negotiating teams prefer directness and use explicit words, while other teams prefer indirectness and use circumlocutions. For example, one side may say, "Our objective in this investment phase of our agreement is to achieve cost neutrality." The other side may word the same idea this way: "Our consulting services to help you set up the new operation will be free of charge, but you will pay our expenses." The terms "investment phase" and "cost neutrality" may not have meaning for the team that is listening for explicit wording, and an agreement may not be reached because the team didn't hear those explicit words. Misunderstandings can result from different preferences for wording, compounding difficulties already present when one side or both are speaking a language in which they are not fluent.

Form

Form is very important in high-context cultures, as we have seen in Chapter 4, and nowhere more so than in negotiation sessions. In Arab cultures, for example, sessions begin with small talk, and communication is indirect. In some situations, negotiators may sit on cushions on carpets, not on furniture. In other situations, the negotiations may take place in a restaurant or club owned by someone other than the negotiators. Visitors will be offered hospitality, such as a small cup of strong coffee, and the offer should not be refused. Proper respect is due older members of the Arab team, and that means not using too much familiarity. Visitors should use titles to address people and should not ask about female family members. (If you ask how many children a businessman has, he may give you the number of his male children.)

In Russia, negotiators must follow the protocol of correctly using Russians' names. This means using the full name: the given name, the patronymic or father's name, and the family name. Proper respect is shown when all three names are used to refer to someone. This may require a bit of effort on the part of a foreigner who is unfamiliar with the name system. The names change, depending upon whether the person is male or female: Alexei Fyodorovitch Melnikov is the son of Fyodor; his married sister is Irina Fyodorovna Dunayeva. A naming system that incorporates one's mother's family name is used by Mexicans and other Latin Americans to varying degrees (see Chapter 4).

Danes, by comparison, use informal address, speaking to each other with the familiar pronoun *du*. They follow the *Jantelov*, the "Law of Jante," in social interactions. This egalitarian principle says one shouldn't try to be "above" someone else. Modest about putting themselves forward, Danes are not hierarchical, and they observe little protocol in negotiation situations. However, they are monochronic and expect punctuality. Negotiations with Danes proceed without interruption.[20] Denmark provides a contrast with Arab, Asian, and Latin cultures, and points out how important it is to know the culture on the other side of the negotiating table.

New Zealanders of British descent are keen to avoid being "tall poppies." They learn from an early age that someone who stands above the others because of self-promotion will be ostracized. The "tall poppy syndrome" comes from the saying that in the field, the tall poppies are mowed down by the farmer's equipment; their bright heads are cut off if they have grown too high. Lower-growing poppies retain their blooms.

Emotion

In some high-context cultures, public display of emotion is a sign of immaturity and a potential cause of shame to the group. Japanese negotiators will close their eyes, or look down, or rest their heads against their hands and shade their eyes in order to conceal an emotion such as anger. Similarly, Thais have learned to keep potentially disruptive emotions from showing on their faces. Koreans, Taiwanese, and other Asians along with Japanese and Thais have earned the descriptor *inscrutable* from Westerners because of their learned cultural practice of avoiding a facial display of strong and disruptive emotion. High-context cultures value harmony in human encounters, and their members avoid sending any nonverbal messages that could destroy harmony. Other high-context cultures, for example in the Middle East, put a high priority on displays of emotion (although not anger) to emphasize the sincerity of the position being put forward.

In low-context cultures, the deliberate concealment of emotion is considered to be insincere. Members of low-context cultures have learned a large vocabulary of facial expressions that signal the emotions a speaker feels. When they see none of the expected indicators of emotion on the faces of negotiators on the opposite side of the table, they assume that an emotion is not present. If this assumption is discovered to be wrong and the speaker is indeed feeling an emotion such as anger, the members of the low-context culture feel deceived.

Silence

Similarly, silence as a nonverbal communication tool can be very effective in negotiations. As was discussed in Chapter 6, in low-context cultures where ideas are explicitly encoded into words and unspoken ideas are more difficult to respond to, silence makes negotiators uneasy. Silence often means unhappiness in low-context cultures. Even when no message about unhappiness is intended, silence in low-context cultures indicates a rupture has occurred, a break in the process of communicating. For these reasons, negotiators from low-context cultures generally are uncomfortable with silence. They often feel responsible for starting a conversation or keeping it going.

Japanese speakers are comfortable with silence in negotiations and do not hurry to fill it up with speech. After a speaker from one side speaks, Japanese listeners pause in silence to reflect on what has been said and consider the speaker's feelings and point of view. This is how Japanese show consideration for others in oral interpersonal communication, as we have seen in Chapter 6. Similarly, to interrupt a negotiator who is speaking is to show disrespect. Because of this protocol—and the Japanese value of silence—negotiators with Japanese counterparts must be careful not to speak too hastily or too much.

The Phases of Negotiation

The foregoing aspects of communication style are employed in specific phases of negotiation. Exchanges proceed according to four phases of negotiation in all cultures;[21] the emphasis and the time spent on any one phase are what differ:

1. **Development of a relationship** with the other side
2. **Information exchange** about the topic under negotiation
3. **Persuasion**
4. **Concessions and agreement**

Some see the process as involving as many as seven steps.

1. *Preparation.* This precedes the first step just listed. As we will see, preparation is an important key for successful negotiation.
2. *Building the relationship.* This corresponds to the first step.
3. *Exchanging information/first offer.* This corresponds to the second step.
4. *Persuasion.* This corresponds to Step 3.
5. *Concessions.* Step 4.
6. *Agreement.* Step 4.
7. *Implementation.* This follows the agreement, and points to the fact that many cultures, such as Japanese and Chinese, use a *holistic* approach to negotiation. Nothing is ever closed until the agreement is signed, and even then some issues may be reopened.

In a holistic negotiation, managers from the United States negotiating with the Japanese, for instance, may think they have decided a key point, only to find the Japanese bring that point up again when they are addressing something else in the negotiations. Westerners approach matters to be negotiated in a more linear way, going through the points sequentially and checking them off as they are settled. Easterners approach the items as discussion points within the context of the relationship they have formed with the other side. The relationship is what makes agreement possible. If a better solution arises for both sides following the negotiation of a point, they do not hesitate to revisit the item and offer a different solution.

The Development of a Relationship

Cultural priorities differ about how much time is spent on each phase; for example, Chinese spend much longer on phases 1 and 2, while Canadians want to get to phase 3 more quickly.

In the first phase, where the relationship between negotiating teams is being established, trust is the critical factor. In cultures where relationships have high priority, time may be spent in nonbusiness activities so the negotiators can get to know each other. Sight-seeing and a welcome banquet are two typical activities in Chinese business interactions with foreigners. In Argentina, the visiting team may be treated to an elaborate cocktail party in someone's home or to a barbecue, called a *parrilla,* in a home or restaurant; at the successful conclusion of negotiations, the teams may enjoy a celebratory meal, usually less formal in dress.

One way to establish a relationship is to identify the common goal both sides have in reaching an agreement. Once the desire or need for the other side to come to an agreement is on the table—in words—along with your desire, you can both refer openly to the common goal.

In order to develop trust, you need to have openness in your communication and to experience openness from the other side. This usually involves some gentle questioning by each side to see how willing the others are to reveal themselves. Often, the answers are already known to the questioners, and the probes are not so much for gathering information as for testing the openness of the other side. Usually each side displays apparent candor in these exchanges; whether it can be trusted or not is what each side has to determine.

Face is an important consideration in developing a relationship with someone from a high-context culture, especially someone from Asia.

Face may be lost as a result of many developments: a premature or overeager overture that is rebuffed by one's opponent; exposure to personal insult, in the form of either a hurtful remark or disregard for one's status; being forced to give up a cherished value or to make a concession that will be viewed by the domestic audience as unnecessary; a snub; failure to achieve predetermined goals; the revelation of personal inadequacy; damage to a valued relationship. The list is endless, for in the give-and-take of a complicated negotiation on a loaded subject, anything can happen.

Since face can be lost even without the awareness of the other party, negotiators need to take care. Asking questions that seem designed to expose weakness, or making comments that assume familiarity, or giving responses with the wrong degree of coolness can all lead to loss of face for the other party and, with it, loss of trust.

Information Exchange about the Topic under Negotiation

Frank disclosure often can work in your favor and generate trust. For example, if the negotiators from the Canwall company had said, "We're very glad to be talking with you about a sale of our product because we have a long-term interest in business with China," their Chinese counterparts would likely have considered this a frank admission of Canwall's aims. You need to disclose at least some of your positions. You also need to be able to believe what the other side is telling you.

One way to obtain information is to ask questions rather than wait for disclosure. According to Richard Mead,[22] you can ask questions:

1. To determine common ground
2. To clarify information

3. To call bluffs

4. To show you are listening

5. To show your interest

6. To control the direction of the discussion

7. To broach potentially controversial issues (rather than by statement)

Items 1, 4, and 5 particularly have to do with developing relationships; item 2 has to do with understanding facts; items 3, 6, and 7 have to do with managing the negotiation process.

Asking questions can be problematic, however. In order not to seem overly aggressive, you may need to "frame" your questions. Framing is discussed in Chapter 5. It means putting a frame of explanatory language around a request that does not change the meaning but makes it less aggressive: "I hope you don't mind my asking for your unit price, but our estimates were much higher and our head office will ask why we were so far off." The frame softens what could be a very hardnosed question: "Where did you get that unit price?"

Another problem with asking *why* questions if you expect a *cause* answer is that in some cultures the typical response is not a cause but an explanation of a pattern—an organizational structure, or market consumption, or an economic policy, for instance (see also Chapter 1).

Let's assume you want to negotiate a purchase from a supplier from another culture. You'll need to ask about technical information, price, discounts, quantity, shipping dates, insurance, payment method, shipping method, repeat orders, and quality control. You'll ask questions about all those items, and each is potentially an issue to be negotiated. As you ask questions, you are refining your idea about the importance to the other side of reaching an agreement and what the other side's *best alternative to a negotiated agreement* (BATNA) is. You are discovering what items the other team is willing to yield on and what items the other team is inflexible about.

Persuasion

This brings us to the third communication phase: persuasion. By this point, you have established what you need to focus on in order to reach an agreement. In other words, you have a clear idea where the conflicts lie, as well as the concord. Now you will attempt to persuade your counterparts to accept a settlement that ensures you what you need and perhaps more. They will do the same.

The language of persuasion varies among cultures, as was discussed in Chapter 5. You can employ the language strategy of inclusiveness for persuasion. For example, if the individual needs of your counterparts are to appear tough and persistent because those are cultural values that drive individual behavior, you can avoid using language that forces them to back down. Use inclusive language such as *together we can* . . . rather than exclusive language such as *you'll have to accept* . . . and *we absolutely require* . . . Avoid *I*-centered messages and *must, should,* and *ought* messages. In other words, use *you-viewpoint* messages and indicate you understand the others' point of view. Encourage your counterparts to focus on what they can gain, not what they may have to give up.

EXHIBIT 9.1   **Low-Context and High-Context Negotiation Tactics**

Low-Context Negotiation Tactics	High-Context Negotiation Tactics
• Supporting argument with factual data	• Supporting argument with personal connections
• Offering counterproposals	• Offering counterproposals
• Silence	• Silence
• Disagreeing	• Suggesting additional items
• Threatening the opposing side	• Referring to precedent
• Attacking opponents' characters	• Deferring to superiors
• Avoiding certain issues	• Avoiding certain issues
• Expressing emotion	• Avoiding conflict
• Insisting on a final position	• Remaining open and flexible
• Making a final offer	• Revisiting and reopening items previously negotiated

Differences in negotiation tactics between low-context cultures and high-context cultures are shown in Exhibit 9.1.

Obviously, the tactics used by low-context cultures will not work in high-context cultures. For example, as Chapter 5 discusses, many cultures are not persuaded by objective facts. Silence may signal unhappiness to the other side or may be understood as a comfortable pause during which you ponder and meditate. Some disagreement is inevitable, since that is why you are at a negotiating table, but how it is communicated varies culturally. Threats, personal attacks, insistence, and being emotional are all subject to cultural priorities.

When members of low-context cultures communicate with members of high-context cultures, they need to be especially aware of the cultural context of communication: concerns for harmony, for status, and for showing respect. When members of high-context cultures communicate with members of low-context cultures, they need to pay special attention to the words and what the words actually say, not to what can be implied or inferred in the words.

Arab businesspeople need to remember that low-context cultures attach face-value meanings to words, analyze the meanings, and don't usually discount any words as mere rhetoric. Businesspeople from low-context cultures need to remember that members of Arab cultures enjoy the way words can affect people and that literal, face-value meanings may not be intended.

People from cultures that prefer explicit communication that is direct and to the point tend to persuade with facts (see Chapter 5). This is true of businesses in the United States, for example, where arguments that are based on fact have greater credibility than arguments that are based on opinion or inference. Facts just *are;* they do not need to be proven.

Some prefer arguments based on inference, which is a conclusion based on fact but not proven. Inferences are assumptions. Some believe inferences generated from facts are more powerful than the facts themselves. When a negotiator suggests that the plan her opposite party has to create new jobs will actually threaten the environment, the negotiator is inferring consequences.

Asian negotiators often use inference when they refer to history. Asians along with Europeans, Latin Americans, Middle Easterners, and Africans tend to take a long view, placing the negotiation in the context of a history reaching back far, but still having a very real meaning for the present. This enables them to take a long view of the future as well. Americans, Canadians, New Zealanders, Australians, most Argentines, and others have a short history, and even that seems remote and unconnected to the present. They often could use their historical contacts as a persuasive tool, but instead overlook them.

Others prefer arguments based on opinion. Opinions cannot be proven to be true or false. They are usually also emotional. For some, emotion means genuine involvement on the part of the persuader. Without emotion, an argument lacks heart and conviction and is simply cold and impersonal. Obviously, when someone who shuns emotion in favor of facts encounters another person who prefers emotion and finds facts alone unconvincing, the result can be miscommunication that results in a failure to reach an agreement.

The sequence in which items are discussed is often a critical communication factor in negotiations. Research has shown that skilled Western negotiators are more flexible in the sequence in which they communicate about factors than average Western negotiators who stick to a planned sequence.[23] The average negotiator treats items independently, while the skilled negotiator is able to link items. This is called "enlarging the pie"; the negotiator adds issues so the pie is larger, allowing everyone to have a larger piece.

Also, skilled negotiators make more frequent reference to long-term concerns than average negotiators. The negotiator who appears to be after a short-term, in-and-out business deal is less likely to succeed than the negotiator who makes reference to long-term goals.

In Focus

Even with the best motives and the most careful preparation, negotiators who ignore the other culture's priorities can put a foot wrong. In 1983, an article in the *Harvard Business Review* outlined what the authors called the "American John Wayne" style of negotiating, which still has relevance today.[24] Here is a summary.

1. **I Can Go It Alone.** Many U.S. executives seem to believe they can handle any negotiation situation by themselves, even when they are outnumbered in negotiation situations.

2. **Just call me John.** Americans value informality and equality in human relationships. They try to make people feel comfortable by playing down class distinctions.

3. **Pardon my French.** Americans aren't very talented at speaking foreign languages.

4. **Check with the Home Office?** American negotiators get upset when halfway through a negotiation the other side says, "I'll have to check with the home office." The implication is that the decision-makers are not present.

5. **Get to the Point.** Americans don't like to beat around the bush and want to get to the heart of the matter quickly.

6. **Lay Your Cards on the Table.** Americans expect honest information at the bargaining table.
7. **Don't Just Sit There; Speak Up.** Americans don't deal well with silence during negotiations.
8. **Don't Take No for an Answer.** Persistence is highly valued by Americans and is part of the deeply ingrained competitive spirit that manifests itself in every aspect of American life.
9. **One Thing at a Time.** Americans usually attack a complex negotiation task sequentially—that is, they separate the issues and settle them one at a time.
10. **A Deal Is a Deal.** When Americans make an agreement and give their word, they expect to honor the agreement no matter what the circumstances.
11. **I Am What I Am.** Few Americans take pride in changing their minds, even in difficult circumstances. Americans also think it is "phony" to act differently in a negotiation with foreigners than they would act at home.

You can venture a guess about how successful these strategies would be in a high-context culture—or in a low-context culture. Cultural values of the United States that are evident are individual performance, desire to achieve an agreement, preference for informality and for communication in English, emphasis on direct and explicit communication, and unease with silence.

Concession and Agreement

Finally, the negotiators' communication task turns to concession and agreement. When making a concession, skilled negotiators link that to a counter-concession, using "if" language: "We'll accept your shipment dates if you'll agree to a discount on future orders." Many experienced negotiators warn that you can't come back and ask for a counter-concession after a concession has been granted to the other side and the discussion has moved on to another issue. Once you agree without conditions or "ifs," the issue is settled. You attempt to reopen it at the risk of losing what agreements—and trust—you have already gained.

Sometimes the final agreement arrives more quickly than you expect. Many Chinese negotiations, for example, consist of probing the other side's position, testing for firmness and the other side's final position. Then, suddenly, you may find the Chinese side offers a final agreement that solves many of the issues raised without the need to haggle and bargain or persuade. When this is the case, it probably isn't a good idea to offer too many counterproposals or alternatives, because that weakens your position. However, advice to Chinese negotiators is to hold back from commitment to unattractive points to see if the other side will offer counterproposals or if it is really firm. Western negotiators are known to be under pressure from their own cultural priorities. They want to achieve an agreement; in some cases, they seem to feel *any* agreement is better than no agreement. They can be impatient, but they also can be imaginative about solutions.

Some negotiating teams can live with an agreement that at least gives them the *appearance* of having done well. Cohen quotes an Egyptian proverb:

Make your harvest look big lest your enemies rejoice.[25]

The agreement has to *look* good as well as be good.

Some cultures are not interested in settling the negotiations in a way that terminates them. To these context-oriented cultures, the relationship between organizations is what makes negotiations and agreements possible. Each side has an obligation to nurture the relationship and keep it going. Signed agreements don't do that. Japanese negotiators, for example, prefer escape clauses in contracts—when contracts are necessary at all. Western negotiators are dismayed when their Japanese or Chinese counterparts begin making changes immediately after contracts are signed. But in Asian cultures the documents are far less important than is keeping the interdependent, interwoven organizations in a good relationship.

Negotiators from the United States are keen to sign agreements. Contracts are firm and go a long way toward eliminating ambiguities and misunderstandings. They and other low-context negotiators see unwritten and informal agreements as unenforceable. They may allow the other side to conceal something; low-context cultures give openness high priority.

It is important for negotiators to understand their counterparts and balance the need for enforceable agreements on the one hand with the need for nurturing trusting relationships on the other. Agreements do not all look alike. *Time* magazine, over two decades ago, ran this statement:

> The successful negotiation between Japanese and Western businessmen usually ends up looking very much like one between two Japanese.[26]

That is still true today. Sensitivity to the other culture, and satisfying the needs of your own are both needed in the 21st century.

Summary

This chapter has shown how cultural priorities affect specific communication tasks, in this case the task of business negotiations.

- The experience of Canwall in China illustrates cultural priorities and shows an outcome that was not what the Canadians had expected.
- What really happened involved the way culture affects communication. Chinese cultural dimensions (see Chapters 3 and 4) include the following: *relationships;* expectations about *time* and efficiency; the way *obligation* is perceived; the value of *harmony;* the method of *learning;* the performance of tasks *simultaneously;* a preference for protocol and *form, seniority,* and *hierarchy; mediated access* to authority; *interdependence;* and *tolerance of uncertainty.*
- Negotiation teams are one kind of team in the workplace; team members have roles that are the result of culture, and teams communicate according to cultural values.
- Factors in intercultural negotiation include different *expectations for outcomes* and a preference for one of the outcomes of negotiation: win–lose, win–win, or stalemate.
- *The orientation of the negotiating teams is strategic or synergistic,* and they might include:
  - Members with high status
  - Members with special expertise
  - A translator

- *Physical aspects of the negotiations* also can affect the outcomes. Such aspects include:
  - Site and space
  - Schedule and agenda
  - Use of time
  - Host hospitality
- *By far the most important differences are in communication styles:*
  - Verbal communication style may be more explicit and direct or more round-about and indirect. Some circumlocutions (such as "cost-neutral" in English) may not be understood by a team with limited English language.
  - The focus may be on what has already been agreed or on what remains in dispute. Some teams negotiate for the honor of their country or firm.
  - Some teams prefer the observance of more form and specific protocol than others. Some show emotion and even make a deliberate display of emotion, while others show little.
  - Some teams use silence, while others are uncomfortable with silence.
- *Negotiation has four phases:*
  - Development of a relationship with the other side
  - Exchange of information and positions
  - Persuasion and argumentation
  - Concessions and agreement

Notes

1. William Zartman and Maureen Berman, quoted in Raymond Cohen, *Negotiating Across Cultures* (Washington, DC: United States Institute of Peace, 1991), pp. 16–17.
2. Geert Hofstede, *Cultures and Organizations* (New York: McGraw-Hill, 1991), p. 225.
3. Cohen, pp. 31–32.
4. Richard L. Daft and Patricia Lane, *The Leadership Experience*, 3rd ed. (Mason, Ohio: Thomson/South-Western, 2005).
5. John G. Oetzel, "Effective Intercultural Workgroup Communication Theory," in William B. Gudykunst, ed., *Theorizing about Intercultural Communication* (Thousand Oaks, CA: Sage, 2005), pp. 351–371.
6. Robert T. Moran and William G. Stripp, *Dynamics of Successful International Business Negotiations* (Houston: Gulf, 1991), p. 84.
7. Richard Mead, *Cross-Cultural Management Communication* (New York: John Wiley and Sons, 1990), p. 203.
8. Yale Richmond, *From Nyet to Da: Understanding the Russians* (Yarmouth, ME: Intercultural Press, 1992), p. 141.

9. Moran and Stripp, p. 77.

10. Ibid.

11. Tom Getman, "World Vision," *The MacNeil/Lehrer NewsHour,* broadcast June 7, 1993, about Somalia.

12. John Mattock, ed., *Cross-Cultural Communication* (London: Kogan Page, 2003), p. 120.

13. Moran and Stripp, p. 168.

14. Cohen, p. 89.

15. Diane Zior Wilhelm, "A Cross-Cultural Analysis of Drinking Behavior Within the Context of International Business." In *Anthropology in International Business,* Studies in Third World Societies, no. 28, Hendrick Serrie, guest ed. (Williamsburg, VA: Department of Anthropology, College of William and Mary, 1986), pp. 73–88.

16. Linda Beamer, "Toasts: Rhetoric and Ritual in Business Negotiation in Confucian Cultures," *Business Forum* (1994), pp. 22–25.

17. Richard Buchanan, Ron Garland, and Mark Armstrong, "Mañana and Manners May Not Be Enough! The Cultural Interface of New Zealand and Argentinean Negotiating Preferences," *Marketing* bulletin 13, no. 1, http://marketing-bulletin.massey.ac.nz/article13/Manana.asp (retrieved March 17, 2003).

18. Sun Tzu, *Art of War* (S. B. Griffith, Trans.) (New York: Oxford University Press, 1984), (original work published 256 B.C.E.).

19. February 21, 1972, *The White House Years,* pp. 1061–1062; quoted in Cohen, p. 123.

20. Richard R. Gesteland, *Cross-Cultural Business Behavior* (Copenhagen: Copenhagen School of Business Press, 2002), pp. 289–290.

21. Graham and Herberger, quoted by Mead, p. 189.

22. Mead, pp. 196–197.

23. N. Rackham, "The Behavior of Successful Negotiators (Huthwaite Research Group Reports)." In *International Negotiations: A Training Program for Corporate Executives and Diplomats,* E. Raider, ed. (Brooklyn, NY: Ellen Raider International, 1976), pp. 196–197.

24. Philip R. Harris and Robert T. Moran, *Managing Cultural Differences,* 2nd ed. (Houston: Gulf, 1987), p. 59, boldface added.

25. Cohen, p. 131.

26. Robert T. Moran, *Getting Your Yen's Worth: Negotiating with the Japanese* (Houston: Gulf, 1985), p. 67.

CHAPTER TEN

Legal and Governmental Considerations in Intercultural Business Communication

Joe Van West, the president of Appliances Unlimited in Mexico, was sitting in his office in Mexico City, thinking about what he should do. The plant in Mexico manufactured small household appliances such as toasters, electric irons, and coffee machines. In addition, the factory produced parts for washing machines to be assembled by the subsidiary of another American multinational company. The small appliances were mostly for the domestic market; the washing machines were both for the domestic market and for export, mainly to the other North American Free Trade Agreement (NAFTA) countries. Over the last two years, the production lines had been upgraded to make use of the latest manufacturing technology.

For several years, Appliances Unlimited, a company headquartered in Chicago, had had plans to expand the Mexican factory to increase production. This became more urgent after exports to Canada, the United States, and Europe picked up during the two years before. The previous managers had looked for a site for expansion, but nothing had been available. A building site was located next to the factory, but a Japanese firm was going to build there. Recently, however, the Japanese had run into financial problems and were pulling out. The inspector in charge of building permits knew that Appliances Unlimited was looking for a site, but when Van West approached the office, the assistant told him that the site did not meet the new regulations for industrial buildings. Thus, the site would not be available. Van West made some additional inquiries but did not get anywhere.

The site was perfect for the expansion. It would be easy to tie the new building into the existing facility. All other possible locations were several miles away from the existing plant; transportation between the sites would be a problem.

Van West decided to meet with the inspector personally. He tried to set up a meeting in his office, but the inspector was always busy. Finally, he agreed to meet for lunch. The inspector was very pleasant and apologetic that the regulations had changed, but unfortunately there was nothing he could do. He indicated that he also had been approached by a Swiss firm and a Canadian firm about the site. They were very interested and willing to pay top dollar. He would have to tell them *no,* too.

They talked about life in Mexico and the United States. The inspector had traveled to New York and Los Angeles several times. He told Van West that his oldest son was set on studying for an MBA in the United States, but the tuition was very high. He just did not see how he could possibly afford $30,000 for each of the two years plus all the additional expenses. As the lunch went on, Van West got the distinct feeling that the building site would be available "at a price." The inspector made it quite clear that in return for a favor he would see to it that the classification of the site would be altered.

After the lunch, Van West was replaying the conversation. Paying money in return for the site went against everything he believed in. He had always tried to be up front and ethical. How could he justify paying a bribe now? And then there were the legal issues; paying bribes was not an option under the Foreign Corrupt Practices Act of the United States. Yet the site was very important, and a decision had to be made fast. He knew that headquarters was pushing hard for the expansion. If he could get the site, the profits from the Mexican operations could go up considerably. His star at headquarters certainly would go up as well. Considering everything, an additional $60,000 for the site did not seem to be such a big sum.

The next day, the inspector called again and inquired whether Van West was still interested. He needed an answer by the beginning of next week since the other companies were willing to pay the top price. Van West contacted Sr. Sanchez, the Mexican lawyer who represented the firm in Mexico, for advice. However, Sanchez was not very helpful. He conceded that such payments were common practices but made it clear that he preferred not to be involved in this matter.

In this case, Mr. Van West faces both a legal and an ethical dilemma (also see Chapter 8). The Foreign Corrupt Practices Act in the United States was passed in an attempt to stop bribery and make the cost of doing business abroad more transparent.[1] The act is an example of how a low-context culture tries to legislate behavior. The Europeans scoffed at the Foreign Corrupt Practices Act. In most European countries, not only was it legal to bribe foreign officials, the bribes could be deducted as a legitimate expense of doing business. During the last few years, however, the European Union has decided that bribes have been getting out of hand and that in the long run it would be cheaper to do international business if European companies also had to follow a similar law. Therefore, the EU has passed antibribery legislation.

In this chapter, we will examine the legal implications of intercultural business communication. In the course of doing business, managers must communicate with governmental offices, other businesses, employees, and the public. In an international environment, those managers must understand not only the culture of the people they are doing business with, but also the laws that regulate business in a culture. Laws are based on cultural priorities, and cultural priorities influence which laws are developed. It is tempting to argue that lawyers can take care of legal issues, and that managers do not need to know much about the legal situation. However, as we will see in this chapter, the legal framework directly affects intercultural business communication practices. Managers need to understand the legal context of intercultural business communication.

Communication and Legal Messages

What makes sense and is legal in one country may be illegal in another. In the United States, it is illegal to discriminate on the basis of race, sex, national origin, and age. East Asian, Latin American, and many European job advertisements, in contrast, may specify the preferred age and sex of a potential employee. For example, job ads for office staff in Mexico frequently mention that the applicants must be *attractive* young females. Japanese companies may say they are looking for a female employee between the ages of 20 and 24. When establishing corporate policies relating to employment, managers must have an understanding of how the laws of the countries they are working in will influence those policies.

Legal systems come out of cultural values. Laws do not develop in isolation; they are culture-bound. As a result, laws relating to the hiring and firing of employees, property, contracts, dispute settlement, and ownership have cultural roots. The way these laws are formulated, communicated, and enforced is influenced by the communication patterns and priorities of a culture. At the same time, the legal system also acts as a stimulus for gradually changing cultural priorities. The point is that managers working and communicating with employees from different cultures and engaging in international business should have at least some understanding of the legal systems of the countries they are dealing with. That does not mean managers must be international lawyers, but it does mean they need to be familiar with basic legal concepts and must know when to call in the legal experts.

Legal systems are territorial. Laws apply to a particular jurisdiction, and typically lawyers are educated in a particular kind of law. Australian lawyers are educated in Australian law. If they work for an international firm, they bring their background in Australian law. When a dispute with a French firm comes up, they do not automatically know what the French legal situation is. In that case, the Australian firm may hire a French law firm to interpret French law. The problem is that the French lawyers know French law but not Australian law. Thus, to the challenges of intercultural communication are added the challenges of different legal systems.

A French lawyer has no problems discussing aspects of French law with another French lawyer. They speak the same language, have the same cultural background, and have had similar legal training. This scenario changes dramatically if the French lawyer must explain a French legal concept to a business lawyer from Sydney, Australia. The two lawyers speak different languages, have different cultural backgrounds, and have been educated in two very different legal systems.

To avoid serious misinterpretation and miscommunication, the lawyers may use a type of back translation. Back translation, as was discussed in Chapter 2, frequently is used when questionnaires are translated from one language into another to ensure accuracy. Lawyers can use the same techniques. After the French lawyer has explained the French legal situation, the Australian can back translate the explanation to the French to ensure understanding. Rephrasing the same question using different formulations and seeing whether the answers are essentially the same can bring out possible difficulties and misunderstandings.

However, back translation does not guarantee effective communication. For example, the term *force majeure* is part of the legal language in both France and Australia. Both sides may use it assuming that the other side understands the phrase as intended. To minimize misunderstandings in the communication process, both sides must ask questions and probe for hidden or different meanings.

When René Chrétien from Lyon and William Brandon from Sydney discuss a business contract, they cannot just look at the literal meaning of *force majeure,* which is "superior or irresistible force." In the Anglo legal system, the term refers to forces of nature or possibly war. The implications are that the terms of a contract may be changed because risk was not allocated in either the expressed or the implied terms of the contract. In France, the term has a broader meaning. *Force majeure* does not just refer to forces of nature and war but also includes changes in economic conditions and other circumstances that could not have been anticipated reasonably when the contract was made. Therefore, when René Chrétien and William Brandon discuss their contract, they must take into consideration the:

- Literal meaning
- Legal meaning
- Implications of the legal meaning for fulfilling a contract
- Implications of the legal meaning for settling contract disputes

Probing for intended meaning and verification for clarity and accuracy are typical of low-context cultures. Greg Turner from Switzerland has no difficulty insisting on clarity; that's part of his job. His success will be measured in part by how clear the terms of a contract are. Akihito Hosokawa from Japan, in contrast, comes from a high-context culture in which an insistence on clarity and precision can be interpreted as a sign of mistrust. Traditionally, a Japanese person is not so much after precise legal meaning as he is after building trust and a long-term relationship. However, in international business dealings, Mr. Hosokawa may get used to greater precision and clarity.

In Focus

Natalie Prior, a professor at a university in the United States, had been invited to teach a course on intercultural communication in an executive MBA program at the University of Lugano, Switzerland. After her engagement there, she was to go on to a university in Tokyo, Japan, to give several seminars to faculty and graduate students. The Swiss university sent a contract for her teaching engagement. In part, the contract read as follows:

1. Responsibilities
   1.1 Teach a course on Intercultural Business Communication. Main breaks are scheduled in the morning from 9:45 to 10:15 a.m. and in the afternoon from 4:15 to 4:45 p.m.
   1.2 Prepare syllabus, course materials, and handouts.
   1.3 Prepare and grade written exams.
   1.4 Be available to students.
2. Compensation
   2.1 The faculty member will be paid $XXX.
   2.2 Money will be paid upon completion of activities.
   2.3 The following expenses will be covered . . .
3. Other
   3.1 The present contract is effective as of date of signature.
   3.2 University regulation and the provisions of Swiss contract law shall govern all aspects not herein specified.
   3.3 The administration reserves the right to communicate any possible changes in seminar dates or to cancel the program by (specified date). If the program is voided by (specified date), this contract is voided.
   3.4 In the event of controversy relating to this contract, the parties shall seek settlement by means of the Independent Appeal Commission established by Swiss Law. In the event that settlement is not reached in the preceding manner, the parties recognize the exclusive jurisdiction of the Court of the City of Lugano.

The arrangement with the Japanese university was quite different. Natalie had exchanged several e-mails with the Japanese professor who had invited her. They discussed the topic of the seminars, housing arrangements, and the amount of the stipend. To most of Natalie's questions the Japanese professor replied: "We can talk about this once you are here." Shortly before Natalie left the United States, the Japanese professor sent an e-mail in which he almost apologetically asked for some administrative details, such as date of birth and citizenship. That was the extent of the contract.

Natalie had very good experiences both in Switzerland and in Japan, but she found the different approaches to the arrangements fascinating.

International business is concerned with both international law and comparative law. There are two kinds of international law: public international law and private international law. Public international law, sometimes called the law of nations, deals with the relationships between countries. It involves treaties, wars, the sea, diplomats, and expropriations, the taking by government of land and other private assets. Since those aspects can affect businesses, public international law and the way it is communicated and interpreted are important to businesses. Cases in public international law may be taken by a country, not an individual, to the International Court of Justice in Den Haag, Holland.

A major issue in public international law is the question of enforcing judgments. The International Court of Justice can render a verdict but has no real power to enforce the verdict. The majority of the decisions rendered by the International Court of Justice are followed; however, since there is no international sheriff, the enforcement of decisions is always a question. For example, expropriation of assets by national governments was a big issue in the 1960s and 1970s, when, for example, Chile nationalized its copper mines. In the 1980s and 1990s, expropriations rarely happened. That changed when Hugo Chavez from Venezuela nationalized big parts of the oil industry in his country. Even if the International Court of Justice were willing to hear the case and render a verdict, such a decision would be almost impossible to enforce. The only recourse would be to freeze Venezuelan assets abroad. War criminals in the Balkans, like Milošević, who was accused of genocide, are tried under public international law. They are charged with crimes against humanity and war crimes. This case was particularly interesting since a number of nations agreed to the trial. That is not always the case, because a person may be considered a terrorist or criminal by one country but a freedom fighter by another. For example, the case against Osama bin Laden, accused of masterminding the bombing of two U.S. embassies in Africa and the World Trade Center in New York and the attempt to bomb the Pentagon or some other building in Washington, DC, has been brought by the United States. If he were to be captured, he most likely would be tried by the United States under United States law. Saddam Hussein's case was tried before a court in Iraq to emphasize Iraqi sovereignty. Theoretically, he could have been tried under international law, but that would have been more difficult if several countries opposed such a trial. Some countries, including the United States, are reluctant to submit to an international court, arguing that such a move would violate their national sovereignty.

Private international law deals with issues between persons and businesses. It involves the settlement of conflicts and the enforcement of contracts. One of the most important questions in private international law is which court has jurisdiction. For example, in a contract dispute between a Venezuelan firm and a Nigerian firm, the partners have to decide which court will settle the dispute and which law will apply (see the "Dispute Settlement" section later in this chapter).

Most international business is concerned more with comparative and private international law than with public international law. How are contracts handled in various jurisdictions? What are employment laws? What are import–export regulations? An international businessperson will be involved regularly in interpreting the laws and regulations of other countries in the context of doing business. Laws and regulations are specific forms of communication, and international businesspeople are interpreters. Alfredo Luzero, for example, must be able to explain the legal concerns of headquarters in Amsterdam to his managers in the subsidiary in Lima. At the same time, he must interpret employment issues and legal concerns of Peru, the host country, for upper management in Amsterdam.

Specific Legal Systems

Although every country has its own laws and legal system, four major legal systems exist:[2]

- Code law
- Anglo-American common law
- Islamic law
- Socialist law

In many parts of the world, the major legal systems are influenced by indigenous systems and tribal laws. Former colonies frequently have kept the legal system of the former colonial power. The result is a mixture of legal systems. New Zealand, for example, follows British common law but also pays special respect to Māori laws. The intercultural sensitivities arising out of the legal combinations present intercultural communication issues. Contracts may be influenced by the traditional considerations of a culture. India also has retained British common law, but local traditions play a role. Payment for goods or services does not follow the tightly regulated schedules of U.S. business firms. The law takes into account the personal relationships of the parties involved. Businesses typically do not press for payment within a specific time period. The assumption is that one does business with people one can trust, and therefore it is assumed the clients will pay when they can. When local laws are not well developed, local law may be applied in civil cases, but in international business transactions a Western legal system may be used.

Code Law

Western continental Europe follows code law. In code law, the emphasis is on the wording of the law rather than similar cases that have been tried previously. Code law comes out of the French legal tradition. French code law dates back to 1806. It was written under the direction of the Emperor Napoleon in an attempt to clarify the legal situation. Although French code law is based on Roman codes, it also incorporates some of the ideals of the French Revolution, such as the right to private property and the freedom to make contracts. French code law also is known as the *Code Napoléon,* and is written in a clear and concise style meant for the citizen.

German code law (*Bürgerliche Gesetzbuch,* or *BGB*) was enacted in 1896. It is a highly structured, precise, and detailed system. In both the French and the German systems, decisions are made by expert judges who interpret the law. Previous decisions in similar situations have only limited persuasive authority.

Code law is deductive. A student of code law learns to read the law paragraph by paragraph. He or she gets the interpretation of the law from a law professor or judge. Previous cases involving a similar legal issue are not binding and not overly important in the logical thought process.

Anglo-American Common Law

Under common law, decisions are based on precedent in similar cases. Common law grew out of common practices of the courts of the king of England. Most of England's former colonies, including the United States, have retained common law. Two notable exceptions are Louisiana in the United States and Québec in Canada. The state of Louisiana and the province of Québec have maintained their French heritage and French legal system. Both use code law.

Common law is inductive. The last relevant case becomes the source of law; therefore, it is also called case law. The terminology can be confusing. For example, the United States, a common law country, has the Uniform Commercial Code (UCC). The UCC was enacted to guarantee uniform enforcement of commercial law across the 50 states. All the states, except Louisiana, have adopted the UCC. In the first few years after the passing of the UCC, lawyers had a hard time interpreting the code because the case law in this area had not been developed yet. In case law, the meaning of the law comes out of cases rather than the wording of the law itself. The following case is an illustration of the application of common law to a business problem. This case is almost 50 years old, but its age is irrelevant. In fact, the age is an advantage because it shows that this decision has stood the test of time. Every law school teaches this case as an illustration of common law, and it is famous in international business circles. It illustrates the difficulties a company may face if the managers do not communicate clearly. If there is a universal ethical standard, a universal standard of right and wrong, it should be possible to clarify the standards through rules and laws and thus ensure that everyone understands and accepts the standards.

In Focus

Frigaliment Importing Co., Ltd.,
Plaintiff
v.
B.N.S. International Sales Corp.,
Defendant
United States District Court
S.D. New York[3]

B.N.S. International Sales Corp. from the United States and Frigaliment Importing Co. from Switzerland had signed a contract under which B.N.S. would deliver 100,000 pounds of chickens to Frigaliment. The chickens were shipped according to the agreement; however, Frigaliment argued that those were not the chickens that had been ordered and that the American company had promised. Therefore, Frigaliment did not want to pay for the shipment.

Since the two parties could not agree on a solution, Frigaliment went to court. The case was tried in a U.S. district court in New York. The judge decided that the Swiss firm could not collect damages but was bound by the contract and had to pay for the chickens. Two issues that are of interest with regard to intercultural issues in legal communication are translation and the application of common law.

LANGUAGE ISSUES

The entire preceding case hinges on the definition of the word *chicken*. Is the term used for any chicken, young and old, male and female, or does it mean a particular type of chicken? The Swiss company argued that *chicken* meant a young chicken suitable for broiling and frying. It furthermore argued that stewing chickens are referred to as *fowl*. The Swiss firm in its argument contrasted chicken (broiler) with fowl (*Suppenhuhn*).

The American company argued that *chicken* means any chicken. They said that since the Swiss company had not specified what kind of chicken it wanted, the Swiss should be made to pay for the shipment. At issue are the correct translation of terms and the accepted use of terms in the chicken trade.

As we have discussed repeatedly throughout this book, businesspeople must understand what the literal meanings of terms are and how those terms are used in relevant business situations. Clearly, the two sides in the case did not communicate clearly what they wanted. This is particularly interesting because both sides had experience with international transactions.

APPLICATION OF COMMON LAW

In deciding the case, the judge in the United States, Oliver Wendell Holmes, referred to case law, which he then applied to this particular case.

- Holmes, a famous judge in the United States, said that "*the making of a contract depends not on the agreement of two minds of one intention, but on the agreement of two sets of external signs—not on the parties' having meant the same thing but on their having said the same thing.*"[4]
- One of the cases he cites goes back to 1761, *Lord Mansfield v. East India Co.* He uses this case to comment on the credibility of witnesses. One of the witnesses testified that to him *chicken* definitely meant broiler. However, the judge argued that this testimony did not support the witness's own practice; the witness in his business always used the word *broiler* if he wanted to make sure that he would get young chickens. The precedent established that no credit should be given to a witness's testimony if the witness was not consistent in usage.[5] Based on the precedent, the judge decided that the Swiss firm had no case.

Had this case been tried under code law, the references to old legal cases and opinions of previous judges would be irrelevant. It would not matter what the judge said about the credibility of a witness in 1761 in London. What would matter would be the interpretation of current law today by a legal expert.

Islamic Law

Islamic law is known as *Sharia*. It is based on the:

- *Qur'an*, the holy book of Islam
- *Sunnah*, the deeds and sayings of Mohammed
- Interpretations of Islamic scholars
- Consensus of the legal community

In addition, Islamic law has been influenced by indigenous and tribal laws, such as Arab Bedouin law, commercial law from Mecca, agrarian law from Medina, and Jewish law.

In contrast to Western legal systems, Sharia encompasses the totality of religious, political, social, domestic, and private life. Sharia is concerned with ethics and moral issues rather than being limited to commercial law and regulations. Islamic law has been static for several centuries; no new interpretations have been allowed. As a result, Islamic law has almost no provisions to deal with modern international business practices and transactions such as credits and interest payments. Nevertheless, several Islamic countries, including Iran, Pakistan, Saudi Arabia, Sudan, and Libya, have Islamic law as the ruling law. Any international manager doing business in an Islamic country needs to be aware of some of the practices of Sharia, specifically as they relate to contracts, banking, and agency relationships. These aspects are discussed in greater detail later in this chapter. Not every country with a Muslim population follows Sharia. In Turkey, for example, 96 percent of the people are Muslims; however, Turkey does not use religious law. In the 1920s, Kemal Ataturk, the father of modern Turkey, deliberately set that nation on a course of westernization. In the process, he removed Islamic law and replaced it with a mixture of French and Swiss law. Today, this system is modified to bring it in line with the European Union.

Islamic law applies to the practices of all individual Muslims, but it also covers foreigners living in an Islamic country. For example, in Saudi Arabia, women are not allowed to drive. This rule applies to foreign as well as Saudi women. Saudi women typically are not allowed to travel on their own. Similarly, Western women cannot travel alone in Saudi Arabia. The ban on the consumption of alcohol includes everyone, Saudis and expatriates. When Muslims travel abroad, they are not totally bound by Sharia, since Muslims recognize the practical difficulties of living by Sharia in other cultures.

The enforcement of Sharia varies from country to country, and businesspeople need to familiarize themselves with the specific rules for each country. Even in the strict countries, however, the enforcement of traditional Islamic law, such as the cutting off of the right hand for theft, is rare. Yet violating religious law can have severe and unexpected consequences.

Socialist Law

With the political and economic changes in Eastern Europe and Russia, the fourth system, socialist law, is losing importance. However, several of those countries are still struggling to put new legal systems in place. As long as remnants of socialist law remain, it is advantageous to have some understanding of socialist law. In Russia, for example, the legal system is still in flux. Many of the old laws regulating property ownership have been discarded, but new laws, even if they are on the books, are not enforced consistently. The emergence of the Russian Mafia, an illegal network operating outside the law, has made the enforcement of laws even more complicated. The uncertain legal situation and constantly changing government regulations create an uncertain and insecure environment for both domestic and international business.

Similarly, China's legal system is still developing to deal with modern business practices. Foreign firms work in China under a high level of uncertainty. Rules regarding what percentage of a company or joint venture a foreign company may own or what amount of profit a subsidiary may take out of China back to the home country seem to change fairly often. Civil law is changing as more and more Chinese are working for foreign companies or starting their own businesses. Formerly, laws relating to corporate liability insurance and health insurance were not considered necessary. A person's needs were covered through the work unit. The organization took care of expenses. Employees did not have to worry, but they also made very little money.

In the past, Chinese citizens did not need to know anything about insurance; they did not need to know about health care options. This has changed drastically. Today, employees earn more, particularly if they work for private or foreign firms; however, they need to pay much more for health care, insurance, transportation, and housing. Even for employees who work for state-owned companies, the cost for health care has gone up dramatically, and the government no longer covers all the costs. At the same time, the demand for modern and up-to-date care has been growing. To meet this need, private insurance companies, both foreign and domestic, have moved in. The government, private corporations, and insurance companies have been educating the public about the underlying principles of insurance, and they communicate the advantages and disadvantages of various plans.

Dispute Settlement

Direct Confrontation and Arbitration

When disputes arise over a contract (also see Chapter 9), the question is whose courts will decide the outcome and which law will be applied. A manager needs to consider the area of dispute settlement from the very beginning of the negotiations and make it part of the negotiation. Each party probably will want the courts of its own country to settle any disputes in the hope that this will be an advantage. In a dispute between a Japanese business and a U.S. business, the Americans will want a court in the United States—for example, a court in Texas—to hear the case. The Japanese, in contrast, will want Japanese courts—for example, in Tokyo—to hear the case. However, because of the tendency of U.S. courts to award huge settlements (up to millions of dollars), it may be advantageous for the American firm to have the case decided in a foreign court. It is helpful if the parties are aware of past decisions in cases of conflicts. If opposing parties conclude that the courts in the other country have been fair in the past, the nationality of the court may not be crucial.

The two parties also may take into account the nature of the business. If the joint business dealings involve shipping and the law of the sea, it may be advantageous if a British court hears the case. The British have a very well developed law of admiralty and therefore may render the fairest and most objective judgment. As a result, a Portuguese firm and a Thai firm, may agree to use British admiralty law in disagreements over shipping issues, even though both firms are in countries that have their own established legal systems.

Traditionally, high-context cultures place less emphasis on detailing the rules and legal provisions in case of disagreement. They prefer a style that avoids finding out who is to blame and who should be punished (also see Chapter 3 on the cultural dimension of rules-observing versus rule-bending).

In Focus

René Lafontaine, a businessman from Lyon, France, had been appointed as the manager of a department in a French subsidiary in Riyadh, Saudi Arabia. He supervised several French men and women and about a dozen Saudi men. He had never been to Saudi Arabia before, and after a month in the new job he decided to host a party after work on company premises. He arranged for food, soft drinks, and wine. Things went very well, and everyone had a good time, when all of a sudden the religious police entered the premises and arrested everyone in attendance. The entire group was taken to jail, where René learned that the group was accused of illegal consumption of alcohol and prostitution. He could understand the first part but not the second until he was told that the attendance at the party by unmarried French women was considered a form of prostitution. He managed to call the French embassy in desperation. Surely, the French ambassador could clear up the whole mess and get them out within an hour. He was wrong; it took the ambassador 24 hours to resolve the situation.

Two Japanese firms doing business together hardly ever resort to the courts to settle disputes; in fact, a firm that goes to court, even if the law is on its side, may lose face. As we discussed earlier in this book, the emphasis in communicating in Japan is on creating an atmosphere of harmony. A lawsuit would disrupt harmony severely. The firm that brings the suit may lose as much or even more face than will the firm that is being sued.

However, a non-Japanese businessperson also should know that in international contracts the Japanese may insist on as much clarity as do Australians, who come from a low-context culture. Firms around the world may practice one style within their cultural boundaries and another one outside their national boundaries.

In countries where suing is not a culturally acceptable means for settling disputes, mediation and arbitration play important roles. Even firms in low-context cultures are beginning to turn to mediation and arbitration in an attempt to cut legal costs and avoid disrupting business transactions.

Arbitration is generally quicker and more neutral than a lawsuit. In arbitration, both sides agree on certain rules before a dispute occurs. They also agree to abide by the decision of the arbitrator. The win–lose approach of lawsuits is replaced with a communication style that seeks to overcome disagreements and reestablish common goals.

When negotiating contracts and trying to set up new business ventures in a country, a manager must examine the overall business climate and government regulation of business. For example, does the government create a positive atmosphere for doing business? Is the government fair, and does it treat locals and foreigners the same way? Or does the government protect local interests each time a dispute arises?

If a company from Venezuela and one from Thailand have a dispute, they have the following options concerning which courts have jurisdiction (in which country the case will be brought) and which law will be applied.

Which Courts Will Have Jurisdiction?

- If the contract does not specify jurisdiction, the courts in the defendant's country will hear the case. If the firm from Venezuela sues the Thai firm, Thai courts will hear the case.
- The two parties may agree that the courts of the country where the contract is to be performed will hear the case. If, for example, the Venezuelan company is to send component parts for assembly to a Thai subsidiary in Tanzania, the Venezuelan firm and the Thai firm may agree that the courts in Tanzania will have jurisdiction.
- The two sides may agree in the contract that the home of the "stronger" party will have jurisdiction.

Which Law Will Apply?

- The two parties can specify which law they want to apply. As was pointed out earlier, in maritime cases both sides may feel comfortable with British admiralty law because it is very well developed and respected.
- The two parties may agree to apply the law of the country where the contract was signed. For example, if the Thais and the Venezuelans meet in New York to sign the contract, they could decide that American law should apply.
- The two sides may agree that the law of the country where the contract will be performed shall apply.

The legal situation can get even more complicated. The two partners in the example may decide that they will use German law (Tanzania was a former German colony, and German law is still part of the system) in a Tanzanian court. Even though the contract is between firms from Venezuela and Thailand, the dispute may not deal with the laws or courts in either one of the countries.

Communication with Agents

International firms frequently hire agents to represent their interests abroad and sell their products. Depending on the cultural environment of the agent, the relationship between the agent and the foreign firm may go beyond a strict business relationship that can be severed at will. In cultures in which business relationships are based on personal relationships and trust, the firing of an agent can cause loss of face for the agent. The agency laws of most countries are based on cultural attitudes toward business relationships.

Agency law in Brazil almost always favors the Brazilian agent. Once an agent has been hired, it becomes almost impossible to get rid of the agent regardless of performance. A business going into Brazil must move very carefully and cautiously before offering anyone a position as an agent. The same is true in many Islamic countries. In Saudi Arabia, for example, it is also next to impossible to fire an agent once he has been hired. Furthermore, agents must be Saudis. A company cannot bring in agents from other countries, even other Muslim countries.

In Focus

Justin Simons was in charge of the international division at Seedlink, an American seed company headquartered in Bloomington, Illinois. As Brazil expanded its soybean production, he saw great potential in selling seed to Brazilian farmers. His company had worked on a type of seed that would be perfect for weather conditions in Brazil. He had been to Brazil once to explore the market. On the last day of the trip, he was introduced to Jose Menem, a likable man in his thirties. Menem seemed to know the agricultural market. His English was good; this was an important point since Justin did not speak Portuguese. Justin had read somewhere that connections are important in doing business in Brazil, and Menem seemed to know everyone.

Justin did not want to waste any time; he was eager to sell in Brazil well before the competition did. Therefore, during his second trip to Brazil he signed Menem on as an agent. A few weeks later Justin began to wonder what was going on. Menem had been enthusiastic and very optimistic about selling seed, but there were very few orders even though it was the time of year when farmers would buy seed for the new crop. When he talked to Menem, he only got evasive answers that things were difficult. Justin tried to convince himself that those were typical startup problems and that things would get better the next year. But communication with Menem remained slow. Typically, Justin would wait for several days for a response to his e-mails. When they did talk on the phone, Menem kept assuring Justin that things would get better once conditions improved. Simons never quite understood what this meant. From contacts in Brazil he found out that Menem was spending most of his time promoting products from other foreign companies.

When Justin learned that a major competitor had landed a huge order from Brazil, he decided that it was time to replace Menem. He realized that he had to make sure that neither Menem nor Seedlink would lose face. Menem was well connected, and he easily could damage Seedlink's reputation. After talking to several managers at Seedlink, Justin decided to contact a lawyer specializing in international business law. He could not believe what the lawyer told him. Unless Menem agreed to a separation, which probably would be rather expensive, Simons would have a hard time getting rid of Menem. In the meantime, the competition would build a substantial advantage in the Brazilian market.

Although hiring a local agent presents many advantages, it also poses challenges in intercultural communication. The agent may know the local territory very well but may not be that familiar with the business practices of the country where the firm is headquartered. He may have to struggle with language issues, reporting requirements of headquarters, different attitudes toward planning, establishment of priorities, clients, and suppliers. The foreign manager may have a limited understanding of the cultural and legal environment of the agent. He may assume erroneously that the agent shares his attitude toward profit and has the same priorities. A firm from the United States may feel that business will improve if it hires two agents in a country so that the agents will compete. The agents, often supported by the laws of their countries, may, however, insist on exclusivity.

It is not enough to hire an agent and then assume that the agent will represent the company and sell the products. The manager and the agent must work together and communicate on an ongoing and regular basis. Ideally, the manager knows the best way to formulate persuasive and negative messages in the agent's culture. The manager also must understand the role of hierarchy and authority in giving directives. If the manager deals with an agent from a culture that values seniority, a younger manager needs to take care when communicating with an agent who is older to avoid insulting the dignity of the agent. The agent must be able to translate the goals of the firm he or she represents into actions that go along with the appropriate priorities of the culture. He or she must communicate to the firm what accepted practices are in contacting clients, setting prices, requesting payment for goods delivered, and working with government offices.

Trademarks and Intellectual Property

Cultures that emphasize the right to private ownership take trademarks very seriously. The assumption is that a person or group can own something exclusively. Chapter 1, for example, discussed the concept of land ownership among Native Americans. In Native American culture, the concept of private ownership does not make sense; no one person can *own* land. Similarly, one cannot own inventions; therefore, Native Americans traditionally would not be concerned about private ownership of trademarks and patents. In cultures in which individual recognition and rights are emphasized, trademarks are seen as an important tool in protecting those rights.

Rules relating to trademarks vary from country to country. In the United States, for example, one can register a trademark only if there is a product behind the trademark; one cannot register a trademark for a product one might develop in the future. The American firm Babushka Markets, for example, cannot register the trademark Babushka Cookies unless it actually has the cookies. The rules are different in Brazil, where one can register a trademark without a product. A company or person could take the name of a successful product such as Babushka Cookies from the United States and register the trademark in Brazil. If the company from the United States at a later date wanted to sell Babushka Cookies in Brazil, the firm first would have to buy the rights to the trademark.

Trademark regulations have become a major issue in international trade negotiations. The name of a firm or product and the shape of a product are seen as powerful communication tools by businesses. For example, Quaker Oats from the United States protects its trademark, the Quaker; Volkswagen protects its trademark, the Bug; and McDonald's protects its arches. Businesspeople must understand the legal background and cultural ramifications and develop an awareness of trademarks as communication emblems that warrant protection. They need to realize that there is no time limitation for a trademark or brand name.

Recently, some European countries have argued that several regional products should have the protection of trademarks. Under this provision, Parmésan cheese would have to come from the Parma area of Italy to be called Parmesan. Likewise, cheddar cheese would have to come from around Cheddar in the United Kingdom to be named cheddar cheese. Clearly, Canadian cheese makers do not support this effort.

The Internet has spurred a whole new dispute concerning the registering of names. Some people have developed Web sites under names that belong to companies or organizations. As a result, a company that has been slow in developing a Web presence may have to buy the Web name from the industrious Web entrepreneur.

An effective Web name is worth a lot of money. Moldova, for example, recognized that it could use its country designation *.md* for financial gain. Physicians in the United States can purchase the right to use the designation *.md* from Moldova for a fee. Moldova then uses the money to develop its Internet system.

Another area of common disputes in international business is the issue of intellectual property rights. Intellectual property includes patents and copyright. With advancing technology, intellectual property has become an important aspect of negotiations. Who has the rights to what, and for how long does anyone hold rights? Under U.S. copyright law, copyright protection lasts for the life of the author plus 70 years. A movie or another work that has no individual author falls under the collective copyright rule, which protects a work for 95 years beyond its creation. Patent laws are good for 17 years.

Concerns are focused on two areas:

- Countries that violate copyright and patent agreements or have not signed agreements
- Individuals who violate laws in the area of intellectual property rights

In Focus

India has not signed agreements on patents. As a result, an Indian firm manufactures pharmaceuticals developed in the United States and sells them under a different name at a much lower price in countries such as Russia. Russia desperately needs pharmaceuticals but does not have the hard currency to purchase them from the manufacturer in the United States. One could argue that pharmaceuticals are overpriced, that the Russians need the product, and that it is a humanitarian measure to allow the production in India. The point that the firm in the United States makes, however, is that the Indian firm did not incur any of the research and development costs.

An additional problem is that the legal system in the area of intellectual property is still evolving in many countries. It is difficult to keep the laws current because of quickly changing technology and its impact on communication. Concerns about intellectual property have commercial, financial, and cultural roots. A company that has invested money to develop a new product wants to reap the rewards and not share its new product with others, at least for a while. These are the financial considerations. We have already addressed the cultural attitudes. Some cultures emphasize private property; others don't.

Computer software, DVDs, and CDs are another hot topic in international legal communication. Frequently, developing countries have no laws regulating copyright violations, and if laws exist, they often are not enforced. In Rumania, for example, companies regularly use pirated software. Everyone knows it, but nothing is done about it. Office 98 was available in Rumania before it was released officially for sale, and it sold for only a fraction of the price in the United States. Likewise, the first Harry Potter book was available in China in Chinese before it was released in the West in English. Another big international issue is the downloading of music. The technology has made it very simple to put songs on iPods. This practice has huge implications for copyright and royalty payments to the artists.

The laws are fairly clear in Western countries: Copying is forbidden. However, it is very difficult to enforce the law. Furthermore, it is very inexpensive to copy software, DVDs, and music. The courts decided to close down Napster, a site that facilitated the downloading of music. The argument is that artists are entitled to royalties from their work. However, the closing of Napster was not very effective. Other sites opened to provide the same service. Even otherwise law-abiding companies have run afoul of copyright laws. A major insurance firm, for example, found that its employees had copied software illegally. The problem was solved, and the firm established very strict rules on the use of software, but it takes constant vigilance, education, and enforcement of policies to ensure compliance. In developing countries with limited access to hard currency, the temptation to violate copyright laws is much greater. Any business firm must be careful to follow the laws of its own country and those of the host country as they relate to intellectual property rights. Both Napster and the insurance company are U.S. enterprises. How do they illuminate the trademark and copyright issues internationally?

The issue of intellectual property illustrates that all of us bring our cultural priorities and frame of reference to the negotiation table. Furthermore, the laws of our respective countries tend to reinforce our cultural attitudes. To negotiate effectively, we need to know both the laws and the cultural reasons for the laws.

The World Trade Organization (WTO) is attempting to resolve this issue by making compliance with copyright laws a condition of membership. As was discussed earlier under our exploration of international law, enforcement could be difficult, however. In 1995, China agreed to improve compliance with intellectual property legislation, but the problem persists. The situation is further complicated by what is considered selective enforcement of copyright laws. China tends to argue that it is impossible to enforce the law; however, China moved very aggressively in the enforcement of copyright when it came to the mascot for the summer Olympics. The mascot is a brand, and China made a lot of money by controlling its use.

International Enterprise and the National Interests

Nations have an interest in regulating businesses within their boundaries. The national interest is to guarantee the continuation of the nation, and business regulation must be seen in that context. A nation is first and foremost interested in business as a promotion of its national interests.

- It may be in the national interest to promote trade to improve employment and living standards at home.
- It may be in the national interest to curtail exports of certain items to guarantee that the products are available for domestic consumption.

- It may be in the national interest to curtail the importation of certain products to protect domestic industries.
- It may be in the national interest to curtail bribery.

For example, France in the 1980s very consciously regulated the importation of computers. Even though Apple computers had offered to put its computers in schools for free, France rejected the offer. France considered it crucial for the national interest to develop its own computer industry. It was willing to go more slowly in computerization than other countries if that meant the development of a French computer industry. To some extent, the French were successful in building a domestic computer industry. In the late 1980s, many French households had Minitel, a computer system for shopping, booking airplane and train tickets, and researching restaurants and other sites. However, the system was not compatible with the emerging Internet. Since households had access to a variety of information under Minitel, many were reluctant to purchase computers to hook up to the Internet. In many ways, the success of Minitel slowed the acceptance of the technology that is used worldwide. Even today, France is lagging behind other European countries in computer ownership.

The Russians are experimenting with import and export taxes and regulations. Currently the system is changing almost daily. The country has not decided what ultimately will be in its best interest. The result is confusion everywhere. The government does not communicate clearly with its own firms and citizens, let alone with foreign firms. Russia is a good example of how uncertain laws and confusion can affect business communication.

Any nation's government must weigh the short-term and long-term interests of the country. If taxes on foreign businesses are too high, those businesses will not invest in the country and the country may suffer. If Russia puts high export taxes on products, it will hinder the international development of its businesses and endanger the future development of its industries. Currently, the legal uncertainties in that country communicate economic and political uncertainty and instability to other countries and cause serious undervaluation of the currency.

Free trade agreements are very popular around the world—a few years ago, Mexico and Israel led with the most FTAs. They reduce tariffs for trade between members, thereby encouraging exports. But countries have to balance their interests. Imports coming in without tariffs endanger local businesses that can't compete with the cheaper imports, at the same time that lower tariffs in export markets encourage local businesses to sell abroad. The World Trade Organization (WTO) is dealing with many of these trade and tariff issues.

Businesses have interests different from those of the nation-state. In many ways, they have outgrown the nation-state. They increasingly look at the global picture. They want to produce wherever it is most efficient; they want to move employees around the globe regardless of nationality and country boundaries. They want to do business on a global basis without national restrictions. However, many companies have issued rules regulating ethical behavior in their domestic and international dealings.

In Focus

Asaji Hasoi is the Japanese dealer for PowerBikes, a U.S. motorcycle company. He speaks good English and gets along well with the marketing staff at the headquarters in St. Louis. Over the years, he has been in St. Louis numerous times for training and product planning sessions. Hasoi has just received a fax from a new brand manager at headquarters, Patricia Holter. Patricia introduced herself and announced that she would come to visit in a month to meet Mr. Hasoi. Mr. Hasoi is delighted, and as he communicates with Patricia several times during the month before her visit, he is beginning to look forward to meeting her. She seems to understand his concerns and is receptive to his ideas concerning the marketing of PowerBikes in Japan.

At the beginning of their visit, they exchange some small gifts and then start discussing the issues at hand. Mr. Hasoi takes Patricia to several stores that sell PowerBikes and introduces her to the store managers. During the last day of Patricia's visit, they wrap up the discussion. Both are pleased with the outcome. At the very end, Hasoi, as a token of his appreciation and recognition of their successful relationship, presents Patricia with an expensive leather jacket for a motorbike. The jacket is wonderful, and Patricia would love to have it. However, she also knows that under company rules she cannot accept the present. An expensive present like this could be considered a bribe and therefore is not acceptable. At the same time Patricia realizes that Mr. Hasoi's intent has nothing to do with bribery. What should she do? She weighs her options and then politely declines the present.

Mr. Hasoi seems to take her rejection merely as a first polite refusal which would be appropriate under traditional Japanese customs. Therefore, he once more offers the jacket. Patricia realizes that rejecting the present would be a personal rejection of Mr. Hasoi. She explains the situation, but Hasoi does not seem to understand her predicament, and he again insists that she accept the present as a token of their working relationship. Finally, Patricia takes the jacket.

The situation is clear. The present is in violation of company rules. Yet from a cultural viewpoint Patricia is in a predicament. One could argue that Mr. Hasoi should understand the issues involved or at least accept Patricia's explanation. The reality is frequently different, and businesspeople must weigh their actions. In this case, one might say that even though the jacket was expensive, the gift is a far cry from a multimillion-dollar bribe. But the rules do not distinguish between a gift to build or celebrate a relationship and a bribe.

Regulations come out of cultural values and concerns. They are meant to protect the national culture, and each country establishes its own laws and rules for competition, taxation, employment, product quality, and the establishment of new businesses. Typically, countries that don't like uncertainty have more rules than those that do. For example, an entrepreneur in Germany needs approval from many more government offices than an entrepreneur in Finland does, and this approval process takes time.

The United States has tried in the past to enforce its regulations for foreign subsidiaries of U.S. companies. Foreign countries have resisted this attempt in many ways, arguing, for example, that a Brazilian subsidiary of a U.S. firm is a Brazilian firm subject to Brazilian and not U.S. regulations. This issue has come to the forefront in antitrust legislation, employment, and labor laws. A manager who has been sent from the United States to manage the Brazilian subsidiary must take the following into consideration:

- American culture when communicating with headquarters in New York
- Brazilian culture when communicating with Brazilians

- Brazilian laws when dealing in Brazil
- Brazilian legal aspects of the business in communicating with headquarters
- U.S. law and its effect on the company's dealings in Brazil

The national government also can regulate the collection, storage, and dissemination of private information. In the United States, many firms have lists of their customers that detail what products a customer purchased and when. Supermarkets, by using specially coded customer cards, offer lower prices for regular customers, but they also collect information on purchasing patterns. Although a number of people in the United States are concerned about this practice, the majority seem to be willing to accept the practice in return for lower prices at the checkout counter. The governments of the European Union (EU) are more concerned about privacy. Under EU regulations a multinational cannot share its customer list with headquarters without the written permission of the customer. For example, Land's End Europe cannot transfer its customer file from Europe to the computer system at headquarters without the express permission of its individual European customers. From a business viewpoint, this regulation makes it more difficult to develop companywide comprehensive marketing plans.

In many cases, national laws are intended to protect domestic companies from competition. For example, Germany still has stricter legislation on when stores can be open than do most other European countries, and those laws apply across Germany. For many years, German consumers were willing to accept the law. However, as more Germans traveled abroad, they began to question the rules. Nevertheless, the lobby of small store owners was powerful enough to keep the law. And then e-commerce arrived. Even if the German government tried to enforce "store hours" on the Internet, it would not work. With the Internet, Germans can now shop around the clock, including Sundays, and they take advantage of the opportunity. eBay and Land's End have thus become very popular.[6]

When Walmart entered Germany, the law allowed stores to be open between 7 a.m. and 6 p.m. Monday through Friday, and 7 a.m. till 4 p.m. on Saturday. Most German stores opened at about 9 a.m. even though they could have opened earlier. Walmart saw this as an opportunity and decided to open as early and close as late as the law allowed. In addition, Walmart emphasized customer service and a friendly atmosphere. As German stores watched the success of the new arrivals, they were forced to change their hours and communication with customers.

Chains such as Aldi and Lidel have adopted the Walmart practice. In addition, filling stations increasingly sell food items, and many of them make more money selling food than they make selling gasoline or petrol. Officially, filling stations are allowed to sell only items a traveler might need, but enforcement has become very lax. First the law tried to protect small stores, and then it changed the official hours so that now all stores can be open till 8 p.m. Monday through Saturday. However, the change has come too late for most small stores, which effectively have been pushed out by the large stores and the filling stations.

Legal Issues in Labor and Management Communication

Labor laws and attitudes toward labor–management relations have deep-seated cultural roots and are not easily transplanted. The bargaining process influences the communication patterns between the two parties. Labor–management relations in the United States are adversarial. Management tries to give as little as possible, and labor asks for as much as possible. The two sides sit down to bargain and negotiate for a settlement. The adversarial process is culturally determined and is enforced by bargaining rules (also see Chapter 9).

The British believe that the adversarial process protects the rights of workers and gives companies a competitive edge. The idea of cooperation between management and labor is strange to the class-conscious British. The bargaining process both in the United States and in Great Britain emphasizes competition and winning. It is "us" against "them," and the goal typically is to beat "them," whoever "they" are.

The Germans, although also very competitive, have tried consciously to overcome the rift between labor and management and to set common goals. As a result, the German system functions very differently. There labor and management sit down together to determine the future of the company. The so-called *Mitbestimmung* (co-determination) requires that half the members of the *Aufsichtsrat,* or board of directors, be representatives of the employees. The idea is that they are all in the same boat and therefore must work together for the common good.[7] One unintended side-effect of the law is that it can restrict the number of non-Germans on the Board of Directors, thereby limiting the diversity of the board.

Under the German *Mitbestimmung* law, every firm has a *Betriebsrat,* a workers' council.[8] This group is heavily involved in terminating employees and setting work rules and other conditions of employment. Again, management and workers sit down together to review cases. A manager from the United States or Great Britain may find it difficult to adjust to this situation.

Court decisions in the United States have held this German-style cooperative approach to be a violation of the law. The unions argue that this cooperation violates the traditional role of unions and the adversarial relationship. A *Betriebsrat,* they argue, is an illegal company union that essentially is working for management and does not represent the employees.[9]

Tell that to the Japanese. The Japanese system is entirely different. It emphasizes harmony and the group and avoids open confrontation if possible. In Japan, under General Douglas MacArthur's leadership after World War II, company unions were established to stabilize the labor market. In a company union, the interest of the workers and the interest of the company are represented. Workers are very much aware of the fact that unrealistic demands on their part would threaten the profitability and long-range success of the firm. Management realizes that it depends on the workers and that good labor relations will improve the performance of the firm. As a result, they tend to work together. In tough economic times, however, many Japanese firms have had to lay off workers, and those workers feel betrayed by a system they trusted. In addition, foreign multinational companies have introduced different approaches to human resource management.

By Western standards, Japanese unions appear to be docile and not really unions. For Japan, in building the country's economy, they worked very well. Company unions also have been able to build on the group orientation of the Japanese. Although company unions are fairly new post-WWII, they have built on traditional values. With the economic problems Japan is facing, similar to those of other industrialized countries, the bargaining process is changing somewhat. Workers are becoming more outspoken, and companies are reluctant to give in to demands.

Union membership in Japan typically includes everyone up through the lower management and supervisory levels. Masataka Ota at Mitsubishi, for example, will be in the company union until he reaches the management level. Then he will leave the union. As a result, the gap between union and management, so strong in British, Canadian, and U.S. firms, is smaller in Japanese companies. Managers have all been in the union at one time. In fact, very successful managers often have been union officials. Their success in that position is seen as proof that they can work with people who have different opinions and can build consensus and communicate effectively. The Japanese believe that unions develop the communication skills that are vital for harmony in Japanese firms. Union membership is a stepping-stone in the hierarchy because it develops communication skills.

Any manager working internationally must be familiar with the varying rules governing unions, cooperation, and adversaries. The existing structures, laws, and rules greatly influence the way a manager communicates with workers. Lack of knowledge, at best, may be disruptive, and at worst may cost a company a great deal of money.

Labor Regulations

Employment Communication

In day-to-day operations, employment communication may well be the most important issue. Traditionally, U.S. companies have practiced employment at will for nonunion employees. That means a company can hire and fire an employee at will with or without cause. Over the last few years, regulations on affirmative action and discrimination based on the Civil Rights Act of 1964 and the Americans with Disabilities Act of 1992 have started to change some of that, but compared with Japan and many European countries, employment in the United States is a variable cost factor. People are hired when times are good and let go when business is bad. The regulations in other countries are much tighter.

As was discussed earlier, large companies in Japan practice lifetime employment, but the system has been changing. Under lifetime employment, workers are considered a fixed cost, not something that can be changed easily. Regulations in France and Germany are very strict when it comes to terminating employees, and rules and regulations are spelled out clearly. Employees have lengthy written contracts and after a probationary period of a year are essentially on lifetime employment. A business in the United States wanting to buy a German factory needs to be aware of German labor law. In several cases, U.S. companies bought a firm under the assumption that the firm would be very profitable if the number of workers could be reduced. They found out after the purchase that any reduction in the labor force was a complicated and time-consuming process. Former Chancellor Gerhard Schröder was attempting to make the system more flexible, but any changes proved to be very difficult. The Germans, who don't like uncertainty[10] to begin with, have become used to the certainties of the *Sozialstaat* (social welfare state). They agree that something has to change, but they are hesitant to make it easier to fire people, shorten unemployment support, or lose contributions to health care. However, with the economic problems, a growing number of people have lost employment. This is seen by many as a violation of a social contract, and laid-off workers increasingly go to court to fight for their jobs. In view of the economic pressures, the employment laws are beginning to change, but this also requires a cultural change in thought patterns and expectations. In addition, national laws need to be reconciled with laws of the European Union. Under European rules, employees in the service industry are allowed mobility throughout Europe. However, high-wage countries, such as Germany and France, are afraid of an influx of workers from Poland or Slovakia and are determined to keep workers from lower-wage countries out.

In legal considerations, the courts of a country tend to be very protective of their jurisdiction in matters of employment. Any foreign subsidiary must comply with the labor laws of the host country, and any contract clause restricting court authority in this area is held to be invalid.

Different legal regulations of the employment process have a definite effect on job search procedures and employment communication in different countries. A student in the United States who has just earned a university degree will put together a résumé and start writing cover letters. The student may even have taken a class about how to best conduct a job search. Many books give advice on how to land the best job. However, rules are very different in different countries, and with increasing foreign investment in the United States, American students cannot limit themselves to the "American way" of finding a job.

The same development is taking place in other countries as well. Job seekers in Great Britain may apply for a job in a U.S.–based firm. Even though the laws of Great Britain apply, the degree of appropriate assertiveness or the number of follow-up letters and inquiries nevertheless is culturally determined and influenced by the home country, in this case the United States. Also, a firm involved in international business cannot select employees solely on the basis of the home country's employment practices and laws. Any international firm needs to take local employment customs into consideration.

The résumé and the accompanying cover letter are influenced by culture and laws, as was pointed out in Chapter 7. In the United States, personal information on résumés is discouraged. Yet German firms want personal information, and so do the French and the Japanese. Any job applicant in the United States who wants to show sincerity and good business etiquette will laser print the résumé and type the cover letter. In France, either the letter or the résumé should be handwritten so that the firm can conduct a handwriting analysis. In Great Britain, the cover letter may be handwritten. In Japan, the résumé used to be handwritten because nobody owned a typewriter (any typewriter with *Kanji* needed thousands of keys). With the advent of personal computers and word processing, however, today most Japanese résumés are typed. Word-processing programs allow the writer to enter text in *Hiragana*. *Hiragana* is a syllabary, which means that every syllable can be represented by a symbol, just as a letter of the alphabet represents a sound. *Hiragana* consists of about 56 syllables, a number that can be accommodated easily on a keyboard. A software program can transform the syllabary into *Kanji*. *Kanji* are Chinese-based characters. Each *Kanji* represents a word, a concept, or even a sentence. Japanese has thousands of *Kanji*. As a result, typewriters once were expensive and cumbersome to use.

Even the choice of an envelope can influence the chance to get the desired job. In the United States, the résumé and letter typically are folded neatly and placed in a regular No. 10 business envelope. In Germany, all materials are put in a clear plastic cover and then placed in a DIN A4 (about 8½ by 11½ inches) envelope, *unfolded*. A folded résumé and cover letter would be unacceptable.

The job interview also varies greatly from country to country. Americans are taught to be assertive (assertiveness is discussed in Chapter 7). The Japanese, in contrast, want to show that they are adaptable and fit well into a work group. Managers hiring an employee intuitively will look for the traits that bring success in their own culture. It is natural to feel comfortable with the familiar because it facilitates the interpretation of verbal and nonverbal communication signals. In the process of looking for the familiar, many people who are different and could bring new views and insights to the job may be passed over.

Since Japanese companies hire employees on a long-term basis, they are willing to spend a lot of time and money on the interviewing process. Mitsui Trading Company, for example, interviews 3,000 applicants in a total of over 5,000 interviews to select about 200 new employees. All top executives in the company are involved in the process. From a U.S. viewpoint, this makes no sense. Managers don't want to spend more time and money on entry level employees than absolutely necessary. In the United States, it is assumed that new graduates may stay three to five years; therefore, the employment process is supposed to be lean.

In planning for international expansion, managers should be aware of, and understand, the basic employment issues in the target country. They also need to develop a feel for the role of the manager in the lives of the employees. As was pointed out in earlier chapters, American managers do not get involved in the personal lives of their employees. There may be a company picnic or company Christmas party, but generally personal life remains outside the office. This is very different from the situation in Latin American and Asian countries, where the manager is not just the manager but also a father figure who takes care of the employees and is involved in their private lives. Although this involvement may not be specified by law, it is specified by custom, and an international manager needs to act accordingly.

Laws for Safety on the Job

All cultures want to keep their workers safe, but they differ in their communication about how this can be accomplished. Low-context cultures believe that detailed rules and regulations create a safer work environment. Firms operating in the United States and similar cultures often feel burdened by enormously detailed and complex safety regulations that are enforced by the Occupational Safety and Health Administration (OSHA). OSHA has, in fact, made the workplace safer, but some foreigners often think that the rules go too far. The regulations must be seen against the background of the tendency in the United States to believe that all injuries and accidents can be prevented if the regulations are strict enough. That attitude is based on the cultural priority that planning can prevent most problems. Furthermore, there is the assumption that the company must be at fault in the case of an accident and that the remedy is a large lawsuit and additional regulation. In many other countries, the rules are less stringent and common sense is applied more often, in part because going to court is not as profitable and because litigation generally is not practiced.

Safety is considered important in high-context cultures, but members in those cultures are more likely to recognize that not every accident can be prevented. In Arab countries, for example, people believe that fate determines to a great extent what will happen and safety rules ultimately cannot interfere with fate. As a result, lawsuits are rarer in high-context cultures, and if they occur, settlements tend to be lower.

Every country has its own work rules and attitudes toward what constitutes safety on the job. In the United States, for example, construction workers wear steel-toed work boots to protect their toes from heavy objects. In Japan, construction workers traditionally wear cotton leggings with a very thin and flexible rubber sole. This looks absolutely horrifying to a Westerner. When one of the authors discussed this with Japanese construction workers and pointed out the shortcomings of this flimsy footwear, the Japanese were astounded. How could anybody feel safe on a bamboo scaffolding wearing inflexible, rigid boots? The Japanese are interested in the flexibility and the grip, which is better achieved with the Japanese boots. Workers in the United States are more interested in protecting the toes from falling objects. A number of female workers on an assembly line in France were wearing sandals without any socks. The supervisor said that the women knew that they were supposed to wear shoes. If they didn't, that was their choice. Because of the liability laws in the United States, no American manager could tolerate that behavior.

In U.S. construction companies, alcohol is absolutely forbidden on the job. Construction workers may drink their beer after the day's work is over but definitely not during the day. In France, where wine often is considered a beverage like water rather than alcohol, French employees may drink wine during their lunch break. They probably would not agree with the argument of people in the United States that even the moderate consumption of alcohol in this environment is a safety issue. In Germany, in contrast, new laws have drastically changed the behavior of drinking beer during the workday. Based on the law, the insurance company will not pay if a driver has an accident after consuming even one beer.

Foreign companies need to be sensitive to cultural differences. Otis Elevator, for example, has the rule that under no circumstances is an Otis Elevator employee allowed to have any type of alcohol during lunch even if the French counterparts have a glass of wine. To violate this rule lays the employee open to disciplinary action or even dismissal. In this case, we are not talking about drinking alcohol while operating dangerous machinery but about a glass of wine during a lunch meeting of managers in France. This situation does raise the issue of whose standards should be applied.

Equal Opportunity

In the United States, legal protection for the equal opportunity of women is in force, and the law says that women should be allowed to work in any field, including construction and mining. There should be no restrictions on women's working night shifts. Women have the same right to any job as men do. European countries and Japan look at this rather differently. Women in Japan are not allowed to work night shifts. It is considered bad for their health to work at night. They also are restricted with regard to overtime. France and Germany have rules protecting women from dangerous or physically taxing work. What is meant as protection often turns out to be reduced opportunities. A well-meaning manager who comes to Japan and wants to provide equal opportunities for women, following the pattern in the United States, may not only run afoul of the law but also alienate the local workforce. At the same time, foreign businesses coming into the United States often do not take seriously the rules and regulations for equal opportunity. They are surprised that the laws are enforced and that they must abide by them. In their own countries, equal opportunity laws may be on the books but enforcement may be less vigorous.

In Focus

Sylvia Drucker recently graduated from a university with a degree in business. She had had excellent grades and was confident that with her academic background and several internships she would have no difficulty finding a good job in Germany. As she studied the job listings, she was glad to see that many companies encouraged women to apply. Some even said that women would receive special consideration.

She had several interviews, and they all went well, but she was still waiting for an offer. The recruiters had been impressed with her credentials, so where was the problem? She noticed that a number of her female friends had similar experiences. Finally, she decided to talk to a family friend who was a manager to get advice. He informed her that both her age, 24, and her family status, recently married, worked against her. The companies looked at her as a young woman in her best childbearing years. If she were to become pregnant, under German law the company would have to provide paid leave before and after delivery. If Sylvia wanted to stay home with her baby for two years, the company would have to guarantee that she would get the same job once she returned. In the meantime, the company might have to hire a temporary replacement.

As companies weighed the options, most decided that hiring her was too great a risk and too much hassle. Legally they could not discriminate against her, but there were no teeth in the law.

In the Middle East, where the role of women is restricted in a number of countries, Western firms need to keep local laws and traditions in mind. Any attempts to change the role of women would be seen as outside interference and would be rejected in many cases, not just by the men but also by the women. With growing Islamic fundamentalism, women in countries such as Egypt, where they had greater opportunities to study and develop careers in the 1970s, 1980s, and early 1990s, are beginning to withdraw from public life again. In Iran, in contrast, women are emerging as managers in businesses after having been marginalized as a result of the Iranian revolution at the beginning of the 1980s.

The whole issue of equal opportunity is a sensitive one. For example, many major firms in the United States boast in their codes of conduct that they practice equal rights in all their subsidiaries. However, a look at job application forms in some of the foreign subsidiaries of those firms indicates a different picture. The employment application forms for work with a U.S. subsidiary in Germany, for example, comply with German practice and German laws rather than U.S. customs. Many of the forms ask for names and positions of parents and siblings, marital status, number of children, health, and age of the applicant. None of these questions may be asked legally by a firm in the United States. Employment laws are definitely culture-bound.

A firm may have the best intentions, but it also has to deal with the realities of the hiring environment in which a subsidiary operates. The laws of the country influence the way businesspeople communicate with their employees. Some activists in the United States argue that the U.S. government should enforce compliance with equal opportunity regulations in all subsidiaries of U.S. firms. How would those people react if the Japanese came in to enforce Japanese employment law in their American subsidiaries?

Managers need to be familiar with employment laws and with sensitivities both at home and abroad in relation to these laws. If a company says in its code of conduct that it enforces equal employment throughout the company and all foreign subsidiaries, that may be well meant, but it is also unrealistic. Perhaps the communication should point out that the company will promote equal opportunity whenever possible while complying with the local laws and customs. That would be a more honest communication.

Legal Considerations in Marketing Communication

Marketing and advertising are regulated in all countries. Advertising is culture-specific and is subject to local regulations. Aspects that typically are regulated are the role of children in advertising, claims of superiority, standards of decency, standards relating to claims of performance, and the language of an advertisement. Russia, where advertising did not play a role in the past, is developing government regulations, but the process is slow because that country has only a limited understanding of the role of advertisement and marketing. What counted in the past was production, not distribution. Consumer goods were always in short supply. In addition, choice was limited. As long as only one type of flour or jam was available, the manufacturer did not have to advertise a particular brand. Products in a way sold themselves because of the limited supply; as a result, marketing communication did not develop. Today, Russia is experimenting with advertising and marketing legislation. Russians can study what other countries do, but they also must find laws that fit their situation and cultural values.

One of the concerns in Russia is the issue of language in advertising. Driving through Moscow, for example, one can see billboards with Western product names written in the Latin alphabet. The Russian government, fearing being overrun by Western culture, is beginning to insist that all advertising also must appear in the Cyrillic alphabet. McDonald's is complying with the rule. Signs for McDonald's appear both in the Western alphabet and the Cyrillic alphabet in Russia. Like many other countries, Russia also seems to have local content laws when it comes to advertising. There is pressure on foreign firms to produce advertisements intended for Russian television in Russia, but the law is not completely clear.

Uzbekistan, a former Soviet republic, also tries to legislate the use of language in public life. By 2004, all textbooks were to be in Uzbek rather than Russian, and all official communication is supposed to be in Uzbek. This has posed some interesting problems. For the last 70 years, Russian was the official language. Uzbek was spoken mostly by people in the countryside. As a result, Uzbek has not developed the vocabulary necessary in modern business and technology. Even people who speak Uzbek have to use many Russian words in their business communication.

Increasingly, Poland is insisting on the use of Polish in advertisements by foreign companies. To protect the Polish language, for example, Marlboro ads in Poland must give the health warning in Polish.

The French, ever watchful of the preservation of the French language through its official language-protection agency, also have tight rules when it comes to the use of language. They have announced sanctions against the use of terms such as *weekend, sandwich,* and *computer* in advertising. In everyday speech, however, people use those terms even though officially the words are banned. In spite of the legislation, many French universities have developed programs in English. For example, the Ecole Superieure des Sciences Commerciales d'Angers and the Ecole Superieure Internationale de Commerce de Metz both offer an entire business semester in English. The European Union (EU) encouraged students to study in other European countries, but it became clear that most of the students had learned English and were not very eager to learn French. To attract those students to France, French business schools and universities had to offer a sufficient number of courses in English. A similar development is taking place in most other countries in the EU. In an effort to facilitate international student exchanges with European and non-European countries, universities increasingly offer courses or even whole programs of study in English.

In contrast to the French, the Japanese, who are so protective of their culture in other ways, do not have any problems with taking on foreign words. Throughout their history, they have imported terms and "Japanized" them in the process to the point where most Japanese children think that *MacuDonaldu* is a Japanese company. A separate Japanese writing system called *katakana* is reserved for words of foreign origin, however, so Japanese readers understand immediately if a word comes from a foreign language.

Marketing in the United States involves a lot of *hype.* A product is the latest, the newest, the best, better than the competition. In Germany, in contrast, claims to superior performance are regulated strictly. Comparative advertisement is forbidden. The use of a superlative such as *best product* is not allowed either, as it is not a provable claim. For example, the brewery in Warstein wanted to advertise its beer as *Die Königin der Biere (the queen of beers);* however the law did not allow this claim. The brewery had to settle for *Eine Königin unter den Bieren (one queen among beers).* Japan does not forbid comparative advertisement, but it is hardly ever practiced because it would acknowledge the existence of the competition, which in turn could cause loss of face for a firm.

The national concerns and national regulations of advertising and marketing communication have received a severe challenge over the last decade with the advent of satellites, private TV channels, the Internet, iPhones, and BlackBerrys. Some laws for regulating marketing and advertising strike us as quaint today.

In Focus

In the 1970s, Luxembourg, which had much more lenient rules on advertising than did its European neighbors, threatened to park a satellite right over the country and beam its programs with advertising into other European countries. The regulatory agencies, the media, and the businesses of the neighboring countries were concerned because that would challenge and violate national legislation on advertising and might give an unfair advantage to firms from countries with less stringent regulations. For example, the role of children in advertisements was regulated tightly in most European countries. In some countries, children were not allowed to be in commercials or commercials could not be addressed toward children. In Holland, any advertisement for sweets had to show a toothbrush to communicate health concerns. By advertising on the Luxembourg channel, firms could circumvent the regulations of their countries. Today, geographic location has become mostly irrelevant in reaching potential customers.

Henry Williams travels a lot on business, but he can keep up with his favorite programs no matter where he goes. In Uzbekistan, he can watch CNN, the BBC, Al Jazeera, and German and Russian television in addition to several Uzbek channels. In Poland, he has access to the BBC, CNN, and Swiss, Austrian, German, and Polish channels. Although CNN and the BBC may adapt their advertising to various regions of the world, they do not adapt to national laws. In addition, he can access the Internet from anywhere.

Such legislation is irrelevant today. No matter what government regulation in Austria, Holland, Saudi Arabia, New Zealand, or Mexico may be, anyone who gets satellite channels or gets news from the Internet has access to programming and advertising that may violate domestic laws. Governments may regulate advertising on domestic television stations, domestic radio, and domestic print media, but the technology has outrun the power of national governments. This is nowhere more apparent than with the Internet. E-commerce is available to anyone with an Internet hookup. A student in Japan has the same access to Amazon.com as does a student in Mexico. China is attempting to block access to the Internet and regulate companies' use of the Internet, but in the long run this approach is unlikely to work.

The move by Google into China has to be seen in this context. Google, which had prided itself for applying the same rules around the world and providing complete access to the Internet through its service, has been widely criticized for self-censoring in China. In China, Google blocked out a number of Web sites that might be offensive to Chinese government sensibilities. Google's argument is that it is better for the Chinese to have access to most of Google's services than none at all. However, even this self-censorship does not result in blocking out all forbidden sites. People are finding ways around the restrictions and can gain access to the entire Internet.[11] During the Iranian election controversy in 2009, the government tried to limit access to Facebook, Twitter, and the Internet in general; however, a total blackout proved to be impossible.

It seems that the only way to regulate advertising on the Internet or international television is through international treaties and sanctions against countries that do not enforce international agreements. However, as we discussed earlier in this chapter, this would be very difficult to enforce.

This does not mean anything goes. An advertisement that can be seen by millions of people at the same time all over the world presents tremendous opportunities but also great challenges. What may be culturally acceptable in one country may be seen as irreverent, insulting, and insensitive somewhere else. For example, a satellite channel that advertises a refrigerator by displaying a ham may be presenting good illustrative advertising in Western Europe and North America but offend people in Islamic countries.

The whole issue of advertising regulation presents tremendous challenges for international business communication.

Investment Attitudes and the Communication of Financial Information

Attitudes toward investment, finance, and accounting have cultural foundations. Each country has rules regulating the collection, interpretation, and communication of these data. International businesspeople regularly communicate financial information to:

- Domestic and international operations
- Governments and regulatory agencies
- Stockholders/shareholders
- Potential investors

A businessperson who understands the rules and is able to adapt this kind of information to the needs of various audiences around the world will be more successful.

The way people invest is greatly dependent on the laws of a country and on cultural attitudes toward risk. A firm that needs to raise capital in a foreign market has to know how people save and what their attitudes toward risk are. After assessing the attitude toward risk, firms can adapt their communication to the financial community and the people of a culture so they can meet their financial needs. Germans are typically very risk-averse. They tend to save their money in the bank rather than invest it in the stock market. During the height of the dot-com craze even the cautious Germans started to invest in the stock market; however, the crash of the market reconfirmed their risk aversion.[12] Many decided that the potential for loss was too great and that the money would be safer in the bank after all. Many Americans also were burned by the crash; however, as the markets are beginning to go up, more Americans are willing to invest in stocks once more.

The Japanese are known for high savings rates, with much of their savings in post office accounts, but the savings rate in Japan is beginning to decline because of consumerism. People in Singapore save about 35 percent of their income, but the savings are enforced by the government and are dedicated to the purchase of apartments and pensions. People in the United States, if they save at all, seem to want a high return on their investment. Knowing how and why people save in a particular culture will help a business decide how to communicate its plan to raise money for expansion or improve operations.

An understanding of investment patterns also will help in assessing the profitability of a firm. Typically, financial analysts examine the ratio of debt to equity, meaning that they look at the relationship between what a company owns and what it owes. In the United States, much of the stock is held as equities by individuals and pension funds, and that stock is considered an asset. As a result, stock analysts look for a low debt-equity ratio. In Japan, in contrast, few individuals hold stocks. Capital is provided by banks in the form of long-term loans. Loans, however, are not an asset but a debt or liability. A company may be very profitable, but its debt-equity ratio will be very different from that of a profitable American company. To judge the health of a company appropriately, an analyst needs to understand the relationship between attitude toward risk, investment patterns, and a company's balance sheet.

International businesses need to study the various attitudes toward investment of foreigners. People in most countries think it is all right if foreigners buy their products or come and spend money as tourists; however, most countries get nervous if foreigners start investing in real estate and buying up businesses. Cultural prejudices emerge very strongly when it comes to foreign investment. For example, shareholders in the United States were very upset at the prospect of the Chinese buying Maytag, an American company that is known for producing high-quality washing machines and other household appliances. Similarly, the Germans were aghast that the U.S.–based Chrysler car manufacturer might share platforms and parts with the luxury car Mercedes.

In the 1980s, for example, many Japanese firms started investing in the United States. Many people in the United States considered that development acceptable as long as the Japanese built factories and created jobs, but when Japan started buying into the entertainment industry and iconic entities such as the Sears Tower in Chicago and the baseball team in Seattle, cultural defenses went up. The issue became even more charged when the Japanese and other foreigners began buying farmland in the United States. Since that time, many Japanese firms have sold their American holdings, often at a substantial loss. In many cases, the Japanese firms had borrowed the purchase money against their real estate holdings in Japan. As the real estate market in Japan collapsed, companies frequently could no longer finance the debt of ownership in the United States and elsewhere. The ensuing financial crisis brought down several governments and contributed to the crisis in Asia.

Most countries have rules for, and tight regulations on, foreign investment. They specify the level of possible foreign ownership. In India, a foreign investor may own over 50 percent only if the majority of the production is exported to earn hard currency. The formerly communist countries and China for years had laws that forbade foreign ownership altogether. That has changed over the last few years, but the situation regarding foreign ownership is still not settled. China allowed Ford Motors to come into China under condition that Ford build its plant in the underdeveloped interior rather than in the coastal area. Motorola was allowed to expand in China as long as they provided management training for employees so that the Chinese could ultimately take over the management of the company. In Russia, foreigners may now own parts of a joint venture, but the tax situation is unclear and the repatriation of profits from the joint venture may not be permitted. The idea is that Russia wants to have capital reinvested in Russia. A U.S. investor should balance this goal against the perceived climate for investments if the rules become too stringent and hostile.

Frequently, developing countries insist on local participation in foreign investment. The goal is to train and educate local people ultimately to run the businesses and minimize the involvement of foreigners. China, for example, is willing to open its market to foreign companies in return for training opportunities for its people. Saudi Arabia also specifies the percentage of the workforce that must be Saudi and the percentage of the payroll that must go to Saudi employees.

As was discussed in Chapter 3, under Islam the charging and earning of interest are considered usury and therefore constitute a violation of the principles of Islam and a violation of the laws. Western business, in contrast, would collapse totally without the concept of interest. In Islam, a savings account does not draw a predetermined amount of interest. Instead, the owner of the account participates proportionately in the success or failure of the bank. If the bank is doing well, the account shares in the profit. If the bank loses money, the account also loses money. This seems to violate the Western concept of savings accounts as low-return but risk-free investments. Standard Western banking communication with regulatory agencies, businesses, and private citizens concerning interest rates for saving, borrowing, and lending would violate the laws of the Islamic host country. Bernard Lewis, a prominent scholar of Islam, argues that rules in regard to usury have prevented Islamic countries from developing tools for modern business such as stock markets and modern corporations. As a result, Islamic countries have fallen behind in economic development.[13]

Islamic financial leaders argue that freedom from usury has kept their banks free from corrupt practices stemming from greed and speculation.[14]

The picture is complicated further by the fact that Islamic businesspeople tend to accept Western rules when they invest their money abroad. They certainly have no problem collecting interest on accounts in Western banks. Muslims sometimes rationalize that different rules apply to dealings with the "infidel" compared with dealing with other Muslims. Islamic countries may practice a dual system of banking: Western commercial banking and Islamic banking. Any foreign investor must, however, be aware that in Saudi Arabia, for example, a foreign businessperson is subject to the laws of Saudi Arabia. Traditionally, Saudi courts tend to favor Saudi businesses over foreign interests.

Japan also is known for cultural hurdles to foreign investment. It is interesting to note that Western critics of U.S. business practices, for example, tend to criticize American resistance to Japanese investment as self-centered and imperialistic. When Japan does essentially the same thing and resists foreign investment, the same critics tend to argue that under international law Japan has a basic right to protect its culture. The Japanese are very quick to point to the uniqueness of their culture, which might be threatened by too much foreign investment or immigration. Over the last few years, however, a growing number of people in Japan have begun to favor opening the country to foreign investment. DaimlerChrysler and Renault, for example, brought major changes to the Japanese auto industry.

In Japan, many of the hurdles are hidden. The official rules do not necessarily discriminate against foreign investment. In the construction industry, the rules did not officially block foreign investment; it just happened that foreign construction firms were hardly ever given a contract. When foreign firms started to insist on a bigger piece of the action, the Japanese promised that Western firms would be considered. In practice, little has changed, though individual Japanese may sympathize with Western firms. The arguments are as follows: "In order to build in Japan, one must understand Japanese soils, be Japanese" and "Foreigners cannot adapt to Japanese ways." Although foreign firms most certainly should do their homework to be successful when investing in Japan, all the preparation will be of little use if foreign investment is blocked officially or unofficially.

The challenges for intercultural communication in the area of investment are daunting. Sometimes the implications of investment agreements and national rules are not totally clear until a project is under way.

In Focus

A German company was building a pharmaceutical plant in the Middle East. In the negotiations, the firm had promised to use local building materials whenever possible and to stimulate and develop the local economy. That sounded easy enough. However, the architectural prints had been developed in Germany. The German architect had, of course, based the plans on German building materials and German building specifications for the typical pharmaceutical plant.

(Continued)

As a result, the building materials had to be imported from Germany. The locals were outraged and charged "willful deceit" (deceitful by design and on purpose). The Germans argued that it was impossible to build a modern facility with the local materials.

Clearly, the two sides had negotiated in a vacuum and had not considered the ramifications of their decisions. The whole problem could have been avoided if local conditions and materials had been considered at the very beginning of the planning stages. Neither side acted out of ill will; both sides were simply ignorant of the conditions. If the Middle Eastern country had insisted on local materials, the German investor probably would have given up the project rather than redesign it.

The implications of laws, culture, and local conditions have to be discussed at the beginning to lay the groundwork for fruitful cooperation. The problem could have been avoided if both sides had been more aware of the priorities of the other.

A European country was building a hospital in an African country. The African country had asked for a "low-tech" health care facility that would take local traditions into consideration. Since patients generally were accompanied by their relatives, space had to be provided for the relatives, too. Electricity was not supplied reliably, and it was doubtful whether well-educated doctors would want to spend their careers out in the countryside, far away from the city. Therefore, the locals wanted a hospital for basic care with minimum technology. The Western country, in contrast, had its preconceived notion of a hospital and was not going to be accused of building a second-rate facility. It built a modern hospital that could have stood in any Western city. The building was completed; however, even after several years the edifice went unused because the electricity was not sufficient, the air-conditioning could not be employed, and doctors refused to go to the rural area.

Many developing countries have a pair of goals that seem to contradict each other. They want foreign investment to provide maximum employment of local workers, but they also want the most up-to-date technology. By definition, the most up-to-date technology employs a minimum of people. A foreign investor must tread cautiously in this paradoxical state of affairs. Unless foreign investors are very skilled and sensitive, they easily can offend local cultural sensitivities. They need to take into consideration ambivalent cultural attitudes toward technology and change. Some cultures may not want change, and others are eager for technical development; more likely, most cultures hold both attitudes at once. If a culture wants to change, to suggest something less than state-of-the-art technology (that may employ more people) may be seen as an insult, implying that the industrialized country does not want the developing country to modernize but just wants it to continue old colonial and imperialistic practices. The suggestion may have been made with goodwill, seeing the need for employment in the developing country. Or the opposite may occur: The foreign investor may insist on doing "only the best" for the poorer nation.

As these two examples illustrate, engineering, architecture, and medicine have legal as well as cultural aspects that must be taken into account in international negotiations and communication. But there are limits to cultural adaptation. For example, when it comes to aircraft maintenance, objective engineering standards are applied regardless of cultural attitudes. Furthermore, the safety of passengers requires that all pilots speak the same language so they can communicate with controllers at any airport.

In Focus

An African country was training pilots for international flights. Before the pilots took the written test for the license, they asked to get more time than the officially allotted time to complete the test, arguing that English was a foreign language to them. The request was denied.

They were told that they would get more time only if the length of all the runways in the world were doubled first. Because the language of aviation is English, the pilots would have to communicate in English, and once in the air, they would have to act fast in an emergency.

In addition to their expectations of foreign investors and regulations for foreign investments, countries have specific rules and regulations on reporting performance, expenses, profit, depreciation, and other accounting information. The basic accounting concepts may be the same, but the way the statistics are collected, compiled, and communicated may be different from country to country. An Italian branch of a Japanese bank had to explain to headquarters the details of a credit analysis performed on Italian businesses. In the process, the Italian branch had to reclassify figures and explain why a certain ratio was good by Italian standards. German companies, for example, are required to put pension obligations and other social costs required by law under liabilities. This is different in the United States. As a result, a businessperson from the United States may decide that a company from Germany is not doing well enough to invest in because the ratio of assets and liabilities does not lie within the range acceptable in the United States. In fact, the German firm may be doing very well. When businesspeople from different cultures communicate about profitability, assets, liabilities, and depreciation, they need to understand the legal and regulatory environments in which financial statements are prepared.

Accounting practices in the United States and Western Europe rely on detailed records that are collected and entered regularly. The Securities and Exchange Commission (SEC) in the United States requires comparative balance sheets and income statements for all U.S. businesses and their subsidiaries. Companies are audited on a regular basis, and penalties for violations are heavy. Ever since the Depression, financial markets and communication relating to finances and investments in the United States have been regulated tightly. Investments are regulated by strict disclosure rules about the source and use of funds.

The financial markets in the formerly communist countries are only beginning to emerge. Rules and regulations are not very clear yet, and in many ways businesspeople do not totally understand the concepts of business finance. Since businesses in the past received their money from the government as it was available or as companies needed it, and since they turned over all revenue from sales to the government, the concept of the time value of money is underdeveloped. According to that concept, $1,000 today is worth more than $1,000 a year from now. If the money is available today, it can be used and invested; it can earn a return. In the Soviet Union, businesses did not manage money and did not have to worry about the cost of money. As a result, the entire area of cost accounting is underdeveloped. The concept of profit as a legitimate goal of business is alien.

A businessperson who wants to invest in Russia will face great uncertainties in the financial area not just because the Russian partner may not want to share information but also because the Russian partner may not understand the information and does not know how to compile it. As a result, communication between a Russian firm and a Western firm relating to financial matters will be difficult. A foreign firm interested in investing in Russia will improve its chances of success if it can communicate financial considerations clearly. That means the foreign firm needs to:

- Understand the Russian environment and Russian attitudes toward finance and investment.
- Explain Western financial concepts.
- Explain the importance of accurate and timely records.
- Evaluate Russian financial reporting on the basis of Russian accounting practices and compare the reporting to Western standards.

In Focus

Serendipity, a small firm from the United States doing business in Russia, needs regular information on the performance of the Russian operation. The president has set the policies for reporting and discussed them with the Russian managers. The Russian managers now must translate the policies and the goal of accurate business and financial reporting into concrete steps. They must see to it that the president of Serendipity in the United States is informed about all events. The Russian managers also must see to it that information is prepared according to the government regulations of the United States and Russia. The Russian managers translate the goals of accuracy, efficiency, and legal compliance into specific reports and documents. The lower-level employees at Serendipity then prepare the actual reports. The midlevel managers are the crucial link between the broad goals and the specific tasks.

In the case of Serendipity, the changing political and economic environment of Russia requires particularly effective communication. In the past, Russian firms did not prepare Western-style balance sheets and income statements. The Russian managers of Serendipity did not have the background to supervise the preparation of those documents and did not understand the need for that kind of information. The American president repeatedly requested the reports by fax, but the reports were not sent because the Russian managers simply did not understand what he wanted and why he needed the information.

The principles underlying business practices were so different that the Russian managers and the American president had a very hard time communicating effectively. Arguably, they did not engage in a rich enough exchange of communication to clarify ideas and discuss policies and procedures. The fax was not a rich enough channel; personal discussions were necessary. That channel was difficult because of the cost of travel.

Also, the Russians did not understand the role, authority, and responsibilities of midlevel employees. They continued to function as they had in the past. Information represented power and was to be hoarded rather than shared. The concept of open communication channels was alien to them, but effective communication is based on open communication.

Russian managers, to become effective communicators, will require more than an understanding of finance and cost accounting; they will need to rethink the goal and purpose of the business organization and its employees and re-think the role of communication. A U.S. manager may wonder about and even be shocked at the independence of the Russian subsidiary and argue that his or her company would not tolerate such communication behavior. The reality is different. The Russians even today seem to function on the assumption that "Russia is big, and the czar is far away." As a result, they tend to provide only the information they consider necessary.

Communication in the financial sector is influenced by cultural priorities. Good financial communication is based on an evaluation of a culture's laws, regulations, and attitudes.

Summary

In the course of doing business, international firms must be able to adapt to dif-fering expectations, laws, and regulations. In particular, they need to consider:

- *Communication and legal messages.* Laws and legal interpretations are influ-enced by culture. What is considered legal in one country therefore may be il-legal in another.
- *Specific legal systems.* The most common legal systems are code law, Anglo-American common law, and Islamic law. These systems vary in their approach to, and judgment of, legal situations.
- *Dispute settlement.* Culture influences the way managers approach direct con-frontation and arbitration, communication with agents, and trademarks and in-tellectual property.
- *Multinational enterprise and national interest.* Nations are sovereign entities and as such are intent on protecting their national interests.
- *Legal issues in labor and management communication.* Laws regulate employ-ment communication, safety on the job, and access to career opportunities. This has major implications for effective intercultural business communication.
- *Legal considerations in marketing communication.* Governments regulate ad-vertising. International managers need to be aware of these regulations to avoid inappropriate or illegal messages.
- *Investment attitudes and the communication of financial information.* At first glance, finance appears to be culture-neutral; however, culture plays a major role in people's attitude toward risk management, investment strategies, and evaluation of the financial soundness of a firm.

Notes

1. http://www.bisnis.doc.gov/bisnis/fcp1.htm. This site discusses the provisions of the Foreign Corrupt Practices Act.
2. R. August, *International Business Law* (Englewood Cliffs, NJ: Prentice-Hall, 1993).

3. *Frigaliment Importing Co., Ltd. v. B.N.S. International Sales Corp.,* United States District Court, S.D. New York, 1957.

4. Oliver Wendell Holmes, Jr., "The Path of the Law," *Collected Legal Papers* (New York, 1952), p. 178.

5. *Walls v. Bailey, New York Reports,* vol. 49 (Ct. of Appeals, 1872), pp. 464, 472–473.

6. Durk Liedtke, "Der Ebay Hammer," *Stern,* May 28, 2003, pp. 38–52.

7. Iris Varner and Carson Varner, "Mitbestimmung," *Encyclopedia of Management,* 3rd ed. (Gale Research, 1999).

8. Iris Varner and Carson Varner, "Aufsichtsrat and Workers' Councils," *Encyclopedia of Management,* 3rd ed. (Gale Research, 1999).

9. Electromation, Inc., 309 NLRB, no. 163 (December 16, 1992); E. I. du Pont de Nemour & Co., 311 NLRB, no. 88 (May 28, 1993).

10. Geert Hofstede, *Culture's Consequences,* 2nd ed. (Thousand Oaks, CA: Sage Publications, 2001).

11. Geoffrey A. Fowler, "Chinese Censors of Internet Face 'Hacktivists' in US," *The Wall Street Journal,* February 13, 2006, p. A1.

12. Hofstede.

13. Bernard Lewis, *What Went Wrong?* (New York: Oxford University Press, 2002).

14. AME Info, Abu Dhabi, United Arab Emirates, February 24, 2003.

CHAPTER ELEVEN

The Influence of Business Structures and Corporate Culture on Intercultural Business Communication

Roberto Ramirez's family has been farming in Brazil for several generations. About ten years ago, the family decided to grow soybeans because the international demand for soybeans was increasing. In the beginning, the Ramirez family simply sold the beans to the closest commercial buyer. They saw themselves as farmers rather than businesspeople. Over the years, however, things began to change. Expenses for fertilizer and seed went up, and prices were depressed because of oversupply worldwide. Roberto attended several seminars on agricultural marketing and decided to try a new approach. The first step was to grow food-grade soybeans. Rather than selling to the local commercial buyer, he contacted Japanese firms directly to buy his soybeans. The Japanese were interested in the high quality and were willing to pay a premium. The new outlet for the crops brought in more cash but otherwise did not have a great effect on operations. Roberto had to deal with shipping and some paperwork, but he had little regular contact with Japan.

He began to wonder what else he could do to promote his soybeans. After doing some research, he decided to process the beans before selling them. He contacted Japanese businesses to sell his product. Since he had exported his beans to Japan before, he thought that he was familiar with the process; however, negotiations dragged on. He was confused; in the beginning, the Japanese seemed very interested, but then things slowed down.

He did not understand why. He had bought the roasting and packaging equipment and hired people to meet production goals, but he was beginning to wonder when he would be able to ship the first container.

Taste tests had indicated that the Japanese preferred a stronger roast. They also wanted smaller packages; the one-pound package he had envisioned was too big for the Japanese market. As the Japanese venture took more and more of his time, he decided that he needed someone who could work closely with the Japanese, someone who could take care of the day-to-day communication, the negotiation, and the import–export formalities.

As the Japanese market took off, Ramirez decided to enlarge operations and reorganize the business. The one-person international operation had grown to a department of three people. They had daily contact with Japan by fax and e-mail, and several times a year someone would go to Japan to discuss issues personally. As a next step, Roberto was contemplating developing his own distribution network in Japan and exploring other Asian markets. He realized this move would require much more involvement in Japanese business practices and knowledge of international business in general, but he thought the chances for success were good. Several times over the years he had attended seminars on Japanese business practices, but he realized that everyone involved in the international operations could benefit from similar training.

Roberto was following international markets closely to find new opportunities. Since Brazil grew soybeans that had not been genetically modified, European countries were particularly interested. Talks with a European food company moved along rapidly, and Ramirez had to decide how to integrate a European venture into his business. The organizational structure no longer accommodated his growing international ventures, and he realized the structure had to change.

As he was getting ready for the next phase, he started thinking about how much his family farming business had changed.

So far in this book, we have examined the relationship between cultural orientations and business communication. We have looked at values and their influence on the framing and organization of messages, the negotiation process, and the legal framework. We have seen that successful intercultural business communication is based on understanding one's own culture and the culture of the partner. But the process does not stop there. Intercultural business communication also must take into consideration the structure of business organizations. In this chapter, we will explore the implications of a business's structure on its intercultural business communication dynamics.

As the opening case for this chapter illustrates, the emerging need for intercultural understanding influences the organizational structure of a firm. Similarly, the organizational structure of a firm influences the degree of intercultural understanding necessary for successful business dealings. The type of product a company manufactures and the life-cycle stage of the product also have an impact on the communication process and intercultural communication needs. As we will see in this chapter, some structures encourage greater intercultural understanding than others. As the businesses expand internationally, their structures and their communication dynamics change.

Lane et al. discuss how attitudes toward intercultural business communication have changed over time.[1] Through the middle of the 20th century, most companies operated in a domestic environment. As a result, they did not need to develop intercultural sensitivities or understanding on a large scale. After World War II, many industrialized countries had to rebuild their industries, and U.S. firms dominated the market. As other countries recovered, international competition heated up and U.S. suppliers lost much of their previous power. Companies from a variety of countries looked to foreign markets to expand and grow. To be successful in these new markets required a marketing orientation, meaning that firms had to understand what products people in these new markets wanted and would buy. The result was a focus on cultural orientation, both similarities and differences. Managers realized they had to understand people in many different markets and cultures and modify their approach accordingly. They saw that what worked at home did not necessarily work abroad.

Lane and his co-authors argue that this stage was followed by a third phase in the 1980s.[2] By that time, many researchers and businesspeople talked about the convergence of markets. They argued that with mass production cultural differences would soon disappear. There would no longer be a need for cultural sensitivity. The only thing that would matter was price. In this environment, cultural orientation would no longer be necessary. Culture was perceived to be a thing of the past, and companies argued that good managers were good managers regardless of the specific environment. From then on, business would be conducted on a scientific management basis. However, advancing technology and deep-seated cultural orientations led to a fourth phase. At the center of this phase were quality and customization. Technology makes it possible that Jim in South Africa can "design" his car on the Internet. He does not have to take what is on the car lot at the local dealer. He has choices. The push for the "global" citizen and the one global market also revitalized local and regional preferences. Niche markets based on age, geography, profession, and life style became the focus. Once more, culture became a major player that influenced the success or failure of a business.

The changes in business developments and dynamics went hand in hand with a changing view of the relevance and importance of culture. Intercultural business communication acted like a wave. At times it was big and considered important, ebbing only when the environment changed. Then it would rise again, becoming a powerful force once more. Today, we have combination of standardization and customization of both business products and business practices. Some high-tech products, such as chips and computers have similar characteristics around the globe. At the same time, we can also see an attempt to revitalize regional markets. Businesspeople today need to be global and local at the same time, and the local appeal requires cultural understanding.

Corporate Culture and Intercultural Communication

Different cultures prefer different business structures. As Chapter 10 showed, in the United States, for example, there is a tendency to incorporate even small firms to minimize risk. This practice is typical in a low-context culture that attempts to legislate risk and liability. In a culture such as India, which believes people are not necessarily masters of their own destiny and that fate cannot be avoided, businesspeople do not believe that one can escape fate by creating a corporation.

At the same time, large corporations around the world, regardless of national origin, have found that certain structures work better for multinational business than others do.

However, the apparent structural similarities may cover up different underlying cultural approaches to doing business. As Adler points out:

> Organizations worldwide are growing more similar, while the behavior of people within organizations is maintaining its cultural uniqueness. So organizations in Canada and Germany may look the same from the outside, but Canadians and Germans behave differently within them.[3]

Organizational behavior includes communication. If people behave differently within these similar structures, they communicate differently. Structures may converge, but cultures keep much of their underlying uniqueness. But even within countries, organizations are different. Companies in a culture may have similar structures, but they have their own corporate cultures. Intercultural business communication may mean the sending and receiving of messages from corporate culture to corporate culture.

> Organizations create culture; to be renewed and restructured, they alter it. Culture explains the pattern of assumptions and behavior formulated by human systems in response to their environment, whether it is a nation with its macroculture, a local community with its needs and customs, a market with its consumers and suppliers, or an industry with its colleagues and competitors.[4]

Like national cultures, organizational cultures establish rules about how to behave, what attitudes to adopt, and how to rank what is significant. Organizations have their own heroes and symbols, their own vocabulary, and their own histories of events that contain the values, attitudes, beliefs, and behaviors they wish to have employees learn. Rituals and myths also play a role in organizational culture. As defined by author Daniel Carbaugh, an organizational culture is:

> ... a shared system of symbols and meanings, performed in speech, that constitutes and reveals a sense of work life; it is a particular way of speaking and meaning, a way of sense-making, that recurs in the oral activities surrounding common tasks.[5]

Even though this definition refers to oral communication only, the same holds true for written communication and nonverbal communication activities.

Each employee's experience is run through the operating environment of the organization. Things that don't fit don't get processed; for the purposes of the organization, they don't exist. Employees learn correct etiquette for the organization and the customs that indicate relative significance. In other words, they learn the specific priorities of the organization. Every time an employee joins a new organization, he or she has to go through a socialization process that is like growing up in a society. Each employee has to learn all the meanings and behaviors—what is a good achievement, what isn't; whom to address a certain way and when; what to expect in a hundred different work experiences—in short, the corporate culture.

An organizational culture is a particular way of creating meaning. Any workplace is its own little world with its own inner structure. It is peopled by its own cast of characters. It employs a set of words not known outside the organization—its jargon. It has rules and follows traditional observances. For example, Motorola has a unique corporate culture, and the company takes great care to teach that culture to new employees. The corporate culture helps everyone from Jim Hyatt in New Zealand to Masataka Honda in Japan. The corporate culture acts as a glue to connect employees from many different cultures.

Think of the company where you work. What happens in your organization when someone retires? Who is the person to whom you show most respect? Do you and your co-workers have to observe any particular customs about lunch times? Coffee breaks? Is there a department or person everyone has to treat with special care because of his or her reputation as a tyrant? Who are the heroes in your organization's history? Now think of what happens when someone joins the organization who is unfamiliar with these things. It is important for that individual to learn the culture as soon as possible, and it is important for the culture because members who do not share the culture threaten it. What are the stories people tell the new employee? Who is allowed to tell those stories? Are the storytellers only those who were original participants in the event being retold? What values of the corporation do those stories transmit? How are these stories connected to the priorities and values of the culture in which the company is embedded?

In Focus

Maria Sanchez and Karen Bone work for Canopy Products in Sydney, Australia. They have different ethnic backgrounds and very different lifestyles. Maria is married. Every morning she takes her two children to day care. Her husband picks them up in the evening. Holidays are family affairs, and frequently Maria's family gets together with cousins, aunts, and uncles. Karen is single. During vacations she likes to relax and pamper herself. Her parents live in a different state, and she sees them about once a year.

When Maria and Karen come to work in the morning, they enter the company as members with their specific backgrounds. As they go through the lobby, they walk past the bulletin boards for the various sports teams. They see how the receptionist prepares a rose for everyone whose birthday occurs on that day. They listen to the daily announcements about company activities. Everyone greets everyone with a friendly hello. By the time Maria and Karen step out of the elevator on their respective floors, they have become part of the corporate family. They have not given up their individuality, but the common company experiences tie them together.

At the heart of each organization are the goals and objectives defined by the organization, which enable the organization to focus on human activity; everyone is working with shared aims. The cultural norms enable the organization to manage the flow of information, people, events, and energies that feed it.

EXHIBIT 11.1
**The Cultural
Environments of
Businesspeople**

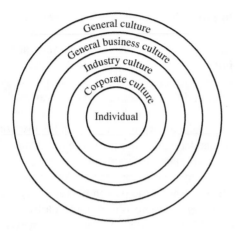

The organizational culture also generates the image of the organization to the outside. It determines how the corporation presents itself. The chief executive officer (CEO) of a corporation identifies its goals in public speeches for customers, shareholders, joint ventures, and the government.

Organizational cultures draw from the culture of their particular industry. The cultures of a particular industry draw from the general business culture for their norms of behavior, values, attitudes, beliefs, and symbols. The business culture in turn draws from the larger general culture of a country.[6] As Exhibit 11.1 illustrates, businesspeople are part of all of these cultures and need to communicate with all of them. That means you may be involved in intercultural communication without ever leaving the country.

A firm that sells strictly in a homogeneous domestic market has less of a need to be aware of foreign cultures and languages.[7] However, given growing diversity in the domestic arena that may change considerably. For example, as the number of people with Latin American, Middle Eastern, Korean, Indian, Vietnamese, and African backgrounds in the United States increases and as their purchasing power increases, more and more companies consider it good business practice to cater to the values and wants of those groups. Twenty years ago American businesses mostly catered to white consumers of European ancestry. Today, that is changing. Catering to different ethnic groups has become big business. Advertisements for food, cosmetics, and fashions zero in on well-defined groups, and technology has made niche marketing a sophisticated communication tool.

The same is true for Europe. Germany, for example, has a growing Turkish population; France has many immigrants from Algeria. The Turkish and Algerian immigrants have had a tremendous influence on the way German and French businesses look at their workers and customers. The government of the Netherlands has considered asking immigrants to pass a culture examination before they can be allowed to come to Holland. Australia has seen growing immigration from China, India, and South Africa. Many firms have developed handbooks and instructions in the various languages of the workers. Managers who once were used to almost all workers being Christian have had to adapt work rules to employees with different religious backgrounds. For example, Muslims have requested time for prayers and food in the company cafeteria that meets Islamic dietary restrictions. Even a domestic firm must be able to communicate with a workforce that is increasingly diverse and have some appreciation for different cultural values.

Stages in Internationalization

In the opening case of this chapter, we looked at the impact of a changing business environment on the need for intercultural competency, and we said that as businesses change and expand internationally, their structures change to meet the growing challenges. In this part of the chapter, we will examine intercultural business communication needs in three major forms of international business involvement: import–export firms, multinational firms, and global firms. One form is not better than another; organizational structures are tools. Businesses change their structures if the environment changes and if the old structures do not meet their needs any longer. In reality, the lines are often fuzzy. Most firms start out as domestic firms. That is true for businesses all over the world. The exception is a specialized import–export business that starts with the specific goal of international business. Most major multinational firms started as domestic firms. Examples are McDonald's; Ciba Geigy, the Swiss chemical corporation; BASF (Badische Anelin und Soda Fabriken), a German chemical firm; Archer Daniels Midland (ADM), a food company in the Midwest in the United States; and Mitsubishi Motors from Japan.

As these companies entered the international arena, their structures changed and their communication changed. They had to develop new communication strategies both for internal and for external communication. As we will see, the import–export stage is often a first step in the internationalization of a business.

In our discussion, we distinguish between a multinational firm and a global firm. A **multinational** firm thinks of itself as a firm that has a nationality; it is a French, Japanese, Chinese, American, or Mexican firm that does business in many nations. Most international firms are multinational corporations (MNCs).

For example, the car maker BMW is a German firm that does some manufacturing in foreign countries. Its cars are sold worldwide. In spite of its international presence, BMW takes great care to ensure that consumers think of it as a German firm. The German connection is important because customers do not want to buy a U.S., Asian, or Latin BMW; no matter where the car is produced, customers want to purchase the German image of reliability, quality, and luxury. The same is true for Swiss watches. A consumer who is willing to spend major money on a Swiss watch wants to be sure that the watch carries the label *Swiss*.

A **global** firm looks at its business as one unit that spans the globe. A true global firm does not think in terms of domestic and international business; its arena is the globe.[8] Very few firms have reached that stage, and the organization of the world into nation states can pose difficulties in the globalization process of companies. Coca-Cola and Microsoft are examples of global firms.

The globalization of a firm is a process that can take a long time. The particular form of development depends on the type of firm, the type of product, the orientation of management, and the political and competitive environments.

International expansion goes hand in hand with the need to deal with different cultures in all aspects of the business. The question that managers must ask is *when* (at what stage) and to *what extent* the international orientation becomes critical and what the communication needs are at each stage.

You may start your career in a domestic company; you may not be particularly interested in doing international business. Yet over time both the firm and you may change. You may see opportunities for selling or even manufacturing your product abroad.

Let us now look at the various stages of international development and the changing communication needs. The stages may overlap. For example, Eike Printing Inc. from Sweden exports printing equipment to Poland, Turkey, and the Baltic countries. In Germany, however, Eike Printing owns production facilities. In Japan, the firm has a joint venture with a Japanese company that produces printing machines for the Asian market.

In Focus

A small Canadian firm is producing scissors and clippers for cutting hair. The founder and owner, Brian Johnson, had no intention of ever going international, but somehow the opportunity to export came up. First, Brian started exporting the product without any modifications. After some time, he realized that the potential for success would be much greater if he studied the foreign markets in more detail. He also realized that the ability to speak some Spanish would be a great asset when talking to his customers in Latin America. In addition, he had to look at cultural attitudes toward cutting hair.

In Canada, the product sold to families that wanted to save money by cutting hair at home. In Latin America, people do not cut hair at home. After some research and visits to his Latin American market, Brian started selling the product to barbers and hair salons. In the process, more people in his firm in Canada needed to learn about the Latin market and the distribution systems within it. He also found that the American "do-it-yourself" attitude had no following in Latin America.

His company's modification to an international business changed communication in the firm. Brian now has to have people with international expertise and awareness of cultural differences in order to communicate successfully with the new market.

The Import–Export Stage

Reasons for Exporting

The first stages of international involvement do not require much international adaptation and involvement in other cultures. For example, most firms start their international experience through market development, by exporting through an import–export firm. In that situation, they are not involved directly with foreign operations. Frequently companies sell abroad because someone abroad wants or needs the product. The attitude tends to be *laissez-faire:* "If it works, fine—if it does not work, not much is lost." As sales grow, the firm may adapt the product to some extent. But if the foreign market really wants and needs the product, the firm's adaptation in terms of culture, language, and product may be minimal.

The firm may want to explore new markets either because the domestic market is saturated or because the firm sees growth potential in other markets and opportunities to expand production capacities. In the beginning exporting stage, the firm typically looks at itself as a domestic firm that also sells some of its production overseas. Some firms may look at exporting as the first step toward more international involvement; others may have no intention of ever going beyond exporting. In this case, the firm will not go through any major changes in its communication. Roberto Ramirez, the soybean producer in the opening case in this chapter, moves easily from a domestic stage to an export stage.

As mentioned, the typical beginning exporting firm exports its products "as is." The firm will make no major changes; perhaps there will be some surface adaptations, but it is not going to spend a lot of money on exporting. An advanced export firm, in contrast, will adapt its products to specific markets and consider the foreign market an integral part of its business. Export firms can be at any point on the continuum.

The Internet and e-commerce have provided international markets to small companies that traditionally might not have thought of exporting at all. As soon as a business has a Web page, people around the world can view its product line and services. This means that a company can become involved in international business without making a conscious decision to sell internationally. The Internet opens the door for everyone, but it also exposes every business with a Web page to potential blunders and missteps. Most e-business is B2B, or businesses selling to other businesses. Whether the customers are businesses or end users, online communication from a Web site has to be constructed with careful attention to cultural priorities to succeed in international markets.

The following example illustrates how a small company is getting involved in exporting:

In Focus

Central Illinois in the United States is known for growing corn (maize in British English) and soybeans. The area has very fertile soils and a climate that is conducive to growing those two crops. With modern soil sciences and fertilizers, production has grown tremendously over the past two decades, and farmers have been faced with the issue of how to get a good price in years of high yields. They have exported part of the production for a long time. The Mississippi River made shipping to seaports economical, and as China, India, and other developing countries grew economically and became more prosperous, they were buying more grain. Even though the export market was good, farmers began to wonder whether they could increase their profits by adding value to the commodity before exporting the grain. As a result, farmers started to export not just grain, but specialty grains as well. Whenever possible, they will export soymeal, and premium food-grade soybeans rather than just generic soybeans.

In another development, corn is increasingly used for alternative fuel production, such as ethanol. A byproduct of this ethanol production is dried distillers grains or DDGs. DDGs can be molded into pallets, highway signs, road surfaces, and packaging materials. DDGs can also be used as feed in aquafarming. Vietnam, Thailand, and Malaysia are all interested in buying raw DDGs for animal feed or processed DDGs. Clearly, this type of exporting is different from exporting the basic commodity. In the process, the exporter has to learn more about the countries they are exporting to. They will need to know about what the specific needs are and develop a detailed marketing strategy.

As we will see in the next section, the change in the exporting strategy has implications for communication practices.

Communication in the Import–Export Environment

If a product is exported without adaptations and is in demand, the need for adaptations in communication is minimal. A small business may go through an import–export firm or hire an agent. The managers of the firm may have little or no contact with the foreign market and may look at exporting as maximizing production capacities or as a market development strategy for expanding the market for the product. If the firm directly hires a foreign agent to represent it and distribute its products in foreign markets, it must at least be familiar with some of the legal issues involved in hiring, maintaining, and firing agents, but direct contact with the foreign market is not extensive (also see Chapter 10).

A beginning exporting firm will hire translators, go to trade fairs and shows, and advertise its products without adaptation to foreign cultures. The firm will be more interested in the technical aspects of exporting, such as letters of credit and shipping methods, than in cultural adaptations to the export country. Communication with the foreign market is filtered through the interpreter or agent. As a company gets more involved in exporting, managers may also attend special export seminars.

The level of adaptation also depends on the product. Coca-Cola often is cited as proof that a product can be successfully marketed globally. Indeed, Coca-Cola has a standardized product—all the syrup for Coke is produced in the United States and shipped all over the world; however, the level of sweetness of the syrup is adapted to specific cultural preferences. In addition, it is this particular adapted product that people in a specific market want. Part of the appeal of Coke is that it is a global product; it looks the same. People don't think in terms of American Coke, German Coke, Indian Coke, or Mexican Coke—they think of Coke, even when it tastes different from country to country!

What works for Coke may not work for other products and firms. Even though the product is Coke, the Coca-Cola Company must adapt its communication style and techniques to the various cultures and communication styles of its bottlers around the world. And even though the product is the same everywhere, the packaging—the bottle sizes and shapes, for example—may vary. In its operations and communication within the worldwide operations, Coca-Cola must adapt to its many varied audiences and take into consideration the expectations and conventions of many cultures.

Similarly, many software programs make only minor adaptations. People the world over use Excel, Word, and PowerPoint. To make this work, Microsoft has added a feature that allows users to select the language of instruction. For example, a user in Italy can choose whether she would like to have the instructions in Italian, British English, American English, German, or French; the software remains the same. Yet, the language option represents a major adaptation in the communication strategy.

Home appliances cannot use the same strategy Coke is using. When it comes to home appliances, people want a product that corresponds to their values, needs, and environment. When Whirlpool did consumer research in France, the company found that buyers wanted a microwave oven that also would crisp food the way a conventional oven does. They developed one and enjoyed great success in Europe.

Washing machines, one can argue, should sell anywhere because they simplify life for everyone, but that does not mean that the same machine will be successful everywhere. Germans want front loaders that heat the water in the washing machine all the way to the boiling point. All Germans "know" that top loaders don't get laundry clean. They also "know" that hot water running into the machine will burn the dirt right into the fabric. The water needs to be heated gradually in the machine to dissolve the dirt. A hookup for running hot water is not necessary. The British, in comparison, prefer top-loading washing machines and extremely hot water. The French use a mixture. In remote areas of Thailand, the needs may be quite different. Electricity may not be readily available, and running water may be rare. As a result, the typical American, British, or German washing machine is not feasible even if the Thai culture were not presenting any hurdles. In order to communicate successfully with potential customers and distributors, managers need to know about these priorities, cultural sensitivities, and resources required to run equipment.

In addition, size and price are factors. If the average wage is $350 per year, very few people will be able to spend $500 on a washing machine or $1,500 on the big refrigerators typical in the United States. A Japanese family that has a small apartment of about 500 square feet (50 m²) in Tokyo may have the money but will not want to buy big appliances from the United States. There simply is not enough room for them. Space is too valuable to clutter up with huge appliances. Culturally based shopping preferences also determine refrigerator choices; in cultures where people value fresh food, and shop every day, large refrigerators are pointless.

Even if the company has excess capacity, and even if the product would make life easier in another culture, the product may not sell unless the firm is willing to research the market in depth, a process that requires a lot of intercultural communication and understanding. A firm needs to research consumer attitudes and preferences, government regulations, and the purchasing power of the people. All this information must be collected, tabulated, evaluated, organized, and then communicated. Only after the research has been completed can the firm work on product adaptation and marketing communication (including advertising). Many firms that see themselves as mostly domestic firms are not willing to expend the energy and money to do that. They may think that adaptation is not cost-effective and that the foreign market is not large enough to justify the effort involved in market research.

U.S. manufacturers of large appliances typically face that problem. The standard kitchen appliances are big. They fit into American homes but are too large for most European and Japanese homes. In addition, U.S. appliances are not considered responsibly "green," and are viewed as wasteful of energy and space. Yet manufacturers frequently argue that the number of consumers who would be willing to buy an adapted product is not large enough to justify the cost of consumer attitude surveys and product adaptation. In Spanish, French, and German stores, one can see samples of refrigerators, dishwashers, and stoves from the United States, but they are considered an oddity and a curiosity. Since they are also very expensive, very few people consider buying them. The Europeans and the Japanese, in contrast, have been willing to adapt to the needs of smaller markets, partly because their own domestic markets are comparatively small.

This example shows that to export successfully, a company must adapt its marketing and product modification strategies to foreign conditions and be aware of consumers' needs and wants. As soon as a decision is made to adapt a product to foreign markets, the need for intercultural communication increases. The company must research the market, the competition, and the market potential. This is a complex communication task. Let us assume you are assigned to research the potential market for motorcycles in Spain. You need to find out the Spanish attitude toward motorcycles. You can interview people; you can design questionnaires. This sounds easy enough, but you must find out whether in Spain people are willing to answer questionnaires and are willing to be interviewed. You must determine their attitudes, preferences, and needs and wants. All these areas are influenced by cultural priorities. What may start out as a simple product adaptation or exporting task may grow into an elaborate intercultural communication task (see also Chapter 8 on gathering information).

If international sales increase, a firm at some point may establish an export department to handle the demand and distribution. Frequently, the export function initially is tacked onto the sales and/or marketing function (see Exhibit 11.2).

EXHIBIT 11.2
Export Structure

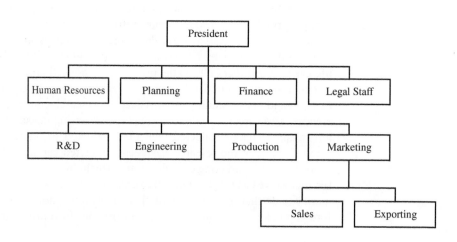

The more the firm gets involved, the greater the need will be to communicate directly with people with different cultural backgrounds. Rather than turning the product over for sale to an agent, the firm will have to have some direct contact with the foreign market. The extent will vary, however, and much will depend on whether the firm sees international expansion as the wave of the future or an ancillary to domestic operations.

In Focus

Yoko Sony is looking for new pots for her new kitchen. She would like something stylish and easy to clean. She has collected several brochures and has been to a number of department stores. Almost all pots are sold in sets of three or five. She likes pots produced by GE, a big American multinational firm; the quality is high, and she likes the color and the form, but the pots look rather big. Even though her new kitchen is larger than the old one, the stove is the same size, and she realizes she won't be able to put four GE pots on the stove at the same time. Ultimately, Yoko purchases a set of five pots from France. They cost a bit more than the GE pots and she doesn't like them as much, but she knows they will fit on her stove.

The need of a firm to be aware of intercultural communication practices and conventions depends on the extent of the international involvement of the firm and the cultural diversity within it. The needs of a firm for intercultural communication skills grow with the increasing globalization of the firm.

The Multinational Corporation

Some multinational firms have national subsidiaries; others have international divisions at headquarters. Each type has its own internal and external communication dynamics.

The National Subsidiary

The Structure of a National Subsidiary Organization

In the national subsidiary structure, a multinational firm has subsidiaries in various countries (see Exhibit 11.3). Those subsidiaries report directly to top management at headquarters without going through regional headquarters or an international division at headquarters. For example, Jesse Hurtado, the president of the subsidiary in Mexico, will direct any concerns or questions to top management in Oslo, Norway. He has access to senior management there and knows he will be heard.

The organization into national subsidiaries takes into consideration the specific needs of the various subsidiaries. It gives importance to local voices and, at least

EXHIBIT 11.3
National Subsidiary
Structure

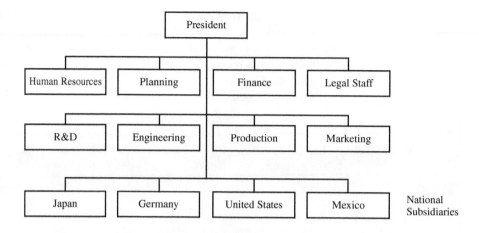

in theory, fosters adaptation to local needs. The top people at the subsidiary can be either home-country employees or host-country employees. If headquarters sends home-country employees, it is in the interest of headquarters to keep those employees at the foreign post for several years to ensure continuation of communication and policy implementation. The successful expatriate typically is in the fourth stage of the model for culture shock, the integration stage (see also Chapter 1). The expatriate is well adjusted and can relate to the concerns of the host-country employees but also understands the concerns of the home country. The expatriate, who at this stage often speaks at least some of the local language, is an effective communicator and negotiator between the two cultures. The foreign subsidiary structure is frequently characterized by "career expatriates." These expatriates will move from one international assignment to the next without coming back to headquarters. If host country nationals are in the leading positions, in all likelihood they will remain in the country of the subsidiary. Their chances of being promoted to leading positions at headquarters are slim. The argument is that they understand the local culture and can communicate effectively in that environment. As with the career expatriates, their value lies in facilitating communication between home-country and host-country cultures.

Communication in a National Subsidiary Organization

The advantage of the subsidiary system is that the managers of the subsidiaries have direct access to top managers at headquarters and don't have to go through several layers of management and the accompanying bureaucracy. The difficulty is that the structure can lead to an overload at top management. If a firm has many foreign subsidiaries, communication between headquarters and subsidiaries becomes time-consuming and it may be difficult to strike a balance between the needs of foreign subsidiaries and concerns at headquarters. Thus, managers at the subsidiary may have to reconcile two options: follow directions from headquarters that may not be appropriate in the host culture or run the subsidiary as an independent unit and lose the synergy a major corporation can provide.

Top management is responsible for directing the concerns of the international subsidiaries to the appropriate departments or sections at headquarters. If managers are overloaded or do not care about the international operations, they can block international involvement and create a bottleneck in international communication. Furthermore, the structure limits communication between subsidiaries. Communication is centralized, with headquarters functioning as the hub of all activity. The subsidiaries function more as autonomous entities that are not effectively linked. In large firms, this structure may become dysfunctional because of the lack of integration of all the entities into one unit. Communication that concentrates on headquarters and subsidiary A, headquarters and subsidiary B, and so on, does not encourage the development of multiple networks and linkages. In the extreme case, the various departments in a company operate as independent units rather than effective teams that work toward the same goals. In Chapter 12, we will discuss the dynamics of diverse teams and how effective management of the intercultural communication process within, and between, diverse teams leads to better output.

In Focus

Susan Carmichael, vice president for finance, has been at RazzleDazzle Luxuries for two months. Before that she always worked in a predominantly domestic environment. As her administrative assistant, Jack Branch, brings in the latest financial analysis figures, the phone rings, and Karl Pracht from Germany is on the line wanting some data about the planned expansion. Francesco Lurati left a message earlier about the financial planning meeting next month. He needs to know what information to prepare. Akihito Koga from Japan is worried about the repatriation of profits from the Japanese subsidiary to headquarters in the United Kingdom. She has heard about his concern before but does not understand all the details. Susan is overwhelmed. When will she ever get to her work?

She is contemplating telling the people in the subsidiaries to communicate with her administrative assistant who then can filter what Susan needs to know, but Susan also realizes that she has to stay in the loop because she will be responsible for what is going on in the financial area. Still, there must be a better way. Perhaps the technician could develop and regularly update a Web site or an electronic bulletin board that would allow for the posting of common questions. That might help with some of the routine communication, but of course they all claim that their problems are unique and need instant attention. Regular videoconferencing might be a useful tool to improve the flow of information; however, the time differences of the various location complicate videoconferencing and conference calls.

People in the field want answers, and Susan has to find a way to get them the answers efficiently.

The International Division

As international operations expand and as the need for effective international communication grows, MNCs typically organize their international activities into an international division.

The Structure of an International Division

An organization with a domestic and an international division looks very efficient (see Exhibit 11.4). On the surface the international division is at the same level as the domestic division. It seems that international operations are considered as important as domestic operations; however, international is separate, and often it is not very well integrated into the rest of the firm. In many firms, the international division is in a different part of the building; sometimes it may even be in an entirely different location. Even though with modern communication systems such as fax, e-mail, phone, instant messaging, and video conferencing, the actual physical location may not be significant, the physical distance can create a mental distance. Frequently international divisions in a multinational firm are organized by product line or geographic location.

What are the results of this international division organization? This situation easily leads to a duplication of efforts. For example, the company may have one research and development (R&D) department as Exhibit 11.4 indicates, but sometimes the domestic and international divisions have their own R&D. The domestic and international division also tend to have their own advertising departments. Ideally, the domestic and international divisions work together, but in many cases they don't. In many cases, the domestic and international divisions compete for scarce resources, and each is more intent on expanding its own power than on maximizing the return and efficiency of the whole.

Trust can become a major issue in that environment. In cultures in which trust is built slowly over a long period, and one does business with people one trusts, the competition between the domestic and international divisions may be particularly destructive of the climate of the firm.

In many cases, the domestic division sees the international division as a drain on resources and may argue, "We would do better domestically if we concentrated on that area rather than running all over the globe." Domestic problems may be attributed to international involvement. The case about Lincoln Electric in Chapter 1 illustrates the way costly international undertakings can threaten workers at home.

EXHIBIT 11.4
**International
Division Structure**

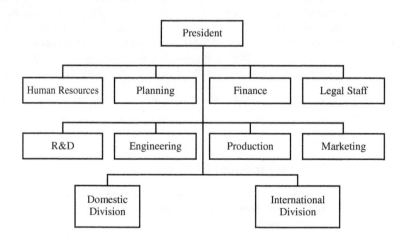

However, the international division also may be seen as a cash cow whose profits can and should be used to improve domestic operations. Profits from international operations often are considered the property of the domestic market. "After all," according to this viewpoint, "international operations are there to support domestic operations, the real concern of the firm, even though the best expansion opportunities may be abroad." This issue surfaces typically in the area of profit repatriation (that is, bringing profits from sales back to the country in which the head office is located). The issue is complex because it also involves transfer pricing and fair prices for transfers between different parts of the company.

Communication in an International Division Organization

The official line of communication goes from the field through the international division to the appropriate areas at headquarters and back. From an operational viewpoint the channel makes sense; communication seems to be efficient because all international communication goes through the international division. However, that channel may be redundant if the person in the field knows the person at corporate who has the answer or is needed to solve a problem.

In Focus

A Japanese subsidiary of an American firm had had another record year. Overall, international revenue had almost doubled over the last three years. The Japanese subsidiary wanted to use the profits for extended R&D activities in its markets. It also wanted to use its excellent performance to improve its standing and prestige in the Japanese business community in which it operated. The subsidiary believed headquarters should consider the effects of repatriation of profits on morale in the subsidiary.

Headquarters and the domestic division saw the picture quite differently. The Japanese subsidiary was expected to repatriate most of its profits to the headquarters in Chicago, where the money would be used to support expansion of the U.S. domestic division. This was to happen through transfer of services from headquarters to the Japanese subsidiary. For example, headquarters can send someone to provide training on the corporate requirements for financial reporting, and headquarters charges the subsidiary for those services. The subsidiary then pays a transfer price set by headquarters for this transfer of services. The transfer price would be adjusted so that the book profits of the subsidiary would look much lower than they actually were. The Japanese subsidiary objected in vain, arguing that the weaker performance would weaken its reputation and its ability to raise money for loans in the Japanese banking community and that the firm would not be as respected in the business community.

This situation illustrates several intercultural communication issues. Headquarters, dominated by managers with mostly domestic backgrounds, used a very patronizing tone: "We know what's best for you and the firm." Headquarters also did not recognize the role profits played in the prestige the subsidiary would gain in its Japanese context. The Japanese subsidiary was not particularly willing to accept a merely supportive role. Managers at the subsidiary had a tendency to look at themselves as an independent unit that did everything better than headquarters did. Rather than pulling in the same direction, the domestic and international divisions tended to try to outmaneuver each other.

This problem has not changed; in fact, with faster and better communications technology, it may have gotten worse. With direct and immediate access to anyone at headquarters or anywhere else in the organization, the temptation to jump channels is great. Why should Pierre from the subsidiary in Seoul waste time contacting the international division if he knows that the manager in Hong Kong can supply him with the answer in five minutes? One could argue that Pierre should at least inform people at the international division. If Pierre writes an e-mail, he could easily copy other people, but he also needs to decide on who actually should be copied and has a need for the information. If he telephones Hong Kong, he may forget to inform the international division or not consider it important.

Who Communicates with Whom

At a very practical level, there is often confusion about who at headquarters should be contacted outside the international division. People in the subsidiary typically know people in the international division but very few people beyond that. They rely on the international division to take care of them. People in the field can send one memo and expect that people in the international division will talk to all the people who need information or can provide information. Headquarters is far away, and so it is tempting to let headquarters take care of any problems.

The feeling of "us versus them" that is typical in the international division organization can be very destructive to the communication climate. Domestic may be condescending and not inform the international division or subsidiaries of new developments. In contrast, in a successful international division the feeling of superiority over the domestic division may create a dysfunctional communication climate. Today, an increasing percentage of the revenues of major companies in many countries comes from international activities. The rivalry and competition over who is best can lead to communication problems and a waste of resources. One group may withhold information from another and endanger the profitability of the whole for the benefit of a subgroup.

Language and Staffing Issues

Language ability is another communication issue. Since international involvement is restricted to the international division, most firms do not see the need for a broad international background among employees outside the international division. Even in the international division, the level of intercultural awareness can be low.

The attitude toward intercultural understanding and language competency (also see Chapter 2) is connected to the type of staffing the company practices. Staffing directly affects intercultural communication effectiveness because staffing influences communication networks. A company that wants to improve its intercultural communication should reexamine its staffing patterns and practices.

Firms that have international divisions tend to practice a mixture of ethnocentric staffing and polycentric staffing.[9] In ethnocentric staffing, the management in the host country comes from the home-office country. The intercultural communication interface takes place at the subsidiary. As a result, communication has been cleaned up by the time it reaches headquarters, and headquarters may not be directly involved in, or even aware of, cultural and linguistic problems in the field. It is the people at the front who have to cope with intercultural communication and language problems. The success of ethnocentric staffing relies on the linguistic and cultural ability of the expatriates.

Headquarters may be interested in having a well-oiled machine rather than open communications. An expatriate may be evaluated on the basis of how smoothly things run. As a result, the expatriate may play down any problems, and headquarters may not get the full picture until it is too late or problems have become major.

In polycentric staffing, management comes from the host country. Here, the culture and communication interface is typically between headquarters and the subsidiary. The international division must deal with intercultural and language issues more directly because the expatriate who formerly filtered all communication between headquarters and the subsidiary is gone.

Practical Communication Options

To minimize the communication problem, firms have a number of options. They can:

- Train everyone in the international division in intercultural communication.
- Create specialists for certain regions.
- Have a mixture of host-country and home-country nationals in the subsidiary.
- Hire host-country nationals who are familiar with the home-country culture.

The first option is expensive, and most firms don't consider broad-based intercultural training practical or necessary. With increasing international competitive pressures, that is changing. Companies are also looking for some international competence in the people they hire.

The mixture of ethnocentric staffing and polycentric staffing creates problems in terms of compensation packages and can create an atmosphere of home-country versus host-country personnel. Expatriates tend to get housing allowances, home leave, tuition support for children, and hardship allowances. The host-country employees who do the same work and work right next to the expatriates invariably have inferior compensation packages. As one engineer in a developing country put it, "Why should an expatriate get more money for having blue eyes and blond hair?"

These days expatriates frequently have dual citizenship. Eileen Zhang, for example, is Chinese. She studied in the United States and received an MBA. She then started work at a U.S. MNC. As soon as she was eligible, she became a U.S. citizen. She rotated through several jobs to become familiar with company procedures and practices. Ultimately, she was sent to Beijing, the city she originally came from, to head the marketing section in charge of marketing coffee in China. Eileen went to China as an expatriate with an expatriate compensation package. Under those conditions, she was eligible for regular home leave, subsidies for educational expenses for her daughter, Western-style expatriate housing, domestic help, and a company car with a chauffeur. Chinese employees in the firm who are well educated but have no expatriate status are upset that they have no access to the same privileges.

In Focus

As long as Bertrand Fowler worked in Delhi, India, he kept headquarters informed of all events and developments at the subsidiary. He had worked in Milan, Italy, for a number of years and knew all the major players in the international and domestic divisions at headquarters. He also knew how to package information effectively and channel it to the appropriate person at headquarters.

Raj Kumatar, an Indian with a business degree from an Indian university, has taken his place. Raj does not know anyone at headquarters, and he has not worked with people from Italy before. It will take some time before he can read the people at headquarters and know what they want and how they prefer to be contacted.

In this environment, the people at headquarters are exposed more directly to the cultural environment of international business. The buffer is gone, and now they must communicate directly with a person who has a different cultural outlook.

George Blair was sent to Tokyo last year from Canada. He is married and has a small child. His wife did not want to leave her friends in Canada, and they recently had bought a nice house in a very good suburb. Why should the couple give up all that to go to Japan? As it turned out, the company picked up the rent for a Western-style apartment in Tokyo, over $6,000 per month. And, of course, George also received other benefits, such as company-paid home leave every year and an allowance for the cost of living in Tokyo. None of the Japanese employees receive any of these benefits.

One could argue that there is a question of fairness of reward, but more is involved. Will the Japanese employees resent the special expatriate package, and will that undermine George's effectiveness, especially in light of the fact that George speaks very little Japanese? Special packages may keep the expatriate separate from the Japanese work group and slow down or even hinder integration into the work group. All this will have an impact on the effectiveness of communication between George and the other Japanese employees, as well as that between the subsidiary and headquarters.

For the expatriate, the argument is that at home he could afford a big house, his wife could continue her career, and his children could stay in their familiar environment. The extra pay and benefits, supporters of the packages argue, are simply compensation for hardships that he would not have had to endure if he had stayed at headquarters.

Attitudes in Different Cultures toward Sending Employees to Other Countries

The extent of the expatriate package depends on cultural priorities. Japanese firms typically send more expatriates to their subsidiaries than do Western firms.[10] However, Japanese expatriate packages are small by Western standards. The international assignment is considered a routine assignment within the company. German firms also don't pay their expatriates as lavishly as American firms do. This was a major issue when Daimler and Chrysler negotiated their merger.

Some firms try to get around the issue by choosing younger, more flexible people to send abroad. Those people are not sent as expatriates but are on the payroll of the subsidiary under the same conditions as host-country nationals.[11] Accounting firms in the United States increasingly are using that model, and it may work if international experience is deemed essential for career advancement. On the whole, however, many firms in the United States still maintain that it is not worth sending younger employees abroad. They feel an employee must be at least middle management before a firm can profit from the employee's time as an expatriate. The average cost to the U.S. company for an expatriate with a family who fails to complete an assignment can be as high as $500,000.

Europeans seem to take a different approach. For example, French firms send many of their younger people abroad. They argue that younger people are less expensive and more flexible in adapting to different cultures. Furthermore, they don't have to worry about schooling for their children. In addition, those employees will bring their international experience back to their jobs at headquarters and be able to use what they have learned throughout their careers. The French are convinced that early international experience will develop international expertise that will enable employees to communicate more effectively with people from many different cultural backgrounds. Those employees will be able to see the partner's point of view and engage in more productive and creative problem solving. They hope that people with early intercultural work experience will be more flexible and better communicators. For example, the French company Schlumberger hires young engineers and moves them around—for example, from Indonesia to Saudi Arabia to Houston.

Mitsui Trading Company also sends employees on international assignments early in their careers. Roughly 30 percent of its workforce is abroad at any given time. As was mentioned earlier, the international assignment is part of the regular career path. The company invests a lot of money in training but fairly little in special compensation. The employee receives intensive language training. Sometimes an employee will spend a whole year in a country to learn the language and the culture. That is the job for that time period. Later, the employee may shadow an experienced expatriate for a year. It is only in the third year that the employee will be involved actively in the actual business of the firm.

Over the last decades, U.S. firms increasingly have withdrawn their managers from assignments abroad because of high early return rates and high costs. They argue that Americans are not good at adapting to different cultures, and host-country nationals educated in the United States are better able to fill the void and establish good communication with host-country personnel.[12] As a result of the economic crisis in 2009, a number of companies froze all international postings and called back most of their expatriates, arguing that they could not afford to keep expatriates abroad.

These arguments are flawed for a variety of reasons. By withdrawing most of their American staff, U.S. firms signal that international involvement is not important to their success or that firms from the United States can be successful without Americans developing intercultural communication skills. In many ways, this is admitting defeat and letting the world know that Americans have given up and are unable or unwilling to deal with the communication challenge. Withdrawing people from international posts also sends the signal that American firms have no staying power and are not interested in doing business over the long run. The competition—the Japanese, the Germans, the French, the Koreans—generally doesn't share that view. Many firms from those countries expect that their employees can adapt, function, and communicate in many different cultural environments. European firms expect that managers will speak at least one foreign language fluently. Increasingly, European companies expect a certain level of intercultural fluency and competence as well. To make sure that employees can function in the global environment, more and more companies provide intercultural training. German companies, for example, conduct regular seminars so that German managers can work effectively with partners from other European Union countries.[13] Volvo in Sweden has a Director for Intercultural Communication. The person has the task of ensuring that employees are interculturally competent.

Assumptions Concerning the Expatriate's Role and Effectiveness

The argument about the need for intercultural effectiveness also raises a question about the role and function of the expatriate. Is the main task of the expatriate to develop and manage opportunities for the firm, or is it to facilitate communication with headquarters so that managers at headquarters don't have to worry about foreign operations?

Another assumption is that a foreign manager in a foreign subsidiary who was educated in the country of headquarters will be more successful than will a citizen of the headquarters country. According to this view, for example, an Indian who was educated in Belgium will be more successful in the Indian subsidiary of a Belgian firm than a Belgian manager will be. But research has shown that a native-born foreign-educated person does not necessarily communicate better with host-country employees than does a person from the home country. The employees at headquarters may develop a false sense of security, thinking that they have taken care of all problems by hiring the Indian-born manager educated in Belgium. They assume that they have someone who is equally at home in both cultures and can communicate with both sides equally well.

They may not realize that the Indian may find himself or herself caught between the native and the headquarters cultures. How well the Indian will do in this setting will depend on professional status, professional skills, family background, intercultural competence skills, and degree of adaptation to the culture of Belgium. The Southeast Asian human resources (HR) manager of Motorola believes that an Indian who has been abroad—either as a student or as an employee—longer than three years will have a very hard time fitting back into the Indian work environment. The employee will have changed, and other Indians will pick up on the changes. Furthermore, in cultures where relationships are important, a manager who has been out of the country for several years may no longer have a network of connections.

Headquarters may select the Indian manager because he can relate so well to the people at headquarters, not realizing that because of that very quality he may have difficulty establishing credibility with Indian businesspeople. What assures the business community in India that the employee has not sold out to the Belgian firm? How can they be certain that he represents the interests of his native culture? In many ways, the better headquarters likes a foreign-born manager, the more his native country may mistrust him. As a result, there may be questions of trust and loyalty. In cultures in which loyalty is important, an employee working for a foreign firm may be somewhat suspect and therefore experience a decrease in his ability to communicate effectively.

In the international division organization, most people agree that:

- Cultural sensitivity and language are important.
- Managers must adapt to the culture.
- Technical expertise is not sufficient.[14]

Valuing Intercultural Communication Competence

Major disagreements occur over how to reach the goal of being a good intercultural communicator. *One of the biggest stumbling blocks in effective commnication is that intercultural sensitivity is considered necessary only for the international division.* The typical attitude in U.S. firms with international divisions is that only the people who are actively involved in international affairs on a regular basis need to be knowledgeable about the cultural priorities of the people they are dealing with. For the rest of the employees, such knowledge typically is not deemed necessary; it does not add to their performance. As a result, the firm remains fragmented into domestic and international divisions. With growing competition, improving global communication systems, and better education, this distinction becomes a hindrance rather than a help.

Businesspeople who have worked abroad often find challenges when they come back to headquarters. To some extent, their reintegration difficulties are related to reverse culture shock, but in many cases a returning expatriate may feel anxious about his or her future with the firm. To capture the knowledge and experience of returning expatriates, firms increasingly plan the return of expatriates in such a way that other employees can benefit from that knowledge.

In Focus

Tim Brandt, the operations manager of a major U.S. firm, has been in Spain for two years. Before that, he set up a joint venture in China and then worked with the subsidiary in Germany for some time. Each time, Tim has tried to learn the language so he can at least function in everyday life.

By any definition, he has been successful in the international field. At times, he is nervous about his career after his foreign assignment, but Tim's firm realizes that he has developed enough valuable expertise to play a major role in the international expansion of the firm. Tim probably will stay in Spain for another year, but headquarters is planning his return and has assigned a mentor to Tim to make the reentry easier. Tim's international experience, ability to speak Spanish and some German, understanding of several other cultures, and ability to adapt to and work in other cultures will be factors in his advancement at headquarters.

As the importance of international operations grows and international competition increases, firms need to reevaluate their view of international operations—in particular, their view of the importance of intercultural communication. The firms that will be successful are the ones that can adapt to different environments and understand the influence of culture on business behavior, such as negotiation.

Several firms are trying to meet that challenge by changing from an international division structure to a global structure.

The Global Firm

The Structure of a Global Firm

The word *global* appears increasingly in the literature in the place of *multinational* and *international,* and a number of companies have changed to a global structure. Confusingly, however, in some cases, the change is simply in the words, and there are no changes in the organizational structures and communication practices; companies refer to themselves as global because it sounds more cosmopolitan.

The differences between an international division structure and a global structure are, however, significant. Going global is not something that can be done overnight or just by changing the name or the stationery. In the change from an international division structure to a global structure, the international division disappears and international operations are integrated into the firm.

In a sense, the organizational structure has come full circle. The global organization chart resembles the organization chart for a domestic firm, with the difference being that the organization encompasses the globe.

The move to a global structure typically begins when international sales consistently account for 35 to 50 percent of overall sales. The move to a global structure is an outcome of a company's international success.

Global firms typically use one of three basic structures: a worldwide function format, a worldwide geographic/regional format, or a worldwide product format (see Exhibits 11.5 through 11.7). The structures can be mixed. For example, a firm may combine regional and product structures. A company also may use a matrix structure for its global approach.[15] The particular global structure a firm chooses depends on the product, the size of the firm, the extent of global operations, and the philosophy of management.

The important point is that regardless of the particular global structure, the firm does not divide operations into domestic and international. Operations are global, and any substructures are an outcome of the needs of the global perspective.

At first glance, the global structure looks very appealing. It does not always work, however, and is not always the optimal organizational form. If the various international and domestic parts of the firm are at different stages of development, production, and technology, the global structure may not get the expected results.[16]

For Shell, Unilever, and Coca-Cola, the global organization works because of the types of products they sell and manufacture. For other companies, the move may be premature or inappropriate because the product needs are different in different markets and because cultural adaptations are important. Wilson Sporting Goods, a firm that manufactures and sells sports equipment, decided that an international division structure was more advantageous because that structure gives more autonomy to the various subsidiaries and allows them to respond to specific market needs and trends more effectively.

For example, golf clubs and tennis rackets in Japan differ in their dimensions, center of gravity, and weight from U.S. dimensions. Exporting equipment from the United States without any modifications does not always work. While some R&D functions may be performed jointly, other operational functions may have different needs and should be developed separately. The products are differentiated enough in various markets to justify different approaches. This is a reality that Coca-Cola does not have to face.

Sometimes the people in a market may reject certain product adaptations for reasons of image. For many years, the Japanese argued that one of the reasons American cars did not sell well in Japan was the location of the steering wheel. American car companies had not moved the wheel to the right side to accommodate driving on the left side of the road. However, when the CEO of a Japanese company who had just bought a BMW was asked whether he would prefer the steering wheel on the right side, he said: "But it is a BMW. Where else would the steering wheel be?" Clearly, having the steering wheel on the left side was a status symbol.

Communication in a Global Organization

What are the implications of a global structure for communication? A shift to a global structure does not make a global person out of a domestic person. A person who in the past exclusively dealt with the domestic market may know Sweden but not know or not care about Hong Kong or Singapore. If the change to a global structure is not prepared carefully, there will be a lot of confusion, bad decisions, and poor communication. The following case illustrates some of these issues.

In Focus

Leisure Wheels Inc., located originally in Dallas, Texas, changed to a global structure in 1991–1992. The change came as a result of the growing importance of the international side of the business. It was an attempt to support further growth and eliminate the "us versus them" feeling that was prevalent in the international division structure. However, a cultural change of this magnitude takes time. Old-timers from the domestic side still had a more domestic outlook at this firm.

In the reorganization, Leisure Wheels Inc. split up the international division. Most of the employees went into specific operations areas, and as a result, the international division was integrated into specific functional areas. Today, employees from the original international division still communicate regularly with each other and keep each other informed; there is still a common bond that is based on common concerns and experiences.

In the old international division structure, a manager knew exactly who needed to receive copies on what issues. Today, a person in marketing research does not automatically send copies to someone in production, sales, finance, or marketing. Karen, the manager of international operations and analysis, for example, came out of the international division. She regularly and automatically e-mailed everyone in the international division. Today, she e-mails only her boss since she is very aware of the number of e-mails that flood everyone's mailbox. It is up to her boss to inform other people who need and could use the information. But the process is no longer automatic. As a result, information is

(continued)

getting lost. Some managers have begun to sense the need for regular and more systematic communication to improve the efficiency of operations. For example, currently, two people from two different units of the same company may go to visit the same dealer in Spain within a two-week time frame. They do not know about each other's visit and do not know about the purpose of each other's trip. There is no central posting on who is going where for what purpose. It is easy to see that this is not very functional. If a marketing person goes, and a few days later a salesperson goes, and after that perhaps a product development person goes, the company spends a lot of effort, time, and money but does not spend resources very effectively and does not communicate with the dealers in Spain effectively.

As the change to a global structure occurred, management realized the need for intercultural communication training, but there was some disagreement about what exactly was needed. The company finally decided that all employees needed training in intercultural business communication and the environment of the foreign subsidiaries. In the first phase of the training program, the company wanted employees to gain a practical understanding of the work and environment in the various foreign subsidiaries. For example, how are dealers in Spain set up? What are their constraints? Who are their customers? What are their concerns?

Research supports this approach. Daft and Lengel found that employees at lower levels need more technical information and training.[17] After the initial training and information, more detailed intercultural communication training is helpful, but the training always should relate to the context of the specific business.

When the executives at Leisure Wheels Inc. first discussed the move to a global corporation, it all looked so easy. Only later did they realize how much work was involved.

Frequently, employees with a domestic background going on their first international trips feel that there is not much to international business, a feeling expressed as, "If you have done one market, you have done them all." These people know the product inside and out, but they have no background in the international market, international distribution systems, international sensitivities, and intercultural communication issues. They tend to evaluate international procedures on the basis of their domestic expertise and their self-reference criterion. They judge everything on the basis of their own backgrounds.

Typically, the instant experts come back with all sorts of ideas for improvement without thinking through the intercultural implications and ramifications of their suggestions. They may think, "If those people in Nigeria would only adopt the way we do things, their problems would be solved easily." They do not realize that this is not the way "they" are doing things and that furthermore there may be very valid reasons why "they" do things differently.

Successful communication in a global firm requires a solid and well-thought-out structure for the communication process, and that structure must be communicated globally. Ramrath, the former president of GE Plastics Pacific Ltd., points out that in globalization a worldwide communication network is essential. He insists that all employees must develop a global attitude and have a sense of adventure; without it, he warns, the venture will not be successful.[18] A global firm requires coordination, communication, and unity of command. It works best if it is supported by a strong corporate culture.

The worldwide **functional structure** does well at unifying command (see Exhibit 11.5). Worldwide operations report to the appropriate functional managers, such as marketing, finance, and personnel, at headquarters. The difficulty is that communication can occur along rather narrow and specialized paths. A functional manager may not have the overview of the whole situation because he or she deals

EXHIBIT 11.5
Global Functional
Structure

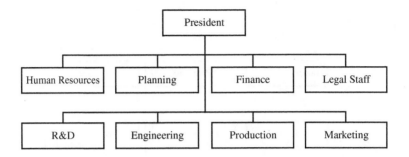

only with one functional aspect. To be successful in this environment, managers from the various functional areas must keep each other informed on a regular basis. They must communicate with the people in their areas of specialization around the globe but also must communicate with managers from other functional areas to coordinate efforts. Many firms spend a great amount of effort on cross-functional training of their management staff to improve operations. The process requires sensitivity and adaptation to the different cultural orientations and goals of the various functional areas.

The **geographic structure** coordinates operations within a region but often does not pay enough attention to coordination between regions (see Exhibit 11.6). This structure facilitates adaptation to local and regional conditions. There are some similarities between a multinational firm that has country subsidiaries and a global company with a geographic structure, but in the latter the emphasis is on regions rather than countries. The individual countries do not report to headquarters but instead report to regional offices. Communication with the various cultural groups within a region improves, but communication between regions may be weak because of different languages and ethnic rivalries. The communication system may be fragmented, and it may be difficult to pull all the regions together to exchange ideas and share resources.

In the worldwide **product structure** (see Exhibit 11.7), global communication relating to one product is efficient, but the communication between various product groups can be weak and duplication of effort is common because each product may have its own sales force and marketing channels. As a result, foreign

EXHIBIT 11.6
Global Geographic
Structure

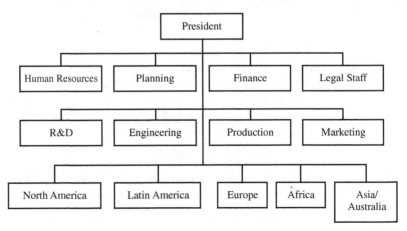

EXHIBIT 11.7
Global Product
Structure

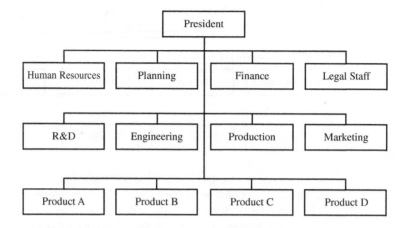

partners may get the impression that the company does not coordinate its efforts very well and that communications are affected negatively by competition and fragmentation.

In Focus

Nestlé, a Swiss company, is an example of a global company with a mixture of product and geographic structure. Nestlé organizes its products into divisions, such as Food and Waters. The Food Division is broken into three zones: the Americas, Europe, and AOA (Africa, Oceana, and Asia). Each of these zones is subdivided into geographic regions run by a Market Head. The Waters Division is totally separate from the Food business. It has its own CEO and management team based in Paris. Nestlé Waters is divided into five zones: North America, Central and South America, Europe, Africa, and Asia with Australia. Country managers report to the Zone Heads. The general manager for the Levant, which includes Lebanon, Jordan, and Syria, reports to the Chief Operating Officer of The Africa–Middle East Zone. The general manager for the Levant is a British national who lived in Australia for many years. His wife is Australian. Before coming to Lebanon, he was the general manager for the food division in Uzbekistan. His current boss, the Market Head for Africa and the Middle East, is an Italian stationed in Dubai.

As a firm becomes a global firm, the changes required for communication will be difficult for personnel at headquarters but even more difficult for people in the field. In the international division structure, employees of the foreign subsidiaries simply had to contact people in the international division; they could expect that the international division would take care of problems. Now employees in the subsidiaries must contact a variety of people: product development, production, marketing, finance, and sales. In many cases, they do not know those people personally. If the company has high turnover in personnel, which is very typical in the United States, the communication problem is exacerbated because a communicator without a background in the company and without intercultural communication skills will have difficulty structuring the message appropriately and selecting the optimal channel.

An effective global structure requires intercultural communication training for many people, at all levels of the organization, over and over again. When the product development team sits down, its members cannot consider just domestic issues; they have to think and plan globally. An advertising campaign cannot be planned with only the domestic market in mind; the team must consider cultural, legal, and regulatory requirements in other markets. Although people may have the major responsibility for a particular segment of the advertising campaign, everyone needs to be aware of the overall strategy and know what is going on worldwide. They all have to overcome their differences and work as a team.

The communication requirements are even more severe if R&D and production are spread over several locations all over the world. A number of firms have R&D labs in several countries. In a global firm, those labs do have to coordinate and communicate with each other. This does not mean they cannot adapt to specific markets, but it does mean they must keep each other informed and cooperate rather than compete for resources. Each segment must have in mind the best interest of the firm as a whole.

Global organizations do not distinguish between domestic and international advertising budgets. The voice of the international side of the business is heard together with the domestic voice, and the money is spent where it will do the most good. This requires that the managers from around the world communicate with each other. They have to understand each other's needs, priorities, and ways of doing things. Without a background in intercultural communication and respect for each other's cultural orientations, this cooperation will not happen.

The people involved in finance, marketing, and product development at headquarters must have a global outlook and understand the thought processes, customs, and values of the cultures in which the firm does business. They need to understand the cultural foundation for saving, investing, and borrowing money. A global structure takes a tremendous amount of commitment. It requires regular meetings, frequent communication, and travel. Only so much can be done by e-mailing, faxing, telephoning, and teleconferencing. A global structure costs money, but the improved strategies can increase profits.

For the global structure to be successful, managers need to have a solid understanding of the dynamics of multicultural groups. In a global firm, people from a variety of professional and cultural backgrounds work together. Unless those people are trained in intercultural communication, the groups may not be effective.[19]

A global structure requires effective communication among the employees at headquarters and then full integration of communication strategies on a global basis. The person getting ahead in this environment is the person who can think and act globally. The staffing in a true global firm is geocentric—the best person will get the job regardless of geographic and national background. The person who will get to the top in that environment needs to have global experience and solid intercultural communication skills. Global experience is no longer an extra, a nice thing to have, but absolutely essential in a global firm.

Few firms today are truly global. Firms must function under the constraints of visas, work permits, government regulations, and import–export restrictions that can hinder globalization. In many ways, the global firm has outgrown the existing political structure, but national laws and different cultural orientations still influence internal and external communications. The North American Free Trade Agreement (NAFTA), ASEAN, and the European Union are examples of how national governments are working with each other and with businesses to remove national barriers and create a global business environment.

Which language should a global businessperson speak (also see Chapter 2)? Many businesspeople in the United States are quick to point out that English is the business language of the world; therefore, English is sufficient. However, a truly global business strategy requires cultural sensitivity, the ability to understand the other side, and the ability to communicate with people from a variety of backgrounds. Being able to speak the native language of the business partner will help even if the foreign counterpart speaks English. For example, one of the author's universities has exchange programs with a business school in Metz, France. Metz is in the northwestern region of France, a traditionally industrial area. Today, the area is known for specialization in logistics. Mercedes is building the Smart car there. The Smart is a very small vehicle designed to take up little space and, therefore, is particularly good for parking in crowded urban centers. Mercedes is headquartered in Stuttgart, Germany. The official language is English. Yet, in the day-to-day activities, most people speak French. Historically, the area went back and forth between Germany and France, and the local language still spoken by many people is a German dialect. To function in this environment, managers need to speak French. English may be the official language, but it is not sufficient. To really get a feel for the area, some German would be helpful as well.

As the chapter on culture and language pointed out, there is a vast difference between being reasonably functional in a language and being bilingual and bicultural. A person who speaks only English will miss much of the background culture and nuances of a conversation. By limiting contacts to people who speak English, a manager will limit his or her exposure to other opinions of native people who do not speak English. The manager may get a very distorted picture of what is going on.

A foreign businessperson who appears fluent in English also may present a problem. The surface knowledge, the speed of speaking, and a good accent may hide the fact that that person may miss many of the fine points that may be important in doing business. An additional problem is the definition of *fluent*. For example, if a businessperson from the United States claims fluency in a language, that can mean anything from being very good to speaking a little. When a businessperson from the Netherlands claims fluency in a foreign language, that typically means excellent use of the language.

The need for language and culture sensitivity is similar in both the international division structure and the global structure. The big difference is that in the global structure many more people need this orientation. In comparison to the international division structure, the need for international knowledge in the global structure is pushed down to lower levels in the organization and encompasses more people.

In summary, to make the switch from international to multinational to global is easy on paper. In many cases, the switch is semantic and nothing changes in the day-to-day operations. Firms that become truly global find that it takes time, training, patience, and detailed attention to communication.

Implications of Cultural Aspects of Business Structures for Communication in an International Firm

So far in this chapter, we have looked at the implications of international expansion and organizational structure for intercultural communication. Some of the communication challenges in this process are universal; a Japanese or a Chilean firm that expands its international operations will face some of the same communication problems.

However, international firms do not communicate only with their own subsidiaries where they still have some control over language, policies, and practices. They also communicate with independent businesses in the countries where their subsidiaries are located. They communicate with third-country businesses. For example, the Thai subsidiary of a firm from the United States may do business with the Thai subsidiary of a French firm. In that case, the communication must take into consideration American, Thai, and French concerns. In addition, subsidiaries communicate with the governments of their countries. Even if a company has a firm company language policy and practices polycentric staffing, the interface with other cultures is ever present, and the firm must deal with different values, attitudes, and practices, not to mention legal requirements.

Different cultures look at organizational purposes and structures differently. The way they view organizational patterns influences their business structures and communication policies and practices. Chie Nakane, a Japanese anthropologist, contrasts U.S. and Japanese firms in that context.[20] She argues that U.S. firms emphasize credentials and qualifications, which she calls attributes, whereas Japanese firms emphasize a common context, which she calls frame. In some countries—Middle Eastern countries are an example—the family is the foundation of business organizations. In the formerly communist countries, an authoritarian centralized system still influences the structure and communication of a firm. Let us look at these organizational patterns and their implications for communication.

Communication in an Organization Based on Credentials

People in the United States, Nakane argues, identify themselves by professional attributes such as job qualifications or credentials; they are accountants, salespersons, engineers, or carpenters.[21] These job labels give Americans their professional identity, and they can take these professional credentials with them. A certified public accountant (CPA) license, for example, is valid in most states in the United States and is recognized in several other countries. More and more workers want to have portable credentials. Recently, for example, salespeople have been talking about a sales certificate that would be based on specific educational and work credentials.

Credentials are influenced by cultural priorities. The labels do not necessarily have the same meaning in different cultures. The label *engineer* does not mean the same educational level and expertise in all countries. Germans make clear distinctions between various levels of engineers. Russians use the term *medical doctor* much more loosely than Western countries do. One credential that is almost universally understood is the MBA. As a result, universities in countries from China to Mexico to Portugal have established MBA programs because the MBA is an internationally recognized credential. Everyone knows that the MBA is a generalist management degree at the graduate level, and as a result, international hiring and evaluation of qualifications are made easier. For example, Germany for many years awarded the Staatsexamen as the official degree at the end of one's studies. As long as most business was domestic, this presented no problems. However, with the growth of international business, people from other countries began to wonder what the Staatsexamen was. They did not have any idea how to categorize the qualifications. During the last few years, several German universities have added the MBA program to their offerings.

In an effort to encourage mobility across Europe and create a European identity, the European Union is encouraging standardization of university degrees: three years for an undergraduate degree and an additional two years for graduate work. The changes were officially announced in the Bologna Protocol in 1999.

Credentials contribute to the identity of an American businessperson. The identification with the firm for which Americans work is only part of their existence; it is not all-encompassing. In the United States, an employee can enter and leave an organization at any level. A person can enter at the beginner level at the bottom or, as has happened at IBM, Kodak, ADM, and Home Depot, at the level of CEO. What counts are the qualifications the employee has, some of which may be credentials.

People want the job that best corresponds to their qualifications. In results-oriented cultures, if that means leaving the firm, that's okay. In fact, most new graduates in the United States stay with their first companies for only three to four years. Career counselors tell them that they should reevaluate their employment situation on a regular basis and jump if a better opportunity presents itself. The emphasis is on individual advancement and individual opportunities, as discussed in Chapter 3. That, of course, has implications for training. In that environment, training will be job-specific and brief. The employer wants to get some work out of the employee before the employee leaves the firm, and the employee wants to develop job attributes that are portable and not just company-specific.

The emphasis on portable credentials and individual achievement influences communication within the firm. For example, if an employee is not absolutely loyal to the firm, how much should he or she be involved in sensitive discussions and issues? The tendency will be to concentrate on job-specific information and limit communication. As a result, it is more difficult to establish teamwork, which requires mutual trust and openness. Firms that operate within a low-context culture try to protect their confidential information through contracts. For example, an employee who has access to confidential information and leaves the firm may have to sign a statement specifying that he or she will not use any of that information. In these circumstances, the emphasis in communication may be on safeguarding information rather than on long-term education, training, and the sharing of information to reach company goals.

In Focus

Rebecca Martin has just finished her degree in international business. She sent out about 50 applications and finally found a job with an import–export firm. It is not exactly what she wanted, but it is a good first job. She really wants to be employed by a big international firm that offers an opportunity to work abroad. She plans to stay with the company for about four years, long enough to get some good practical background in the nuts and bolts of international business. During that time, she also would like to get an MBA with an emphasis on international finance. She believes that the combination of practical experience and a master's degree should set her up very well for her second job. And that one, she is determined, will be with a big international firm.

She will work hard at the import–export firm, but she is not dedicating her life to that firm. Her loyalty ultimately is to her own career. While she is with the firm, she will evaluate regularly whether she is progressing at a rate that will make her competitive for the next job. Networking will help her to be aware of opportunities.

People who come from a cultural environment where relationships, commitment, and loyalty are important values may be puzzled by the constant personnel changes in U.S. firms. If Masataka Hyashi from Nagoya, Japan, talks about the possibilities of a joint venture to Patricia Lesch in Chicago today, there is no guarantee that Patricia Lesch will still be there a few weeks from now. When Hyashi contacts Chicago again, Lesch may have left the firm for better opportunities and someone else will have taken her place. The Japanese, for whom the building of personal relationships is a crucial aspect of doing business, may find the personnel changes in U.S. firms disorienting.

The focus on credentials reinforces a cultural leaning toward equal opportunity, merit, individualism, and merit orientation. Such an orientation influences how people conduct their job search, what they put on their résumés, and how they interact with co-workers (also see Chapter 10).

Communication in an Organization Based on Context

The organization based on context is best exemplified in Japan. Japanese organizations, according to Nakane, are organized on the basis of frame, or group belonging, a concept that goes back to the idea of household, *ie,* and emphasizes the importance of the group over the individual.[22] The Japanese male is first and foremost an employee of his firm. He is a Toyota man, a Mitsubishi man, or a Komatsu man rather than an engineer or an accountant. He identifies with the firm, the corporate household. Credentials are valid within that context but don't mean much outside the context. The lack of portable credentials limits job mobility, but it also provides a certain degree of security.

The employee is part of a family that takes care of its members; in return, the employee supports the goals of the firm. The system is based on reciprocity, or *amae* (see

Chapter 4). The concept of *amae* means that a person willingly takes care of another person but also is willing to be taken care of by that person. *Amae* establishes mutual dependency. Nobody can do things alone. As we discussed in earlier chapters, the Japanese are willing to put personal considerations after group considerations. Harmony of the group is considered more important. As a result, communication avoids the open conflict and confrontation that are common in more individualistic cultures.

Within the frame or context, employees know how to act and behave, and the expectations reinforce cultural priorities. They know their place; they know what to say, how to address someone, and how deeply to bow. As soon as that familiar environment changes, the Japanese are at a loss. The culture has not given them the background or experience to deal with strangers. Japanese are ill at ease in new situations and with strangers. They do not know how to address the other person, and they do not know where they stand in the hierarchy vis-à-vis the other person, aspects that lead to a certain level of insecurity. The result is incongruous communication behavior.

For example, in his group, Ishido Tanaka is polite, considerate, and nonassertive. When he is confronted with the world outside the group, the familiar norms and guidelines are gone. How does he deal with this environment? In a variety of ways. One way is to pretend that the other side does not exist, creating psychological space in crowded conditions. The other way is behavior that is at odds with the principles of behavior within the group. The Japanese on subways can be remarkably aggressive and impolite. Pushing with one's elbows, forcing one's way in, using rude language, and spitting are typical signs of behavior that would be unacceptable within the group but are tolerated outside the group.

When it comes to hiring, a company based on group identity will look for someone who will fit into the group and bring prestige to the firm. Therefore, many Japanese firms pay more attention to the university attended than to the subject studied. A fitting personality is more important than are specific skills. After all, technical aspects can be learned; it is much harder to change or form the personality and character. Even though with economic problems and restructuring of industry the practice of lifetime employment is weakening, the concept is still strong. A Japanese employee is supposed to fit in and take his place. He is part of the firm.

In Focus

Mitsui Trading Company hires about 100 new employees every year. In an effort to select the very best people, meaning the ones who will fit into the company the best, Mitsui Trading interviews 3,000 applicants. All in all, the company will conduct at least 5,000 interviews. In the first round, an applicant will have a half-hour interview. If the candidate advances, he or she will interview with more senior people. In the last round of the selection process, candidates interview with top executives. This process costs huge sums of money, but Mitsui Trading thinks in the long term. The money is well spent if it ensures that the applicant will become part of the Mitsui family.

As we discussed in Chapter 10, this emphasis on fitting in is evident in Japanese résumés and the job interview process. The résumé emphasizes names of schools and universities rather than specific courses and grades on exams. Companies are willing to spend many hours on interviewing potential employees to ensure that they hire someone who fits in and has the "right" character. Specific credentials are seldom highlighted.

There have always been Japanese who would leave a job and go somewhere else, but the professional move was always downward to a smaller and less prestigious firm. This is just beginning to change. When a senior official from Toyota had been hired for a leading position by another major Japanese firm, that made headline news, indicating how rare such changes are even today. However, mobility is on the rise. Increasingly, Japanese executives insist that Japanese firms need to promote on the basis of merit and encourage young talents if Japan is to be a viable competitive player in the future. Joint ventures with foreign firms and foreign buyouts also have contributed to employee turnover. When DaimlerChrysler bought a controlling share in Mitsubishi Motors a few years ago, many Japanese workers were laid off (also see Chapter 12).[23]

Since one can assume in the Japanese context that people will be with the firm for a long time, it is worth training them in a wide variety of jobs. For example, several Japanese firms regularly send employees to the Thunderbird School of International Management in Glendale, Arizona. During their studies, the Japanese employees remain on the payroll of their firms and the firms pay the tuition. These firms have decided that the investment will pay many returns. The firms are not interested primarily in their employees getting a degree, although that is expected. They are willing to support the employees because they hope that the employees will learn how Americans think and are motivated. In addition, they hope that their employees will build relationships with people who will be in leading positions in the United States in the years to come. This kind of investment makes sense only if an employee will remain with the firm.

If employees will stay in the firm for the duration of their careers, it also makes sense to involve them in making decisions and sharing information. After all, they have a stake in the firm. The adversarial labor–management process in American firms is replaced with a more cooperative approach. The feeling is that we are in this together; we must work problems out, and we must cooperate for the benefit of all sides. As we discussed earlier in this book, the building of group cohesiveness frequently occurs after hours in bars. Japanese managers have been known to receive lavish expense accounts to entertain colleagues and partners. Even here changes are occurring. For example, Japan's biggest brokerage, Nomura Securities and Mitsui Company, halved its entertainment budget in the last decade. The Bank of Tokyo-Mitsubishi, formed by a merger, spends less on entertainment now than either of the two banks did as separate businesses.

Although job mobility in Japan has increased, much of the old sentiment remains. The Japanese example of a business organization that is based on group belonging illustrates the connection of culture, organizational structures, and communication. Seniority matters in promotions, and therefore more people tend to reach positions with fairly high titles in the firm. Titles matter; they give face. The differentiation of people is apparent in the job duties rather than the job titles. As a result of cultural influences on promotions, the organizational chart tends to be broader at the top than it is in many American firms. Communication emphasizes the well-being of the firm and harmony between employees rather than individual achievement. Because of these long-cherished values, layoffs in the late 1990s and the early years of the 21st century hit Japanese employees particularly hard. They believed in the company as their family; they were willing to work long hours in return for security. That dream has been shattered for many. It remains to be seen what the long-term effect will be on employee loyalty and dedication to the corporation.

Today one can observe a growing difference between Japanese employees working for Japanese companies and Western companies. Japanese managers working in Japanese firms tend to emphasize the traditional Japanese values of harmony, group orientation, and lifetime employment. They are reluctant to voice criticism openly of co-workers or their companies. Japanese managers working for Western companies, on the other hand, talk more openly about their individual career ambitions, their achievements, and their complaints about work issues. They are much more focused on performance standards and measurements of productivity. The contrast became very clear when one of the authors interviewed managers from both groups in Japan. It will be interesting to see whether these attitudes will influence the general Japanese workplace in the long run.

Japanese firms going into low-context cultures initially were confused by the adversarial approach of employees and the separation of work time and private or family time. U.S. employees, and Europeans too for that matter, were not willing to sacrifice their evenings and weekends for the betterment of the firm. In Japan, in contrast, employees are expected to spend time with co-workers after business hours. Typically, Japanese expatriates take this practice with them. At a Japanese subsidiary in the Midwest in the United States, for example, the Japanese employees tend to stay at the office long after the American employees have left for the evening.

The organization based on context reinforces cultural orientation toward collectivism, blending in, obligations, and loyalty rather than individual rights.

Communication in an Organization Based on Family Orientation

Business in the Middle East is based on the concept of the family. According to the *Qur'an,* a family must take care of its members. A family has a holy obligation toward its members. The family orientation seems to fit the Japanese group structure, but the group in Japan does not necessarily include the blood family. The Middle East looks at the family as including all blood relatives.

In contrast to a Japanese firm, which emphasizes the group and consensus building, a firm in the Middle East is ruled by the senior male member of the family. It is much more authoritarian and autocratic than is seen in the harmony-based approach of Japan. Even when a senior manager asks for advice, family members understand that the senior member has the cultural right to make decisions. He may listen but does not have to. Americans hire on the basis of specific qualifications; the Japanese, on the basis of character; a Middle Eastern firm must take care of family members first. If outsiders come into the company, they need to be part of the same social network, and they are expected to bring the necessary connections to other firms and government agencies.

These firms do not have official organizational charts. For outsiders, it is therefore impossible to determine who reports to whom and who holds what positions. Female family members may have indirect power but may not show up in any official capacity. Unless an outsider develops close relationships over a long period of time, he or she may not understand the dynamics of the communication patterns and may miss crucial elements of the business activities and negotiation processes.

A successful businessman may start several new businesses, one for each son, rather than expand the existing business. By doing this, he can ensure that after his death each son will be the senior member in his firm. This setup creates clear lines of ownership and communication and prevents squabbles over who is entitled to do what. It also can create a unique communication code that is difficult for outsiders to decipher. In American firms, communication codes are more readily transferable. Pezeshkpur, a well-known author, states that Middle Easterners function best if the lines of authority and power are clear.[24] The uncertainty connected with negotiating and compromising is culturally more difficult.

Businesspeople in the United States like to toss ideas back and forth and reach a compromise or consensus after arguing. Middle Easterners prefer for someone to be in charge and make the final decisions. The family orientation and the emphasis on seniority meet these expectations. In this environment, the establishment of authority through appropriate introductions, credentials, and connections is crucial for success. Business is conducted at a personal rather than an institutional level. The development of trust and personal relationships is necessary. To develop these relationships, potential partners exchange gifts and favors resulting in a whole network of complicated connections. The practice of reciprocal gift giving can lead to bribery and extortion; however, traditionally gifts tended to be fairly small. It seems the problem is not so much the gift itself but the interpretation of the gift by those who do not understand the cultural reason for it.

One could argue that the pattern of family businesses is similar throughout the world; however, in Western countries the family business is one model among many. In Middle Eastern countries, it is the predominant business form and therefore represents the business environment and climate to a much greater extent.

In Focus

Esa Ali just received his undergraduate degree in marketing from an American university and is ready to go back to Jordan where his family owns a small company that manufactures souvenirs. During his studies, Esa had two internships with companies that cater to tourists. He also did a study on marketing channels and market research. He would have liked to stay a few more years in the United States, but the family told him they needed him. His father was getting

(continued)

on in years, and business was down. Esa was a bit nervous; he had not seen his family in over four years. What would they be like? What did they think? He knew that he had changed, but what about his brothers? Had they changed, too? Esa had prepared himself well. He was enthusiastic and saw a number of opportunities that could be developed.

In the first meeting of the male members who were involved in the business, everyone welcomed him back but nobody asked for his advice. When he finally spoke up, it became clear that they did not listen to what he had to say: "They would think things over"; "Yes, they had tried that and it did not work"; "Theories might be good, but this was reality." As the meeting went on, he was wondering why he had come back.

During the next few weeks, his brothers voiced their concerns that he did not seem to have learned anything. Why did he not contribute? Now he was totally confused. First they did not listen, and now they were accusing him of not contributing. As time went by, he began to be more conscious of the dynamics in the group. The father and the oldest brother clearly had the say, but another of his brothers managed to get his suggestions out on the table, and frequently the father and the oldest brother would go along. Esa decided that he would talk unofficially and in private to both his father and his oldest brother to lay some groundwork for changes. Esa was convinced that some of the family members were poorly prepared to perform the jobs they held. They needed some training. Most of the communication with suppliers and customers went through old established channels. Although Esa knew that the personal relationship was important, he also was convinced that modern technology could speed up some things. This was a family business, but not everyone contributed. One of his brothers hardly ever came to work. They desperately needed someone to take over the finances, but nobody in the family was very interested in that side of the business. Esa suggested hiring someone who was not a family member, but that did not get very far. His father would not hear of it. Finally, a cousin who had studied finance was asked to do the job.

During his studies, Esa had become used to voicing his opinions openly and questioning others. He liked to analyze problems and examine possible solutions. It was not easy to accept his place in the family, but he realized that was the only way he could ever be effective.

Communication in an Organization Based on Political Principles

Organizational principles in formerly communist countries are different altogether. Some people argue that there is no point discussing the communist system since most of those countries are not communist any longer. However, the influence of the communist system has been so strong and has shaped organizations to such an extent that the results will endure for a long time. People doing business in that part of the world will have to deal with the remnants of communist attitudes. For example, China, a major trading partner of the United States, Europe, Japan, and the Middle East, is still communist even though on the surface economic centralization has given way to a market-oriented economy.

In the communist system, the business organization is based on the concept of collective ownership and the absolute right to a job. In the case of China, this was formerly expressed in the concept of the iron rice bowl. Twenty years ago, although the rewards were minimal, an employee of a firm did not have to worry about unemployment or the basic needs of life. Furthermore, except for top party people, nobody had much. The business organization was not governed by business principles but first and foremost by political considerations. The system created a mentality of dependency in which people had little motivation and were not willing to take risks. The iron rice bowl is really a thing of the past in China. The biggest practitioners—the huge state-owned enterprises in heavy industry—have laid off and retired many workers. The old support systems no longer function, but new institutions such as insurance companies have been slow to develop.

Today, the Chinese economy has three parts. One is represented by the risk-oriented entrepreneurs who seize every business opportunity that presents itself. This group is fast-growing. Another group consists of those who work for foreign firms and joint ventures. Many of those people are well educated, and they aim at attaining a Western affluent lifestyle. The third group consists of those who are still working for the state-owned sector; this remains by far the largest sector of the economy, including village, township, county, provincial, and national organizations. Increasingly, these people have less and less access to economic resources. So far, employees have had job security in most cases, but they are falling behind in their standard of living.

Communication in these three sectors is very different. In the private companies, Chinese managers and employees are beginning to take greater responsibility for their work. They are expected to show initiative and be flexible. They earn easily ten times what a worker in a state-run enterprise gets, but they also have more responsibility and incur greater risks. Frequently, Chinese employees in private firms and joint ventures are Western-educated. They want the trappings of a Western lifestyle. Young urban Chinese wear fashionable Western clothes, they have breakfast at Starbuck's, and their apartments are equipped with air conditioners.

The typical traditional top-down communication of the state-run enterprise is giving way to a more open communication style. An outsider who goes to China to do business needs to examine what kind of firm she or he is dealing with and adjust her or his communication pattern to the specific circumstances.

One cannot talk about Chinese employees in general; one needs to specify the term more clearly. Is an employee a Chinese-educated person working for a state-run enterprise? Is she or he working for a Western firm? Is she or he Western-educated but working for a private Chinese firm? Is she or he Western-educated but working on an expatriate contract for a Western firm? Is she or he Western-educated, and has returned to China where she or he currently works for a Western firm? In the last case, the employee would not receive the same pay as the expatriate. All these Chinese employees have different expectations, different communication styles, and to some extent different priorities.

At the same time, a Western businessperson needs to realize that even in private companies business practices are influenced strongly by the government. On the surface, business may be Westernized; in reality, the Communist party still has a lot of power.

As the formerly communist economies become more market-oriented, people are eager to reap the profits but are not necessarily willing to accept the responsibility for efficiency and take the risk of failure. A number of Western firms that have gone to countries of the former Soviet Union must deal with that attitude. In the case of one firm, the American owner found it was very difficult to get information from the employees in Russia—even the most factual and neutral information. Information is power, and to part with it may not be wise, as was discussed in Chapter 8. Employees may also fear that the information they give to the owner could be used against them.

Because in the past the Soviet government provided raw materials and took care of selling the manufactured products, their accounting and financial systems are underdeveloped. It is not just that the technical systems are weak; more importantly, the concepts are not clear. Generally, employees understand the term *profit*, but they have a hard time seeing that a profit must be earned, that the production and the sales must be there before one can enjoy the profits. The laws of the Soviet Union contributed to that lack of understanding. For example, in the 1930s a law was passed that declared that anyone who bought a product from the state and sold it for a higher price was engaging in *speculation*. Speculation was considered not business but immoral profiteering. No wonder the distribution of goods was a huge problem. The definition of profit as profiteering is deeply engrained even today. It goes through all age groups and educational levels. There is always something suspicious about a person who makes a living in the distribution channel. In addition, people have a hard time understanding that one has to invest and build capital before one can reap profits. The following case illustrates how difficult it can be to explain basic business concepts to people who are new to a market economy.

In Focus

When Nestlé entered Uzbekistan a few years ago, it formed a joint venture with NAFOSAT, a local state-run dairy company. The Soviet dairy production had collapsed totally, and Nestlé had to build the dairy industry from nothing. The farmers have a contract with Nestlé to deliver milk that meets Nestlé's strict standards. In return, Nestlé helps the dairy farmers with the raising and feeding of cattle. The Uzbek farmers own 50 percent of NAFOSAT, or about 2.5 percent of the joint venture. Nestlé business will show a loss in the early years of establishment until the volumes grow. NAFOSAT's business was not and is not in good shape. Before the joint venture was formed, NAFOSAT was close to bankruptcy.

In July 2002, the shareholders' annual general meeting was held for NAFOSAT. Since Nestlé is the largest shareholder, it was agreed that the meeting would take place in the company's factory in Namangan. At the meeting, the local shareholders became very angry and wanted to know where their profits were. Martin Woolnough, the manager for Nestlé in Uzbekistan, faced the crowd. He knew this was not going to be easy, but Nestlé was in Uzbekistan for the long haul. It was absolutely crucial that these farmers understood the concept of profit and realize that nobody had stolen their money. Martin likes to tell stories that his audience can relate to. Here is what he said.

"Let's all build a restaurant in the field next door. Please look out the windows at the field across the road. Let's imagine that all of us in this room were friends and we decided that it was worth building a restaurant there. Let's imagine it would cost USD 100 to build this restaurant and that in order to raise the money, we all contributed $1 each. Okay?

"So, it takes us one year to build our restaurant . . . Would we expect our $1 investment to have made any money for us yet? No, of course not. To attract customers, we hire a good chef, but business is a bit slow to start with and we find that after the first year, instead of making a profit we make a loss. How will we pay for the loss? I guess we could borrow money from the bank, or maybe each of us could provide additional funds. Since we do not have any extra money, we decide to get a loan at the bank. What about our initial $1? Has it made us any money yet? Of course not.

But we still own a restaurant, and if it were sold, *maybe* we could get our dollar back. However, we have worked very hard, and we don't want to sell it now, do we?

"As each year goes by, our restaurant becomes more and more popular, and after about three years we make our first profit. Does that mean that every owner can now get a share of the profit? Of course not; we still have to repay the bank the money we needed when we were making a loss. What about our initial investment of $1 each? What's it worth now? Well, that depends on the *value* of our business—do we just own a restaurant building and equipment, or do we also have a proven way of earning profit? What if our chef is the best in the region and people have started coming from miles around to eat our *plov* [a local Uzbek rice-based dish]? We have become famous for our restaurant. Now we own more than just buildings, don't we? Maybe other people would see our restaurant, and a rich local man might come and offer us a great price for our restaurant.

"What if he offered us $200 for the lot? Excellent! If we sell it, we would each get USD 2. Great, but does it mean we have really made USD 1 yet on our initial investment? *Only if we sell* . . . but we don't want to.

"Clearly, in the years ahead, if our restaurant continues to do well each year, then we can expect to make a good profit each year as well as keep our initial investment safe (and growing). We could expect a share of the profit to be paid to us as the owners each year, but would this be the best use of the profit? What if we decided to keep investing the profit to redecorate and expand our restaurant? Why would we do that? Well, our primary interest is to see our business grow both in the physical buildings and equipment but also in the unseen value that our business is worth—the price someone else would pay for it. But to make the restaurant grow, we need to use a big part of the profit to improve and update it." The crowd listened and nodded. Martin was successful in explaining a complicated principle because he was able to see the issue from the Uzbek side. They could relate to the story; it made sense to them.[25]

Summary

An international firm, no matter what its own organizational structure is, must deal with a variety of business structures around the world. As companies expand internationally, their communication needs change. A domestic firm has communication needs very different from those of an international firm. An international firm with an international division faces the challenge of competition between domestic and international divisions. A global firm integrates international operations throughout the firm. As a result, a global firm needs people with intercultural communication expertise at all levels.

In addition to adapting communication to the growing internal diversity, international firms must adapt to the varying communication practices of other firms around the world. We examined the following areas:

- *Corporate culture and intercultural communication.* Companies develop their own unique corporate cultures. The corporate culture is embedded in the national culture.

- *Stages in internationalization.* Typically, the internationalization starts with an import–export stage, followed by the multinational firm and then the global firm. Each stage has its own organizational structure and communication environment.

- *Implications of cultural aspects of business structures for communication* in the international firm. Effective intercultural communication in a firm is influenced by the structure of the firm, which in turn is influenced by cultural priorities. Priorities for credentials, context, family, and political considerations influence the way people are hired, trained, and promoted. As a result, communication patterns depend on the specific organizational context.

Notes

1. Henry W. Lane, Joseph J. DiStefano, and Martha L. Maznevski, *International Management Behavior,* 5th ed. (Malden, MA: Blackwell Publishing, 2006).

2. Ibid.

3. Nancy Adler, *International Dimensions of Organizational Behavior* (Boston: Kent, 1986).

4. Philip R. Harris, Robert T. Moran, and Sarah V. Moran, *Managing Cultural Differences: Global Leadership Strategies for the 21st Century,* 6th ed. (Burlington, MA: Elsevier, 2004).

5. Donald Carbaugh, "Cultural Communication and Organizing." In *Communication, Culture, and Organizational Processes,* Intercultural and Intercultural Communication Annual, vol. IX, William B. Gudykunst, Lea P. Stewart, and Stella Ting-Toomey, eds. (Newbury Park, CA: Sage, 1985), p. 37.

6. Vern Terpstra and Kenneth David, *The Cultural Environment of International Business,* 2nd ed. (Chicago: Southwestern, 1985).

7. Nancy Adler and F. Ghadar, "International Strategy from the Perspective of People and Culture: The North American Context." In *International Management Behavior,* H. Lane and J. DiStefano, eds. (New York: Kent Publishing, 1991).

8. S. J. Kobrin, "Is There a Relationship between a Geocentric Mind-Set and Multinational Strategy?" *Journal of International Business Studies* 25, no. 3 (1994), pp. 494–512.

9. H. Lane and J. DiStefano, *International Management Behavior* (New York: Kent Publishing, 1991).

10. Kimio Fujita, "Letter from Samoa," *Japan Economic Review,* November 2001. Mr. Fujita was the adviser to the foreign minister of Samoa and former president of the Japan International Cooperation Agency.

11. Teresa Palmer and Iris Varner, "Leveraging the Knowledge of Expatriates to Enhance Organizational Performance: What Can HRM Do?" In *Proceedings of the 2002 Conference of the North American Management Society and the Midwest Society for Human Resources/Industrial Relations,* R. Greenwood, ed. (Chicago, 2002).

12. S. J. Kobrin, "Expatriate Reduction and Strategic Control in American Multinational Corporations," *Human Resource Management* 27, no. 1 (1988), pp. 63–75.

13. Till Hein, "Das Kommt den Chinesen Spanisch vor," *Die Zeit,* no. 41 (September 30, 2004), p. 41; Andreas Unger, "Auf Tuchfuehlung Gehen," *Die Zeit,* no. 48 (November 24, 2005), p. 86.

14. R. L. Tung, "Selection and Training of Personnel for Overseas Assignments," *Columbia Journal of World Business* 16 (1982), pp. 68–78.

15. Simca Ronen, *Comparative and Multinational Management* (New York: Wiley, 1986).

16. Adler and Ghadar, "International Strategy."

17. R. Daft and R. Lengel, "Information Richness: A New Approach to Managerial and Organizational Design." In *Research in Organizational Behavior* (Greenwich, CT: JAI, 1984), pp. 191–233.

18. H. Ramrath, "Globalization Isn't for Whiners," *The Wall Street Journal,* April 6, 1992.

19. Joseph DiStefano and Martha Maznevski, "Creating Value with Diverse Teams in Global Management," *Organizational Dynamics* 29, no. 1 (2001), pp. 45–63.

20. Chie Nakane, *Human Relations in Japan* (Ministry of Foreign Affairs, Japan), 1972. Also see Makoto Ohtsu and Tom Imanari, *Inside Japanese Business* (London: M. E. Sharpe, 2002).

21. Nakane, *Human Relations.*

22. Ibid.

23. Chester Dawson, Jeff Green, Larry Armstrong, Christine Wheatley, and Jonathan Wheatley, "Mr. Fix-It," *BusinessWeek,* May 14, 2001, pp. 66–67.

24. C. Pezeshkpur, "Challenges to Management in the Arab World." *Business Horizons,* 21 (1978), pp. 47–55. Also see Bernard Lewis, *What Went Wrong?* (New York: Oxford University Press, 2002).

25. Cited with permission from Martin Woolnough, manager of Nestlé Uzbekistan. Nestlé Uzbekistan LLC was formed as a joint venture in which Nestlé S. A., the Swiss parent, owns approximately 95 percent and NAFOSAT owns 5 percent. Additionally, Nestlé Uzbekistan LLC owns 35 percent of NAFOSAT, and the government of Uzbekistan owns 15 percent of Nestlé Uzbekistan LLC. The balance of the NAFOSAT shares is owned by about 100 private individuals who have little or no experience owning shares and would best be described as traditional country people.

CHAPTER TWELVE

Intercultural Dynamics in the International Company

On May 7, 1998, Daimler-Benz AG and Chrysler stunned the world by announcing that they had agreed to merge the two companies. There had been rumors for some time, yet when the news came, it made headlines. This was the first megamerger of two big international companies, and it would make DaimlerChrysler the fifth-largest maker of cars and light trucks in the world.

Juergen Schrempp, chief executive officer (CEO) of Daimler-Benz, and Robert Eaton, CEO of Chrysler, had met at Chrysler's headquarters on January 12, 1998, to explore possible cooperation. That meeting, which lasted just 17 minutes, resulted in a decision to merge the two companies. The two CEOs met a number of times in Germany, London, New York, and South Africa in the following months, but their meetings were always kept secret. They never appeared together in public, and only a few trusted executives knew about the talks. In fact, each person who was told about the talks also was told that so far no information had leaked to the outside; therefore, any leaks in the future could be traced very easily and be punished accordingly. The threat worked, and everyone kept quiet.

When the merger was announced, Eaton and Schrempp hailed it as a "merger of equals." They were to be co-chairs for three years. After that, Eaton would step down and Schrempp would become the sole CEO. There would be headquarters both in Auburn Hills, Michigan, and in Stuttgart, Germany. The company language would be English. Economies of scale and the sharing of technology and other information would result in huge savings—USD 400 million in the first year alone—and higher profits. Daimler would contribute engineering know-how, and Chrysler would contribute creativity and marketing savvy.

The merger was made official on November 17, 1998. On that day, Eaton and Schrempp together rang the opening bell on Wall Street. In Stuttgart, employees celebrated with an

American-style party that included turkey. In Auburn Hills, Chrysler employees ate potato salad and sauerkraut. Each member of the integration teams received half a share of stock in the new company.

From the very beginning, the merger required a reconciliation not only of big issues but also of seemingly unimportant points. For example, a committee had to sit down and decide whether a brochure encouraging employees to accept global assignments should have the shape of a globe or a rectangle. The choice of color was another stumbling block. After several months of regular meetings the committee finally decided on the globe shape, but the color was still unresolved. Ultimately, the group agreed on yellow and blue. The Germans immediately thought of Lufthansa Airlines, and the Americans, all from the Detroit area, thought of the University of Michigan.

The negotiations for expatriate pay were tough as well. American expatriates are used to lavish compensation packages, much larger than what their German counterparts were used to. The Germans, on the other hand, were used to long vacations. The proposal that finally was hammered out included the following: Expatriates from Germany and the United States would stay on the home-country payroll and would be paid in the home-country currency. That meant no more special pay packages. The Americans were used to a three-month lump sum at the beginning of an expatriate assignment to cover costs; the Germans wanted none of that. The two sides finally compromised on one month's pay. The company offered to pay for housing in the new location and upkeep of the expatriate's house in his or her old location, including snow removal and lawn care. Expatriates from both countries would be given 25 days of vacation and a plane trip home for themselves and their families once a year. The company offered to help spouses find employment in the new location. German expatriates in the United States would get Chrysler automobiles at discount rates; American expatriates in Germany would get Mercedes vehicles at discount rates.

None of those issues dealt with the company product, marketing strategies, or customer relations. At times, the discussions went nowhere. Compromises frequently left both sides disappointed.

Less than two years after the merger, the company bought a controlling share of Mitsubishi. Now there were three corporations and three national cultures involved. Chrysler had had an unsuccessful joint venture with Mitsubishi in 1980, when together they built an automobile assembly plant in Normal, Illinois. Ultimately, that joint venture was dissolved, to some extent at least because of different approaches to doing business. In the joint venture, Chrysler had been the junior partner; Japanese headquarters had the ultimate say on most issues. In the new formation, Chrysler was aligned with the majority merger partner, Daimler; however, the earlier relationship between Chrysler and Mitsubishi did not seem to affect the ties to DaimlerChrysler.

Mitsubishi was in trouble when DaimlerChrysler acquired the majority interest; it had lost money in 2000, and the Japanese were deeply unhappy at the measures taken by DaimlerChrysler to bring it back to profitable figures, including firing many of the top executives at Mitsubishi.

Schrempp and Eaton had emphasized the potential savings and economies of scale that the merger of Daimler and Chrysler would create. On that expectation, the stock rose to a high of USD 108. When reports of culture clashes between Auburn Hills and Stuttgart began to emerge, sales problems and production issues made headlines, and the stock dropped to a low of USD 26.

During the following years the road for the merger was rather bumpy, and the expected savings and market growth never materialized. Daimler had been seen as the stronger partner that would pull Chrysler along; however, under Zetsche, who had worked for Daimler in Stuttgart, Chrysler stabilized while Daimler ran into problems. Among other things, the Smart became a drag on the profitability of Daimler. The Smart is a sub-compact car that was designed for city traffic. It is easy to park because it takes up very little space. In congested European cities, this was seen as a huge advantage. However, the Smart was expensive. Production was plagued by quality issues, and the Smart never quite attracted enough people to make it profitable.

At the same time, Mitsubishi Motors ran into major problems as well. The company had covered up defects in its cars over several years. Quality problems led to financial problems, and the question was whether DaimlerChrysler would support Mitsubishi financially. This would be a further drag on the profitability of DaimlerChrysler. Mitsubishi Motors is one company in the Mitsubishi Keiretsu, a conglomerate of companies that traditionally would help each other in case of problems. The companies composing the Mitsubishi Keiretsu are Mitsubishi Bank, Mitsubishi Corp., Kirin Brewery, Mitsubishi Rayon, Mitsubishi Electric, Mitsubishi Heavy Industries, and Mitsubishi Motors. Traditionally, all companies in the *keiretsu* would do business with each other whenever possible. Each *keiretsu* has a bank at its center, and all companies in the *keiretsu* use this bank for their financial and banking needs.

The question was whether the Mitsubishi Keiretsu would bail out a company that was controlled by a foreign firm. When DaimlerChrysler bought a controlling share of Mitsubishi Motors, this was seen as proof that the traditional *keiretsu* was breaking apart. As the crisis deepened in the spring of 2004, DaimlerChrysler decided not to put more money into Mitsubishi Motors.[1] Ultimately, the *keiretsu* followed tradition and bailed Mitsubishi Motors out. As a result, DaimlerChrysler's shares in Mitsubishi Motors fell to 22 percent.[2] In November 2005, DaimlerChrysler sold its remaining shares of Mitsubishi Motors to Goldman Sachs.[3] The big auto conglomerate was back to two companies.

For 2005, DaimlerChrysler posted an 84 percent rise in income, but most of that came from the financial service area of the company rather than the production side. While Chrysler announced a profit for 2005, sales slumped as high gasoline prices scared buyers away from trucks and SUVs. The Mercedes division posted a loss of 505 million euros for 2005, its first annual loss in over ten years. In addition, Mercedes announced layoffs for 8,500 employees and a restructuring of the unprofitable Smart division.[4] At the end of 2005, Schrempp, the CEO of DaimlerChrysler announced that he would step down. Many observers felt that effectively he was ousted. The Board of Directors had voiced doubts about Schrempp's continuing effectiveness. Zetsche, who had turned Chrysler around, followed Schrempp as the new CEO. In March 2006, the stock traded at USD 46, up from the low of USD 26 but only a shadow of the height of USD 108 at the excitement over the merger.

On August 3, 2007, DaimlerChrysler sold the Chrysler Group to Cerberus Capital Management. The Chrysler Group became Chrysler Holding LLC, and 81.1 percent of the new company was owned by Cerberus. DaimlerChrysler changed its name to Daimler AG and kept 19.9 percent in the new Chrysler Holding Company. "Daimler AG paid Cerberus USD 650 million to take Chrysler and associated liabilities off its hands. This is a remarkable reversal in fortunes on the USD 36 billion paid to acquire Chrysler in 1998. Of the USD 7.4 billion purchase price, *Cerberus Capital Management* invested USD 5 billion in Chrysler Holdings and USD 1.05 billion in Chrysler's financial unit. The de-merged Daimler AG received USD 1.35 billion directly from Cerberus but directly invested USD 2 billion in Chrysler itself."[5] Thus ended a celebrated merger after only eight years.

Throughout this book we have emphasized the importance of cultural awareness in international business. We have discussed the foundations of culture and various cultural priorities. Chapters 3 and 4 examined five categories of questions that can help you assess the cultural priorities of the cultures in which you are working. In Chapters 2, 5, 6, 7, 8, and 9, you learned about the impact of culture on verbal and nonverbal communication, specific business tasks such as the collection of information, the organization of information, decision making, conflict resolution, and negotiation. In Chapters 10 and 11 you learned about the impact of culture on the organizational setup of a company and the importance of understanding the legal environment in intercultural business communication.

With this foundation, you are now equipped to identify cultural issues in international business ventures. You also know that when you read a newspaper or watch a television program, there is no signal that flashes to let you know: "Here is a particular cultural problem—pay attention," or "In Japan, the traditional corporate structure is based on seniority and group cohesiveness, which in turn are related to a high-context society. The Japanese function on a base of relationships that is developed over a long period. Change therefore is slow, and individuals should fit into the group rather than stick out." Since this cultural signal is not flashing, many people believe culture is not relevant. However, when you talk to expatriates and other businesspeople who are active in international business, they will tell you that an understanding of culture is one of the greatest contributors to success, while lack of understanding is one of the greatest contributors to failure.

This book has given you a framework for learning the *why* of other cultures. We also have shown how to apply cultural understanding to writing correspondence and negotiation. It is now up to you to put this knowledge to use. In this chapter, we will apply this knowledge by discussing the 1998 merger of Daimler-Benz AG and Chrysler Corp. into DaimlerChrysler. In the process, we will:

- Identify cultural issues that affected the merger.
- Examine the role of intercultural business communication as a strategic tool for success.

In the Appendix, we give you two additional cases for practice. We encourage you to use this book as a guide. Good luck in this adventure that is just beginning.

Cultural Issues in the DaimlerChrysler Merger

Before we discuss the cultural issues that surfaced in the merger, we present an overview of the history of the two companies.

In Focus

THE HISTORY OF CHRYSLER
Chrysler started when Maxwell Motors became Chrysler Corp. in 1925, with Walter Chrysler as the president. In subsequent years, Chrysler bought Dodge and produced De Soto, Plymouth, and Chrysler cars. During World War II, Chrysler produced tanks and combat vehicles. After the war, Chrysler became best known for big powerful cars, but with the Arab oil embargo in the 1970s, it ran into trouble. Consumers wanted smaller, fuel-efficient cars, and Chrysler could not deliver. Lee Iacocca became president of Chrysler in 1978. When the company faced bankruptcy, Iacocca was able to secure federal loan guarantees of USD 1.5 billion. Under Iacocca's leadership, Chrysler thrived and was able to repay the loans seven years ahead of schedule. In the 1980s, Chrysler's fortunes soared with the introduction of the minivan. Chrysler and Mitsubishi Motors started a joint venture in the mid-1980s under the name Diamond Star Motors Corp. In 1987, Chrysler bought the Jeep brand, thereby adding another popular vehicle to the Chrysler lineup. The cooperation with Mitsubishi ended in 1991, and Iacocca stepped down in 1992.

Chrysler, the smallest of the Big Three car companies (General Motors and Ford are the other two), was best known for its creativity and ability to overcome obstacles. Under Eaton, Iacocca's successor, Chrysler made significant progress in quality and efficiency, and the company became the world leader in profitability per vehicle.

The merger with Daimler seemed to open up worldwide opportunities, but the merger did not last. Chrysler was eventually sold to Cerberus, a private equity group.

HISTORY OF DAIMLER-BENZ
Daimler and Benz merged in 1926 to become Daimler-Benz AG. The company is best known for the Mercedes car, named after the daughter of a race car driver who ordered 30 cars with the stipulation that they be named Mercedes. During World War II, Daimler-Benz became a leading arms maker for Hitler, and it used slave laborers during that time. In the 1990s, the company paid huge sums of money as compensation and published a book about its role in World War II. In 1997, it had revenues of USD 70 billion. It employed 300,000 workers worldwide. More than two-thirds of its revenue came from outside Germany, and in the 1990s the company built plants in the United States and France.

In the 1980s, Reuter, the CEO, started on a path of diversification; however, when the company started losing money, Schrempp ousted Reuter and took over. He reversed the diversification efforts and went back to Daimler-Benz's core business: luxury cars and big trucks. Schrempp alienated the Daimler Board and the shareholders with his flamboyant and arrogant style. He was ousted and replaced by Zetsche. After the end of the DaimlerChrysler merger, the company became Daimler AG. The company still has a 19.1 percent stake in the Chrysler Holding Company.

Preparation and Training

It was one thing to announce the merger; it was an entirely different thing to make the merger work. Three international accounting firms, four investment banks, and six corporate law partnerships worked on the merger. Clearly, both sides focused on financial, regulatory, legal, and business issues. As we will see, those issues played a major role; however, the merger almost was derailed over cultural issues.

To deal with internal merger issues, the company appointed 28 integration teams that set out to mesh the two corporations. The integration teams started their work in 1998 and officially finished in 1999; however, in a global company, integration is an ongoing task. The members received some intercultural training, but they complained that the training was not very helpful and got stuck in stereotypes. For example, the Germans were told that Americans are superficial and that an invitation does not mean anything. When a German executive came to Auburn Hills, he therefore booked a hotel room even though his American counterpart had invited him to stay at his house. He was very surprised that the American not only picked him up personally at the airport but actually took him to his home. The Americans had been told that Germans are stiff and that form and politeness are crucial: "Never, never greet a German with your hands in your pocket if you want to be taken seriously." When the Americans met the Germans in Stuttgart, they were surprised that quite a few of the Germans had their hands in their pockets.[6]

It seems that most of the training focused on cultural stereotypes and aspects that can be observed rather than the underlying reasons for behavior. The resulting stereotypes did not foster a systematic approach to studying and observing other cultures. Both German and American employees of DaimlerChrysler were frustrated because they did not learn *why* Germans or Americans behave as they do.

Since many employees from the other side did not behave as the trainer had said they would, both Americans and Germans concluded that the training was not helpful. However, effective cultural training could have helped them understand a number of business and management practices that slowed the merger process.

Attitudes toward Management

There were numerous cultural differences that the training did not address at all. The Germans came to meetings with thick folders and a detailed agenda. They prepared very detailed minutes of every meeting, whereas the Americans preferred free-flowing discussions and wanted agendas as general guidelines. The Germans wanted detailed summaries of previous meetings at the beginning of every session; the Americans wanted none of that.

After studying the role of culture in international business communication, you know that the German attitude toward meetings and agendas is related to a dislike for uncertainty. Agendas provide order and minimize the risk that something unexpected will happen. Americans, who are generally more willing to accept uncertainty, prefer a more flexible approach.

As the case at the beginning of the chapter pointed out, a decision was made to make English the official company language. The Americans who would deal with Germans on a regular basis were relieved because there was no need to learn the German language. When John Craig and Daniel Wilson went to their first meeting in Stuttgart, they were in for a surprise. During the official meeting everyone spoke English; however, as soon as the meeting was officially over, all the Germans switched to German. John and Daniel did not understand a word and decided that a few German lessons might be helpful after all.

The Americans were worried that the Germans would discuss the important points in German and leave the Americans out of the process of the discussions. The Germans, who spoke very good English, nevertheless were worried that their English might not be good enough to get all the nuances of the language.

The two sides also had to come to terms with different approaches to formality. The German members of the integration team called each other *Mr.,* using last names. The Americans, being used to first names, thought the Germans were stiff and unfriendly. The issue did not disappear when the Germans agreed to use first names because in German there is also the distinction between the informal *you* (*Du*) and the formal *you* (*Sie*). Typically, the informal *you* is used with persons one knows well. At the workplace, first names and *Du* hardly ever are used. The Germans tried the awkward combination of *Sie* and first names when the Americans were around. Gradually the Germans eased up and used first names with *Du* on a more regular basis.

The corporate cultures were very different as well. At Chrysler, executives ate in the executive dining room; in Stuttgart, executives ate in the same cafeteria with the workers even though generally Germans are more formal than Americans. In contrast, the Americans did not use titles, whereas in Stuttgart titles were important. Almost all top managers at Daimler had international experience. In fact, international assignments were considered a must on the way to the top. They had been in South Africa, South America, North America, and all over Europe. Also, they all spoke English and frequently a second foreign language. At Chrysler, in contrast, almost nobody even had a passport, and nobody at the top spoke a foreign language.

The majority of upper management at Daimler-Benz had been with the company for a long time. Schrempp, for example, had started his career as an apprentice at Daimler. Most managers had a technical and/or engineering background. As a result, they focused on technical designs and technical quality. Typically, engineers at Daimler decided what a new car would look like. It was almost unheard of to collect information relating to design from consumers. After all, the crucial aspect was technical perfection. Driving was a serious business; there was no place in cars for cup holders, for example. Chrysler managers, by contrast, came from a variety of backgrounds, including marketing and finance. Although some had been at Chrysler for a number of years, many had gained experience at other automobile companies or even in other industries before joining Chrysler.

The different approaches to cars and their design had an impact on views of corporate reputation. At the beginning, there had been talk of sharing technology and platforms. However, Daimler engineers were concerned about giving their first-class technology to a mass-market car company. Purchasing was to be consolidated, but it turned out that the differences were so huge that little consolidation would be possible.

Attitudes toward Compensation

In the summer of 1998, the German magazine *Stern* ran an article comparing the pay of a Daimler employee to that of a Chrysler employee. The article showed pictures of the houses of employees and talked about their vacations, hobbies, and work schedules. It also compared the pay of two supervisors, both before and after taxes.[7]

The German employees knew that they were among the highest-paid workers in the world. There was some fear that the merger would have a negative impact on German pay. By showing that the two supervisors in the story had comparable pay packages, the article helped reduce or eliminate that concern. It was interesting to note, however, that the German and American supervisors had very different priorities for spending their money. The German employee spent much of his money on his house, garden, and furnishings. The American employee also had a nice house but spent most of his disposable income on short vacations and eating out.

The difference in pay at the employee and supervisor levels might not have been that great; however, this was not true at the expatriate level. Daimler saw an expatriate assignment as a regular and required step on the ladder to the top. Expatriate packages therefore were small by American standards. However, on international flights, Daimler executives went first class. At Chrysler, only a few top executives were allowed to go first class, but compensation for foreign assignments was lavish by German standards. As the case at the beginning of this chapter pointed out, expatriate compensation became a big issue in the merger process. Ultimately, both sides gave a little. The attitude toward expatriate pay speaks volumes about attitudes toward international business. At Daimler, international experience was considered a prerequisite for success, whereas at Chrysler it was considered something unique that merited special compensation.

The difference in compensation, however, was most pronounced at the executive level, particularly for the CEO. At the time of the merger, Eaton received about USD 11 million a year, including stock options. Schrempp, by contrast, received about USD 2 million. In fact, the top ten people at Daimler-Benz made USD 11.3 million together, about the same as Eaton made by himself. In addition, under German law, individual executive pay does not have to be disclosed. Publication of the aggregate pay of the top earners is sufficient. Under American law, however, individual compensation must be disclosed. Rumors in Germany were flying that Schrempp's main goal for the merger was to receive an American-style salary under German disclosure laws.

After the merger of Daimler and Chrysler, compensation for German CEOs and upper management went up considerably, a development that received much negative press in the German media. As a result, employees, stockholders, and the public began to ask for more transparency and more disclosure of executive pay. While some changes have occurred, the debate is ongoing with no clear solution in sight.

Regulatory Issues

Because of government regulations, the new company was incorporated in Germany. That had some unintended consequences. Since DaimlerChrysler was incorporated under German law, the Standard & Poor's (S&P's) 500 no longer listed the company. Under existing law, U.S. pension funds no longer were allowed to invest in the company. The pension funds therefore sold their holdings in Chrysler.

DaimlerChrysler stock was listed on 12 international stock markets, becoming the first truly international stock. It was traded around the world in local currencies rather than as repository receipts. When traded as repository receipts, shares are deposited in the bank and then dollar-denominated receipts are issued against them. The rate of currency fluctuation therefore always plays a role in trading.

With the trading of common shares in the local currencies, the conversion cost can be avoided. The shares can be traded at 12 different stock markets without incurring conversion costs.

Under German law, labor and banks sit on the board to look at the long-term health of the firm. Since the bank is not going to sell the stock, it is not concerned when a stock goes down, as long as the company seems to be healthy in the long run. American investors, in contrast, look for returns and fast results. As a result, American investors follow the stock market very closely and require explanations when a stock goes down. When Schrempp became CEO, he asked the board members of Daimler what the Daimler stock price was. Only one of the members gave an answer, and his estimate was not close to the actual price. None of the others even ventured a guess. In the American context, it would be unethical and irresponsible for a board member not to have the latest information on a company's stock price.

Germany requires two financial reports a year, whereas the United States requires four quarterly reports each year on a timely basis. Usually, U.S. corporations announce expected results two weeks before the end of the quarter and actual figures right at the end of the quarter. Since American investors want fast and timely information, they would not accept two reports per year as sufficient information. The timing of reports and announcements created a problem as well. For example, Stuttgart would make announcements in the morning, when it was still night in the United States. By the time the Americans got the information, it was old news. The time lag became a big issue and was seen as proof that the Germans were excluding the Americans intentionally in an effort to gain total control.

Reports on the Merger

In this section, we will look at attitudes toward the merger over time as reported in the media. As you will see, those attitudes varied.

Throughout 1998, views of the merger were generally positive even though cautionary voices spoke as well. From the beginning, there was concern that the merger was not a merger of equals but a takeover of Chrysler by Daimler. There also were articles in the business press in both countries warning of major culture clashes, but most of those articles talked in general terms rather than giving specifics.

That changed fairly dramatically in 1999. Increasingly, reports were critical of the slow speed of integration. For example, it took 25 percent of 300 managers' time to work out the details of the merger, time that those managers did not spend producing and selling cars. Schrempp came under criticism as well. He was seen as tyrannical and dictatorial by the American public and by Chrysler employees in Detroit, where he was firing executives at Chrysler to gain complete control. The board of directors, which had started out with an almost even split between American and German members, increasingly looked German. By October 1999, the board had eight Germans and five Americans.

Critics charged that there was a war of cultures and that Schrempp was not able to build a new culture. Rather than the promised merger of equals, Chrysler was organized as an American subsidiary of Daimler. Some voices went so far as to recommend dissolving the merger.[8]

By fall 2000, the stock had dropped from a high of USD 108 to USD 45. Forecasts were gloomy, and Chrysler had run into serious problems. Sixty percent of the value of the stock had been wiped out since its high. Eaton had left before his three years as Co-CEO were up, and his replacement, Holden, was fired by Schrempp, who sent his own person, Zetsche, to Auburn Hills in the United States. Critics talked of a cultural drama of Shakespearean proportions and the selling of an American icon to dictatorial and power-hungry Germans.[9]

Morale at Chrysler took a nosedive. Suppliers were unhappy when Zetsche, in an attempt to cut costs, asked them to lower their prices. Gradually, there was a realization that Chrysler's problems were not all of Schrempp's making. The company had been heading for trouble before the merger. Some people felt that Eaton had known about it and was glad to get out of a potential mess. He took his money and left.

Up to that point, Schrempp had been criticized for being high-handed. Now he also was criticized for not being decisive enough and not moving fast enough. The merger had been mismanaged, and the intercultural communication was disastrous. Know-it-all Germans had been greedy for Chrysler's distribution system and marketing ability. But it was clear now that there seemed to be irreconcilable differences in marketing and engineering philosophies.

The conclusion at the end of 2000 was that the merger had failed miserably, that there was no synergy, and that the cultures were too different to be able to work together.

While DaimlerChrysler was still trying to merge as one company, Schrempp bought a controlling share of 34 percent of Mitsubishi Motors, arguing that the company needed a presence in Asia if it wanted to be a global player. Earlier, he had toyed with the idea of buying Nissan, but Renault took that company.

In May 2001, after DaimlerChrysler had bought a controlling share of Mitsubishi, Mitsubishi, one of the smallest Japanese automakers, reported USD 750 million in pretax losses on sales of USD 31 billion for the year 2000. Mitsubishi sales had dropped 17 percent in the first part of the year. Quality problems, lack of a clear production focus, and a cash crunch had contributed to the problem. Schrempp had known about the problems at Mitsubishi when he bought parts of the company. He had sent Rolf Eckrodt to Japan to reverse the fortunes of Mitsubishi Motors. Eckrodt had a tough task ahead when he arrived at Mitsubishi Motors in Japan in January 2001.

Eckrodt had experience in restructuring ailing carmakers. In particular, he had been the key player in restructuring Daimler's subsidiary in Brazil, where he had earned a reputation for being ruthless in laying off workers and reorganizing the company. The Japanese, aware of his tough style, were apprehensive when he arrived and made it clear that they were not just going to take orders from Germany. Sonobe, Mitsubishi Motor's CEO, was no pushover. He had been responsible for Mitsubishi's turnaround in the United States, and he felt that he could do the same for the parent company in Japan. When Eckrodt first arrived in Japan, he and

Sonobe had long talks about the best strategy for solving the problems. They were going to work together; however, when Mitsubishi had to recall 1.36 million cars because of quality defects, Eckrodt decided that the time had come to act decisively.

In March 2001, Eckrodt replaced five Japanese top executives with Germans. The Japanese were stunned, particularly since four of the Germans were under 40 years of age. He then decided to cut costs, lay off 9,500 workers, sever ties with one-third of the suppliers, and reduce the number of automobile models on the production line.[10]

In March 2002, Eckrodt ousted Sonobe as CEO of Mitsubishi Motors and took the job himself. In the same month, the company announced that Mitsubishi Motors had returned to profitability, made steady progress in its turnaround efforts, and surpassed the targets set for cost reduction. The company was determined to accelerate the turnaround plan on the basis of the positive results.[11] The Japanese had mixed reactions. Some saw the changes as a violation of fundamental cultural values that value lifetime employment and seniority. Others saw the changes as necessary if the Japanese company was to survive. Most of the Japanese agreed that the changes could not have been made by a Japanese manager. As the opening case in this chapter mentioned, the union between DaimlerChrysler and Mitsubishi was dissolved in 2005. The Japanese Mitsubishi Keiretsu circled the wagons and supported its own member when DaimlerChrysler refused to put more money into Mitsubishi Motors.

When the merger of Daimler and Chrysler was first announced, newspapers, magazines, television, and radio ran numerous stories about this new company. Toward the end of the merger the stories no longer celebrated the "sexy" global merger but concentrated more on the problems. The dissolution of the merger received comparatively little coverage.

The stock, as the opening case pointed out, had been on a roller coaster. After an all-time high of USD 108, it slumped to a low of USD 26 and finally recovered to USD 46 in 2006. However, the stock price was not just a result of the merger issues; it must also be seen in the context of the general pattern of the stock market since 2000. Some manufacturing processes in DaimlerChrysler merged successfully, and production managers from the two companies did become comfortable with each other. Zetsche, who had been greeted in Auburn Hills with great suspicion, seemed to fit in after all. Even Yokich, the boss of the United Auto Workers labor union, liked him in spite of the fact that 26,000 hourly and 6,000 salaried jobs had been lost. Gradually, Zetsche seemed to turn Chrysler around. At the same time, Schrempp lost his power. Layoffs in Stuttgart did not help. Zetsche replaced Schrempp, but to the very end Schrempp stood by the merger and insisted that it would eventually be very successful in spite of any difficulties. However, in 2007 Daimler sold the Chrysler company and the merger ended.

Today, following the economic crisis of 2008–9, the Chrysler company is in bankruptcy; its stock is not traded. The future of Chrysler is uncertain; it might continue, be bought by another auto company, or disappear completely. The Daimler AG stock trades in the low USD 30 range.

Intercultural Business Communication as a Strategic Tool for Success

As the DaimlerChrysler case illustrates, businesspeople are members of their national cultures. Eaton, CEO of Chrysler, and Schrempp, CEO of Daimler, brought their cultures to the negotiation table, and so did the members of the integration teams. In addition, they brought their respective corporate cultures, which are influenced by the national culture. The two corporate cultures also are embedded in the culture of the automobile industry. The web of cultural connections goes all the way down to the line workers in the two companies. A worker on the assembly line may not always be aware of the cultural context, but the influence is there nevertheless. One of the biggest tasks is to bridge the culture gap so that work teams can focus on business tasks.

All international companies face cultural issues, particularly in mergers and joint ventures. To build on the potential synergies of cultural diversity, companies need to:

• Create awareness of the process of intercultural business communication and understand ways to communicate about culture and to communicate by using culture.
• Develop an understanding of the dynamics of culturally diverse groups.
• Place the communication process and the dynamics of diverse teams in the context of corporate strategy.

The Process of Intercultural Business Communication

Intercultural business communication has three parts, as illustrated in Exhibit 12.1: cultural strategy, business strategy, and communication strategy.[12] The list of variables in each circle is not complete. You may think of additional aspects that influence each circle, but the variables listed are the major ones. A company may have influence over some of those aspects, whereas others are beyond its control.

For example, national laws concerning mergers, government regulations concerning the listing of foreign companies and stocks, and reporting regulations affect the business strategy but are beyond the direct influence of a company. The company has to understand the rules and regulations to avoid violating them, but it cannot change them. They are a given. DaimlerChrysler had to comply with German reporting rules. Even if American investors want more information, the company is not bound by their requests. DaimlerChrysler may agree that four quarterly reports are good for investor relations but may decide that two reports provide all the necessary information.

The particular business strategy a company develops also is influenced by the competition the firm faces and the position of its products. For example, Daimler wanted to get a foothold in the broader automobile market in addition to the luxury market. It hoped to do that by joining with a company like Chrysler. Schrempp furthermore hoped that a broader product line with lower-cost products would help

EXHIBIT 12.1 **Intercultural Business Communication Strategy**

Desired Level of
Internationalization

Competitive
Position

Size of Firm

Corporate
Culture

Economic
Climate

Business Strategy

HR Practices

Position of
Product

Government
Regulation
and Laws

Structure
of Firm

Financial
Health of
Firm

Rules Adhering/Bending

Role of
Individual

Role of
Hierarchy

Form and
Status

**Intercultural
Strategy**

Role of
Gender

Attitudes
toward
Uncertainty

High Context/
Low Context

Cultural
Sensitivity

Willingness
to Take
Risks

**Intercultural Business
Communication Strategy**

Corporate Communication
Policy

Individual
Goals

Corporate
Goals

Availability of
Technology

Position
in Firm

Language
Verbal/Nonverbal

Corporate Strategy

Purpose of
Communication

Personal Preference
of Channel

Technical
Background

Awareness
of Audience

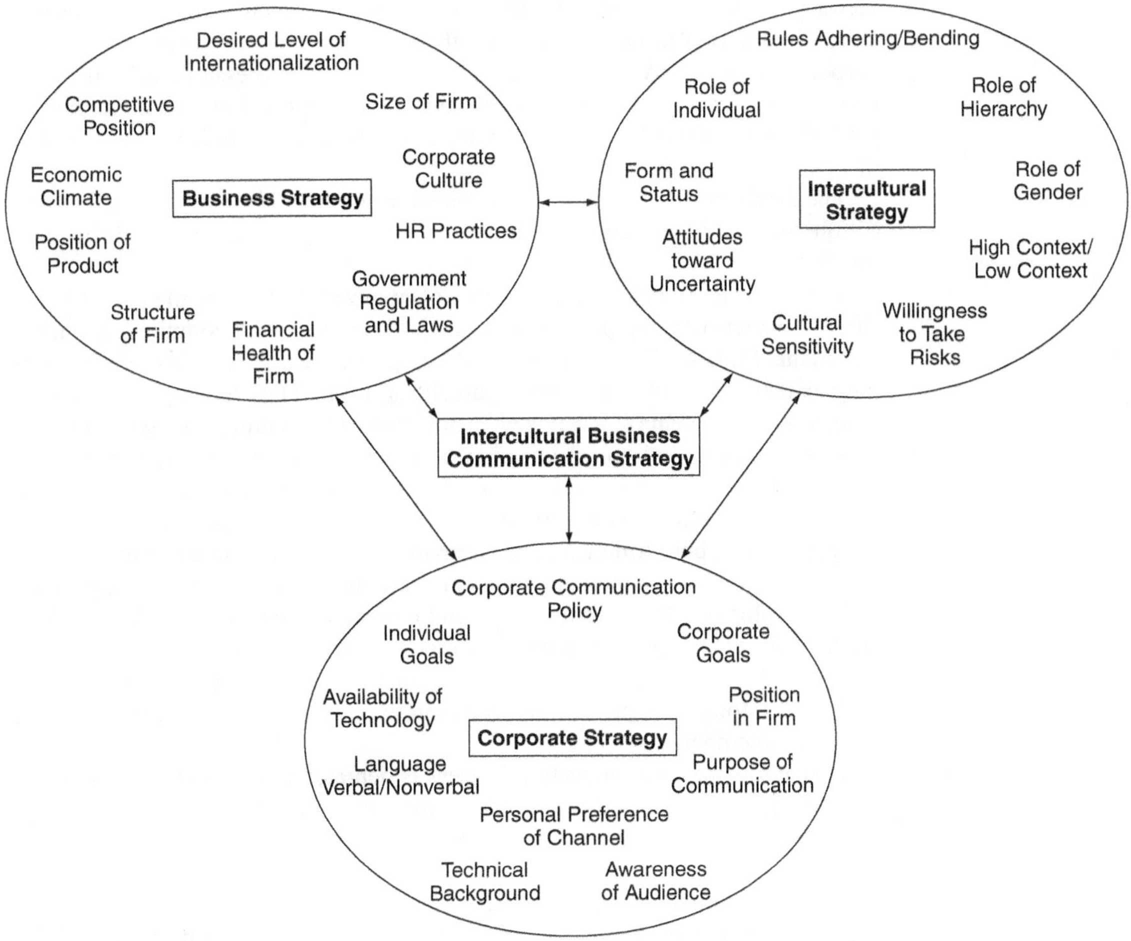

the company's expansion into Asia. Eaton saw international expansion as a way to stay competitive. Daimler offered an opportunity for Chrysler to become a player in Europe, with Daimler's high-quality products that appealed to a luxury market.

At the time of the merger, both companies seemed to be in sound financial positions. Their practices were different, as we discussed earlier, and so were their corporate cultures, but both sides thought that those differences would not present major obstacles. Overall, the two companies seemed to be a good fit for a merger.

In the circle identifying intercultural strategy in Exhibit 12.1, we list ten variables. You have learned about cultural attitudes relating to hierarchy, change, risk, and the individual versus the group, among many others. The DaimlerChrysler case shows that the Germans and the Americans had different cultural priorities. When Mitsubishi joined the mix, the cultural factors became even more complex.

The cultural differences find expression in the role of rules and formalities and views on risk and uncertainty, the promotion of women, and communication styles. In addition to national culture, there are other cultural variables, such as corporate culture and professional culture. Different professions have different cultures. For example, accountants have a different culture than do human resources (HR) managers. To some extent those cultures overlap, but they are also distinct.

The third circle focuses on communication strategy. The particular communication strategy is influenced by ten factors that we have discussed throughout this book.

The dynamics of communication in a company are shaped by the people in the firm. Managers develop policies and standards on corporate communication, but within that framework individuals can develop their own styles and preferences as long as they stay within corporate guidelines. In the DaimlerChrysler situation, members of the integration teams were not allowed to communicate with anybody outside the team, and communication between teams was heavily regulated as well. Confidentiality was seen as crucial so that team members would not be influenced by outside pressure groups. However, outside the specific issues of the merger process, both American and German companies are more transparent than Japanese companies. American companies are the most transparent. Legislation enforces rules on corporate reporting and communication with all stakeholders. German firms are less transparent, as reporting requirements for executive pay illustrate. Japanese firms are the least transparent in this group. Also, when Mitsubishi Motors ran into serious problems, the *keiretsu* stepped in to support one of its own members.

Frequently, the communication process is depicted in the model illustrated in Exhibit 12.2, which identifies a sender, a message, and a receiver of the message (see also the Process Model of Communication, Exhibit 5.1, in Chapter 5). A feedback loop indicates that communication is an interactive two-way process. However, the model does not provide details of the complexity of the relationships between people, businesses, and cultures. It merely shows that there are at least two parties involved.

In the case of the merger of Daimler and Chrysler, the model should show that representatives from Daimler and Chrysler discussed the merger; however, there is nothing in the traditional model that specifically relates the process to business or deals with group dynamics. In Chapter 1, we discussed the roles of perception and schemata in communication. Since we cannot enter the mind of a person we are communicating with, we ultimately communicate with our schema of that person. Now imagine this process involving not just two people but a group of ten

EXHIBIT 12.2
A Traditional
Communication
Model

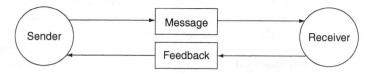

people who all bring their own cultures to the business at hand. The potential conflict between reality and perception is multiplied. The approaches to solving conflicts, establishing goals, and collecting information, to name just a few regular business tasks, combine to become a huge endeavor. In the case of Daimler-Chrysler, the situation became even more difficult because the players of the integration teams were expected to step outside their own cultural orientations and create a new company with a new culture that fit into both the German and the American national cultures.

Frequently, businesses sidestep a discussion of the communication process and focus on the way a business strategy affects corporate goals, work units, and individual employees (see Exhibit 12.3). This model shows as a corporate strategy that Daimler and Chrysler decided to merge. At the upper-management level, the goals for the merger were spelled out, such as economies of scale in production, access to new markets, and greater international competitiveness. The specific business units and the individuals in these units then worked out the details. However, we do not learn anything from this model about the interaction of people or the cultural variables of the interaction. In this case, it seems at times that the CEOs thought they could simply decree the merger by saying that it would be done because that was the strategy. But the case also makes it clear that this approach does not work unless business strategy and intercultural business communication are connected.

For an international businessperson, it is the interaction of the three circles in Exhibit 12.1 that is the exciting part. Throughout this book, we have shown the connections between those three variables. When Juergen Schrempp from Stuttgart, Germany, and Robert Eaton from Auburn Hills, Michigan, discussed a possible merger of their companies, they brought their cultural backgrounds with them, but in the process of discussion they also started the potential growth of a new corporate culture. They took something from both environments and hoped to create something new. In that effort, both Schrempp and Eaton needed to understand how businesses function in the other country; they needed to understand the relationships between culture and business and needed to understand the dynamics of communication in both cultures. They needed to understand their own

EXHIBIT 12.3
Strategy Model

Corporate Strategy

↓

Corporate Goals

↓

Unit Goals

↓

Individual Goals

national and corporate cultures and where differences could be significant. The same process is at work when a joint venture is formed.

As the three variables interact, a new construct, an intercultural business communication strategy, emerges.[13] Intercultural business communication means we have to be aware of the role of each circle. At DaimlerChrysler, for example, the participants in the merger negotiation had to look at the strategic goals of the two companies, the cultural environments of both companies, and the communication practices of both companies. Building upon that background, they then could start to develop an intercultural strategy to achieve the goals of the merger.

As the case has illustrated, the two companies came from different realities in all three circles. Germans and Americans both lean toward egalitarianism rather than hierarchy. Germans tend to use titles, and protocol is important, but advancement tends to be based on skills and merit. However, they are very different when it comes to acceptance of uncertainty and the role of the individual versus the group. Americans have an orientation toward individuality and are willing to tolerate uncertainty to a much greater degree than Germans are. Germans therefore want tight rules and regulations and formalized work processes.[14] A background in a technical field such as engineering, and an academic title guarantees that a person is an expert and has the background to do the job. This view is reflected in the corporate officers. Of the nine officers in 2006, one was Canadian, two were from the United States, and six were Germans. Among the six German executives, three had Ph.D. degrees. Americans are less impressed with academic titles.

It is noteworthy that there were no women in top management or on the Supervisory Board. In the initial merger negotiations, the Americans at times felt like unsophisticated country cousins. As the case points out, hardly anyone at Chrysler had a passport prior to the merger, and although the executives had college degrees, nobody had a Ph.D.

Because of their dislike of uncertainty, Germans rely on form. From an American point of view, they appear stiff. Americans, in contrast, appear insincere in their informality. The German executive arriving in Auburn Hills thought that the invitation to stay at the American's home was a mere figure of speech without any meaning. Zetsche, however, had had work experience in America. He knew how to read signals more effectively and made it a point to adapt to American informality, a move that helped his acceptance in Detroit. For example, he joined civic organizations and mingled socially at community affairs. The case also illustrates the problems of stereotyping and focusing on the visible how-to culture. It seems that much of the training did not go beyond a list of dos and don'ts. The participants were not taught to look behind the façade and become familiar with the backstage culture, or the *why* of the culture.

In the beginning, the differences almost derailed the merger, and it took time to see any synergy that could result from cooperation. In the end, the new company never was able to overcome the cultural differences even though Zetsche tried hard. As the environments change, the intercultural business communication strategy will change as well. When Zetsche came to Detroit, Chrysler was in bad shape. He had to develop a strategy that fit that particular situation. Although he left no doubt that he was the boss, he also worked to establish his credibility and gain the trust of the American workers. Zetsche proved that he could adapt his communication strategy. He listened to the people around him, and he observed the communication process and practices. Schrempp, on the other hand, was widely criticized for not being able to adapt to the changing communication dynamics around him. In the beginning, Schrempp was hailed as a great and decisive leader, but increasingly his critics pointed out that he did not listen and could not see that his style might alienate employees, the public, and the Board of Directors. Zetsche had better intercultural communication knowledge and skills, and the ability to implement them, but the two sides could not overcome the problems.

The news reports of the merger tended to concentrate on the key players, but it is clear that much of the work had to be done by people below the executive level. Employees at both Daimler and Chrysler worked on the merger. They worked within their companies and then in joint teams. Before Daimler's and Chrysler's cultures could be truly merged, Schrempp had brought in Mitsubishi, and a third and very different culture became part of the company. We have discussed how Exhibit 12.1 models the German–U.S. interaction; consider how it models the German–U.S.–Japanese interaction.

Dynamics of Culturally Diverse Teams

In an era of globalization, most people work in an environment of cultural diversity. Increasingly, companies rely on teamwork, arguing that diverse teams make better decisions than do homogeneous teams; however, better performance does not come automatically. Culturally diverse teams face many challenges.

As you have learned, people from different cultures have different approaches to making decisions, solving problems, and negotiating deals. They view the world differently. Westerners tend to have a linear view of the world with an either-or approach, whereas Asians have a more holistic worldview that is inclusive of contradictions. Although the top executives at both Daimler and Chrysler were either German or American, the employees and managers had a variety of backgrounds. Daimler employs many Turks and people from Eastern Europe. Chrysler in many ways reflects the cultural diversity of the American population at large. You can see similar situations in almost all major corporations around the world. For example, in one Swiss multinational company, all work teams are culturally diverse. In a team of ten people, it is not uncommon to have four or five nationalities represented. Even if the majority of the team members are Swiss, the cultural diversity still can be a major issue. The Swiss Germans, Swiss French, and Swiss Italians all come from different cultures and speak different languages. The cultural and communication dynamics in such groups are complex and at times confusing.

Three areas of cultural difference are especially likely to be sources of problems:

- Direct versus indirect communication
- Different attitudes toward hierarchy and authority
- Different norms for decision-making (when it is time, who makes a decision, how)

Several things are sure:

- Multicultural teams will be more and more common
- Well-functioning multicultural teams are important to organizations
- Culture is the most significant difference among team members, because culture determines how people interact, and how they deal with conflict
- Cultural differences have the potential to add value to organizations and the potential to create divisions among people.
- Therefore, Cultural Intelligence (CQ) can play an important role in the way culturally diverse teams operate.

To harness the potential of culturally diverse groups, businesses need to spend time developing those groups by creating cultural awareness, understanding, respect, and appropriate behavior—in other words, CQ. The material in this book is at the heart of that process.

As you probably know from your own experiences in group projects, groups do not become productive automatically. It can be a long process. For example, it took months for the team at DaimlerChrysler to develop a brochure for expatriation strategies. For nearly a decade, the two entities tried and failed to be one cohesive unit, and they finally split. During the entire time of the merger, some people argued that the integration teams did not work fast enough, whereas others argued they did not take enough care to work out important details. It was a no-win situation.

On the surface, the team-building phase is not always productive. Talking about building a cohesive team seems to get nowhere. Critics, for example, charged that managers were wasting 25 percent of their time on integration aspects rather than building and selling cars. From that viewpoint, bringing together culturally diverse teams takes attention away from the actual business task.

Most managers do not receive training in developing culturally diverse teams that communicate effectively; they do not see culture as a variable that has a huge impact on business functions. According to this view, training in intercultural competence may be a nice add-on but is not a crucial element in success. This view is represented by the attitude that a good manager at home is a good manager anywhere. Goal orientation and focusing on the task at hand are seen as the ingredients that guarantee success. In the case of DaimlerChrysler, this became clear when German managers thought that an American company could be run the same way as a German company, and the Chrysler people thought that they certainly could not learn anything from a foreign manager. In fact, the perception by each side that its way was the right way contributed to many of the problems of the merger. Both sides may have paid lip service to understanding cultural differences, but deep down both "knew" they were right.

With this view, a manager usually assembles a team and gives a charge to the team. Particularly in low-context cultures, a manager may expect the team to focus on the task at hand and not get "personal." The belief is that a rational and analytical discussion, which is culturally value-free—as if such a thing exists—will get the fastest and best results. In the DaimlerChrysler case, both companies were from Western cultures, yet they faced huge problems in their discussions. If companies from very diverse cultures are involved, the approaches to task orientation and problem solving are likely to be even more different.

Not all culturally diverse teams are the same. We can identify destroyer teams, equalizer teams, and creator teams.[15]

Destroyer Teams

Destroyers are teams that cannot agree about what to do, and even more importantly, how to do it. Members of these teams do not trust each other. When team members are from results-oriented cultures, they may not pay enough attention to relationships. They may be disappointed at what appears to be not enough attention to building good relationships. When team members are from relationship-oriented cultures, they may be disappointed that members of other cultures devote most of their attention to results rather than relationships.

When people do not trust each other, they tend to think in negative stereotypes. Team decisions in destroyer teams are often made by leaders without team members' participation.

In one extreme, the destroyers will argue that nothing is possible and that there is no way to cooperate. In the beginning of the DaimlerChrysler merger, for example, there had been talk about synergies in the areas of sharing technology, automobile parts, and marketing. Destroyers on both sides of the Atlantic, however, argued against this. Daimler did not want to risk its reputation of luxury and high quality by putting its parts into "cheap" cars, and Chrysler did not want to contribute its marketing knowledge. As a result, team members representing both sides blocked the team effort and thus the intercultural integration efforts.

Equalizer Teams

The equalizer teams have few or no disagreements and come to decisions without conflict. They are more difficult to spot because everything they do seems to go according to schedule and plan. They work together and make decisions. However, the decisions may come too fast, and then the team does not build on the unique opportunities and different viewpoints that the team members bring to the table. They want to get along. As a result, groupthink takes over. Groupthink is a term for a willingness of teams to agree that is so strong it leads people to close their minds to problems. The desire to conform and avoid disagreements is so great that people do not think critically or point out problems with what others are saying. In trying to keep disagreements at a minimum, these teams also keep innovative ideas at a minimum. Organizations are disappointed that their work is ordinary, and not better than monocultural teams.

Why do these smoothly operating teams disappoint? Sometimes people who would like to offer different points of view feel they never get a chance. They may be unsure of how to present an alternative opinion, or they may worry others will criticize them for being uncooperative. Some cultures value harmony to the point where speaking against something is viewed very negatively. Some people take time to work through ideas in their minds, then have something to say, only to find the group has moved to some other point. They do not feel comfortable speaking up after everyone else has moved on.

Typically, equalizer groups say: "There is nothing to this culture bit. It is hugely overblown. We are all people with the same interests, and we all agree." After the first few months, some managers at DaimlerChrysler felt that team members from the two sides were working together just fine. They said the cultural differences had been exaggerated. Perhaps a few had different ideas, but overall there was no problem. By not admitting that there are differences, equalizer teams never openly face their differences and build on their different expertise. They tend to be satisfied with mediocrity.

Creator Teams

Creator teams are high-performance teams that acknowledge and make use of cultural differences. They take the time to work through their differences, a time-consuming process but one that is well worth the effort in the long run. Creator teams, as authors DiStefano and Maznevski argue, go through several stages.[16] Culturally diverse teams in an international business environment face additional challenges.

Creator teams are rarer than the other two types, but they are most valued by organizations because their work is better than teams without diversity. The members are not necessarily better on their own, but the way they interact brings out the best in everyone.

The creator teams succeed because they respect cultural differences, and keep them in focus while they work. Members try to understand one another, bringing knowledge and learning to the teamwork. This corresponds to the *knowledge* component in CQ. Team members also try to find ways to connect with each other. Team members try to use their cultural differences, not ignore them, and see how differences can contribute to better teamwork. The desire to connect corresponds to the *motivation* component in CQ.

Finally, creator teams use communication behavior that makes sure everyone has a voice and each voice is taken seriously. They urge participation by everyone. They explore reasons why some people are not speaking: shyness, taking time to reflect, unwillingness to say something that is contrary to others' opinions. Creator teams also take time to resolve conflict, and try to use an integrating communication style in a collaborative mode. We could say each member has concerns for everyone else's face. This communication style corresponds to the *behavior* component of CQ.

Obviously, it takes time to learn and understand other team members' cultures; it takes time to listen and draw out opinions, and it takes time to resolve disagreements. Successful teams do not operate well automatically. It can be a long process.

Often the teams who are responsible for complex cultural management, such as teams formed when two companies with different cultures merge, are pulled in different directions. Some people may say they are taking too long to merge two companies, while other people may complain that they are not taking enough time to do it carefully.

EXHIBIT 12.4   **Stages in the Building of Culturally Diverse Teams**

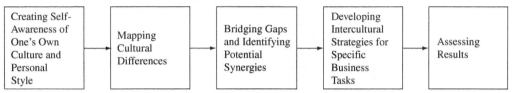

Now let us examine in more detail the factors that make creator teams more successful than equalizer or destroyer teams. Five factors that make good multicultural teams are:

- Creating self-awareness
- Mapping differences
- Bridging gaps and identifying synergies
- Developing communication strategies
- Assessing results

Exhibit 12.4 illustrates the stages for developing successful multicultural creator teams.

Creating Self-Awareness

At the beginning, team members need to become aware of their own cultural priorities. In earlier chapters, we discussed this process in the context of the self-reference criterion. Since a culture is normal to a native of that culture, few people consciously develop critical understanding of their own culture. CQ calls this reflection and awareness *meta-communication*. It is almost a kind of thinking about thinking. A word that helps describe it is mindfulness. When we are mindful of our own culturally based ideas, we are more open to the ideas of others.

Frequently, the development of such awareness is undervalued because it is assumed that people know their own priorities and cultural inclinations. However, a lack of self-awareness can hinder a solid understanding of the cultural priorities of the other group members.[17] Conscious self-awareness also can help identify and overcome one's self-reference criterion, in which a person judges somebody else on the basis of his or her own cultural priorities (also see Chapter 1).

Members of the integration teams at DaimlerChrysler needed to develop a conscious understanding of their own cultural priorities by asking questions such as the following: What does it mean to be a manager at Chrysler? What are the values of a manager at Daimler-Benz? How do my personal values fit into this corporate setting? What is important to me? How do we make decisions?

Mapping Differences

In the second stage, group members map their differences. They literally plot the intensity of their cultural priorities on a piece of paper and compare the orientations of the various group members. This is a graphic illustration of where team

EXHIBIT 12.5 **Mapping Differences**

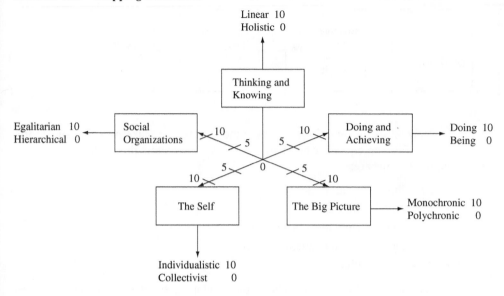

members stand in relation to values. For example, one team member may value hierarchy, whereas another may dislike hierarchy very strongly. It may be helpful if each team member enters his or her own value positions on the chart.

The chart resembles the spokes of a wheel (see Exhibit 12.5). Each spoke represents one of the five value categories we discussed in Chapters 3 and 4.

For each of those categories, we discussed several questions. Ideally, we would include each question in the mapping diagram, but the amount of detail would get confusing. Therefore, it might be more useful to select one or two of the questions that are most relevant to the task at hand. For the integration teams at Daimler-Chrysler, we could decide on the following questions for each of the categories:

- Thinking and Knowing
  - How do people learn, from authoritative sources or from hands-on experience?
  - In what patterns do people reason?
- Doing and Achieving
  - Is uncertainty avoided or tolerated?
  - Are rules bent or observed?
- Are results or relationships more important?
  - The Big Picture
  - How is time understood?
  - Are tasks done sequentially or simultaneously?
  - Is change positive or negative?
  - Who is in control of events, people or deities?

EXHIBIT 12.6   Mapping Questions

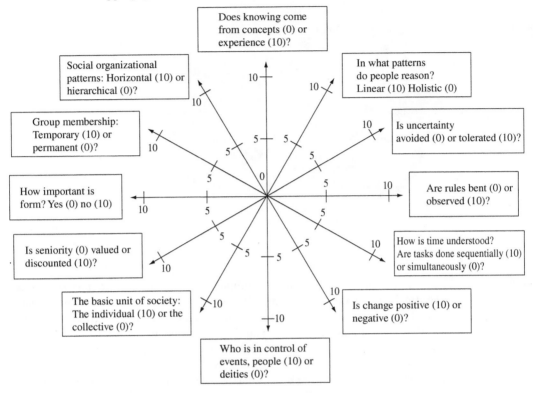

- The Self
  - Is the basic unit of society the individual or the collective?
  - Is seniority valued or discounted?
  - How important is form?
- Social Organizations
  - Is group membership temporary or permanent?
  - Are social organizational patterns horizontal or hierarchical?

If we include the two or three questions for each spoke, the diagram will look like Exhibit 12.6.

For each question, team members can now enter their priorities on a scale from 0 to 10. The individual ratings carry a subjective judgment of a team member's priorities, but the completed diagram will indicate priorities and differences among the team members.

The Diversity Wheel in Exhibit 12.7 is another way of picturing each team member's cultural identity, so differences and similarities among members can be identified.

EXHIBIT 12.7 The
Diversity Wheel

Source: Adapted from *Diverse
Teams at Work*, Gardenswartz
and Rowe (Irwin, 1995), p. 33.

It is interesting to note that the emphasis on laying out differences may be acceptable in low-context cultures. High-context cultures, however, may be much more reluctant to identify differences explicitly. As we have pointed out repeatedly, we all bring our cultures with us, and the researchers who established these steps come from a low-context environment. It makes sense in low-context cultures to state differences explicitly. If the discussion involves low- and high-context cultures, this approach may not be acceptable. The members may want to find a more subtle way to identify different cultural priorities. For example, one-on-one discussions in an informal setting after work may be a better venue to talk about differences in opinions and priorities than in group meetings at work.

Bridging Gaps and Identifying Synergies

After the differences have been mapped, group members are ready to bridge the gaps. In this stage, they acknowledge their differences. The bridging is an important step in the establishment of cultural synergy because it entails building on the strengths that the various cultures represent.[18] The DaimlerChrysler teams at this stage verbalized their differences and acknowledged them publicly. For example, team members openly acknowledged that they approached expatriation differently. As we discussed earlier, at Daimler, expatriation was a regular step in career advancement, whereas at Chrysler it was seen as a special assignment.

In this stage, team members don't yet have a way to overcome the differences, but they know where the issues are. In the beginning of the merger process, there was a lot of talk about sharing technology and platforms. If both sides had gone through a team development program, they would have been able to see that their approaches to technology, sharing information, and the importance of corporate reputation management were different. They could have worked on overcoming the obstacles much earlier if they had not pretended that there was no problem.

Developing Communication Strategies

At this point, team members are ready to integrate their knowledge, approaches, and backgrounds, and develop an intercultural business communication strategy that will build on the strengths of the members and is aligned with organizational strategies and goals. (Chapter 9 discusses communication strategies on teams.)

Team members at DaimlerChrysler at this stage would develop a detailed strategy for cooperation and integration. Ideally, the team now speaks with one voice, but only after all the differences have been explored and assessed. Because the viewpoints on sharing technology were different, they would have developed a strategy for determining areas for cooperation and integration and developed specific plans for reaching the goals. For example, they could have decided to develop a timeline for evaluating proposals for sharing technology and evaluating joint research projects.

Assessing Results

Throughout the entire team-building process, teams assess their progress, and at the end the members assess the results. The assessment also is done by the managers who formed the group. Management, in conjunction with the group, collects the process knowledge that has been gained. It stores that knowledge to have it ready for retrieval for future use.[19]

Managers who have created a team assess its work, what it has accomplished for the organization. Some organizations use formal assessment tools such as periodic reports and the record of the team's work. Other teams have informal assessments, such as informal meetings to talk to the manager who has created the team. These assessments focus on how the team is progressing toward its goals, how closely the time schedule is followed, and how much work remains before the product will be available.

Over time, the process should be less time-consuming, but it should never be automatic. As soon as it becomes automatic, there is a danger of equalizing rather than maximizing the potential.

Culture in the Context of Corporate Strategy

After examining the process of creating effective culturally diverse teams, we are ready to place the team process in the context of the organization as a whole. After all, group work is not an end in itself. The people at Daimler and Chrysler did not meet to perfect group dynamics or group processes. They had a specific business goal: to bring two different companies together and shape them into one unit. Teamwork has to be seen against that background. Exhibit 12.8 illustrates the interaction between the business strategy and the intercultural business communication work of the various players. In the model, two members come from culture A, two from culture B, and one from culture C.

The model is recursive, meaning that at any stage participants will verify that they are on track and that their activities are contributing to the reaching of the identified goals. If the activities do not contribute, the participants either realign the activities or reexamine the strategies and the stated goals. By integrating the

EXHIBIT 12.8
**Intercultural Teams
and Business
Communication
Strategy: Process
Involving One
Diverse Team in
One Company**

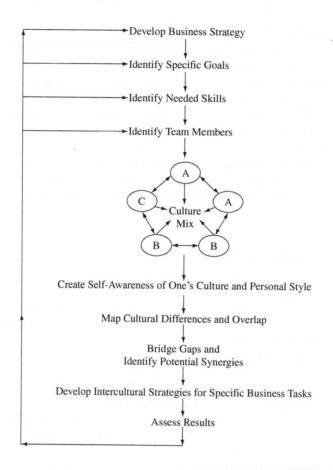

Develop Business Strategy

Identify Specific Goals

Identify Needed Skills

Identify Team Members

Create Self-Awareness of One's Culture and Personal Style

Map Cultural Differences and Overlap

Bridge Gaps and
Identify Potential Synergies

Develop Intercultural Strategies for Specific Business Tasks

Assess Results

team and group activities into the broader context of the organization, the model overcomes a major shortcoming of the conventional communication model.

The model separates activities into discrete steps; however, some of the steps can occur simultaneously. Before the multicultural group can start its work, the organization must have a clear strategy in place and identify the organizational goals to which the multicultural group will contribute. After the strategy and the goals have been identified, the organization needs to identify the skills that the participants should bring to the task so they can work effectively and efficiently. The types of skills depend on the goals at hand. As a result, different goals may require different skills. Once the desirable skills have been identified, managers can go to the next step and select the players or group members who have the necessary mix of skills and attributes.

The process depicted in Exhibit 12.8 is simplified insofar as it shows only one culturally diverse group in one company. An example is a culturally diverse team at Caterpillar (CAT), a U.S. company. Its global marketing division develops marketing strategies for many different markets. To ensure that the diverse markets have input, CAT appoints employees from a variety of cultural backgrounds to the team; however, all team members are CAT employees. In that sense, they all work toward the same goal.

Today, all international businesses and many domestic businesses have culturally diverse teams. For example, teams in U.S.-based companies have members who are European-American, Latino-American, African-American, Asian-American, and many other combinations. In many European companies, the team members in a particular company may be German, French, Scandinavian, Italian, Turkish, Algerian, Dutch, and Polish. For those teams to be effective and add value to the company, they need to become creator teams.

In international business, however, we typically deal with several companies and many intercultural teams. This process is illustrated in Exhibit 12.9.

**EXHIBIT 12.9   Intercultural Teams and Business Communication Strategy:
Process Involving Two Companies**

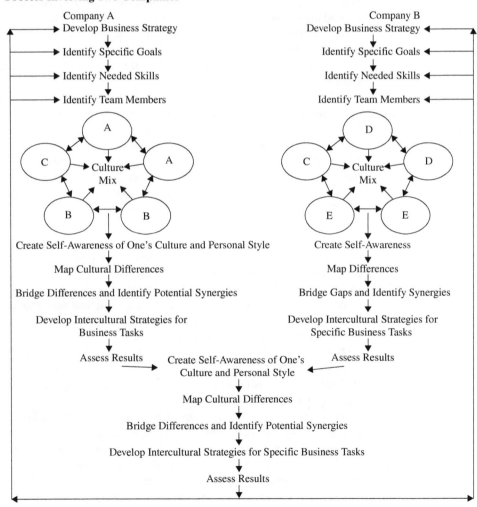

When two international companies enter negotiations as buyers or sellers of goods, they work together for a specific purpose but remain distinctly separate companies. The negotiation for the wallpaper contract between a Canadian company and a Chinese company discussed in Chapter 9 falls into this category. The two sides came together for one particular project, but there were no plans to unite the companies. The two sides evaluated their international interaction against their own goals and objectives. The Chinese ultimately decided that a contract with the Canadians would not be in their interest and discontinued the talks. In other instances, a relationship may be formed and go on for many years—for example, the company may use the same supplier over a long period, or the company may negotiate with many different groups and any relationship may be for just one specific project.

Most international companies work with local businesses and other international firms but keep their own identity. For example, Nestlé has subsidiaries around the world. The firm regularly needs to work with suppliers, interest groups, and governments in many different countries, and many of those groups have a culturally heterogeneous workforce. Nestlé works with those groups, but it keeps its own identity. Cooperative efforts would resemble the dynamics depicted in Exhibit 12.9.

When two companies decide to form a joint venture or explore the possibility of a merger, their beginning discussions may resemble what is depicted in Exhibit 12.9. At this stage, they explore possibilities for closer cooperation, but they still evaluate any proposal on the basis of their own goals. When Daimler and Chrysler first started their discussions for a merger, their interaction probably looked similar to what is depicted in Exhibit 12.9. Two distinct companies planned to come together with players from different backgrounds. There was diversity within and between groups. The goal was to see how a merger would fit into the strategy of either company. Teams from both companies also would work together and provide feedback to their respective companies in Detroit and Stuttgart.

Once the merger was finalized, however, the picture changed. At this stage, there was one company with culturally diverse teams. It no longer was a question of whether the two sides wanted to cooperate; they had to cooperate if the merger were to be successful. Chrysler and Daimler now had the same goals, and it became the task of the integration teams to help develop cultural synergies. This situation is illustrated in Exhibit 12.10.

Some people argue that Schrempp and Eaton decided to merge before both sides had thoroughly evaluated the issues involved in a merger and that many of the problems that surfaced after the merger could have been avoided if the merger had been prepared more thoroughly.

However, once the merger had been agreed on, DaimlerChrysler had one corporate strategy. But as the case illustrates, the announcement of a merger does not eliminate the need for intercultural integration. In fact, it became even more crucial because now both sides had to work together; they could not walk away from each other. Furthermore, intercultural communication was no longer an isolated

EXHIBIT 12.10
**Intercultural Teams
and Business
Communication
Strategy: The Process
after a Merger**

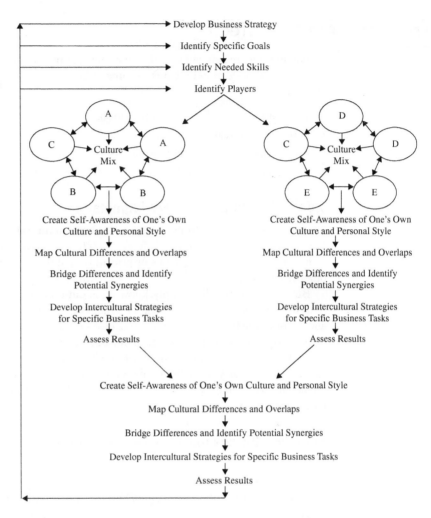

occurrence, but a daily reality. The difference is that under the merger, the culturally diverse teams do not represent different companies but different entities
within the same company.

A merger results in one company with different players and groups, but all the
groups strive to achieve the same corporate goals. You can see that it may take a
long time before any merger gets to this point, and DaimlerChrysler ultimately did
not get there. Successful international companies are able to build on the cultural
diversity of their employees. In the process, they frequently build strong corporate
cultures. The corporate culture does not eliminate the cultural backgrounds of the
players, but it does facilitate the overcoming of one's self-reference criterion in
view of the overall corporate goal and mission.

When Teams Are Not Effective

Although no team sets out to fail, sometimes teams do fail. Four alternative measures exist; three can help teams become effective—in other words, become creator teams.

- Try to adapt to each other's expectations
- Subdivide the team and tasks
- Have a manager intervene
- Remove member(s), or disband

Try to Adapt to Each Other's Expectations

Earlier, we discussed self-awareness and taking cultural differences into account. We looked at mapping cultural differences, so every team member would be aware of his or her own cultural values or priorities, and the cultural priorities of every other team member.

But we can agree that simply knowing about other people's cultural priorities does not automatically mean a team member can overcome his or her own biases and accommodate or adapt to someone else's cultural priorities.

We have been talking throughout this book about ways to understand and connect with people from other cultures, but when it is no longer abstract, and instead is right in front of you, with people who have different views and opinions, that connection is a challenge. This is where we can return to the idea of cultural intelligence for some specific help.

Specific Abilities that Make up Teamwork CQ

CQ in teamwork includes specific abilities. We will look at them in the three areas of CQ: cognition, motivation, and behavior.

In the *cognition/knowledge* component of CQ, team members need the ability to:

- Gather knowledge about other cultures and reflect upon it
- Recognize different information-processing styles
- Anticipate others' expectations

The *motivation* component of CQ calls for the ability to:

- Be open to difference
- Tolerate ambiguity

The *behavior* component of CQ calls for the ability to:

- Communicate in an appropriate style for conflict management
- Adjust behavior according to others' expectations
- Manage emotion

We will look briefly at each of these eight abilities.

Gather Knowledge about Other Cultures

Scholars agree that the more one knows about another culture, the easier it is to communicate with members of that culture. However, on a team with a great deal of diversity, it is hard to know about every culture. That is why this textbook gives you a way to know about all unfamiliar cultures, using the 24 questions. When you have answers to them, you will have an understanding of the key aspects of another culture.

Reflection about what you know about any other culture is important, since it suggests differences and similarities. In teamwork, for example, two important cultural priorities are the communication style (how direct? how indirect?)—and the approach to authority (is it direct? is it mediated?). Reflection about what you know of a teammate's views of these two priorities can make you consider other cultural dimensions that may be part of your teammate's views, such as hierarchy or horizontality in management structures, and which one your team-mate might prefer to operate in your team. You may see a results-orientation or a relationship-orientation.

Recognize Different Information-Processing Styles

In Chapter 3 of the textbook, you learned about some general ways to process in-formation that are related to culture. For example, in Western European societies, the ancient Greek tradition of reasoning is common. It is based on the concept that every individual thing has a unique identity, which can be discovered through probing and research. Each item individually relates—or doesn't relates—to each other item. A key principle in Western thinking is that two opposing things cannot both be true.

Reasoning in results-oriented cultures involves a linear sequence of logical steps that include and exclude items from categories. Cause-and-effect patterns of reasoning result from the Western approach, and most Western cultures use cause-and-effect reasoning without being aware of it. Commonly, they approach prob-lems as effects and look back to the causes in order to solve problems.

Non-European ways of processing information, or of reasoning, are based on concepts of interrelatedness. Items are points in a whole network, and when one point is engaged, others in the network are also affected. The identity of any one item depends on its relationships with other items.

A key principle in Asian thinking influenced by ancient Chinese authors is the importance of opposing ideas being held together in balance. Both exist, and influence each other, because they are related to each other.

Reasoning in relationship-oriented cultures involves taking into account an entire web or network of things or people, and finding what leads to balance. This principle often is at work in teams where members from Asian cultures seek to rec-oncile opposite ideas held by different members. They are not simply trying to patch up differences; they are trying to arrive at a conclusion where balance is achieved between opposing points of view, as the most desirable outcome.

Decision-making processes differ, depending on culture, as we have seen in Chapter 8. Members of results-oriented cultures make decisions based on outcomes or ends. Members of relationship-oriented cultures make decisions based on means, or relationships. When decisions have to be made about disagreements, we have seen that people from different cultures have different conflict-management modes and styles of communication.

Anticipate Others' Expectations

This involves *mindfulness*. Mindfulness is a concept from Buddhism. It means considering other team members' values and ways of processing information, and *trying to imagine what they are thinking*.

This involves putting yourself in another's position and thinking about how that other team member sees the world. Even more, this is thinking about what your team members' expectations are. They will have expectations for you and the other team members, and expectations for the way the team works, and expectations for the kind of work the team will produce. The more you can imagine what your teammate expects, the better prepared you will be to cooperate.

This thinking leads back to what you know about your teammate's values and attitudes, and how culture affects them.

Two CQ abilities refer to the motivation component of CQ.

Be Open to Difference

Being open to difference is more than simply opening your ears to hear about it. Openness means being willing to take a different value or behavior into your own heart and mind. Openness means holding a different alternative as a possible change in your own thinking.

Learning is the process by which change in one's thinking occurs. Being open to difference means being willing to learn and take as one's own something new.

One additional outcome of this willingness to be open is that sometimes people are surprised to find a difference is not really very different at all, and they have actually discovered a similarity. Give yourself and your teammates time to think about and get used to difference. Some people respond immediately with closed minds to difference, but upon reflection they later come to accept it. Openness of mind can increase with practice.

Tolerate Ambiguity

Another motivation aspect of the CQ of teamwork is being willing to live with a little confusion and lack of black-and-white clarity. Members of some cultures are unhappier with ambiguity than members of other cultures. They are not comfortable with uncertainty, and want teammates' positions and thinking spelled out clearly.

Members of other cultures tolerate ambiguity, and are able to go with the flow. They are less likely to pressure teammates to say exactly what they mean. Being willing to give teammates space to think and time to find ways to express their views will lead to better team communication, ultimately.

Now we can turn to three factors that contribute to CQ in team behavior.

Communicate in an Appropriate Style for Conflict Management

We have talked already about the communication styles—integrating, bargaining, and obliging—that take teammates' concerns into account and also protect teammates' face. Conflicts in teams are inevitable, unless the team is an equalizer, which is only going to produce mediocre work and is not valued by organizations. Because teams meet regularly, conflicts have the potential of causing damage to the work and to relationships.

Conflict management may sound rather remote and abstract, as it was discussed in Chapter 8. But when it is conflict between team members, who are work colleagues and meet regularly, conflict is immediate and a cause for worry. Conflict communication behavior is important.

Adjust Behavior According to Others' Expectations

This behavioral ability follows on from the cognitive ability to anticipate the expectations of teammates. Once you have an idea what your teammate may be thinking and expecting, you adjust your behavior to meet those expectations.

One way of adjusting your behavior is to match or mirror the behavior of your teammate. By behaving in a way that is familiar to your teammate, you can put him or her at ease. You mirror or show back to your teammate a corresponding behavior. The behavior may be nonverbal or verbal.

Adjusting behavior is also picking up cues from your teammate and responding accordingly. This can work when your teammate has negative expectations that you can counteract. For example, if you think a teammate expects you to respond negatively to a statement, you can adjust your behavior to take the statement positively. Your teammate will feel more comfortable, having the negative expectation overturned.

Manage Emotions

As we have previously discussed, emotional expression varies according to culture. In relationship-oriented cultures, too much emotion—especially disapproval, disappointment, and anger—can threaten the face of the one who displays emotion and the face of those to whom the expression is directed. Face damage leads to a loss of harmony in the group, and threatens relationships.

Sometimes, perhaps surprisingly, too much positive emotion can cause discomfort. People from different cultures may not know how to interpret outbursts of laughter. They may wonder, "Have I missed a joke?" "Should I laugh too?" "Is the laughing person mentally unbalanced?"

Of course, teams that work together well can often experience spontaneous amusement and pleasure in each other's company. They have confidence in each other's respect and consideration.

These eight CQ elements are specific ways teammates can contribute to the development of a creator team.

Another solution when teams are in need of help is to make changes in the team structure. This usually means subdividing the team.

Subdivide the Team and Tasks

So far in looking at what to do when teams are not effective, the focus has been on individual team members. Some authors suggest another solution: Restructure the team by subdividing it.

When teams encounter disagreement, and cannot move forward, a sub-team can work on trouble areas while other sub-teams work on other things. This is a way around a disagreement that seems to deadlock the team, and stop it from functioning. It is also a strategy for destroyer teams, when two or three people on each side want to win the conflict.

Additionally, creating sub-teams can help non-participating members feel more comfortable about making a contribution. Some members of equalizer teams may not want to speak up in a larger group, but are able to express their opinions easily to a small group.

Sometimes team members do not participate because they do not want to be alone in supporting a position. While the other team members seem to be moving together in one direction, an individual may not want to be isolated. Putting a non-participating team member in a sub-team can encourage involvement.

Sub-teams can also help move the team forward by taking specific tasks. Several sub-teams can work through tasks at the same time, and then each can report back to the larger team, enabling the team to be more efficient. Team members can decide to break into sub-teams, or the manager who created the team can make this change to the team structure.

In fact, when teams fail to operate well, they often turn to managers (or teachers, in class teams) for help.

Have a Manager Intervene

Managers represent the organizations' aims of having better problem-solving, creativity, and innovation than they get from individual employees. They want teams to function well so those aims are reached, and often look to managers to turn around failing teams.

However, most managers have not had training in how to create and manage multicultural teams. Many managers do not even see culture as an important factor in having multicultural teams work well. Managers tend to focus on the specific skills of each team member, and choose each one for that reason. Sometimes, however, managers decide who to put on teams using cultural stereotypes, rather than thinking about expertise.

Managers may have the attitude, something fairly widespread, that a good manager is a good manager anywhere in the world. In other words, managers may see their task of management as culture-free. What they do not realize is that their idea of management and of the role of manager is the product of their own culture. Managers may even *say* they think culture is important, but what they could *mean* is that they think their own culture is "right." When managers do have knowledge and skill about creating and assisting multicultural teams, they often come in as brokers in conflicts (third-party intervention). Such a mediator has an authority that surpasses the team leader's authority.

Team members' own cultures probably supply different attitudes toward authority. They may not all welcome third-party assistance from the manager, or believe the manager has superior ability to solve the problems of a team that is not working well. This can be an obstacle to a third-party settlement.

However, managers often do help teams turn around and function well after doing poorly. They can set the example for members to adapt to each other's cultural expectations. They can model the individual CQ abilities that are important for good teamwork.

One other alternative exists for teams that do not function well: removing individuals or disbanding the team.

Remove Member(s) or Disband the Team

Sometimes the problems between people do not go away, even with efforts to resolve them. Sometimes an individual believes his or her views are the only correct views, and if the other team members disagree, then the individual leaves the team. Although this is a failure of teamwork, nevertheless it is sometimes the best solution. The team may be able to work as a creator team after the exit of a member who was a source of conflict. Of course, the source of conflict is not always the person who leaves.

Teams begin their lives believing they will work together to accomplish the organization's goals. Team members generally feel positive in the beginning. They sort out roles, and get to know one another. Relationships develop as individual team members spend time and effort understanding each other.

When teams fail, everyone feels partly responsible for the failure. After someone leaves a team, roles have to be reassigned and a period of readjustment is necessary. Shock, dismay, or anger can prevent the remaining team members from working well. Some teams never recover. On the other hand, as people adjust to new roles and relationships, teams can restart and operate better than before.

When a team goes on to work well after someone has left, the judgment is that the loss was for the better. If a team goes on to work poorly, the judgment is that the person who left was a sad loss, and the team is worse off because they are no longer on it.

The ultimate recourse for a team that is not working well together and cannot achieve its goals is to disband altogether. Obviously, disbanding is an unhappy conclusion since it means the team's failure has let down the organization.

Applying Your Cultural Knowledge to Business Situations

Throughout this book, we have focused on how understanding cultural priorities can facilitate communication and make international business more productive. An understanding of the relationship between effective intercultural business communication, the dynamics of culturally diverse groups, and the overall business strategy will prepare you to become a player in an exciting global environment.

In the Appendix, there are two more cases that give you an opportunity to apply cultural principles to international business situations. As you prepare these cases for discussion, we encourage you to review the previous chapters. It will be helpful if you consider the cultural aspects, the specific business communication tasks, and the impact of culture on legal systems and organizational structures as you explore solutions to the problems at hand.

Summary

This chapter applied the principles of intercultural communication in the global workplace to the case of DaimlerChrysler. Since there is no red flag indicating cultural problems in international business, it takes some practice to identify cultural issues. This chapter has given you the opportunity to examine a real case in view of what you have learned.

- After the presentation of the case, we identified the major cultural hurdles that DaimlerChrysler needed to overcome to be successful. The two sides had different approaches to dealing with uncertainty, the role of formality, conducting meetings, and compensation.
- We discussed the variables of the intercultural business communication process: the intercultural strategy, the business strategy, and the communication strategy. The interaction of these three variables creates new synergies that help establish an intercultural business communication strategy.
- As companies increasingly rely on teamwork, an understanding of the dynamics of culturally diverse teams is necessary. We identified the stages in developing teams that can take advantage of diverse viewpoints within the groups: self-awareness, mapping of differences, bridging gaps and identifying synergies, developing communication strategies, and assessing the results of teamwork.
- Teams function in the context of corporate strategies and goals. We examined the ways teams fit into the corporate process and identified three situations: diverse teams within one company, diverse teams in two different companies that are working together but keep their own identity, and diverse teams in two companies that have merged or formed a joint venture.

Notes

1. "DaimlerChrysler Dumps Mitsubishi," BBC News, April 23, 2004.
2. Fuso Press Release, "Mitsubishi Fuso: Top Management Change Effective End of June 2005."
3. DaimlerChrysler Press Release, May 31, 2005.
4. Stephen Power, "Daimler Net Soars 84%, Lifted by Financial Arm," *The Wall Street Journal,* February 17, 2006, p. A3.
5. Sholnn Freeman and Tomoeh Murakami Tse, "DaimlerChrysler Nearing Deal to Sell U.S. Auto Unit," *Washington Post,* May 14, 2007, p. A1.
6. Peter Schneider, "Scenes from a Marriage," *New York Times Magazine,* August 12, 2001, pp. 44–48.

7. *Stern,* May 15, 1998.

8. *Forbes,* May 31, 1999.

9. *Ward's Automotive,* July 2000.

10. Chester Dawson, Jeff Green, Larry Armstrong, Christine Tierney, and Jonathan Wheatley, "Mr. Fix-It," *BusinessWeek,* May 14, 2001, pp. 26–27.

11. DaimlerChrysler Top Stories, "Mitsubishi Motors Announced Return to Profitability: Mitsubishi Motors FY 2001 Business Results and FY2002 Forecast," http://www.daimlerchrysler.com/ index_g.htm (retrieved June 21, 2003).

12. Iris Varner, "The Theoretical Foundation for Intercultural Business Communication: A Conceptual Model," *Journal of Business Communication* 37, no. 1 (2000), pp. 39–57.

13. J. M. Perkins, "Communication in a Global, Multicultural Corporation: Other Metaphors and Strategies." In *Exploring the Rhetoric of International Professional Communication,* C. R. Lovitt and D. Goswami, eds. (New York: Baywood Publishing, 1999), pp. 17–38.

14. Geert Hofstede, *Culture's Consequences,* 2nd ed. (Thousand Oaks, CA: Sage Publications, 2001).

15. Joseph DiStefano and Martha Maznevski, "Creating Value with Diverse Teams in Global Management," *Organizational Dynamics* 29, no. 1 (2000), pp. 45–63.

16. Ibid.

17. J. Gresser, "Breaking the Japanese Negotiation Code: What European and American Managers Must Do to Win," *European Management Journal* 10, no. 3 (1992), pp. 286–293.

18. J. M. George, G. R. Jones, and J. A. Gonzales, "The Role of Affect in Cross-Cultural Negotiations," *Journal of International Business Studies* 29, no. 4 (1998), pp. 749–772; P. Guptara, "The Impact of Culture on International Negotiation," *European Business Review* 92, no. 2 (1992), pp. xi–xii; Y. Paik and R. L. Tung, "Negotiation with East Asians: How to Attain 'Win-Win' Outcomes," *Management International Review* 39, no. 2 (1999), pp. 103–122.

19. Teresa Palmer and Iris Varner, "Integrating Knowledge Management into HRD to Improve the Expatriate Process." In *Proceedings of the HRD Academy National Convention,* P. Kuchinke, ed. (Academy of Human Resource Development, 2000), pp. 921–926.

CASE 1: WHAT ELSE CAN GO WRONG?[1]

Joe Van West, President of Appliances Unlimited in Mexico, was thinking about his arrival in Mexico City and his life during the last six months as he was sitting in his office. He remembered getting the phone call late one evening while sitting in front of the TV in his house in Taipei, Taiwan, where he was Operations Manager of the local subsidiary of Appliances Unlimited, a Belgian firm. The phone call was to tell him that Mr. Brian Hodges, the President of the Mexican subsidiary of Appliances Unlimited, had had a major heart attack and would retire immediately. Mr. Van West had met Mr. Hodges several times at meetings, but he did not know him very well. The caller, his friend at headquarters, Stijn Verckens, indicated that management at headquarters was looking for a speedy replacement for Hodges, and that Joe Van West should talk to the President of the International Division at headquarters immediately. Van West had always wanted to run a subsidiary. It would be a great opportunity, and he did tell Verckens that he would think about it.

Van West had gotten excellent reviews for his work as Operations Manager in Taipei. He was ready for the next step. He had hoped there would be an opportunity in Canada or the United States, but he, an American citizen, and his wife, a native of Belgium, had decided a number of years ago that they would go wherever the opportunity presented itself. Van West talked to several people at headquarters, including the president for International. He applied for the job in Mexico, and was excited when he got the appointment. Being president of a subsidiary in a major market like Mexico was a big promotion and also financially rewarding. He looked forward to the new assignment.

When Van West arrived, he met with all the major players at the plant. He listened carefully and asked lots of questions about production, marketing, and sales. He sent e-mails to headquarters as well as had lengthy conversations on the phone with executives there. He went to Brussels twice to discuss the plans for the plant in Mexico.

By all accounts, his family had adjusted well. Antonio Hernandez, the Vice President for Manufacturing, had been wonderful in helping his family get settled. Mr. Hernandez and his wife had introduced Van West and his wife to one of the best clubs in the city, as well as many influential families in business and politics. The two women had become good friends. Mrs. Hernandez had helped with the everyday orientation, which consisted of things like shopping, schools, and household personnel. Mrs. Van West was grateful for all the assistance. The adjustment to Mexico City had been so much easier than the one to Taipei a few years earlier.

Everything had started so well that Van West had a hard time figuring out just what had gone wrong. Now he was facing major production problems and the threat of a strike! Looking back, he could see the signs of problems building, but when they first appeared they had not seemed like major issues. Well, he had to

[1] The case is an update and adaptation by Iris Varner of: J. B. Schnapp, "Crisis in Caribia," *Harvard Business Review* (November–December, 1968).

get a handle on this, or he might as well pack his bags and look for another job. He reviewed each problem in turn.

Production Issues

The plant in Mexico manufactured small household appliances, such as toasters, electric irons, blenders, and coffee machines. In addition, the factory produced parts for washing machines to be assembled by the subsidiary of an American multinational company. The small appliances were mostly for the domestic market, while the washing machines were both for the domestic market and for export, mainly to other NAFTA countries. Over the last two years, the production lines had been upgraded to make use of the latest manufacturing technology. Projections called for future expansions and increasing profits.

A few weeks ago Van West had received a phone call from the production manager of the American subsidiary manufacturing the washing machines. He voiced concern over the quality and the delivery schedule of the washing machine parts. The number of defective parts had increased considerably over the last three months, and five times the parts had been delivered late enough to affect production schedules for the washing machines.

Van West had talked to Hernandez about the issue, but Hernandez did not seem to think it was a big deal. Just the same, he promised to look into it. Even with Hernandez's reassurances, Van West was concerned, and he started checking a bit on his own. He went to the factory floor. In the past, he had never gone by himself; Hernandez had always been with him. Van West felt a bit uncomfortable and intimidated. His Spanish was limited; he had had three years in high school, and although he had started taking private lessons after his arrival in Mexico, it was slow going and he was self-conscious about making mistakes. The line supervisor, Duarte Gonzales, spoke enough English to lead him around.

Gonzales mentioned some difficulties with some of the new machines and the reasons they had broken down several times. He also indicated that some of the newer employees were different and not as dedicated as the long-time employees. Gonzales did not talk about Hernandez, but Van West picked up that their relationship was a bit tense. He grew concerned that Hernandez had never mentioned any of these problems, and he decided to talk to Hernandez again to emphasize the importance of quality and timeliness of delivery.

He phoned Hernandez, who was out of the office and would not be back until the next day. As he was walking back to his office, it occurred to Van West that Hernandez was gone frequently. He had never paid much attention to this before but decided to keep a closer watch on Hernandez in the future. When Van West talked to Hernandez the next day, Hernandez brushed the issue with the washing machine parts aside. Gonzales was exaggerating the problems. Sure, there had been some problems in the past, but nothing to worry about. Things would be just fine. However, he also pointed out that Van West would have to make some concessions to local work attitudes. He said: "You know things are looser here. You just cannot expect the same performance you are used to. Take it easy; everything will be fine. Just don't worry. Leave it to me. I know how to take care of things."

Hernandez came from a distinguished Mexican family. His grandfather had been a prominent surgeon, and his father was a well-known lawyer. Hernandez himself had gone to the best schools in Mexico and had received an MBA from the University of Michigan. He knew everyone of importance in the business circles of Mexico City. But Van West was increasingly concerned about his nonchalant attitude toward day-to-day affairs at the plant. At the same time, he did not know how to best approach Hernandez. Their close social contacts made it difficult to criticize his performance. Van West was also wondering how involved and how knowledgeable Hernandez was about the production process and the new technology.

In the following weeks, Van West went several times to the factory floor when Hernandez was absent. He started to get a clearer picture of the production issues even though his limited Spanish slowed the discussions with Gonzales and the line supervisor.

After Van West had first arrived in Mexico and received a thorough briefing, he had asked Hernandez to deal with the day-to-day issues until he was settled and comfortable. He had shared his management philosophy with the management at the plant: to delegate as much as possible and include employees in the decision-making process. He felt that he could use his expertise and talents best by paying attention to the big issues. Everyone had agreed with him and thought that this was a good approach.

Worker Unrest

As Van West was contemplating what to do, Vincente Garcia, in charge of Human Resources, came to inform him that the workers were getting agitated and had started to meet in small groups to discuss their opposition to the implementation of new computer programs to monitor the quality of output, evaluate production costs, and track efficiency. While the updating of production equipment over the past few years had improved the quantity of output, cost overruns had remained a problem. Furthermore, efficiency levels and quality of output had not improved as much with the new equipment as headquarters had hoped. As a result, headquarters had been pushing for the installation of state-of-the-art computer systems to monitor all phases of operations.

Van West's predecessor had not been very familiar with computer programs. In fact, he had been very apprehensive about all the software and programs headquarters had been pushing. Finally, a year ago, headquarters had sent an expert to supervise the installation and implementation of the latest technology. Hodges had announced that Jones would be at the plant for a while and that he would work on installing technology to track performance. Frank Jones, the technician, was in his thirties. He certainly knew his stuff and was happiest when he could talk about computer technology. He had little direct contact with the workers. Whenever he had to talk to employees, he would go through the Vice President for Manufacturing. If Hernandez was not available, he would talk to Gonzalez.

Hodges had not paid any attention to Jones. When Van West arrived, he was briefed about the technology update, but with everything else going on, he had not taken the time to familiarize himself with any of the details. Things seemed to run just fine. Jones indicated that the system would soon be ready for testing and be fully operational in a few more weeks. However, as employees learned a bit more about what Jones was doing, they grew concerned and uneasy. Some of the senior workers talked to Raoul Cortez, who worked with Jones, about their concerns and the new system. Cortez hinted that the new system could certainly be programmed to identify specific production problems and track individual work performance. Jones was not aware of the workers' concerns and their talks with Cortez. When an article in a local newspaper discussed layoffs after the introduction of new technology at another plant, the employees at Appliances Unlimited became very alarmed. They were not going to sit there and wait to lose their jobs. Several of the leaders were talking of forming a union and perhaps even calling a strike. Van West was not familiar with the Mexican union process and union legislation, but any disruption sounded terrible.

Thinking about the possible strike, Van West was in disbelief. He had been told that the workers at the plant were happy and dedicated. Nobody had ever talked about a union, at least not in public. Labor relations had been good, and Appliances Unlimited was known for excellent pay and benefits. A shutdown at this point would seriously affect delivery contracts. It would also affect negotiations with new clients.

Van West knew he had to do something. But what? He decided to call a meeting to discuss options. He asked the following people to attend a meeting the next morning at 9 a.m.: Hernandez, Gonzales, Garcia, Jones, Cortez, and Sanchez.

Questions for Discussion

In your discussion you may want to examine the following questions. Look at them in light of the cultural knowledge you have gained.

- What are the underlying cultural issues contributing to the problems?
- What should Van West have done when he first came to Mexico?
- How should Van West deal with Hernandez? Address the role of the boss in Mexican culture. Address the relationship between superiors and subordinates.
- How can Van West deal with the labor issue? How does this relate to attitudes toward change, the relationship between the individual and the group, and hierarchy?

CASE 2: HANA, A JOINT VENTURE BETWEEN HEALTH SNACKS AND TOKA FOODS[2]

When Health Snacks and Toka Foods formed a joint venture four years ago, the future looked very promising. Health Snacks was looking for opportunities to enter the Japanese market, and Toka Foods was well positioned in Japan to facilitate that

---

[2] This case is an update and adaptation by Iris Varner of the Showa case, which is published by the President and Fellows of Harvard College.

process. Toka Foods, on the other hand, was interested in gaining access to new technology. Since Health Snacks was a leader in the adaptation of new technology to business processes, the joint venture seemed ideal. At the time the joint venture was established, executives both from Health Snacks and Toka Foods had spent many hours hammering out an agreement that would help both sides realize their objectives.

Each side was excited about the new opportunities; however, after the first six months, several disagreements surfaced regarding the management of the joint venture. One of the issues was who should get copies of written communication regarding production schedules and marketing plans. The Americans felt they were not sufficiently included in discussions relating to the joint venture. The Japanese managers, on the other hand, were frustrated with the number of requests for reports from the American side.

At first these disagreements seemed rather superficial, but as time went by, both sides became increasingly unhappy and started to blame each other for any difficulties.

Health Snacks had tried to solve the problems via electronic communication, faxes, and e-mails. They even had organized a teleconference to meet "face-to-face" so each side could hear the other's viewpoint, but the problems remained. After much soul-searching, Ron Carter decided it was time to fly to Nagoya and face the problems head-on.

Mr. Carter had joined Health Snacks as President of International Operations only nine months earlier. In this position, he also served as vice president for the joint venture with Toka Foods. He had received a thorough briefing at the time and had also studied the history of the joint venture on his own. He had been an expatriate in Australia and France managing international subsidiaries in both countries, was 40 years old, and was expected to have a bright future.

Health Snacks was a major manufacturer of convenience foods and health food products. The company had registered several patents for extending shelf life while maintaining quality. The company had sales of roughly $3 billion and had subsidiaries in 30 countries around the globe. In the last year, roughly 34 percent of corporate sales had come from international sales. Tim Davis, President for International Operations at Health Snacks, and Mr. Carter's predecessor, was given the task of exploring the expansion into the Japanese market.

Health Snacks had never had any major presence in Japan; however, top executives believed that Japanese consumers were increasingly interested in convenience foods and health foods. Many Japanese still went shopping for food daily, but the number of people making weekly food purchases was increasing. Toka Foods, a traditional food processor, had attempted to move into this market but ultimately decided it lacked the processing and packaging technology, as well as the quality control to establish a major presence. As a result, Toka Foods started looking around for a potential partner. In the beginning, Health Snacks and Toka Foods had explored licensing agreements. Toka Foods, in particular, was interested in getting a license for using Health Snacks' processing and packaging technology. Health Snacks, however, felt that a joint venture would provide better opportunities for their establishing a presence in the Japanese market. Upper management knew that the Japanese market was difficult to enter, and they hoped they would not have to develop an entire distribution system.

The negotiations had been very difficult and took much longer than executives from Health Snacks had anticipated. The Japanese were slow and deliberate in their approach to the negotiation, and once the Japanese side had made up its mind on a point, it was difficult to agree on any changes since everything had to go back and be rediscussed by Japanese executives.

The composition of the negotiation team also became an issue. Based on initial contacts, Health Snacks knew that Toka Foods was interested in technical details. To speed up the process and provide technical details, Health Snacks had initially sent an engineer from production and one from packaging, both in their early thirties with no international experience. The two engineers took detailed reports, diagrams, and illustrations with them. They knew the technology inside out, but the Japanese, while asking many questions, did not move toward any agreement. When the two engineers from Health Snacks could not answer questions relating to projections of production and sales, the Japanese became impatient. The two engineers found the talks tiring, and sitting across from a team of eight Japanese managers was intimidating and exhausting. Furthermore, the Japanese repeatedly asked the same questions. It was only after the President of the International Division at Health Snacks, Tim Davis, participated in the negotiations that progress was made. He visited several times, and an agreement was finally signed.

The final agreement had the following provisions: The ownership of the joint venture was equally divided. Toka Foods was to provide facilities for processing of food and packaging. The Japanese side was also to provide its marketing network and develop new marketing channels where necessary. Health Snacks was to provide the latest technology and assist with the production setup. The joint venture was to be called Hana, and products from the joint venture were to be marketed under the brand name, Hana.

The management of the joint venture posed some special issues as well. Given that the joint venture would be located in Japan, the contract specified that the joint venture would have a board of eight people, four from each partner; however, all employees working for the joint venture would come from Toka Foods. The joint venture would have a president and a vice president. The president was to be Japanese, nominated by Toka Foods but subject to approval by the entire board. The Vice President of International Operations at Health Snacks would serve as the American vice president for the venture. Health Snacks would send a Health Snacks executive to serve as Technical Director and board member. This person would be the only American posted full-time to the joint venture in Japan.

The Composition of the Board

The board composition was as follows:

- Health Snack representatives: the CEO of the parent company, the CFO of the parent company, the President of International Operations and Vice President of the joint venture, and the Technical Director.
- Toka representatives: the CEO of Toka, the Vice President of Production of Toka, the President of the joint venture, and the CFO of the joint venture.

The establishment of the first board and the selection of president, vice president, and technical director had not posed any problems, and everything seemed to go according to schedule.

About ten months ago, Mr. Carter's predecessor left the company and Mr. Carter was hired to fill his place. Shortly after Mr. Carter assumed his position at Health Snacks, the Japanese president of the joint venture, Mr. Hyashida, died at the age of 63. Mr. Carter was waiting to discuss possible successors with Toka Foods' President, Mr. Sony, when he received an e-mail from Mr. Sony informing him that the Japanese had nominated Mr. Hiromitsu Ota for the position. Mr. Carter was upset because he had expected that even though the Japanese could select their nominee, they would have consulted him before making the nomination public. More importantly, Mr. Carter did not think that Mr. Ota was the right person for the position. His judgment was reinforced when he discussed the issue of the joint venture in Japan with Mr. Russell, the technical director and board member.

Mr. Ota had joined Toka Foods right after graduating from Waseda University 35 years earlier. For the past 20 years he had held staff positions at Toka Foods. He was manager of administrative services at a major company plant and after that was personnel manager at headquarters. In the latter position, he joined the board of directors at Toka Foods. Currently, he was general manager of several staff departments. Mr. Carter simply was at a loss as to why Mr. Sony would nominate someone without line experience for the position of president of the joint venture.

Mr. Russell filled him in on traditional Japanese corporate practices, and it began to dawn on Mr. Carter that he had little understanding of the management of Japanese corporations. Many of the major companies still practice a form of lifetime employment. With economic difficulties, increased competition from abroad, and increasing foreign ownership of Japanese corporations, the practice is not as common as it once was; however, lifetime employment is still seen as the ideal, particularly when it comes to older employees. Under lifetime employment, employees, almost all males, are recruited right out of college. They move slowly up the corporate ladder until the age of about 60. At that stage, most people retire and only selected people move into executive positions. Competence and performance play a role in the promotion to upper management and executive level positions, but seniority is a major factor throughout. Even though under Japanese law board members are elected by shareholders for two-year terms, in reality they are appointed by the president of the company and/or the chairman of the board. Frequently, a seat on the board is a reward for loyal and faithful company service rather than exceptional performance. Board membership is typically rotated every two years to make room for more junior managers; however, at that time of scheduled rotation many board members targeted for leaving the board are still quite young and not ready to retire. Therefore, it is quite common to appoint outgoing board members who have no chance of further promotion at the company to positions in subsidiaries, affiliated companies, or joint ventures. It became clear to Mr. Carter that Mr. Ota was not going to be promoted to President of Toka Foods and would, therefore, be rotated off the board. He had served Toka Foods loyally and with great dedication but was considered unsuitable by the company to occupy the top positions. However, he was considered appropriate for president of the joint venture.

Mr. Carter was upset. He wanted the best person for the job and was convinced that other candidates were available. In fact, he had met Mr. Katsuki from Toka Foods only a couple of months ago in Chicago. He seemed to have the qualities that Mr. Carter was looking for and expecting in the president for the joint venture.

After talking to Mr. Russell, he informed Mr. Sony that he objected to Mr. Ota. At the same time, he proposed Mr. Katsuki for the position and gave his reasons for his choice. Mr. Katsuki was 48 years old and had been with Toka Foods during his entire career. Currently, Mr. Katsuki was the marketing director for the joint venture. He had made quite an impression at Health Snacks headquarters in Chicago. He spoke excellent English and seemed to have the characteristics and the energy for moving the joint venture forward. Mr. Katsuki seemed to be straightforward in his communication and very dynamic compared to many of the other Japanese Mr. Carter had met.

As Mr. Carter reflected on the joint venture, he came to the conclusion that the joint venture was run almost exclusively as a Japanese corporation. The American side had little input, and Mr. Carter felt that Health Snacks was increasingly marginalized. In addition, it always took weeks before he received responses to inquiries, and he was convinced that management needed to be more responsive to queries from the American side. He realized that the time difference and language issues posed a hurdle to communication; it was all the more reason to get someone like Mr. Katsuki who could relate to the American side. He carefully worded his opposition to Mr. Ota and his suggestion of Mr. Katsuki. Only after he was convinced that the message was tactful, courteous, and constructive and had gone through several revisions, did he send it off. He was, therefore, rather surprised when he received a letter from Mr. Sony totally rejecting his suggestions. Mr. Sony was polite but made it quite clear that Toka Foods had carefully considered all options and that Mr. Ota was the right person, and Mr. Katsuki was out of the question. He further explained that a promotion for Mr. Katsuki would be totally unacceptable and would ruin Mr. Katsuki's career. In his letter, Mr. Sony gave no explanation as to why the appointment of Mr. Katsuki would ruin his career. When Mr. Carter asked Mr. Russell for more information, Mr. Russell talked about traditional Japanese management practices that would be next to impossible to change.

Mr. Carter was wondering how things could have progressed to such a state without Mr. Russell's informing him about the discussions at the joint venture. How effective was Mr. Russell in his job, and how well did he understand the Japanese and Japanese practices? Mr. Carter had assumed that Mr. Russell was well integrated into the running of the joint venture and actively participated in the discussion of management issues.

When Health Snacks was hiring a technical director, the company had looked for someone with Japanese experience and language ability. Such a person, however, was difficult to find, and Mr. Russell had been a compromise candidate.

He spoke some Japanese and had been a student at a Japanese university 15 years earlier. From comments by the Japanese, Mr. Carter figured that Mr. Russell's Japanese language ability was rather limited. Furthermore, he did not seem to have established a close working relationship with the Japanese managers of the venture. Mr. Russell had his family with him in Japan, his wife and two teenage sons. He preferred to spend evenings and weekends with his family rather than go out with colleagues. In fact, he found the evening entertainments and visits to bars unproductive and exhausting.

Mr. Sony was not looking forward to Mr. Carter's visit. He hated confrontations and was worried that the meeting would not be very pleasant. He had not met Mr. Carter before. He never did understand why American companies were hiring top people from the outside. The frequent changes in personnel were rather unsettling to him since it seemed he had to adjust to new faces all the time. He also was not quite sure how much Mr. Carter understood about Japanese management practices. And the message from Mr. Carter concerning the nomination of Mr. Katsuki added to his suspicions.

Mr. Sony was convinced that Mr. Ota was the best and most appropriate person for the position in the joint venture. He was owed the position for his loyal and dedicated service. Given that several new board members needed to be appointed, a reappointment of Mr. Ota to the board was not a viable option. Mr. Sony was well aware that Mr. Ota was not a dynamic person or visionary manager, but he got along with people and always put the company first in all his business dealings. Therefore, the position of president of the joint venture was suitable and appropriate. He could see why Americans might not think so, but the president had to function in a Japanese environment and have the appropriate stature and seniority to represent the company well. In the Japanese environment, it was not necessary to have a strong leader or enthusiastic promoter. Someone who could build consensus and move the entire group along was much more important, and Mr. Ota had a proven track record in that area.

Clearly, Mr. Sony thought that Mr. Carter had no knowledge of Japanese business practices. If he did, he would have never even suggested Mr. Katsuki. Sure, Mr. Katsuki was dynamic, and he would have a bright future particularly with the internationalization of businesses. However, to promote him now would ruin his career forever. He would not be accepted by his peers, and his seniors would deeply resent his promotion over them. The only way to guarantee Mr. Katsuki's ultimate success would be for him to take his time and move up the ladder slowly.

As he was thinking the joint venture over, he was also focusing on Mr. Russell. What did Mr. Russell do to represent the Japanese viewpoint in Chicago? In fact, he had not seen much of Mr. Russell lately. Communication was difficult because he had a hard time understanding Mr. Russell when he spoke Japanese, and he himself did not speak very fluent English. It also occurred to him that Mr. Russell had not attended many of the social functions and had rarely participated in weekend outings and golf games. He just did not seem to be part of the joint venture family. Perhaps the joint venture had not been such a good idea after all.

As the plane was getting closer to Nagoya, Mr. Carter was wondering whether it was all worth it. Mr. Sony had very similar thoughts as he was preparing to meet Mr. Carter.

Questions for Discussion

Consider the following questions in your discussion of the case and pay special attention to the cultural dimensions.

- What are the underlying cultural issues?
- What could both sides have done to avoid the current problems? Relate your discussion to the cultural priorities in Chapters 3 and 4.
- Given that there is a problem, what can/should both sides do to overcome the problems?

Can the joint venture be saved?

Index